THIRD EDITION

SOCIOLOGY IN ACTION

A CANADIAN PERSPECTIVE

THIRD EDITION

SOCIOLOGY IN ACTION

A CANADIAN PERSPECTIVE

Diane G. Symbaluk, PhD
Sociology Department
Grant MacEwan University

Tami M. Bereska, PhD
Sociology Department
Grant MacEwan University

NELSON

NELSON

Sociology in Action: A Canadian Perspective, Third Edition
by Diane G. Symbaluk and Tami M. Bereska

Vice President, Product Solutions:
Claudine O'Donnell

Publisher, Digital and Print Content:
Leanna MacLean

Marketing Manager:
Claire Varley

Content Manager:
Lisa Berland

Photo and Permissions Researcher:
Carrie McGregor

Production Project Manager:
Jennifer Hare

Production Service:
SPi Global

Copy Editor:
Holly DIckinson

Proofreader:
SPi Global

Indexer:
SPi Global

Design Director:
Ken Phipps

Higher Education Design PM:
Pamela Johnston

Interior Design:
Sharon Lucas

Cover Design:
Sharon Lucas

Cover Image:
Simon Ritzmann/Getty Images

Compositor:
SPi Global

Printed and bound in Canada
1 2 3 4 21 20 19 18

For more information contact Nelson Education Ltd., 1120 Birchmount Road, Toronto, Ontario, M1K 5G4. Or you can visit our Internet site at nelson.com

Additional credits for recurring images: Sociology in My Life: franckreporter/iStock; Sociology in My Community: PatCamera/iStock; Sociology in Words: filadendron/iStock; Sociology Online: Rawpixel.com/Shutterstock; Sociology in Practice: iStock/Thinkstock; Sociology On Screen: iStock/Thinkstock; Sociology in Music: PeopleImages/iStock.

Library and Archives Canada Cataloguing in Publication Data

Symbaluk, Diane, 1967-, author
Sociology in action : a Canadian perspective / Diane G. Symbaluk, PhD, Sociology Department, Grant MacEwan University, Tami M. Bereska, PhD, Sociology Department Grant MacEwan University. — Third edition.

Includes bibliographical references and index.
Issued in print and electronic formats.
ISBN 978-0-17-672506-8 (softcover).
—ISBN 978-0-17-685376-1 (PDF)

1. Sociology—Canada—Textbooks. 2. Sociology—Textbooks. 3. Textbooks. I. Bereska, Tami M. (Tami Marie), 1968-, author II. Title.

HM586.S95 2018 301.0971
C2017-907529-2
C2017-907530-6

ISBN-13: 978-0-17-672506-8
ISBN-10: 0-17-672506-7

For those who have yet to discover sociology and those who have already come to appreciate it.

Brief Table of Contents

Detailed Table of Contents

A Unique Learning System

THE SOCIOLOGICAL TOOLKIT

The essence of sociology lies in the sociological imagination, a cognitive skill that enables individuals to identify the links between the micro level of individual experiences and choices and the macro level of larger sociocultural forces. This textbook highlights the tools that are necessary to develop that skill: empirical research methods that create verifiable knowledge, sociological theories that explain that knowledge, and critical thinking that enables us to evaluate and to extrapolate from that knowledge.

Empirical Research Methods and Sociological Theories

Representative of the discipline of sociology, academic research based on empirical research methods and sociological theories constitute the foundation for each chapter.

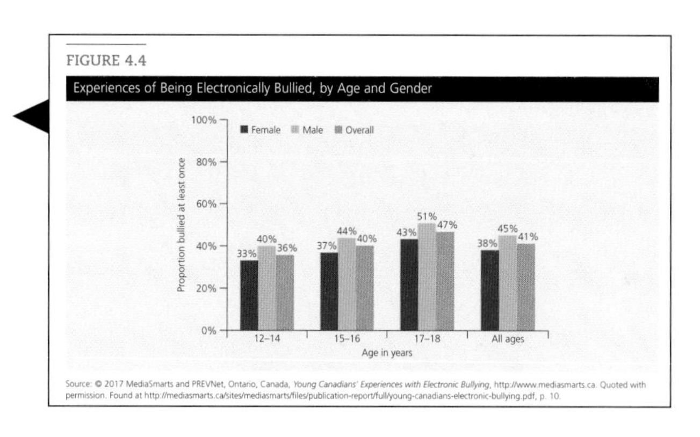

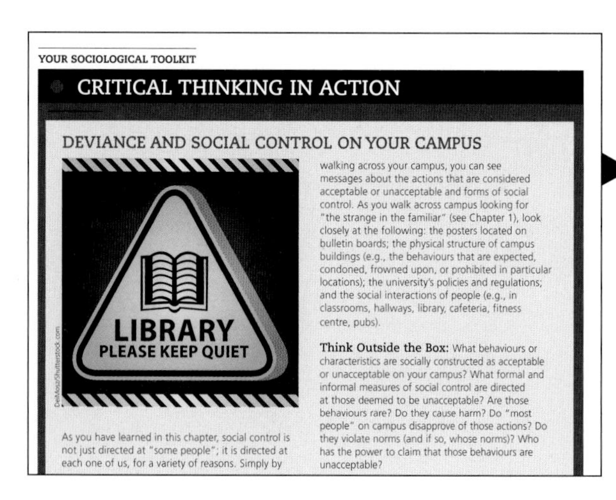

YOUR SOCIOLOGICAL TOOLKIT

CRITICAL THINKING IN ACTION

DEVIANCE AND SOCIAL CONTROL ON YOUR CAMPUS

As you have learned in this chapter, social control is not just directed at "some people"; it is directed at each one of us, for a variety of reasons. Simply by walking across your campus, you can see messages about the actions that are considered acceptable or unacceptable and forms of social control. As you walk across campus looking for "the strange in the familiar" (see Chapter 1), look closely at the following: the posters located on bulletin boards; the physical structure of campus buildings (e.g., the behaviours that are expected, condoned, frowned upon, or prohibited in particular locations); the university's policies and regulations; and the social interactions of people (e.g., in classrooms, hallways, library, cafeteria, fitness centre, pubs).

Think Outside the Box: What behaviours or characteristics are socially constructed as acceptable or unacceptable on your campus? What formal and informal measures of social control are directed at those deemed to be unacceptable? Are those behaviours rare? Do they cause harm? Do "most people" on campus disapprove of those actions? Do they violate norms (and if so, whose norms)? Who has the power to claim that those behaviours are unacceptable?

Your Sociological Toolkit: Critical Thinking in Action

Research has found that critical thinking does not automatically develop with a postsecondary education—it requires practice. In each chapter, a box titled **Your Sociological Toolkit: Critical Thinking in Action** provides students with specific opportunities to think critically about particular issues by evaluating, questioning, or deconstructing certain pieces of knowledge or claims to truth or by extrapolating from the material addressed in the body of the chapter to a broader question or social problem.

Four distinct but complementary ways of practising sociology

Unique to this textbook, four different settings within which the sociological toolkit can be used are highlighted: **in theory**, **in practice**, **in my community**, and **in my life**. This approach is especially effective for helping students understand how sociology relates to their everyday lives and how academic sociology (i.e., based in theoretical and empirical research) applies to real life.

Your Sociological Toolkit: Sociology in Theory sections highlight certain pieces of research by formally trained academics.

YOUR SOCIOLOGICAL TOOLKIT
SOCIOLOGY IN THEORY

LO7 EXPLAINING DEVIANCE AND SOCIAL CONTROL

A variety of theories are used to analyze criminalized and non-criminalized forms of deviance. Like

YOUR SOCIOLOGICAL TOOLKIT

SOCIOLOGY IN PRACTICE

MONITORING CHILDREN'S EXPOSURE TO VIOLENCE

Various efforts have been made to try to monitor children's exposure to violence, including the use of V-chips and other program-blocking technology designed to allow parents to customize what their children view at home. All Canadian stations (even if they air an American show) include show ratings and blocking technology embedded in the broadcast signal. Symbols and icons appear on screen to denote program content that includes violence, coarse language, sexuality, and/or mature themes. This practice, which has been in effect since 1997, demonstrates how collective efforts can promote social change because the ratings were first developed by a group called the Action Group on Violence on Television (AGVOT) (Canadian Broadcasting Standards Council, 2017).

Think Outside the Box: In what ways does the Internet pose challenges for monitoring children's exposure to violence?

Your Sociological Toolkit: Sociology in Practice boxes consist of applications of sociological concepts for policy development.

Your Sociological Toolkit: Sociology in My Community boxes demonstrate how sociological principles can be transmitted to nonacademic audiences.

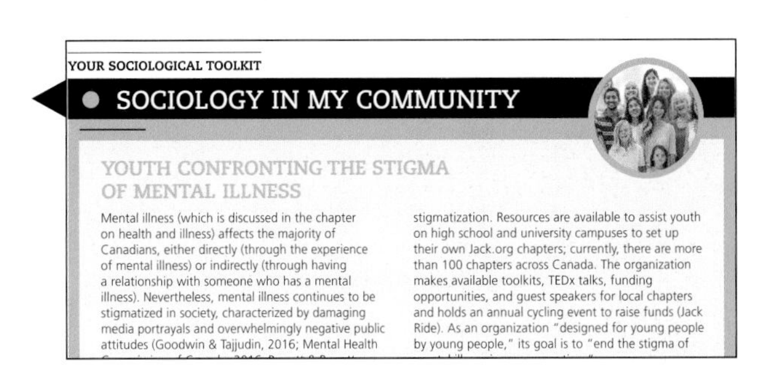
YOUR SOCIOLOGICAL TOOLKIT

SOCIOLOGY IN MY COMMUNITY

YOUTH CONFRONTING THE STIGMA OF MENTAL ILLNESS

Mental illness (which is discussed in the chapter on health and illness) affects the majority of Canadians, either directly (through the experience of mental illness) or indirectly (through having a relationship with someone who has a mental illness). Nevertheless, mental illness continues to be stigmatized in society, characterized by damaging media portrayals and overwhelmingly negative public attitudes (Goodwin & Tajjudin, 2016; Mental Health

stigmatization. Resources are available to assist youth on high school and university campuses to set up their own Jack.org chapters; currently, there are more than 100 chapters across Canada. The organization makes available toolkits, TEDx talks, funding opportunities, and guest speakers for local chapters and holds an annual cycling event to raise funds (Jack Ride). As an organization "designed for young people by young people," its goal is to "end the stigma of

YOUR SOCIOLOGICAL TOOLKIT

SOCIOLOGY IN MY LIFE

MY FAMILY

The opening quotation in this chapter suggests that families are of the utmost importance in determining who we are, creating the frameworks on which our lives are built. Families are at the core of our socialization experiences throughout our lives. In childhood, our parents and other family members are key socializing agents, providing us with some of the knowledge and life skills we will carry with us throughout our lifetimes. We undergo further socialization in the context of family life if and when we marry or enter a common-law relationship, have children, get divorced, remarry, acquire additional children through remarriage, have our children move out of the family home, and become grandparents. We spend a considerable amount of time and energy interacting with and thinking about our families.

Think Outside the Box: How would you describe your family?

Your Sociological Toolkit: Sociology in My Life boxes are applications of sociological knowledge to one's own personal life experiences.

ADDITIONAL FEATURES

The Sociological Toolkit is the organizing framework of the text. The following special features also characterize it:

- ***Learning Objectives and Outcomes*** are numbered statements about the intended knowledge and/or skills students should be able to demonstrate following a thorough reading of the chapter. The Learning Objectives and Outcomes run throughout the body of the chapter to encourage critical, focused reading.

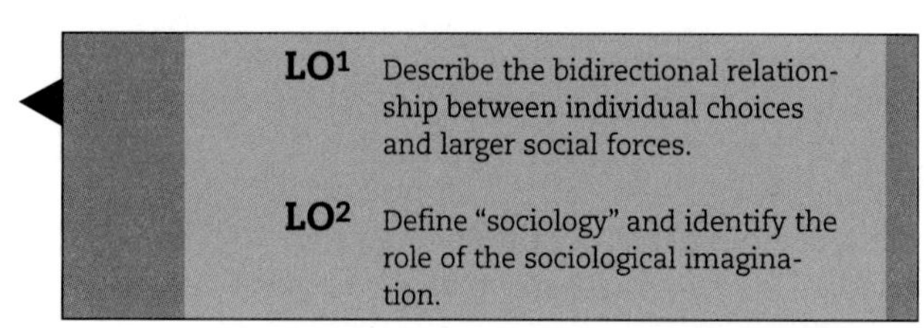

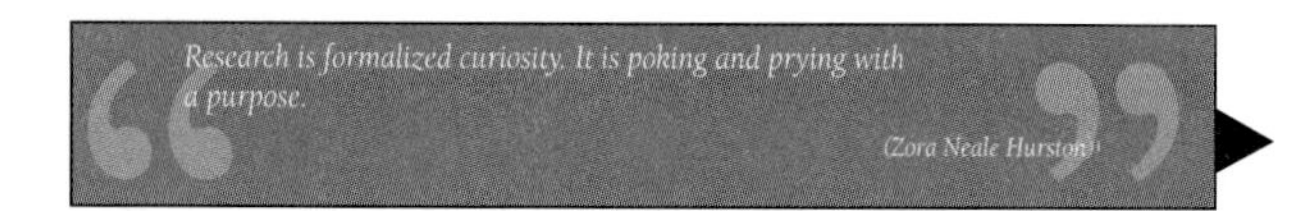

- ***Opening quotations*** begin each chapter; they are intended to spark the reader's interest and set the tone for the chapter by highlighting a central concept, issue, or paradox that is pertinent to the topic covered in that chapter.

- ***Sociology on Screen*** boxes discuss documentaries and/or fictional films that illustrate key concepts and processes.

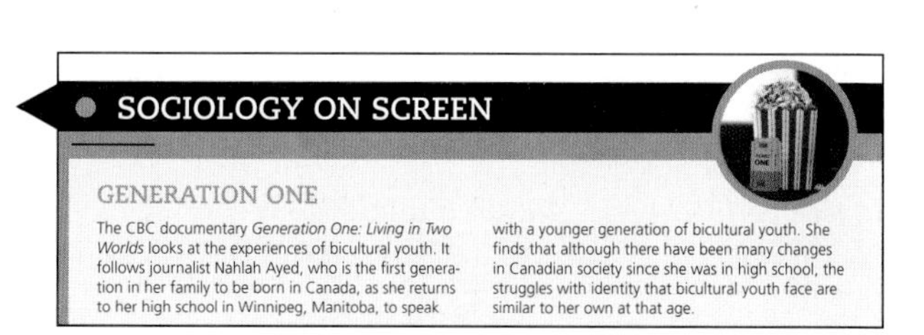

- ***Sociology in Music*** boxes look at music that illustrates the importance of sociological concepts in everyday practices.

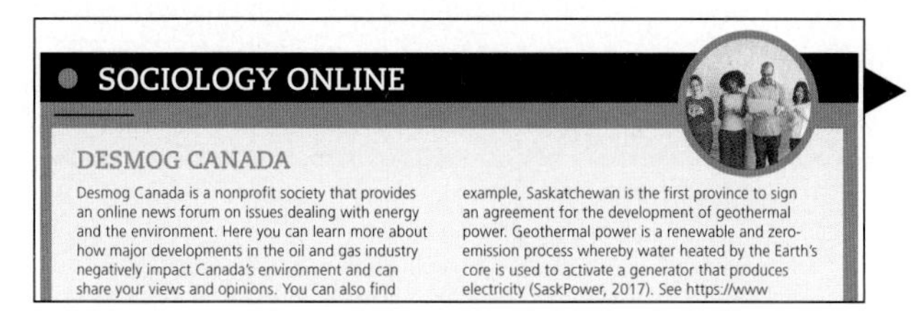
SOCIOLOGY ONLINE

DESMOG CANADA

Desmog Canada is a nonprofit society that provides an online news forum on issues dealing with energy and the environment. Here you can learn more about how major developments in the oil and gas industry negatively impact Canada's environment and can share your views and opinions. You can also find

example, Saskatchewan is the first province to sign an agreement for the development of geothermal power. Geothermal power is a renewable and zero-emission process whereby water heated by the Earth's core is used to activate a generator that produces electricity (SaskPower, 2017). See https://www

- ***Sociology Online*** boxes highlight particular websites that demonstrate key concepts and provide in-depth examples of topics discussed in the chapters.

- ***Sociology in the News*** boxes contain media coverage illustrating how sociological concepts and processes are presented in statements made to the public.

SOCIOLOGY IN THE NEWS

FROM THE DAVIS INLET TO NATUASHISH

Until 1967, the Innu in Labrador lived nomadic lives. In 1967, the federal government relocated them to a permanent settlement in order to better provide services for them. Told that they would be given comfortable homes and schools and access to healthcare, they were relocated to a distant island off the coast, where their way of life completely changed.

The government did not keep its promises. Instead, the Innu were left to endure overcrowded

also formed to help resolve the community's social problems.

However, critics point out that to this day, many social problems persist. Within just a period of a few months in 2017, two youth committed suicide (in a population of only 936 people). Although the community voted to ban alcohol back in 2008, recently RCMP officers reduced the frequency of baggage checks with people coming into the community (via ferry in the

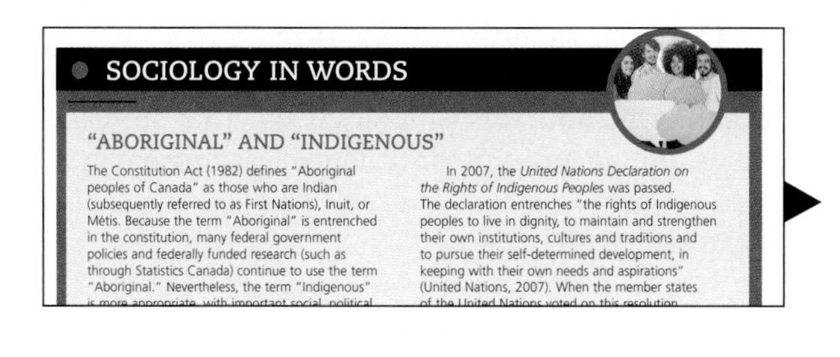
SOCIOLOGY IN WORDS

"ABORIGINAL" AND "INDIGENOUS"

The Constitution Act (1982) defines "Aboriginal peoples of Canada" as those who are Indian (subsequently referred to as First Nations), Inuit, or Métis. Because the term "Aboriginal" is entrenched in the constitution, many federal government policies and federally funded research (such as through Statistics Canada) continue to use the term "Aboriginal." Nevertheless, the term "Indigenous"

In 2007, the *United Nations Declaration on the Rights of Indigenous Peoples* was passed. The declaration entrenches "the rights of Indigenous peoples to live in dignity, to maintain and strengthen their own institutions, cultures and traditions and to pursue their self-determined development, in keeping with their own needs and aspirations" (United Nations, 2007). When the member states

- ***Sociology in Words*** boxes include either the testimony of people who experience sociological concepts first-hand or in-depth explanations by theorists who study sociological issues.

Also included for student review are the following features:

- ***Chapter Summaries*** are succinct examples of the kinds of responses students are expected to provide in relation to the learning objectives and outcomes.
- ***Time to Review*** questions at the end of each main section highlight key points and provide students with a built-in test of their mastery of the material before they proceed to the next section.
- ***Margin Definitions*** provide definitions conveniently located in the text margin beside the section where the term is first introduced. Students can practise their understanding by accessing the interactive flashcards online.
- ***Recommended Resources*** provide references for additional readings, films, and other sources related to the issues pertinent to a given chapter.
- ***For Further Reflection*** questions present opportunities to examine chapter content in more detail and to demonstrate a personal understanding of the key concepts and processes discussed in the chapter.
- A ***Glossary*** of all key terms is included at the end of the text.

Preface

INTRODUCTION

Sociology is about the real world. It can be thought of as the most comprehensive social science[1]—one that provides a systematic means for understanding the interconnectedness among people, among institutions, and between individuals and the society in which they live. A major objective of our textbook is to give you the tools to help you develop your sociological imagination[2] so that you can see how you (and other people) influence and are influenced by society; so that you can view social issues from a variety of different perspectives and critically evaluate those perspectives (including your own); and so that you can extrapolate from the empirical and theoretical research presented in this textbook to the real-world issues you or others experience every day. The sociological imagination is not merely an intellectual exercise; it is the foundation for social action. We hope that by the time you finish this textbook, you will be better equipped to engage in effective social action in the context of your own families, communities, and professions, as well as in the context of larger social problems, such as social inequality and environmental degradation.

OVERALL GOAL OF THIS BOOK: HELPING STUDENTS ACQUIRE THE FUNDAMENTALS OF SOCIOLOGY

Persell, Pfeiffer, and Syed[3] surveyed 44 preeminent leaders in sociology (including American Sociological Association [ASA] presidents, regional presidents, and national grant recipients in sociology), asking them what students need to know by the time they finish a course in introductory sociology. The following nine themes emerged as overall directives for what students should learn about in an introductory sociology course:

1. The "social" part of sociology, or learning to think sociologically
2. The scientific nature of sociology
3. Complex and critical thinking
4. The centrality of inequality
5. A sense of sociology as a field
6. The social construction of ideas
7. The difference between sociology and other social sciences
8. The importance of trying to improve the world
9. The important social institutions in society

Our goal as authors was to provide a foundation on which those objectives can be met by those teaching introductory sociology, whether in classrooms, online, or in other distance learning environments. The feedback of our reviewers was invaluable to our efforts.

ORGANIZATION

Part 1: Practising Sociology: Your Sociological Toolkit provides students with a framework for how to think sociologically. Beginning in Chapter 1, you will start to see the fundamental connection between individual choices and larger social forces, a connection that lies at the heart of the sociological imagination. Chapter 1 explains why the sociological imagination is important—in the 21st century, perhaps more important than ever before—and outlines the tools that will help you build your own sociological imagination (empirical research methods, sociological theories, critical thinking). Empirical research methods are presented in detail in Chapter 2. These methods help us move beyond commonsense ideas to appreciate the scientific nature of sociology as a discipline that provides answers to important questions.

Part 2: Society and the Self: The Foundations has four chapters that constitute a foundation of sociology as a discipline. Chapter 3 highlights the cultural context of our social experiences and outlines

[1] G. Delanty, Social Science: Philosophical and Methodological Foundations, 2nd ed. (Buckingham: Open University Press, 2005); G. Delanty, "Sociology," in Blackwell Encyclopedia of Sociology, ed. G. Ritzer (Malden, MA: Blackwell, 2007), http://www.blackwellreference.com.

[2] C.W. Mills, The Sociological Imagination, 40th anniversary ed., ed. C.W. Mills (New York, NY: Oxford University Press, 2000), 3–24.

[3] C.H. Persell, K.M. Pfeiffer, and A. Syed, "What Should Students Understand After Taking Introduction to Sociology?" Teaching Sociology 35, no. 4 (2007): 300–14.

the basic components of culture. Chapter 4 addresses the role of socialization in the emergence of our own identities and the identities we ascribe to others, as well as the social structure within which socialization occurs. Chapter 5 discusses social inequality as a challenge for many people and as a stable feature of Canadian society. In the 21st century, the mass media are a key source of information and have come to play a central role in connecting members of society to one another. So this section of the textbook ends with a chapter about the mass media, including a critical look at how they shape our perceptions.

Part 3: The Micro and Macro of Our Everyday Experiences has six chapters that focus on various aspects of students' own experiences. Chapters 7 and 8 consider the implications of sex, gender, and sexualities, as well as ethnicity, for who we are and who others say we are, as well as for socioeconomic status, discrimination, and family life. Chapter 9 helps us appreciate the influence, diversity, and changing nature of Canadian families. Chapter 10 focuses on the various ways we come to know what is "true"—through religion, science, and the modern education system—and the ways in which all three are socially constructed. Chapter 11 explores the myriad ways that people (including ourselves) are subjected to measures of social control on a daily basis, such that we are identified as deviant—sometimes in noncriminal ways, other times in criminal ways. Chapter 12 describes patterns of health and illness, with an emphasis on "lifestyle" factors and social determinants of health, as well as the prevention and treatment of illness in the broader context of health care systems.

Part 4: Our Changing World discusses the importance of collective action, social movements, and globalization for effecting widespread change. Chapter 13 discusses social change as brought about by various forms of collective behaviour and social movements. Chapter 14 focuses on ecological issues and environmental sociology as part of a global call to action for sustainable development. Chapter 15 describes historical precursors to globalization; outlines technological, economic, political, cultural, and social characteristics of globalization; and assesses the relative merits and drawbacks of globalization.

UNDERLYING THEMES

- *The impetus for social action.* All introductory sociology textbooks mention C. Wright Mills's concept of the *sociological imagination.* However, they tend to treat the sociological imagination as an end in itself rather than as a means to an end. When Mills spoke of the sociological imagination, he emphasized its centrality in creating informed and active citizens. By focusing on the sociological imagination and social action, this textbook provides the impetus for students to become more socially aware and more active as citizens in their communities, in society, and in the world. Whether they become parents, teachers, community league soccer coaches, entrepreneurs, or social activists trying to create meaningful social change, students will see the value in utilizing their own sociological imaginations.
- *The prevalence of social inequality.* From the stratification of Canadian society into distinct and unequal social classes to the differential treatment of men and women based on socially constructed gender differences, this book teaches students about the centrality of social inequality. Throughout, we emphasize how social inequality is built into Canadian society and how various processes and structures lead to its reproduction in subsequent generations.
- *The socially constructed nature of society.* Whether we are debating how to define the family, how to describe deviance, how to measure poverty, or even how many sexes exist, this book highlights ways in which key concepts we tend to take for granted are actually social constructions contingent on specific historical contexts and the needs or interests of particular groups.
- *Ways to engage students and instructors.* Students need to see the relevance of sociology in their everyday lives as well as how this translates into related careers. Similarly, instructors need to find ways to embed sociological concepts in students' interests and course curriculum paths. We include particular pedagogical features to help bring sociology alive; we then translate social issues from theory into practice and finally into the public and personal domains. A variety of boxes are included to help students and instructors see the links between individuals and society and the overall applicability of the discipline of sociology as a means for facilitating social change. These boxes highlight films, music lyrics, websites, media stories, first-hand testimonies, and the actions of individuals or groups.

- *Built-in skill development tools for students.* In each chapter, we begin with a set of learning objectives and outcomes and end with a chapter summary that refers back to those objectives and outcomes. Throughout the chapter, indicators draw students' attention to which learning objective is being addressed in any given section. We also provide Time to Review questions throughout each chapter (with answers provided online as part of MindTap) so that students and instructors can gauge how well the main points are understood before moving on to a new section. We end each chapter with a set of recommended resources (readings, films, Internet resources) and critical reflection questions.

CHAPTER HIGHLIGHTS AND WHAT'S NEW TO THIS EDITION

A key change in the third edition is that in all chapters, a critical thinking question (*Think Outside the Box*) has been added to the Critical Thinking in Action box, as well as the other toolkit boxes: Sociology in My Life, Sociology in My Community, and Sociology in Practice. These questions enable students to engage more deeply with the material, and instructors might use the questions to facilitate class discussion or as short written assignments. For users of MindTap, sample answers or points to consider are provided for each of these questions. Listed below are some of the topics and issues covered in specific chapters along with descriptions of key changes integrated into the third edition.

Chapter 1 Seeing and Acting Through the Lens of Sociology

- What is sociology?
- What can I do with a degree in sociology?
- Comparing sociology and other disciplines
- The value of the sociological imagination
- The beginner's guide to critical thinking

NEW TO THE THIRD EDITION . . .

This chapter introduces the idea of the sociological toolkit. Just as a hammer and a saw enable an individual to build a shed in the backyard, empirical research methods, sociological theories, and critical thinking enable students to develop their sociological imaginations. The chapter has been updated to include a discussion of Peter Berger's emphasis on seeing the "strange in the familiar" and the "general in the particular," as well as expanded material on Canadian feminist scholar Dorothy Smith and a new Sociology in Words box (When Is the Time to "Commit Sociology"?). The chapter continues to emphasize research on critical thinking, which shows that most students enter university with lower order thinking skills and that a significant number graduate without having had sufficient opportunities to develop higher order thinking skills. Critical thinking skills require practice, and this chapter outlines for students how this textbook will give them opportunities for that practice.

Chapter 2: Applying Sociological Research Methods

- Goals of sociological research
- Steps for conducting sociological research
- Ethical conduct for research involving humans
- Distinguishing between qualitative and quantitative methods

NEW TO THE THIRD EDITION . . .

This chapter has been updated to include new studies demonstrating the array of approaches used in sociology (e.g., evaluation research, empowerment research, decolonization research, and participatory action research). It now includes current research on social media (e.g., Facebook, Instagram), distracted driving (texting), organized crime, fear of cancer recurrence, and rights involving end-of-life circumstances.

Chapter 3: "I Am Canadian": What Is "Canadian" Culture?

- Language as a precursor to shared understandings
- Norms as regulators of shared behaviours
- Values as shared ideas
- Popular culture and high culture

NEW TO THE THIRD EDITION . . .

Additional information on language diversity and usage in Canada is provided, including recent attempts to preserve Cree via immersive schooling, the use of unique "Canadianisms," and the incorporation of gender-neutral pronouns in public institutions. This chapter also expands on cultural relativism and multicultural debates. including Quebec's Bill 62, "An Act to foster adherence to State religious neutrality." Finally, at the request of reviewers, information on culture shock and cultural omnivores has been introduced.

Chapter 4: Socialization: The Self and Social Identity

- The self and its connection to socialization and social interaction
- Primary agents of socialization
- Master status and the looking-glass self
- Components of the social structure
- Social institutions and bureaucracy

NEW TO THE THIRD EDITION . . .

At the request of reviewers, a new section on socialization and genetic influences has been included, with an emphasis on how epigenetics blur the distinction between nature and nurture influences on the developing self. Additional information is provided on agents of socialization, including what effective parenting and schooling entail and how peers contribute to bullying. New information is also included on child rights and child welfare in Canada.

Chapter 5: Social Inequality in Canadian Society

- Connections between social stratification and social inequality
- Slavery in the past and human trafficking in the present
- Class structure and social mobility
- Blaming the poor for their plight
- Consequences of social inequality

NEW TO THE THIRD EDITION . . .

Updated information and statistics are provided throughout this chapter on stratification, wealth, net worth, poverty, and poverty reduction, with an emphasis on Canada's income-based class structure. At the request of reviewers, the sections on measuring poverty and Canada's poor are expanded. In addition to the low-income cutoff, information is provided on two other measures of poverty (the Low-Income Measure and the Market Basket Measure) and more information is included on the intersectionality of age, gender, and race.

Chapter 6: Mass Media: Living in the Electronic Age

- Media prevalence and forms
- "Being alone together" in public spaces
- Agenda setting: the media are not neutral
- How the media shapes our perceptions
- Media literacy: thinking critically about the media

NEW TO THE THIRD EDITION . . .

In the 21st century, the media are in a constant state of evolution. So in the third edition, this chapter provides important updates regarding the nature of contemporary media (e.g., media consumption, media concentration, and media violence, as well as termination of cable and satellite subscriptions, increased prevalence of simultaneous media, Bitcoin's latest status, popular apps, and the prevalence of augmented reality). At the request of reviewers, additional information is included on privacy and regulation and on the repercussions of continual online connectivity with others.

Chapter 7: Sex, Gender, and Sexualities: Deconstructing Dualisms

- Elite discourses of sex, gender, and sexuality
- Spectrums of sex, gender, and sexualities
- The educational, occupational, economic, and familial consequences of being born male or female

NEW TO THE THIRD EDITION . . .

At the request of reviewers, this chapter is updated to include a discussion of Alfred Kinsey's work on sexuality as a continuum, and the concepts cisgender, gender non-conformity, and pansexuality are introduced. There is new material about non-traditional gender socialization by parents and the resistance they often encounter and, conversely, the way that some parents' identities are threatened when they are faced with raising a gender non-conforming child. The section on the household division of labour is expanded to include discussions of domestic outsourcing, younger couples in cohabitational relationships, and LGBTQ couples. Statistics on gender performance in education, gender segregation (in education and occupation), and gendered economic experiences are updated. At the request of reviewers, the section on theories of gender is expanded to include a discussion of Indigenous feminisms, intersectionality and the matrix of domination, and more material on Judith Butler's work. In addition to revised boxes, there are several new boxes as well: movies and television shows that deconstruct dualisms; Plan International's "Because I am a Girl" campaign; and how gender non-conformity is supported with Bill C-16.

Chapter 8: Race and Ethnicity: Defining Ourselves and Others

- Ethnicity, race, racialization, and visible minorities
- Contemporary ethnic patterns
- Bicultural adaptation patterns
- Media frames of ethnicity
- Prejudice and discrimination

NEW TO THE THIRD EDITION . . .

In the third edition, the statistics on current ethnic patterns, the economic experiences of Indigenous people and immigrants, and hate crimes are updated. New examples of discrimination include the Saskatoon police starlight tours, police carding of racialized groups, and the hashtag activism of Black Lives Matter. In addition to revised boxes, there are three new boxes: Spencer Wells's TED talk ("A Family Tree for Humanity") and the affiliated genographic project of the National Geographic Society; a CBC documentary about bicultural youth in Canada; and the macro-level implications of using the term "Indigenous" in place of "Aboriginal."

Chapter 9: Canadian Families: Past, Present, and Future

- Contemporary trends in Canadian families
- Is the family declining?
- The commodification of children arising from new reproductive technologies
- The effects of colonization on Aboriginal families

NEW TO THE THIRD EDITION . . .

In addition to updated statistics on contemporary trends in Canadian families, the chapter includes expanded discussions of family violence and social exchange theory (within the context of dating and relationships between adult children and their parents, especially when adult children live in the family home). New examples include the money that families spend on their pets and debates over when it is appropriate to use reproductive technologies. In addition to revised boxes, there are several new boxes: parallels between the overrepresentation of Indigenous children in the child welfare system today and residential schooling in the past; agencies that help newcomer families with parenting; and Parenting After Separation (PAS) courses that are required of divorcing parents in some provinces.

Chapter 10: Learning What is "True": Religion, Science, and Education

- The origins and meaning of "truth"
- Implications of religious affiliation
- The transition to scientific truth
- Scientific knowledge as constructed
- The role of education in modern society

NEW TO THE THIRD EDITION . . .

The chapter includes new examples, such as Stephen Harper's and Donald Trump's muzzling of government scientists and reduced funding for climate change research and epigenetics as a paradigm shift affecting sociology. There is new material on debates over religion in public schools, current research questioning whether religiosity is associated with greater philanthropy, expanded discussion of Indigenous education and curriculum, and updated statistics on religious patterns. In addition to revised boxes, there are several new boxes: Indigenous science, petitions for an inclusive education in Quebec, and the group People for Education.

Chapter 11: Social Control, Deviance, and Crime

- Are you socially controlled?
- Social control and deviance
- Forms and patterns of crime
- Racialization within the criminal justice system
- Theories of deviance and crime

NEW TO THE THIRD EDITION . . .

The concept of social control serves as the frame for this chapter, emphasizing the myriad ways in which we are all subjected to social control on a daily basis—and correspondingly, the ways in which we are all socially typed as deviant in some way. In the third edition, new examples include WannaCry ransomware, extremist groups, and the carding of black youth in Toronto. Material on summary and indictable offenses, crime rates, crime severity, and empirical applications of various theories to criminal and non-criminal behaviour is updated. In addition to revised boxes, there are several new boxes: family violence and restorative justice; a critique of imprisonment as a form of punishment (using the United States as an illustration); and the youth group Jack.org (which works to end the stigmatization of mental illness).

Chapter 12: Health and Illness: Is It "Lifestyle" or Something More?

- Patterns of health and illness
- "Lifestyle" behaviours and health
- Social inequality and health
- Health care systems

NEW TO THE THIRD EDITION . . .

There are extensive updates to statistics on causes of death, patterns of morbidity and mortality, tobacco use, alcohol use, diet, physical activity, health inequalities, food insecurity, and health care expenditures. New topics include the illness identities of children with cancer and youth with eating disorders as well as privileged medical discourses involving physician and nurse power over health care assistants. In addition to revised boxes, there are two new boxes: the causes and implications of new viruses spreading to humans from other animals and the World Health Organization's recommendations for controlling the impact of the tobacco life cycle (from cultivation to disposal) on the environment and human health.

Chapter 13: Social Change: Collective Behaviour and Social Movements

- Collective behaviour in crowds
- Rumours, gossip, and urban legends
- Widespread panic and moral panic
- Claims and claims making
- Types of social movements

NEW TO THE THIRD EDITION . . .

This chapter has been extensively updated to provide recent examples of various forms of collective behaviour (e.g., Pride Parades, new fads and fashions, disasters [oil spills, Fort McMurray fires]) and moral panic (Islamic extremist groups). The section on social movements has been expanded to include current research on recent social movements (e.g., the Arab Spring and Winter, People Against Distracted Driving, and Idle No More).

Chapter 14: "Going Green": Environmental Sociology

- Social factors posing environmental challenges
- Growing awareness of environmental issues
- Strategies for better environmental choices

NEW TO THE THIRD EDITION . . .

This chapter includes important updates to environmental issues and patterns of environmental degradation. A number of concepts are clarified and expanded on (e.g., the ecological footprint, ecological overshoot, and climate change), and new information is introduced on how individuals and members of society can contribute to sustainable growth in the future, including the United Nations' 17 Sustainable Development Goals.

Chapter 15: Globalization: The Interconnected World

- Neoliberalism and its implications
- The vision of globalization and its reality: the good, the bad, and the ugly
- Global justice movements

NEW TO THE THIRD EDITION . . .

In this chapter, there are several new examples, such as the softwood lumber dispute, global terrorist networks, the downward transfer of power from nation-states to alliances of cities working toward common goals (such as sustainability), and the global assembly line involved in manufacturing the iPhone. New topics include global child labour and the 2030 Agenda for Sustainable Development. In addition to revised boxes, there are several new boxes: the five flagship programs of the International Labour Organization, the organization Global Citizen, and the uneasy alliances between government leaders and the global banking industry.

ANCILLARIES

Our textbook has several supplements for instructors and students.

INSTRUCTOR RESOURCES

The **Nelson Education Teaching Advantage (NETA)** program delivers research-based instructor resources that promote student engagement and higher order thinking to enable the success of Canadian students and educators. Visit Nelson's **Inspired Instruction** website at nelson.com/inspired/ to find out more about NETA.

The following instructor resources have been created for *Sociology in Action*, Third Edition. Access these ultimate tools for customizing lectures and presentations at nelson.com/instructor.

NETA Test Bank

This resource was written by Vincent Sacco of Queen's University. It includes over 1100 multiple-choice questions written according to NETA guidelines for effective construction and development of higher order questions. Also included are over 350 true/false questions, 100 short-answer questions, and 100 essay questions.

The NETA Test Bank is available in a new, cloud-based platform. **Nelson Testing Powered by Cognero®** is a secure online testing system that allows instructors to author, edit, and manage test bank content from anywhere Internet access is available. No special installations or downloads are needed, and the desktop-inspired interface, with its drop-down menus and familiar, intuitive tools, allows instructors to create and manage tests with ease. Multiple test versions can be created in an instant, and content can be imported or exported into other systems. Tests can be delivered from a learning management system, the classroom, or wherever an instructor chooses. Nelson Testing Powered by Cognero for *Sociology in Action* can be accessed through nelson.com/instructor.

NETA PowerPoint

Microsoft® PowerPoint® lecture slides for every chapter have been created by Tami Bereska of Grant MacEwan University. There is an average of 25 slides per chapter, many featuring key figures, tables, and photographs from *Sociology in Action*. NETA principles of clear design and engaging content have been incorporated throughout, making it simple for instructors to customize the deck for their courses.

Image Library

This resource consists of digital copies of figures, short tables, and photographs used in the book. Instructors may use these jpegs to customize the NETA PowerPoint or create their own PowerPoint presentations. An Image Library Key describes the images and lists the codes under which the jpegs are saved.

NETA Instructor Guide

This resource was written by Karen Taylor of NorQuest College. The Enriched Instructor's Manual provides strategies for engaging students actively and deeply in the study of sociology. Each chapter addresses key educational concerns, such as typical stumbling blocks students face and how to address them, as well as engagement strategies and assessment tools. "What Can I Do Online" is a new section in each chapter. Our intention is to provide instructors with ideas they may choose to include in their teaching toolkit.

MindTap

Offering personalized paths of dynamic assignments and applications, **MindTap** is a digital learning solution that turns cookie-cutter into cutting-edge, apathy into engagement, and memorizers into higher-level thinkers. MindTap enables students to analyze and apply chapter concepts within relevant assignments, and allows instructors to measure skills and promote better outcomes with ease. A fully online learning solution, MindTap combines all student learning tools—readings, multimedia, activities, and assessments—into a single Learning Path that guides the student through the curriculum. Instructors personalize the experience by customizing the presentation of these learning tools to their students, even seamlessly introducing their own content into the Learning Path.

STUDENT ANCILLARIES

MindTap

Stay organized and efficient with **MindTap**—a single destination with all the course material and study aids you need to succeed. Built-in apps leverage social media and the latest learning technology. For example:

- ReadSpeaker will read the text to you.
- Flashcards are pre-populated to provide you with a jump start for review—or you can create your own.

- You can highlight text and make notes in your MindTap Reader. Your notes will flow into Evernote, the electronic notebook app that you can access anywhere when it's time to study for the exam.
- Self-quizzing allows you to assess your understanding.

Visit nelson.com/student to start using **MindTap**. Enter the Online Access Code from the card included with your text. If a code card is *not* provided, you can purchase instant access at NELSONbrain.com.

ADDITIONAL RESOURCE

MAKING WOMEN COUNT

The Canadian Centre for Policy Alternatives is an independent, member-based research institute that works on various projects of interest to Canadians (e.g., climate change, economic security, seniors care). A current focus is *Making Women Count*, which highlights how gender inequality impacts the economy, politics, and well-being of Canadians. Here you can find publications and news releases about gender inequality, including information on how women continue to bear much of the burden for unpaid and undervalued work. Find out why Victoria is considered the best and Windsor is considered the worst place to live as a woman in Canada based on indicators of economic security, education, health, leadership, and personal security by accessing *Making Women Count* at **https://www.policyalternatives.ca.**

ACKNOWLEDGMENTS

We express our gratitude to the following reviewers, who offered candid opinions and suggestions that helped shaped this third edition of *Sociology in Action: A Canadian Perspective*:

Francis Adu-Febiri, Camosun College

Dawn Anderson, University of Regina

Clayton Cobb, Seneca College

Sara Cumming, Sheridan College

Tara Gauld, Confederation College

Sarah Knudson, University of Saskatchewan

Timothy MacNeill, UOIT

Karen Taylor, NorQuest College

Publishing a textbook is a team effort, and we also wish to acknowledge the support, feedback, and assistance provided by everyone we worked with at Nelson: Leanna MacLean, Publisher; Claire Varley, Marketing Manager; Jennifer Hare, Production Project Manager; Carrie McGregor, Photo and Permissions Researcher; and Holly Dickinson, Copy Editor. We would especially like to acknowledge our Content Manager, Lisa Berland, who had the challenging assignment of keeping two academics on task and within the word limit. It brings to mind the movie *Wonder Boys*, starring Michael Douglas, in which Professor Tripp's manuscript is 1,000 pages, and the book is still not finished—clearly, he needed a good developmental editor!

A question often asked at interviews for academic positions is about the links between research and teaching. It seems that all candidates easily refer to how their research influences their teaching by providing a body of knowledge they can bring to the classroom. Less common are responses that emphasize how teaching influences their research—how much they, as academics, are able to learn from their students. We have learned more from our students than can be easily expressed. Our students, past and present, are the most important part of the team that has created this book. They have inspired us, given us profound ideas at times when our own ideas are in short supply, and shown us how students today *really* learn. The students at Grant MacEwan University, in particular, have shown us the amazing things that can happen when people use their sociological imaginations in their own lives, in their communities, and in the world. Above all, this book is for the students.

About the Authors

Diane G. Symbaluk

Like many students, I found sociology quite by accident. While trying to find a course that would fulfill a Canadian content requirement for a B.Ed. degree en route to a teaching career, I stumbled across an introduction to sociology course advertised with descriptive words such as "people," "society," "families," and "deviance" that sounded interesting. I could never have known then that my tendency to say "don't assume" and "don't take people for granted" underscored the beginnings of the development of my sociological imagination. After completing an Introduction to Sociology, my interest was piqued; I switched to the sociology program, where I earned a B.A., followed by an M.A. and a Ph.D. I went on to teach sociology full-time at Grant MacEwan University, where I continue to teach a range of courses: introductory sociology, social psychology, criminology, and social research methods. I love teaching, and I appreciate my students even more. They have inspired me to write resources that will contribute to their success, including study guides, manuals, Web-based course tools, and especially this textbook. I am also interested in student ratings of instruction and student assessments of instructors' character strengths—the focus of my current research interests. I constantly re-evaluate my initial assumptions of people and social situations while maintaining allegiance to the Chinese proverb: He who says it cannot be done should not interrupt the person who is doing it.

Tami M. Bereska

I began university as a psychology major. I had never even heard of sociology. But then I made my discovery. A discipline in which you could study families, teenagers, television shows, popular music, crime, and white supremacists—wow! Who could have ever believed that learning could be so interesting? Sociology grabbed me and has never let me go. Since obtaining my M.A. and Ph.D. in sociology, I've studied all sorts of interesting topics: adult and adolescent series romance novels (e.g., *Harlequin*, *Sweet Valley High*), what being a "real man" means in young adult novels for boys, and representations of Scientology in movies and on TV. Popular culture, deviance, and youth fascinate me. Along with my love of sociology is a love for teaching undergraduate students. I had my first opportunity to give a university lecture as a teaching assistant while working on my M.A. My supervisor had to be away, and he asked me to lecture in his Social Organization class, with 180 students. As someone who had always hated giving presentations in class, I was terrified. But 10 minutes into my lecture, I knew this was what I wanted to do with my life. I've since taught courses ranging from deviance to social psychology, with class sizes as small as four and as large as 400. The pleasure I derive from connecting with students has also led me to write textbooks—first, a book on deviance and social control and now this book, one that will bring the fascinating world of sociology to those students who, like me, may have never even heard of sociology.

ESB Professional/Shutterstock

01 PART

Practising Sociology: Your Sociological Toolkit

CHAPTER 01

Seeing and Acting Through the Lens of Sociology

Arthimedes/Shutterstock

It can be said that the first wisdom of sociology is this—things are not what they seem.

(Berger, 1963, p. 23)

LEARNING OBJECTIVES & OUTCOMES

After completing this chapter, students should be able to do the following:

LO1 Describe the bidirectional relationship between individual choices and larger social forces.

LO2 Define "sociology" and identify the role of the sociological imagination.

LO3 Elaborate on the similarities and differences between sociology and other related disciplines.

LO4 List and describe the tools that are used to develop the sociological imagination.

LO5 Contrast positivist, interpretive, and critical approaches to theorizing.

LO6 Outline the core assumptions of the functionalist, conflict, symbolic interactionist, feminist, and postmodern perspectives.

LO7 Identify what critical thinking is and explain its importance.

LO8 Describe the four different ways that sociology can be practised.

LO1 THINGS ARE NOT WHAT THEY SEEM

"I'll believe it when I see it!" How many times have you heard someone say this or used that phrase yourself? Although we often come to trust in what we can see for ourselves, sociology asks us *not* to automatically trust what we see. Consider, for example, a television screen like the one in the photo below. If you were asked what you see when you look at that screen, your initial response might be, "I see a road." But if you took a closer look—presuming that there is more than meets the eye—you might see something very different. Walk up to a television screen and look at it from a centimetre or two away, and now you'll realize that what first looked like a road is really rows and columns of pixels, tiny squares of coloured light. If you looked even more closely, you would see that what first appeared to be a dark grey road is really a combination of red, green, and blue pixels. *Things are not what they seem.*

Now shift your attention to yourself and to the clothes you wore to class today. Initially, you might say personal choice led you to wear those particular clothes. But if you now look at your classmates, you can see that many of them are wearing clothes that are very similar to yours (e.g., jeans and a T-shirt). You and many other people have made a similar choice today, suggesting that there is something more than just individual preference operating here. If I were to go on to ask you why you are a university or college student, you might give me a similar answer—personal choice. And indeed, unless someone registered you as a student against your will, physically dragged you to class this morning, and tied you into your chair, it most certainly *is* your choice. But remember, there is more than first meets the eye. If you examine these circumstances more closely, you will start to realize that just as pixels of coloured light underlie the televised image

Ruslan Ivantsov/Shutterstock

If we look closely, we can see that there is more than meets the eye in this image.

of a road, an array of social factors and experiences has contributed to your choice to become a university or college student. When you begin to consider the ways that society shapes your personal choices, you are starting to practise sociology by seeing the **strange in the familiar** (Berger, 1963).

When examining your choice to become a student, you might first consider specific people who influenced your decision, such as the family members and friends who supported, encouraged, or demanded that option. You could then go on to look at some of the more personal social and economic resources that enabled you to become a university or college student—a student loan, a Registered Education Saving Plan (RESP), or parents who support you. The personal resources you have available are important factors that underlie your ability to pursue a postsecondary education. But using a sociological perspective requires you to analyze even beyond your own family, friends, and resources. In much the same way that many of your classmates chose to wear similar clothing to you, many others have elected to attend university or college alongside you. In the 2014–2015 academic year, more than 2 million students were registered in undergraduate programs in Canadian universities and colleges (Statistics Canada, 2016). That means more than 2 million people—with different families, sets of friends, and personal resources—all made the same personal choice that year! Explaining this fact requires you to extend your sociological gaze beyond your own life to larger sociocultural and socioeconomic forces affecting many people simultaneously, or seeing the **general in the particular** (Berger, 1963).

Strange in the familiar: Instead of assuming that people's actions are determined solely by personal choice, looking for the ways that society shapes those choices.

General in the particular: The broader social patterns that are reflected in the actions of individuals.

Norms: Society's expectations for how we are supposed to act, think, and look.

Normative: Behaviours, appearances, and thoughts that correspond to society's norms.

Micro level: The level of individual experiences and choices.

Macro level: The level of broader social forces.

Agency: People's capacity to make choices, which then have an impact on other people and on the society in which they live.

For instance, after the worldwide economic recession in 2008 that limited job opportunities, undergraduate enrollments increased by 4.1 percent in 2009 and by another 3.6 percent in 2010 over the previous year; economic downturns motivate people to improve their educational qualifications and skills (Association of Universities and Colleges of Canada, 2009). The impact of the economy on postsecondary enrollment is readily apparent. But more subtle influences on the decisions we make come from society's expectations, or **norms**. By virtue of growing up in a specific family in a particular society at a certain time in history, we learn how we are supposed to act. Whether or not we actually behave in accordance with those norms, we are still aware of what those expectations are.

In Canada today, a postsecondary education is **normative** in that it corresponds to norms about the kind of education people need before entering the workforce. In contrast, had you been a young Canadian woman in the 1950s, a university education would *not* have been normative; instead, society's expectations were that you should marry young, have children, and be a full-time homemaker. Sometimes society's norms are so powerful that they influence formalized rules, such as policies and even the law. For example, if you were a Jewish Canadian before the end of the Second World War, the doors of many universities would have been closed to you, regardless of your academic ability and desire to pursue a university education. Similarly, if you were an Indigenous person in the early 20th century, the residential school that you would have been forced to attend by law would not have given you the education necessary to gain entrance to a university. And although the opportunity for a university education is available to everyone in the 21st century, sociologists point out that the ability to take advantage of that opportunity is not equally available to all (see *Sociology in My Life*).

The essence of sociology is this connection between individual experiences and larger social forces that exist outside the individual (see *Figure 1.1*). This is also known as the relationship between the **micro level** and the **macro level**. Thus far, we have examined ways that larger social forces (the macro level) influence individual experiences (the micro level). However, the relationship is bidirectional, in that your personal choices also have an impact on the people around you, your community, and your workplace—what sociologists refer to as **agency**. When enough people make similar choices or acquire support for particular decisions, the macro level is affected—either the status quo is supported or social change occurs. Social movements can occur, and school practices and policies, workplace culture and policies, social programming, legislation, and larger cultural norms can all be affected.

For instance, when the authors of this book were in elementary school in the mid-1970s, it was rare for children to eat lunch at school; children either had to go home for lunch (regardless of whether there was an adult there to supervise them), or they walked to a

SOCIOLOGY IN MY LIFE

THE IMPACT OF LIFE CHANCES

Think about your own background for a moment—the neighbourhood you lived in while growing up, your parents' jobs, your lifestyle. If the two photos below represent two ends of a continuum, where would you locate your own childhood background—closer to the photo on the left (i.e., extreme poverty) or to the photo on the right (i.e., attending a private school)? Do individuals who grow up in these very different types of neighbourhoods have the same freedom to go to university? Is that opportunity equally available to both of them? Think about the resources it takes to go to university or college and the obstacles that can prevent it. Perhaps you enjoyed similar resources or encountered similar obstacles in your path. Max Weber (1864–1920), one of the founders of the social sciences as a distinct area of study, referred to these varying opportunities that people face as **life chances** (1978). Social stratification, inequality, race, ethnicity, and gender are just some of the factors that affect one's life chances. You will learn more about all of these factors in later chapters.

Think Outside the Box: What other areas of life, in addition to education, might be affected by the life chances reflected in the above photos?

Discha-AS/Shutterstock

SpeedKingz/Shutterstock

FIGURE 1.1

Personal Choices and Social Forces

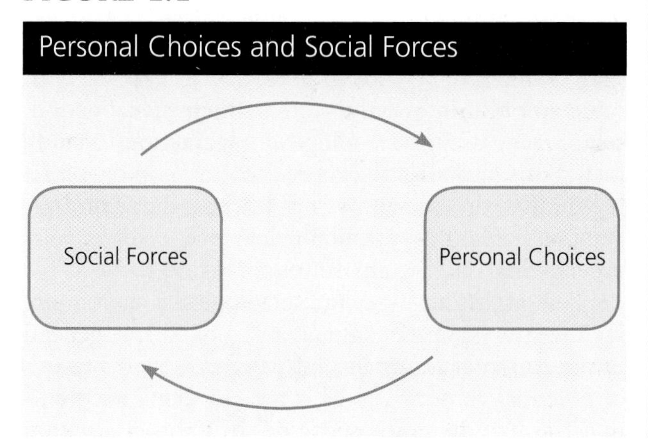

nearby care provider's place. If there was an unusual circumstance (e.g., the caregiver had to be at an appointment), then the parent would write a note to the teacher and request that the child be permitted to eat lunch at school that day under the teacher's supervision or be sent to a classmate's home. Less than a decade later, processes and procedures had been developed around the need for lunch-hour supervision. Why did such a dramatic change occur in such a relatively short time? Because economic and social factors changed the lives of parents, and then the changing lives of parents made changes in school practices necessary.

Life chances: The opportunities an individual has in life based on various factors, including stratification, inequality, race, ethnicity, and gender.

The assumption that mothers were at home to make lunch for their children was based on family patterns that existed in previous decades, when most middle-class married women were full-time homemakers. This began to change in the 1960s and 1970s, when more married mothers began to enter the paid labour force. The changing choices of parents elicited changes in the environment outside the family. But at the same time, larger sociocultural factors were contributing to parental choices. More mothers were entering the workforce because of changes in the economy that necessitated dual incomes for many families, as well as the influence of the women's movement, which emphasized the importance of female equality. The media also played a role in the evolution of a "risk society" through their coverage of missing children cases, which contributed to growing concerns about children being sent home unsupervised.

Thus, when we look at people's experiences, the micro level and the macro level are intertwined. Recognizing the myriad ways in which they are intertwined requires using something sociologists distinctively call the "sociological imagination."

TIME TO REVIEW

- What do sociologists mean when they say that "things are not what they seem," and what are some examples?
- What type of relationship exists between the micro level and the macro level? Provide some examples of this relationship.

LO2 WHAT IS SOCIOLOGY?

Sociology is the systematic study of society using the sociological imagination. The connection between the micro level and the macro level is the essence of the sociological perspective. C. Wright Mills (1916–1962) defined the discipline of sociology on the basis of the **sociological imagination**, which involved looking for the "intersections of biography and history" (1959/2000, p. 7), tracing the linkages between individual experiences and larger sociocultural forces. For example, we can use the sociological imagination to explore body modification. If we consider why a particular person gets a tattoo or a piercing, the answer may tell us something specific about that one individual, such as that he or she is a risk taker. But when we consider the nature of body modification in general, we learn about larger social relationships. We learn about workplace norms, in that people must hide their body art in certain workplaces but not others (Timming, 2015). We also learn about interpersonal relationships, such as in the historical and contemporary practice of memorial tattoos (DeMello, 2016). Similarly, we learn about norms governing gender. Women with tattoos are perceived more negatively than men with tattoos, especially if they are middle-aged (rather than younger) and their tattoos have masculine designs (Musambira, Raymond, & Hastings, 2016). We identify allegiances to certain subcultures since tattoos can indicate membership in particular gangs. We even learn about the ideologies of subcultures—for example, a "Poison-Free" tattoo on a member of the Straightedge subculture signifies commitment to a substance-free lifestyle (Straightedge Worldwide, 2017).

Sociology: The systematic study of society using the sociological imagination.

Sociological imagination: The ability to perceive the interconnections between individual experiences and larger sociocultural forces.

Mills (1959/2000) did not see the sociological imagination as an intellectual tool to be used solely by sociologists (or even by students in sociology classes); he proposed that society as a whole *needed* its citizens to look for the links between the macro and micro levels. In fact, Mills criticized many of his fellow sociologists for spending their time intellectualizing in the ivory towers of academia and for not assuming any personal responsibility for improving society. The sociological imagination is not just about *thinking*; it is also about *action*. That action might be at the level of your everyday life, where paying attention to the relationship between individual choices and larger social forces will make you a more informed parent, voter, teacher, office manager, or team member. But it might also be at a more macro level of social action, trying to improve some aspect of your community or even society as a whole (see *Sociology in Words*).

Berger (1963) describes sociologists as professional people watchers who are gripped by curiosity whenever they find themselves "in front of a closed door behind which are human voices" (p. 21). In order to build knowledge and facilitate social action, sociologists use the sociological imagination to study just about anything that is related to people—social inequality, the economy, politics, media, families, gender, sexualities, ethnicity, deviance, crime, social movements, and the environment, just to name a few.

The ability to use your sociological imagination, see the strange in the familiar, and look for the general in the particular translates into a considerable breadth of potential careers. Unlike some university programs that train students for specific jobs upon graduation

SOCIOLOGY IN WORDS

WHEN IS THE TIME TO "COMMIT SOCIOLOGY"?

What are the root causes of terrorism? This question was asked by Justin Trudeau in April 2013. He asked it because of two recent incidents—a terrorist bombing at the Boston Marathon and the arrest of two men for conspiring to attack a Via Rail train in Canada. Prime Minister Stephen Harper criticized Trudeau for raising this question, saying, "... this is not a time to commit sociology" (Fitzpatrick, 2013). In Harper's view, understanding the causes of terrorism was of less value than apprehending and punishing individual terrorists. Of course, since that time, there have been many more terrorist attacks in countries around the world, such as Kenya, Iraq, France, and England.

One year later, Harper made a similar point regarding another social issue. In response to demands for a national inquiry into missing and murdered Indigenous women, he "urged Canadians away from understanding missing and murdered aboriginal women as a 'sociological phenomenon' and instead suggested Canadians 'view it as a crime'" (Kaye & Béland, 2014). Once again, he argued that understanding the reasons why Indigenous women are overrepresented as victims of violence was of less value than apprehending and punishing individual criminals.

Why is it important to "commit sociology"? Fletcher (1971) argued that sociology is of "central importance in and for our time" (p. 5). Several decades later, his argument is stronger than ever:

> We would like to eliminate from society war, poverty, crime and delinquency.... We would like to improve matters; to remove these obstacles to social justice; and would therefore like to know the underlying *causes* of these social facts. Then, on the basis of this knowledge, if we could get it, we would like to formulate effective social policies and institute political reforms.... [We must] establish reliable knowledge *on the basis of which to act*. For we quickly learn that we can only effectively change the nature of society ... *if we know what that nature is*.*

*R. Fletcher, *The making of sociology: A study of sociological theory*, Vol. 1. London, UK: Thomas Nelson and Sons, pg. 36, 1971.

"I love our lunches out here, but I always get the feeling that we're being watched."

© Love, Jason, jlvn685, CartoonStock.com

(e.g., teacher, accountant), an education in sociology provides its graduates with a knowledge base and a set of skills that apply to a variety of careers (beyond sociology professor). Graduates have a deep understanding of community, social, and cultural issues; knowledge of group dynamics, public policies, and community development; skills in gathering and analyzing data; and the ability to problem solve and think critically. Graduates may work with clients of community or social service agencies, develop or administer programs for community agencies or governments, conduct research in the public or private sector, and much more.

LO3 COMPARING SOCIOLOGY AND OTHER DISCIPLINES

As you may have already noticed in some of your classes, similar topics are covered in different disciplines. For example, you may have studied families in a psychology, anthropology, or even political science course—and you will also learn about families in your sociology course. Many of the topics studied by sociologists are also analyzed by researchers in other social science disciplines—culture and cultural variations (anthropology and cultural studies), political forces (political science and development studies), occupational and economic forces (economics and political economy), families (family studies and social work), and media (psychology, cultural studies and communications). What are the differences, then, between sociology and the other social science disciplines?

Scholars within the discipline of sociology were not the first to study society. Arab scholar Ibn Khaldun's work (1332–1406) is recognized as a significant forerunner to sociology. He studied the structures and processes of power in different societies (ranging from desert tribes to nations). He proposed that as societies grew in size, labour was no longer used for survival but rather for the pursuit of luxury for society's wealthy and powerful (Weiss, 1995). Sociology as a discipline later emerged in a particular context of place and time. It can be traced to a historical period that includes the French Revolution (1789–1799) and the accompanying Enlightenment. This was a time of rapid social, political, and economic change—cities increased in size, there was the transition to a wage economy, absolute monarchies were threatened, the power of religion declined, and the power of science grew. For some more politically and socially active scholars, these social, political, and ideological changes illustrated that ordinary citizens could create large-scale transformations in society. For other scholars, the question was one of how it was possible for society not to crumble in the midst of these massive changes. Intellectuals sought to understand and explain social change and its consequences.

Auguste Comte (1798–1857), who coined the term *sociology*, suggested that empirical research and theory should be used in pursuit of this goal. The sociological perspective developed out of philosophy, economics, history, psychology, and law. Many of the well-known scholars who are referred to as "sociologists" because their work is central to sociology (and whose work will be presented at various points in this book) were, in fact, not "sociologists" by training. For example, Max Weber's training was in economic history, Karl Marx's in philosophy, and Émile Durkheim's in educational thought and philosophy. With that knowledge, they sought to understand social change and what made "society" possible in the face of change.

The sociological perspective emerged in the 19th century; the formation of distinct disciplines is a more recent phenomenon. In the 20th century, distinct boundaries were constructed around bodies of knowledge and the subject matter of specific disciplines (Delanty, 2005, 2007). Thus, while historians studied the past, anthropologists studied premodern societies, political scientists analyzed structures of governance, and economists studied the production and consumption of goods and services. The attention of scholars within each of these disciplines was focused on a certain part of society. In contrast, sociologists studied *all* of these parts of society while using a wider range of research methodologies and theories (Delanty, 2005, 2007). Hence, sociology can be thought of as the most *comprehensive* of the social sciences.

However, sociology goes a step further and proposes that society is more than a compilation of history plus government plus the economy (and so on). There is a web of interconnectedness *among* its parts—they interact in particular ways, and the nature of that interaction contributes to any social phenomenon, such as social problems (e.g., terrorism and environmental destruction) or even more mundane aspects of everyday life (e.g., tattooing and social media use). What governs a sociological approach is an analysis of these interactions and an emphasis on tracing the linkages between individual experiences and larger sociocultural forces.

Although distinct disciplines were formed in the early 20th century, the 21st century is characterized by greater *postdisciplinarity* (Urry, 2000). This means that the differences among disciplines are less apparent. For example, today sociology and anthropology both study premodern and modern societies, although in varied ways (Delanty, 2005, 2007).

In addition to blurred boundaries between disciplines, the 21st century is also characterized by greater *interdisciplinarity* (Delanty, 2005, 2007), where scholars in a variety of disciplines work together to better understand social phenomena. For instance, globalization is not associated with a specific discipline but rather brings together diverse groups of scholars, including sociologists, economists, and political scientists (you will learn more about globalization in Chapter 15). Interdisciplinarity has created new disciplines as well, such as women's studies, cultural studies, and family studies. University departments that are affiliated with these areas of study will often include faculty members who are sociologists, economists, political scientists, historians, social psychologists, and philosophers.

TIME TO REVIEW

- What is sociology, and what is the role of the sociological imagination?
- Who should be using the sociological imagination, and for what purpose?
- How is sociology related to other disciplines?

LO4 BUILDING YOUR SOCIOLOGICAL IMAGINATION: YOUR SOCIOLOGICAL TOOLKIT

If the sociological imagination is the foundation of sociology, and if it is necessary for effective social action from your own personal micro level to society's (or the world's) macro level, where does it come from? In the same way that you need a variety of tools to build a shed in your backyard (e.g., hammer and saw), several tools, when used in an array of settings, will enable you to develop your sociological imagination: empirical research methods, sociological theories, and critical thinking.

EMPIRICAL RESEARCH METHODS

As was pointed out earlier, "reliable knowledge" (Fletcher, 1971, p. 36) must serve as the basis of social action. **Empirical methods** are used to create that knowledge. Sociological research methods are empirical because, through direct observation of the social world, they generate findings that can be verified by other members of the academic community. In Chapter 2, you will learn more about the steps in the sociological research process and the systematic procedures that comprise its empirical methods.

LO5 SOCIOLOGICAL THEORIZING

The data gathered using empirical methods are explained using sociological theories. Sociological theorizing was central to explaining changes during the French Revolution and continues to be crucial to understanding and explaining society.

A **theory** is a set of propositions intended to explain a fact or a phenomenon. Theorizing can be thought of as "puzzle-building" (Bengston et al., 2005, p. 5), trying to fit the pieces of some social phenomenon together in order to reveal a cohesive picture. There are three different approaches to theorizing: *positivist, interpretive,* and *critical* (White, Klein, & Martin, 2015).

Positivist approaches stem from the natural sciences and have an interest in objective *explanation and prediction.* In the social sciences, such approaches are used to examine relationships between variables in an effort to learn more about how society works, enabling subsequent improvements in the social environment (Ashley & Orenstein, 2001). For example, knowledge of factors that contribute to hate crimes can lead to the development of more effective prevention and intervention efforts. In contrast, interpretive theorizing and critical theorizing reject the positivist assumption that there are objective "laws" governing the way society works. Instead, they emphasize the cultural and historical specificity of all processes.

Interpretive approaches focus on *understanding*—the ways that people come to understand themselves, others, and the world around them. They presume that human beings are "self-interpreting animals" (Taylor, 1985, p. 45), constructed and shaped through culture. Here, the goal of sociology is to describe the role culture plays in creating people and societies and how people come to think about their positions within that culture and their relations with other people. For instance, interpretive theorizing might explore what masculinity means to men who have been convicted of hate crimes.

Critical approaches explore the role that *power* plays in social processes, the reason why some people's understandings of the world become dominant (such as through being reflected in legislation); it then ties that knowledge to *emancipation*—empowering subordinated groups in society. For example, critical theorizing might analyze how members of certain social groups are subordinated in society in many ways, including through being victimized by hate crimes—and emphasize the importance of changing society in order to end that subordination.

Positivist, interpretive, and critical approaches to theorizing give rise to a number of specific theoretical perspectives (or frameworks) in sociology. Some address the micro level, emphasizing individuals as the basic component of society, whereas others emphasize the macro level, focusing on social institutions as the basic component of society.

LO6 CORE SOCIOLOGICAL THEORETICAL PERSPECTIVES

The core theoretical perspectives in sociology are the functionalist, conflict, symbolic interactionist, feminist, and postmodern perspectives. One easy way to help you consider

Empirical methods: Data collection that produces verifiable findings and is carried out using systematic procedures.

Theory: A set of propositions intended to explain a fact or a phenomenon.

Positivist: An approach to theorizing that emphasizes explanation and prediction.

Interpretive: An approach to theorizing that focuses on the ways people come to understand themselves, others, and the world around them.

Critical: An approach to theorizing that explores the role power plays in social processes and emphasizes the importance of knowledge being tied to emancipation.

these perspectives is to think of them as different "lenses" through which one can view the world. Some perspectives are similar to lenses that become darker or lighter when exposed to different levels of light. When we identify patterns of subordination and inequality in a critical way, society looks somewhat "darker"; however, because these perspectives also provide for the possibility of emancipation, the "brighter" side of society can be seen as well. Other theoretical frameworks are more like "rose-coloured" glasses, where society is viewed in a positive, cohesive manner, and the goal is to keep everything running smoothly. You will also encounter perspectives that seem more like regular "clear" glasses, wherein the nature of the viewpoint depends on the person who is wearing them. Finally, some lenses are nontraditional, such as those created through laser surgery or the fragmented lens of a kaleidoscope.

Zerbor/Shutterstock

According to the functionalist framework, every structure in society plays a necessary role in keeping society together.

THE FUNCTIONALIST PERSPECTIVE

Functionalism, also known as structural functionalism, takes a positivist approach to theorizing. It has its origins in the early development of sociology. Its overriding concern is with how social order is maintained, especially during times of significant societal change. Through this "rosy" lens, everything in society works to restore order and balance. It is a macro-level perspective, in that society is perceived as comprising a number of *structures* (e.g., institutions such as the family, economy, education, government, and religion), each of which fulfills important *functions* that keep society running smoothly—similar to the manner in which in a house of cards, each card plays an important role in maintaining the stability of the stack as a whole.

Manifest functions: An intended function of one of society's structures.

Latent functions: An unintended function of one of society's structures.

Values: Collectively shared criteria by which we determine whether something is right or wrong.

Dysfunctional: One of society's structures no longer fulfills its function effectively.

Anomie: A feeling of normlessness.

Some of the functions served by each structure are **manifest functions**, those that an institution is intended to fulfill; for instance, the manifest function of postsecondary education is job training. Other functions are **latent functions**, those that are less obvious; a latent function of postsecondary education is mate selection. All of society's structures are necessary to maintain social order. Should something go awry with one of the structures (e.g., the economy), the entire social order is at risk of collapsing, just as accidentally touching a single card can cause a house of cards to fall apart.

A core assumption of the functionalist perspective is that consensus and cooperation are fundamental to the maintenance of social order. Society is made up of norms and **values** (i.e., criteria by which we determine whether something is right or wrong, such as the *principle of equality*), and those norms and values exist because most people agree they *should* exist. When problems emerge with one or more of the main foundational structures (i.e., should it become **dysfunctional**), consensus is threatened, which puts society as a whole in peril. Since the focus is on stability and social order, the functionalist perspective assumes that in most cases, other structures will adapt to restore order, just as when the education system started to assume responsibility for the noon-hour supervision of children.

Émile Durkheim (1858–1917) is recognized as one of the founders of sociology and of the functionalist view. Moving from a smaller community to the large city of Paris during the peak of industrialization, he saw rapid social change first-hand and elaborated on what happens when society changes too rapidly. Rapid social change, such as what was seen in Europe after the French Revolution and later during industrialization, creates what Durkheim labelled **anomie**, a mass feeling of normlessness, or uncertainty about what the rules are in this unfamiliar situation (Durkheim, 1933, 1951). The concept of anomie can also be applied to the aftermath of large-scale natural disasters that have an impact on a region's infrastructure; examples of this include Japan's earthquake in 2011, the Fort McMurray wildfire in 2016, and the flooding in many parts of Canada in 2017.

You may recall stories in the media of how disasters are sometimes followed by violence and looting and wondered what would cause people who have just gone through such traumatic experiences to act in that way. Durkheim's work provides an answer. He proposed that a consequence of anomie is deviant behaviour: when we are no longer certain about which rules do or do not apply, we may act in ways that are dysfunctional for society, such as looting in the aftermath of a natural disaster.

In Durkheim's own life in France, he saw anti-Semitism gain strength in the midst of rapid social change. But he also noted that being subjected to such prejudice, the Jewish community (of which he was a part) developed closer bonds; its solidarity was enhanced by this collective experience (Jones, 1986). In a later chapter, you will learn more about how, in some contexts, deviant behaviour (such as anti-Semitism) can actually help maintain social order. In later chapters, you will see other functionalist theories applied to specific topics as well—for instance, Parsons' and Bales' theorizing about gender roles (e.g., Parsons & Bales, 1955), as well as Merton's work on the normative structure of science and the causes of deviance (Merton, 1938, 1968, 1973).

THE CONFLICT PERSPECTIVE

Like the functionalist perspective, the conflict perspective is a macro-level view that focuses on large institutions. However, whereas the functionalist perspective takes a positivist approach that looks for the causes of social phenomena, the conflict view takes a critical approach that emphasizes power and emancipation. Through a darker lens, the conflict perspective proposes that society is characterized by conflict and competition over scarce resources. You might recall playing "king of the castle" as a child, where each child strives to reach the top of a piece of playground equipment and then prevent other children from reaching that position. In this game, the child at the top would sing out to the other children, "I'm the king of the castle and you're the dirty rascals!" The king might even use physical force to keep other children from reaching the top by pushing their hands away as they reach for the top of a climbing apparatus or shoving them back down a slide as they climb it.

Similarly, the conflict perspective views society as comprising a small group of powerful people at the top of society and a large group of powerless people at the bottom. Those at the top control the resources and hence have a vested interest in structuring society in such a way as to keep the large group of powerless people at the bottom. Allowing more people to reach the top would mean having to share resources with them.

Karl Marx (1818–1883) is credited as one of the founders of the conflict perspective. As someone who was perceived as having radical political views, he experienced oppression by the government in power. At various times, he had to flee (or was expelled from) Cologne, Paris, and Brussels for his political activities and publications. Marx emphasized the economic sphere as the driving force of inequality—more specifically, the power differentials and conflict between the owners of the means of production (i.e., the **bourgeoisie**) and those who are employed by those owners (i.e., the **proletariat**) under capitalism. Other conflict theorists look to other sources of social inequality. Although Max Weber (1864–1920) concurred that capitalism was intertwined with inequality, he maintained that the source of that inequality was not economic but ideological. In a later chapter, you will learn more about the changes in religious doctrine that Weber argued were necessary for the emergence of capitalism.

Resources are distributed unequally not only between groups but also within them;

Bourgeoisie: In Marxist conflict theory, the owners of the means of production.

Proletariat: In Marxist conflict theory, the people who work for the owners of the means of production.

arleksey/Shutterstock

Conflict theorists propose that society comprises a small group of powerful people at the top of the social hierarchy and a large group of powerless people at the bottom.

thus, conflict occurs within groups as well (Engels, 1884/1972). In workplaces, some individuals have more power than others to control aspects of the work environment. Even within families, some members have more power than others by virtue of controlling the economic or emotional resources.

In later chapters, various conflict theories will be applied to specific topics. For example, conflict theorists highlight how education reproduces the existing social order and poses significant disadvantages for particular groups in society (see the chapter on religion, science, and education). And in the chapter on globalization, *dependency theory* proposes that relationships of exploitation have emerged between developed nations and underdeveloped nations, which have been exploited for their natural resources, such as gold, coffee, and oil.

Conflict theories do more than merely analyze social inequality. Just as some lenses may become lighter under certain conditions, conflict theories propose that conditions of inequality can be changed to eliminate that inequality; this draws attention to a "brighter" view of society. In his description of the evolution of world economic systems, Marx described a time in the future when the proletariat would rise up to unite and fight their oppressors. The notion of **praxis**—the responsibility that scholars have to provide subordinated groups in society with the knowledge they need to end their powerlessness—was emphasized in Marx's early work. Thus, the conflict framework is tightly linked to practice, such as large-scale social movements (e.g., the Civil Rights, women's rights, and LGBTQ rights movements).

The conflict and functionalist perspectives both emphasize the macro level. Other frameworks focus on the micro level—that is, the *people* who make up society rather than the institutions. One of these perspectives is the symbolic interactionist perspective.

Praxis: The responsibility that scholars have to provide subordinated and marginalized groups in society with the knowledge they need to be able to end their powerlessness.

Significant others: People who are important to us.

Generalized other: An overall sense of people's expectations.

THE SYMBOLIC INTERACTIONIST PERSPECTIVE

The symbolic interactionist perspective (also known more simply as the *interactionist* perspective) takes an interpretive approach that analyzes how we develop understanding. It is attributed to the pioneering work of George Herbert Mead (1863–1931) and Herbert Blumer (1900–1987). You can think of the interactionist perspective as a way to look at the world through regular, clear lenses. Society is depicted as comprising individuals who are engaged in various forms of communication, through words, facial expressions, gestures, and clothing (Blumer, 1969; Mead, 1934). These symbolic forms of communication come to mean particular things to certain people based on common shared understandings that develop between them—much like after many years of marriage, spouses can often finish one another's sentences.

Communication can be direct, such as between people who are in the same room, talking on the telephone, texting one another, or having an email exchange. It can also be indirect, such as when actors, directors, writers, journalists, news anchors, and musicians communicate to an audience at home. During our lifetimes, as we communicate with others, we come to attribute meaning to our experiences and thereby develop particular perceptions of, understandings of, and reactions to ourselves, other people, and the world around us. Our understandings grow and change over time and from situation to situation depending on with whom we are communicating.

Significant others—the specific people who are most important to us, such as parents, partners, children, close friends, or maybe even our favourite professors—play an important role in our socialization, the lifelong process by which we acquire the knowledge and skills for everyday life in society. We can say we have passed through all of the main stages of socialization once we have developed what Mead (1934) called a *generalized other*. The **generalized other** is not a specific person but rather an overall sense of people's expectations; even if we are not in the presence of someone who is important to us, we may still care about what "others" think of the way we look or act. This reflects our ability to take into account more than just our individual perspective, or the perspectives of specific people we care about, but also the perspectives of a multitude of nameless, faceless people. For example, when getting ready for a date, you might wonder what your best friend would say about your new fragrance (i.e., significant others) or what "people" (none of whom you personally know) will think when you walk into the restaurant in the clothes you are considering wearing (i.e., generalized other).

Within sociology, the symbolic interactionist perspective has been applied to an array of topics, from how we come to develop a particular ethnic or gender identity to how being labelled in a negative way can influence deviant behaviour. This array of topics shares an emphasis on how we come to understand our own lives and the lives of others.

FEMINIST PERSPECTIVES

Feminism is "the system of ideas and political practices based on the principle that women are human beings equal to men" (Lengermann & Niebrugge, 2007a, para. 1). This may be a taken-for-granted assumption for most of you, but as you will see in a later chapter, it is a relatively recent idea in world history and is still not accepted by all. Feminism includes social and political practice, as well as academic work, both empirical and theoretical. Feminism and sociology have had a relationship since the discipline's beginnings, and that relationship rests on feminist social and political practice.

Bettmann/Getty

Feminism is represented not only by academic theories but also social and political activism.

FEMINISM AND SOCIOLOGY: THE EARLY YEARS

A history of sociology often reads as if it were a history of male scholarship. However, women have played an important role in the development of the discipline. During the "first wave" of feminist sociology (1830–1930), women who were engaged in feminist practice were attracted to this new social scientific field. Their practical efforts at emancipation (e.g., the right to vote) and a discipline that used scientific methods to solve social problems seemed a natural fit (Lengermann & Niebrugge, 2007a, 2007b).

Female sociologists of this time were well-known public figures and were recognized by their male peers in sociology. The scholar most commonly recognized as a female founder of sociology is Harriet Martineau (1802–1876). In addition to her sociological research and writing, she was an essayist and intellectual critic; she also wrote novels and children's books. She translated Auguste Comte's work into English and wrote the first major statement of method in sociology. In her career, she wrote eight major books, published more than 200 articles, taught sociology, and was a member of the American Sociological Society. At the time of its writing, her book *Illustrations of Political Economy* (1832/2004) even outsold Charles Dickens' books. Her scholarly work was strongly intertwined with practice. She was a speaker for social reform, not only for women but also for trade unionists, immigrants, blacks, and the working class (Lengermann & Niebrugge, 2007b).

A generation later, Martineau was followed by a long list of female scholars who associated themselves with the discipline of sociology: Beatrice Potter Webb (1858–1943), Anna Julia Cooper (1858–1964), Jane Addams (1860–1935), Charlotte Perkins Gilman (1860–1935), Ida B. Wells-Barnett (1862–1931), Marianne Weber (1870–1954), and more. Like Martineau, besides being scholars, they were socially and politically active.

Feminist sociologists in the early years viewed sociology as "a project of social critique in which research and theory had a morally necessary focus on the description, analysis, and correction of social inequality" (Lengermann & Niebrugge, 2007b, p. 10). But they were also highly diverse in terms of the forms of inequality they focused on, the research methodologies they used, and the balance of empirical research and theory in their work. Feminist sociology is equally diverse today (if not more so); this is evident when we focus our attention on feminist theory.

FEMINIST SOCIOLOGY TODAY

Because of the diversity that characterizes feminist theory, feminist perspectives are difficult to discuss in an overview. Various feminist theories are labelled liberal, radical, socialist, or post-colonial, and the list goes on (Ritzer & Stepnisky, 2014). They can differ considerably. Some propose that men and women are inherently similar, with differences emerging only due to socialization; others claim that men and women are inherently different, highlighting female "nurturance" and male "aggression." Some focus exclusively on the experiences of women, whereas others emphasize the ways that traditional gender roles and **patriarchy** (i.e., legal and/or social power vested in males) affect both men and women. Feminist theorizing is done *within* other theoretical perspectives as

Feminism: The system of ideas and political practices based on the principle that women are human beings equal to men.

Patriarchy: Legal and/or social power that is vested in males.

well (e.g., symbolic interactionist). But despite the differences in feminist theorizing, there are some areas of widespread agreement, described below. Like the conflict perspective, feminist perspectives draw attention to the "darker" side of society (i.e., inequalities based on gender), while also highlighting the "brighter" possibility of social change to reduce these equalities.

First, feminist perspectives contend that academic research has traditionally been **androcentric** (or male-centred) and that it has failed to adequately study women's experiences, instead treating men's experiences as the normative "human" experience. The androcentric bias is also evident in the manner in which the prolific work of female sociologists in the early years was subsequently erased from the histories of sociology that were developed in the mid-20th century and that were reproduced in Introductory Sociology books for many decades to come (Lengermann & Niebrugge, 2007a, 2007b). Second, these perspectives assume that society is structured on the basis of gender, and therefore that people's experiences are also structured on the basis of gender. Males and females are often treated differently (e.g., parents buy trucks for their sons and dolls for their daughters) and often face differing expectations regarding their behaviour (e.g., women should not get tattoos, and if they do, they should not have masculine designs). And third, these perspectives attest that research and theory must be intertwined with practice—the fundamental objective underlying all critical theories.

Canadian sociologist Dorothy Smith (1987, 2005) is a foundational figure in contemporary feminist theory, with her work reflecting all three of these assumptions. As a young scholar in the 1960s, trying to balance her work in the male-dominated academic world with her role as a single parent, she realized that her experiences and view of the world differed from those of her male colleagues. Based on that experience, she proposed that because men and women have occupied different positions in society, they have developed different viewpoints. The standpoints of women, as a marginalized and oppressed group, have been ignored or derided. Smith argues that central to feminist theory and practice is listening to women's voices and experiences. More broadly, she proposes that because people's experiences of larger social structures are dependent on their standpoints (e.g., women's compared to men's), the only way to understand (and change) those structures at the macro level is to understand people's everyday lived experiences at the micro level. The assumption that scholars must explore the social relations that structure people's everyday lives has expanded beyond feminist theory and practice and is now integrated into other areas of study and practice as well, such as education, human services, and policy development.

Androcentric: Male-centred, failing to account for women's experiences.

Feminist practice ranges from the micro level to the macro level. At the most micro of levels, it can inform how individuals make choices and carry out their everyday activities, as well as the ways in which they interact with their partners or socialize their children. At the community level, feminist practice is the foundation for various programs, such as "women in science" summer camps that encourage girls to pursue further education in science. At a more macro level, it underlies changes in school curricula, such as the courses that are made available to male and female students, as well as the content of school textbooks. At the most macro of levels, feminism is the foundation for large-scale social movements, such as those that resulted in some women attaining the right to vote in federal elections (1918) and being legally declared "persons" (1929).

Feminist research and theorizing have been conducted on topics that will be addressed throughout this book, including the portrayal of women in the media, feminist critiques of science, feminist perspectives on religion, and analyses of globalization. But even more fundamentally, because gender is one of the bases on which all societies are structured, gender is often addressed even when a specific "feminist" theory is not being applied.

There is a considerable range of work within feminist perspectives. Similarly, the last theoretical perspective to be presented—the postmodern framework—also comprises many divergent viewpoints and is even less cohesive than the feminist framework (Downes, Rock, & McLaughlin, 2016).

THE POSTMODERN PERSPECTIVE

The discipline of sociology emerged from the significant social change that accompanied the French Revolution and the Enlightenment, with the functionalist perspective explaining how social order could be maintained during such times. The postmodern perspective emerged from another time of significant social change, the post–Second World War era. Postmodernists point out the ways in which our lives have dramatically changed since the war. Before and during the war, Western societies were industrial, based primarily on manufacturing products (e.g., tables and refrigerators). Since that time, they have largely lost their industrial base and now primarily produce ideas and images. As we go about our daily lives, we are bombarded by an endless array of ideas and images communicated through movies, music, advertisements, and other forms of media. There are so many messages that it can be difficult to know where to turn our attention! In this regard, it might be easy for you to think of the postmodern perspective as viewing the world through coloured contact lenses of your choosing, a technologically modified lens (e.g., via laser surgery), or even the fragmented lens of a kaleidoscope.

Arising from this view of postwar society are two forms of postmodernism: skeptical and affirmative (Rosenau, 1992). *Skeptical* postmodernism proposes that these social changes have created inescapable chaos and meaninglessness; because this form of postmodernism precludes the possibility of any meaning in the world, it has not played a significant role in sociology. In contrast, *affirmative* postmodernism suggests that the manner in which society has changed means that we cannot rely on grand, overarching theories of society (such as functionalist and conflict) or broad categories of people (such as generic labels such as "man" or "black"). Instead, affirmative postmodernists focus on the local and specific, deconstructing what is perceived as "knowledge" and asking questions of that knowledge.

In addition to skeptical and affirmative postmodernism, *post-structuralist* theories are sometimes categorized as belonging to the postmodern framework, although this is widely disputed (in this book, the category "postmodern" includes post-structuralist theories). Post-structuralist theories are exemplified by the work of Michel Foucault (1978, 1980, 1977/1995), who was one of the most influential social scientists of the late 20th century. Making the claim that truth is not "objective" but rather historically produced, Foucault emphasized the relationship between knowledge and power. There are many different **discourses** in society—that is, ways of understanding a specific subject or social phenomenon. Which of those discourses is perceived as valid depends on where the competing discourses are located within the structure of power. When a discourse emerges from a structural location of power, it becomes an *elite discourse* and is widely accepted. Consider the role of the media "expert." When significant social issues or news events are presented on a daytime talk show or the evening news, a sound bite from a token "expert" is often included. The role of that "expert" is to explain the phenomenon to us, and we have a tendency to accept that explanation as valid knowledge simply because an "expert" has conveyed it. At a broader level, certain types of knowledge are granted more legitimacy by the public than others. In 21st-century Canada, scientific claims to knowledge hold this role; however, in pre-Enlightenment Europe, as well as in some cultures today, religious claims to knowledge were granted the most legitimacy in the eyes of the public.

Throughout this text, the postmodern perspective will be represented in diverse forms, such as in relation to the media, religion, science, and education. In practice, postmodern ideas underlie some forms of social activism (e.g., environmental and anti-globalization) as well as media literacy efforts. For a review of the key assumptions of the core theoretical frameworks, refer to *Figure 1.2*.

TIME TO REVIEW

- What tools are used to develop the sociological imagination?
- What are the differences among positivist, interpretive, and critical approaches to theorizing?
- What are the core assumptions of the functionalist perspective, and what happens when society changes too rapidly?
- What are the core assumptions of the conflict perspective, and what is the role of praxis?
- What are the core assumptions of the symbolic interactionist perspective, and how are significant others and the generalized other involved?
- What is the relationship between feminism and sociology, and why is it more appropriate to refer to feminist theoretical perspectives in the plural?
- What are the different forms that postmodernism takes?

LO7 CRITICAL THINKING

In addition to empirical research methods and sociological theories, the process of critical thinking will help you develop your sociological imagination. To think "critically" about a source of information or a particular issue does not mean to *criticize* it, as a parent may have once criticized the music you were listening to. Rather, "critical thinking is that mode of thinking—about any subject, content, or problem—in which the thinker improves the quality of his or her thinking by skillfully taking charge of the structures inherent in thinking and imposing intellectual standards upon them" (Scriven and Paul, cited in

Discourses: Ways of understanding a particular subject or social phenomenon.

FIGURE 1.2

The Core Theoretical Frameworks of Sociology

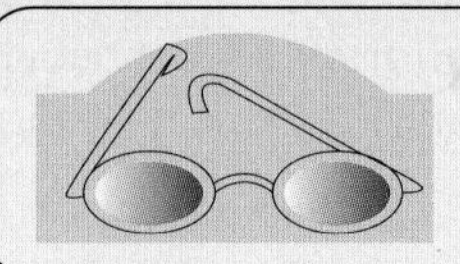

Functionalist Framework—Émile Durkheim

- A macro-level perspective that views society as comprising a number of structures, each of which fulfills important functions that keep society operating smoothly.

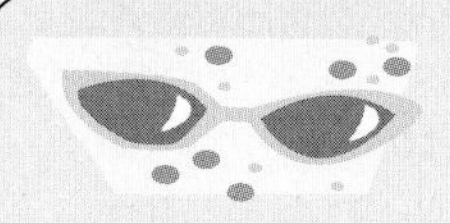

Conflict Framework—Karl Marx/Max Weber

- A macro-level perspective that describes society as characterized by conflict and competition over resources that are distributed unequally.

Interactionist Framework—George Herbert Mead/Herbert Blumer

- A micro-level perspective that depicts society as consisting of individuals engaged in various forms of communication that come to have particular meanings.

Feminist Framework—Harriet Martineau

- A micro- or macro-level perspective that assumes society is structured on the basis of gender.

Postmodern Framework—Michel Foucault

- Skeptical postmodernism proposes that the nature of social change has created inescapable chaos and meaninglessness, while affirmative postmodernism suggests that we can no longer rely on overarching theories of society or categories of people.

Foundation for Critical Thinking, 2015). But what, in practice, does that actually mean? How do you do it? And in what ways is it different from the "thinking" we do from the time we are small children?

Most of us are not born with the inherent knowledge of how to think critically. Instead, we tend to think dualistically and evaluate information or arguments as true or false, as accurate or inaccurate (Massengill, 2011). This is referred to as *lower order thinking*, based on memory, recall, and paraphrasing. This stands in contrast to critical or *higher order thinking*, where we extrapolate information from one domain and apply it to another. For example, with higher order thinking, you would be able to take your knowledge of Durkheim's concept of *anomie* and apply it in your volunteer work with the Red Cross following a local flood. Similarly, you could extrapolate conflict theory's discussion of the mechanisms of inequality and oppression in order to evaluate issues of homelessness in your city.

Several empirical studies have found that most students begin university with lower levels of thinking (Arum & Roksa, 2010; Gerwing et al., 2007; Rickles et al., 2013). Furthermore, half the students haven't developed a higher order of thinking after two years in university, and one third show no improvement in thinking after four years (Arum & Roksa, 2010). In other words, the development of critical thinking is not inherent in a university education. Rather, critical thinking requires practice, takes time to build, and needs a classroom environment that facilitates such practice; if the curriculum in a university classroom does not provide opportunities for critical thinking, students will find it difficult to develop (Arum & Roksa, 2010). But those students who are exposed to environments that give them the opportunity to practise it over an extended period of time *do* show significant growth in higher order thinking (Rickles et al., 2013).

At a micro level, the ability to think critically helps you succeed in your classes and get as much out of them as possible. *Figure 1.3* provides a list of starting questions you can use to critically evaluate the material in your class readings and lectures, as well as any information you may use for assignments. But to become a skilled critical thinker, practice is necessary outside the classroom as well. If you practise critical thinking regularly, it will eventually become second nature to you (see *Sociology Online*). At the macro level, critical thinking is linked closely to social action, in the form of *critical societies* containing a mass of higher order thinkers:

> There has never been a more important time to foster and develop critical societies. With the dwindling of the earth's resources, with vast declines in natural habitats, with impending extinction of growing numbers of animals, with the melting arctic ice, with wars and hunger and hopelessness on the part of so many, with all of the monumental problems we face, it is vital that we turn things around and get them right. Whether and to the extent to which they do will depend directly on our ability to solve the complex problems before us, to follow out the implications of our actions, to develop and use our collective intelligence in doing so. (Foundation for Critical Thinking, 2015)*

As you progress through this book, we ask you to try to think critically about the materials you are reading, the social issues being addressed, and, perhaps most importantly, your own reactions to those materials and issues. And because critical thinking requires practice, in each chapter you will find a *Critical Thinking in Action* box that gives you a specific opportunity to think critically about a particular issue.

FIGURE 1.3

The Beginners' Guide to Critical Thinking

Summarize the information

- What is the *topic area* of the information?
- What are the *main ideas*?
- What are the *conclusions*?

Evaluate the information

- Who is the *target audience*? How does the nature of the audience affect the presentation of the material?
- Are the ideas or points that are being made supported by *evidence*?
- Is the argument *balanced*, or is it one-sided?
- Are you being *persuaded* to adopt a certain view?
- Does language or tone reveal any *biases*?
- Is the material *well organized* and *well communicated*?

Respond to the information

- What is *your position* on the topic? Upon what is your position based?
- Are there any *other ways* of looking at it?
- Can the main points or conclusions be applied to *other situations/events*? In other words, are there other "places" where you can see this same thing happening?
- What are some of the potential real-world *consequences* of the conclusions?
- What *images of the subject matter* are presented in the argument? What might some of the *consequences* of those types of images be?
- What did this argument *make you think of*? Did it bring to mind something you have experienced? Something else you have read? Something you have learned in another class? Something you have observed?

LO8 USING YOUR SOCIOLOGICAL TOOLKIT

Practising sociology means using your sociological imagination, a skill that is built using a variety of tools. Empirical research methods are the means for creating verifiable knowledge. Sociological theories provide a larger context of explanation for that knowledge. And critical thinking enables us to evaluate and extrapolate that knowledge, as well as other forms of knowledge we encounter in our daily lives (e.g., through the media).

These three tools, and the resultant sociological imagination, are used in an array of settings; in other words, there are different ways you can practise sociology (Clawson et al., 2007). Beginning in Chapter 3, you will see the various settings within which the sociological toolkit is used. *Academic sociology* comprises the empirical research methods and sociological theorizing conducted by formally trained researchers; this type of sociology will be apparent throughout the bulk of each chapter, with certain pieces of work highlighted in *Sociology in Theory. Policy sociology* refers to the use of research, theorizing, and critical thinking for policy development in governments, other public organizations (e.g., public universities), and private organizations (e.g., community agencies); within each of the substantive chapters, policy sociology will be highlighted in boxes titled *Sociology in Practice. Public sociology* transmits sociological knowledge to nonacademic audiences; for example, information about same-sex parents may be presented to daycare employees as part of their training package, or a sociologist might be interviewed on the evening news about a recent case of bullying. Public sociology will be highlighted in *Sociology in My Community* boxes. Finally, *private sociology* is the application of sociological knowledge to one's own personal life; at various

*Linda Elder & Rush Cosgrove, Critical Thinking, the Educated Mind, and the Creation of Critical Societies...Thoughts from the Past, Foundation for Critical Thinking, 2015. Found at: http://www.criticalthinking.org/pages/critical-societies-thoughts-from-the-past/762.

SOCIOLOGY ONLINE

THE CRITICAL THINKING COMMUNITY

The Critical Thinking Community (**http://www.criticalthinking.org**) is an online community operated by the Foundation for Critical Thinking, "an educational nonprofit organization, to promote essential change in education and society through the cultivation of fairminded critical thinking" (Foundation for Critical Thinking, 2015). Besides offering an array of research on critical thinking, it provides resources for researchers, teachers (K–12), university professors, people in nursing and health care professions, and college and university students. You can find a wide range of specific information to help you become a skilled critical thinker: the intellectual standards that are the essence of critical thinking; nine strategies for practising critical thinking in your everyday life; how to study and learn; and the art of close reading.

points, you will encounter boxes titled *Sociology in My Life*, in which you are asked to consider some aspect of your own experience in the context of the academic material that has been presented.

TIME TO REVIEW

- What is critical thinking, and why is it important?
- What are four different ways that sociology is practised?

Sociology is the study of society using the sociological imagination, and you can practise sociology in myriad ways. You can analyze and evaluate any aspect of society, including the films, music, websites, and news events that are part of your daily life. Sociology is everywhere around you—the difficulty you may come to face is learning to occasionally turn off your sociological imagination so that you can simply enjoy a movie or a song without analyzing it!

As you begin seeing and acting through the lens of sociology, remember Berger's (1963) message: *Things are not what they seem.*

CHAPTER SUMMARY

LO1 Describe the bidirectional relationship between individual choices and larger social forces.

Although we think of many of our own actions in terms of personal choice, those choices are embedded in and influenced by larger social forces. At the same time, the choices we make can have an impact on the people around us and on society itself.

LO2 Define "sociology" and identify the role of the sociological imagination.

Sociology is the systematic study of society using the sociological imagination. The sociological imagination refers to the ability to see the interconnectedness of individual choices and experiences (i.e., the micro level) and larger social forces (i.e., the macro level).

LO3 Elaborate on the similarities and differences between sociology and other related disciplines.

Many disciplines, such as political science, history, and economics, study specific "parts" of society. Sociology is a more comprehensive discipline in that all of those "parts" of society, and the interactions among them, are studied by sociologists. However, the social sciences and humanities have become increasingly characterized by interdisciplinarity and what some scholars call postdisciplinarity; this means that there are fewer distinctions between various disciplines in the 21st century than there were in the past.

LO4 List and describe the tools that are used to develop the sociological imagination.

When used in an array of settings, the following tools help us develop the sociological imagination: empirical research methods, sociological theories, and critical thinking.

LO5 Contrast positivist, interpretive, and critical approaches to theorizing.

Positivist approaches have an interest in explanation and prediction, whereas interpretive approaches have an interest in understanding ourselves, others, and the world around us, and critical approaches have an interest in emancipation.

LO6 Outline the core assumptions of the functionalist, conflict, symbolic interactionist, feminist, and post-modern perspectives.

According to the functionalist perspective, society comprises structures that fulfill various functions that are necessary to the smooth running of society. The conflict perspective proposes that society comprises a small group of powerful people at the top of society and a large group of powerless people at the bottom. The interactionist perspective states that society is made of people who are engaged in continual communication that influences our understandings. Feminist perspectives are diverse but have some shared assumptions: that academic research has been androcentric; that society is structured on the basis of gender; and that research and theory must be intertwined with practice. Postmodern perspectives focus on the ways society has changed in the post–Second World War era; post-structural approaches, in particular, explore the relationship between knowledge and power.

LO7 Identify what critical thinking is and explain its importance.

Critical thinking is a mode of thinking that uses intellectual standards to carefully evaluate information and ideas and extrapolate them to a variety of situations. We become skilled critical thinkers only through practice. Critical thinking is important from our own personal micro level (such as in succeeding in university) to the macro level (such as in solving social problems).

LO8 Describe the four different ways that sociology can be practised.

Academic sociology is the theoretical and empirical research conducted by formally trained researchers. Policy sociology refers to the use of the results of theoretical and empirical research for policy development. Public sociology transmits sociological knowledge to nonacademic audiences. Private sociology refers to the application of sociological knowledge to one's own personal life.

RECOMMENDED RESOURCES

1. For an illustration of how something that seems as personal as tattooing actually tells us stories about social structures and processes, refer to D. Davidson (Ed.), *The Tattoo Project* (Toronto, ON: Canadian Scholars Press, 2016).
2. To explore whether sociology is sufficiently "radical," see M. Porter, "You Call Yourself a Sociologist and You've Never Been Arrested," *Canadian Review of Sociology and Anthropology* 32, no. 4 (1995): 415.
3. To see an example of public sociology, go to *The Society Pages* (https://thesocietypages.org/), an open-access social science project that applies the sociological imagination to current issues and events. It includes articles, podcasts, and videos on crime, politics, gender, race, and more.

FOR FURTHER REFLECTION

1. Using your sociological imagination, how has your choice of clothing today *been influenced* by larger social forces? In what ways might your choice of clothing also *influence* larger social forces?
2. What current event or issue would you like to explore using the sociological imagination? Why do you think it would be useful to look at that issue through the lens of sociology?
3. Consider your role as a postsecondary student. How would you view that role using each of the theoretical perspectives reviewed in this chapter: functionalist, conflict, symbolic interactionist, feminist, and postmodern?

CHAPTER

Applying Sociological Research Methods

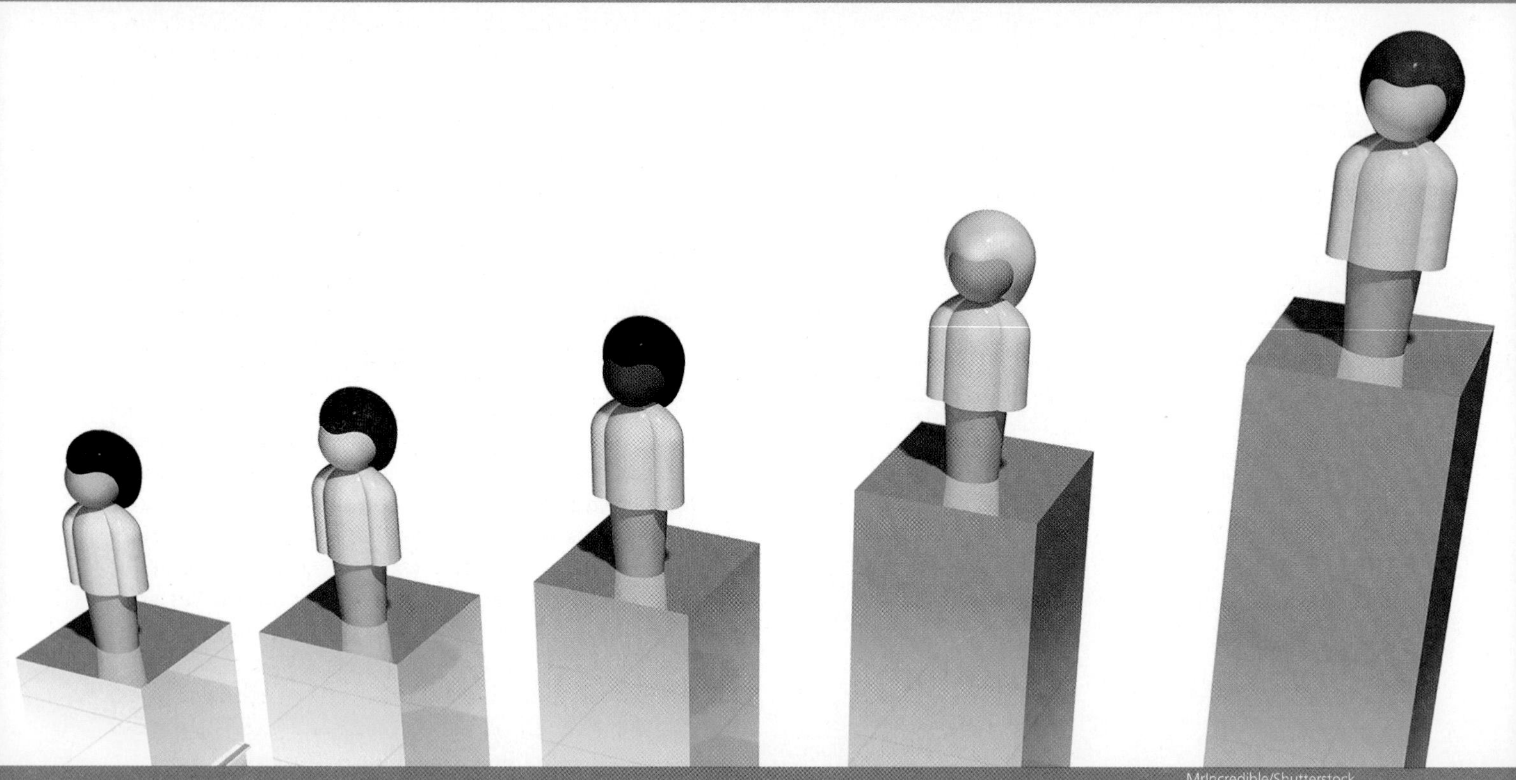

MrIncredible/Shutterstock

Research is formalized curiosity. It is poking and prying with a purpose.

(Zora Neale Hurston)[1]

LEARNING OBJECTIVES & OUTCOMES

After completing this chapter, students should be able to do the following:

LO1 Explain why sociological reasoning is important.

LO2 Differentiate between deductive and inductive approaches to reasoning.

LO3 Demonstrate an understanding of the goals of sociological research.

LO4 Identify steps for conducting sociological research.

LO5 Identify the ethical principles that underlie research involving human participants.

LO6 Differentiate between qualitative and quantitative research methods.

LO7 Describe the main use of each of the following research methods: experiments, surveys, interviews, focus groups, secondary analysis of existing data, content analysis, ethnography, systematic observation, and participant observation.

LO1 WHY SOCIOLOGICAL RESEARCH IS IMPORTANT

In Chapter 1, you learned that things are not always as they seem and that it is therefore important to delve beneath the surface of an issue in order to understand the complexities that are not readily apparent. As implied by the opening quotation, in this chapter, you will find out how sociological research methods provide a systematic design for learning about real-life issues that are too complex to be left to other ways of knowing, such as following commonsense assumptions. You will also learn why it is important to conduct research involving humans in an ethical manner and how you can go about studying topics of interest to you.

COMMON SENSE AND SCIENTIFIC REASONING

Since the subject matter of sociology is society and we already know a lot about how our world works, sociology is often perceived to be nothing more than a body of common sense and personal opinions. For instance, consider this question: Does money buy happiness? As a student, you already know it is difficult to balance all of the demands on your time, such as going to class, studying for exams, working on assignments, spending time with family or friends, and trying to earn a living. Tens of thousands of dollars would certainly help ease some of this burden. Using your "common sense," you might be inclined to assume that by virtue of giving *you* greater personal freedom or making your life more comfortable or less stressful, money probably buys happiness in general. Don't assume! Your own commonsense ideas and observations may serve you well in your immediate experience, but scientific ways of knowing can better help you understand under what circumstances your ideas about everyday life may (or may not) be accurate in the wider context of society. With even a basic understanding of the scientific side of sociology, you will be equipped with skills that will help you avoid some of the pitfalls of "common sense" and find more accurate answers to life's questions, such as whether money can buy happiness.

SOCIOLOGY AS A SCIENTIFIC METHOD

Sociology is considered a social science because as a discipline it seeks to enhance our knowledge of people and society using empirical methods (i.e., data collection methods that produce verifiable findings). As with the natural sciences, such as biology and chemistry, the social sciences also use *systematic procedures*. This means that the steps taken to design and carry out research are organized, methodical, and standardized in such a way that they are recognized by other researchers. Generally, the procedures must be so clear that another researcher could verify the decisions and processes undertaken and possibly even replicate (i.e., precisely duplicate) the study based on how it is described in writing. Although some scholars equate the scientific method exclusively with positivism, others (including the authors of this book) have a broader view of what the scientific method is, viewing it more as a rigorous means of developing new knowledge through various approaches.

SOCIOLOGICAL REASONING

Recall that a theory is a set of principles or propositions intended to explain a fact or phenomenon. Empirical research and theory are intertwined, with each informing the other. Its interrelationship with empirical research distinguishes sociological theory from commonsense hunches: theories inform research, can be tested and verified using scientific methods, and may develop out of research as an explanation for the findings. The principal components of any theory are concepts. A **concept** is an abstract idea expressed as a word or phrase used to categorize a particular feature of the social world. For example, the concept "social class" helps us categorize Canadians into similar economic levels based on indicators such as income and may be used in a theory explaining why certain groups are more likely to pursue a university education than others. Concepts used in research take the form of variables. A **variable** is a categorical concept that refers to properties of people or entities that can differ and change over time or from situation to situation. An easy way to find a host of variables is to visit an online dating site such as Tinder or eHarmony. Just about everything contained in a match's profile is a variable (e.g., single, female, and outgoing). "Single" refers to one category of the variable "marital status," where the remaining possibilities include married, common law, divorced, or widowed. "Female" is a category for the variable "sex," and "outgoing" is a personality trait.

Concept: An abstract idea expressed as a word or phrase.

Variable: A categorical concept for properties of people or entities that can differ and change.

Deductive reasoning: A theory-driven approach that typically concludes with generalizations based on research findings.

LO2 DEDUCTIVE AND INDUCTIVE REASONING

The scientific method entails a cyclical process that is ongoing and can include inductive or deductive forms of reasoning (see *Figure 2.1*). **Deductive reasoning** starts with theories and follows a "top-down" approach that ends with research findings. For example, Döring, Reif, and Poeschl (2015) hypothesized that selfies posted to Instagram would be less gender-stereotyped than depictions in magazine ads because selfies are created by a broad range of people. The researchers started with existing theories, developed a new hypothesis, and then carried out their own study as follows:

- *Prior Research Lesson 1*: Media advertising depicts people in gender-stereotyped ways using features such as gaze, posture, and body display (e.g., Goffman, 1979).
- *Prior Research Lesson 2*: Gender stereotyping is also evident in social media, including Facebook, wherein males post profile pictures that enhance their status through objects such as cars, whereas females post profile pictures that highlight their emotionality (e.g., Tifferet & Vilnai-Yavetz, 2014).
- *New Research Project*: Döring et al. (2015) conducted a content analysis of 500 selfies to see if displays on Instagram are as gendered as those

FIGURE 2.1

Deductive and Inductive Reasoning

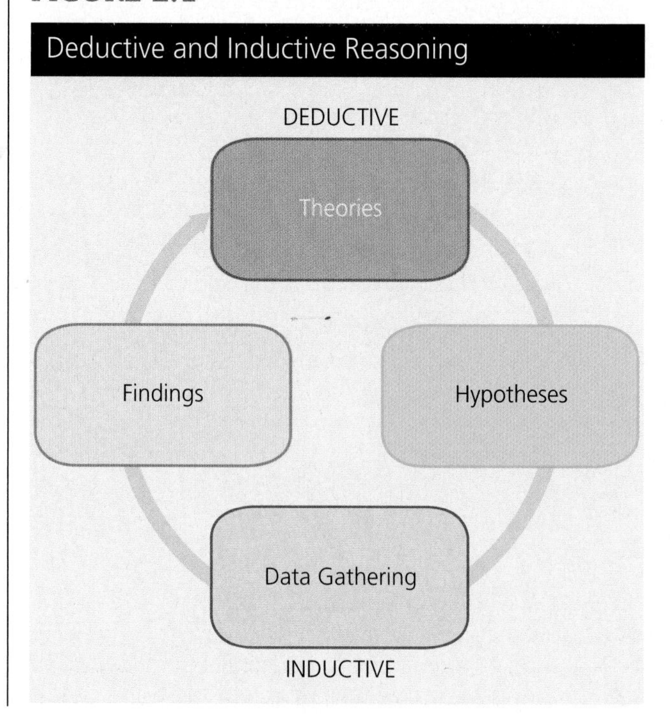

in magazine ads. The results showed that Instagram selfies reproduce the same stereotypes as those found in magazines. Moreover, in selfies, females were more likely to include a kissing pout face or just their bodies, whereas male selfies contained more muscle presentation than magazine counterparts.

Inductive reasoning, in contrast, is data driven or "bottom-up," beginning with observations and ending in theory construction (although existing theory can be used to inform all stages of research). For cancer survivors, fear of cancer recurrence (FCR) is an ongoing reality. However, for some, the fear may be so high that professional help is required. Mutsaers et al. (2016) sought to differentiate between clinical and nonclinical fear levels based on the experiences of cancer survivors. Their inductive approach can be summarized as follows:

- *Locating suitable participants*. Participants met a number of criteria (e.g., they had been diagnosed with cancer). In addition, they were chosen based on their scores in a larger study that identified them as having nonclinical (low) or clinical (high) fear levels.
- *Data gathering*. Semi-structured interviews were then used to learn about the extent to which cancer survivors' fear led to impairment and distress.
- *Findings*. Researchers uncovered 10 features of high FCR, including death-related thoughts, feeling alone, thoughts or images lasting 30 minutes or more, daily recurrent thoughts that are difficult to control, more thoughts as time goes on, beliefs that the cancer will inevitably return, distress, impairment in functioning, and intolerance of uncertainty. Comparing patterns that appeared in the statements from participants with high and low FCR helps assess clinical FCR and lays the foundation for a theory about the experience of clinical FCR.

Inductive and deductive reasoning may take different paths to finding answers to questions about the social world, but both play a part in reaching the goals of sociological research.

LO3 GOALS OF SOCIOLOGICAL RESEARCH

Sociological research generally rests on one of five main purposes: to explore, to describe, to explain, to evaluate an area of interest, or to help empower a disadvantaged social group. The goal of **exploratory research** is to help us understand more about an area that is not well established. You can think of exploratory research as answering these questions: *What is it like to be X?* (where X is a category of people, such as cancer survivors) or *What is X like?* (where X is a social phenomenon, such as the recurrence of cancer). As another example, consider text messaging (i.e., a social phenomenon) or even people who text message (i.e., a category of people). Although text messaging is as common today as are lengthy lineups at Tim Hortons, the first Short Message Service (SMS) was sent just 25 years ago (i.e., in 1992), making this mode of communication ripe for exploratory research.

Exploratory research into the potential uses and misuses of text messaging has shown us positive and negative implications of sending and receiving text messages. For example, we know that distracted driving was responsible for 25 percent of driving fatalities in 2013 (Traffic Injury Research Foundation, 2017). We also discover that "commonsense" assumptions about how text messaging impairs users' ability to have face-to-face relationships are not borne out by research. Text messaging does not diminish relationships; rather, it supplements and even helps maintain them (Bryant, Sanders-Jackson, & Smallwood, 2006). Text messaging is also not associated with poor written-language outcomes (Plester, Wood, & Bell, 2008) or spelling ability (Varnhagen et al., 2010; Wood, Kemp, & Plester, 2014). Recent research finds that the use of "textese" (abbreviations for words such as "brb" for "be right back") has a positive effect on grammar development in children (van Dijk et al., 2016).

Inductive reasoning: A data-driven approach that begins with observations and ends in theory construction.

Exploratory research: Explores an area of interest that very little is known about.

gazmandhu/Shutterstock

Distracted driving is responsible for more deaths than impaired driving.

Text messaging is now being examined as an intervention tool for promoting human papillomavirus (HPV) vaccination (Lee et al., 2016), inhibiting self-harming (Owen & Charles, 2016), and establishing healthier eating habits (Pedersen, Grønhøj, & Thøgersen, 2016) among adolescents.

The goal of **descriptive research** is to note features and characteristics of a group, event, activity, or situation (Adler & Clark, 2003). Statistics Canada collects information on Canadians every five years in order to describe the Canadian population on a variety of characteristics, such as age. From the 2016 census, we learn that there are now more than 5.9 million seniors (age 65 and older) and that the proportion of seniors is steadily increasing. By 2036, we can expect seniors to comprise between 23 and 25 percent of the population (Statistics Canada, 2017a). Census data also tell us that there are more people age 55 to 64 (the age group where people start to leave the workforce) than between 15 and 24 (the group entering the labour force) (Statistics Canada, 2016). This descriptive information is especially informative for decision-making and plans involving retirement funds and Canadian pension reform. Although retirement might be a long way off for you, a lack of available funds for retirees over their remaining life course will directly impact the Canada Pension Plan deductions taken off your paycheque for the duration of your employment.

Explanatory research is designed to clarify aspects of a particular social phenomenon so that we can better understand what kind of effects it has (or doesn't have). Deters and Mehl (2012) conducted an experiment to find out whether posting Facebook updates reduces loneliness. First, Facebook posts were monitored for two months; also, the participants' level of loneliness was assessed using the UCLA loneliness scale. Next, half the participants (i.e., the experimental group) were sent daily email requests to update their posts. All participants were asked to regularly report on their mood (i.e., happiness) and level of social connectedness. At the end of the week, loneliness was measured again. The findings showed that individuals who posted more frequently on Facebook were less lonely (Deters & Mehl, 2012).

Descriptive research: Describes features and characteristics of a group, event, activity, or situation.

Explanatory research: Clarifies aspects of a particular social phenomenon.

Evaluation research: Assesses the need for or effectiveness of a social program.

Empowerment research: Examines social settings and conditions to identify key issues and involves stakeholders for the purpose of improvement.

David M G/Shutterstock

Posting updates on Facebook reduces loneliness by providing a sense of connectedness.

Evaluation research is conducted in order to help assess the need for or effectiveness of a social program. Evaluation research conducted to examine a social condition prior to the establishment of a program is called a *needs assessment* (Symbaluk, 2014). A needs assessment asks, "*What is the nature of this social problem?*" and "*What resources are necessary to address this problem?*" Evaluation research used to examine existing programs is referred to as *program evaluation* (Symbaluk, 2014). A program evaluation is interested in whether a program is working as intended. For example: "*Did the program achieve its goals?*" and "*Were the costs justified given the outcomes?*" The Aboriginal Skills and Employment Training Strategy, in operation from 2003 to 2012, was designed to maximize employment for Indigenous people in a variety of sectors (e.g., oil and gas, mining, and construction). The federal government plans to renew and expand this initiative based on findings from program evaluations (Government of Canada, 2016). An early evaluation demonstrated justification of expenditures based on the objectives met (e.g., skill development and enhanced employment opportunities) (Human Resources and Skills Development Canada, 2009). A more recent evaluation indicated positive outcomes for participants (e.g., increased employment and increased earnings) and noted areas for improvement (e.g., higher priority on current market demands and specific areas of industry) (Employment and Social Development Canada, 2013).

Finally, **empowerment research** is undertaken in order to improve conditions within a particular social setting or for a particular group in society. *Action research* is one such strategy that generates knowledge about an area of interest in order to bring about social change. Action research is "carried out by a team that encompasses a professional action researcher and the members of an organization, community or network (stakeholders) who are seeking to improve the participants' situation" (Greenwood & Levin, 2007, p. 3). Action research starts with observation and measurement designed to identify key issues, is followed by some kind of action (i.e., a strategy is put in place), and then includes an evaluation component in order to determine whether improvement resulted (McNiff, 2017). Action research is carried out by researchers in a diverse range of fields (e.g., sociology, education, and health) and contexts (e.g., in classrooms, as part of community-based research, via social services) using a variety of methods (e.g., interviews, observations, and analysis of existing documents). Action research is sometimes called **participatory action research** (PAR). Although all action research strives to identify and solve a problem within a collaborative setting, PAR places more emphasis on the target group and stakeholders—viewing a problem as one that originates within the community and one that can only be resolved by its community members via an active collaboration process that involves the stakeholders at every stage of the research process (Selenger, 1997). This is especially important in research undertaken to learn more about vulnerable groups (see *Critical Thinking in Action*). In this sense, community members are not objects of study but are active contributors (co-researchers) in the research process and the reality created from it (MacDonald, 2012). For example, Penrod et al. (2016) demonstrated how PAR could be used to improve end-of-life care in prisons. In their study, researchers worked alongside staff from all areas (e.g., nurses, chaplains, security guards, counsellors) to empower them to identify what end-of-life care currently looks like for prisoners, to help them see new opportunities within their existing structures, and to assist them in developing means for improving it.

TIME TO REVIEW

- Why is sociology considered a science?
- What is a "concept"?
- How can inductive reasoning be distinguished from deductive reasoning?
- What are the five main purposes of sociological research?
- Which type of research is best suited to answering the question: What is it like to be X?

THE SOCIOLOGICAL RESEARCH PROCESS

If you choose to major in sociology, at some point, you may be required to conduct research on your own initiative. This section provides an overview of the steps you need to go through to carry out sociological research.

LO4 STEPS FOR CONDUCTING SOCIOLOGICAL RESEARCH

1. *Research question: What interests you?* The best place to start any research project is with a research question or issue you wish to learn more about. As an example, let's return to the question posed at the beginning of the chapter: *Does money buy happiness?*
2. *Literature review: What is already known about this topic?* Sign in to the library to find academic articles on your area of interest using sociology-related databases (e.g., SocINDEX or Sociological Abstracts). Databases help you find research-based articles on your topic when you insert key terms such as "money" and "happiness." Research articles inform you about ways that money and happiness are defined (e.g., yearly employment income and life satisfaction ratings), about studies that have already been conducted (e.g., cross-cultural comparisons and surveys of university students), and about previously known findings (e.g., money is related to happiness, but the relationship depends in part on how happiness is defined). The literature review is also important for identifying central concepts and framing a research interest in the most relevant theoretical context.
3. *Narrowed focus. How can you transform your research interest into a study?* A research question identifies an area of interest but is often too general or abstract to allow for empirical testing. One way to clarify your research question is by *operationalizing* the main variables. **Operationalization** refers to the process of defining variables in a precise manner that is measureable. Income, for example, might be defined as yearly dollars earned after taxes and other deductions. Researchers

Participatory action research: A field method involving stakeholders as co-researchers in a collaborative process designed to improve outcomes.

Operationalization: The process whereby variables are defined in a precise manner that is measureable.

strive to use measures that are reliable and valid. **Reliability** refers to the consistency of a measure. To show reliability, two different researchers should be able to come up with the same value for someone's employment income. **Validity** has to do with how well the measure represents the intended concept (i.e., is it measuring what it is supposed to?). Employment income is a fairly valid measure of how much money a person makes but may not be a good indicator of how much money a person has because someone could inherit money, win a lottery, have savings but no longer work for an income, receive a pension in lieu of an income, or have a very high debt load.

Once you've worked out the measurement issues, you can develop your research question into a hypothesis. A **hypothesis** is a testable research statement that includes at least two variables. For example, a hypothesis for the relationship between money and happiness might be: *People who net a yearly salary of $100,000 or more experience higher life satisfaction than people who take home $35,000 or less per year*. After you've defined your interest in a manner that is amenable to testing, you need to develop a research design.

4. *Research design: What is your proposed research design?* A **research design** is a detailed outline of all the proposed components of a study. At a minimum, it should identify the research interest, whom or what will be studied, and how data collection will take place (i.e., a description of the research method, as discussed in the latter part of this chapter). A research design usually contains other relevant details, such as how ethical guidelines will be adhered to (more on this shortly) and, in some cases, how a data site will be accessed and left once the study is concluded.
5. *Data collection: How will you collect your data?* The next stage involves collecting the data (or observations) that form the basis of a study. In a study on money and happiness, you might survey 100 people to obtain their incomes and reported levels of life satisfaction.
6. *Data analysis: What can you do with the data?* After you have the observations (or empirical facts), what do you do with them? **Data analysis** involves compiling observations into a format that helps us learn more about the research problem. The exact process depends on the research method used. If interviews are used, then data analysis involves carefully recording all of the verbal responses (*transcription*) and then going back over them to identify common themes (a procedure called *indexing* or *coding*). For example, it may turn out that people with higher incomes say similar things about life satisfaction (e.g., they report having happy marriages and liking their jobs). If the data are numerical (e.g., happiness ratings), analysis is conducted using a statistical software package (e.g., SPSS or PSPP) that provides descriptive information, such as the number of people at each income level, or compares the average life satisfaction ratings for high- versus low-income earners. Statistical software can also be used to compute correlation coefficients that quantify the linear relationship between two variables. For example, a Pearson r of .83 would depict a strong positive relationship between money and happiness (i.e., as income goes up, correspondingly, so does a person's self-perceived happiness). There are also software programs such as NVivo for nonnumeric unstructured data that can be used for coding the content of interview responses into categories and themes (Bazeley & Jackson, 2013).
7. *Draw conclusions: What do the data tell you?* Once the data have been collected and analyzed, researchers *draw conclusions* by revisiting their original research question. Data on money and happiness help us better appreciate how complex the relationship is. For example, a study using the first Gallup World Poll, which was based on a representative sample of people from 132 countries, tells us that money does buy some degree of happiness because increases in income are associated with increases in life satisfaction; however, after a certain point, money no longer contributes to greater life satisfaction. Essentially, once all of our basic needs are met (i.e., adequate food, shelter, clothing, and some extras, such as entertainment), increasingly greater amounts of income begin to play a lesser role in happiness compared to nonmonetary considerations, such as respect, autonomy, social support, and having a fulfilling job (Diener et al., 2010). Note that a correlation does not prove causation. People with a lot of money might be very happy due to other factors, such as better health or the attainment of higher education, which may impact earning ability and influence happiness. You will

Reliability: There is consistency in the measure for a variable of interest.

Validity: A measure is a good indicator of the intended concept.

Hypothesis: A testable research statement that includes at least two variables.

Research design: A detailed outline of all of the proposed components of a study.

Data analysis: Compilation of observations into a format that helps us learn more about the research problem.

FIGURE 2.2

Steps in a Research Process

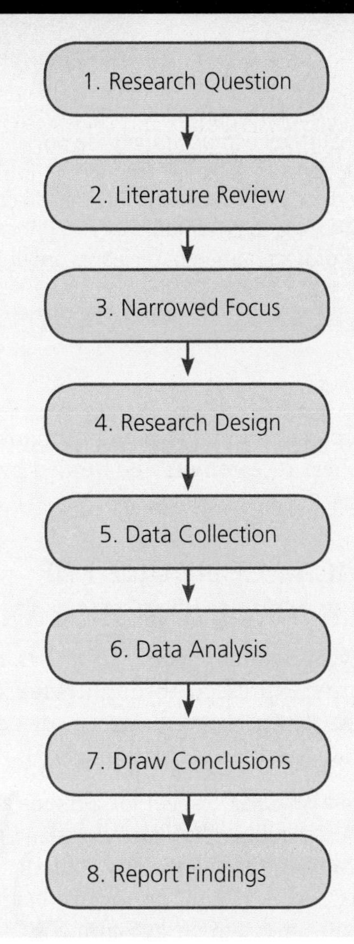

learn more about the role of wealth in subsequent chapters as those who make more money benefit substantially (e.g., they have higher educational attainment, more fulfilling jobs, better social supports, superior health, and longer life expectancies). Sociological research does not always prove something so much as it helps us better *understand* it.

8. *Report findings: How can you share the findings?* A research process concludes with a *dissemination of findings*. To further knowledge in an area of interest, researchers may present their findings at academic conferences or write articles about their studies for publication in peer-reviewed journals such as the *Canadian Journal of Sociology*. Each subsequent study adds another dimension of knowledge to the general area of interest.

A research project may vary slightly from the process described here depending on the exact nature of the issue, the type of design selected, and the approach followed. For example, qualitative approaches use broad research questions and therefore do not operationalize variables or test specific hypotheses. Nonetheless, you can use these eight steps as a starting framework for any project, as summarized in *Figure 2.2*.

TIME TO REVIEW

- What are the main steps in a research process?
- What do sociologists mean when they claim that a measure is "reliable"?
- What sorts of information should you include in a research design?

THE IMPORTANCE OF ETHICS IN RESEARCH

HUMAN MISTREATMENT

History is replete with examples of how people have been mistreated in a variety of medical, military, and research contexts. For instance, atrocious medical experiments were conducted in Germany on men, women, and even children who were prisoners of war in the Nazi era (1933–1945). In a well-known case, about 1,500 sets of twin children were taken against their will to a physician named Josef Mengele (the "Angel of Death") in Auschwitz, where they were subjected to abusive procedures and surgeries (e.g., removal of organs, attempts to change eye colour, blood transfusions, injections of germs), often without the aid of an anesthetic. Most of these children died (Lagnado & Dekel, 1991). Although Mengele fled to South America and managed to evade capture, many other physicians, military officials, and political leaders were later tried in Nuremburg for their abusive actions and were eventually sentenced to death or long prison terms. Another outcome of the trials was the development of the Nuremberg Code, the first set of directives for human experimentation that detailed the importance of obtaining prior consent, protecting participants from harm, and acknowledging subjects' right to end participation (National Institutes of Health, 2017).

The unethical treatment of humans extends beyond medical and military contexts to research in the social sciences, as evidenced by a series of experiments on obedience to authority conducted by Stanley Milgram in the 1960s. In these experiments, participants believed they were giving harmful electric shocks to another participant and were told by the researcher

SOCIOLOGY ON SCREEN

THE STANFORD PRISON EXPERIMENT

The famous Stanford prison study designed by Philip Zimbardo, Craig Haney, and Curtis Banks in 1971 to examine how participants would behave as "prisoners" or "guards" was recently reproduced as a Hollywood film. *The Stanford Prison Experiment* (2015), directed by Kyle Patrick Alvarez and starring Billy Crudup, Tye Sheridan, and Ezra Miller, gives viewers chilling insight into the original study demonstrating the powerful effects of situational forces on individuals. It also illustrates the need for researcher accountability in carrying out research projects to ensure that ethical principles established to protect human participants are upheld.

that it was essential they continue. Milgram's (1963) procedures were highly criticized for making participants undergo unnecessary and unreasonable amounts of psychological harm (e.g., see Baumrind, 1964). Similarly, Philip Zimbardo's simulated prison experiment that took place in 1971 also caused harm, in this case to college students, who in their roles as "prisoners" suffered physical and psychological distress for several days (Haney, Banks, & Zimbardo, 1973). Even those serving as "guards" suffered in the knowledge that they were behaving in sadistic ways toward fellow students (i.e., prisoners). Seeing what was happening, Zimbardo himself finally halted the study. Although ethical review processes at universities grew more stringent over time as a result of well-known experiments such as these, highly standardized research ethics policies and review practices came into being only recently.

THE TRI-COUNCIL POLICY STATEMENT

In an effort to reclaim public confidence, promote research with humans, and, at the same time, defend the dignity of those who serve as participants, Canada's three federal research agencies—the Canadian Institutes of Health Research (CIHR), the Natural Sciences and Engineering Research Council of Canada (NSERC), and the Social Sciences and Humanities Research Council of Canada (SSHRC)—jointly adopted the "Tri-Council Policy Statement: Ethical Conduct for Research Involving Humans" (TCPS) in 1998. The TCPS outlines ethical principles and includes a set of guidelines that regulate research carried out by sociologists as well as researchers from other disciplines. The policy has been updated several times since 1998, and the TCPS 2 (2014)[2] now serves as the official policy for these agencies and universities throughout Canada where research is conducted using humans as participants and where research may be funded by one of the three agencies.

LO5 ETHICAL CONDUCT FOR RESEARCH INVOLVING HUMANS

The underlying value of the TCPS 2 is respect for human dignity expressed through three main principles: respect for persons, concern for welfare, and justice (CIHR, NSERC, & SSHRC, 2014):

1. *Respect for persons.* Respect for persons "recognizes the intrinsic value of human beings and the respect and consideration they are due" (CIHR, NSERC, & SSHRC, 2014, p. 6). This means that research participants are granted "autonomy" or the right to decide whether and how they will be involved in research. Voluntary participation or consent is generally obtained from research participants ahead of time as a means to respect autonomy. In order for consent to be valid, the participant must be capable of freely giving it and must be aware that consent is ongoing and can be withdrawn at any time without penalty. Someone who is serving time in jail, for example, may be informed that participation is purely voluntary, but that person may believe that noncompliance will have a negative impact on obtaining early parole. The onus is on the researcher to protect those who may have limited or impaired autonomy. Voluntary participation is usually secured via a signed consent form that details what the study is about, what participation entails, what the risks and benefits of participation are, and how anonymity and confidentiality are to be maintained. An early study by Laud Humphreys (1975) has been described as somewhat of an ethical nightmare in its failure to obtain informed consent from

men who unknowingly became research participants after having sexual relations with other men in public washrooms. The researcher pretended to be part of the action, serving as a voyeur lookout; later, he followed those men to their vehicles to obtain their licence plate information. Almost a year later, the researcher used that information to obtain the men's home addresses and showed up at their doors to conduct interviews with them about their prior sexual behaviours!

Where possible, participants should be anonymous, and if this is not possible, their identity should be kept confidential. *Anonymity* exists if a researcher cannot link any individual response to a participant. Participants are anonymous when their names are left off questionnaires. *Confidentiality* has to do with agreements regarding what will be done with the information once it is collected (Sieber, 1992). Confidentiality is upheld when a participant is not identifiable in any way to the public. A researcher may know the identity of an interviewee, for example, but the participant's name will not be included in any published findings. Similarly, no information will be released that might allow others to infer the identity of the respondent, such as a job description at a company where there is only one person in a particular role (e.g., director of sales). In rare cases, participants cannot be informed of all of the essential details at the time of consent. For example, suppose that a researcher is interested in whether students would be willing to lend their notes to a fellow student who claimed he missed class due to a work emergency. Disclosing this information ahead of time to obtain consent would render students more likely to help and would negate the naturalism of the helping behaviour that is the focus of the study. **Debriefing**, or the later disclosure of all relevant details, is mandatory in cases where participants cannot be told all of the information ahead of time. Debriefing should occur as soon as possible and be treated as a "two-way educational process" wherein participants can receive further clarification of any aspect of the study (Eyde, 2000, p. 61).

2. *Concern for welfare*. The well-being of research participants is also a foundational ethical principle, and researchers need to design studies carefully so as to minimize the potential for harm. This is not always easy to anticipate in advance. Although we can appreciate how a physical activity, such as doing push-ups, might lead to possible injury, it isn't always clear how someone might be affected psychologically (e.g., by something he or she disclosed during an interview, by something an experimenter said, by one's own performance results). Also, broader social, economic, and cultural issues may need to be considered. For example, colonialism has had profound effects on Indigenous cultures. In addition, Indigenous people tend to have a collective or group orientation rather than an individual one. Hence, the well-being of a research participant may extend beyond one person to an entire community.[3]
3. *Justice*. Finally, ethical principles include the prioritization of justice. Justice in this sense means that people will be treated fairly and equitably and with respect. In some cases, we may wish to conduct research with vulnerable groups such as prison populations (especially if we want to learn more about crime processes, the criminal justice system, or people who have been labelled as criminals), children (e.g., to examine specific developmental phases in intelligence or socialization), and certain other social groups (e.g., many Indigenous cultures are plagued by high rates of violence and suicide and by high dropout rates from school). In such cases, researchers may need to be especially careful to secure consent, explain the nature and purpose of the study, and ensure that safeguards are built into the study to minimize potential harm and to uphold dignity.

To familiarize yourself with the guidelines for conducting research with humans, try working your way through the introductory tutorial (TPCS 2 Tutorial) provided at the Government of Canada's Interagency Advisory Panel on Research Ethics site; visit https://tcps2core.ca/welcome.

TIME TO REVIEW

- What is the underlying value of the TCPS 2 (2014), and how is this expressed through its principles?
- What is the difference between anonymity and confidentiality as they relate to the ethical treatment of human research participants?

LO6 QUALITATIVE AND QUANTITATIVE METHODS

Sociologists distinguish two main approaches to research depending on the underlying purpose of the research, the type of reasoning used to frame the study, and

Debriefing: The later disclosure of all relevant details in cases where research participants cannot be told all of the information ahead of time.

the type of data collected. With **qualitative methods**, the goal is most often to better understand the nature (i.e., "quality") of some phenomenon as framed by inductive reasoning and data in the form of words or images. **Quantitative methods**, *by contrast*, are usually employed to test hypotheses and measure (i.e., "quantify") social phenomena based on deductive reasoning and numerical data.

The difference in methods is reflected in the techniques most relevant to them. For example, quantitative researchers might want to learn more about whether teaching evaluations should be made public at postsecondary institutions. For this, they could use a survey to test a number of hypotheses, including one that predicts that students would be in favour of published ratings, whereas faculty would be opposed. Researchers might also ask instructors to rate how they feel about some of the potential disadvantages or have students rate how they feel about certain perceived benefits of published ratings (e.g., see Howell & Symbaluk, 2001). Note that a quantitative researcher already knows what she or he is looking for and uses a technique that specifically addresses the hypothesis that has been developed. A qualitative researcher, by contrast, might be interested in finding out more about students' perceptions of instructors more generally. With this broader, more inclusive research question in mind, the qualitative researcher might interview students to learn more about what they think of their instructors and the classes they take. Maybe particular themes will emerge in the feedback, such as a tendency to comment about instructor knowledge, organization, and appearance. Further in-depth interviews with students might help us better understand the nature of the comments. Is it more important to have an organized instructor or a knowledgeable one? Rather than start with a foundational theory, qualitative researchers may provide room for a theory to emerge from the observations (i.e., the data), using a technique called **grounded theory**.

Quantitative methods: Methods usually employed to test hypotheses based on deductive reasoning and numerical data.

Qualitative methods: Methods most often employed to better understand social phenomena using inductive reasoning and non-numerical data.

Grounded theory: A systematic strategy for moving from specific observations to general conclusions about discourses, actions, interactions, and practices.

Grounded theory "is a systematic strategy for moving from specific observations to general conclusions about discourses, actions, interactions, and practices" (Scott & Garner, 2013, p. 88). A qualitative researcher applies a series of steps to make sense of the data in a manner that unveils the theory that ultimately explains the findings. You can learn more about data interpretation and analysis in a research methods course. For now, consider that existing theories are important for informing data collection processes and that new theories sometimes develop out of research findings.

The Canadian Press/Mark Spowart

Dance is a key feature of Indigenous cultures.

Note that qualitative and quantitative methods differ with respect to how data are collected and what the data consist of. A qualitative researcher is likely to be the research instrument that collects data (e.g., as an interviewer who gathers opinions in the form of statements), whereas a quantitative researcher is likely to use some kind of instrument, such as a questionnaire (to obtain opinions in the form of ratings, such as levels of agreement) or some other measurement device (such as a stopwatch to time endurance for an exercise). Quantitative research generates numerical data that are amenable to statistical analysis. Since quantitative approaches tend to be deductive in nature, the research process is apt to be linear, with data collection followed by data analysis. Qualitative research, in contrast, often follows an inductive approach that involves gathering observations in the form of statements or images. The relationship between data collection and data analysis is more circular; while collecting the data, the researcher may make note of an interesting phenomenon (e.g., the interviewee brings up a

YOUR SOCIOLOGICAL TOOLKIT

CRITICAL THINKING IN ACTION

DECOLONIZATION AND INDIGENOUS RESEARCH

Research methods are not neutral in and of themselves; rather, they are data-gathering techniques created by people with particular beliefs and cultural orientations. Researchers, in turn, interpret findings obtained through methods by applying their own personal orientations, which in turn help construct reality and inform future research. As Gegeo and Watson-Gegeo (2001) eloquently put it:

> When outside researchers including anthropologists write ethnographic accounts of people's knowledge(s), or construct theories of other people's cultures, they certainly constitute an epistemological community. But it is not the epistemological community that created the knowledge they are theorizing. In other words, anthropological theories of other people's cultures are not indigenous theories of those cultures. Anthropological accounts of other people's cultures are not indigenous accounts of those cultures, even though they may be based on interviews with and observations of indigenous community's individuals and societies. All of the foregoing activities, while they draw on indigenous cultural knowledge, are imagined, conceptualized, and carried out within the theoretical and methodological frameworks of Anglo-European forms of research, reasoning, and interpreting. (p. 58)

Although researchers may not be able to carry out research in a truly neutral manner or ever gain a true insider's perspective when learning about colonized groups and communities, they can choose to "decolonize" the research methods used to study them. Decolonization is a process whereby research is conducted in a manner that allows colonized, oppressed, or otherwise marginalized groups to express their views and concerns in whatever form is most relevant to them (Chilisa, 2012).

Think Outside the Box: In what ways might participatory action research serve as a good starting point for decolonizing research methods?

Source: D. W. Gegeo & K. A. Watson-Gegeo, "How we know": Kwara'ae rural villagers doing indigenous epistemology, *The Contemporary Pacific*, 13 (1), pp. 55–88, 2001.

point that the researcher hadn't thought of), and then the researcher may integrate that point into subsequent interviews with the remaining participants.

As with assessments of reliability and validity, qualitative approaches must demonstrate **rigour**—that is, the trustworthiness of the research process and data collected. One of the main ways to achieve rigour is through **triangulation**, that is, the use of multiple data-gathering techniques within the same study (e.g., participant observation, interviews, and focus groups) in order to verify and substantiate the findings (e.g., a participant says something in an interview that is also brought up by members of a focus group and that was earlier observed by the researcher). Rigour in qualitative research is also established through the "credibility" of the research findings—that is, research is credible when the participants' views of reality closely align with how the researcher has conveyed them (this is akin to validity) (Symbaluk, 2014; Tobin & Begley, 2004). Finally, similar to reliability, rigour is enhanced using "audit trails," which are transparent, verifiable, and detailed documents outlining how research decisions were made and how conclusions were reached throughout the research process (Liamputtong, 2013; Symbaluk, 2014).

Although it is common practice to determine in advance whether you will be using a more qualitative or quantitative approach, generally, it is the goal of the research (e.g., to explore the experiences of cancer survivors), the type of reasoning to be employed (e.g., inductive or deductive), or some other factor (e.g., the availability of existing data or the willingness of participants) that determines the exact method(s) used. In the next section, you will learn about the specific research techniques characteristic of quantitative and qualitative methods.

Rigour: Trustworthiness of a qualitative research process and the data collected.

Triangulation: The use of multiple data-gathering techniques within the same study.

TIME TO REVIEW

- How does the purpose of quantitative methods differ from that of qualitative methods?
- What are some other differences between qualitative and quantitative methods?

LO7 SOCIOLOGICAL RESEARCH METHODS

EXPERIMENTS: WHAT IS CAUSING THIS?

An **experiment** is a deductive research method for testing a hypothesis through the use of a carefully controlled environment and random assignment to conditions. Experiments are a means for carrying out explanatory research based on positivist theorizing, which emphasizes objectivity. Experiments, which are used infrequently in sociology, typically take place in a laboratory. *Any* controlled environment (such as a classroom or an office) can be considered a laboratory. For example, in Symbaluk et al.'s (1997) study on pain endurance, the lab was a seminar room at the University of Alberta in which participants completed an isometric quadriceps exercise. This exercise involved sitting against a wall without a seat, legs positioned at a 90-degree angle, which causes lactic acid to build up in the thigh muscles and produces pain. The hallmark of experimental designs is the ability to test cause–effect relationships. This is possible owing to careful control over the environment (which rules out extraneous, or unintended, variables that could affect behaviour, such as distracting noises) and random assignment to conditions (which eliminates any individual differences that may be present among participants). For example, some people are naturally more athletic than others. Random assignment spreads a relatively even mix of athletic and nonathletic participants across all of the conditions.

Experiment: A deductive research method for testing a hypothesis through the use of a carefully controlled environment and random assignment to conditions.

Independent variable: The presumed cause or variable that is manipulated in an experiment.

Control group: Participants in an experiment who are not exposed to the independent variable.

Dependent variable: The outcome or variable that is measured in an experiment.

In an experiment, at least one variable is manipulated in order to see what effect it produces. An **independent variable** is the presumed cause; this is the variable that is manipulated in an experiment. In Symbaluk et al.'s 1997 study, the social modelling of pain was one of the independent variables. In this case, social models were actors posing as previous participants who demonstrated how to perform an isometric quadriceps exercise. Before completing the exercise, participants were randomly exposed to a pain-tolerant social model, a pain-intolerant social model, or a control group social model. Three different versions of the videotape constituted the experimental manipulation (i.e., the independent variable). In each version, the person demonstrating the exercise was believed to be a previous participant; however, that person was actually a social model who appeared to be either pain *intolerant* (i.e., dropped a switch that stopped a timer indicating the first sensation of pain at about 10 seconds into the exercise, displayed signs of pain throughout the exercise, such as moaning and rubbing his legs, and stopped early) or pain *tolerant* (indicated feeling the first instance of pain later on and displayed similar signs of pain during the exercise but lasted much longer).

There was also a **control group**, which included subjects who were not exposed to the independent variable. Participants in this condition received the same instructions via a videotape, except there was no information on the experience of pain or on how long the social model lasted (instead, they saw a freeze-framed social model on the screen in the isometric sitting position, and a voice-over simply reiterated how to complete the exercise). The control condition helps establish what would normally happen in the absence of the independent variable (i.e., how long the average person lasts at isometric sitting).

The **dependent variable** is the outcome or variable that is measured in an experiment. In this case, pain endurance was the dependent variable and was measured in minutes and seconds. As it turned out, participants who were exposed to the pain-tolerant model lasted significantly longer than those in the control and pain-intolerant conditions (Symbaluk et al., 1997). Note that exposure to a pain-tolerant model increased pain endurance and that exposure to a pain-intolerant model lessened the ability to withstand pain. Since the environment was carefully controlled (i.e., there was only one participant in the room at the time, the assistant monitoring the exercise did not know what the research hypothesis was or which condition the participant was assigned to, etc.), the only possible influence on the outcome was exposure to social models (the independent variable).

STRENGTHS AND LIMITATIONS OF EXPERIMENTS

The greatest advantage of an experimental design is that it allows for tests of causality. Robust effects can often be established even with fairly small numbers of participants, and the findings are generally definitive. The most serious limitation of this method is artificiality. Rarely in a lab can you study the precise real-life concepts or processes you wish to learn more about. For example, suppose you are interested in severe acts of violence committed against strangers. It is unethical and impractical to imagine you will be able to control the variable you are most interested in. Instead, you might have to develop a simulated environment such as an opportunity to enact violence against a stranger in a video game. But will this really tell you about your original research interest? Simulated acts of violence are clearly not the same as actual ones; for example, participants may be much more willing to commit acts of simulated violence against fake video game opponents than they would ever be to harm someone in real life. To overcome the artificial nature of a lab, which produces findings that are difficult to generalize to the real world, researchers sometimes opt for field experimentation.

Field experiments are experimental designs constructed in real-life settings where the variables of interest are more likely to occur naturally. However, the closer to the real world the research setting is, the less able the researcher is to control the environment, and factors other than the independent variable can have implications for the findings (e.g., the weather might influence how participants behave, or persons other than the participants might enter the field of study).

SURVEYS: WHAT IS YOUR OPINION ON THIS?

Surveys are as common in social science research as they are in everyday life. You have probably completed some kind of survey by filling out a form on customer service in a restaurant, by giving opinions over the phone to someone collecting views on an issue such as the health care system, or by rating instructors and classes you have taken as part of a larger process of faculty evaluation. A **survey** is a quantitative research method for gathering opinions or other details about topics of interest from the perspective of respondents using a questionnaire.

A *questionnaire* is an instrument that typically contains a series of close-ended or "forced choice" questions; participants are prompted to choose from a list of answers. This is similar to what you encounter on a multiple choice exam. Answers are later coded and

computed into percentages and other group statistics. A 2015 Supreme Court of Canada decision gave Canadians certain rights regarding their end-of-life circumstances. Researchers from the University of Lethbridge used an online questionnaire to examine opinions on the practice of assisted death (Karesa & McBride, 2016). Among other items, psychologists were asked for their opinion on individuals' rights to receive assistance by choosing one of the following responses: "Yes, I believe every competent adult should have this right," "Yes, but I believe it should be allowed only in certain cases and situations," or "No, I do not believe anyone should have this right." Ninety-three percent were in favour, with 52.4 percent of the participants reporting that everyone should have this right and 40.5 percent indicating that it should only be allowed under certain circumstances. Interestingly, close to 50 percent also said they lacked confidence in their perceived ability to assess the competency of an individual who was terminally ill and about 45 percent felt they lacked sufficient training (Karesa & McBride, 2016). These findings suggest that end-of-life decisions will pose unique challenges for physicians and psychologists in the years to come.

Questionnaires can be administered in a number of ways, including in person or over the telephone; they can be facilitated by a researcher or an assistant. They can also be self-administered, as in the case of mail-outs and online questionnaires. In a face-to-face or telephone survey, the person administering the survey asks questions of another (the respondent) and records the answers. **Respondents** are persons who consent to provide answers to surveys.

Survey: A method of gathering opinions using a questionnaire.

Respondents: Persons who consent to provide survey answers.

FIGURE 2.3

An Important Note to Students

A common exam error made by students is to confuse random assignment with random selection. Try to remember that random assignment has to do with how participants are put into the conditions of an experiment, whereas random selection refers to how participants are obtained, primarily for use in survey research.

A researcher sometimes tries to select a **representative sample** of respondents—that is, a small group that closely resembles the population of interest. For instance, if the population of interest is a university's student body, which consists of 18,000 people, a representative sample might include 100 randomly selected students: most who attend full-time days, some who attend part-time days, and some who take classes on weekends and evenings. *Random selection* means that every person in the population of interest has an equal chance of selection (see *Figure 2.3*). A registrar's office, for example, may maintain a listing of all the students who are currently enrolled in at least one course at a particular university. Using a software program or other suitable method (such as putting every name into a container, from which names are drawn one at a time until 100 have been obtained), the researcher could end up with a randomly selected representative sample of students. In some cases, the population of interest is not fully identifiable (as might be the case if you were interested in people who commit certain crimes because many crimes go unreported, and even those that are reported may not result in a conviction). When it is not practical or even possible to obtain a representative sample that is randomly selected, researchers may opt for a *sample of convenience*. For example, a researcher interested in the area of sexual offending might administer a questionnaire to a specific group of inmates in a particular maximum security facility who are undergoing treatment for commission of sexual assault crimes.

Representative sample: A group that closely approximates the population of interest.

Interview: A verbal question-and-answer technique used for obtaining information on a topic of interest.

STRENGTHS AND LIMITATIONS OF SURVEY RESEARCH

Survey methods are commonly used for descriptive purposes and have fairly high response rates. Survey approaches are great for collecting a lot of rich, detailed information in a relatively short time. If each question represents a variable of interest, think about how many relationships can later be examined from answers given on a five-page questionnaire. Face-to-face and telephone surveys are especially useful in situations where establishing rapport may help acquire participants or where questions require further clarification (i.e., lack of understanding may be evident in the respondent's facial expressions or tone of voice). Self-administered surveys make it easy to use a wide range of respondents (e.g., known offenders attending a local program as part of their sentencing might consent to complete a questionnaire, or Internet users from all over the world might consent to participate in an online questionnaire). Because anonymity can be ensured with ease, surveys are also a good method for obtaining information on very sensitive subjects (e.g., crimes or sexual behaviour).

The biggest limitation of surveys is that it is difficult to verify the accuracy of the findings given that some respondents might lie or otherwise misrepresent the truth (e.g., exaggerate, forget things, or omit important information). Another potential problem begins with the wording of a survey. In face-to-face and telephone surveys, a researcher may get the opportunity to clarify a question that has been posed; by contrast, the instructions and wording on a questionnaire are fixed. If respondents cannot properly follow the directions for how to complete the questionnaire, if they cannot understand certain questions, if some questions are poorly worded, or if response categories don't closely approximate the actual experiences and views of respondents, the responses obtained may not be valid measures of the concepts being investigated.

INTERVIEWS: WHAT CAN YOU TELL ME ABOUT THIS?

An **interview** is a verbal question-and-answer technique used to gather rich, detailed, first-hand information about a phenomenon of interest. Structured interviews are often conducted for descriptive research purposes. For example, a researcher interested in video gaming might ask questions about frequency or duration of use, preferred type of games, and game features that a player likes or dislikes. Interviews range in structure from highly standardized to completely unstandardized. A *standardized* or highly structured interview follows a set format of predetermined questions with no additional questions or clarification allowed. The interviewer reads a question, waits for the response, and records it (e.g., "When was the last time you played a video game?" Pause. The person says "last week," and the interviewer goes on to the next question: "What type of game was that?"). A standardized interview is similar to a face-to-face survey, except with an interview, the respondent gives whatever answer he or she wishes instead of responding in the limited-choice fashion imposed by most questionnaires. Hence, the answer to "What type of game was that?" as part of an interview could be "a video game," "a shooting game," a "war game," or "Call of Duty: Infinite Warfare" (and the researcher will later figure out how to code that information). A person completing a survey usually chooses from among a range of responses provided (e.g., "Which one of the following best describes the kind of game you last played: an action game, a shooter game, or an adventure game?").

An *unstandardized* interview has no set format, so the order or wording of questions can be modified and the interviewer can add, change, or delete items as warranted by the process (Lune & Berg, 2017). Unstructured interviews are most likely to be conducted for exploratory and explanatory purposes. In this case, an interviewer might begin with something very open-ended and subjective, such as "Can you tell me about your experience with video gaming?" The nature of the response received will largely determine what sort of question the interviewer poses next (e.g., a response such as "Well, I'm currently addicted to Halo 6" might be followed by a question such as "Why do you consider yourself addicted to that particular game?"). Unstructured interviews, also called qualitative interviews, tend to rely on interpretive theorizing because the emphasis is on how the respondents perceive and explain their own experiences. Semi-standardized interviews fall somewhere between these two versions and allow for some clarification of items as well as flexibility in the order and wording of questions.

USE OF FOCUS GROUPS: HOW DOES THE GROUP VIEW THIS?

Another way to conduct interviews is with *focus groups* of six to 10 participants. Focus groups are especially useful for gathering information at one time from a small group that shares some trait that is relevant to the topic of interest. Focus groups are commonly used for empowering or exploratory purposes and can be based on interpretive or more critical forms of theorizing. For example, based on an interpretive framework, a researcher might include students in a focus group designed to learn more about effective study habits, instructors in a focus group on best teaching practices, or recently retired employees in a group designed to learn more about disengagement from work roles. The main difference between focus groups and interviews is that the responses obtained in a focus group are generated through group discussions rather than individual responses stemming from individual interviewees. For example, one person in the focus group might make a comment that changes another respondent's line of thinking to generate a response that would not have resulted in an individual interview with that person. In focus groups, the interviewer is usually called a *moderator*. A moderator is responsible for introducing the purpose of the focus group (e.g., what the research interest is, what information is being sought, and what is expected of participants), outlining the rules for how the interview session will unfold (e.g., a question might be asked aloud, and then participants may be asked to respond in a particular order, one at a time), managing short question-and-answer sessions (e.g., coaching to ensure that each participant gets a chance to speak and that others do not interrupt), and dealing with any unforeseen issues that might arise (e.g., someone might appear upset by something that is said). A highly organized and skilled moderator is essential for creating and maintaining positive group dynamics (Lune & Berg, 2017).

STRENGTHS AND LIMITATIONS OF INTERVIEWS

Like surveys, interviews generate high response rates. They also have this added advantage over questionnaires: the answers provided better reflect the respondents' actual views. In addition, confusing questions can be clarified during an interview to further increase the validity of responses. However, interviewing is a two-way process, and for that reason, responses can be greatly affected by a number of considerations pertaining to both the interviewer and the interviewee. For example, how comfortable is the interviewee with the interviewer? How does the interviewee feel about the subject matter, and how much of her or his time is the interviewee willing to contribute to the research project? Establishing good rapport with a participant is essential and may be accomplished using extra questions designed to put the respondent at ease and get him or her talking (e.g., "Have you heard about the new video game that was just released?"). In addition, an interviewer needs to be mindful of how questions are communicated and how information is elicited from the interviewee (e.g., by speaking at a level that is appropriate to the respondent's educational attainment and discussing issues in terms that can be readily understood by the interviewee).

The order of questions is also important. It is best to begin an interview with a few easy-to-answer questions that are less central to the research, such as background information (e.g., "Can you please tell me how old you are?" "What do you do for a living?"). Sensitive questions should come later in the interview, once rapport is established. Interviewers sometimes use probe questions such as "Can you tell me more about that?" or "And then what happened?" to try to obtain additional information. Subsequent questions may develop and change as a result of feedback from the respondent. This is why consent to participate is actually an ongoing social contract and an especially important ethical concern when using interview methods.

SECONDARY DATA ANALYSIS: WHAT INFERENCES CAN BE MADE FROM THESE DATA?

Secondary analysis of existing data (also known as *archival analysis*) is a research method used to examine information on a topic of interest that was originally collected or created by someone other than the researcher for an unrelated purpose. Secondary analysis may be carried out for any number of research purposes (e.g., for descriptive purposes using a quantitative orientation, for exploratory purposes using a qualitative approach, and for evaluation purposes using qualitative or quantitative approaches). Data sources already exist everywhere: in printed materials such as newspaper articles, reports, books, novels, diaries, letters, children's stories, and magazines; online, in databases and on home pages and social media websites; in the graffiti left on buildings and structures; and in what Webb et al. (2000) call the "physical traces" people leave behind through their impact on the environment. Note that this content has been created for purposes other than research (e.g., a television series was developed to make money in the entertainment business, graffiti might be used in order to denote territory) and that it is referred to as "secondary data" once it is used for research purposes.

Secondary analysis of existing data: A research method used to examine information on a topic of interest that was collected or created by someone other than the researcher for an unrelated purpose.

Content analysis: A secondary analysis technique used to systematically examine messages contained in text or portrayed in images.

dmitro2009/Shutterstock

Graffiti can be considered a form of artistic expression, a type of vandalism, and even a source of data for sociologists.

Secondary analysis is often conducted using existing statistics from government agencies. The government has mandated Statistics Canada to provide statistical information on Canada's population, resources, economy, society, and culture as a whole as well as for each province and territory (Statistics Canada, 2017b). Statistics Canada collects information from a representative sample of Canadians every five years using a census. Statistics Canada also regularly receives information from a number of individual agencies, including the criminal justice, health care, and education systems. Information is tabulated in aggregate (grouped) format and presented in reports that contain statistical information, tables, and graphs. Besides informing Canadians about their country, these reports help the government and other stakeholders analyze performance, develop policies and programs, and determine how best to allocate resources. Statistics Canada has a wealth of information to share about a range of topics, including business performance and ownership, education, training and learning, crime and justice, the environment, and much more. Statistics Canada now partners with postsecondary institutions to help researchers obtain access to data through the Data Liberation Initiative (DLI). The DLI offers access to public-use files from various surveys, including the Canadian Community Health Survey and the General Social Survey. Ask a reference librarian how you can access this information or visit the DLI page on Statistics Canada's website at http://www.statcan.gc.ca. Most levels of government also provide publicly accessible "open data" covering a broad range of topics (e.g., elections, fuel consumption, average rents, citizenship).

Content analysis is a secondary analysis technique for systematically examining messages contained in text or portrayed in images. Content analysis may be carried out using qualitative or quantitative methods for a variety of research purposes. For example, to better understand how the public health risks of mad cow disease in Alberta in 2003 and *E. coli* water contamination in Ontario in 2000 were portrayed in the Canadian media, researchers looked at newspaper

Vladimir Gjorgiev/Shutterstock

Selfies are even more gender explicit and stereotyped than advertisements in magazines.

articles following initial outbreaks. The results indicated that how an incident was reported in the first 10 days "framed" subsequent media coverage (Boyd, Jardine, & Driedger, 2009; Driedger et al., 2009). Researchers also used content analysis to examine unsafe-driving messages contained in 200 Canadian print and television advertisements. One study revealed that 18 percent of all ads, especially television ads, included unsafe or aggressive driving practices, suggesting a need for government-imposed regulation (Watson et al., 2010). Content analysis is an especially well-established technique for examining how men and women are portrayed in the media. Döring et al.'s (2015) content analysis on Instagram selfies discussed earlier showed that men and women choose to portray themselves in highly gender-stereotyped ways.

If the goal of the research is to examine how language is used (e.g., in the media to convey stereotypes or to represent power), then the researcher is conducting **discourse analysis**—the critical examination of the ways in which language is used to convey social constructions and social relations. Language is not seen as a simple or neutral medium for communicating information but rather as a domain in and through which our knowledge about the world is actively shaped. Discourse analysis can involve the use of one or more methods, such as transcribed conversations (conversational analysis), oral narratives (narrative analysis), and messages within images from specific genres (e.g., media discourse analysis). Because discourse analysis is concerned about context—that is, how language shapes meaning—secondary sources are almost always included. For example, a researcher may examine medical descriptions of an illness and media portrayals of that illness besides carrying out qualitative interviews with individuals who have the illness in order to learn more about how that illness is represented.

Finally, **historical analysis** involves examining and interpreting historical forms of data in order to better understand past practices or groups and/or relationships between the past and the present. Sources for historical analysis can include any number of existing resources, such as documents, photographs, journal entries, folklore, films, and life histories (Lune & Berg, 2017).

STRENGTHS AND LIMITATIONS OF SECONDARY ANALYSES

With secondary analysis, the data have already been collected and are available. This saves a researcher many long hours and probably dollars that would otherwise have been spent collecting first-hand data. Besides being convenient, secondary analysis is one of the few methods that is nonreactive and unobtrusive—in other words, it does not involve gathering information directly from people whose responses may be affected by the very fact that they are taking part in a study (e.g., a respondent might falsely state that she does not smoke in order to be perceived more favourably by the interviewer). The main drawback to this method is that the data were collected for a purpose other than the intended study, so it may be biased or incomplete (i.e., missing variables of interest). This is especially likely when newspaper articles written from a particular perspective for a specific audience are later used in content analysis. Because the researcher has no control over how the data were collected in the first place, it is difficult to verify the accuracy of the information and—in the case of existing statistics—to determine how variables were originally measured, collected, and coded.

ETHNOGRAPHY: WHAT IS IT LIKE TO BE A MEMBER OF THAT GROUP?

Since most qualitative approaches try to get at the nature and meaning of events, it only makes sense that some methods are needed for gathering data in natural settings. **Ethnography** is the broad term for various forms of fieldwork designed to describe everyday behaviour in natural settings. In some cases, fieldwork is carried out in order to learn more about a

Discourse analysis: The use of multiple methods to critically examine the ways in which language is used to convey social constructions and social relations.

Historical analysis: The examination and interpretation of historical forms of data.

Ethnography: Fieldwork designed to describe everyday behaviour in natural settings.

SOCIOLOGY IN PRACTICE

EXPLORING ORGANIZED CRIME

Sally Atkinson-Sheppard (2016) spent more than three years engaged in participant observation in order to learn more about Bangladesh's organized crime structure. As part of her fieldwork, the researcher conducted 80 interviews and two focus groups with a range of participants, including police officers, prison officers, nongovernmental organization workers, and community members. She also spent time with a support organization in which she conducted workshops and carried out group interviews with children involved in organized crime. Her findings revealed that organized crime in Dhaka operates in a hierarchical fashion, with crime bosses (*mastaans*) at the top operating clearly defined businesses with political protection, followed by street gangs, who are used by the bosses to control areas of the city, and street children at the lowest echelon, where they are used as "illicit labourers" to carry out a multitude of crimes, such as selling drugs and committing murder (Atkinson-Sheppard, 2016).

Think Outside the Box: What are some of the research benefits and drawbacks of spending long periods of time engaged in fieldwork?

particular subculture; in other cases, it is used to assess a social problem within a particular group with the objective of bringing about needed change. An ethnographer is a social scientist who uses multiple methods over time in order to gather information about a group or culture while participating (to a greater or lesser degree) in that group. Typical methods used by ethnographers include observing people and practices, making detailed notes, taking pictures, participating in events and activities with members of a group, and conducting interviews. Refer to *Sociology in Practice* to learn more about a cross-cultural ethnographic study of organized crime.

SYSTEMATIC AND PARTICIPANT OBSERVATION: WHAT IS HAPPENING?

In a **systematic observation**, a researcher directly observes a social group or process but does not interact with the participants (this is also sometimes called *nonparticipation observation*). Observational research is used by both qualitative and quantitative researchers and can take place anywhere a group of interest is located. For example, for a researcher who is interested in learning more about the play stage of development, a daycare facility or structured play group might be an appropriate place to observe children engaged in play. Another way to conduct qualitative research in the field is through participant observation. In **participant observation**, a researcher collects systematic observations while taking part in the activities of the group being observed. Some groups and activities are not particularly amenable to investigation by outsiders. For example, members of an outlaw motorcycle gang are generally unwilling to allow nonmembers access to their business deals or initiation rituals. Hence, a researcher may have to join a group (or already be a member of that group) in order to carry out a study.

Systematic observation: A naturalistic but nonparticipatory method for collecting data on a social group or process.

Participant observation: A naturalistic method for collecting systematic data while taking part in a social group or process.

STRENGTHS AND LIMITATIONS OF FIELD APPROACHES

The greatest advantage of field approaches is that they allow researchers to study areas of interest in natural settings. It doesn't get more realistic than that! Describing what a group is like is best done if a researcher has gained an accurate understanding of the members' own points of view. Participating in a group is one of the most straightforward ways to develop rapport and to ensure that a researcher is around when important events and behaviours take place. However, participation poses special challenges for researchers, who need to be skilled in observing variables and people of interest while taking accurate field notes. Even if a researcher is only observing a group (i.e., systematic observation), he or she will need to be where the group is in order to code variables of interest.

Another special consideration regarding this form of data collection is that the data are generally compiled by a single researcher whose own traits and life experiences impact his or her perceptions and make the researcher stand out as an "outsider" to the group being studied. As a result, the researcher might need to spend long periods of time in the field in order to "fit in" and become accepted by the group before beginning to gain an insider's perspective and find ways to verify data collected on the group. Another difficulty with field studies, one that poses a special challenge for researchers, is how to access and then later exit a research setting. Gaining permission to join a group, establishing contacts and trust while in the group, and then leaving that group are tricky because the researcher now has social relationships with members of that group. Clearly, field approaches reiterate the importance of developing and following ethical guidelines. *Table 2.1* summarizes the main research methods discussed in this section, including key features, strengths, and limitations.

TABLE 2.1

Sociological Research Methods

Method	Question	Key Features	Strengths	Limitations

• Experiment
  • Lab
  • Field
	• What is causing this?	• Control
		• Random assignment
		• Manipulation and measurement of variables
			• Can test causality
			• Can isolate variable
				• Artificiality and low generalizability (lab)
				• Realism but low control (field)

• Survey • Questionnaire	• What is your opinion on this?	• Sample • Series of questions	• High response rate • Rich, detailed information • Relationships among many variables	• Validity • Respondent accuracy
• Interviews • Focus groups	• What can you tell me about this?	• Series of questions	• Can clarify questions (during interviews) • Participation in the process	• Establishing and maintaining rapport • Group dynamics
• Secondary analysis of existing data • Content analysis • Discourse analysis • Historical analysis	• What inferences can be made from these data? • What messages are being conveyed?	• Statistics, text, or images • Quantitative: predetermined categories and use of indicators • Qualitative: looks for patterns and themes	• Convenient • Large data sets • Reliability of measures • Nonreactive measures	• Validity • Incomplete measures
• Ethnography • Systematic observation • Participant observation	• What is it like to be a member of that group? • What do the actions mean to the members of the group?	• Interviews • Participant observation • Secondary analysis of existing data	• Natural settings • Rich, detailed information • Insider insight	• Accessing and exiting research settings • Bias • Reactivity

MULTIPLE METHODS AND MIXED METHODS

Thus far, we have discussed each method in isolation in order to help you appreciate its use, merits, and limitations. Researchers routinely investigate phenomena of interest using multiple methods. In fact, certain methods typically use more than one data collection technique and can be considered multiple-method approaches. For example, case study research typically employs a number of research methods. A **single-case design** "refers to case study research that focuses on only one person, organization, event or program as the unit of analysis as emphasized by the research objectives" (Symbaluk, 2014, p. 268). A researcher carrying out a single-case organizational study might wish to investigate the overall purpose of a reintegration program, such as that of the John Howard Society, which oversees services and programs for at-risk youth and men and women involved with the criminal justice system. A case study on how the programs and services correspond to the organization's mandate, core values, and mission might include secondary analysis of existing data (e.g., documents about the organization, meeting notes, website information, and publications) as well as interviews with the board of directors, trained staff, and individuals participating in the offered programs. Similarly, evaluation research, action research, and ethnographic research typically entail a combination of methods, such as participant observation, interviews, and secondary analysis of existing data.

Single-case design: Case study research that focuses on only one person, organization, event, or program as the unit of analysis, as emphasized by the research objectives.

Convergent design: Employs at least one qualitative and one quantitative method at the same time in order to compare different perspectives as part of the overall data integration.

Separate from studies that involve multiple methods of various kinds (where the methods could all be qualitative or all quantitative), there are studies that have designs that specifically entail the use of qualitative and quantitative methods with equal priority (Creswell, 2014; Creswell & Clark, 2011). For example, in a **convergent design**, qualitative and quantitative methods are employed in the same phase of the study so that the researchers can compare different perspectives when assessing the overall findings. Wilson et al. (2012) used a convergent design to examine care setting transitions in the last year of life for rural Canadians. They relied on quantitative secondary data (e.g., in-patient hospital and ambulatory information) and survey data (completed by individuals who knew details about the deceased) alongside qualitative interviews with bereaved family members. Their findings indicated that rural Canadians undergo more transitions than their urban counterparts (i.e., they are moved eight times on average) and that this process is especially difficult on family members, who must travel frequently to visit and take the patients to and from various appointments (Wilson et al., 2012). Mixed-method designs are beneficial for overcoming the limits of any particular approach while benefiting from the combined strengths of various approaches.

TIME TO REVIEW

- Which variable is manipulated in an experiment?
- What are some of the ways that questionnaires can be administered?
- In what ways are focus groups different from interviews?
- What is the main drawback of secondary analysis of existing data?
- How does participant observation differ from systematic observation?

CHAPTER SUMMARY

LO1 Explain why sociological reasoning is important.

Common sense is limited as a result of the individual's selective perception. Sociological reasoning uses empirical methods and systematic procedures to study the social world and enhance our understanding of people and society.

LO2 Differentiate between deductive and inductive approaches to reasoning.

Deductive reasoning starts with theories and ends with research findings, whereas inductive research begins with observation and ends in theory construction.

LO3 Demonstrate an understanding of the goals of sociological research.

Exploratory research helps us understand an area that is not well established; descriptive research helps denote features and characteristics of a group; explanatory research clarifies aspects of a particular social phenomenon; evaluation research assesses the need for or effectiveness of a social program; and empowerment research is undertaken in order to improve conditions within a particular setting or for a particular group.

LO4 Identify steps for conducting sociological research.

Steps in conducting research include identifying an area of interest, determining what is already known about the topic, narrowing the research focus, developing a research design, collecting data, analyzing data, drawing conclusions, and disseminating the findings.

LO5 Identify the ethical principles that underlie research involving human participants.

Research involving humans should always be carried out in a manner that demonstrates a concern for welfare, respects dignity and the decision to participate in research, and prioritizes justice.

LO6 Differentiate between qualitative and quantitative research methods.

Qualitative methods help us better understand or describe something and typically uses inductive reasoning, whereas quantitative methods are generally more focused on counting things or testing hypotheses based on deductive reasoning.

LO7 Describe the main use of each of the following research methods: experiments, surveys, interviews, focus groups, secondary analysis of existing data, content analysis, ethnography, systematic observation, and participant observation.

An experiment is a deductive method used to test causality as a function of control and random assignment. Surveys are used to gather opinions from respondents using questionnaires. Interviews use question-and-answer techniques to obtain first-hand opinions. In-depth interviews conducted on small groups are called focus group interviews. Sometimes data originally collected for other purposes, such as statistics collected by government agencies, are used for secondary analysis to investigate topics of interest. Content analysis is a secondary analysis technique used to examine messages contained in images and print. Ethnography refers to field approaches that allow researchers to study people in natural settings. Observations can entail no involvement (systematic) or direct involvement (participant) by the researcher with the people being studied.

RECOMMENDED RESOURCES

1. For open data sets in Canada, visit the Government of Canada's online site http://open.canada.ca. For open government data from around the world, visit the Open Data Index at https://index.okfn.org.
2. A resource for designing and using survey methods is D. A. Dillman, J. D. Smyth, and L. M. Christian, *Internet, Mail, and Mixed-Mode Surveys: The Tailored Design Method* (4th ed.) (Hoboken, NJ: John Wiley and Sons, 2014).
3. To learn more about qualitative research and to appreciate how power and privilege pose implications for research, we recommend S. A. Tilley, *Doing Respectful Research* (Nova Scotia: Fernwood, 2016).
4. For more information on the Stanford Prison Experiment and to view a slide show with original footage, visit http://www.prisonexp.org.

FOR FURTHER REFLECTION

1. Suppose you are interested in studying how people adjust after being released from prison. How might you refine this research problem? What kinds of ethical issues need to be addressed before you can conduct this research? What research method do you think is best suited to this type of research interest?
2. A health care provider wishes to survey patients to determine whether the facility is meeting the needs of its clients. The health provider contracts you to develop a questionnaire that can be given to patients who come to the lab for blood tests. What kinds of questions would you include on the questionnaire? How might you word the questions? What other issues need to be addressed in order to obtain useful findings?
3. Consider the content of a typical course or instructor evaluation form. List five key traits you feel an award-winning instructor would possess (e.g., is knowledgeable, fair). Visit the popular site RateMyProfessors.com. Choose a school other than the one you are currently attending and randomly select an instructor. Print the ratings for that instructor. Conduct a content analysis of the ratings to answer the following questions:
   a. Is the selected instructor rated positively by his or her students?
   b. What qualities of the instructor are emphasized in the ratings?
   c. Can you discern any main themes or patterns to the ratings?
   d. Given the traits you listed as important prior to accessing the site, do you think the posted ratings are a valid measure of the instructor's teaching effectiveness? Why or why not?
   e. What other factors might influence ratings of instruction provided on this site?

ENDNOTES

1 Retrieved August 24, 2016, from thinkexist.com

2 The TCPS (2014) further clarifies a number of issues regarding research, the consent process (e.g., alterations to consent), privacy and confidentiality (e.g., secondary use of nonidentifiable information), and governance (e.g., criteria for determining when Research Ethics Board involvement is no longer required).

3 Chapter 9 explains how to interpret the ethics framework in Indigenous contexts, discusses concerns particular to Indigenous peoples, delineates how to apply provisions in Indigenous contexts, and explains how the research and ethical review processes operate therein.

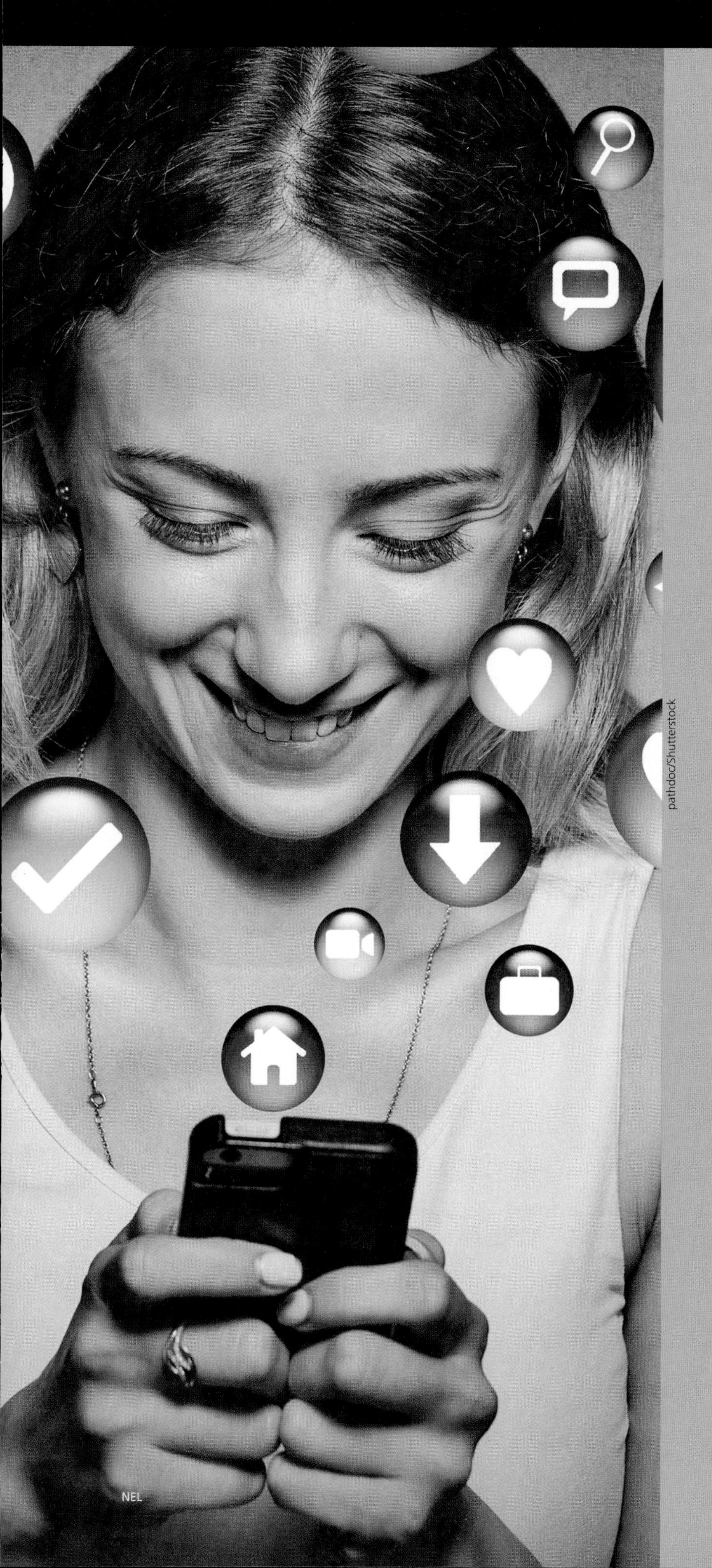

pathdoc/Shutterstock

02 PART

Society and the Self: The Foundations

CHAPTER 03

"I Am Canadian": What Is "Canadian" Culture?

Ink Drop/Shutterstock

I am Canadian, a free Canadian, free to speak without fear, free to worship in my own way, free to stand for what I think right, free to oppose what I believe wrong, or free to choose those who shall govern my country. This heritage of freedom I pledge to uphold for myself and all mankind.

(John Diefenbaker, from the Canadian Bill of Rights, July 1, 1960)[1]

LEARNING OBJECTIVES & OUTCOMES

After reading this chapter, students should be able to do the following:

LO1 Define culture and distinguish between material and nonmaterial forms.

LO2 Explain why language is viewed as a precursor to shared understandings and explain how language confers gender expectations.

LO3 Explain why norms are considered to be regulators of shared behaviours.

LO4 Identify shared values and debate the correspondence between cultural values and norms using functionalist and conflict perspectives.

LO5 Explain why values exist alongside contradictory norms.

LO6 Describe features of Canadian culture that make it unique.

LO7 Outline the main assumptions of critical views of popular culture.

TYPES OF CULTURE

LO1 DEFINING CULTURE

If you were asked to describe what is distinct about "Canadian culture," what would your response include? Would you emphasize similarities or differences among Canadians? Is shovelling snow worth mentioning as a typical expectation for most Canadians? Do you think Canadian culture is distinct because it includes traditions maintained by various groups of Indigenous peoples? Would you mention the Quebec sovereignty movement? Would your portrayal refer to well-known Canadian symbols such as the flag, the Maple Leaf, Molson Canadian beer, hockey games, or the Tim Hortons franchise? Would you locate Canadian culture in music by Leonard Cohen, Celine Dion, Justin Bieber, or Drake or in paintings by Emily Carr or Robert Bateman? Would you reference any of the "cultured" Canadians from the upper classes, such as the Irving or Thomson families, who maintain a disproportionate share of wealth? Your response could include some, all, or none of these accounts. Indeed, the concept of "culture" is interpreted in so many incompatible ways that some describe it as one of the most complicated words in the English language (Williams, 1976, p. 87).

For sociologists, **culture** encompasses the sum total of the social environment in which we are raised and continue to be socialized throughout our lives. This means that culture entails a wide assortment of ideas, customs, behaviours, and practices. Although all societies and even groups within the same culture differ in how they develop and carry out specific practices, they also share certain features. For example, all societies find ways to secure food, clothing, and shelter; all societies develop forms of communication and familial structures; all societies implement ways to use tools; and all societies come up with means for self-expression—practices that anthropologist George Murdock (1945) termed **cultural universals**.

The postmodern framework you were introduced to in Chapter 1 emphasizes the changing nature of society and is therefore a useful lens for examining the diversity and ever-changing nature of Canadian culture. By recognizing the spectrum of cultural differences among divergent groups that make up Canada, the postmodern lens affirms that we are discussing what can be described as multiple simultaneous Canadian "cultures" that are constantly being created and re-created, rather

Culture: The sum total of the social environment in which we are raised and continue to be socialized throughout our lives.

Cultural universals: Common practices shared by all societies.

Iurii Osadchi/Shutterstock

Hockey is one of the defining symbols of Canadian culture.

than a single, unified Canadian identity (Sumara, Davis, & Laidlaw, 2001). For the sake of simplicity, however, we will continue to use the singular term *culture* in this chapter. Basic elements of culture include the foundations of our expectations, which are rooted in geography, climate, language, norms, and values, as well as the existing artifacts of "our" time and the traditions passed down to us from previous generations. In this chapter, we discuss basic elements of Canadian culture and try to locate features that contribute to its uniqueness, beginning with the distinction between different forms of culture.

Material culture: Tangible or physical items that people have created for use and give meaning to in a given culture.

Nonmaterial culture: Intangibles produced by intellectual or spiritual development; also, the use of artifacts in a given culture.

Culture shock: A sense of disorientation and confusion that results when placed in unfamiliar surroundings where aspects of the material and nonmaterial culture are new or unknown.

MATERIAL AND NONMATERIAL CULTURE

We are where we live and who we live among! Although many of our decisions in life involve some level of individual "choice," engaging our sociological imaginations means that we look for the ways those choices are intertwined with larger sociocultural forces, such as the culture in which we are raised. It is precisely this culture that informs many (but not all) Canadians about the pleasures of eating poutine or pizza on a Friday night and similarly fails to teach just as many (but not all) Canadians to prefer black pudding (a type of sausage usually made with the coagulated blood of pigs that is popular in Britain) or balut (a hard-boiled egg containing a fertilized duck embryo that is a delicacy in Asia). Similarly, through socialization practices, Canadians come to share cultural ideas about what is important (e.g., securing a job) and what the appropriate means are for obtaining desired goals (e.g., going to school to learn skills associated with legitimate forms of employment).

Sociologist William Fielding Ogburn (1922) used the term *social heritage* to describe the common cultural world into which children of a particular group are born. He also noted the importance that people attach to material objects and the central role that material belongings take on in any given culture. **Material culture** includes all of the tangible or physical items that people have created for use, such as pizza and poutine, along with works of art, various forms of housing, means of transportation, clothing, tools, and countless electronic gadgets. In contrast, intangibles that are the end product of intellectual and/or spiritual development, or the meanings that people attach to artifacts, are considered aspects of **nonmaterial culture**. Examples of nonmaterial culture include language, knowledge, symbols, customs, morals, beliefs, and practices that help organize and give meaning to our social world. Material and nonmaterial culture both contribute to our understandings of ourselves and the world around us. This is why individuals who travel abroad or immigrate to new countries experience what is known as **culture shock**, a sense of disorientation and confusion that results when placed in unfamiliar surroundings where objects, practices, language, and rules are new or unknown. International travellers may even experience "reverse culture shock" upon returning home, where once familiar aspects of material and nonmaterial culture now appear very different. Recommended coping strategies for adapting to a new culture include learning the language, becoming familiar with the rules, getting involved in the new culture, and developing social relationships (Government of Canada, 2016).

farbled/Shutterstock; iStock/Thinkstock; Michael Gray/Thinkstock; igor kisselev/Shutterstock; iStock/Thinkstock; Subbotina Anna/Shutterstock; NoirChocolate/Shutterstock; iStock/Thinkstock; MJ Photography/Alamy; iStock/Thinkstock; iStock/Thinkstock; C. McGregor

From butter tarts to maple syrup, sockeye salmon, dulse seaweed, and bannock bread, Canada's culinary heritage is diverse.

TIME TO REVIEW

- How do sociologists define culture?
- What is the distinction between material and nonmaterial culture?

HOW CULTURE SHAPES OUR UNDERSTANDINGS

LO2 LANGUAGE AS A PRECURSOR TO SHARED UNDERSTANDINGS

Language is the primary facilitator of culture because it is the main channel through which people express themselves and pass acquired knowledge on from one generation to the next. Sociologists define **language** as a shared system of communication that includes spoken, written, and signed forms of speech as well as nonverbal gestures used to convey meaning. Ninety-eight percent of all Canadians can speak English or French, and most households have adopted one of these two official languages as their primary language at home (Statistics Canada, 2016). English is the most prevalent language spoken in most provinces and territories. Exceptions are Quebec (where almost three quarters of people are French-speaking) and Nunavut (where 70 percent of the population speaks an Inuit language) (Statistics Canada, 2016). However, a multitude of languages coexist in Canadian society.

Canada consists of divergent groups, including Indigenous peoples (i.e., First Nations, Inuit, and Métis), early colonizers (i.e., the English and the French), and millions of immigrants (e.g., Chilean, East Indian, Japanese, South Korean, Lebanese, Iranian, Syrian, German, Chinese, American, Italian, Polish, Ukrainian, Russian, Dutch, and Filipino). Significant portions of these groups and their descendants speak languages other than English and French and engage in a variety of traditional cultural practices. For example, more than 50 Indigenous languages exist in Canada stemming from 11 language

Language: A shared system of communication that includes spoken, written, and signed forms of speech as well as nonverbal gestures used to convey meaning.

families. Whereas some Indigenous languages have become extinct over time, others are being maintained as second languages (Norris, 2014). Even unilingual English-speaking parents in Onion Lake Cree Nation (straddling the border between Alberta and Saskatchewan) send their children to Kihew Waciston Cree Immersion School to ensure that this language remains vibrant in subsequent generations (Besner, 2016). Language is a central component of culture as it contributes to identity, cultural diversity, and freedom of expression.

Mother tongue refers to the first language learned at home in childhood that is still understood by an individual at the time the information on language is collected. If a person learned two languages in childhood (and still understands them), the mother tongue is the language that was spoken most often at home prior to starting school (Statistics Canada, 2015a). Canada's linguistic diversity is evident by the more than 200 languages reported as mother tongues and the 4.7 million Canadians (14.2 percent of the population) who continue to speak a language other than French or English on a regular basis (Statistics Canada, 2015b). About 20 percent of Canada's population speaks a language other than French or English at least on occasion. Within this population, immigrant languages are more prevalent than Indigenous languages or sign languages. In recent years, the numbers have especially increased among groups speaking Tagalog (a Philippine language), Mandarin, Arabic, Hindi, Creoles, Bengali, Persian, and Spanish (Statistics Canada, 2015b).

Mother tongue: The first language learned at home in childhood that is still understood by an individual.

YOUR SOCIOLOGICAL TOOLKIT
SOCIOLOGY IN THEORY

THE SAPIR–WHORF HYPOTHESIS

Language serves as a referent such that aspects of material and nonmaterial culture come to take on particular meanings and to be understood similarly by people who share a common culture and speak the same language. Hence, to English-speaking people living in Canada, the concept "dog" clearly represents a four-legged, fur-covered, domesticated animal that barks and makes for a loyal pet. But language is even more fundamental than this because it also helps construct abstract forms of cultural reality. Anthropologist and linguist Edward Sapir (1884–1939) first became intrigued by how language shapes people's world views when he came across Franz Boas's (1911/1976) early study of Hopi Indian language and noted the absence of an objective sense of time. For instance, where we might say "the light flashed," a Hopi Indian would say *Reh-pi* or "flash," without a subject (i.e., the light) and with no reference to time (Carroll, 1956, p. viii). Because of how they use and understand

SOCIOLOGY ON SCREEN

ATANARJUAT (THE FAST RUNNER)

© Aboriginal Peoples Television Network/ Collection Christophel/Alamy

Based on stories passed down from generation to generation by Igloolik elders, *Atanarjuat (The Fast Runner)* is considered one of Canada's best films of all time for its depiction of Inuit culture and its emphasis on the importance of oral history in the transmission of cultural values. The story centres on a community beset by imbalance, jealousy, and revenge. *Atanarjuat* is Canada's first-ever full-length feature film written, produced, directed, and acted exclusively by people of Inuit heritage. The film won numerous awards, including Caméra d'Or for Best First Feature Film, six Genie Awards, and Best Canadian Feature Film. *Atanarjuat* was released in 2001 as part of a trilogy, which also includes *The Journals of Knud Rasmussen* (2006) and *Before Tomorrow* (2008). To learn more about these films and to view them online, visit Isuma Productions at http://www.isuma.tv/atanarjuat.

language, the Hopi likely experience the world quite differently from other groups that use languages that make references to time—for example, with past, present, and future verb tenses. This revelation led Sapir to believe that language helps establish thinking—a phenomenon we now refer to as the principle of *linguistic determination*.

Benjamin Lee Whorf (1897–1941), Sapir's student, found that how language is used to label and code events and objects is also important for understanding what those things mean in a particular culture. In Whorf's words: "We cut nature up, into concepts, and ascribe significances as we do, largely because we are parties to an agreement to organize it in this way—an agreement that holds throughout our speech community and is codified in the patterns of our language" (Carroll, 1956, p. 213). In the Hopi language, only some events reflecting a brief duration, such as "lightning," "wave," and "flame," are represented as verbs, whereas in Nootka (a language native to Vancouver Island), every word is a verb; hence, a "house" (which would be a noun in the English language for a shelter) is stated more in terms of its functional properties, as in "it houses" (or provides a shelter); similarly, a "flame occurs" (Carroll, 1956, pp. 215–216). Whorf's position that language has particular meaning within the given culture in which it occurs is commonly referred to today as *linguistic relativism*. Taken together, the principles of linguistic determination and linguistic relativism form what is called the **Sapir–Whorf hypothesis**. That hypothesis, named after its two proponents, then, is the assertion that language helps shape reality for those experiencing it.

Language helps us appreciate how vastly different cultures may be from one another. This is especially evident in the language used to describe prevalent aspects of climate, geography, and material culture. Inuit languages, for example, have different words for snow (e.g., to depict crunchy snow, soft snow, old snow); the Italian language differentiates among types of

Sapir–Whorf hypothesis: The assertion that language helps shape reality for those experiencing it.

© Aurora Photos/Alamy

Not all translations appropriately convey an intended meaning.

pasta (e.g., spaghetti, vermicelli, and penne), and there are a variety of Arabic words delineating subtle differences in camels and camel equipment (Bryson, 1990, pp. 14–15). Words and phrases unique to Canadians and Canadian culture are called "Canadianisms," such as "tuque" (a peaked woollen winter hat), "washroom" (public toilet), "chesterfield" (a type of sofa), and "eh" (an expression at the end of a sentence used to turn it into a question) (Dollinger, Laurel, & Fee, 2013).

The nuances of language and meaning are especially apparent in blunders that occur when products are marketed in foreign countries. As Ricks (1999) notes, "cultural differences are the most significant and troublesome variables encountered by the multinational company" (p. 4). For example, when the Coca-Cola Company began marketing in China, it introduced Chinese characters that sound similar to the English pronunciation of the product's name (i.e., "ke-ke-ken-la"). However, the literal meaning of those sounds, "bite the wax tadpole" or "a wax-flattened mare" (depending on the dialect), did not resonate well with customers, and the characters were soon changed to "ko-kou-ko-le" to fit a more pleasant interpretation: "happiness in the mouth" (p. 38). Likewise, video game software developer Sega Corporation ran into an issue when it began marketing in Italy because "say-ga" as pronounced in English refers to male masturbation in Italian. Hence, to disassociate itself from any potential misinterpretation, the company goes by "see-ga" in Italy (Texin, 2011).

YOUR SOCIOLOGICAL TOOLKIT
SOCIOLOGY IN THEORY

GENDERED LANGUAGE

Language enables cultural diversity; it also imposes constraints on individuals and groups in society. The feminist framework can help us better appreciate how language confers cultural constructions. These begin even before birth with the names selected for boys versus girls, followed by the qualitatively different adjectives used to describe males versus females later on. For example, a baby boy may be "strong" and sometimes "cute" but not "pretty," just as an adult female may be "beautiful" but never "handsome." Language continues to shape differential expectations and experiences for males and females as they enter school and form relationships (e.g., boyfriend and girlfriend) and take on adult roles (e.g., husband and wife). Feminist theory is especially concerned with the ways in which language differentiates between males and females in ways that perpetuate and even produce inequalities. For example, certain terms can denote that a male is assumed to be present and serves as the head of a household (e.g., by use of "his" rather than "their" home) or that a female is expected to play a central role in child rearing (e.g., "her" rather than "their" children"). Similarly, in the case of employment, language is often used to denote who is expected to hold a particular title (e.g., "chairman" or "city councilman") or a given position (e.g., "mailman," "fireman," "stewardess," and "cleaning lady"). Finally, the use of *androcentric* or exclusively male terms to represent both sexes (e.g., consider the United States Declaration of Independence: "all men are created equal") may inadvertently reinforce sexism by emphasizing the male term over the female one.

Folkways: Informal norms based on accepted traditions.

As a result of feminist activism and increased female participation in the paid workforce, this use of the English language has started to shift. There are now more "gender-neutral" terms, such as the North American occupational titles of "chairperson," "city councillor," "mail carrier," "firefighter," "flight attendant," and "house cleaner." Also, language has become more "gender-inclusive" to ensure that one sex is not left out, as evident in the use of "Dear Sirs/Mesdames" or the even more neutral "To whom it may concern" in written correspondence. Gender equality is also evident in the use of "Ms." rather than "Miss" or "Mrs." when addressing a female in reference to her surname (as in Ms. Smith). Similarly, there is an increased tendency to use inclusive, nonprescriptive language when denoting relationships; thus, "friend," "partner," or "spouse" could pertain to an individual of the same or the opposite sex. Public institutions (including universities) now recognize the need to give individuals the right to choose whether they wish to be referred to by gendered pronouns such as "he" or "she" or more neutral ones such as "ze" or "they" (see *Sociology in my Community*).

LO3 NORMS AS REGULATORS OF SHARED BEHAVIOURS

Language is often used by members of a given culture to communicate expectations about appropriate conduct. This is another way that language places restrictions on individuals. How many times did a parent nag you to brush your teeth, wash your hands, or finish your supper before starting your dessert? Have your teachers ever reminded you to stay seated, sit quietly, or raise your hand before answering in class? Recall from Chapter 1 that *norms* are expectations for how we are supposed to act, think, and look. For sociologists, **folkways** are informal norms based on accepted

YOUR SOCIOLOGICAL TOOLKIT

SOCIOLOGY IN MY COMMUNITY

GENDER-NEUTRAL PRONOUNS

Most North American universities encourage the use of gender-neutral pronouns if preferred by students in reference to their personal identity. This practice may now be required by law in Canada with the recent passing of Bill C-16, which incorporates "gender identity" and "gender expression" into the Human Rights Act and Criminal Code.

Think Outside the Box: Why do you think universities encourage the use of terms that move beyond traditional pronouns?

Gender Pronouns

Please note that these are not the only pronouns. There are an infinite number of pronouns as new ones emerge in our language. Always ask someone for their pronouns.

Subjective	Objective	Possessive	Reflexive	Example
She	Her	Hers	Herself	She is speaking. I listened to her. The backpack is hers.
He	Him	His	Himself	He is speaking. I listened to him. The backpack is his.
They	Them	Theirs	Themself	They are speaking. I listened to them. The backpack is theirs.
Ze	Hir/Zir	Hirs/Zirs	Hirself/ Zirself	Ze is speaking. I listened to hir. The backpack is zirs.

Courtesy of Trans Student Educational Resources transtudent.org. Design by Landyn Pan

traditions and centre on acts of kindness or politeness that demonstrate respect for the generalized other. For example, unless you have been specifically told to do otherwise, you probably address your instructor with his or her formal title (e.g., "Doctor" or "Professor"), and wait your turn in a lineup to purchase coffee. Note that culture is always changing, and that is why you are much more inclined than your parents to begin an email or answer the phone with the greeting "hey" rather than "hello." Note that aspects of culture are also "contested" (i.e., disputed), and that is why some of your instructors may still frown on the use of "hey" as an appropriate conversation starter. Failure to comply with cultural expectations in the form of folkways generally results in informal sanctions (i.e., punishments), such as expressions of disapproval from others.

Mores refer to institutionalized norms that are considered to embody fundamental values. Mores are a formalized means for maintaining social control in society (this is discussed in more detail in the chapter on social control, deviance, and crime). Examples of mores in Canadian culture include formal legislation (i.e., laws) stating that no one is allowed to trespass, commit theft, or sell prohibited drugs. **Taboos** are mores that have such strong moral connotations attached to them that the acts are considered wrong in and of themselves (e.g., cannibalism and incest). Transgression of mores and taboos generally results in formal sanctions, such as the loss of personal freedom (i.e., a prison term).

Sociologists also distinguish between prescriptive and proscriptive norms. **Prescriptive norms** are rules depicting behaviours we are expected to perform, such as covering one's mouth while coughing, respecting the rights of others, and following the appropriate authority structures in the workplace. **Proscriptive norms** are rules outlining behaviours we are expected to *refrain* from doing, such as speaking with one's mouth full, swearing in church, or taking drugs that impair one's ability to perform in the workplace.

NONVERBAL COMMUNICATION AS A CONVEYER OF CULTURAL MEANING

Signs of disapproval and other informal sanctions are often applied through nonverbal communication. For example, a person who joins a friend at the front of a lineup at Tim Hortons may receive disapproving looks from other patrons.

Mores: Institutionalized norms embedded in laws used to help maintain social control.

Taboos: Mores that are considered wrong in and of themselves.

Prescriptive norms: Rules concerning behaviours we are expected to perform.

Proscriptive norms: Rules concerning behaviours we are expected to refrain from doing.

© Candy Davis. Courtesy of Icon Experience Photography

This gesture is common to Canadians and is used to display pleasure.

Similarly, when someone cuts in front of you in traffic, you might blow your horn or perhaps even give the other driver a hand gesture, such as the well-known middle-finger "salute," to communicate displeasure. Use caution while travelling in a foreign country and attempting to communicate using a gesture from your homeland. There are no universal gestures. Even commonplace Western gestures, such as waving hello or showing a peace sign, can mean different things in other cultures. All cultures, however, possess similar *categories* of gestures. For example, they have gestures (albeit different ones) for displays of friendship or anger. Also, some facial expressions are widely recognized across cultures (e.g., happiness, sadness, anger, surprise, disgust, and fear).

Nonverbal gestures with direct verbal equivalents are known as **emblems**. Emblems are typically used in place of words, an example being the traffic salute ("flipping a bird") mentioned earlier, or where someone motions by pulling an index finger toward him or her to represent "come here." Gestures are also used for greetings or displays of pleasure. Canadians display what looks like sideways "horns" with the index finger and pinky extended and *pointing sideways* or even down (see the grad photo) to indicate that they are having "fun." A similar gesture with the extended index finger and pinky *pointing up* is often displayed as "devil horns" by fans and band members at heavy metal concerts.

LO4 VALUES AS SHARED IDEAS

Recall that *cultural values* are collectively shared ideas about what is right and wrong. In 1990, the federal government created a task force to gather opinions from Canadians about their views on Canada's future and what it means to be Canadian. By the end of an eight-month data-gathering process, 75,069 calls had been received via an idea line, more than 13,000 group discussions had taken place involving 315,000 participants, 7,056 letters had been received, and more than 300,000 elementary and secondary students had participated in various forums (such as the Citizens' Forum on Canada's Future, 1991). Extensive analyses revealed that, taken together, participants identified seven common unifying Canadian values*:

Emblems: Gestures with direct verbal equivalents.

1. *Belief in equality and fairness in a democratic society.* The participants identified equality and fairness as a core value. One group, from Newfoundland, told the commission: "We believe that most Canadians want a society that ... protects national interests while remaining responsive and accountable, to individual rights; ... protects freedom, so that individuals can live in the manner of their choice, so long as they do not infringe on the rights of others; ... protects the rights of all Canadians to fair and equal treatment: women, ethnic minorities, different linguistic groups, aboriginal peoples, various religions, etc." (p. 35).
2. *Belief in consultation and dialogue.* Canadians regarded themselves as "people who settle their differences peacefully and in a consultative rather than confrontational manner" (p. 37) at both the level of individuals and the level of government. Participants noted that relations could be vastly improved if there were more opportunities for educational visitor exchanges, particularly those designed to illuminate issues involving Quebec's place in Confederation.
3. *Importance of accommodation and tolerance.* "Forum participants recognize the existence of different groups in societies and their need to sustain their own cultures while attaching themselves to the country's society, values, and institutions. As well, they acknowledge the existence of various legitimate competing regional and cultural interests in Canada" (p. 40). Acceptance and support were expressed especially in relation to overall ethnic diversity and the need to accommodate Indigenous self-government.
4. *Support for diversity.* Repeatedly, participants noted the importance of retaining and celebrating Canada's rich diversity in terms of language, region, ethnicity, and culture. This value is the overarching principle for the Canadian Multiculturalism Act as described in *Sociology in Practice*.
5. *Compassion and generosity.* Canadians recognized the importance of supporting the collective in the form of "universal and extensive social services, our health care system, our pensions, our willingness to welcome refugees, and our commitment to regional economic equalization" (p. 42).

*Citizen's Forum on Canada's Future – Keith Spicer Commission Report (1991). *Citizen's Forum on Canada's Future: A Report to the People and Government of Canada*. Permission granted by the Privy Council Office

Krishna.Wu/Shutterstock

Canadians value Canada's natural beauty.

6. *Attachment to Canada's natural beauty*. Canada's natural environment was identified as important. This was summarized by one person, who said, "All Canadians love the land" (p. 42). Widespread concern for the environment was best captured by a group in Nova Scotia: "The beauty of our country … must be preserved through stricter laws regarding pollution and other environmental hazards" (p. 43).

7. *Our world image: Commitment to freedom, peace, and nonviolent change*. Finally, the maintenance of a progressive but free and peace-keeping country was expressed by forum participants who felt that "Canadians are generally respected throughout the world," that "resorts to violence … have no rightful place in Canada," and that "a Canadian is a person, regardless of ethnic origin, who … feels free to develop in his or her own, individual way" (p. 44).

CORRESPONDING VALUES AND NORMS

Cultural values and norms are closely related in that values reflect group ideas, whereas norms are those ideas translated into expectations about actions. For example, Canadians value freedom and equality, including the right to choose marital partners (e.g., based on things such as love and mutual respect); this translates into laws recognizing same-sex marriages and laws permitting the adoption of children by same-sex couples. Similarly, people agree that diversity is important; the Government of Canada officially sanctions diversity, and this is stated in various policies.

YOUR SOCIOLOGICAL TOOLKIT

SOCIOLOGY IN PRACTICE

THE CANADIAN MULTICULTURALISM ACT

The Canadian Multiculturalism Act, as a policy of Canada, is to be carried out in ways that reflect core values, as illustrated by these excerpts:

> It is hereby declared to be the policy of the Government of Canada to
>
> (*a*) recognize and promote the understanding that multiculturalism reflects the cultural and racial diversity of Canadian society and acknowledges the freedom of all members of Canadian society to preserve, enhance and share their cultural heritage; …
>
> (*e*) ensure that all individuals receive equal treatment and equal protection under the law, while respecting and valuing their diversity;
>
> (*f*) encourage and assist the social, cultural, economic and political institutions of Canada to be both respectful and inclusive of Canada's multicultural character; …
>
> (*i*) preserve and enhance the use of languages other than English and French, while strengthening the status and use of the official languages of Canada; and
>
> (*j*) advance multiculturalism throughout Canada in harmony with the national commitment to the official languages of Canada.

Multiculturalism as a core Canadian value assumes that all groups are inherently equal within a culture. Sociologists, however, recognize the existence of a "dominant" Canadian culture—one that has the entrenched economic strength and political influence to impose its own cultural preferences on the rest of society.

Think Outside the Box: Who comprises Canada's dominant culture (i.e., what are some attributes of this group)? Why and how might this group serve to undermine multicultural values?

Source: Canadian Multiculturalism Act, 1985, c. 24 (4th Supp.), pp. 3–4.

For example, diversity is specifically recognized in the preamble to the Canadian Multiculturalism Act: "AND WHEREAS the Government of Canada recognizes the diversity of Canadians as regards race, national or ethnic origin, colour and religion as a fundamental characteristic of Canadian society" (Canadian Multiculturalism Act, 1985, p. 4).

So far, you have learned that culture is a broad concept that encompasses both tangible and intangible aspects of life that come to have particular meanings for a given group. Language plays an important role in creating and shaping reality as experienced by the members of a given culture. Language in verbal and nonverbal forms contributes to cultural diversity; it also helps regulate members of a culture through collectively shared ideas, referred to as values and behavioural expectations (i.e., norms). This next section takes a closer look at the correspondence between cultural values and norms and examines how well Canada lives up to its multicultural aims. Also see *Critical Thinking in Action* to learn more about Bill 62—a proposed law that highlights the contradictory nature of multiculturalism in theory versus practice.

Social facts: Observable social phenomena external to individuals that exercise power over them.

YOUR SOCIOLOGICAL TOOLKIT
SOCIOLOGY IN THEORY

FUNCTIONALIST AND CONFLICT PERSPECTIVES

Functionalists contend that shared cultural values are the foundation of society and what holds it together. According to Émile Durkheim, cultural values and norms are **social facts**—observable social phenomena external to individuals that exercise power over them (Durkheim, 1895/1938). For example, Durkheim posits: "When I perform my duties as a brother, husband or citizen and carry out the commitments I have entered into, I fulfil obligations which are defined in law and custom and which are external to myself and my actions. Even when they conform to my own sentiments and when I feel their reality within me, that reality does not cease to be objective, for it is not I who have prescribed these duties; I have received them through education" (p. 50). Durkheim argued that people display a *collective conscience,* that is, a recurring pattern by which they respect norms and follow them, because they have internalized them through early socialization practices (Durkheim, 1893/1933).

YOUR SOCIOLOGICAL TOOLKIT

CRITICAL THINKING IN ACTION

IS DIVERSITY SUPPORTED IN CANADA?

In 2015, Minister of Justice Stéphanie Vallée introduced Bill 62 in the legislature. Bill 62 is "An Act to foster adherence to State religious neutrality and, in particular, to provide a framework for religious accommodation requests in certain bodies." This bill, ostensibly to ensure religious freedom and equality in the province, requires public employees to "demonstrate religious neutrality" and not to act in ways that "favour nor hinder" others based on their religiosity (or nonaffiliation). The ambiguity of the wording implies (similar to controversial Bill 60, which was struck down) that all public employees in the province need to refrain from publicly displaying their faith—not just elected officials but also police, teachers, doctors, soldiers, transport workers, and so on. In practice, this means people have to refrain from wearing conspicuous religious attire. Thus, women who follow certain Islamic traditions would no longer have been permitted to wear the face veil known as the *burqa.* Similarly, men would be forbidden to wear turbans (e.g., Sikhs and Muslims) or *kippahs* (the cloth skullcap worn by Jewish men). In addition, it also implies that students in public schools might require special accommodations on a case-by-case basis because teachers would no longer be allowed to endorse practices that reflect particular religious beliefs (e.g., absences for religious reasons).

Think Outside the Box: Which of the seven core Canadian values discussed earlier in this chapter does Bill 62 most closely support, and which does it negate?

Internalization of norms means that as time goes on, people come to accept cultural norms and follow them without even being aware they are doing so. This is akin to how you habitually come into every sociology class shortly before it begins, then sit facing the front of the room and take notes during the lecture. Similarly, Talcott Parsons (1951) contended that culture is a generalized system of internalized symbols and meanings, along with role expectations (i.e., norms) and general values held by the collectivity. In this case, norms and values work together at a more general level in the form of social institutions (e.g., the family and school) to keep society running smoothly.

In contrast, the conflict framework highlights the lack of correspondence and the apparent contradictions between cultural values and norms. For example, even though equality is valued in Canadian society, not all groups are treated equally, as illustrated by the more than 150,000 Indigenous children who were mistreated in residential schools, which had been established to integrate them into a predominantly English-speaking Canadian culture. To learn about those residential schools and the Truth and Reconciliation Commission that has helped to rebuild the relationship between Indigenous peoples and Canadian society, refer to the later chapter on race and ethnicity.

LO5 IDEAL VERSUS REAL CULTURE

To explain the existence of common values alongside practices that appear to contradict these values, sociologists sometimes distinguish between "ideal" and "real" culture. **Ideal culture** encompasses the cultural values that most people identify with; **real culture** refers to the actual practices engaged in. For example, Canadians value equal rights, and although men and women are treated similarly under the law, this is not always the case in practice—women are still disadvantaged by inequities in pay (see Chapter 7). Similarly, Canadians highly value the natural environment and the need to protect it (ideal culture), yet they also engage in practices that harm it. For example, the oil sands in northern Alberta, where thousands of Canadians have found work, have also been found to destroy forests, pollute rivers, and emit toxins into the environment (real culture). Finally, although multiculturalism is highly valued by the majority of Canadians (ideal culture), it is also met with skepticism and fear (real culture) because it encourages groups to maintain divergent cultural beliefs and practices that may serve to fragment Canada's unity. That said, although minority groups do sometimes assert their interests (e.g., by participating in political discussions and by expressing their freedom of religion), they do so while abiding by the laws of the country and, in the case of immigrants, by upholding the oath of citizenship (Adam, 2008).

These discrepancies between real and ideal culture are not an exclusively Canadian phenomenon. Gannon's (2008) GLOBE study of 62 national or societal cultures found the same paradox: cultural values are consistently associated with cultural practices, but those associations are often contradictory. This means that, more often than not, groups behave in ways that go against cultural values. Why does this happen? Beyond the ongoing quest for control over scarce resources and the desire for profit discussed throughout this book, cultural variations in the existing beliefs and practices of particular groups also help explain the discrepancy.

TRADITIONAL BELIEFS VERSUS MODERN PRACTICES

Although discovery and invention often serve as precursors to cultural change, change is sometimes resisted when modern technology and science advocate for practices that are inconsistent with traditional beliefs that are highly regarded and continue to be part of a group's cultural heritage. For example, despite the well-established health benefits of breastfeeding for both mothers and infants in developing countries, cultural beliefs continue to discourage women from engaging in this practice. Osman, El Zein, and Wick's (2009) study of 353 first-time mothers recruited from 17 hospitals spread over five regions of Lebanon revealed that family members were a primary source of discouragement and that numerous cultural beliefs inhibited breastfeeding altogether or led to its discontinuation within a few months. In this case, cultural views included the belief that a mother can harm her infant through her breast milk (e.g., the baby could be poisoned by bad milk, or abdominal cramps could be transferred from a mother to her child via breast milk). In order to think like a sociologist, you need to employ the nonjudgmental principle of **cultural relativism**—contending that beliefs and practices are best understood from within

Ideal culture: Cultural values a majority of people identify with in a given society.

Real culture: Practices engaged in by the majority of people in a given society.

Cultural relativism: An ability to understand another culture in its own terms sympathetically enough so that the culture appears to be a coherent and meaningful design for living.

the culture in which they occur. According to Lavenda, Schultz, and Zutter (2016), we demonstrate cultural relativism when we are "understanding another culture in its own terms sympathetically enough so that the culture appears to be a coherent and meaningful design for living" (p. 30).

The recruitment of child soldiers is another example of a phenomenon that is viewed and practised very divergently depending on the culture in which it takes place. Although the United Nations and various human rights organizations call for worldwide bans on the recruitment of all individuals under the age of 18 for military purposes, a range of countries still allow it. Many of the larger and wealthier states recruit for the military beginning at age 17 (e.g., China, France, and the United States) and some as young as 16 (e.g., Brazil, Canada, and the United Kingdom). Afghanistan, Democratic Republic of Congo, Myanmar, Somalia, South Sudan, Sudan, and Yemen are considered among the seven "worst" recruitment countries for enlisting children under the age of 15 (Child Soldiers International, 2016). If you consider it wrong to recruit a 13-year-old in the Republic of the Sudan or in the Republic of South Sudan but not a 16-year-old in Canada, it is likely because you are viewing this practice from the perspective of the culture in which you were raised. Sociologists use the term **ethnocentrism** to refer to the tendency to believe that one's cultural beliefs and practices are superior and should be used as the standard to which other cultures are compared.

Sudanese children often end up in the military as an escape from extreme poverty. Thus, by declaring the cultural practice inhumane or by taking steps to abolish child soldiers, little improvements may actually come about in the lives of those most affected. The reintegration of former child soldiers into Sudanese communities following demobilization efforts has generally led to the reinstatement of the factors that promoted recruitment in the first place. Demobilized soldiers face lives of poverty because many families live off the equivalent of less than a dollar a day, with no access to running water or electricity and no means to feed additional members (CBC Radio, 2010). According to the deputy head of the Southern Sudan Demobilization, Disarmament and Reintegration Commission (SSDRC), "Getting food is very difficult.... So when a child moves from where he's getting food easily and whatever [in the military], then he goes and he fails [to eat] for something like two days, a day without food, then he has to think of going back" (Baddorf, 2010). Sociologist Ann Swidler (1986) points out that we have a tendency to focus too much on trying to explain actions (e.g., the employment of child soldiers) as based on cultural values (e.g., it is not okay to exploit children), and by doing so, we may neglect to focus on the distinct cultural phenomenon (e.g., widespread poverty) that may be more important as an explanatory agent for why such ideologies persist.

Ethnocentrism: The tendency to believe that one's cultural beliefs and practices are superior and should be used as the standard to which other cultures are compared.

Subculture: A group that can be differentiated from mainstream culture by its divergent traits involving language, norms, beliefs, and/or values.

Counterculture: A type of subculture that strongly opposes central aspects of mainstream culture.

SUBCULTURES AND COUNTERCULTURES

Even within Canada, cultural variations exist in beliefs and practices. A **subculture** is a group that can be differentiated from mainstream culture by its divergent traits involving language, norms, beliefs, and/or values. For example, Hutterites choose to live communally as colonies and work on cooperative farms that are owned by the entire group, sharing a distinct system of traditional beliefs concerning religion, dress codes, and rules for conduct that is unlike that of mainstream society. Individuals can belong to more than one subculture simultaneously, and various subcultures can exist within the larger context of Canadian culture at any given time. Subcultures are identified by shared traits, which can include food preferences (vegans and vegetarians), music interests (techno, Indie pop, and alternative rap), clothing and hairstyles (emo, punk, and gangsta), forms of body art (e.g., tattoos and piercings), shared recreation (e.g., Internet groups), and even age (baby boomers, Gen-Xers, and millennials).

A **counterculture** is a type of subculture that strongly opposes core aspects of the mainstream culture. Hells Angels are classified as a counterculture because of their involvement in criminal activities such as prostitution, drug trafficking, weapons trafficking, and extortion (Siegel, Brown, & Hoffman, 2006). The hippies were another counterculture; in the 1960s, these youth joined together to share their alternative value system, love of music, and drugs such as marijuana and LSD. Canadian culture continues to include a blend of diverse groups and traditions coexisting in what sociologists describe as a "cultural mosaic." The many subcultural cuisines that make up the Canadian food landscape today have their roots in the diffusion

The Canadian Press/Jonathan Hayward

Bountiful is a countercultural community in southeastern British Columbia that practises plural marriage (i.e., one man with multiple wives) as part of its religious doctrine.

of cultural traits across subcultures. Close to three quarters of Canadians (72 percent) report that they have a particular preference for Chinese, Italian, and Latin American/Mexican dishes (Gregoire, 2017).

TIME TO REVIEW

- What two assumptions make up the Sapir–Whorf hypothesis?
- In what ways do folkways differ from mores?
- How is nonverbal communication used to convey meaning?
- Why is it important to use cultural relativism when viewing cultural practices?
- What is the difference between a subculture and a counterculture?

LO6 HOW IS CANADIAN CULTURE UNIQUE?

THE ABUNDANCE OF CANADIAN SYMBOLS

At the beginning of the chapter, you were asked what comes to mind when you think of Canadian culture. Among other things, you probably thought of various symbols of the country, both material and nonmaterial. A **symbol** is an object, image, or event that represents a particular concept. For example, a heart is regularly used as a symbol for love. Similarly, a flag is

Mariemily Photos/Shutterstock.com

An RCMP officer in dress uniform.

often used to symbolize a country. The Canadian flag, then, serves as an important, uniquely "Canadian" symbol. Similarly, the RCMP is recognized throughout the world as a symbol of Canada's unique identity.

The Maple Leaf is one of Canada's more salient symbols, one that is recognized throughout the world. Canadians travelling abroad sometimes wear a Maple Leaf pin to identify themselves as Canadian or to distinguish themselves from Americans. As Ferguson and Ferguson (2001) put it in their playful book *How to Be a Canadian*, "the two central axioms of Canadian identity, the mantra and motto of an entire nation [are]: a. I. Am. Canadian. b. I am not American" (p. 159). Other well-accepted symbols underscore Canada's cultural diversity. For example, *inukshuks* (stone cairns built to look like people with their arms outstretched) remind us of Inuit traditions, whereas totem poles (carved from Western Red Cedar) are associated with the Indigenous peoples of the Pacific Northwest.

Even nonmaterial aspects of culture can serve as symbols, such as sports originating in Canada: hockey, lacrosse, basketball. Symbols also reflect values, including attachment to Canada's distinct natural beauty (the Canadian Rockies) and to

Symbol: An object, image, or event used to represent a particular concept.

Regien Paassen/Shutterstock

Totem poles in Stanley Park, Vancouver, BC.

Reprinted with permission of Orchestre Symphonique de Montréal

The Montréal Symphony Orchestra

its wildlife (the loon, Canada goose, beaver, moose, and polar bear). Finally, symbols are especially evident in popular forms of material culture: Canadian beer, maple syrup, Tim Hortons, and poutine. Note that although many Canadians still associate Molson Canadian breweries with Canada and the slogan "I. Am. Canadian" with Molson beer, Molson is actually produced by a multinational brewing company, Molson Coors.

THE PREVALENCE OF HIGH CULTURE AND POPULAR CULTURE

HIGH CULTURE AND THE SOCIAL ELITE

Canada's distinctiveness is also evident in its high culture and popular culture. For sociologists, **high culture** refers to activities shared mainly by the social elite, who supposedly possess an appreciation for this culture and the resources necessary to immerse themselves in it (i.e., wealth and higher education). High culture consists of the many forms of creative and performing arts (e.g., visual, theatre, and music). Famous Canadian examples from the performing arts are the Canadian Opera Company, the Stratford Festival, the Montréal Symphony Orchestra, and the Royal Winnipeg Ballet.

According to French sociologist Pierre Bourdieu (1930–2002), cultural and educational practices lead to the *social reproduction* of classes. Those in the higher classes have more financial resources, and this allows more exposure to high culture; also, they have been socialized by their elite families and by their education to understand and appreciate various aspects of that culture. Members of the social elite then pass on their shared understanding and appreciation of high culture to future generations as a social asset (Bourdieu, 1973). Participants in this elite culture can be distinguished from lower classes on the basis of status symbols. **Status symbols** are material indicators of wealth and prestige. Examples include imported luxury cars (Ferrari, Porsche, and Rolls-Royce), designer clothing and jewellery (Gucci, Chanel, and Hermès), and paintings by highly praised artists (Van Gogh, and Picasso, Cèzanne).

High culture: Activities shared by the social elite.

Status symbols: Material indicators of wealth and prestige.

Popular culture: Well-liked everyday practices and products.

POPULAR CULTURE AND THE MASSES

High culture is often contrasted with **popular culture**, a term used to describe the everyday cultural practices and products that are most desired by the masses. Canadian popular culture encompasses movies and television series, Internet sites such as Facebook and YouTube, cellphone apps, and heavily marketed products that may or may not originate in Canada (e.g., iPhones, drones, DreamWorks Trolls, Lego, Barbie, True Religion jeans, and Canada Goose parkas). Popular culture also includes well-established spots to eat, drink, or shop, such as McDonald's, Tim Hortons, Starbucks, American Eagle, and Lululemon. Popular culture, sometimes called "pop culture," is sometimes equated with "youth culture." A distinct youth culture emerged following the Second World War, a time characterized by a significant increase in births as well as by economic prosperity, which gave people more disposable income to spend on leisure, fashion, and the mass media (e.g., music). Since that time, specific eras have even been referred to by the popular culture prevalent at the time (e.g., hippy, disco, punk, and hip-hop) (Danesi, 2008).

But although pop culture is now often associated with youth culture, it extends further back in history; in fact, when fictional "novels" first emerged in the 15th century, they were considered to be the popular culture of the masses rather than the high culture of the elite. In contemporary society, much of pop culture is promoted and even constructed via the mass media (e.g., music idols, television and movie celebrities, and sports icons).

YOUR SOCIOLOGICAL TOOLKIT
SOCIOLOGY IN THEORY

LO7 CRITICAL VIEWS OF POPULAR CULTURE

Popular cultural theorist John Storey (2009) describes popular culture as an "*empty* conceptual category" that can be filled in a number of potentially conflicting ways. For example, popular culture can be viewed as whatever is left over from the categorization of high culture, as a power struggle involving dominant and subordinate classes, and as a venue for distinguishing various social groups from the dominant one (pp. 1–13). Critical approaches view pop culture from the perspective of ideology. **Ideology** refers to a set of ideas that support the needs and views of a particular group. Conflict theorists generally view popular culture as a means for the ruling class to control the masses.

The Frankfurt Institute for Social Research (later known as the Frankfurt School) was founded in 1923 as a research organization made up of critical scholars, including pop culture critics Theodor W. Adorno (1903–1969), Erich Fromm (1900–1980), and Max Horkheimer (1895–1973). Supporters of the Frankfurt School claim that popular culture serves the dominant class while exploiting the lower class (Danesi, 2008). Adorno (1991) points out how the price of commodities forms the basis of most social relations: "This is the real secret of success ... what one pays in the market for the product.... The consumer is really worshipping the money that he himself has paid for the ticket.... But he has not 'made it' by liking the concert, but rather by buying the ticket" (p. 38). Adorno further explains how the costs of advertising preclude the lower classes from ever getting a chance to make money in the culture industry. Although he refers to the culture industry as a form of "mass deception," he does not suggest that the consumer is naive; rather, the consumer is brought under the spell of advertising in such a way that he or she feels compelled to participate in consumerism even with a full understanding that capitalists are benefiting in ways that go well beyond the value of the product being sold.

Not everyone, however, views materialism as a form of exploitation. As Goldthorpe et al. (1969) note in *The Affluent Worker in the Class Structure*:

> It is not to us self-evident why one should regard our respondents' concern for decent, comfortable houses, for labour-saving devices, and even for such leisure goods as television sets and cars, as manifesting the force of "false" needs; of needs, that is, which are "superimposed upon the individual by particular social interests in his repression." It would be equally possible to consider the amenities and possessions for which the couples in our sample were striving as representing something like the minimum material basis on which they and their children may be able to develop a more individuated style of life, with a wider range of choices, than has hitherto been possible for the mass of the manual labour force. (pp. 183–184)

Even if consumerism is viewed as personal "choice" rather than a form of exploitation, it is important to note that many Canadians' choices are constrained by socioeconomic and other macro-level factors that are largely beyond their control.

In *Understanding Popular Culture*, John Fiske (2010) suggests that viewing culture from either a solely exploitive framework or a solely personal choice framework is too limiting. Popular culture is intricately tied into capitalism because it is the producers who determine what exists for the masses to consume. But this is not a one-way relationship, and the links between the two are important for understanding how the masses themselves help shape popular culture (see *Sociology in My Life*). Fiske differentiates between "mass culture" and "popular culture," noting that mass culture refers to the material products produced by the capitalists to exploit the masses, whereas popular culture includes the intangible components of culture experienced by the masses, components that in turn shape mass culture. Specifically, the masses impart their own meanings to the objects created by the capitalists and in doing so play an important role in shaping the face of consumerism. When asked why jeans are so popular, Fiske's students explained that jeans allowed them the freedom to "be themselves." In yet another paradox of values and norms, the students felt they were expressing their own individuality even while they were conforming to the same dress patterns as the wider group. Although producers of jeans are obviously out to make a profit, capitalism as an ideology is not directly transmitted into

Ideology: A set of ideas that support the needs and views of a particular group.

the commodities it produces. By purchasing jeans en masse, consumers contribute to capitalism and enable it to thrive. For example, producers can use profits to expand manufacturing and locate means to further exploit the profit potential of the market. But in addition, by paying attention to the meanings of their products for consumers, producers can expand into various styles and designer labels; these allow for greater profit but also build upon individuality and the need to maintain group allegiance.

Finally, it is important to note that although we continue to distinguish between high culture and popular culture, the original emphasis on an elite class consuming and reproducing high culture versus the masses engaged in more popular forms of culture accessible to those with lower educational attainment and a modest income bears little resemblance to today's cultural consumption habits. Someone with a low income may forego buying tickets to the symphony but can still enjoy the very best symphony performances free via YouTube. And anyone may purchase trending songs spanning an array of genres from iTunes. Sociologist Richard Peterson (1992) notes that although those in the upper classes are still more likely than those in the lower classes to appreciate certain features of high culture (e.g., symphonic music) and to participate in some of the more traditionally elite activities (e.g., attending the opera and owning art collections), they are also very likely to enjoy a variety of genres of music and participate in popular culture activities. Rather than view the elite as "snobs," Peterson used the term "*cultural omnivores*" to describe those of high social standing who enjoy high culture *and* are just as likely to participate in non-elite activities.

TIME TO REVIEW

- In what ways do symbols contribute to Canadian culture?
- What is the difference between high culture and popular culture?
- In what ways does the conflict perspective present a negative view of popular culture?

In this chapter, we emphasized different kinds of culture and explained how culture shapes our identity through language, values, and norms. We also explored cultural diversity and the implications posed by contradictions between norms and values. Canadian culture, although diverse, also includes shared cultural features, as evidenced by the abundance of widely recognized symbols and the established nature of high culture shared by the social elite and popular culture consumed by much of Canadian society.

All of the elements of culture discussed thus far help form the basis of the social structure of a given society. We rely on language, norms, and values to help us make sense of our everyday lives, to guide our behaviour, and to facilitate social interactions with others around us. In the next chapter, you will learn about how the elements of culture continue to shape our social identity and contribute to our unique self, which develops through our interactions with others in a lifelong process of socialization.

YOUR SOCIOLOGICAL TOOLKIT

SOCIOLOGY IN MY LIFE

IN WHAT WAYS DO YOU INFLUENCE POPULAR CULTURE?

Consider the many items you possess that are indicative of popular culture. Most students, for example, have a cellphone. Without making reference to its basic functions (to make and accept calls or to send and receive text messages), how would you describe what your phone *means* to you? Fiske (2010) has suggested that we should view popular culture as something that is in part negotiated by the masses, which help shape what becomes popular at a given point in time.

Think Outside the Box: In what ways is the meaning your phone has for you shaped by the wider mobile phone industry? Conversely, in what ways does the meaning it has for you shape that industry?

CHAPTER SUMMARY

LO1 Define culture and distinguish between material and nonmaterial forms.

Culture is the sum total of the social environment in which we are raised and in which we continue to be socialized throughout our lives. Material culture includes all of the tangible or physical items that people have created for use and give meaning to, whereas nonmaterial culture includes intangibles produced by intellectual or spiritual development and the use of artifacts in a given culture.

LO2 Explain why language is viewed as a precursor to shared understandings and explain how language confers gender expectations.

Language determines how we think and what we think about, thereby shaping the reality experienced by those who share a common language. Cultural constructions are embedded in language, as in the case of different words commonly used to describe males and females.

LO3 Explain why norms are considered to be regulators of shared behaviours.

Norms inform members of a culture about appropriate and inappropriate forms of conduct; violations of norms result in sanctions.

LO4 Identify shared values and debate the correspondence between cultural values and norms using functionalist and conflict perspectives.

Core Canadian values include a widespread belief in equality, consultation, accommodation, support for diversity, compassion, a concern for the environment, and world peace. A functionalist perspective highlights the existence of shared values, such as support for diversity. Functionalists emphasize how shared ideas translate into widely followed practices such as respect for the diversity of languages spoken in Canada. In contrast, a conflict perspective highlights the lack of correspondence between values and norms, as in the case of Indigenous children who were not allowed to speak their mother tongue in residential schools.

LO5 Explain why values exist alongside contradictory norms.

There are a number of reasons why values and norms do not always correspond. Traditional beliefs passed from one generation to the next may prevent groups from engaging in particular behaviours and may also condone behaviours that go against cultural ideals. Also, cultural variations exist within and between various subcultures and countercultures operating in a larger cultural context.

LO6 Describe features of Canadian culture that make it unique.

The uniqueness of Canada's culture is evident in the abundance of symbols (e.g., the Maple Leaf and the RCMP) and many forms of high culture and popular culture. High culture refers to activities shared by the social elite. Popular culture refers to well-liked, everyday cultural practices and products that are widely engaged in and/or used by the masses.

LO7 Outline the main assumptions of critical views of popular culture.

Critical perspectives generally view popular culture as a means for the ruling class to control the masses, although some theorists see popular culture more as a matter of personal choice than exploitation. Fiske's (2010) framework rests on the assumption that the masses give meaning to commodities created by the ruling class; this in turn shapes popular culture.

RECOMMENDED RESOURCES

1. To learn more about words and phrases that are uniquely Canadian, you can access *A Dictionary of Canadianisms on Historical Principles* at http://faculty.arts.ubc.ca/sdollinger/dchp2.htm.
2. To watch *Atanarjuat (The Fast Runner)*, visit: http://www.isuma.tv/atanarjuat.
3. To learn about Indigenous terminology, culture, and identity and to better understand Indigenous issues in Canada, we recommend C. Vowel, *Indigenous Writes: A Guide to First Nations, Métis & Inuit Issues in Canada* (Winnipeg, MB: Highwater Press, 2016).
4. For an excellent discussion of popular culture in capitalist societies, refer to J. Fiske, *Understanding Popular Culture* (2nd ed.) (New York, NY: Routledge, 2010).

FOR FURTHER REFLECTION

1. Reflect on how language shapes culture. Suppose you or a close friend were raised to only speak English, whereas your parents (or grandparents) speak a different mother tongue. Are any aspects of your parents'/grandparents' cultural heritage now lost as a result of having to translate meanings from one language to another?
2. Take a minute to reflect on the seven shared Canadian values identified in this chapter. Is there a value you strongly believe in that is not listed here? Which of the items listed here do you perceive would generate the most agreement among Canadians? Which would receive the least amount of support? Why do you think this is the case? Does our government support these values? Why or why not?
3. Can you identify one item you possess and are especially fond of that would be considered an example of Canadian popular culture? How might your reasons for owning this item be viewed as supporting the interests of capitalists?

ENDNOTE

1 Retrieved March 18, 2017, from "Discover Canada: Memorable Quotes," http://www.cic.gc.ca.

Socialization: The Self and Social Identity

Rawpixel.com/Shutterstock

I know you are, but what am I?

(Paul Reubens, as Pee-Wee Herman)[1]

LEARNING OBJECTIVES & OUTCOMES

After reading this chapter, students should be able to do the following:

LO1 Explain how our own unique sense of "self" includes traits that fall along a personal–social identity continuum.

LO2 Define "self" and explain its connection to socialization and social interaction.

LO3 Describe the continuum of nature versus nurture assumptions.

LO4 Describe Mead's stages of development of the self and differentiate between the "I" and the "me."

LO5 Identify the ways in which the perceptions of others affect our individual identities.

LO6 Identify primary agents of socialization and describe their main contributions to the development of the self and/or social identity.

LO7 Outline the basic components of social structure.

LO8 Explain how social institutions contribute to social structure and assess the merits of Weber's ideal type of bureaucracy in modern society.

LO1 IDENTIFYING OURSELVES AND IDENTIFYING OTHERS

The opening quotation was often used by a 1980s children's TV and film character, Pee-Wee Herman. He would use it as a child-like retort whenever another character called him an unpleasant name; the phrase may even bring back schoolyard memories of your own childhood. But those words also reveal a more basic aspect of social life—the fact that we are in a constant process of both identifying ourselves and being identified by others. Countless characteristics are integrated into this process, ranging from physical attributes (e.g., 5′ 10″, brown-haired, green-eyed) and ascribed characteristics (e.g., Indigenous, male) to abilities (e.g., visual-spatial, athletic), likes/dislikes (e.g., rock versus country music), preferences (e.g., vegetarian, taking the bus to work), and group affiliations (e.g., church member, full-time student, chess club). When integrated into your own sense of self, those traits fall along a **personal–social identity continuum** (Tajfel & Turner, 1986). The personal–social identity continuum refers to the range of traits you possess that emphasize the way you see yourself as a unique individual on one end and those that underscore your membership in a group on the other end. Precisely which traits stand out the most to you at any given time can vary across contexts. "Lousy dancer" may become more dominant when you are at a wedding, "Canadian citizen" when you are crossing an international border, and "father" when you are attending a parent–teacher interview at a school. Identities are always in flux as we change throughout our lives, developing new interests and abandoning some old ones, getting a new job, meeting new people, having children, aging, and accumulating life experiences that influence our view of the world and ourselves.

Among the myriad characteristics that contribute to our individual sense of self, some constitute *master statuses* (defined and described in more detail later on), ones that are so fundamental to who we are that they shape almost every aspect of our lives and take precedence over other characteristics. Sex and gender and race and ethnicity (addressed in later chapters) are some of these characteristics; you may view them as essential to your identity, but even if you don't, they are still central to how *others* categorize you, and they affect your life in a multitude

Personal–social identity continuum: The range of traits you possess that emphasize the manner in which you see yourself as a unique individual on one end and those that underscore your membership in a group on the other end.

of ways. And even if the way that others identify you corresponds to the way you identify yourself, there can still be divergent views about the **auxiliary traits** that are presumed to accompany that master status. Auxiliary traits refer to *other* characteristics that a person associates with a particular master status. For example, you might associate "parenthood" with qualities such as nurturance and patience; someone else, though, might associate that same master status with discipline and authority. Similarly, the interests, skills, and abilities that one person associates with being "female" might be quite different from those that another person associates with being "female."

LO2 THE SUBJECTIVE AND SOCIAL NATURE OF THE SELF

Although our identities undergo a multitude of changes over time, we still think of our core self as somewhat "stable" and "knowable" (O'Brien, 2011). Sociologists use the term "self" to refer to our knowledge of ourselves as entities separate and distinct from others and the term **self-concept** to refer to the totality of various traits, feelings, and values that underlie our own unique personalities and preferences (Schieman, 2007). We recognize where our abilities and some of our challenges lie, and we can also identify ways in which we compare to others and "fit in" or "stand out from" our families, circle of friends, and others in society. From a social psychological perspective, this sense of self is both "subjective" and "social" (Charmaz, 2007). Our self-concept is subjective because each of us has our own perception of the unique collection of traits, talents, and experiences we possess (e.g., one of the authors perceives herself to be "friendly," "impatient," "generous," "responsible," "directionally challenged," "clever," and "physically active"). The crux of the self-concept is also social because it is only through our interactions with others that we come to develop the meanings, shared understandings, and bases of comparison that ultimately create our subjective selves (Charmaz, 2007). For example, the same author perceives herself to be generous largely because others have pointed this out (e.g., students and colleagues express their appreciation for help obtained, friends and family tease her for being "too generous" with gifts). Similarly, you might consider yourself to be "attractive" or "talented" based on the amount and kind of attention you have received from others in various social environments. Self-understanding, then, is an individual's sense of who he or she "is" at a given time, based on perceived similarities to and differences from others. It is formed through **socialization**, the lifelong process through which people learn about themselves and their various roles within society and in relation to one another. Socialization includes learning the norms, values, and language of a shared culture, as well as the knowledge, understandings, and experiences that help shape our **social identities** (who we are in terms of the social groups we consider ourselves to be a part of) and our **personal identities** (the ways we consider ourselves to be unique individuals). From a sociological perspective, this learning is contingent on other people—that is, it is a function of social interaction. This chapter explores how our personal and social identities form, develop, grow, and change over time and how we, in turn, have socializing effects on others.

Auxiliary traits: Characteristics presumed to accompany a specific master status.

Self-concept: An individual's sense of who he or she is based on perceived similarities to and differences from others.

Socialization: The lifelong process through which people learn about themselves and their various roles in society and in relation to one another.

Social identity: The portion of an individual's sense of self derived from membership in social groups.

Personal identity: The portion of an individual's sense of self that renders him or her unique from others.

Biological determinism: The belief that human behaviour is controlled by genetics.

Sociobiology: The belief that social behaviour evolved from the need to reproduce and survive.

LO3 NATURE AND NURTURE: MAJOR INFLUENCES ON THE DEVELOPING SELF

Early philosophers questioned whether a newborn possesses inborn (biological) influences that predetermine who he or she will eventually become or whether a newborn is a "blank slate" on which society imposes its influence. Traditionally, this consideration was labelled the nature versus nurture debate, implying that identity is wholly the result of one or the other.

BIOLOGICAL INFLUENCES

On the extreme end of "nature," evolutionary theorists advocate **biological determinism**, the belief that all human behaviour is controlled by our genetic makeup. Biological determinism underlies a controversial concept called **sociobiology**, which claims an evolutionary origin for people's social behaviour based on a species' need to reproduce and survive (Wilson, 1975). To explain differences in mate selection strategies, for example, sociobiology points out how it is advantageous for males to have multiple partners and to seek out young, attractive potential partners who symbolize fertility, whereas it is more advantageous for females to select a male on the basis of power and resources (Bailey et al., 1994). Whereas sociobiology has been widely criticized for its dependence on ultimate causes rooted in natural selection processes, other biosociological theories based on more proximal causes, such as genes, enzymes, or hormones, continue to show merit for explaining social behaviour (Machalek, 2007). For example, researchers in Toronto have identified the presence of certain enzymes in children with clinically diagnosed aggression (Beitchman et al., 2004). Prison studies find high levels of testosterone in males who commit violent and sexual crimes (Dabbs et al., 1995). Twin studies also find more congruence in the criminality of identical twins compared to nonidentical twins (Raine, 1993). Of course, based on similarity in looks, parents and significant others might treat identical twins more alike than fraternal ones to create this outcome. However, the Minnesota Twin Study examined the influence of genetics in twins who were raised apart and found that biology helped explain similarities in their personalities and behaviours (Segal, 2012).

SOCIETAL INFLUENCES

The other side of the debate is typified by **behaviourism**, a school of thought centred on external influences and attributed to psychologist John B. Watson, who claimed that all behaviour was the result of learning: "Give me a dozen healthy infants, well-formed, and my own specified world to bring them up in and I'll guarantee to take any one at random and train him to become any type of specialist I might select—doctor, lawyer, artist, merchant-chief and, yes, even beggar-man and thief, regardless of his talents, penchants, tendencies, abilities, vocations, and race of his ancestors" (Watson, 1924, p. 82). B.F. Skinner (1938) later developed "radical behaviourism" (also known as "behaviour analysis"), which similarly downplayed the importance of biology but also emphasized how learning is a function of the consequences that follow behaviour. Specifically, reinforcement in the form of positive consequences strengthens the likelihood of future responses, whereas negative consequences decrease them. However, social psychologist Albert Bandura's early research on aggression led him to conclude that a lot of learning takes place in the absence of immediate or obvious consequences, where people simply observe and then imitate the actions of others (Bandura, 1962; Bandura & Walters, 1959).

Today, most academics (including sociologists) recognize the interrelationships between nature (biology) and nurture (socialization and social interaction) as important for influencing people's lives and their developing selves. Although children inherit particular genes from their parents, their families of origin also provide a context within which socialization takes place. The interaction between biological factors (e.g., hereditary predispositions) and the environment (e.g., interactions with others) helps a child reach his or her potential. As discussed in the earlier chapter on culture, language is the primary means by which we interact with one another, experience life, and convey meaning. Case studies of lost or abandoned children who have been raised in isolation and lack human contact teach us that in the absence of socialization processes, humans fail to develop social behaviours we consider fundamental to being human, such as communicating with language (see *Sociology in the News*). Similarly, children born with genetically inherited disabilities may develop only limited social functioning even with high levels of social engagement. Thus, both nature and nurture are necessary for human development, growth, and potential and are equally important.

AGENCY AND HUMAN DEVELOPMENT

Furthermore, individuals actively shape their own environments over time. This view is best captured by the **bio-ecological theory of human development**, which stresses the importance of human agency and considers human development to be an ongoing, evolving, and reciprocal process between individuals and their wider structural environments. Many layers of influence and reciprocal interaction help shape (or, conversely, hinder) human potential, including micro-level influences, such as parents, teachers, and peers, as well as larger,

Behaviourism: A school of thought that denies free will, emphasizes observable phenomena, and claims that all behaviour is learned from the environment.

Bio-ecological theory of human development: A theory that views human development as a dynamic process of reciprocal interaction in which individuals play an important role in shaping the environment in which they develop.

more removed forces (e.g., the economy, social services, political ideology) (Bronfenbrenner, 2001). Moreover, these forces operate on individuals who are themselves active agents. Children may resist or embrace the attempts made by their parents, teachers, and friends to teach them life lessons. Adolescents make choices about who they wish to spend time with, and those choices help shape the experiences that unfold from there. Young adults associate with particular groups, date certain individuals, and work for specific employers. Within the ensuing interactions, existing ideas and meanings are brought to light, new meanings develop, traits are shaped, and various characteristics are adopted to create the identities that comprise the self. Bronfenbrenner (2005) summarizes this process as follows: "Human beings create environments that shape the course of human development. Their actions influence the multiple physical and cultural tiers of the ecology that shapes them, and this agency makes humans—for better or worse—active producers of their own development" (p. xxvii).

SOCIALIZATION AND GENETIC INFLUENCES

Lastly, research suggests that socialization itself is influenced by a complex interplay between genetic preconditions and environmental factors. Avinun and Knafo-Noam (2015) explain how a child's genotype can affect his or her temperament to impact the type of parenting received, which ultimately influences how that child experiences the world. For example, fearful children (as indicated by various neurological and endocrine responses) are at risk for negative parenting, which can lead to long-term negative outcomes in children exposed to negative parenting that can still be present by the time they reach adulthood. Some reactions from early caregivers are now believed to change how genes are expressed in offspring via epigenetic processes, blurring earlier distinctions made between nature and nature and working to shape the developing self. *Epigenetics*, originally coined by Waddington (1942), refers to the study of the mechanisms that bring about changes in gene expression.

SOCIOLOGY IN THE NEWS

FERAL CHILD: THE CASE OF NG CHHAIDY

In 2012, the world discovered a "feral child" named Ng Chhaidy, who was reunited with her family after 38 years of separation, during which she spent much of her life living in isolation in an Indian forest. Ng Chhaidy went missing from her village in Saiha in the southernmost district of Mizoram, which borders Myanmar, when she was only four years old (Edwards, 2012). Chhaidy and her cousin Beiraku, who was also four at the time, disappeared while playing in a field shortly before a heavy rainstorm. Although Beiraku was later found beside a stream, there was no sign of Chhaidy (Edwards, 2012). Over the years, there were a few purported sightings of "a jungle girl," but her father was unable to find her. After a visitor from Myanmar told Chhaidy's father that he resembled a woman she had adopted after finding her "naked and half dead" in the village cemetery, he raised the money to travel to Aru to see if this might be his long-lost child. As it turned out, she was (Edwards, 2012). Since her reunion with her family in 2012, Chhaidy, now in her late 40s, has received no professional help and remains an untapped goldmine of scientific discovery. Although she is still childlike and unable to use language in a conventional sense, Chhaidy is described as having adjusted to her new life remarkably well and is full of emotion, demanding regular "impromptu hugs and kisses" from those close to her (Dixit, 2015).

Chhaidy with her mother.

TIME TO REVIEW

- What is the personal–social identity continuum, and how do master statuses and auxiliary traits fit into it?
- What is included in one's self-concept?
- In what ways is the self both subjective and social?
- What is the main assumption underlying biological determinism?
- Which school of thought best typifies the nurture side of the development debate?

YOUR SOCIOLOGICAL TOOLKIT
SOCIOLOGY IN THEORY

DEVELOPMENT OF THE SELF

An emphasis on meanings and subjective understandings is at the foundation of the symbolic interactionist perspective. According to Blumer (1969, p. 2), that perspective rests on three assumptions:

1. Human beings act toward things (such as other humans or objects) on the basis of the meanings the things have for them.
2. The meaning of things is derived from social interactions.
3. These meanings are handled and modified through an interpretive process.

For Mead (1934), the uniquely human capacity for acting and reacting in relation to others on the basis of shared meanings is the essence of the development of the social self. This "reflexive" self can take into account itself (as an object), itself in relation to others (as a subject), and the views of wider society (i.e., the generalized other). Mead (1934) pointed out that we are not born with a self; rather, the self develops within and through our interactions with others. This is especially evident in children's play and games.

LO4 I, ME, AND THE GENERALIZED OTHER

Shortly after birth, an infant is able to recognize significant others. A baby also begins to see himself or herself as an object—an entity that exists with fingers and toes that can be moved around and even put into a mouth. In this *preparatory stage*, babies do little more than imitate others. For example, an infant will wave "bye-bye" in response to someone else waving "bye-bye." In the next stage, called the *play stage*, children start to take on the role of others. Here, a child begins to see that people exist in relation to one another. A common form of play at this stage is to play "house," where the child takes on the role of one other person in a household, such as pretending to be "the mommy." Or a child might listen to someone's heart with a toy stethoscope, pretending to be a "doctor," or place items in a toy basket, pretending to be a "shopper," or place fake food in a little pot, pretending to "cook supper," in response to visits to the family physician, going on trips to the grocery store, and/or observing parents prepare meals. During this phase, a child can only focus on one role or perspective at a time (e.g., "I am the doctor" or "I am the mommy"). However, the child can switch back and forth between roles and demonstrate an understanding of temporal order (e.g., a child pretends to be a cook to make a meal and then, when the meal is ready, pretends to be the person at the table eating the meal) (Angus, 2007). It is not until the *game stage* that a child is able to take into account several different roles simultaneously.

Mead (1934) used the analogy of a baseball game to explain how the actor in the game stage must be able to understand different roles and perspectives and be able to think about them simultaneously before making a move. For example, a pitcher will need to consider the score, the inning, and the various players and their relative positions (e.g., on the bases) before making a decision about where to throw a ball retrieved while in play (see *Figure 4.1*). The ability to engage in role taking and account for multiple perspectives at once is what Mead meant by the socialized self or the "generalized other."

Mead further distinguished between two parts of the self: the "I" and the "me" (see *Figure 4.2*). The "I" is the relatively uninhibited and spontaneous self that is unique to the person (i.e., the constellation of one's personality traits that form the basis of the self-concept, along with subconscious desires and creative potential). In contrast, the "me" represents the socialized self that acts in accordance with societal expectations. For example, one of the authors notes that her spontaneous "I" who is in a hurry to get to class might desire to join a colleague she recognizes at the front of a long lineup at Tim Hortons, but the more socialized "me" is either going to wait at the end of the lineup for the appropriate turn to purchase coffee or forgo a coffee purchase altogether in order to reach class early.

FIGURE 4.1

Mead's Stages in the Development of the Self

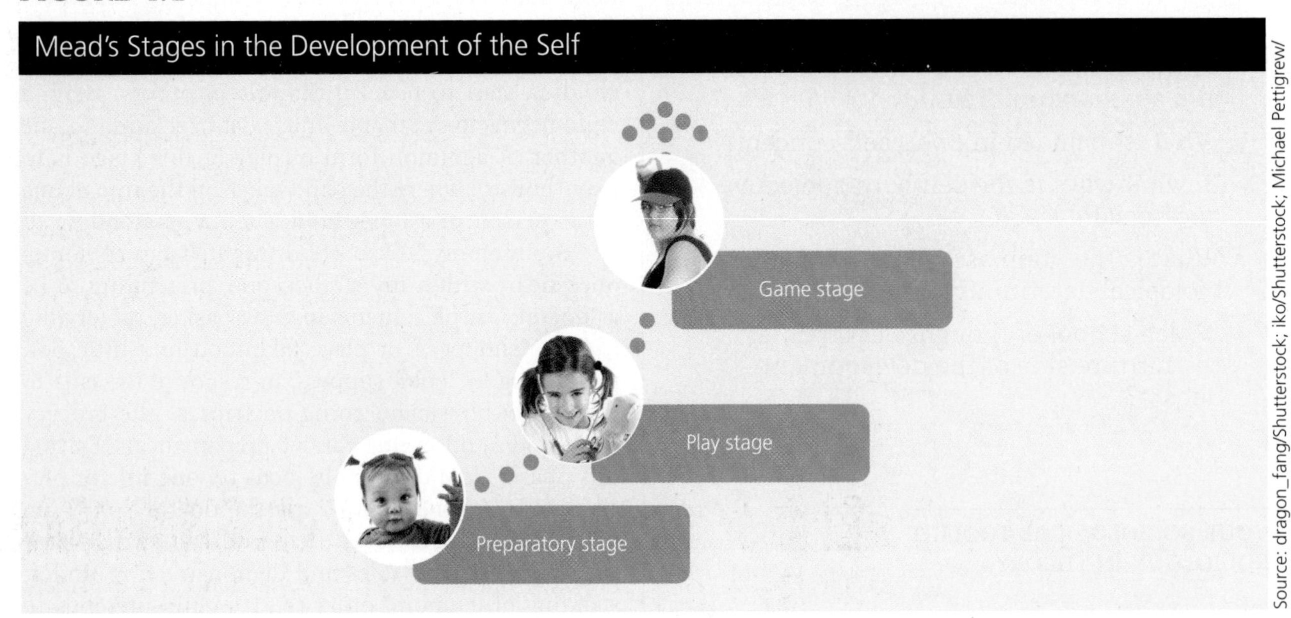

Source: dragon_fang/Shutterstock; iko/Shutterstock; Michael Pettigrew/Shutterstock

FIGURE 4.2

Mead's Representation of the Self: The "I" and the "Me"

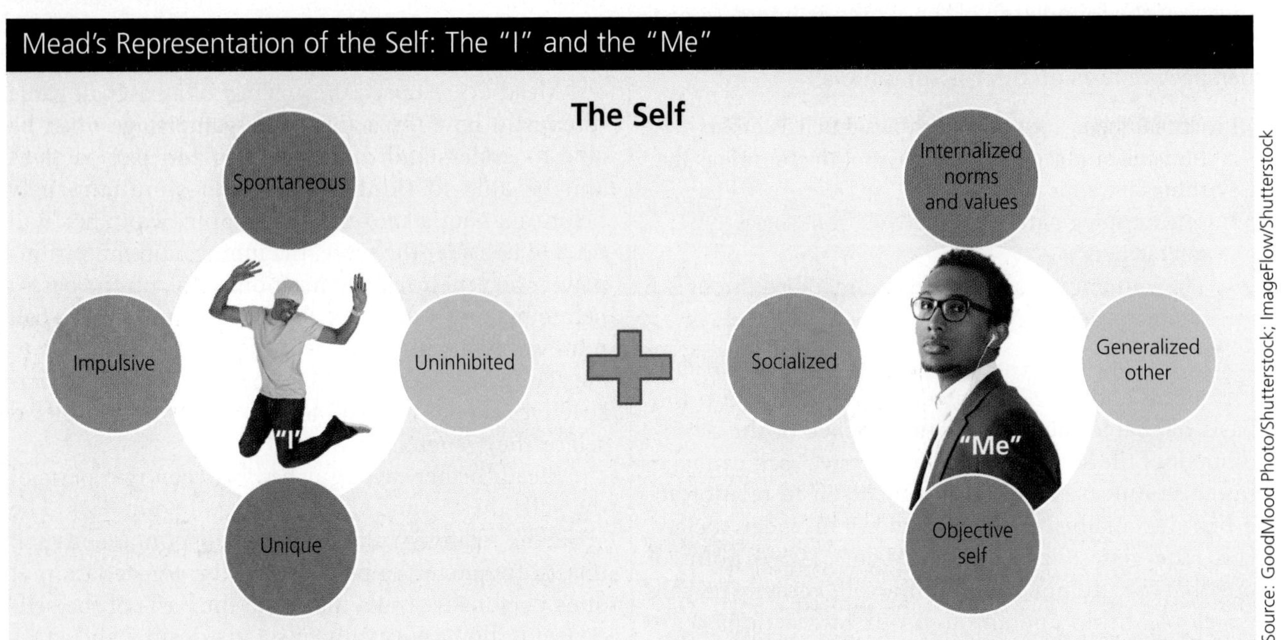

Source: GoodMood Photo/Shutterstock; ImageFlow/Shutterstock

LO5 SELF-PERCEPTION: THE LOOKING-GLASS SELF

Note that not everything we learn about ourselves from others is positive or even accurate, yet these views still have an impact on the developing self. Inevitably, children get into disagreements with their peers that sometimes culminate in an exchange of insults, such as name calling. When this happens, parents and teachers often tell children that what others think of them shouldn't matter—that "sticks and stones may break my bones, but names will never hurt me." In fact, what others think of you *does* matter and can have significant implications. Interactionist theories explain how the way that others identify and label us affects our self-perception. An important

FIGURE 4.3

Cooley's Looking-Glass Self

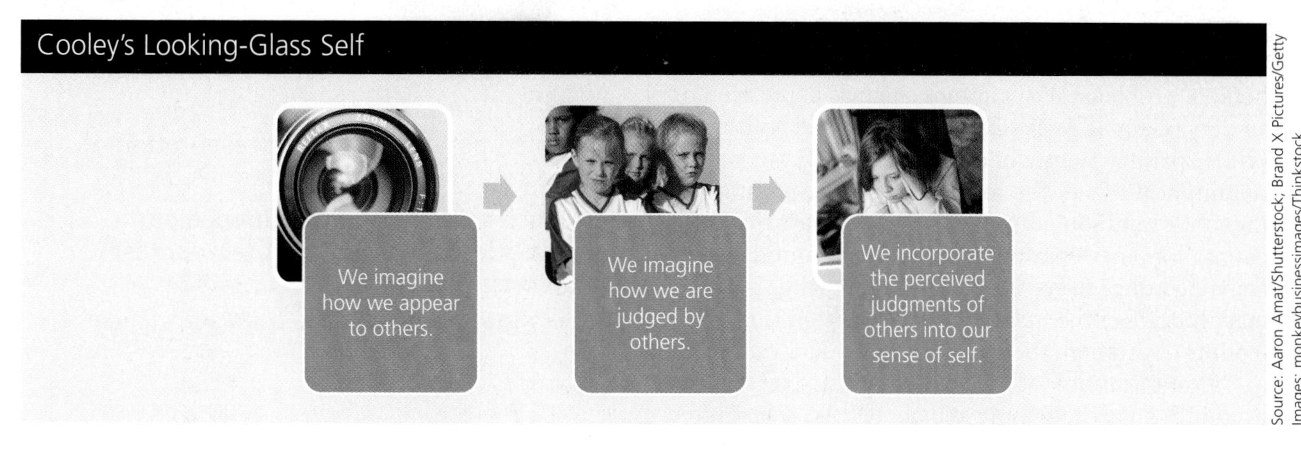

Source: Aaron Amat/Shutterstock; Brand X Pictures/Getty Images; monkeybusinessimages/Thinkstock

concept within the interactionist perspective is the **looking-glass self**. The looking-glass self refers to the sense of ourselves that we develop based on our perceptions of how others view us. Charles Horton Cooley (1864–1929) proposed that people in our lives serve as a "looking glass" (a historical term for mirror) (Cooley, 1902). When we interact with them, we "see" ourselves reflected back. There are three core components to the looking-glass self (Yeung & Martin, 2003). First, we imagine how we appear to others. Second, we imagine how they judge that appearance. Third, we incorporate the perceived judgments of others into our own sense of self (see *Figure 4.3*).

For instance, if we think our parents consider us intelligent, capable, and attractive, we will come to see ourselves in the same way; similarly, if we think they perceive us as incompetent and unattractive, we begin to see ourselves that way as well. Note that it is the *perceived* judgment of others that is significant. Hence, we may *incorrectly* believe that our parents consider us incompetent, and this will still become incorporated into our looking-glass self. In addition, when others identify us on the basis of master statuses such as sex or ethnicity, which they then associate with certain auxiliary traits, our own identities may be affected by the assumed accompanying auxiliary traits. For example, if parents continuously act in an overly protective manner toward a daughter who is "vulnerable" and "needs protection," that daughter may come to view herself as vulnerable and in need of protection.

The influence of others on our personal and group identity is neither direct nor certain. First, the extent of influence may depend on how important those others are to us. The perceptions of significant others (e.g., family members) may have more of an impact

"Of course you're big and clumsy but don't forget one thing: you're supposed to be big and clumsy."

Farris, Joseph, jfa1521, Cartoonstock.com

than those of more distant people in our lives (e.g., coworkers) or the generalized other (Cooley, 1902; Gamble & Yu, 2008; Yeung & Martin, 2003). Second, there are individual differences in the extent to which the looking-glass self is utilized (Hartner, 1999; Hartner & Whitesell, 2003). That is, some people have more of a *looking-glass self-orientation (LGSO)*, whereas others have more of a

Looking-glass self: The sense of ourselves that we develop based on our perceptions of how others view us.

"core" self-orientation. A person with more of a LGSO is more dependent on others' perceptions for his or her sense of self. A stronger LGSO is associated with less stability in one's identity, as well as a greater likelihood of problematic symptoms, such as depression or anxiety (Gamble & Yu, 2008). Maruna and colleagues (2004) paint a picture of even more significant potential implications of the looking-glass self, pointing to the subtle (and sometimes not so subtle) ways that drug counsellors may communicate a lack of confidence in convicted drug users' ability to really change—which may then affect the likelihood of **recidivism** (i.e., reoffending). Although there may be individual variations in the implications of the looking-glass self, there is no doubt that the way in which at least *some* other people see you has an impact on how you, in turn, see yourself and, in turn, how you present yourself, including your virtual self (see *Critical Thinking in Action*).

Recidivism: Committing further crimes after having been convicted of a crime.

TIME TO REVIEW

- According to Mead, what three stages make up the development of the social self?
- Which part of Mead's representation of the self includes the generalized other?
- How do other people influence our identities, according to interactionist theorists?
- Do others influence everyone equally?

People learn, grow, and change over time with age, through new experiences, and in response to others. Thus, socialization takes many different forms and is enacted in various ways throughout the life course. Sociologists use the term *primary socialization* to refer to the earliest form of socialization,

YOUR SOCIOLOGICAL TOOLKIT

CRITICAL THINKING IN ACTION

SELF-TRACKING AND THE CREATION OF A VIRTUAL SELF

Have you ever kept track of how much weight you lost or how much progress you made in the gym over time? In *The Virtual Self: How Our Digital Lives Are Altering the World Around Us*, Nora Young (2012) describes the culture of "self-tracking," wherein we create digital records of ourselves. For example, people keep track of how fit and healthy they are by recording their dietary intake, energy expenditure, and weight gains and losses using Internet-based programs such as Weight Watchers® online, mobile apps (e.g., MyFitnessPal, SparkPeople Mobile), and gadgets such as the Fitbit Blaze or Withings Go. The act of monitoring ourselves is not new. But as Young (2012) points out, we are now creating data about ourselves in volumes that never existed before, and we are sharing this information as part of our "digital reality." Think about what you share with others using social media such as Facebook, Twitter, and LinkedIn. Our digital selves can include postings about our daily thoughts and moods, our likes and dislikes, our current job and relationship statuses, the events we plan to attend, the places we've been, and even compilations of our personal achievements and our connections to others.

What image is conveyed in your digital self?

Think Outside the Box: In what ways has your virtual self changed over time? How does your virtual self illustrate what sociologists refer to as "agency"?

which begins the moment an individual is born into a culture and experiences socialization "for the first time" (Wasson, 2007). Primary caregivers in a newborn's family are the central socializing forces and continue to play an important role throughout childhood.

LO6 AGENTS OF SOCIALIZATION

Much of the information we receive about ourselves comes from agents of socialization. **Agents of socialization** are the groups, social institutions, and/or social settings that have the greatest amount of influence on the developing self. Principal agents of socialization include the family, the school, the peer group, and the mass media. Other important agents of socialization can include parenthood, the workplace, religion, sports, marriage, and correctional services (e.g., prison, probation, and parole).

THE FAMILY

In every society without exception, the family is the first and often the most important agent of socialization. Children are the offspring of parents, and this family unit is part of a biosocial system that is designed to love, protect, and care for them (Grusec & Davidov, 2007). Families also provide most aspects of early socialization, from language acquisition to what and how to eat, personal grooming, and wider societal expectations regarding how to behave. Many of the lessons learned are based on observations made during family routines and rituals. Society places the responsibility for children in the hands of their parents, who also have the authority to make decisions on their behalf and who are expected to maintain long-term relationships with them. From a functionalist perspective, the family's role is to provide support (e.g., love, protection, economic well-being) and guidance along the path to becoming productive and responsible adult members of society. Effective parenting enhances child attachment and improves child outcomes; by contrast, dysfunctional parenting impedes socialization and causes insecure attachment in children (Swenson, 2004). For resources on effective parenting, refer to *Sociology in My Community*.

Duff and Peace (2013) explain that children learn two important attitudes through their early interactions with primary caregivers. First, through the emotional reactions they receive from their parents, children develop self-esteem. Since **self-esteem** is an evaluation of one's self-worth, parents who engage in favourable interactions with their children (e.g., smile at them, encourage them, show approval) help instill high self-esteem in their offspring.

Agents of socialization: The groups, social institutions, and/or social settings that have the greatest amount of influence on the developing self.

Self-esteem: An evaluation of one's own self-worth.

YOUR SOCIOLOGICAL TOOLKIT

SOCIOLOGY IN MY COMMUNITY

PARENTS MATTER

The Canadian Association of Family Resource Programs (FRP Canada) is a national organization that promotes the well-being of families by providing consultation and resources to caregivers. For example, parents can access downloadable resource sheets in a variety of languages (e.g., Arabic, Chinese, Hindi, Punjabi, Somali, Tagalog, Urdu) on building active habits, singing through the day, developing family routines, and connecting through stories. Other resources include links to financial information (e.g., the Canada Education Savings Program), information on positive discipline, brochures from the Centre of Excellence for Early Childhood Development on a range of topics, such as aggressive behaviours, breastfeeding, and parent–child attachment, as well as access to encyclopedias and handbooks on child development (FRP Canada, 2017).

Think Outside the Box: What resources would you like to see made available for Canadian parents?

Conversely, parents who often show indifference or behave in disparaging ways (e.g., ignore or constantly criticize their children) are likely to instill a sense of low self-worth, making their children feel unloved or unlovable (Duff & Peace, 2013). Parents also play a central role in helping an infant develop **interpersonal trust**. This attitude also affects self-worth as it involves the perception that one can trust and rely upon others who have his or her best interests at heart. Children who have low self-esteem and low interpersonal trust have later problems developing secure attachments in adulthood. As adults, they tend to adopt fearful and avoidant interaction styles that inhibit the development of meaningful close relationships (Aronson et al., 2017).

Although no two families are exactly alike, the feminist perspective points out the many ways in which traditional families re-create existing patterns in society. For example, females are expected to become primary caregivers who look after children and elderly parents, whereas males are expected to become primary breadwinners in the economic sphere. The differential treatment of males and females is also evident in the treatment of boys and girls by their parents, wherein girls learn about caring and the need to be cared for, whereas boys learn the importance of problem solving and becoming independent. Clearfield and Nelson (2006) found that mothers of daughters spoke to and interacted with their infants more overall than did mothers of sons. Even while the children were playing independently or exploring the room, mothers of daughters were more likely to talk to them and offer them comfort if they became upset. With three- and four-year-olds, fathers were found to stand closer to their daughters during a risk-taking activity (i.e., traversing a small obstacle course), and both mothers and fathers offered more help to daughters when they reached an especially difficult part of the obstacle course—in this case, girls needed to be "rescued," or helped through the activity, whereas boys were encouraged to do it themselves. Differential experiences in the family, education, and employment for males and females are discussed in greater deal in a later chapter on gender.

For a conflict theorist, the family is a hub of disagreement where there are ongoing struggles that demonstrate power differences among individual members. Many children have at least one sibling (i.e., a brother or a sister), and siblings contribute to socialization independent of parent–child interactions. Relationships with siblings can be an important source of support, but at the same time, sibling conflict and poor-quality relationships are associated with negative developmental outcomes (Dunn, 2007; Rathus, 2018). Children also find themselves in conflict with their parents, especially during *adolescence*, when a teenager prefers the company of friends to that of family members. The main thrust of this phase is a quest for independence as teens begin to acknowledge their individuality apart from the family unit. It might seem to a teen that it is his or her "right" to talk to friends until 2 a.m. and to stay out late, but such actions may not be acceptable to parents, who feel it is their duty to constrain the impulses of a teen until he or she has demonstrated a capacity to assume greater responsibility and make sensible choices.

Interpersonal trust:
A perception that another person can be relied upon and has your best interests at heart.

Parents may be able to exert control and authority over their children (e.g., by implementing "time-outs," or taking away privileges for breaking rules); however, as the interactionist perspective reminds us, children are just as likely to influence their parents. This highlights the importance of human agency and the bidirectional nature of socialization within families (Kuczynski & Parkin, 2007). The child is an active agent with intellect, purpose, feelings, and a host of traits that constantly influence the parents as they act and react in novel ways in different situations over time. Thus, the decision of whether or not a particular child gets to stay out late on a particular night will depend on many factors, most of which originate within unique and dynamic parent–child contexts (see also Kuczynski, 2003).

Given the myriad family forms and dynamics, it is difficult to identify exactly what would constitute a "normal" versus an "abnormal" family environment. Instead, a family is usually assessed in terms of how well that family performs *functions* and how well that family *communicates* with its individual members (Zastrow & Kirst-Ashman, 2016). From this perspective, a "healthy" family is one that provides a high level of support for its individual members (e.g., material and emotional support) and has good communication skills (e.g., conflicts are resolved through consultation and rational decision-making) (Zastrow & Kirst-Ashman, 2016). Unhealthy family environments, in contrast, fail to adequately support group members and are characterized by poor parenting skills that foster child maltreatment, including child abuse (i.e., injuries to a child) and child neglect (e.g., improper health care, lack of supervision, poor nutrition) (Zastrow & Kirst-Ashman, 2016). In extreme cases, child welfare services may intervene and even remove children from dysfunctional families (see *Sociology in Practice*).

YOUR SOCIOLOGICAL TOOLKIT

SOCIOLOGY IN PRACTICE

CHILDREN'S RIGHTS AND CHILD WELFARE IN CANADA

Children's rights are a subject of debate and discussion. Although parents maintain the primary responsibility for their children, citizens and government representatives (including parents) have determined that all Canadian children have certain basic rights, such as the right to protection from physical and emotional harm. "Child welfare" refers to a system of government and private services aimed at protecting children from abuse and neglect (Canadian Child Welfare Research Portal, 2017). Child welfare agencies throughout the provinces and territories investigate alleged cases of child abuse and neglect and, where necessary, make temporary and permanent alternate care arrangements for children (e.g., placing a child in a relative's home, foster care, or a permanent adoptive home). In 2013, an estimated 62,428 Canadian children (or about 8.5 per 1,000 in the population) were removed from their families of origin (Jones, Sinha, & Trocmé, 2015). Indigenous children are disproportionately represented among those in child protective services. In many of these cases, children are removed because welfare agents believe caregivers pose a "potential risk of harm" to children (e.g., via caregiver substance abuse and a lack of social supports) (Sinha et al., 2011).

Dir. Melisa Brittain, 2017, Vtape.org; Painting: Blue by Tyler Blackface

This 2016 documentary highlights the voices of Indigenous youth who have had negative experiences with child welfare in Canada.

Think Outside the Box: How might higher rates of Indigenous children in foster care reflect broader structural disadvantages that place Indigenous families at risk?

THE SCHOOL

When apart from their families, children spend much of their time in school, where they learn to read and write, along with various other lessons based on processes of socialization. For example, within the class environment, students learn from their teachers and classmates about personal management (e.g., how to cooperate with others, respect the rights of others, assume personal responsibility, and work independently). Social interactions with teachers and peers play a central role in the transmission of cultural values and norms that are deemed important. Because schools tend to reinforce existing structures, processes, and practices in society, they also help maintain the differential treatment of particular social groups based on gender, socioeconomic status, and ethnicity (see later chapters). This is, in part, achieved by teachers' prior expectations about their students' abilities and their subsequent behaviours toward students as a function of these expectations (Wentzel & Looney, 2007). Positive socialization experiences stem from "effective" school environments that include elements such as a positive school climate (e.g., students feel safe and supported, teachers and the principal work together collaboratively), the promotion of high standards (e.g., challenging academic work and appropriate curriculums), and clear classroom management objectives (e.g., clearly stated expectations and consequences for rule violations) (Rathus, 2014; Shaffer & Kipp, 2013).

THE PEER GROUP

Another primary agent of socialization is the peer group—a group of individuals who share particular characteristics, such as grade level at school, age, and extracurricular activities (e.g., sports). Peers enact various socializing functions, teaching us to share, to think about the well-being of others, and to be a good sport even when we lose a game. We learn through our interactions with peers what it feels like to be accepted or rejected. Also, the peer group is a principal source of **social comparison**, in

Social comparison: Refers to how individuals evaluate themselves in terms of appearance, merit, and abilities based on how they compare to others.

SOCIOLOGY ON SCREEN

MODERN FAMILY

Postmodern perspectives point out how diverse and complex families are. *Modern Family*, a popular ABC comedy that debuted in 2009, provides a glimpse into the complex relationships within families sharing the same dwelling, as well as between family members related by blood and marriage. The series' characters include Phil and Claire Dunphy and their three children (Haley, Alex, and Luke) and Claire's brother Mitchell Pritchett, his husband Cameron Tucker, and their adopted daughter Lily. A third family unit consists of Claire's father (Jay Pritchett), who is married to Gloria Delgado-Pritchett, his second wife, her son (Manny) from a previous marriage, and their son (Joe). From Claire and Mitchell's lingering childhood rivalry to Jay's reconstruction of marriage, parenthood, and grandparenthood to Mitchell and Cameron's journey into married life and parenthood, the series depicts an endless array of challenges that require the characters to learn, rethink, and transition through various roles and stages in a complicated web of interrelated and reciprocal relationships.

Bob D'Amico/ABC via Getty Images

ABC's *Modern Family* is all about socialization.

that individuals evaluate their own appearance, merit, and abilities in comparison with others (Festinger, 1954). For example, based on the class average for a mid-term exam, you can determine whether you are below average, average, or above average in your ability to demonstrate your knowledge of sociology relative to your peer group. Similarly, comparisons with peer groups inform us whether we are "good-looking," "fat," "smart," "short," or "athletic." The peer group also exerts a great deal of influence over individuals, who are pressured to conform to group expectations regarding appearance, activities, and views of others; sometimes this culminates in inappropriate forms of exclusion and aggression, including bullying. Salmivalli and Peets (2009) note that bullies and victims are often in the same school classroom and that bullies gain status when peer groups witness acts of bullying. About 40 percent of Canadian youth are likely both to be bullied (i.e., as victims) and to bully others (i.e., as aggressors) (Craig & McCuaig Edge, 2012). Bullying takes a variety of forms, including verbal bullying (e.g., name calling, spreading rumours, making negative references to one's culture), social bullying (e.g., excluding others from a group, humiliating others with public gestures), physical bullying (e.g., hitting, shoving, destroying another's belongings), and electronic bullying (also called cyberbullying) (Bullying Canada, 2017).

As shown in *Figure 4.4*, electronic bullying (i.e., being threatened, embarrassed, gossiped about, or made to look bad online) is more prevalent among older youth, and boys are slightly more likely than girls to fall prey to it (Li & Craig, 2015). Whether

FIGURE 4.4

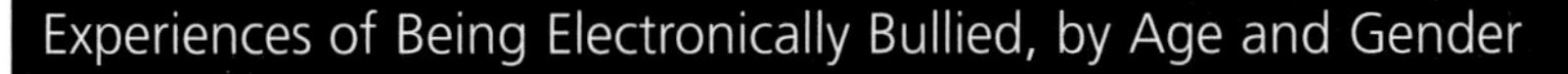

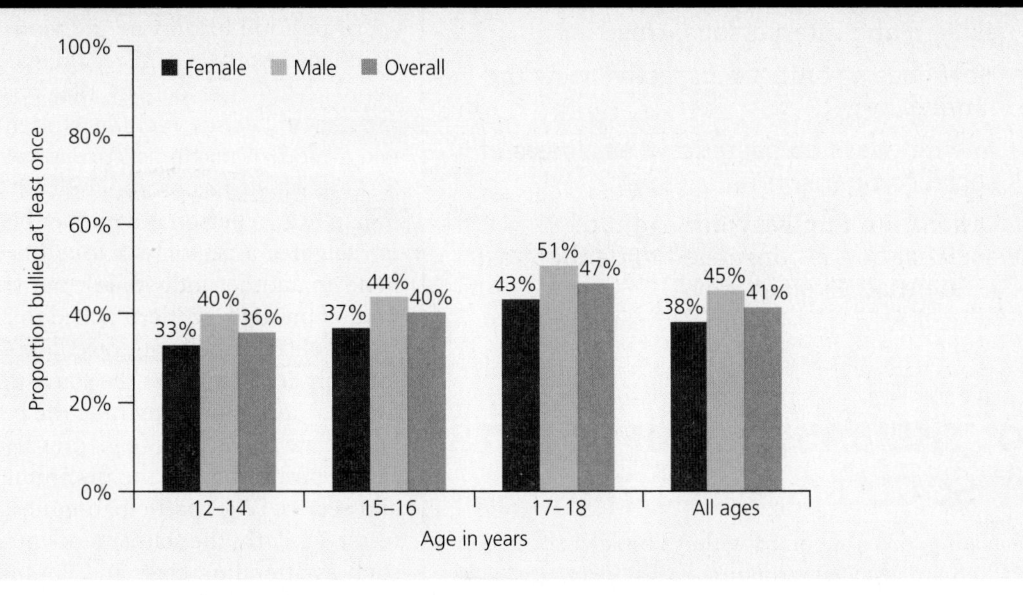

Source: © 2017 MediaSmarts and PREVNet, Ontario, Canada, *Young Canadians' Experiences with Electronic Bullying*, http://www.mediasmarts.ca. Quoted with permission. Found at http://mediasmarts.ca/sites/mediasmarts/files/publication-report/full/young-canadians-electronic-bullying.pdf, p. 10.

electronic bullying is substantively different from other forms of bullying continues to be a point of debate; however, the Internet does amplify the visibility of bullying, which can worsen bullying if others join in, or it can lessen bullying because this also increases the chances of intervention (Boyd, 2014). All forms of bullying have the potential to produce negative outcomes for both bullies and their victims, including changes in thought patterns (e.g., they are more likely to become depressed and think about committing suicide) and an increase in health issues (e.g., they experience sleep problems and anxiety) (Zastrow & Kirst-Ashman, 2016).

MEDIA

Media are communications formats that target mass audiences in print (e.g., newspapers, magazines, and books) or electronic format using audio and/or images (e.g., movies, radio, television, the Internet). Some consider the media to be the most influential socialization agent of our time, trumping even the family, given that they now permeate all aspects of our lives (including families) and will continue to do so throughout our lives (e.g., see Bereska, 2018; Jhally & Katz, 2013). Canadians spend more time on the Internet than anyone else in the world (about 37 hours per month) (Canadian Internet Registration Authority, 2016). While on the Internet, they engage in any number of activities: watching television, viewing YouTube videos, using social media (Facebook, Twitter), texting and emailing others, listening to the news, shopping, banking, playing games, and possibly even committing criminal activities—all of which are socializing influences. The media are often highly beneficial because they connect us with others, help maintain social relations, inform us about important local and international events, and provide us with entertainment. However, as you will learn more about in Chapter 6, the media are not neutral—media companies are profit-based and construct reality and shape our perceptions in particular ways so that we come to believe certain messages (e.g., about politics, gender, violence, and consumerism), often with negative implications and outcomes for both individuals and society as a whole.

Media: Communications that target large audiences in print or in electronic format using audio and/or images.

TIME TO REVIEW

- How do interactions in the family influence the development of one's self-esteem and interpersonal trust?
- How does a conflict perspective view the family?
- In what ways do peers serve as a basis of social comparison?
- Other than family, which agent of socialization is considered to be the most influential? Explain why.

LO7 THE BASIC COMPONENTS OF SOCIAL STRUCTURE

Socializing forces act on us within a broader social context known as social structure. **Social structure** is the framework of cultural elements and social patterns in which social interactions take place. Without social structure, you would arrive at your school and have no idea what comes next. There are structural guidelines operating in postsecondary institutions. These interactions include norms (e.g., students attend classes, students are expected to take notes), values (e.g., getting an education is important), and social patterns (e.g., the professor creates a course outline, teaches course content, and evaluates students, who in turn are expected to attend class, complete assignments, and obtain any needed additional help during scheduled office hours). Like cultural elements, social patterns help us make sense of social situations. Patterned social arrangements exist within three main areas of social structure: statuses and roles, social groups, and social institutions.

Social structure: The framework of cultural elements and social patterns in which social interactions take place.

Status: A recognized social position that exists independently of any given individual who may occupy it.

Role: The behavioural component of a given status.

Anticipatory socialization: The process by which individuals learn about the roles associated with a particular status before taking on that status.

STATUSES AND ROLES

Usually, when you think of "status," you consider things such as titles (e.g., president, chief), which denote power or authority, or the prestige associated with expensive houses and fancy cars. These forms of status have to do with social classes, which are discussed in the chapter on social inequality. This chapter is concerned with **status** as it relates to *any* recognized social position held by an individual in society, a position that exists over time regardless of which individual people happen to occupy that position at any given moment. Statuses include student, professor, caretaker, mother, machinist, prime minister, and brother. A status is a social position in that it exists in relation to others (e.g., a person is a mother because she has a son or daughter, a person is a friend because of his or her bond to another individual), not because it has some kind of prestige or title attached to it.

A **role** is the behavioural component of a status. For example, a person with the status "professor" will perform the accompanying role; the behaviours expected here relate to teaching (e.g., preparing notes), research (e.g., contributing to the discipline via publications), and service (e.g., participating on university committees). Similarly, the status "student" entails behaviours such as attending class and completing assignments on time. We *hold* statuses, but we *enact* roles. Statuses and their accompanying roles are essential elements of our identities; they provide us with purpose, fulfillment, and meaning. At the same time, our statuses can create problems and even damage our sense of self. In interviews Minaker (2012) conducted with women about what parenthood meant to them, one mother noted: "Being a mom is love, amazing, and rewarding" (p. 130), whereas another admitted: "Being a mom is exhausting and challenging" (p. 132).

Parenthood is rewarding in infinite ways, but it is also an extremely stressful period of adjustment for many parents. Few individuals contemplating parenthood have an accurate notion of the time and the financial and emotional demands their children will place on them, and most would benefit from anticipatory socialization. Through **anticipatory socialization**, individuals learn about the roles associated with a particular status *before* taking on that status. Controlling for existing social supports, prior life experiences, and other factors, such as health, education, and income, Gage and Christensen (2001) found that anticipatory socialization gained from a variety of sources—participating in child care, observing others engaged in child care, taking parenting classes, talking with others about child care (e.g., doctors, nurses, friends, spouses), speaking to parents and relatives, caring for pets—was associated with positive outcomes for males and females making the transition to parenthood.

We are born with some statuses (i.e., son or daughter), acquire other statuses over time (e.g., aunt, mother, or grandmother), work to achieve certain statuses (e.g., BA graduate, sociologist, and master electrician), inadvertently end up with some statuses through our actions (e.g., impaired driver, and prison inmate), lose statuses (e.g., widow and unemployed person), and exit some of our statuses (e.g., through divorce or retirement). The sum total of all of the statuses a person holds at any given time is called a **status set**.

ACHIEVED AND ASCRIBED STATUSES

Sociologists also distinguish between statuses that are ascribed and statuses that are achieved. **Ascribed statuses** are social positions that people inherit at birth or acquire involuntarily over the life course (e.g., male, son, brother, and widower). **Achieved statuses** are social positions that people obtain through personal actions (e.g., husband, graduate, lawyer, and criminal). Although the term "status" is neutral when it refers to a social position, particular statuses are not neutral in the sense that some are more important than others. Being a devout Latter-day Saint (i.e., Mormon), for example, may necessitate behavioural guidelines, such as going on a mission at age 19 (if you are a male), that take precedence over other expectations afforded by concurrently held statuses such as those related to friendships, school, or employment.

A **master status** is the most influential of all of the statuses in a person's status set. Sociologist Everett Cherrington Hughes (1945) first used the term "master status" to refer to a status that "tends to overpower, in most crucial situations, any other characteristics which may run counter to it" (p. 357). A master status affects both the individual and his or her choices relative to that status, as well as how others accept and interact with that person. As an African American raised in the early 20th century, Hughes discussed how being black could be considered a master status, as could one's professional standing. He noted that when two powerful statuses coincided, as in the case of a black physician, it posed a dilemma for white Americans, who found themselves having to choose whether to treat "him as a Negro or as a member of his profession" (p. 357). Note that individuals can have more than one master status at a time (e.g., race/ethnicity, occupation, age) and that those statuses can operate simultaneously (e.g., "male teenager with prior DUI conviction" or "elderly female with heart condition") and that those statuses may be relevant only in particular situations (e.g., when trying to qualify for vehicle or medical insurance) or may be salient across most situations (e.g., dangerous offender). A master status has exceptional importance for a person's identity and life experiences. Consider how your life and the various identities that make up your self-concept would change tomorrow if you suddenly acquired the master status of single parent, Canadian prime minister, multimillion-dollar lottery winner, dangerous offender, or patient with a terminal illness (see *Sociology in My Life*).

Status set: The sum total of all of the statuses held by a person at a given time.

Ascribed statuses: A social position conferred at birth.

Achieved statuses: A social position obtained through personal actions.

Master status: The most influential status in an individual's status set.

ROLE CONFLICT AND ROLE STRAIN

Sometimes the competing demands of different statuses pose challenges for individuals. Think about what might happen to Taylor (a fellow student),

YOUR SOCIOLOGICAL TOOLKIT

SOCIOLOGY IN MY LIFE

WHAT COMPRISES YOUR STATUS SET?

Try to write down 10 statuses you currently hold. To assist you, consider your relationship relative to people in your family (e.g., Do you have a brother or sister? Are you a niece or nephew?). Also think about some of the activities you currently engage in or memberships you hold (e.g., Do you attend school full-time? Do you play any sports? Are you employed? Are you part of any social groups?).

Think Outside the Box: Of the statuses you listed, which one would you consider to be your master status? Explain why this is the case.

who has a final exam scheduled at a time when she is supposed to work her regularly scheduled shift at her job. **Role conflict** refers to a situation in which incompatible role demands exist as a result of two (or more) statuses held at the same time. In this case, Taylor is both a student and an employee (i.e., the two statuses); the roles associated with these statuses require her to be in two different places at the same time. Hopefully, she can find a replacement to work her job on short notice, or her university's policies consider work obligations to be a valid excuse for missing an exam. Role conflict is often experienced by students who are also parents (e.g., a child may get sick and require care on the same day as a final exam) and students who are athletes (for whom competitions, playoff games, and matches may require travel away from classes and/or otherwise interfere with study time).

Sometimes conflicts even occur between role requirements of a single status. **Role strain** refers to a situation in which incompatible role demands exist within one status. For example, as a student, you will likely experience role strain in the last few weeks of class: the "typical" student may be required to complete a research project, prepare for a class presentation, write a paper for one or more courses, and study for final exams.

Role conflict: A situation in which incompatible role demands exist between two or more commonly held statuses.

Role strain: A situation in which incompatible role demands exist within a single status.

Social group: Two or more people who share relevant cultural elements and interact with regular frequency.

Social network: An interrelated system of social relationships of varying purpose, relevance, intimacy, and importance.

Social facilitation: The tendency for people to do better on simple tasks, but worse on complex tasks, when they are in the presence of others and their individual performance can be evaluated.

Social loafing: The tendency to put in minimal effort on simple group tasks when individual performance cannot be evaluated.

SOCIAL GROUPS

Social groups are another part of the broader social structure from which we create social identities. A **social group** consists of two or more people who share relevant cultural elements and interact with regular frequency. Social groups you might identify with include coworkers, your family, teammates in a sport, your peer group at school, members of your church, and people in clubs you are associated with. Social groups contribute to the social structure by delineating various statuses and roles. For example, there are various positions in retail sales work (e.g., sales associate, assistant manager, manager). Each status corresponds to various rules, expectations, and obligations. As a part-time sales associate, you might be expected to help customers, report to an assistant manager, and take breaks only at times designed by a manager, and you may not be entitled to any vacation pay or sick leave benefits. Note that roles always exist in relation to other roles to which they are oriented (Turner, 1962). A sales associate cannot perform his or her job in the absence of customers. Similarly, an assistant manager's duties exist because there is a corresponding manager role. Social groups and the individuals who comprise them are sometimes linked together through social networks. A **social network** is a system of social relationships of varying purpose, relevance, intimacy, and importance. If you use social media such as Facebook, Twitter, or LinkedIn, you are already part of a social network that brings you into contact with family members, close friends, coworkers, acquaintances, and other social groups, such as professional associations and charitable organizations.

POSITIVE AND NEGATIVE GROUP INFLUENCES

Besides teaching us about statuses, roles, and their accompanying norms, social groups have profound effects, positive and negative, on individual group members. For example, in the presence of others, an individual's performance on a task that is well learned or fairly easy to begin with will be enhanced. **Social facilitation** is the "tendency for people to do better on simple tasks, but worse on complex tasks, when they are in the presence of others and their individual performance can be evaluated" (Aronson et al., 2017, p. 221). According to Robert Zajonc's (1965) early drive theory of arousal, the presence of others arouses us, and this brings out our dominant responses. To the extent that a skill is new or a task is difficult, the most dominant responses are likely to include errors. This helps explain why an ice skater can complete a complicated jump during some of his or her training sessions but falters during an Olympic skate in the presence of thousands. The presence of others can also lead to reduced effort, as is often the case in group presentations. **Social loafing** is the tendency to put in minimal effort on simple group tasks when individual performance cannot be evaluated (Aronson et al., 2017). To prevent this, you need to find ways to motivate your group mate (e.g., by explaining that he or she has unique talents that the group is relying on) or to make each individual's contribution apparent (e.g., assign clear and distinct tasks so it will be evident who is and is not contributing).

Sometimes individuals follow group norms or give in to group pressure in order to fit into a group or to not stand out as different. **Conformity** is a form of social influence in which individuals change their behaviour in order to adhere to group norms. In one of a series of classic experiments, Solomon Asch (1956) demonstrated how group pressure could be used to persuade students to give incorrect answers on a simple line test (see *Figure 4.5*). Based on eyesight alone, the correct answer on the second card could be readily discerned. However, the participants were asked to provide an answer after the rest of the members of the group gave their response. The group members were actually "confederates" (i.e., research assistants pretending to be other participants). For the first few trials, the confederates gave the correct answer and so did the participants, who were always seated next to last. However, on the third trial, the confederates gave an incorrect response. Much to the confusion of the participants, confederates continued to give incorrect responses on 12 of the 18 trials. Of the 123 actual participants in the study, 27 percent gave incorrect responses along with the group most of the time! About 50 percent gave in to group pressure some of the time. Only 24 percent answered error-free, as a minority of one against the unanimous majority (Asch, 1956).

The tendency to want to maintain agreement while in a group can pose special problems for decision making. Irving Janis (1972) coined the term **groupthink** for the process in which members of a group come to favour consensus over critical thinking and rational decision making, producing poor and even disastrous outcomes. Janis (1972) identified many historical examples of groupthink in American political decision making, including the U.S. government's failure to anticipate the Japanese attack on Pearl Harbor and the botched Bay of Pigs invasion, a U.S.-backed attempt by Cuban exiles to overthrow the Cuban dictator Fidel Castro. Strategies for avoiding the pitfalls of groupthink include having a nondirective leader (i.e., someone who doesn't state his or her view at the onset), inviting out-group individuals with expertise on the subject matter to provide alternative and challenging viewpoints, and having the leader assign the role of "critical evaluator" to each member of the group to encourage discussion and debate (Janis, 1972).

FIGURE 4.5

Asch's (1956) Experiment on Group Conformity

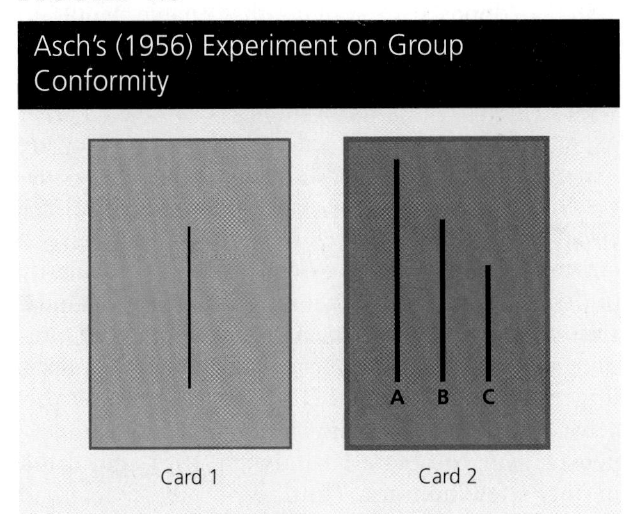

Source: Adapted from Asch, S. E. (1956). Studies of independence and conformity: A minority of one against a unanimous majority. *Psychological Monographs*, *70*(9),1–70.

LO8 SOCIAL INSTITUTIONS

Thus far, we have mainly discussed patterns of interaction at the micro level. Established social patterns also exist at the macro level of institutions. **Social institutions** are relatively permanent societal structures that govern the behaviour of groups and promote social order. Some examples of social institutions are the family, religious institutions, schools, the political system, the economy, and the media. Each institution serves a main purpose (i.e., the family provides support and is the primary agent of socialization, education is a mechanism for transmitting important cultural beliefs). To accomplish these purposes, social institutions are composed of various structures, processes, and rules that exert control over individuals and come to shape their identities.

A highly structured social institution is referred to as a *formal organization* owing to the presence of a specific type of organizational structure known as a bureaucracy. A **bureaucracy** is a formal organization model consisting of an explicit chain of authority and a set of procedures

Conformity: A form of social influence in which individuals change their behaviour in order to adhere to group norms.

Groupthink: A process in which members of a group favour consensus over rational decision making, producing poor and even disastrous outcomes.

Social institutions: Relatively permanent societal structures that govern the behaviour of groups and promote social order.

Bureaucracy: A formal organization model consisting of an explicit chain of authority and a set of procedures and protocols that guide the relationships and processes that exist within it.

and protocols that guide the relationships and processes that exist within it.

YOUR SOCIOLOGICAL TOOLKIT
SOCIOLOGY IN THEORY

MAX WEBER'S IDEAL TYPE OF BUREAUCRACY

Sociologist Max Weber developed an ideal-type model to illustrate the key features of bureaucracy. An **ideal type** is an analytical construct that depicts all the main features of some social phenomenon but is not found in reality (Weber, 1903–1917/1949). Thus, an ideal type is the perfect example from which we can compare real-life cases to see how well they fit the model (or don't). Weber's ideal type of bureaucracy includes a division of labour, a hierarchy of authority, written rules and regulations, impersonality in decision making, and employment based on qualifications (Murray, Linden, & Kendall, 2017, pp. 191–194).

A *division of labour* entails people carrying out different sorts of tasks. In a university, there are people who work as faculty, staff, or administrators in separate areas, such as facilities, finance, and the department of sociology. A *hierarchy of authority* refers to a "chain of command" where positions are arranged according to levels of responsibility and power. In a university, a faculty member is supervised by a department chair, who is under the supervision of a dean, who is under the authority of a vice president (academic), who is under the authority of the president. All academic institutions include *rules and regulations* that govern the behaviour of staff, faculty, and students, as you already know from student codes of conduct, course outlines, and procedures for borrowing resources, paying tuition, registering in courses, and even graduating. Displays of emotion and special considerations are discouraged. *Impersonality* means that all people working within bureaucracies are supposed to perform their duties as a matter of principle (e.g., a sympathetic professor should not give a certain student an extension on a term paper but instead should consistently apply the deductions for lateness that are listed in the course outline). Finally, all people employed in a bureaucracy are hired on the basis of *qualifications*. Hence, faculty members with the highest or most specialized degrees (e.g., a PhD) are typically hired over those with a master's degree.

Ideal type: An analytical construct that clearly depicts all of the main features of some social phenomenon but is not an entity that can be found in reality.

Bureaucracies have many advantages, including efficiency, which translates into things getting done through various delegated divisions of labour. Hierarchies of authority help establish where someone goes first to resolve an issue (e.g., a student must first see his or her instructor about a class before going to the department chair). Similarly, clear rules indicate precisely what is or is not allowed (e.g., a student may be granted a deferred exam for a religious holiday but not for a personal vacation or a relative's wedding). Impersonality and employment based on technical qualifications can result in opportunities for individuals who work hard and continue to upgrade their skills, as opposed to systems that enable people to advance based on connections, as in "who you know."

The bureaucratic model has proven to be a highly successful approach to business. Ritzer (2015) explains how four main features of bureaucracy are exemplified by McDonald's, the world's most successful franchise. First, self-service increases the *efficiency* or speed with which a consumer can satisfy a craving for a Big Mac, as evidenced by the popularity of drive-thru windows. Second, *calculability* "emphasizes the quantitative aspects of products sold (portion, size, and cost) and services offered (time it takes to get the product)" (p. 14). Consumers readily perceive that the "extra value" meal is a relatively inexpensive way to obtain a sandwich, fries, and drink in only a few minutes. Third, *predictability* refers to the "assurance that products and services will be the same over time and in all locales" (p. 15). Fourth, part of the success of McDonald's can be attributed to its *control* over customers. As Ritzer puts it, "lines, limited menus, few options, and uncomfortable seats all lead diners to do what management wishes them to do—eat quickly and leave" (p. 15).

Ritzer (2015) argues that these four principles now represent values operating in contemporary society more generally, which he refers to as the *McDonaldization of society*. We see the viability of these principles in the sheer number of McDonald's restaurants—there are 1,400 in Canada and more than 33,000 worldwide in 119 countries (McDonald's Restaurants of Canada Limited, 2017); we also see them in the adoption of the same doctrine by competitor franchises (e.g., Burger King, Wendy's), successful variant franchises (e.g., Tim Hortons in Canada), and even casual dining franchises (e.g., Red Lobster, Olive Garden). The core features of efficiency, calculability, predictability, and control can now be seen in a wide range of successful businesses (e.g., IKEA, Walmart, PetSmart); they have even come to govern the exotic dancing industry (Deshotels, Tinney, & Forsyth, 2012). Bureaucratic principles serve the business sector well, but they also tend to have shortcomings that are especially apparent to individuals. If you have ever tried to change classes or obtain a tuition refund, you can probably relate to "the slowness, the ponderousness, the routine, the complication of procedures and the maladapted responses of the bureaucratic organization to the needs which they should satisfy" (Crozier, 1964, p. 3). Bureaucratic processes take a lot of time and require many steps to completion. Not only that, but also in most bureaucracies, the rules, hierarchy of authority, and division of labour are not as clear-cut as implied by Weber's ideal type. This is why in academic institutions, students are not sure whether they should go to an instructor or the department chair first to handle a class matter and why some employees, such as "instructional assistants," may carry out functions, such as providing administrative support to department chairs, that bear little or no resemblance to their stated job titles.

RESOCIALIZATION: MORE THAN STARTING OVER

Just as socialization can occur at any stage in the life process, an individual may undergo resocialization. **Resocialization** involves a person radically altering his or her identity by giving up an existing status in exchange for a new one. Resocialization can be voluntary, such as when a person decides to leave a place of employment in order to retire, raise a family, or care for elderly parents. This process can also be involuntary if the individuals involved have little choice but to undergo resocialization. For example, someone might end up divorced after leaving an unfaithful partner, whereas another individual may end up a widower after the death of a loved one. Involuntary forms of resocialization also take place in settings referred to as "total institutions."

A **total institution** is an isolated social system in which certain individuals are housed, looked after, and socialized apart from the wider society. In a collection of essays called *Asylums*, Erving Goffman (1961) described a total institution as "a place of residence and work where a large number of like-situated individuals, cut off from the wider society for an appreciable period of time, together lead an enclosed, formally administered round of life" (p. xiii). An example of a total institution in Canada is any prison in the federal correctional system (e.g., Edmonton Institution, Willow Cree Healing Centre). A prison is designed to reform and rehabilitate inmates to become law-abiding citizens while protecting the rest of society from the potential harm they pose. Goffman (1961) notes that the inmates in a total institution are closely supervised at all times (e.g., by staff members and surveillance systems), that they are subject to strict schedules and standardized procedures (e.g., meals

Resocialization: A process that involves radically altering one's identity by giving up an existing status in exchange for a new one.

Total institution: An isolated social system in which certain individuals are housed, looked after, and socialized apart from the wider society.

Millhaven is a maximum security prison in Bath, Ontario, that houses dangerous offenders, including Canadian serial killer and rapist Paul Bernardo.

take place at a certain time, only a certain amount of time is allotted for exercise, and cells are searched on a regular basis), and that they operate as bureaucracies (e.g., they have explicit chains of authority and protocols). Given the strict control, it is next to impossible for inmates to maintain their former personal or social identities, which rely on meaningful interactions and agency. Instead, the self is stifled by the processes that remove individuality and diminish self-worth. Although the intent is usually to help individuals learn new values, ideas, and identities, high rates of reincarceration (return) after release from correctional facilities suggest that the new, more compliant identities formed in the absence of meaningful interactions are not likely to endure outside of the institutional structures that created them.

TIME TO REVIEW

- What are the three main elements that make up social structure?
- What is the difference between role conflict and role strain?
- What is groupthink, and what can be done to prevent it?
- What are some advantages and disadvantages of Weber's ideal type of bureaucracy for businesses and individuals?
- What is a total institution? Provide an example of one.

CHAPTER SUMMARY

LO1 Explain how our own unique sense of "self" includes traits that fall along a personal–social identity continuum.

The personal–social identity continuum is the range of traits you possess that emphasize the extent to which you view yourself as "unique" (e.g., I am driven, I am clumsy, I am happy) versus part of a social group (e.g., I am a student, I am a daughter, I am a Christian).

LO2 Define "self" and explain its connection to socialization and social interaction.

The self is an individual's reflexive sense of her or his own particular identity, constituted vis-à-vis others in terms of similarity and difference, without which she or he wouldn't know who they are and hence wouldn't be able to act. Through the process of socialization, people learn about themselves and their various roles within a particular culture. Most of the learning takes place during social interactions with others.

LO3 Describe the continuum of nature versus nurture assumptions.

On the extreme nature side, theorists advocate biological determinism, that is, the view that behaviour is the end result of genetics. Sociobiology points to evolutionary origins for social behaviour (i.e., the need to reproduce). Moving toward the centre of the continuum, sociologists highlight the importance of biology and socialization in the development of the social self. For example, the bioecological theory of human development stresses the importance of human agency and the reciprocal nature of social influences. Finally, on the extreme nurture side, the school of behaviourism posits that behaviour is the end result of learning, especially through the use of rewards and punishment.

LO4 Describe Mead's stages of development of the self and differentiate between the "I" and the "me."

Mead explained how the self develops through stages evident in children's play. In the *preparatory stage*, the focus is on motor skill mastery and imitation; in the *play stage*, children begin to take on the role of others, one at a time; in the *game stage*, the actor must be able to understand different roles and perspectives and be able to think about them simultaneously, demonstrating the generalized other. Mead also described two parts of the self: the "I" and the "me." The "I" is the spontaneous self that is unique to the person, whereas the "me" is the portion of the self that responds during interactions based on cultural norms (i.e., the generalized other).

LO5 Identify the ways in which the perceptions of others affect our individual identities.

We are constantly identifying ourselves, being identified by others, and identifying others.

Master statuses may be essential to your identity, but even if they aren't, they are still central to how others identify you. Through the looking-glass self, we imagine how we appear to others, imagine how they judge that appearance, and then incorporate those perceived judgments into our own sense of self.

LO6 Identify primary agents of socialization and describe their main contributions to the development of the self and/or social identity.

Primary agents of socialization include the family, the school, the peer group, and the mass media. The family is a source of social support and encouragement, structure and discipline, imbalances in power, and conflict. Similarly, the school is a highly supportive mechanism for teaching skills, norms, and values, and it is also a foundation for perpetuating social inequalities. The peer group is a powerful source of social support, social comparison, and social pressure, with positive and negative outcomes for one's self-identity. Finally, the mass media inform us, entertain us, and teach us a multitude of lessons, with positive and negative implications for individuals and society as a whole.

LO7 Outline the basic components of social structure.

Social structure consists of statuses and roles, social groups (e.g., peer groups, coworkers), and social institutions (e.g., the family, the school) that provide a framework within which social interactions take place.

LO8 Explain how social institutions contribute to social structure and assess the merits of Weber's ideal type of bureaucracy in modern society.

Social institutions are relatively permanent societal structures that govern the behaviour of groups and promote social order, as in the case of the family as the primary agent of socialization or religion as an institution that provides people with a sense of purpose. According to Weber, an ideal type of bureaucracy includes a specialized division of labour, a clear hierarchy of authority, written rules and regulations, impersonality in dealings, and employment based on technical qualifications. A bureaucracy can be highly successful, largely because of its efficiency, objectivity, and clear directives, but it can also lead to very time-consuming, inefficient processes that become ends in themselves.

RECOMMENDED RESOURCES

1. For a comprehensive look at the ecology of socialization agents and socialization outcomes, refer to R.M. Berns, *Child, Family, School, Community: Socialization and Support*, 10th ed. (Belmont, CA: Wadsworth, Cengage Learning, 2016).
2. To learn more about self-identification, categorization of others, and communal identity, we recommend R. Jenkins, *Social Identity*, 4th ed. (New York, NY: Routledge, 2014).
3. For a critical look at Canada's child welfare system, we recommend *(Dis)placed: Indigenous Youth and the Child Welfare System*, a 2016 documentary directed by Melisa Brittain. Go to http://www.kingcripproductions.com/displaced.html.
4. For downloadable parenting resources, visit the Canadian Association of Family Resource Programs at http:www.parentsmatter.ca.

FOR FURTHER REFLECTION

1. Do you have a virtual self? What sorts of information could a stranger obtain about you from Internet searches?
2. Which agent of socialization do you consider the most influential?
3. Would the diagnosis of a terminal illness such as cancer be considered a master status? Explain your answer.
4. Does your university or college fit Weber's notion of an ideal bureaucracy? Why or why not?

ENDNOTE

1 Retrieved March 26, 2017, from thinkexist.com.

CHAPTER 05

Social Inequality in Canadian Society

Prazis Images/Shutterstock

The history of all hitherto existing society is the history of class struggles.

(Karl Marx & Friedrich Engels,1848/2010, p.14)

LEARNING OBJECTIVES & OUTCOMES

After completing this chapter, students should be able to do the following:

LO1 Define social stratification and differentiate between caste and class systems.

LO2 Explain what social inequality looks like in Canada using measures of wealth.

LO3 Describe Canada's class structure and social mobility.

LO4 Critically assess the low-income cutoff as an estimate of poverty.

LO5 Identify groups most at risk for poverty in Canada and discuss how poverty is linked to negative outcomes.

LO6 Critically assess Canada's social safety net as a means for reducing poverty.

LO7 Debate why there are social classes and whether stratification is helpful or harmful to Canadian society.

LO1 SOCIAL STRATIFICATION: SANCTIONED SOCIAL INEQUALITY

According to *Maclean's* magazine (2013), there are at least 99 reasons why it is better to live in Canada than anywhere else in the world, including these: Canadians live a long time, enjoy a high quality of life, have high life satisfaction, are highly educated, and are fairly well off financially. As a highly developed nation with an advanced economy, universal access to health care, and publicly funded education, Canada does boast one of the best standards of living in the world. But this does not mean that everyone in Canada is "well off"—something that readers of the Maclean's article might be led to assume. All nations, including Canada, are characterized by social inequality, meaning that citizens range from very poor to extremely wealthy, with corresponding levels of quality of life. Like culture and social structure, social inequality plays an important role in shaping who we are, what we experience, and who we become. If your parents are wealthy, your life chances are considerably better than if they are poor. If your parents are poor, you face challenges securing basic necessities, such as suitable winter clothes and a nutritious diet. **Social inequality** refers to the unequal distribution of resources such as wealth, prestige, and power. That inequality affects personal outcomes, such as educational and occupational attainment, and also health. In this chapter, we examine social inequality in Canada and consider features of Canadian society that help sustain it.

Social inequality is intertwined with **social stratification**, which refers to socially sanctioned patterns of social inequality that persist in society and are based on distinguishable attributes such as race, age, gender, income, and occupation. Social stratification systems hierarchically rank entire categories of people so that some hold "higher" or "lower" social positions than others.

CLOSED SYSTEMS OF STRATIFICATION

In a *closed system of stratification*, there is little or no movement between social rankings. This means that someone located in a low social position will remain in that position throughout his or her life.

Social inequality: An unequal distribution of resources.

Social stratification: Socially sanctioned patterns (or classes) of social inequality that exist in society and that are based on distinguishable attributes such as race, age, gender, income, or occupation.

SOCIOLOGY ON SCREEN

I AM NOT YOUR NEGRO

I Am Not Your Negro (2016), written by the late James Baldwin and directed by Raoul Peck, is an illuminating documentary that provides a historical and personal account of social stratification based on race in America. The film originated with a biography Baldwin started that outlined the deaths of his three close friends: Medgar Evers, Malcolm X, and Martin Luther King, Jr. Although he never completed the book, it posthumously provides the foundation for this film.

SLAVERY

Slavery is the most extreme example of the lowest possible position in a closed system of stratification. Individuals classified as slaves are not considered "citizens" of a nation; rather, they are owned by others as property and have no legal rights and no means for accumulating wealth. Slavery is based in economics but is historically associated with race, involving the categorization of people based on perceived ancestry and physical traits such as facial features, skin colour, and hair texture. There was slavery in Canada for more than 200 years, which ensured that some groups of people would never acquire sought-after resources (e.g., land and capital). Most slaves in Canada descended from Indigenous peoples, including the Labrador Inuit and the Sioux around the Great Lakes. Before colonization, Indigenous groups would take enemy groups as "subjugated war captives." With the arrival of the French, Indigenous slaves were often offered up as "tokens of friendship" in political exchanges (Canadian Museum of History, 2017a). Under European colonization, Indigenous slaves were also routinely kept by early settlers in order to work the land or be traded for goods and services. In addition to the slavery of Indigenous peoples, other social groups were brought to Canada for the purpose of slavery. Most of the slaves that were brought into Canada in the 17th and 18th centuries were of African descent and served as farm hands and domestic servants. Between 1783 and 1865, after the American Revolution, some American slaves fled to Canada.

The Upper Canadian Act Against Slavery of 1793 freed slaves who entered Upper Canada (i.e., Ontario) from the United States, the West Indies, and Africa. Other jurisdictions followed suit. Former slaves coming to Ontario as immigrants were thereafter promised freedom, yet all existing slaves in Canada remained the "property" of their owners, who could do with them as they wished. This is evident in the Preamble to Chapter VII of the abolition bill, which reads: "Whereas it is unjust that a people who enjoy freedom by law should encourage the introduction of slaves, and whereas it is highly expedient to abolish slavery in this province, so far as the same may gradually be done without violating private property" (Nickalls, 1831, p. 41). Slavery was finally abolished throughout Canada in 1833 (Canadian Museum of History, 2017b).

Slavery has been illegal in Canada for almost two centuries, yet it still exists in a nonsanctioned but highly lucrative form: human trafficking, mainly of women and children, who are bought and sold internationally, usually for the purpose of exploitation in the sex trade. Some of them are misled into believing they are going to another country for legitimate full-time employment; others, especially underage girls, are coerced into prostitution through force, confinement, isolation, and the withholding of identification documents (RCMP, 2014). According to the 2016 Global Slavery Index, around

songpholt/Shutterstock

Human trafficking in Canada is monitored by the Human Trafficking National Coordination Centre at RCMP Headquarters in Ottawa.

45.8 million people in the world today are enmeshed in "modern slavery"; the numbers are especially high in India, China, Pakistan, Bangladesh, and Uzbekistan. Modern slavery includes human trafficking as well as forced labour, servile marriage, and the sale or exploitation of children.

THE CASTE SYSTEM

Another example of a closed system of stratification is the **caste system**, which is based solely on inherited social standing. People are born into social ranks that remain fixed throughout their lives. Caste systems have been identified in many parts of the world historically and continue to exist today in countries such as India and Pakistan (Luce, 2007). The caste system in India has its origins in ancient Hinduism and consists of four hierarchical layers or strata that coincide with historical occupations: the Brahmins (the upper caste, consisting of priests), the Kshatriyas (the second caste, consisting of warriors and kings), the Vaishyas (the third caste, consisting of merchants and traders), and the Shudras (the fourth caste, consisting mainly of labourers) (Dirks, 2001). A fifth group, the Untouchables, is viewed as so lacking in standing that its members are not even recognized in society (Jaffrelot, 2005). Untouchables are similar to slaves; they lack rights and are predestined to carry out unclean, often unpaid, tasks in society, such as cleaning toilets and sweeping debris. As an author from the Kshatriyas caste put it, "The [Untouchable] sweeper is worse off than a slave, for the slave may change his master and his duties and may even become free, but the sweeper is bound forever, born into a state from which he cannot escape and where he is excluded from social intercourse and the consolations of his religion. Unclean himself, he pollutes others when he touches them" (Anand, 1935, p. 6).

Caste reproduction serves to accentuate social inequality and persists because cultural practices, norms, and beliefs reinforce the existing divisions. For example, marriage occurs within castes; also, the higher castes are generally the only ones with the resources necessary to acquire the education for better-paying jobs and social advantages they pass on through family and community connections (O'Hanlon, 2017). Religious beliefs also play an important role in maintaining the caste system; for example, it is believed that deeds in a past life account for the occupation/caste in the present one. Governments have attempted to raise up the lowest castes—for example, by allowing a small percentage of those in the lowest groups to attend school. But given the sheer number of impoverished people in India, these efforts have helped little. Even though the state now prohibits discrimination based on the basis of caste, widespread violence in some regions along caste lines continues to reproduce the subordination and exploitation of the lower castes (Rai, 2009). And although the privileged nature of the hierarchical caste may be disavowed publicly, it tends to be "assiduously maintained in private" (O'Hanlon, 2017, p. 438) and is passed on through a complex web of cultural, religious, and familial practices.

OPEN SYSTEMS OF STRATIFICATION: THE CLASS SYSTEM

Some forms of stratification, such as slavery and caste systems, are closed. Others are open, in that it is possible to move from one level to another. One such form is the class system, which is the dominant system of stratification in the world today, including in Canada. A **social class** is a group whose membership is based on economic measures such as annual income. In a **class system** of stratification, individuals are born into a social class, but unlike in a caste system, it is possible for them to move into higher or lower classes over time based on effort and achievement, life stages, personal circumstances such as illness and disease, and broader societal conditions (e.g., an economic depression). Although some of these factors may be perceived as characteristic of individuals, various macro-level forces ensure that certain groups of people are more apt to end up in the higher and lower classes. The higher classes are better able to access the opportunities that enhance life chances and overall quality of life.

SOCIAL MOBILITY IN CANADA

The movement within and between classes in open systems of stratification is referred to as **social mobility**. Vertical mobility relates to movement up or down the social ladder, whereas horizontal mobility relates to changes within the same social location (e.g., moving from one job to another with a similar income and level of authority).

Caste system: A hierarchical system of stratification based on inherited social standing.

Social class: Shared membership in a group based on economic standing.

Class system: A hierarchical system of stratification based on achieved and ascribed economic measures such as annual income or the possession of resources.

Social mobility: Movement that occurs within and between social classes in a stratification system.

William Albert Allard/National Geographic Creative

"Untouchables" are persons of such a low status that they fall outside the caste system in India.

Intragenerational mobility refers to changes in social class that occur within a person's lifetime. Most university students have incomes that place them in the low class (i.e., you work, if at all, for a low wage and probably only part-time). After obtaining a degree, you are likely to secure a full-time position with a modest annual salary that moves you into the lower end of the middle class; this demonstrates intragenerational mobility. As your skills and qualifications grow with experience, you may obtain more senior positions within your field, along with corresponding increases in salary and shifts in your class status. At times, these shifts may result in a large-scale change in class status (e.g., from middle class to upper class); however, changes in occupational status most often occur within existing social classes (e.g., from lower middle class to mid-middle class).

Intragenerational mobility: Changes in social class that occur within a person's lifetime.

Socioeconomic status: Social standing based on a combined measure of education, income, and occupation.

Intergenerational mobility: Changes in the social class of children relative to their parents.

Patterns of social mobility tend to be stable across generations (Wanner, 2004). This is especially evident when we compare the occupational status of fathers and sons. For example, a son whose father is a welder is more likely to also secure a position in the trades (although it may be of higher rank and pay) and less likely to become a physician. Occupation is often used as a measure of social class because it is closely tied to the other relevant indicators (e.g., income and education). **Socioeconomic status** refers to social standing based on a combined measure of education, income, and occupation. Educational attainment is the most influential contributor to socioeconomic status because it is a prerequisite for many qualifications-based occupations and is strongly associated with income. Although mobility patterns tend to be stable across generations, with greater educational attainment, sons and daughters may be able to secure higher class positions than their parents. **Intergenerational mobility** refers to changes in the social class of children relative to their parents. Intergenerational mobility is a good indicator of equality because it demonstrates that social position can be achieved through individual merit.

Chen, Ostrovsky, and Piraino's (2016) analysis of Canadian mobility based on earnings and income comparisons between fathers and their children at similar points in middle age showed a weaker intergenerational transmission for daughters compared to sons and greater earnings persistence for males with high-income earning fathers, who pass on a significant advantage to their offspring. Where social

YOUR SOCIOLOGICAL TOOLKIT

CRITICAL THINKING IN ACTION

BLAMING THE POOR FOR THEIR PLIGHT

Blaming the poor for their social standing often reflects a lack of understanding about the life chances that emerge from patterns of social stratification and social mobility. In response to a question posed by a reporter who wished to know if the federal government was going to do anything to end child poverty in the near future, then Industry Minister James Moore stated: "Is it my job to feed my neighbour's child? I don't think so" (Norman, 2013).

Think Outside the Box: In what way might Moore's own social standing influence his beliefs about poverty and even hinder attempts to end child poverty in Canada?

mobility did occur, it was greatest for sons of low-earning fathers. The earning potential of women is less pronounced, in part because they tend to leave the labour market at various intervals in relation to childbearing. Moreover, women with higher incomes may marry individuals with comparable standing and then opt to work less in the paid sector (Chen et al., 2016). Overall, patterns of social mobility in Canada are fairly stable over time and are subject to only modest increases owing to changes in education and occupation from one generation to the next. These opportunities are both enabled and constrained by social forces, including family background, the social definitions attached to ascribed traits (e.g., gender, ethnicity), and structural factors (e.g., shifts in population demographics) (see *Critical Thinking in Action*). A closer look at the nature and structure of Canada's class system, especially its relationship to wealth and net worth, reveals more about how social inequality is maintained in open systems of stratification.

TIME TO REVIEW

- What is the term for socially sanctioned patterns of social inequality?
- In what ways has slavery existed in Canada?
- How can a caste system be differentiated from a class system of stratification?
- What contributes to social mobility in Canada?

LO2 WEALTH AS A MEASURE OF SOCIAL CLASS

To gauge social inequality and discern distinct classes in Canada, it is most useful to examine economic measures such as financial wealth and poverty. **Financial wealth** corresponds to economic assets derived from income, real estate, savings, income-generating investments (such as stocks and bonds), and other sources of revenue or capital. The most common measure of financial wealth is income from employment. Information on Canadians' income is drawn from Revenue Canada tax returns and Statistics Canada surveys about economic assets. The median after-tax yearly income in Canada for economic families (i.e., groups of two or more) and persons not in an economic family (e.g., individuals who live alone or with others they are unrelated to, such as renters) was $55,600 in 2014 (Statistics Canada, 2016a). *Median* is an indicator of the middlemost value, meaning that half of the population has an income above that amount and the other half have an income below it. This is a good indicator of what "middle class" means by Canadian standards. By lining up all of the after-tax incomes for Canadian economic families and persons not in an economic family from lowest to highest and then partitioning them into 10 equal groups, each containing 10 percent of the population (called deciles), we can see how income denotes class structure (see *Table 5.1*).

Financial wealth: Corresponds to economic assets derived from income, real estate, savings, stocks, bonds, income-generating investments, and other sources of revenue or capital.

TABLE 5.1

After-Tax Income and Share of Total, by Decile, 2014

Decile	Upper Limit	Average Income	Income Share	Class
Lowest	$17,600	$9,300	1.4 percent	Impoverished
Second	$26,600	$21,800	3.2 percent	Low
Third	$35,500	$31,100	4.6 percent	Low
Fourth	$44,700	$40,200	5.9 percent	Lower-Middle
Fifth	$55,600	$50,000	7.4 percent	Middle
Sixth	$67,100	$61,300	9.0 percent	Middle
Seventh	$82,000	$74,300	10.9 percent	Upper-Middle
Eighth	$100,900	$90,900	13.4 percent	High
Ninth	$131,500	$114,400	16.8 percent	High
Highest	—	$186,500	27.4 percent	Ultra-rich

Source: Adapted from: Statistics Canada. (2016e). Upper income limit, income share and average market, total and after-tax income by economic family type and income decile, Canada and provinces. CANSIM Table 206-0031.

LO3 CANADA'S INCOME-BASED CLASS STRUCTURE

HIGH CLASS

Starting at the top, the highest 30 percent of income earners in Canada can be considered "the high class" or the "well-off." Note that although the deciles are defined on the basis of economic family types, individuals who hold particular income-generating jobs and/or have income-producing investments either singularly or jointly with spouses produce these incomes. Those in the top deciles earn well over a $100,000 a year after taxes (Statistics Canada, 2016e). This group is only 30 percent of the population, yet their earnings constitute 57.6 percent of the total income reported—a disproportionate share of Canada's overall wealth. Those in the high classes can afford large homes in "good" neighbourhoods, purchase luxury vehicles, take regular vacations to exotic destinations, and manage the costs associated with sending their children to top-tier universities. At the very top of the deciles is an extremely small group consisting of less than 1 percent of the population, who make up the "ultra-rich," or what Gilbert (2015) calls the "capitalist class." Families in the ultra-rich or capitalist class are assured social reproduction because their incomes rise more quickly than those of other Canadians. Canada's top-paid CEOs hit an all-time high in 2015, earning an average income of more than 9.5 million, or 193 times the national average wage (MacKenzie, 2017).

The ultra-rich include people born into the wealthiest families. That said, most of Canada's ultra-rich are self-made millionaires, including Mark Scheinberg, who founded the online gambling site *PokerStars*, and Susan Niczowski, whose *Summer Fresh Salads* business earns more than $100 million annually (Basa, 2016; Harris, 2013). Outside of the ultra-rich "outliers," the high class in Canada includes families headed by the CEOs of large corporations, university-educated individuals employed in the professions (e.g., engineers, physicians, and lawyers), individuals with industry certifications in the trades (e.g., welders, electricians, and heavy-duty mechanics), professional athletes, and the self-employed (e.g., business owners and executives). Families in the high class tend to have salaried positions with benefits (e.g., pensions and paid sick leave) as well as high levels of job security. With the exception of the high-paying trades, occupations in this class are regularly rated as high in prestige (Marger, 2014); also, they include a high level of autonomy as well as considerable power and authority over others (Hodson & Sullivan, 2012).

THE MIDDLE CLASSES

Most Canadians perceive themselves as "middle class." Taken as a whole, the middle class has incomes ranging from about $40,200 to $74,300. Canada's middle classes include families with semiprofessionals and managers who have at least a four-year university or college degree (e.g., teachers, social workers, and police officers), as well as those in nonretail sales (e.g., insurance representatives) and families headed by people who work in the trades (e.g., pipefitters and machinists). The middle class also includes individuals with a high school diploma who are employed in lower-paid "semiskilled" positions more commonly held by males (historically known as "blue collar" jobs) in areas such as trucking or manufacturing, administration, or retail sales.

Perhaps you have read in the papers something about a "shrinking middle class." That term refers to the growing income inequality in Canada (and in many other parts of the world); that is, incomes are becoming more polarized. Middle-class incomes are shrinking as a result of the loss of many full-time jobs in areas such as construction and manufacturing, the creation of low-paying jobs in the service industry, and corporate "downsizing," "outsourcing," and "part-timing" (Kerbo, 2012). This trend is even common in the upper-middle range; many academics are now part-time instructors who are paid an hourly wage on a term-by-term basis, with little job security and minimal benefits.

THE LOW CLASS: POOR

In the lowest deciles, we find the bottom 30 percent of the population, who earn less than $35,500 (Statistics Canada, 2016e). The low class includes families headed by those who have some high school education and hold the lowest paying jobs in the labour force, earning minimum wage or slightly more, as well as various individuals who live alone or with other unattached persons. This class is sometimes referred to as the "working poor" (Gilbert, 2015). The occupations of the working poor are often referred to as "unskilled labour." *Unskilled labour* includes physically demanding jobs and ones that require little or no previous experience (e.g., landscape labourer, construction labourer, fast-food server, and telemarketer). There is little or no social mobility among unskilled workers (Hodson & Sullivan, 2012). The low class also includes Canada's impoverished—a group that is extremely poor, relatively uneducated, and often unemployed or employed only part-time.

In every province and territory, families span the social classes. However, income also varies considerably both within and between Canada's cities, provinces, and territories.

REGIONAL INCOME DISTRIBUTION

High median family incomes do not reflect the absence of social inequality. In fact, the opposite is true. Alberta, for example, has a high median family income (i.e., $100,750) (Statistics Canada, 2016c) as well as the most pronounced gap between those who are wealthy and those who are poor. Since 2011, Alberta has also experienced the greatest growth in inequality largely attributable to the top 10 percent of earners (Flanagan, 2015). Comparably, there is less social inequality but a much lower median family income in New Brunswick ($69,290), Nova Scotia ($72,270), and Prince Edward Island ($72,380) (Statistics Canada, 2016c), where a greater overall percentage of the population is less well off. With the demise of the fishing and mining sectors over the past several decades, many workers left the Atlantic region to secure gainful employment in other provinces—for example, in Alberta, where high-paying jobs in construction, trades, and energy were plentiful prior to the drop in oil prices. *Figure 5.1* shows the regional variations in family income in Canada by province and territory for 2014.

Annual earnings also reflect regional differences in employment rates and opportunities as well as in the **cost of living**—that is, average prices for essential goods and services such as food, housing, transportation, and health care. In Nunavut, Yukon, and the Northwest Territories, the cost of living is higher because commodities need to be flown in, which drives up their prices (see *Figure 5.2*). In addition, because a small population resides on a vast land mass with an extreme climate, communication and transportation infrastructure is expensive to build and maintain. To offset the disadvantages and to attract workers to the region, employers sometimes offer wage bonuses or higher-than-average wages (especially in the mining and health sectors of Yukon and the Northwest Territories). Also, the federal government allows a northern residency tax deduction (Canada Revenue Agency, 2017). This helps attract workers to these areas but does little to improve conditions for residents who have no industry benefits. Consequently, there is a higher level of poverty and a lower median income in places such as Nunavut.

NET WORTH AND CLASS STRUCTURE

A second financial measure for gauging social inequality is **net worth**, which refers to the dollar value of all financial assets after liabilities

Cost of living: A measure of the average price for essential goods and services in a given area, including transportation.

Net worth: Total assets calculated by subtracting all existing financial liabilities from assets.

FIGURE 5.1

Regional Variation in Annual Family Income, Canada, 2014

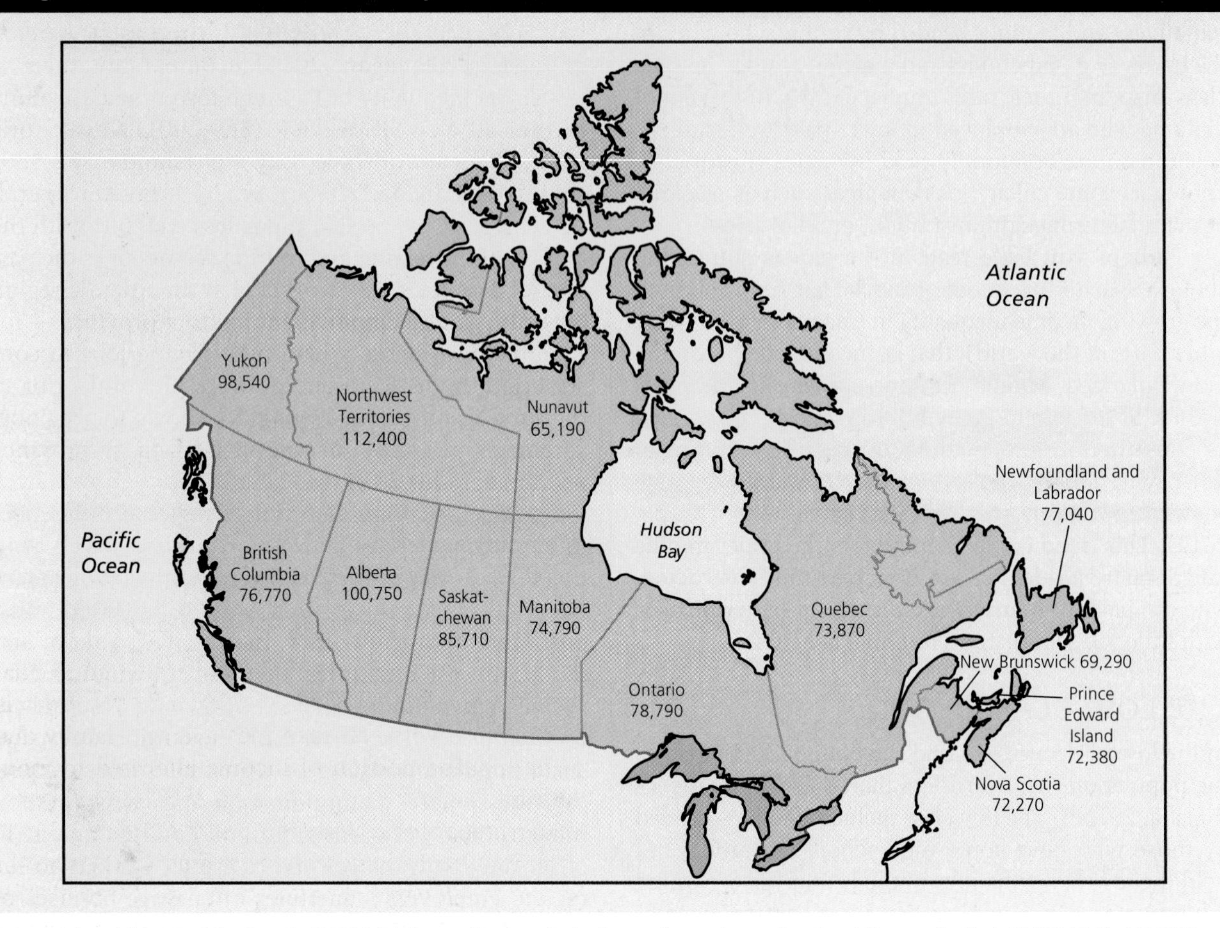

Source: Adapted from: Statistics Canada. (2016c). Median total income, by family type, by province and territory (all census families). CANSIM Table 111-0009.

are subtracted. Net worth is calculated by subtracting all existing financial debts (e.g., mortgages and loans) from assets (e.g., savings, home equity, and investments). In 1999, the median net worth of Canadian families was $225,400, whereas the median debt was $36,700. By 2012, median net worth had risen to $405,200, but debt had also climbed to $60,100 (Uppal & LaRochelle-Côté, 2015). More than 35 percent of Canadian families have a debt that is at least twice the level of their annual after-tax income. Those most likely to incur debt are younger families, families whose major income earner has a university education, couples with children, and families in the top 20 percent of earners. Net worth increases more for certain family types than for others. Between 1999 and 2012, the greatest gains in net worth were for top-earning families ($472,700), home owners without a mortgage ($357,400), families whose major income earner had a university degree ($198,500), families with a major income earner ($190,300), and couples without children ($185,000) (Uppal & LaRochelle-Côté, 2015).

Net worth increases as income goes up because those in the higher classes have access to a broader range of earning opportunities, such as private investments and employer pensions, whereas the smaller percentage of those in the lower classes who see gains in net worth only do so through increases in real-estate investments (Uppal & LaRochelle-Côté, 2015). According to Oxfam Canada's (2017) latest research, the Thomson family and the Weston family together have as much wealth as 30 percent of all Canadians combined. Refer to *Table 5.2* for a list of Canada's 10 richest families by net worth.

FIGURE 5.2

Food Prices in Nunavut

cherries/Shutterstock

Nunavut average price compared to Canada's average retail price shown in brackets

1 L fresh milk (2%)	=$3.63 (2.30)
450 g butter, salted	=$7.26 (3.28)
1 kg celery	=$12.44 (3.38)
1 kg carrots	=$6.90 (2.25)
4.54 kg potatoes	=$12.86 (5.84)
450 g soda crackers	=$7.43 (3.02)
500 g peanut butter, smooth	=$6.16 (3.68)
1.36 L apple juice	=$8.95 (2.12)
1 L tomato ketchup	=$9.09 (3.61)
2.5 kg flour, all purpose, white	=$13.70 (5.00)
2 kg sugar, white	=$9.65 (2.69)

Sources: Nunavut Bureau of Statistics, 2016 Nunavut Food Price Survey, Comparison of Nunavut & Canada CPI Food Price Basket Items. Found at: http://www.stats.gov.nu.ca.

POVERTY AND CLASS STRUCTURE

A final way to gauge social inequality is to focus on the opposite end of the spectrum by estimating the number of people in society who lack wealth. One challenge in determining how many poor there are in Canada is how to measure poverty consistently. The federal and provincial governments have yet to reach a consensus about what it means to "be poor." In the absence of such a definition, most researchers, academics, and social analysts rely on Statistics Canada's

low-income cutoff as an indicator of poverty. This tool marks a threshold below which families assuredly experience financial difficulties.

LO4 MEASURING POVERTY: LOW-INCOME CUTOFF

The **low-income cutoff** (LICO) refers to an annual family income value in dollars below which a family is considerably worse off than the "average" family due to the high proportion of income allocated to food, clothing, and shelter. Families at the LICO spend a greater proportion of their income (i.e., about 63 percent) on these basic necessities relative to the average family, which spends about 20 percent less (i.e., 43 percent) (Statistics Canada, 2015b). For example, imagine that a lone parent named Joe earns $1,920 a month based on $12.00 per hour working full-time to support himself and his son. If Joe spends $750 on rent, $300 on food, and $100 on clothing, he will not be below LICO because the basic needs for his family constitute about 60 percent of his regular earnings. However, Joe also has to pay at least 10.77 percent of his income as federal taxes, which reduces his earnings by $207 per month. This means that Joe is "poor" (i.e., below LICO) because 71 percent of his "available" income is allocated to the basic necessities. See *Sociology in My Life* to determine how you fare in comparison. An *after-tax LICO* is commonly used because it provides the most accurate reflection of accessible income. This example is based on Joe's after-tax yearly income

Low-income cutoff: An annual family income value in dollars below which a family is worse off than average due to the high proportion of income allocated to food, clothing, and shelter.

TABLE 5.2

Canada's 10 Richest Families by Net Worth (in Billions), 2017

Rank	Name	Net Worth	Residence	Industry	Companies
1	Thomson Family	39.12	Toronto	Media, information distribution	Thomson Reuters, Woodbridge Co.
2	Galen Weston	13.22	Toronto	Food, groceries, real estate, retail	George Weston Ltd., Loblaw Cos. Ltd., Holt Renfrew
3	Saputo Family	10.61	Montreal	Dairy	Saputo, TransForce
4	Rogers Family	9.13	Toronto	Cable TV, communications, professional sports	Rogers Communications Inc.
5	Garrett Camp	8.93	San Francisco	Transportation, social media	Uber, StumbleUpon
6	Joseph Tsai	8.27	Hong Kong	E-commerce	Alibaba
7	Irving Family	7.65	Saint John	Oil, gas stations, forestry products, media, transportation	Irving Oil Ltd., J.D. Irving, Ltd.
8	Paul Desmarais Sr.	6.71	Montreal	Financial services, energy	Power Corporation of Canada
9	Richardson Family	5.95	Winnipeg	Wealth management	James Richardson & Sons, Ltd.
10	James (Jimmy) Pattison	5.74	Vancouver	Auto sales, food, media, forestry products, entertainment, export services	Overwaitea supermarket group, Save-On-Foods, Ocean Brands seafood

Source: Adapted from *Canadian Business*, "Canada's 100 Wealthiest People, 2017." Found at: http://www.canadianbusiness.com. Used with permission of Rogers Media Inc.

of $20,556 (or $1,713 per month). After covering basic needs, Joe only has $563 each month to divide across all remaining expenses, including transportation, personal care, and child care, suggesting that he would struggle to pay his bills at $12.00 per hour. The minimum Canadian hourly wage currently ranges from $10.72 to $13.60, moving to a high of $15.00 for Alberta in 2018 (Government of Canada, 2017a).

Statistics Canada calculates multiple LICOs, adjusting for family and community size. As shown in *Figure 5.3*, an average after-tax LICO for a two-, four-, and six-person Canadian family in 2017 was $30,625, $45,712, and $58,473, respectively (Government of Canada, 2017b). The LICO is criticized for not taking into account regional differences in costs of living, and as an estimate of poverty, the LICO is also conservative in that it fails to take into account much of what Canadians actually pay for on a regular basis. Living expenses include shelter, food, and clothing, but they also include other necessary expenditures, such as costs associated with operating a household, raising children, obtaining health care, taking care of personal

Fred Lum/The Globe and Mail/The Canadian Press

More than 850,000 Canadians visit a food bank every month.

FIGURE 5.3

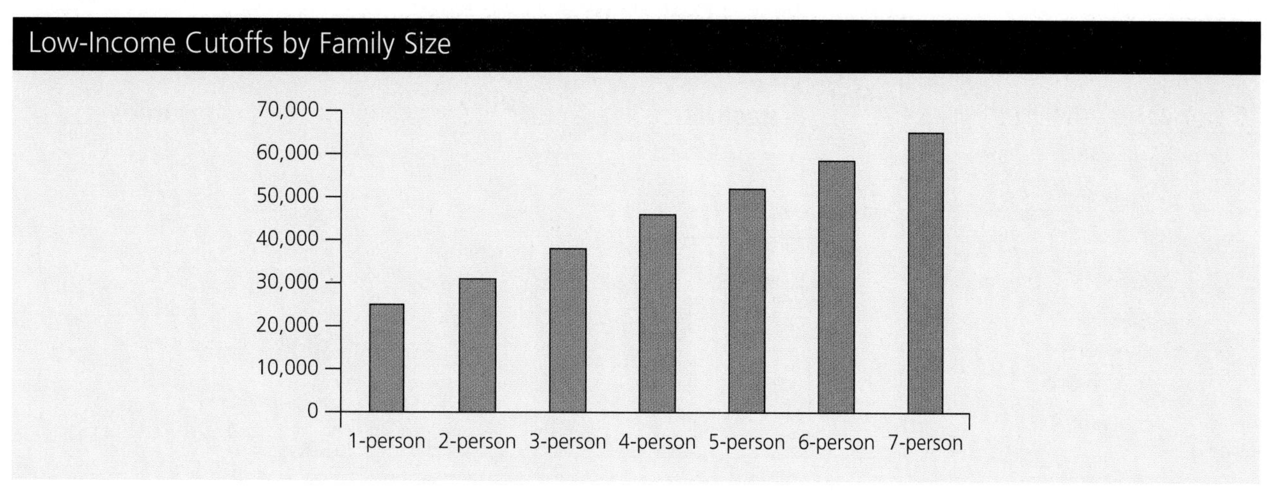

Source: Government of Canada (2017b)

needs, getting an education, acquiring personal insurance, and using transportation.

Statistics Canada computes two other measures of low incomes: the Low-Income Measure (LIM) and the Market Basket Measure (MBM). The LIM, used for international comparisons, is based on incomes less than 50 percent of the national median adjusted for family size. The MBM is based on an actual cost of purchasing a needed "basket" of goods and services (e.g., nutritional food, shelter, clothing and footwear, necessary personal items, and transportation) across the country (Statistics Canada, 2015a). Although the 2016 Statistics Canada Census data on income have yet to be released, based on the LIM, 13 percent of the population was classified as "low income" in 2014 compared to 8.8 percent using the LICO and 11.3 percent with the MBM (Statistics Canada, 2016b). As with regional variations in family income, there is disparity in poverty across Canadian cities and provinces, with the largest concentrations of families with low incomes in the larger urban areas of Vancouver, Toronto, and Metropolitan Montreal (Federation of Canadian Municipalities, 2010).

LO5 WHO ARE CANADA'S POOR?

For most Canadians, low income is a temporary state. Younger individuals tend to earn low wages when they first enter the workforce, but their wages increase over time with experience. Similarly, employed individuals of all ages may experience a short-term drop in income during an economic downturn, particularly when there are widespread layoffs, but their incomes tend to bounce back once circumstances improve. Certain groups of people, however, remain at high risk for "persistent" low-income states, including single, unattached individuals, people with physical and mental disabilities, visible minorities who are recent immigrants, and individuals living in households headed by a lone parent (Lamman & MacIntyre, 2016) (see *Figure 5.4*). The same

YOUR SOCIOLOGICAL TOOLKIT

SOCIOLOGY IN MY LIFE

ARE YOU ABOVE LICO?

Make a list of all of your "typical" monthly expenses. Comparing your expenses to your monthly income, what proportion of your available money is spent on the three basic needs: food, essential clothing, and shelter? Does this put you above, at, or below LICO?

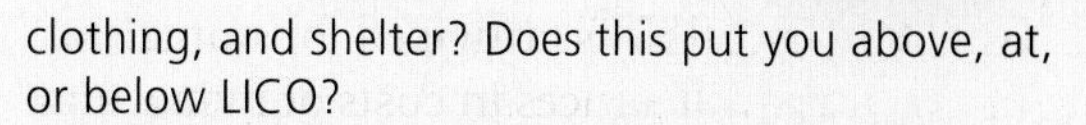

Think Outside the Box: Is the LICO an accurate reflection of poverty? Why or why not?

FIGURE 5.4

Low-Income Rates of Vulnerable Groups, Total Population, 2014

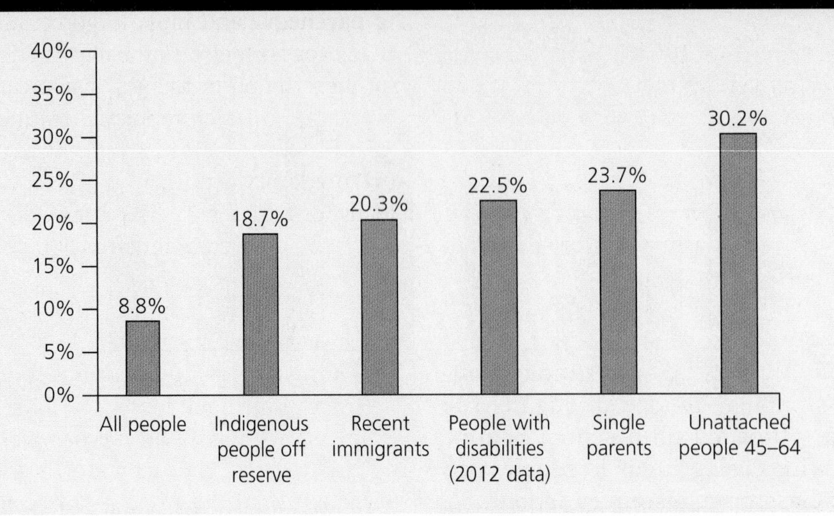

Source: Statistics Canada, custom tabulation based on Canadian Income Survey, 2014. Data for people with disabilities are only available for 2012.

groups (not counting children) are also at greater risk for unemployment, and poor people with jobs are more likely to have nonstandard work arrangements, such as temporary, part-time, or self-employment (Hay, 2009).

Poverty is also linked to the intersectionality of age, gender, and race. That is, individuals who occupy any of the categories listed above and are children, females, or Indigenous peoples are especially prone to poverty. Females in many groups (e.g., those 18 to 64, and especially women who are lone parents) experience a higher-than-average risk known as the *feminization of poverty*. Around 14.7 percent of all children in Canada live in low-income families, with an incidence of 44.9 percent for children who live in female-headed lone-parent families (Statistics Canada, 2016d). Imagine trying to manage the additional cost of child care if you were a single mother living in Toronto, where it costs an average of $1,649 per month to put your infant in daycare (Macdonald & Friendly, 2016). The intersectionality of risk characteristics is especially evident in the case of Indigenous children, more than half of whom (51 percent living off reserves and 60 percent on reserves) live in a state of persistent poverty (Macdonald & Wilson, 2016).

SOCIOLOGY ONLINE

MAKING WOMEN COUNT

The Canadian Centre for Policy Alternatives is an independent, member-based research institute that works on various projects of interest to Canadians (e.g., climate change, economic security, and seniors care). A current focus is *Making Women Count*, which highlights how gender inequality impacts the economy, politics, and well-being of Canadians. Here you can find publications and news releases about gender inequality, including information on how women continue to bear much of the burden for unpaid and undervalued work. Find out why Victoria is considered the best and Windsor is considered the worst place to live as a woman in Canada based on indicators of economic security, education, health, leadership, and personal security by accessing *Making Women Count* at **https://www.policyalternatives.ca**.

NEGATIVE CONSEQUENCES OF SOCIAL INEQUALITY

EDUCATION AND POVERTY

Children born into poverty are further disadvantaged once they enter the school system. Recall that the greatest portion of poor children in Canada are those living on reserves. Chronic underfunding by the federal government for students on reserves (compared to those off reserves, which have provincially run systems) has led to substandard levels of schooling and educational opportunities on many First Nation reserves (e.g., a lack of supplies, library books, and no access to extracurricular activities) (Laboucane, 2010; Macdonald & Wilson, 2016). Although off-reserve schooling is publicly funded through Grade 12, many costs are offloaded onto school boards. Parents are tasked with raising funds to supplement library resources, classroom resources, computer equipment, field trips, and playground equipment. Wealthier parents have more resources to contribute in the form of financial donations, fundraising purchases, and unpaid volunteer efforts. Families living in poverty are less able to participate in fundraising programs and are less able to utilize many enrichment activities, such as school field trips, band equipment rentals, organized sports, and hot lunch programs. Those who are impoverished tend to do less well in school, and this creates a cycle of poverty because those who do poorly in school are more likely to drop out and are more likely to end up being poor as adults.

Educational attainment is a significant determinant of future employment. In 2016, about 85 percent of Canadians between the ages of 25 and 44 who had a postsecondary degree were employed, compared to 75 percent with a high school diploma and 48.5 percent with less than Grade 9 (Statistics Canada, 2017b). Similarly, educational attainment is an important contributor to future earnings. Individuals who complete high school even without continuing on to postsecondary earn significantly more than those without a Grade 12 diploma (Frenette, 2014), and those with successively higher levels of education (e.g., a graduate degree versus an undergraduate degree) earn correspondingly higher incomes. A TD economics study found that it costs about $84,000 to obtain an undergraduate degree in Canada (including tuition, books, and living expenses), but a recent graduate can only expect to earn between $35,000 and $43,000 (Deveau, 2013).

HEALTH, HARDSHIPS, HOMELESSNESS, AND POVERTY

Many Canadians living in poverty live from paycheque to paycheque and must forgo certain health care practices because they lack the means to cover plans that pay for prescription medicines, vision care, or supplemental provisions (e.g., chiropractic treatment, orthotics). The poor often resort to using high-interest financial services, or "predatory lending," wherein they obtain payday loans for basic necessities, including food, and are subsequently charged as much as 500 percent in annualized interest rates (Fantauzzi, 2016). The poor also often go hungry and suffer malnutrition because they do not have enough money to regularly purchase groceries, which limits their access to nutritious foods. Lack of regular access to nutritious foods also poses long-term health implications, including the prevalence of higher rates of diabetes, heart problems, hypertension, and cancer (Phipps, 2003). The chapter on health and illness provides a more detailed discussion of the links between socioeconomic status and health.

The most extreme hardship associated with poverty is homelessness. A recent report called *The State of Homelessness in Canada* indicates that as many as 235,000 Canadians are currently without a home (Gaetz et al., 2016). **Homelessness** can be succinctly defined as a state in which a person is unable to secure a permanent residence. However, there is much more to this state, as evidenced by the definition provided by the Canadian Homelessness Research Network (2012):

> Homelessness describes the situation of an individual or family without stable, permanent, appropriate housing, or the immediate prospect, means and ability of acquiring it. It is the result of systemic or societal barriers, a lack of affordable and appropriate housing, the individual/household's financial, mental, cognitive, behavioural or physical challenges, and/or racism and discrimination. Most people do not choose to be homeless, and the experience is generally negative, unpleasant, stressful and distressing.
>
> Homelessness describes a range of housing and shelter circumstances, with people being without any shelter at one end, and being insecurely housed at the other. That is, homelessness encompasses a range of

Homelessness: A state in which a person is unable to secure a permanent residence.

SOCIOLOGY IN THE NEWS

WATER INSECURITY AND INDIGENOUS COMMUNITIES

On June 7, 2016, Human Rights Watch released a 92-page report titled "Make it Safe: Canada's Obligation to End the First Nations Water Crisis" about water insecurity in Indigenous communities (Klasing, 2016). Although water shortages and a lack of safe drinking water are often considered to be global issues faced by impoverished and developing countries such as those found in Africa and Western Asia, a sizeable portion of Indigenous people in Canada currently live in communities without any running water or flush toilets. Compared to Canada as a whole, Indigenous homes are 90 times more likely to lack running water (UN Department of Economic and Social Affairs, 2009, p. 25).

And although most Indigenous communities in Canada have access to running water, it is not always safe for drinking. As of March 31, 2017, there were 137 Indigenous communities under a drinking water advisory (Health Canada, 2017). More than half of these communities are deemed "high risk" and have been under advisory for many years owing to major deficiencies in available water sources and/or in waste management systems. Even communities with new treatment plants are not guaranteed access to safe drinking water, as evidenced by the long-term advisory for the Serpent River First Nation in Ontario (McClearn, 2017).

Several structural issues have contributed to the slow progress Canada has made toward remedying water problems on reserves. Water and waste management for Canadians is overseen by the provincial and territorial governments, whose regulations do not apply to Indigenous communities on reserves. Instead, regulatory authority falls under the federal Indigenous and Northern Affairs Canada, which receives funding for water services; Health Canada, which regulates the safety of drinking water; and Environment Canada, which plays a role in the regulation of wastewater. Indigenous communities are responsible for the water systems themselves and for the monitoring of drinking water quality, along with some of the costs incurred (Simeone, 2010). The largest obstacles to progress are funding, infrastructure, and the availability of trained operators. The Liberal government vowed to improve water conditions for Indigenous Canadians and has committed 1.8 billion dollars toward addressing the ongoing health and safety issues and ending long-term water advisories by 2021 (Indigenous and Northern Affairs Canada, 2017).

skhunda/Shutterstock

Thousands of Indigenous peoples living on reserves in Canada lack access to running water in their homes.

physical living situations, organized here in a typology that includes (1) Unsheltered, or absolutely homeless and living on the streets or in places not intended for human habitation; (2) Emergency Sheltered, including those staying in overnight shelters for people who are homeless, as well as shelters for those impacted by family violence; (3) Provisionally Accommodated, referring to those whose accommodation is temporary or lacks security of tenure, and finally, (4) At Risk of Homelessness, referring to people who are not homeless, but whose current economic and/or housing situation is precarious or does not meet public health and safety standards.*

There is a range of homelessness in Canada, from people living on the street, staying in emergency shelters, or sleeping in vehicles to those staying "temporarily" with friends and/or relatives. Note that even more Canadians (as many as 3 million households) live in "precarious" forms of housing (e.g., their current housing is unaffordable, below standards, and/or overcrowded) (Canada Without Poverty, 2017).

*Canadian Observatory on Homelessness (2012), Canadian Definition of Homelessness. Found at http://www.homelesshub.ca.

Philip Arno Photography/Shutterstock

More than a million Canadians are at risk for homelessness.

Risk factors for homelessness can be identified at the micro and macro levels. The two main structural factors that increase the risk of homelessness are inadequate incomes and a lack of affordable housing (Echenberg & Jensen, 2009). Individual-level factors include unemployment, divorce, substance abuse, and mental illness (Canadian Mental Health Association, 2003).

TIME TO REVIEW

- What is financial wealth, and how is it measured in Canada?
- What do measures of financial wealth tell us about social inequality?
- How is poverty estimated in Canada?
- Who is at greatest risk for poverty in Canada?
- What are the consequences of poverty?

POVERTY AS A FEATURE OF CANADIAN SOCIETY

Except during the recession of 2008–2009, there has been very little change in the overall rate of poverty over the past several decades, indicating that poverty is a persistent and enduring characteristic of Canadian society (Hay, 2009). A **recession** refers to a general economic decline that persists for two or more three-month periods. A recession is often identified by a drop in a country's gross domestic product. **Gross domestic product (GDP)** is an indicator of a country's economic productivity based on goods and services as measured by household consumption, government spending, and investments. Canada's GDP dropped 3.3 percent between the fall of 2008 and the summer of 2009 (CBC News, 2010). The economy is one of the main structural factors leading to fluctuations in poverty rates because it represents changes in business cycles, which in turn correspond to employment rates, income levels, and the overall cost of living. Although Canada made its way out of the 2008–2009 recession, the economic plight is ongoing. Record-low interest rates have made it more attractive to borrow and spend rather than save, and this is the main reason many Canadians are now carrying substantial debt loads they may never be able to repay. From 2009 to the present, Canada's economy has seen only minimal growth due to the large drop in commodity prices owing to the low price of

Recession: A general economic decline that persists for two or more three-month periods.

Gross domestic product (GDP): An overall indicator of a country's economic productivity based on goods and services as measured by household consumption, government spending, and investments.

SOCIOLOGY ON SCREEN

FOUR FEET UP

Written and directed by award-winning photographer Nance Ackerman and produced by Annette Clarke (2009), *Four Feet Up* is a National Film Board documentary that takes a critical look at poverty in rural Canada. Ackerman spent two years with a rural family in order to depict the experience of poverty through the eyes of an eight-year-old boy named Isaiah Jackson. For more information and a short clip from the film, visit the home page for the National Film Board at https://www.nfb.ca.

oil. At present, Canada's economy is considered to be "resilient" but "vulnerable" as a result of high housing prices (e.g., Vancouver) and high household debt (Organisation for Economic Co-operation and Development, 2016).

LO6 POVERTY REDUCTION

Federal policies and programs designed to provide income security are highly effective for reducing poverty, as evidenced by the fact that elderly Canadians as a group are not considered at risk for poverty. This is partly because Canadians over 65 currently have access to ongoing sources of income in the form of Old Age Security (since 1951), the Canada Pension Plan (since 1964), and/or the Quebec Pension Plan for those living in Quebec. Since the first baby boomers turned 65 in 2011, however, Canada now has more people than ever retiring and drawing pension, with comparably fewer workers paying into pensions and contributing via income tax (Statistics Canada, 2017a). The difficulty, then, also lies in sustaining measures that reduce poverty, particularly when several groups are at risk for poverty and one or more costly social programs are needed for each group to keep them above the low-income cutoff.

Social safety net: Services and programs designed to lessen financial burdens experienced by low-income groups.

Poverty reduction strategies are generally incorporated as part of a society's broader social safety net. A **social safety net** consists of services and programs designed to lessen the financial burdens experienced by low-income groups.

Federal and provincial initiatives usually take the form of supplemental financial supports (such as income benefits for seniors and child tax benefits for families) and employment benefits (such as EI to cover periods of unemployment) (see *Sociology in My Community*). Other programs, such as housing allowances, food allowances, and daycare allowances, address specific issues related to inadequate income. Still other measures, such as fee waivers, target groups at greatest risk for poverty, including Indigenous peoples and recent immigrants (Hay, 2009). Although they do help reduce poverty, these initiatives cost money that is not readily available in government budgets and that must be funded through cutbacks, increased taxes, or deficit expenditures.

TIME TO REVIEW

- What is a recession, and how is it related to a country's gross domestic product (GDP)?
- Is poverty decreasing over time in Canada?
- What kind of measures help reduce poverty?

YOUR SOCIOLOGICAL TOOLKIT

SOCIOLOGY IN MY COMMUNITY

POVERTY REDUCTION STRATEGIES

All provinces and territories in Canada have a poverty reduction strategy plan in place, with the exception of British Columbia. Although each plan is somewhat unique, most plans centre on provisions for ending homelessness, reducing child poverty, increasing food security, improving health care and education spending, and providing income security. For example, Ontario's five-year plan includes initiatives directed at reducing child poverty through direct financial support to families with low to moderate incomes, school nutrition programs, after-school programs, and programs for youth transitioning out of care programs once they reach adulthood (Province of Ontario, 2017).

Think Outside the Box: If you lived in a remote community in Nunavut, how might poverty look different from a smaller community in Ontario?

YOUR SOCIOLOGICAL TOOLKIT
SOCIOLOGY IN THEORY

LO7 WHY ARE THERE CLASSES IN SOCIETY?

STRATIFICATION IS BENEFICIAL

Functionalists point out that inequality exists in all societies, which suggests that it is inevitable and even necessary. According to Davis and Moore (1945), stratification is beneficial because it leads to **meritocracy**, a condition of advancement based on worth derived from experience, skills, and educational attainment. Social stratification is functional because it motivates people to achieve higher education and develop their skills to their potential for success. It also ensures that the most capable people (i.e., those with the highest intellect and the utmost abilities) end up occupying the most important social positions in society (e.g., those that require the greatest amount of skill, the longest period of training, and the highest intellect) (Brym, 2016).

Poverty also persists because the poor carry out many functions that benefit those who are not poor. According to Herbert J. Gans (1971), every society has low-paying, demeaning, and undesirable jobs; therefore, poverty helps ensure that society's "dirty work" gets done. We see this today in the growing population of unskilled temporary foreign workers in Canada in a variety of areas, including agriculture, food processing, hospitality, long-haul trucking, and live-in caregiving. Gans (1971) also pointed out how the poor are especially likely to foster social mobility in groups just above them, noting that "members of almost every immigrant group have financed their upward mobility by providing slum housing, entertainment, gambling, narcotics, etc., to later arrivals" (p. 23). The poor also serve as scapegoats for "laissez-faire" capitalism, wherein to the extent that the poor can be painted as a "deprived population that is unwilling to work," there is less political pressure to change the system or employ measures to reduce poverty (Gans, 1971, p. 23).

STRATIFICATION IS A BY-PRODUCT OF CAPITALISM

Most theoretical models used to describe how social classes originate or why they persist have foundations in the conflict perspective, given that the very notion of classes necessarily implies inequity in terms of resources and power. The epigraph to this chapter suggests that a class-based system of stratification is inevitable. In the *Manifesto of the Communist Party* (1848/2010), Karl Marx and Friedrich Engels observed that people are essentially cooperative by nature when attempting to secure basic needs (i.e., food, shelter, and clothing). However, once basic needs are met and a division of labour emerges in society, class struggles become apparent (Coser, 1977). As production moves away from individuals to factories, workers become exploited by capitalists, who pay the workers less than what they deserve for their efforts.

MARX'S VIEWS ON STRATIFICATION

From a Marxist perspective, the materialistic nature of a *capitalist society*, as rooted in the private ownership of property and the generation of surplus, fosters competition and creates a distinction between owners and workers that leads to the emergence of social classes. The economy is the central institution in society, and this, like a master status, has a far-reaching impact on all the other sectors (e.g., religion and politics). Cultural values and practices, then, are more apt to be considered by-products of capitalist dominance, as in the case of religion, which Marx (1843–1844) deemed "the sigh of the oppressed creature, the heart of a heartless world and the soul of soulless conditions. It is the opium of the people" (Cowling et al., 1970, p. 127). According to Marx, although religion is beneficial in that it provides temporary relief to the masses, who are long sufferers of exploitation, it primarily serves to maintain the existing social order.

Thus, social stratification, like religion, is a means used by the most powerful to retain their position in the upper echelons of a society. From Marx's perspective, stratification benefits the bourgeoisie (i.e., the owners of the means of production) and disadvantages those who work for the owners (i.e., the proletariat). Marx used the term **alienation** to refer to the detachment that exists between the worker and his or her labour as perpetuated under capitalism. Canada's migrant workers are especially prone to exploitation and abuse by their employers due to their precarious status stemming from a range of vulnerabilities, including language barriers, isolation, and overreliance on their employers to meet basic needs (Canadian Council for Refugees, 2016).

For Marx, workers are alienated from productive activity (because they do not work for themselves), from the product (because it belongs to the bourgeoisie), from their fellow workers (especially when they are forced into competition with one another), and from their own human potential (they have been reduced to something akin

Meritocracy: A condition of advancement based on worth.

Alienation: The detachment that exists between the worker and his or her labour as perpetuated under capitalism.

© Historical image collection by Bildagentur-online / Alamy

Karl Marx (1818–1883).

to machines) (Ritzer & Stepnisky, 2014). Marx saw the increasing alienation of workers as culminating in a revolution that would eventually overthrow the bourgeoisie and pave the way for communism. *Communism* is a classless economic system in which there is group (or communal) ownership of the means of production.

WEBER'S VIEWS ON STRATIFICATION

Max Weber's views on capitalism are quite different from Marx's. In *The Protestant Ethic and the Spirit of Capitalism* (1904/1958), Weber emphasizes how the emergence of rationality in the West coincided with the rising "spirit" of capitalism within Protestantism; both promoted ideas that emphasized the importance of economic success, such as "time is money," "be industrious," "be punctual," and "earning money is a legitimate end in itself" (Ritzer, 1992, p. 150). Hence, religion also contributes to the influence of capitalism. Although Weber also focused on economics, he did not view the mode of production as necessarily the only key influence in society. Things such as religion (or even race) could also be significant contributors to social inequality between groups. In addition, instead of discussing just two main groups in conflict with each other, Weber recognized a broader range of strata, which he discussed in terms of status differences (rather than class differences). This is a very different use of status than that described in Chapter 4; in this particular case, status does depict hierarchical ranking.

For Weber, status referred to social standing as based on similarities in upbringing and lifestyle that could be attributed to wealth, power, and/or prestige. *Wealth* in this case refers to economic assets such as income, *power* is the ability to enact one's will, and *prestige* refers to the social advantage conferred by a particular position. The elements of status often correspond to one another. For example, as a group, physicians are fairly autonomous and thereby share a high level of prestige, while their knowledge and skills translate into high salaries (wealth). In addition, they possess power in terms of the level of control over their own work environment (which also relates to prestige), and they have authority in relation to patients and coworkers, such as nurses (which also illustrates power). Whereas Marx emphasized the differences between two classes based on those who owned the means of production and those who worked for the owners, Weber viewed class differences as based on differences of lifestyle and interests afforded by similar social standing.

THE CAPITALIST CLASS

Some conflict theorists have focused exclusively on the "ultra-rich" capitalist class in an effort to describe who this group is, how it exerts influence, and how it maintains its position of power in society; this focus has come to be known as elite theory. *Elite theory* explains power relationships in society as residing in a small group that holds positions of authority in economic and political structures. Weber's contemporaries, sociologists Vilfredo Pareto (1848–1923), Gaetano Mosca (1858–1941), and Robert Michels (1876–1936), wrote extensively about the same small group that possessed wealth and power, which they called the "governing elite," the "elite," and/or the "ruling class." Similarly, C. Wright Mills (1956) wrote about "the power elite," a very cohesive group of top corporate officials from the government, military, and economic structures who share similar backgrounds and play a central role in decision making in the United States (Marger, 2014). John Porter (1921–1979), a highly influential sociologist and economist, was the first to demonstrate that Canadian society also consists of hierarchically ranked social classes that are headed by what he termed the "corporate elite." In *The Vertical Mosaic: An Analysis of Social Class and Power in Canada,* Porter (1965) explains how Canada can be divided into a "vertical mosaic" of social classes based on measures of inequality (e.g., wealth and power) identified by the early conflict theorists. In addition, membership in certain ethnic groups confers more or less status. Specifically, those of British origin tend to fall into the highest social classes, where power and privilege are concentrated, whereas Indigenous peoples tend to be in the lowest classes, which correspond to lower education attainment, income, and occupational prestige. The *corporate elite* are highly influential Canadians who head up the economic and political spheres and who both compete and cooperate with one another as central decision makers. Although their interests may differ (and, hence, create competition), there is also substantial overlap because they are from the higher social class, intermarry, form business partnerships, belong to elite social clubs, and hold similar positions on corporate boards (Helm-Hayes & Miller, 1998). Hence, the elite also tend to support one another when necessary in order to maintain the overall structure.

STRATIFICATION PRODUCES SURPLUS VALUE

Not all theories assume that stratification is as beneficial as functionalists claim or as self-serving for capitalists as the conflict theorists make it out to be. Sociologist Gerhard Lenski's (1966) theory of social stratification is based on the assumption that societal rewards are distributed according to *both* societal needs (the functionalist perspective) and power (the conflict view). In his view, "men will share the product of their labors to the extent required to ensure survival and continued productivity of those others whose actions are necessary or beneficial to themselves" (p. 44). According to Lenski, although there will always be stratification, there should be less inequality in modern industrial societies compared to nonindustrial ones because some of the accumulated "surplus value" will be shared with workers in order to manage the system (i.e., control the working class) and prevent loss of productivity due to things such as strikes (Marger, 2014). This is true of advanced countries with lower social inequality, including Sweden, where all workers are entitled to good social benefits and wages, unions support workers but also form strong partnerships with industry leaders, and workers are directly involved in decision making.

YOUR SOCIOLOGICAL TOOLKIT

SOCIOLOGY IN PRACTICE

HUMAN RIGHTS AND A NATIONAL STRATEGY FOR POVERTY REDUCTION

Several years ago, Bill C-545, "An Act to Eliminate Poverty in Canada," was introduced into the House of Commons. This bill recognized poverty as "the condition of a human being who does not have the resources, means, choices, and power necessary to acquire and maintain economic self-reliance and to facilitate their integration into and participation in society." It described poverty in a context of human rights, clearly delineated the negative outcomes of poverty (e.g., on the health of individuals and on the economic and social development of society), and declared the elimination of poverty a federal government obligation (i.e., to develop and implement a strategy that would strengthen the social and economic safety net, promote participation, respect human rights, and reflect the needs of local communities with specified short- and long-term outcomes) (Bill C-545, 2010).

Although the act did not become law, various proponents of poverty reduction (e.g., policymakers and academics) have maintained this approach, seeing poverty as a violation of human rights whereby all Canadians are deemed worthy of the right to food, water, and housing security. From this perspective, "the right to food means freedom from hunger and should be understood as the right to feed oneself rather than to be fed" (Canada Without Poverty, 2015). Human rights–based approaches are considered to be more effective for breaking the intergenerational cycle of poverty compared to more temporary measures (Smith-Carrier & Lawlor, 2017) because they call for an investment in actual food security to enable self-sufficient (and ongoing) access to affordable, nutritional foods as opposed to the periodic use of food banks. The Government of Canada is committed to developing a national strategy for poverty reduction and is encouraging public discourse. To learn more about how you can participate, search "poverty reduction strategy" at http://www.canada.ca.

Think Outside the Box: From a human rights approach, what is one initiative you would recommend to the Government of Canada for reducing poverty?

However, in the absence of widespread sharing of surplus by the corporate elite in Canada (or, conversely, an uprising of the poorest classes), the gap between the wealthy and the poor continues to persist and widen. This is because the rich incur greater and greater amounts of profit from capitalism and use those profits to increase their own power and profit at the expense of the classes below them. The existence of surplus is what Lenski claimed was most problematic about stratification because when there is a lot of surplus (as in the case of capitalism), power determines how that surplus gets distributed in almost every instance (Lenski, 1966, p. 44). A lessening of social inequality requires considerable change and will probably not come about until it is addressed more fully at the federal level of government. The lower classes are the least inclined to vote but would benefit most from representation that specifically targets improved quality of life for all low-income earning groups. Although poverty has been conventionally measured in Canada using the LICO, it is increasingly being viewed in the context of social stratification and as a violation of a basic human right to a reasonable standard of living (see *Sociology in Practice*).

TIME TO REVIEW

- In what ways is social inequality beneficial to society?
- How do social classes emerge, according to Karl Marx?
- How does Max Weber's view of capitalism differ from that of Karl Marx?

CHAPTER SUMMARY

LO1 Define social stratification and differentiate between caste and class systems.

Social stratification refers to sanctioned patterns of social inequality. Castes are closed systems that rank groups based on inherited and relatively permanent social standing. Class systems rank order groups on the basis of economic measures, such as income, and are more open, providing for horizontal and vertical social mobility.

LO2 Explain what social inequality looks like in Canada using measures of wealth.

Social inequality refers to an unequal distribution of resources, including wealth, which is measured by income from employment and net worth. Social inequality is most evident in the widening gap between those with the most versus those with the least amounts of wealth. For example, those in the highest deciles earn a greater share of the overall income in Canada, are better able to save and invest, and have a disproportionately high net worth.

LO3 Describe Canada's class structure and social mobility.

Based on income, Canada's class structure can be divided into low, middle, and high classes. Although there is significant social mobility in Canada, much of it occurs *within* classes and is largely based on educational and occupational attainment.

LO4 Critically assess the low-income cutoff as an estimate of poverty.

The low-income cutoff is based on the proportion of income spent on only three basic needs (i.e., food, clothing, and shelter). Most Canadians pay other essential costs associated with transportation, child care, and household operation that are not addressed by the low-income cutoff, which suggests that the LICO is too conservative and therefore vastly underestimates the number of poor Canadians.

LO5 Identify groups most at risk for poverty in Canada and discuss how poverty is linked to negative outcomes.

Groups most at risk for poverty include children, recent immigrants, lone-parent families (especially those headed by females), people with disabilities, and Indigenous peoples. Impoverished children are at a disadvantage in the school system as their families typically cannot afford to pay for additional enrichment, such as field trips or hot lunches. The poor also may forgo regular nutritional diets, and this poses additional health risks, such as an increased risk of heart disease and diabetes.

LO6 Critically assess Canada's social safety net as a means for reducing poverty.

The existing social safety net is insufficient for keeping at-risk groups at or above low-income cutoffs. This is partly due to the sheer number of low-income Canadians, a lack of affordable housing, and a high cost of living relative to low and minimum wages.

LO7 Debate why there are social classes and whether stratification is helpful or harmful to Canadian society.

There are distinct social classes in Canada largely because capitalism supports the disparity and the top-earning Canadians tend to benefit most from the existing system in a manner that leads to social reproduction. Conflict theorists highlight the negative consequences of exploitation, especially in the form of low wages and differences in power that prevent the lower classes from succeeding, whereas functionalists suggest that social inequality is necessary to ensure that the most capable individuals are sufficiently motivated to undertake the more difficult, challenging, and/or more important positions in society.

RECOMMENDED RESOURCES

1. To learn more about modern slavery, we recommend the *Global Slavery Index 2016*, published by the Walk Free Foundation and available for download at https://www.globalslaveryindex.org.
2. For a discussion of the underlying contributors to water insecurity for Indigenous peoples living on reserves in Canada, refer to Human Rights Watch's (2016) report: *Make it Safe: Canada's Obligation to End the First Nation Water Crisis*, available at https://www.hrw.org.
3. To better appreciate how poverty affects the working poor, how Canada's corporate elite benefit from political control and tax benefits, and how tax-funded social welfare practices in Ireland and Sweden are used to eradicate poverty, we recommend Babin and Deveaux's (2008) award-winning documentary *Poor No More … There is a Way Out*.
4. You can read and compare poverty progress profiles for 2016 on each of Canada's provinces and territories by accessing Canada Without Poverty at http://www.cwp-csp.ca.

FOR FURTHER REFLECTION

1. Do you think Canada needs a national poverty reduction strategy? Why or why not? What do you think should be the focal point of a national strategy for ending *world* poverty? How does this differ from measures that address poverty in Canada?
2. Is the middle class shrinking in Canada? Consider why answers to this question rest on how "middle class" is defined in Canada.
3. Provide examples of occupations in Canadian society that you feel best demonstrate how social stratification leads to meritocracy as predicted by Davis and Moore's functionalist theory. Can you also think of specific examples that can serve as exceptions to this rule (e.g., important positions that are underpaid or occupations that attract salaries that are not warranted by their respective skill levels or value to society)?

Mass Media: Living in the Electronic Age

sibsky2016/Shutterstock

In a culture like ours, long accustomed to splitting and dividing all things as a means of control, it is sometimes a bit of a shock to be reminded that, in operational and practical fact, the medium is the message.

(Marshall McLuhan, 1964, p.7)

LEARNING OBJECTIVES & OUTCOMES

After completing this chapter, students should be able to do the following:

LO1 Describe the history of the traditional forms of mass media.

LO2 Describe the role of new media forms, including whether they make traditional ones obsolete.

LO3 Differentiate among media assumptions provided by the core sociological frameworks.

LO4 Evaluate the relevance of media ownership for agenda setting.

LO5 Demonstrate a critical understanding of ways that media shape our perceptions.

LO6 Debate whether violence in the media causes viewers to become violent.

LO7 Illustrate what it means to be "media literate."

MASS MEDIA PREVALENCE AND FORMS

From Facebook updates to iPhone text messaging to the latest episode of our favourite television show captured on high dynamic range playback or streamed live on Netflix, most of us spend a considerable portion of our available time plugged into some form of communications technology. Because we are constantly bombarded with information and imagery in news stories, advertisements, and a multitude of entertainment venues, such as movies, video games, and music, it is especially important for us to use the sociological imagination to understand our connection with mass media. What forms of media do we use, and how often do we use them? Who controls the content of mass media, and why does it matter? What central themes and ideas are represented in the messages and images conveyed by the media? In what ways do mass media content affect our thoughts, feelings, and behaviours? What can we do to become more media-literate as consumers? These are all questions of interest to sociologists that you will learn more about in this chapter.

MEDIA CONSUMPTION

Canadians are world leaders when it comes to spending time engaged in online activities. Canadians ranked first in 2016, spending close to 37 hours per month accessing the Internet for email (92 percent), banking (68 percent), social media (59 percent), news (55 percent), general browsing (49 percent), and shopping (46 percent) (Canadian Internet Registration Authority, 2016). Of those interacting with social media, Facebook is most preferred, followed by YouTube and Twitter (Insights West, 2016). Facebook continues to gain momentum, especially among those age 35 and older, whereas YouTube, Instagram, and Twitter are growing at a faster rate among millennials (i.e., those 18 to 34) (Insights West, 2016).

iStock/Thinkstock

Canadians are world leaders when it comes to Internet use.

Before global mass communication via the Internet, media were concentrated in seven main areas: books, newspapers, magazines, cinema, recordings, radio, and TV.

LO1 TRADITIONAL FORMS OF MASS MEDIA

As noted in the earlier chapter on socialization, *mass media* refers to communications that target large audiences. Early forms of pictographic writing and cuneiform words can be traced back to the Sumerians of Mesopotamia, who scratched them onto clay tablets in 3400 and 3000 BCE, respectively (Encyclopaedia Britannica, 2017). Nelson Education, a leader in the Canadian book industry and the publisher of this textbook, has been in business since 1914 (Nordal, 2010). You are probably familiar with the Harry Potter book series by British author J.K. Rowling. But are you also familiar with the novels and other works by highly acclaimed Canadian authors, such as Margaret Atwood and Yann Martel?* Printed books continue to persevere despite online competition. According to recent research, print books are still more popular than e-books or audio books (Perrin, 2016).

Newsprint originated in Canada in Halifax, Nova Scotia, in 1752, when John Bushell sold his first copy of the *Halifax Gazette* from his print shop on Grafton Street (Province of Nova Scotia, 2017). Today in Canada, there are 90 Canadian paid-subscription daily newspapers, with more than 5 million copies (printed and digital) in circulation (Newspapers Canada, 2015). Newspaper advertising is declining in many parts of the world, including in North America, where circulation now accounts for more industry revenue (Marketing Charts, 2016).

The first Canadian magazine also originated in Nova Scotia: *The Nova Scotia Magazine and Comprehensive Review of Literature, Politics, and News*, first published in 1789 (McCann, 2012). Canada's most popular magazines today are *Chatelaine, Canadian Living*, and *Reader's Digest* (Agility PR Solutions, 2016). Most of the top-circulating magazines worldwide originate in the United States, including *National Geographic*, with a circulation of 6.8 million in 2013, and *People*, with a readership of more than 45 million (Briscoe, 2016). Print magazine sales have been steadily declining, whereas digital copies, with much smaller markets, have been increasing in popularity (Maloney, 2014).

*Margaret Atwood (born in Ottawa in 1939) is a highly acclaimed Canadian author, poet, and feminist. She has written several award-winning novels, including *Life Before Man* (1979), *The Handmaid's Tale* (1985), and *Alias Grace* (1996), along with poetry collections, children's books, short fiction, and nonfiction. Canadian Yann Martel (born in Salamanca, Spain, in 1963) won the 2002 Man Booker Prize for his novel *Life of Pi* (2001).

Cinema includes the movie industry, which originated in the late 1800s. As with the magazine industry, our neighbours to the south dominate the film industry. The American film industry is credited with the two highest-grossing movies of all time: *Titanic* and *Avatar*, although James Cameron (the writer and director of both) is Canadian! He was born in Kapuskasing, Ontario (Filmmakers Magazine, 2017). The movie industry continues to thrive, with increased global box office sales and increased cinema screens worldwide (particularly digital). More than two-thirds of North Americans went to the cinema at least once in 2016, whereas those ages 18 to 24 went an average of 6.5 times (Motion Picture Association of America, 2017).

Music has been integral to Canadian culture since colonial times and even before. Early sound recording is generally traced back to Thomas Edison's phonograph (1877) and Emile Berliner's gramophone (1878) (Library and Archives Canada, 2014). Vinyl long-playing records first came to market in 1948 and were followed by 8-track cartridges in the 1960s, cassettes in the 1970s, and compact discs in the 1980s (Taintor, 2004). Interestingly, whereas 8-tracks have gone out of circulation and cassettes and CDs have become scarce, vinyl records have survived and even grown in popularity, with more than 3.2 million records sold in 2016, reaching a 25-year high. Record sales are flourishing for a number of reasons,

Tibor Kolley/The Canadian Press

Canadian filmmaking produced the comedies *Trailer Park Boys: The Big Dirty* (2006), *Countdown to Liquor Day* (2009), *Don't Legalize It* (2014), and *SwearNet* (2014). The *Trailer Park Boys* series regularly airs on Netflix.

including the recent deaths of various music legends (e.g., Leonard Cohen, Prince, and David Bowie). David Bowie became the best-selling vinyl artist in 2016 as five of his albums posthumously topped the charts (Ellis-Petersen, 2017).

In 1901, Guglielmo Marconi transmitted the first wireless radio signal across the Atlantic Ocean, from Poldhu, Cornwall, to St. John's, Newfoundland. The following year, he established the first licensed wireless telegraphy station at Grace Bay, Nova Scotia. The radio operators on the *Titanic* were Marconi employees; in 1912, while that ship was sinking, they sent out distress messages using the early technology (University of Oxford, 2017). In 1919, the first broadcasting licence was issued to Marconi's company to operate an experimental radio station out of Montreal, Quebec, originally called XWA (Hammond Museum of Radio, 2004). By 2015, there were 704 radio stations in Canada (Government of Canada, 2016).

Television was introduced to Canada in 1952. By the end of that decade, most Canadian households had one. Canadian households today still have TVs, albeit 85 percent are digital, and more than half (53 percent) have PVRs (Statista, 2017). From cable TV to direct broadcast satellites, bigger screens, sharper screens (e.g., 4K Ultra High Definition), and 3D screens, the industry is constantly improving its technology to remain competitive. TV is still the most heavily consumed form of mass media: the average Canadian adult watches about 28 hours per week compared to 19.5 hours doing other things on the Internet and 16.8 hours listening to the radio (Thinktv, 2016b). Even millennials, who spend only 18 hours per week watching television, do so at a rate that is 5.5 times that of their time spent on YouTube and 3.8 times that of their time on Facebook, Instagram, Snapchat, and Twitter combined (Thinktv, 2016a). Given the choice between online viewing and regular TV viewing, most people still prefer a TV screen. Still, 2016 was a record year for "cord cutters," with about 202,000 Canadians terminating their cable and satellite subscriptions, opting for streamed content instead (Jackson, 2017).

Another significant shift in how TV is consumed is the increasing prevalence of simultaneous media. According to an Accenture report, as many as 87 percent of television viewers use a second screen while watching television (Mann et al., 2015). For example, viewers might use a smartphone or tablet to look up an actor who is on the TV show being watched, or to vote for a particular contestant on a special Twitter feed during *The Voice*, or to access special content during *The Walking Dead*. Simultaneous media most often occurs with a TV and smartphone, and this form is especially common among younger viewers. The dual use of a TV and laptop/desktop is more prevalent among middle-aged viewers (Mann et al., 2015). See *Figure 6.1* for the frequency of simultaneous media by device and age of viewer. The Internet is having a profound effect on all traditional mass media.

FIGURE 6.1

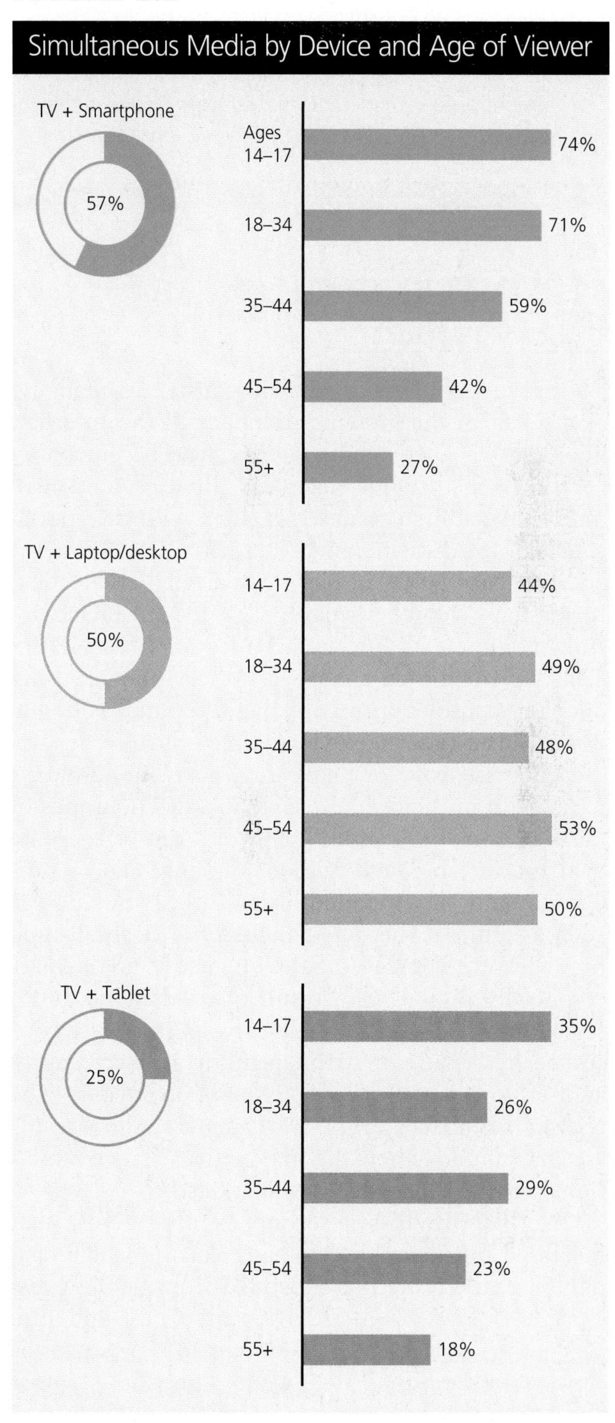

Source: 2015 Accenture Digital Consumer Survey, https://www.accenture.com/t20150523T021027__w__/us-en/_acnmedia/Accenture/Conversion-Assets/Microsites/Documents17/Accenture-Digital-Video-Connected-Consumer.pdf, page 7.

SOCIOLOGY ON SCREEN

INSIDE RUSSIA'S CREEPY, INNOVATIVE INTERNET

Bloomberg's (2016) *Inside Russia's Creepy, Innovative Internet* is an illuminating documentary produced by Bernadette Walker and directed by Grant Slater on inventors of advanced technology and how that technology is controlled in modern Russia. Russia is unique in that it has its own Internet, search engines, email systems, game platforms, and even social networks (similar to Facebook). In this manner, a very small group of people, referred to as an oligarchy, are able to monitor and control virtually all of the information individuals are exposed to. One app, called "Find Face," can instantly recognize any person simply from a photo taken on a cellphone.

THE INTERNET CHANGES EVERYTHING

The seven traditional media are constantly changing as a result of the growing influence of the Internet. Books, newspapers, and magazines can be purchased (or accessed through electronic libraries) and read online. We still go to movies (albeit with the special effects of IMAX, Panoramic, and UltraAVX 3D views) and purchase DVDs in Blu-ray or Digital HD format. Increasingly, though, we pay to view and stream movies from commercial Internet venues such as Netflix Canada, which even enables us to view movies using our game consoles or smartphones. People also illegally download and stream movies for free from torrent sites.

Likewise, you don't have to own a radio nowadays to listen to music over a live broadcast. Thousands of radio stations from around the world can be accessed over the Internet, and millions of songs can be purchased and downloaded from online businesses such as iTunes. The music industry is at an all-time high despite decreased sales in nearly all formats (especially digital) as a result of on-demand audio streaming. Drake's *Views* album was the most consumed in Canada in 2016, spending 12 weeks at #1 and setting a record for over 290 million streams (The Nielsen Company, 2017). On-demand audio streams are an example of how the Internet has changed traditional media *and* created new markets.

Netflix provides a second example. Now that increased broadband access has created a viable residential market, Netflix expanded from being a distributor of TV and film content to a producer as well. The show *House of Cards* is exclusive to Netflix, as are the new seasons of *Travelers, Stranger Things, Orange Is the New Black,* and more. The Internet has revolutionized how viewers consume media content, including videos, and has also brought with it new competitors, such as Amazon and TalkTalk TV, which are, in turn, producing and distributing that content in alignment with the changing needs of "on-demand" customers.

Bitcoins: A form of digital currency mined on the Internet and later exchanged for goods and services.

The Internet has even led to the development of new cryptocurrencies. **Bitcoins** were the first form of digital currency that could be mined on the Internet and later exchanged for material goods (e.g., games and books) and services (e.g., transportation). The price of Bitcoin

Christopher Morris/Getty Images

The world's first Bitcoin ATM appeared in Waves coffee shop in downtown Vancouver.

is predicted to reach $100,000 USD by 2027 (Kharpal, 2017). Besides revolutionizing the traditional media, the Internet itself is considered to be a form of mass media.

LO2 NEW MEDIA

Modern media technologies are often categorized as "new" or "emerging." These new media encompass everything on the Internet, from educational resources (library archives) to communication services (email), social networking applications (Twitter and Facebook), search engines (Google Chrome), e-commerce businesses, and audio and video streams. On the Internet, you can visit a vast array of sites for everything from chatting to banking, gaming, reading, and gambling. One of the most popular Internet sites today is YouTube, owned by Google.

YOUTUBE: A MEDIA DISRUPTOR OR A FORCE TO BE RECKONED WITH?

YouTube, founded in 2005, is the leading media outlet for public expression through its video-sharing platform. It is best understood as a "reach business," in that it enables users to expose themselves to a vast number of visitors (Burgess & Green, 2009). Those who access the site can find debates on a range of topics from religion to politics; they can learn how to do things such as beat a level in a favourite video game or put up drywall; they can watch controversial sports and celebrity moments. All of this is uploaded by individuals who have captured events on video. Scenes from just about every major movie, concert, video game, and TV series can be found on YouTube. This has helped shape public perceptions of YouTube as an acceptable platform for the widespread sharing of illegally reproduced materials.

AP Photo/Lynne Sladky/CP Images

Luis Fonsi and Daddy Yankee's "Despacito" is the most viewed video in YouTube history.

YouTube is both a distributor of popular culture and a creative outlet. That is the essence of its success *and* its controversy. According to Burgess and Green (2009), YouTube is a disruptive force because it "is variously understood as a distribution platform that can make the products of commercial media widely popular, challenge the promotional reach the mass media is accustomed to monopolizing, [and] at the same time is a [powerful] platform for user-created content where challenges to commercial popular culture might emerge, be they user-created news services, or generic forms such as vblogging—which might in turn be appropriated and exploited by the traditional mass media" (p. 6). Copyright controversy notwithstanding, YouTube has established itself as one of the most popular forms of Internet-based media available today.

SMARTPHONES TAKE OVER

New media also include the latest electronic gadgets, from games to gaming consoles (i.e., Nintendo's Switch, Sony's PlayStation VR, and Microsoft's Mixer on Xbox One), digital audio/players (e.g., Apple iPod touch, Apple iPod nano, and Apple iPod shuffle), and, of course, cellphones. Tomi T. Ahonen (2008), one of the world's experts on how money is made in the mobile telecom industry, combines all types of print (i.e., newspapers, magazines, and books) into one main form of media; these, along with recordings,

"It's not your traditional report. I've done it in the form of a YouTube video."

Marc Bruxelle/Alamy

Will augmented reality prove to be the next new best thing?

radio, cinema, TV, and the Internet, comprise what he calls the six "old" forms of mass media. Due to the increasing prevalence and unique capabilities of smartphones produced by leaders such as Apple and Samsung, Ahonen argues that mobile deserves a separate distinction as the seventh mass media. For example, he points out that mobile offers a digital interface to the real world and enables augmented reality (Ahonen, 2013). Moreover, he notes how mobile has superseded traditional forms of media in numbers (e.g., mobile subscriptions exceed newspaper circulations) and value (i.e., the mobile market is estimated at $407 billion annually). He even suggests that it is now in a position to "cannibalize" the other six forms, including the Internet (Ahonen, 2017b).

More recently, Ahonen considers augmented reality to be the eighth mass media. Not to be confused with virtual reality (computer technology that creates realistic images using specialized headgear), **augmented reality (AR)** is "an enhanced version of reality created by the use of technology to overlay digital information on an image of something being viewed through a device (such as a smartphone camera)" (Merriam-Webster, 2017). Ahonen (2017a) claims that AR is a standalone industry from mobile as it can be utilized via various devices, such as game consoles and tablets, and is already worth billions of dollars. In a 2012 TED talk, he predicted that one billion people would be using AR by 2020. This prediction might come true sooner rather than later when you consider the unprecedented success of Pokémon Go, the first game app to combine virtual reality with geographic space and promote social interactions (Clark & Clark, 2016). In the first two weeks of its release, it was downloaded 30 million times (Grubb, 2016). At the seven-month mark, Pokémon Go had surpassed its 650 millionth download and had generated $1 billion in revenue, breaking several world records as the most successful AR venture, app ever launched, game ever sold, and new digital service (Ahonen, 2017a; Ahonen, 2017b).

Augmented reality (AR): An enhanced version of reality created by the use of technology to overlay digital information on an image of something being viewed through a device (such as a smartphone camera).

THERE'S AN APP FOR THAT

Uber-company Apple changed the media world by creating Web-based applications (apps) for its wireless devices (iPhones, iPads, and some iPods). Apps allow mobile users to obtain the functional benefits of traditional forms of media with the ease of accessibility, anywhere and at any time. You can now do so many things with apps and spend so much time using them that this is raising concerns that electronically mediated communication may cause people to stop interacting in real life. According to Sherry Turkle (2011), a psychologist and expert on mediated culture, we are now connected to more people than ever before, but we tend to maintain relationships with those people using the Internet as an intermediary (e.g., we are more likely to send an email than encroach on our "real time" with a phone call or an in-person visit). Also, we opt for the company of our personal online network over that of the strangers around us—a phenomenon she refers to as being "alone together" in public spaces. Because we have ongoing and relatively permanent access to the Internet, infinite sources of information are with us at all times. This continual

"Hold on a minute. I'm downloading an app to monitor my app downloading."

Cable, Carole, ccan239, www.cartoonstock.com

connection to others via online ties has many repercussions, including preoccupation to the point of exhaustion, overreliance on technology and the creation and maintenance of virtual selves, a tendency to overshare online, and a disinclination to give others our full attention in real life (Turkle, 2011).

NEW FORMS OF MEDIA ARE UNIQUE

Newer forms of mass media often improve on features of previous forms, but surprisingly, they rarely make older forms obsolete. Recall the chapter's opening quotation, which ends with these words: "the medium is the message." So wrote Canadian-born Marshall McLuhan (1911–1980) in his book *Understanding Media: The Extensions of Man* (1964). McLuhan claimed that with each new technological invention or medium, a change is introduced that fundamentally alters the way we experience life. As he explained, the railway "did not introduce movement or transportation or wheel or road into human society, but it accelerated and enlarged the scale of previous human functions, creating totally new kinds of cities and new kinds of work and leisure" (p. 8). Each new media form has properties that may not in themselves be unique (e.g., cameras existed before smartphones with cameras in them) but that fundamentally change how we now experience things by introducing new possibilities and changes in pace, which in turn create a different world.

Consider this example: we used to experience audio with a radio; then the Walkman was invented, and we were able to transport that audio with us; then came the iPod, which was even more portable. Other examples: with the advent of big-screen TV, we didn't stop going to movies, and although TV allowed us to see music videos, it didn't end the enjoyment we got from hearing songs played on the radio, especially while driving. Clearly, new media may provide us with markedly new experiences, but the older ones retain their appeal. Cellphones, for example, have several features that do not exist elsewhere, such as ringtones and specialized apps. Also, despite their small screen size, cellphones are much more advanced than home computers, especially when it comes to multiple simultaneous inputs (e.g., camera, video, and GPS) (Ahonen, 2009).

Mobile is unique in other ways as well. People who use smartphones are permanently connected to the Internet and can personalize their experiences as a function of the particular apps they download. Recall the earlier discussion of second-screen TV watching. "Companion" apps are now being developed to more easily enable user interaction. For example, there were various Superbowl LI apps that enabled second-screen viewers to customize news highlights, view behind the scene photos, and comment on posts by other fans.

PRIVACY AND REGULATION

Have you set up your smartphone so that it is password protected? When is the last time you checked the privacy policies for the social networking sites you use? Every time you open Facebook, visit a website, or order merchandise online, you leave an information trail behind you that can be tracked and used in various ways by other individuals and businesses and even by governments. In 2016, the Privacy Commissioner of Canada commissioned research into the general public's knowledge of privacy-related issues and discovered that Canadians consider themselves to be knowledgeable about privacy matters and are very concerned about the protection of their privacy. In particular, Canadians are worried about how their online personal information might be used by organizations such as health or insurance companies for decision making or marketing firms to determine their preferences and make them targets for online advertising. Most mobile users said they enact privacy precautions such as limiting the amount of information shared online and uninstalling or not installing apps that access personal information (Phoenix Strategic Perspectives Inc., 2016).

Privacy concerns raise the question of whether the Internet should be regulated and, if so, how. Broadcasting and telecommunications in Canada are regulated and supervised by the Canadian Radio-television and Telecommunications Commission (CRTC). The CRTC is an independent tribunal that oversees more than 2,000 broadcasters (e.g., TV services, and radio stations), including companies that operate as service providers and telecommunications carriers (i.e., phone companies). The CRTC's mandate is to ensure access to diverse, affordable, high-quality communications that serve the interests of Canadians by following the objectives of the Broadcasting Act, the Telecommunications Act, and Canada's anti-spam legislation. The CRTC's main activities include issuing, renewing, and amending licences; approving (or not) mergers and changes in ownership; and promoting regulation compliance (CRTC, 2017).

The CRTC supports the principle of net neutrality as a governing framework. **Net neutrality** refers to a principle of equality and detachment with respect to how

Net neutrality: A principle of equality and detachment with respect to how information on the Internet is treated by network providers.

information on the Internet is treated by network providers. Net neutrality prevents Internet providers from manipulating how Internet traffic gets prioritized (Gordon, 2014). Otherwise, major media providers (discussed in the next section) could prioritize their own stations and channels, restrict access to competitors' products, and/or charge additional fees for access to competitor stations. In support of net neutrality, the CRTC recently enacted a policy regulating telecom pricing to ensure that Canadians are being treated fairly by their Internet providers (CRTC, 2017).

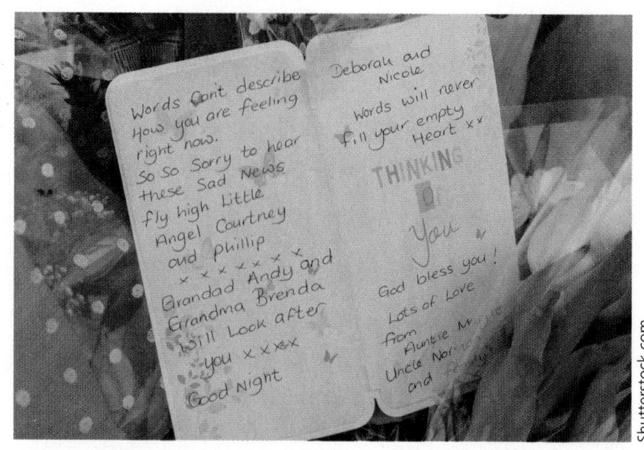

Tribute note left at the feet of the Angel of the North in memory of Courtney Boyle and stepdad Philip Tron, who died in the 2017 Manchester terror attack.

TIME TO REVIEW

- Prior to the Internet, in which seven areas were the media concentrated?
- Why is YouTube considered to be both a media disruptor and a force to be reckoned with?
- What does Tomi T. Ahonen consider to be the seventh and eighth mass media?
- Why don't new forms of mass media make traditional forms obsolete?
- Why is net neutrality important to Internet consumers?

YOUR SOCIOLOGICAL TOOLKIT
SOCIOLOGY IN THEORY

LO3 FUNCTIONALIST FRAMEWORK

Different sociological frameworks help us better understand how the mass media influence us and how we, in turn, influence the mass media. Since the main concern of a macro-level functionalist framework is social order, this perspective helps us see how the media contribute to social stability. For example, a manifest (or intended) function of the media is to provide us with current, up-to-date communications. By listening to or watching a live news broadcast, we can learn about practical matters of local interest, such as the weather and traffic conditions, as well as global events, such as the recent terrorist attacks in Paris, Manchester, and Kabul. Within seconds of each attack, tweets, photos, and videos were being sent out by spectators using social media (such as Facebook, Twitter, and Instagram), allowing the rest of the world to experience the events as they unfolded.

The media play a key role in connecting us to other people and to information and in that way help us become more socially aware—of ourselves, our communities, other people, diverse cultures, current events, and a plethora of issues facing society. In that sense, the media help us function in relation to one another (see *Critical Thinking in Action*). Social media in particular expose us to a range of individuals we might not otherwise be in contact with and in this sense provide platforms for shared experiences and meaningful connections with individuals and groups of all ages and characteristics. The mass media have many socializing effects, some of which are less obvious than others and some of which may be harmful, as the conflict framework demonstrates.

CONFLICT FRAMEWORK

Like the functionalist framework, the conflict framework focuses on large-scale institutions such as the media, but it suggests that society is characterized by disparities and power struggles linked to the unequal distribution of resources. The media are an essential source of information, and because most of the media are in the hands of a small group of powerful corporations, a handful of people have the power to shape the messages contained in the media.

MEDIA OWNERSHIP IS CONCENTRATED

Whether it is newspapers, TV, music, or the media industry more broadly, the concentration in ownership is apparent. For example, Quebecor Media owns companies that together control a sizeable portion of Canada's publications, including daily newspapers such as *Le Journal de Montréal* and *Le Journal de Québec*,

CRITICAL THINKING IN ACTION

MASS MEDIA AS A SOCIAL INSTITUTION

In an earlier chapter, you learned that social institutions are relatively permanent societal structures that govern the behaviour of groups and promote social order. Families, religion, education, the economy, and the political system all serve a variety of functions for individuals and for society. In countries where the media are state-owned (e.g., China, Ethiopia, Iran, and Syria), the content tends to be more prescriptive (e.g., it often serves political functions by providing particular perspectives and censoring others). Silverblatt (2004) contends that the media emerged as a social institution in state-owned countries largely because it has taken over many of the functions once performed by other institutions.

In Western countries where media operates under private ownership (e.g., Canada, the United States, and Australia), it was never intended to serve as a social institution. Instead, its main purpose was to generate profit, and this is why the content is heavily laden with sexuality and violence, because this is what appeals to broad audiences (Silverblatt, 2004).

Think Outside the Box: Do you think new media in Western countries operate collectively as a social institution? Why or why not?

over 75 magazines (e.g., *Clin d'oeil* and *Chez Soi*), and books. Quebecor also controls TV programming and TV specialty services through TVA Group as well as cable distribution, Video on Demand, and Pay Per View through Videotron. And it holds interests in music, new media, and production and marketing (CRTC, 2016). Brunswick News, a private newspaper publisher owned by James K. Irving, can be considered a **monopoly** because it owns all three of New Brunswick's English-language daily newspapers, most of its weeklies, and 18 of the 25 community papers in the province. Concentrated ownership permits highly selective reporting as evident in the *Telegraph-Journal's* recent failure to report problems with Irving Oil's pollution control equipment and emissions (Livesey, 2016).

Similar patterns are evident in the music industry. As the beginning of any season of *The Voice* demonstrates, an infinite number of individuals with various amounts of musical talent hope to be discovered. Recording companies are the main agents of power when it comes to determining who gets to produce a song and ultimately which songs will be played, purchased, and streamed. Although it may appear that the number of record labels is endless, Canadian recording companies are all owned by one of three international parent companies (i.e., Sony BMG, Universal Music Group, and Warner Music Group). These large corporations are known in the recording industry as *the Big Three* because together they control 80 percent of the entire music industry (McDonald, 2017).

Canada has its own TV networks, including the CBC, a Crown corporation; private networks (e.g., City, CTV, and Global Television Network); a French-language network, TVA; and the Aboriginal Peoples Television Network (APTN) (see *Sociology in Practice*). Still, Canada is the largest importer of U.S. content, where the most popular TV series originate. American TV was historically concentrated in three main networks: ABC, CBS, and NBC. Eventually, two other networks emerged: HBO and Fox. Together they are often referred to as the *Big Five Networks* given their overwhelming market share. These five networks are linked to five major conglomerates: *Time Warner* (HBO), *Disney* (ABC), *National Amusements* (CBS and Viacom), *News Corp* (Fox), and *Comcast* (NBC Universal) (Straubhaar, LaRose, & Davenport, 2014).

A **conglomerate** is a corporation made up of several widely diversified companies. For example, *Disney* owns major broadcasting (e.g., Walt Disney Television, ABC Television Network with shows such as *How to Get Away with Murder, Dancing with the Stars*, and *The Bachelor*), cable networks (e.g., ESPN Inc., Disney Channels Worldwide), studio entertainment (e.g., Walt Disney Studio Home Entertainment, Walt Disney Animation Studios, Marvel Studios), studio production (e.g.,

Monopoly: A company that has exclusive control over a particular product or service.

Conglomerate: A corporation made up of several different widely diversified companies.

YOUR SOCIOLOGICAL TOOLKIT

SOCIOLOGY IN PRACTICE

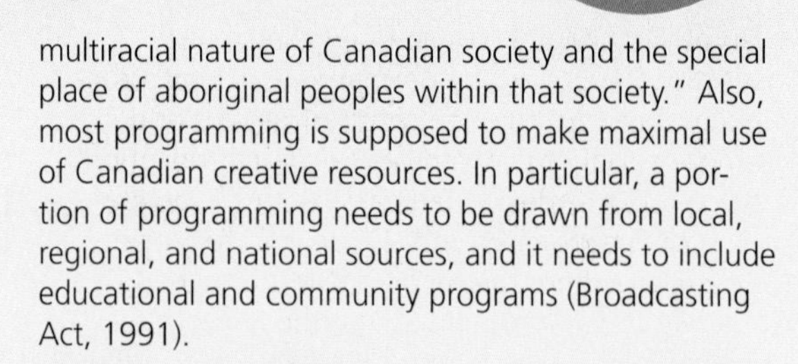

CANADIAN BROADCASTING POLICY

Under the Broadcasting Act, all Canadian broadcasting systems must be owned and controlled by Canadians and the content of broadcasts must include a wide range of programming that reflects the interests of Canadians. For example, entertainment program content needs to display Canadian talent, and information on Canada must be presented from a Canadian point of view. In addition, programming and the employment affiliated with it must serve "the needs and interests, and reflect the circumstances and aspirations, of Canadian men, women and children, including equal rights, the linguistic duality and multicultural and multiracial nature of Canadian society and the special place of aboriginal peoples within that society." Also, most programming is supposed to make maximal use of Canadian creative resources. In particular, a portion of programming needs to be drawn from local, regional, and national sources, and it needs to include educational and community programs (Broadcasting Act, 1991).

Think Outside the Box: How do digital technology and the Internet pose challenges for this broadcasting policy?

Walt Disney Studios), music (Walt Disney Records, Hollywood Records), books and magazines (e.g., ABC Daytime Press, Marvel Comics), interactive media (e.g., Disney Online, Disney Games, Disney Mobile), parks and resorts (e.g., Disneyland Park, Shanghai Disney Resort), cruise lines (e.g., Disney Fantasy), and various consumer products (Walt Disney Company, 2017).

LO4 AGENDA SETTING: THE MEDIA IS NOT NEUTRAL

Corporate giants such as Disney and Comcast selectively determine which issues we will be exposed to as we read the papers, watch TV, or listen to the radio. Will the focus be on the economy (e.g., the deficit), the environment, health care, or crime? Messages we are repeatedly exposed to become relevant and thereby important to us. So the media also tell the public which issues they should be most interested in. There are links between agenda setting in the media, what the public thinks is important, and the policies developed to deal with the issues (Soroka, 2002; Wanta & Ghanem, 2007). As political scientist Bernard Cohen (1963) noted, "The press may not be successful much of the time in telling people what to think, but it is stunningly successful in telling its readers what to think about" (p. 13).

Several theorists in a variety of disciplines have highlighted the implications of private, centralized ownership of the mass media for agenda setting. In *Manufacturing Consent: The Political Economy of the Mass Media*, Herman and Chomsky (1988) explain how the news media are controlled by a concentrated elite. That elite creates propaganda (i.e., biased persuasive communications) about international affairs that becomes the basis of what the public is repeatedly exposed to as daily news. Herman and Chomsky's ideas have become known more widely as *the propaganda model*. In contrast to what the general public perceives to be true about a democratic system (e.g., free and open press), Herman and Chomsky (1988) contend that the media serve the interests of those in power by filtering the messages the public receives in a way that generates (i.e., manufactures) consent for particular political and economic agendas. In this manner, the news media are able to manufacture consent for government policies (such as Canada's role in

© Schwadron, Harley, hsc5858, www.cartoonstock.com

YOUR SOCIOLOGICAL TOOLKIT

SOCIOLOGY IN MY COMMUNITY

FAIRNESS & ACCURACY IN REPORTING

Fairness & Accuracy in Reporting, Inc. (FAIR) is a not-for-profit organization that serves as a national media "watch group" advocating for more diversity and less bias in media reporting. FAIR works from the assumption that the for-profit nature of the media, combined with their highly concentrated ownership, compromises independent journalism. Thus, FAIR contends that reform should be directed at breaking up conglomerates and establishing not-for-profit, publicly owned broadcasting sources (FAIR, 2017). FAIR identifies marginalizing media practices and offers the public alternative viewpoints. For example, an article in its monthly magazine *Extra*! pointed out various ways in which a potential merger between Comcast and Time Warner would negatively impact the general public beyond higher cable bills and restricted options for subscribers. Summarizing the work of media researchers and critics, Yu (2014) explains that media consolidation on this scale limits the access that women and communities of colour have to TV and radio licences. It also leads to further reductions and "broken promises" with respect to the amount of diversity and local programming shown on TV and reduces the amount of say communities have in determining their own media needs.

Think Outside the Box: Can you identify any positive outcomes of media convergence for individuals and society?

the Afghan and Iraq wars) or for particular politicians' political platforms during election time.

Karen Dill-Shackleford (2016), a leading social psychologist in the area of media influence, notes an interesting paradox: we live in a culture that is powerfully influenced by media messages, yet we fail to recognize or downplay that influence, feeling we are invulnerable. We may accurately perceive that particular shows, messages, and advertisements are fictional and that they contain paid actors and models who are endorsing specific products for the benefit of corporations. Yet we also falsely believe that the media are transparent—that news programs simply present us with "the facts" and that fictional programming's only function is to entertain us. On the one hand, the media are an effective resource for conveying news, providing entertainment, sharing views, offering outlets for discussion, disseminating information, and networking. But on the other hand, the media are profit-centred businesses, and some become so successful that they come to dominate and control the market as monopolies and conglomerates (see *Sociology in My Community*). Rather than downplay media influence or polarize it as mainly positive or negative, Dill-Shackleford (2016) recommends we recognize its various effects, particularly the "deeply personal" ones, such as social affirmation and fandom, and be mindful in our media use to maximize the benefits while minimizing the harm.

TIME TO REVIEW

- How does a functionalist perspective view the mass media?
- How does a conflict perspective view the mass media?
- What do sociologists mean when they say that mass media ownership is concentrated?
- What are the implications of media ownership concentration for agenda setting?
- What main paradox exists in relation to mass media influence?

LO5 HOW THE MEDIA SHAPE OUR PERCEPTIONS

THE INTERACTIONIST FRAMEWORK

The micro-level interactionist theoretical framework helps us appreciate how we are individually and uniquely influenced by the people around us, from the significant others who are important to us and central to our well-being (e.g., family members, our intimate partners, and our close friends), to those from whom we take cues or learn particular skills in more temporary or isolated situations (e.g., a manager who trains you to perform the basics of your job or a professor who teaches you sociology), to the more abstract generalized other that reflects an understanding of group attitudes and norms. In the case of media influence for any given individual, bear in mind that as consumers, people choose to indulge in certain forms of media (e.g., TV and social networking) and select particular versions of those media (e.g., SportsNet and Facebook). Also, people can opt in or out of forms of media, although in some cases, they may face social sanctions, such as when friends are suddenly unable to reach them through Facebook. Moreover, people may selectively spend a lot of time, a moderate amount of time, or very little time exposed to any or all of the various media. Although we will discuss some of the common messages that may result from media socialization shortly, because of individuals' unique experiences with the media, the impact of mass media socialization on any one individual is quite difficult to establish.

The symbolic interactionist perspective is interested in communication, interpretation, and meaning. In *Frame Analysis* (1974), Canadian-born sociologist Erving Goffman (1922–1982) explained that *how* an interaction or event is depicted or "framed" is integral to its perceived meaning. Similarly, sociologist Stuart Hall (b. 1932) uses the term *representation* to describe how meanings are attributed to media images. There are multiple interpretations for the media images we see; hence, the meaning of a particular image emerges from an interaction between the characteristics of the image itself and the nature of the individual's own interpretation of that image (Hall, 2009).

Entman (1991) maintains that the essential determinant of framing is "sizing" because this helps the general public interpret the importance of an event. *Sizing* refers to "the overall salience of the event in the flow of the news" based on "how much material on the event is available" and "how prominently it is displayed" (Entman, 1991, p. 9). So an event that receives a lot of coverage (e.g., is the leading story in multiple mass media for many days) will be interpreted as most important, whereas other issues will be deemed less relevant, mainly because the public is not as aware of them. Clearly, "if it bleeds, it leads," but for how long? Interestingly, although disasters make front-page news, after a few days, the media often move on to the next big story, sometimes erroneously leading the public to perceive that the issue has been resolved.

In addition to sizing, Entman (1991) identifies four other properties of news narrative that contribute to frames and help create meaning by making certain aspects of news media more salient: agency, identification, categorization, and generalization.*

1. *Agency* refers to the inclusion of particular words that suggest where responsibility for an event lies. For example, *Newsweek's* cover headline "Murder in the Air" and *Time's* "Shooting to Kill The Soviets Destroy an Airliner" helped frame the 1983 downing of Korean Air Lines Flight 007 as an intentional event with a clearly guilty party (p. 6).
2. *Identification* includes the use of words that encourage (or discourage) identification with the central characters in a news story. Entman suggested that the inclusion of names of victims or "humanizing" phrases, such as "innocent human beings" or "loved ones," encourages identification, whereas use of neutral terms, such as "those who died" or "civilians," discourages identification (p. 17).
3. *Categorization* refers to the overall framework used to label an event by the media. The Korean Air Lines incident mentioned earlier was most often categorized in the print media as an "attack" rather than a "tragedy."
4. Lastly, *generalization* refers to the extent to which a media story is generalized to a larger political system or issue. Reporting of recent terrorist attacks in Europe is generalized to the rise of the Islamic State of Iraq and the Levant (ISIL), also known as the Islamic State of Iraq and Syria (ISIS).

On TV, framing centres on the main characters who deliver messages, such as the lead anchor on the national news or the outspoken judge on a reality series—consider Simon Cowell and his role on *America's Got Talent*. Also, framing includes the overall objectives of particular shows: the tough guy wins the Ultimate Fighting Championship title, the best-looking young woman becomes America's Next Top Model. Together, the characters and themes perpetuate common but unrealistic cultural beliefs, such as anyone can achieve success, celebrity status, and popularity.

The same messages are present in product advertisements: buy this beer, and you too will be lounging on a beach surrounded by swimsuit models! Print advertisements are laden with descriptive words, background colours, and images placed in particular ways to draw our attention; in much the same way,

*Adapted from: R. Entman, "Symposium Framing U.S. Coverage of International News: Contrasts in Narratives of the KAL and Iran Air Incidents," *Journal of Communication*, Vol. 41, Issue 4, pp. 6–27, 1991.

SOCIOLOGY ON SCREEN

STATE OF SURVEILLANCE

HBO's (2016) VICE documentary *State of Surveillance* educates viewers on the various ways the U.S. government and outside sources (such as the police, FBI, and CIA) can impinge on the privacy rights of others through their cellphones. VICE travelled to Russia to learn more about spy techniques from Edward Snowden, who claims that surveillance has gone from the exceptional cases involving suspected terrorists to the ongoing surveillance of everyday people using IMSI catchers (spyware), which track cellphone use and collect "metadata." Specialized software can now be used to turn a phone on, record calls made, reveal the history of Internet searches, and indicate locations travelled. Edward Snowden is a former American CIA employee and whistleblower who went public with information on invasive spying with information he gathered while employed by the National Security Agency and Central Intelligence Agency. He is currently living in Russia under temporary asylum.

pop-up ads on the Internet grab our attention by claiming we've won something and encouraging us to click on a tab for more information. For academics (and viewers), the three prevailing concerns about the mass media are (1) consumerism, (2) stereotypes, and (3) violence.

CONSUMERISM: THE MEDIA TEACHES US THAT WE NEED TO BUY PRODUCTS

"It's not fair!" was the response from the (then) eight-year-old son of one of the authors who learned he could not have his own credit card, nor would he be given access to his mother's Visa. He explained that he needed a credit card to purchase "sand dollars" in the Facebook game *FishVille*, which he accessed via his mother's Facebook account. He further protested that the awesome fish and specialty items he wanted to purchase for his virtual tank exceeded the number of sand dollars he could ever earn playing the game for free. Not surprisingly, the same child wanted to shop only at a store called West 49, carrying designer-labelled jeans, T-shirts, hoodies, and runners, for his back-to-school clothes. The power of advertising is the second most researched area in media studies, after research on the effects of media violence. Many decades of research have found that repeated exposure to advertising increases brand recognition, which results in positive associations with particular brands and a desire to select those products (Desmond & Carveth, 2007). From a corporate standpoint, the influence on youth is profitable enough to warrant investing billions of dollars targeting children in commercials. This has garnered the attention of parents, educators, and media critics.

FEMINIST FRAMEWORK

Besides fostering consumerism, the mass media present us with certain types of messages, repeatedly. One negative implication of this practice is that the mass media show stereotyped depictions of various groups, such as men, visible minorities, people with disabilities, gays, lesbians, the elderly, and, especially, women. A **stereotype** is an overgeneralization about a group that is often based on faulty assumptions. Many feminist perspectives point out that most differences between men and women are socially constructed rather than the result of biology. Traditional gender roles are emphasized in the media in ways that continue to teach females to be nurturing and submissive and males to be aggressive and independent. Part of this occurs through repeated exposure to mass media generalizations about how women and men behave or how they ought to behave in society.

THE MEDIA REINFORCES STEREOTYPED IMAGES OF WOMEN AND MEN

The media teach us, for example, that popular women are tuned into the latest consumer trends (i.e., they wear brand-name clothing, own many pairs of shoes, and celebrate the joys of new appliances). The media also emphasize the importance of women's beauty—especially the ultra-thin, busty Barbie doll form of beauty. Although women's images in the media are changing—partly as a result of more

Stereotype: An overgeneralization about a group, often based on faulty assumptions.

Bloomberg/Getty Images

Even as monsters, these dolls teach girls about the importance of beauty and fashion.

women achieving higher positions of media power, for example, as producers—the overall cultural messages remain. Anderson and Gray (2008) note that "the most common representation of women in the media is as victims, most commonly of sexual violence. Other consistent media images include women as overly feminized or sexualized; women as nurturing and caring, based on their role as mothers; and women as inscrutable and dangerous" (p. 462). Many studies have examined and substantiated the effects of stereotyped portrayals of women in the media. By the time girls reach the age of four or five, they have already internalized the narrow ideal of female beauty we get in media messages. Compared to those who watch less TV, girls who are heavy TV viewers have more restricted notions of female beauty, share more common perceptions of beauty, and place more emphasis on the importance of beauty (Stern, 2004).

Males are also portrayed in negative, stereotyped ways by the mass media. In an analysis of how men were depicted in newspapers, magazines, and TV shows in the United States, the United Kingdom, and Australia, Macnamara (2006) found that men are consistently portrayed in relation to violence or aggression. In fact, more than 75 percent of media depictions show men as one of four main stereotypes: villains, aggressors, perverts, or philanderers (i.e., womanizers). Besides stereotyped depictions of groups in society, the media repeatedly present us with messages that contain acts of violence.

VIOLENCE IS THE NORM IN THE MASS MEDIA

Given its prevalence in the media, violence is the most researched topic in media studies. Much of our daily dose of violence comes from TV—through sports, from hockey to boxing; as news, from local shootings to international warfare; in our favourite prime-time dramas; and even in children's programming, especially in animation, where the Teenage Ninja Mutant Turtles demonstrate their martial arts skills and Pokémon fight each other to enhance their trainer's skills. Violence is also integral to many of the movies we see in theatres (e.g., *Hacksaw Ridge, War of the Worlds, Silence*). Many of the most popular video games, such as *Call of Duty, Halo, Assassin's Creed,* and *Grand Theft Auto*, also contain violent content, which is built into the main plots and themes.

Grand Theft Auto, a highly successful series of video games, has been accused of promoting a subculture of violence and lawlessness among youth by glorifying car theft, drug use, random acts of killing, and driving under the influence of alcohol and by offering negative depictions of women. Both sex and violence are found in many video games, but some game developers have taken it to extremes. For example, in 2006, the game *RapeLay* was released in Japan. In this game, players take the role of a male character who, based on the players' choices, stalks, sexually assaults, and even gang rapes a mother and her two daughters. As you have already likely guessed, outrage ensued over the release of this game, and it was eventually removed from the market.

Given that we are exposed to so much violence in so many ways, we have to wonder what happens to viewers as a result of all this exposure. Does this violence have any real effect on consumers? Should the newest *Call of Duty*, or some other equally violent video game, be banned from distribution or even censored by the government? Most people would say no, and to date, no games have been banned in Canada. So the more appropriate question is: *Who should be allowed to play them?* Common sense suggests that we should not allow young children to play violent video games rated M (for mature). But what if all 8-, 9-, or 10-year-old kids are already playing such games? Is it okay as long as the child has parental consent or knows the content is fictional? See *Sociology in Practice* for ways that parents monitor television. Will early exposure to first- and third-person shooter-based war simulation games create violence-prone adults? What does the research tell us? Studies on the links between media violence and aggression are the most prevalent and debated area of research in literature on the effects of the mass media.

LO6 SOCIAL LEARNING THEORY

In the 1960s, in his now classic studies on observational learning, Canadian-born social psychologist Albert Bandura (b. 1925) and his colleagues conducted a series of experiments demonstrating how children learn to imitate aggression displayed by adults. In the first experiment, children who had earlier witnessed a social model (i.e., an adult research assistant) act aggressively toward an inflated "Bobo the Clown" doll later imitated the behaviour when engaged in free play (see Bandura, Ross, & Ross, 1961). The same process was enacted when children observed the behaviour of an aggressive adult on film (see Bandura, Ross, & Ross, 1963, and refer to the series of photos shown on the next page). A later study showed that aggressive imitation can be eliminated through the use of positive incentives and lessened through the subsequent use of punishment (Bandura, 1965). *Social learning theory* proposes that people learn by observing the behaviour of others (as well as its consequences) (Bandura, 1978) and then go on to imitate that behaviour. Hence, an immediate effect of viewing violence is that in the absence of other forms of intervention, it can lead to subsequent acts of aggression.

This theory has been used to explain real-world acts of violence, such as a school shooting in Taber, Alberta (1999), where a 14-year-old boy walked into school and shot two of his fellow students with a rifle; one of the victims was killed, the other seriously injured. This event occurred only eight days after a highly publicized school shooting at Columbine High School in Colorado, where two students shot and killed 12 of their fellow students and one teacher and wounded 24 others before committing suicide. The similarity of these two incidents prompted many people to speculate that the Taber shooting had been a "copycat" crime that had been primed by news exposure and imitated through social learning, much like the children who had beaten up the Bobo doll several decades earlier.

We learn not only about acts of violence in the media but also about how to enact aggression. Lieutenant Colonel Dave Grossman, who trains elite military and law enforcement officers, noted that he could remember no military skill achievement comparable to that of Michael Carneal, a 14-year-old boy who had never fired a real gun before but managed to fire eight shots from a .22 pistol into a group of students at Heath High School in West Paducah, Kentucky, hitting eight of them, five with head shots and three with hits to the upper torso. Grossman indicates that Michael Carneal learned these skills playing simulated shooter games at home and in video arcades (Grossman & Degaetano, 1999).

DESENSITIZATION THEORY

Desensitization theory proposes that repeated exposure to violence lessens its emotional impact. Compare the very strong emotional reaction of a young viewer who sees someone murdered on television for the first time to one who has already seen hundreds of acts

TAKE THAT BOBO. In Bandura's classic experiment, children were shown a movie (top four frames) of a model hitting a Bobo doll. If they saw the model rewarded for this behaviour, they treated the doll similarly (middle and bottom rows).

SOCIOLOGY IN MUSIC

VIOLENCE IN MUSIC

Violence is also prevalent in the music industry, incorporated into the lyrics of songs that top the Billboard charts. Although violent lyrics can be found in all popular music genres (from country to metal to pop), rap and hip-hop have been the focus of considerable attention. Popular rapper Eminem has topped the charts various times with songs such as "Not Afraid," "Lose Yourself," and "Love the Way You Lie," featuring Rihanna. Much of Eminem's music contains references to violence between males, and some songs include references to acts of violence committed by males toward their girlfriends. For example, "Love the Way You Lie" contains the confession "I laid hands on her," and in the now-notorious suicide song "Stan," featuring Dido, we hear the line "Hey, Slim, that's my girlfriend screamin' in the trunk," shortly before Stan drives his car off a bridge. In a study by Burgess, Dill, and Wright (2009), college students reported that the most common representations of women in rap songs they listened to were "ho" (or "whore"), "bitch," and "slut" and that rappers were most likely to rap about "sex," "drugs," "money," "women," and "violence."

of violence in movies, on TV programs, and in video games. The nightmares children may initially have when they see something scary are real. But over time, the same children will be less emotionally impacted by observing on-screen violence and, in all likelihood, will eventually join the masses who don't think twice about the violence they may be seeing in movies, in video games, or even on the evening news. Research now shows that desensitization is physiological as well, in that people who view more media violence have lower rates of blood pressure when faced with media violence compared to people with less exposure to media violence (Mrug et al., 2015).

In a video called "Killing Screens: Media & the Culture of Violence," George Gerbner pointed out that media producers know about the effects of desensitization and thus need to come up with new techniques for gaining attention. So in order to maintain consumer interest, movie sequels tend to have more killings presented in more dramatic, highly sensationalized ways as we move from earlier versions to the more current ones (e.g., the *Saw* and *Scream* series) (Dinozzi, 1997). If you don't believe this, try counting the number of murders in the first movie in a violent series compared to one of its sequels. More people will die and/or be killed in much more gruesome ways in the sequels. The effects of violence over time are also accounted for by the cultivation theory.

Pe3K/Shutterstock.com

Do video games promote violence?

CULTIVATION THEORY

Unlike desensitization theory, which focuses on diminished emotional reactions, cultivation theory explains how our thinking changes in specific ways as a result of repeated exposure to violence. *Cultivation theory*

"That's two dimensional violence. What I worry about is three dimensional violence outside."

© Farris, Joseph, jfa0300, www.cartoonstock.com

purports that repeated exposure to television violence has cumulative effects on viewers. It begins with fear and a sense of vulnerability that one will become a victim of violence, then progresses to the point where people believe that the world is more dangerous than it really is, termed the *mean world syndrome*. This can lead people to seek out more protective measures than are actually warranted, such as greater government intervention (Gerbner et al., 2002), and explains in part why some Canadians endorse things such as curfew bylaws to keep adolescents off the streets at night and perhaps why some people feel they need to carry handguns for protection.

SUMMING UP LESSONS LEARNED ABOUT MEDIA VIOLENCE

Taken together, research shows us that exposure to media violence teaches people about violence (e.g., how to enact it), can lead to desensitization (where we are less affected by it), and can lead to the eventual acceptance of violence. The propensity to become violent develops over time with media exposure. For example, short-term effects include increased physical and verbal aggression as well as increased aggressive thoughts and emotions. Long-term effects include an increased risk of engaging in physical assaults and even spousal abuse (e.g., Anderson et al., 2003).

Most video games contain violence, and the vast majority of youth ages 12 to 17 play them (Lenhart et al., 2008). A task force on violent media composed of leading research scientists was created in order to review and synthesize the literature on violent video game use. The task force examined previous meta-analyses (studies that combine the effects of multiple studies) along with various types of research conducted since 2009, such as experimental and longitudinal studies. Taken together, the findings show a consistent relationship between violent video use and increases in aggressive behaviour, aggressive thoughts, and aggressive feelings. Moreover, violent video game use is associated with decreases in prosocial behaviour, empathy, and sensitivity toward aggression (APA Task Force on Violent Media, 2015).

Although a sizeable body of research finds short- and long-term negative effects of media violence, other related questions and issues continue to somewhat undermine these results. For instance, are we certain we have a handle on what exactly constitutes an act of aggression in the media? Does it need to include intent to harm? Do we include all psychological and physical forms of aggression—the coworker who starts a nasty rumour about someone in order to get ahead; the athlete's game play? Is violence in a video game the same as violence on TV? Is a stabbing the same as a shooting? Besides the issue of how violence should be defined or measured, most of the effects are indirect and are difficult to establish for any given person. In many cases, other unmeasured risk factors could be accounting for the increases in aggression. Also, although most people are exposed to considerable amounts of media violence on a regular basis, relatively few people behave aggressively in the real world. Hence, some scholars continue to argue

YOUR SOCIOLOGICAL TOOLKIT

SOCIOLOGY IN PRACTICE

MONITORING CHILDREN'S EXPOSURE TO VIOLENCE

Various efforts have been made to try to monitor children's exposure to violence, including the use of V-chips and other program-blocking technology designed to allow parents to customize what their children view at home. All Canadian stations (even if they air an American show) include show ratings and blocking technology embedded in the broadcast signal. Symbols and icons appear on screen to denote program content that includes violence, coarse language, sexuality, and/or mature themes. This practice, which has been in effect since 1997, demonstrates how collective efforts can promote social change because the ratings were first developed by a group called the Action Group on Violence on Television (AGVOT) (Canadian Broadcasting Standards Council, 2017).

Think Outside the Box: In what ways does the Internet pose challenges for monitoring children's exposure to violence?

that the evidence is not conclusive (e.g., see Taylor & Huesmann, 2014, for a review), whereas others point out that the real challenge lies in trying to explain the actual process by which exposure to violence creates subsequent violence (Potter, 2014). Beyond trying to delineate the causal path, we also need to start thinking about how best to mitigate the outcomes since the owners of the media are unlikely to be persuaded to stop producing what the general public continues to consume in high demand.

In this regard, some researchers have opted for a more holistic approach, one that moves beyond the arguments that seek to condemn or support views of media violence to consider violence in a broader context, such as the social and political factors that encourage it (Trend, 2007). Other approaches consider opposing viewpoints, look at violence as a social problem, or consider a range of views on how society should best respond to media violence (e.g., Dudley, 1999). The APA Task Force on Violent Media (2015) suggests that all stakeholders (e.g., parents, video game makers, the legal system) work together to answer the question: "What cost is necessary to produce (or prevent) the effect?" (p. 16). We won't resolve the media debate here, and we'll leave you to consider your own position on this. Perhaps by turning to the postmodern view in closing, you can appreciate more fully why any given perspective will likely be inadequate for explaining the influences of today's ever-changing media.

POSTMODERN FRAMEWORK

The postmodern framework is probably best suited to helping us appreciate the many ways that our lives change with each new medium. Recall that postmodern ideas tend to underlie social action. The popularity of YouTube attests to the ability of consumers to influence the media and one another in ways that reshape cultural trends. Similarly, the ability to communicate quickly and widely via the Internet on the social networking platform Facebook helped students in Egypt successfully mobilize to overthrow the government in a monumental revolution in 2011 and helped remobilize protesters in 2013. From the terrorist attacks in Paris that killed 130 people in 2015 to the more recent attacks in Kabul, we are kept abreast of each new development as it unfolds through the media. Postmodern approaches to the media also encourage consumers to be aware of media ownership objectives, to think critically about the messages they take in, and to make informed choices about the kinds of messages and media they choose to engage with.

Media literacy: The ability to recognize, critically assess, and make informed choices about the messages contained in mass media forms.

LO7 MEDIA LITERACY: THINKING CRITICALLY ABOUT THE MEDIA

Media literacy refers to the ability to recognize, critically assess, and make informed choices about messages contained in mass media forms. According to Media Smarts (2017), media understanding includes an acceptance of these five concepts*:

1. *All media are constructions.* Media content is created by individuals who choose to convey a particular message by virtue of what is included and what is left out of the message. Since media messages represent the views of the capitalist class, the messages also underrepresent the views of less powerful groups in society. Media literacy works toward deconstructing (or taking apart) media messages to expose built-in assumptions, stereotypes, and misrepresentations and to show how or why they were made this way.
2. *Audiences negotiate the meaning in media.* Individuals interpret meanings in a variety of ways depending on their own life experiences, familial and cultural background, age, gender, ethnicity, and social class. So the same media message may be interpreted positively by one person and negatively by another.
3. *Media have commercial interests.* Media literacy aims to encourage an awareness of how the media are influenced by commercial considerations and how these affect content, technique, and distribution. Most media production is a business and must therefore make a profit. Questions of ownership and control are central. As we noted earlier, a small number of conglomerates own most of the leading recording companies, television networks, newspapers, radio stations, film production companies, and other forms of mass media.
4. *Media have social and political implications.* Media have a great influence on politics and social change by giving us an intimate sense of national issues and global concerns. At the same time, mass media have the power to set agendas and limit who and what we will be exposed to (e.g., national leaders, health issues, environmental concerns), and they determine how particular groups are represented (e.g., in a positive or negative manner).
5. *Each medium has a unique aesthetic form.* Each medium, be it a TV show, a radio program, or a video game, has its own way of storytelling, and it

*Source: © 2017 MediaSmarts, Ottawa, Canada, Key Concepts for Media Literacy, http://www.mediasmarts.ca. Adapted with permission.

YOUR SOCIOLOGICAL TOOLKIT

SOCIOLOGY IN MY LIFE

DEMONSTRATING MEDIA LITERACY

Reflect on what you have learned in this chapter about the mass media and its influence on individuals. In particular, consider ways in which the media is concentrated among a few major conglomerates, such as Disney and Comcast, and how these giants have the power to manipulate various media functions, such as the news or entertainment venues.

Think Outside the Box:
In response to media concentration, what is one way you demonstrate media literacy?

is important to understand how a particular media form is getting your attention and conveying its message.

To become media literate, we need to accomplish several things. First, we need to understand the nature of the media (i.e., that the mainstream media is a profit-centred, highly concentrated industry that uses techniques that construct reality for viewers). We also need to appreciate the wider implications of media (e.g., how the media expose us to large doses of violence, how they portray stereotypes, and how they promote consumerism). Finally, we need to develop critical viewing skills. For example, we need to be aware that we are being influenced, we need to consider who is sending the message and how the message is coming across, and we need to think about what that particular message is designed to accomplish (see *Sociology in My Life*).

TIME TO REVIEW

- How do individuals' unique experiences influence the kind of socialization provided by the mass media?
- In what ways is media news framed to make messages more apparent?
- What is the main assumption of social learning theory?
- According to cultivation theory, how does violent media exposure result in cumulative effects over time?
- What shared assumptions about the media comprise media education?

CONCLUSIONS

Much of the research that has been done on the media has focused upon the various concerns that have been voiced over aspects of its production and content. But this certainly does not mean that the media does nothing but corrupt humankind. New forms of electronically mediated communications, such as tweets, Instagram posts, and Facebook updates, play a central role in many of our lives, particularly for providing us with real-time information. Traditional forms of media eventually led to the development of new media, which includes smartphones, augmented reality, and even apps that have yet to be developed. Although it is sometimes demonized because of its inherent consumerism, as well as the presence of violence and gender stereotypes, the media also serve important positive functions. It is only through the media that we can sometimes learn about events affecting our close and more distant friends or relatives (e.g., what issues they support), our communities (e.g., local events happening here), and our world (e.g., the destruction of the Twin Towers on 9/11, the revolution that changed Egypt's political structure, the nuclear disaster in Japan, the fighting in Libya, and the unrest in Russia and Ukraine).

The media can keep us safe, such as by broadcasting a tornado warning or a flood alert. Cellphones and texting enable parents to keep closer tabs on their children and intimate partners to touch base during their busy days. Facebook enables friends and family members who are separated by long distances to have a greater presence in each others' everyday lives. The Internet brings virtual communities together—whether you are a new parent, someone suffering from a debilitating disease, someone too busy to find a potential date any other way, or an

LGBTQ (i.e., lesbian, gay, bisexual, transgender, queer/questioning) youth, you can find an online group of similar others who provide each other with support and suggestions for life's challenges. And, of course, the media also entertain us (even if this is not their primary purpose), and human beings have been creating means of entertainment for thousands of years. Even the authors of this book have been known to occasionally escape into the violent mass-mediated worlds of *Blacklist*, UFC, and boxing on Pay Per View and first-person shooter games such as *Call of Duty*.

CHAPTER SUMMARY

LO1 Describe the history of the traditional forms of mass media.

Prior to the Internet, the mass media consisted of books, newspapers, magazines, cinema, recordings, radio, and television.

LO2 Describe the role of new media forms, including whether they make traditional ones obsolete.

Modern forms of media are referred to as new media and include the Internet, video and computer games, and cellphones with downloadable applications. The Internet changed all of the traditional forms of mass media (books are now available online, radio audio streams can now be accessed over the Internet, etc.), but new forms of media didn't eliminate the traditional ones, which have features we still enjoy for their own unique experience (e.g., watching a movie on a big screen or listening to a radio). However, new forms are also unique and are sometimes better for other reasons—for example, they allow us to experience augmented reality and to multitask (with the latest smartphones).

LO3 Differentiate among media assumptions provided by the core sociological frameworks.

A functionalist framework points out ways that the media help us find out about important events and better communicate with one another to become more socially aware and connected. The conflict framework notes that the mass media are profit-based businesses with concentrated ownership, which influences the kind of information we are exposed to. The interactionist framework helps us understand how individuals uniquely interpret media messages. Feminist frameworks highlight how the mass media portray stereotyped images of certain groups, such as women, and emphasize particular messages, such as the importance of beauty. Finally, the postmodern framework helps us better appreciate the many ways our lives have changed with technology and how the media facilitate social action.

LO4 Evaluate the relevance of media ownership for agenda setting.

Media ownership is highly concentrated. A small number of large corporations own most of the ways we receive information and thereby largely determine which issues the public is exposed to and what it comes to think is important.

LO5 Demonstrate a critical understanding of ways that media shape our perceptions.

As a major agent of socialization, the mass media teach us to hold particular political views, teach us to be fixated on consumerism (i.e., the need to buy things), reinforce stereotypes, including beauty standards, and expose us to a large amount of violence.

LO6 Debate whether violence in the media causes viewers to become violent.

On the one hand, research shows that we become less sensitive to media violence over time so that we require greater amounts for stimulation. Eventually, we suffer cultivated cumulative effects, including an increased fear of victimization, and we come to believe that the world is more dangerous than it actually is. Importantly, increased exposure to violence leads to an increased likelihood of behaving and thinking in aggressive ways. On the other hand, research has failed to provide conclusive evidence of a direct link between exposure to violence and subsequent acts of violence. There is not even consensus on what constitutes violence.

LO7 Illustrate what it means to be "media literate."

We can help diffuse some of the potential negative effects of media viewing by varying our media exposure, by becoming more aware of media influence, and by improving our ability to deconstruct media messages through media literacy education.

RECOMMENDED RESOURCES

1. For more information on print and electronic media, how media and society interact, and the role of advertising and public relations, refer to R. Hanson, *Mass Communication: Living in a Mediated World* (8th ed.) (Thousand Oaks, CA: Sage, 2017).
2. For a critical examination of how social media have changed how we relate to one another, we recommend S. Turkle, *Alone Together: Why We Expect More from Technology and Less from Each Other* (New York, NY: Basic Books, 2011).
3. You can visit Ahonen's daily blog to check out his latest technology forecasts, or you can view his TED talk on augmented reality given at TEDxMongKok by visiting his website: http://www.tomiahonen.com.
4. The Media Education Foundation's bestseller *Consuming Kids: The Commercialization of Childhood* is an excellent resource for anyone who wants to learn more about how corporations create a consumer culture. You can find out more about this film and others like it by visiting http://www.mediaed.org.
5. To find out what how video games are rated (e.g., easy of play and educational value) as well as things to watch out for, such as violence, online interaction, language, and consumerism, see Common Sense Media (https://www.commonsensemedia.org).

FOR FURTHER REFLECTION

1. Should the Internet be regulated? Why or why not?
2. Select a full-page advertisement from any magazine of your choice and bring it to class. Record answers to the following questions and be prepared to share them in class:
   a. What product (or service) is the focus of this ad?
   b. Who owns or is responsible for this ad?
   c. What techniques are used to attract attention to this ad?
   d. Who is the primary targeted audience for this product?
   e. What is the main message depicted in this ad?
   f. What other representations are evident in this ad?
3. Interview someone in a different generation from you (e.g., your mother, an uncle, a grandparent, or an elderly neighbour) about the media. What was the principal medium in his or her youth? What was the primary function of that medium? What was the "leading-edge" medium of that time, and how was that new form expected to change things?

carlosseller/Shutterstock

03 PART

The Micro and Macro of Our Everyday Lives

07 CHAPTER

Sex, Gender, and Sexualities: Deconstructing Dualisms

ekmelica/Shutterstock

But let me tell you, this gender thing is history. You're looking at a guy who sat down with Margaret Thatcher and talked about serious issues.

(George Bush, Sr.)[1]

LEARNING OBJECTIVES & OUTCOMES

After completing this chapter, students should be able to do the following:

LO1 Describe the elite discourses that equate sex, gender, and sexuality.

LO2 Explain the ways in which sex, gender, and sexualities are socially constructed.

LO3 Discuss the different educational experiences of males and females in childhood and in postsecondary studies.

LO4 Describe the occupational sex segregation within the labour force.

LO5 Discuss the ways that economic experiences are gendered and the reasons why.

LO6 Identify the gendered nature of family life for children and adults.

LO7 Outline the various sociological theories that address gender.

In the above quotation, President George H.W. Bush made a sweeping claim, "this gender thing is history," suggesting that in the late 20th century, gender no longer mattered. A woman (Margaret Thatcher) could become prime minister of Britain. Women were capable of discussing "serious issues." Men were capable of discussing serious issues with women. But is it actually the case that in the 21st century, gender is irrelevant? Have the constraints (and privileges) of traditional gender roles been relegated to the past? As we progress through this chapter, we will see that although society has undergone significant changes, gender continues to operate as one of the master statuses by which others identify us and we identify ourselves. The elite discourses of gender and their connections with the elite discourses of sex and sexuality influence individual thoughts and feelings, the nature and content of social interactions, and the structure and functioning of society's institutions.

LO1 ELITE DISCOURSES OF SEX, GENDER, AND SEXUALITY

You may recall the concept of *elite discourses* from Chapter 1. Foucault (1980) proposed that there are multiple ways of understanding any social phenomenon. Those understandings emerge from different locations of power. When particular understandings emerge from positions of authority, those understandings become elite discourses and are widely accepted. Through socialization, elite discourses become so deeply ingrained that many people have difficulty even imagining alternative possibilities. The power of elite discourses is especially evident when we consider sex, gender, and sexualities. Being identified as female or male affects every facet of people's lives. However, "female" and "male" do not refer to *gender* but point to *sex*; this distinction is one between social forces and biological forces. **Sex** describes biology, which in Euro-Canadian cultures has traditionally been equated with the **dualism** of

Sex: Biological characteristics that include sex chromosomes, primary sex characteristics, and secondary sex characteristics.

Dualism: A contrast between two opposing categories.

female/male; we often hear references to the "opposite sex." Sex is determined at the moment of conception and is followed by the development of primary and secondary sex characteristics.

Gender describes the social world, the behavioural, cultural, or psychological traits associated with a specific sex, within a certain culture, at a given point in history. Gender is socially determined through socialization processes in the context of cultural norms. Because sex is based on a dualism, gender is presumed to be as well; the traits associated with being female are labelled **femininity**, whereas those associated with being male are labelled **masculinity**.

Traditionally, masculinity has been equated with action, aggression, independence, dominance, athleticism, and self-reliance. In contrast, femininity has been equated with passivity, kindness, shyness, sensitivity, loyalty, and compassion (Bem, 1974).

The dualisms of sex and gender are related to yet another dualism, this one in the realm of sexuality. Attraction to members of the "opposite sex" is referred to as **heterosexuality**, whereas attraction to members of the "same sex" is considered **homosexuality**. Both terms are dependent on the view of sex as consisting of only two "legitimate" sexes—female and male. The belief that sex can (or should) be equated with gender, and then with sexuality, has become an elite discourse to the extent that it is difficult for many people to even imagine other ways of thinking about the issue or organizing their lives.

Gender: The behavioural, cultural, or psychological traits associated with a particular sex, within a certain culture, at a given point in history.

Femininity: The behavioural, cultural, or psychological traits associated with being female, within a certain culture, at a given point in history.

Masculinity: The behavioural, cultural, or psychological traits associated with being male, within a certain culture, at a given point in history.

Heterosexuality: Sexual attraction to members of the "opposite sex."

Homosexuality: Sexual attraction to members of the "same sex."

Intersexed: A person whose physical sex characteristics fall outside the boundaries of the male/female dualism.

Disorders of sexual development or **differences in sexual development (DSD):** A term used in place of *intersexed*, referring to physical sex characteristics that fall outside the boundaries of the male/female dualism.

LO2 MOVING OUTSIDE ELITE DISCOURSES

In fact, there are other ways of thinking about these concepts. Even a concept that appears to be as straightforward as sex is more complex than we might think. It is more accurate to think of sex as a *spectrum*, similar to the colour spectrum (Ainsworth, 2015). There is a wide range of physical sex differences, just as there are a multitude of possible combinations of primary, secondary, and chromosomal characteristics. The dualism female/male is an oversimplification of sex, just as the colour "blue" is an oversimplification of a portion of the colour spectrum. In some circumstances, such as when choosing a paint colour for our walls, we will speak with greater precision—we want a "muted greyish-blue" rather than "tropical turquoise." In the context of sex, attention is sometimes drawn to this spectrum. An individual may have the external genitalia of a female but the internal reproductive organs of a male, ambiguous external sex organs, or the chromosomal variation XXY (and the list could go on). When a person's sex characteristics do not neatly fit into the dualism of male/female, that person may be labelled **intersexed**. However, a growing number of scientific experts and advocates have moved away from that term and instead use the terms **disorders of sexual development** or **differences in sexual development** (both of which use the acronym **DSD**). They argue that the term DSD more correctly emphasizes a characteristic of the body ("Jo *has* a difference in sexual development), whereas intersexed was a label applied to the entire person and thereby conflated with identity ("Jo *is* intersexed).

How many people do not fit neatly into the dualism of female/male? Because sex falls along a spectrum, this is a difficult question. Some individuals may be labelled as having a DSD at birth because of ambiguous external genitalia. Other people may not be categorized as such until adulthood—for example, when seeking medical attention because of difficulties in having children. Some people live their entire lives without knowing that some aspect of their internal biology falls outside that dualism. Although there is some disagreement among medical doctors about precisely which characteristics should be labelled as a DSD, there is no doubt that it is a characteristic of

TIME TO REVIEW

- What are the dualisms that constitute the elite discourses of sex, gender, and sexuality?
- In what ways are the dualisms of sex, gender, and sexuality connected to one another?

many people in the world, with estimates ranging from 1 in 4,500 births to 1 in 100 births depending on which specific characteristics are included (Ainsworth, 2015; Arboleda, Sandberg, & Vilain, 2014). Just as the dualism of male/female is a social construction, so is the label of intersexed. As the Intersex Society of North America (2008) points out, "nature doesn't decide where the category of 'male' ends and the category of 'intersex' begins, or where the category of 'intersex' ends and the category of 'female' begins. Humans decide" (para. 4).

When children are diagnosed with differences in sexual development, parents face pressure from doctors (among others) to choose whether they want their child to be raised as a male or a female; then, in some cases, surgery is performed to fit that decision. The elite discourse of the medical community views DSDs as problems that must be fixed, even though they are often not associated with any physical health problems. In fact, the evidence is stronger that in the 20th century, early genital surgeries caused more psychological and sexual problems than they resolved (Koyama & Weasel, 2003). Thus, although sex is a biological reality, the recognition of two, and only two, "legitimate" sexes is a *social construction*—one that emerges from social processes, not just biology.

The manner in which gender is socially constructed is even more apparent (see *Sociology in My Life*). There is greater gender variation within sexes than there is between sexes, and the idea that females are "naturally" feminine whereas males are "naturally" masculine was refuted long ago by cross-cultural research. In some cultures, women are aggressive and men are nurturing; in others, men and women are expected to embody similar traits. Furthermore, many cultures have recognized multiple sex/gender combinations. Between 100 and 150 Indigenous cultures in North America have recognized multiple sex/gender combinations in biological males, and between 27 and 75 have recognized multiple combinations in biological females (Nanda, 2000). The Cree use the term *aayahkwew* ("neither man nor woman") and the Inuit the term *sipiniq* ("infant whose sex changes at birth") to refer to male-bodied persons with a female essence; the Ojibwa use the term *okitcitakwe* ("warrior woman") and the Zuni the term *katotse* ("boy-girl") to refer to female-bodied persons with a male essence (NativeOUT, n.d.). People so named were traditionally associated with spiritual power and often performed specialized roles in their communities: name giver, healer, or spiritual leader (Nanda, 2000). European explorers referred to these individuals as *berdaches*, from the French word *bardaches*—which, loosely translated, means "male prostitutes." For many decades, anthropologists used this term as well. Because of its derogatory origins, at a 1990 conference for Indigenous people, participants adopted the anglicized term **two-spirited**, referring to individuals who have both male and female spirits (Roscoe, 1998).

In contemporary society, individuals whose gender identity (i.e., how they see themselves) or expression (i.e., how they look or act) corresponds to elite, dualistic discourses are referred to as **cisgender**. Those

Two-spirited: In Indigenous cultures, individuals who have both male and female spirits.

Cisgender: Individuals whose gender identity or expression corresponds to their birth sex.

YOUR SOCIOLOGICAL TOOLKIT

SOCIOLOGY IN MY LIFE

MY GENDER

Because elite discourses equate gender with sex, when others identify you as female or male, they may subsequently expect you to embody femininity or masculinity, as appropriate for your sex. The ways that they identify your sex, and then your gender, may or may not correspond to the way that you identify your own sex or gender. When your appearance or behaviours contradict people's expectations of sex or gender, you are likely to face some social disapproval.

Think Outside the Box: In what ways do you conform to, or contradict, traditional notions of male or female, masculinity or femininity? What consequences have you faced from others for either conforming to or violating those norms?

who step outside dualisms of sex and gender may consider themselves two-spirited, **transgender**, or **gender nonconforming**; other terms can include gender variant, gender creative, gender nonbinary, or gender fluid.

Historical research on Euro-Canadian cultures reveals the socially constructed nature of gender. For instance, with industrialization, the female role came to be that of the nurturing parent and homemaker, the creator of a *haven in a heartless world* (Lasch, 1977). At that time, employment legislation removed children and women from workplaces, making the "private" world of families and the "public" world of paid employment increasingly separate. Men came to be associated with the public sphere, whereas women and children were associated with the private sphere. Concerns about the moral dangers of an urban world were growing. Because men spent most of their day in the public sphere, they were considered especially vulnerable to those perceived dangers. So, it was important that when they returned home, they entered an environment that would recharge their physical health, psychological well-being, and moral strength. Because women were largely relegated to the home, femininity came to be associated with qualities that could create this "haven." They were to ensure that every aspect of the home—from the decor of the rooms to the meals that were prepared—contributed to a nurturing environment. Media told them exactly how to achieve this goal; a plethora of cookbooks, housekeeping manuals, guidebooks for women, and popular women's magazines were released, contributing to the emergence of what was known as the *cult of domesticity*. However, this industrialized vision of the ideal female homemaker applied only to the lives of middle-class women (and particularly white, middle-class women); working-class women (especially those who were ethnic minorities) continued to be workers and income earners. In fact, working-class women were often the ones enabling middle-class women to transform their homes into havens by working as domestic servants (e.g., maids, nannies, and cooks), taking in laundry, and more. An image of the cult of domesticity

Transgender: Individuals whose gender identity or expression corresponds to that of another sex.

Gender nonconforming: Individuals whose gender identity or expression falls outside elite, dualistic discourses. May also be referred to as gender variant, gender creative, gender nonbinary, or gender fluid.

http://lookbook.nu/jocelyn_m

Jocelyn M. uses social media to challenge society's elite discourses of gender.

is reflected in *Figure 7.1*, a document that has made its rounds online. This was also the image reflected in the most popular television shows in the 1950s and 1960s (e.g., *Father Knows Best*).

During the same era, the male role emphasized characteristics viewed as necessary in the industrialized world—traits that would enable men to achieve economic success in the free market and compensate for the perceived feminizing influence boys faced in the private sphere of the home. These characteristics are now viewed as "traditional" masculinity (David & Brannon, 1976):

- *The Big Wheel*: Compete for success and achievement (economically and physically).
- *The Sturdy Oak*: Be stable, tough, and in control at all times.
- *Give 'em Hell*: Be dominant and aggressive.
- *No Sissy Stuff*: Avoid anything associated with femininity, such as emotions or sexual attraction to men.

More than a century later, anti-violence educator Jackson Katz argues that although alternative masculinities have become more common, traditional masculinity has also become more extreme—what may be called **hypermasculinity** (Jhally & Earp, 2016). Changes in media images over the last several decades illustrate hypermasculinity, such as larger guns in Hollywood action movies, bigger muscles and more unrealistic body types in male action figures, more aggressive

Hypermasculinity: Traditional masculinity in an extreme and exaggerated form.

FIGURE 7.1

The Good Wife's Guide

Housekeeping Monthly 13 May 1955

The good wife's guide

- Have dinner ready. Plan ahead, even the night before, to have a delicious meal ready, on time for his return. This is a way of letting him know that you have been thinking about him and are concerned about his needs. Most men are hungry when they come home and the prospect of a good meal (especially his favourite dish) is a part of the warm welcome needed.
- Prepare yourself. Take 15 minutes to rest so you'll be refreshed when he arrives. Touch up your make-up, put a ribbon in your hair and be fresh-looking. He has just been with a lot of work-weary people.
- Be a little gay and a little more interesting for him. His boring day may need a lift and one of your duties is to provide it.
- Clear away the clutter. Make one last trip through the main part of the house just before your husband arrives.

Housekeeping Monthly 13 May 1955

- Gather up schoolbooks, toys, paper etc and then run a dustcloth over the tables.
- Over the cooler months of the year you should prepare and light a fire for him to unwind by. You husband will feel he has reached a haven of rest and order, and it will give you a lift too. After all, catering for his comfort will provide you with immense personal satisfaction.
- Prepare the children. Take a few minutes to wash the children's hands and faces (if they are small), comb their hair and, if necessary, change their clothes. They are little treasures and he would like to see them playing the part. Minimise all noise. At the time of his arrival, eliminate all noise of the washer, dryer or vacuum. Try to encourage the children to be quiet.
- Be happy to see him.
- Greet him with a warm smile and show sincerity in your desire to please him.
- Listen to him. You may have a dozen important things to tell him but the moment of his arrival is not the time. Let him talk first – remember his topics of conversation are more important than yours.
- Make the evening his. Never complain if he comes home late or goes out to dinner, or other places of entertainment without you. Instead, try to understand his world of strain and pressure and his very real need to be at home and relax.
- Your goal: Try to make sure your home is a place of peace, order and tranquillity where your husband can renew himself in body and spirit.
- Don't greet him with complaints and problems.
- Don't complain if he's late home for dinner or even if he stays out all night. Count this as minor compared to what he might have gone through that day.
- Make him comfortable. Have him lean back in a comfortable chair or have him lie down in the bedroom. Have a cool or warm drink ready for him.
- Arrange his pillow and offer to take off his shoes. Speak in a low, soothing and pleasant voice.
- Don't ask him questions about his actions or question his judgment or integrity. Remember, he is the master of the house and as such will always exercise his will with fairness and truthfulness. You have no right to question him.
- A good wife always knows her place.

The Advertising Archives/Alamy

Source: Image Courtesy of The Advertising Archives

SOCIOLOGY ON SCREEN

DECONSTRUCTING DUALISMS IN THE MEDIA

The creative arts have long been an arena for social commentary and critique, whether about specific public figures, current events, or social issues such as inequality. Furthermore, their framing of people and issues has an impact our own interpretations of the social world. As such, the creative arts have been at the forefront of deconstructing dualisms of sex, gender, and sexualities. For example, transgender characters have been present in film for several decades (although they are frequently played by cisgender actors). Just a few of the more well-known films include *The Crying Game* (1992), *Boys Don't Cry* (1999), *Hedwig and the Angry Inch* (2001) (also a current Broadway production), Kinky Boots (2005) (also a current Broadway production), *Transamerica* (2005), *The Danish Girl* (2015), and *Tangerine* (2015). Transgender characters have been less common on television until relatively recently (although the 1970s comedy *The Jeffersons* did include an episode with a transgender character, which was highly controversial at the time). Today, television series with transgender characters include *Orange Is the New Black, Transparent, The Fosters, American Horror Story: Freak Show, and Sense8*. In several cases (such as *Transparent*), the shows include multiple transgender characters and may also represent characters who fall outside dualisms of sex, gender, and sexualities in other ways.

In addition to transgender characters, other gender nonconforming characters are now being featured in film and television (although less often). Actor Asia Kate Dillon (who identifies as gender nonbinary) is the first to play a gender nonbinary character on television, in the series *Billions*. In film, Kelly Mantle plays a nonbinary character in *Confessions of a Womanizer* (2016); Mantle was the first person in Hollywood whose work was submitted for Oscar consideration in both the Best Actor and Best Actress categories.

The creative arts play an important role in deconstructing dualisms of sex and sexualities as well. For instance, fluid sexualities (e.g., pansexuality) are presented as a normal state of affairs on television shows such as *Schitt's Creek, Pretty Little Liars, Sense8, House of Cards*, and *How to Get Away with Murder*. Similarly, differences in sexual development have been explored in films such as XXY (2007) and the television series *Faking It*. However, the sex dualism of female/male has been addressed the least in the creative arts, which suggests that elite discourses of sex are the most pervasive of all.

postures by male music artists in music videos, and more extreme violence enacted by male characters in many video games (Jhally & Earp, 2016).

Turning to sexualities, we can analyze the ways they are socially constructed as well. Similar sexual desires and acts exist throughout the world, but the meanings attributed to those desires and acts, and the ways they are treated, emerge from social processes. For instance, in the language of the Sambian culture (in New Guinea), words that categorize people as heterosexual, homosexual, or bisexual don't exist; instead, Sambian culture utilizes concepts that refer to different times in the life cycle, when varied types of sexual relationships are considered appropriate or inappropriate (Herdt, 1984). Even in North America in the mid-20th century, pioneer sexuality researcher Alfred Kinsey contended that sexualities were not represented by a dualism but rather by a spectrum. Building upon earlier models developed by scholars in the 1920s, Kinsey developed a scale that reflected a continuum of sexualities, with exclusively same-sex desires and activities at one extreme end and exclusively opposite-sex desires and activities at the other (Kinsey, Pomeroy, & Martin, 1948). Nevertheless, at that time, Kinsey's ideas faced resistance on many fronts, and traditional discourses of sexuality prevailed for many decades (Drucker, 2010).

Bisexuality: Sexual attraction to both males and females.

Pansexuality: Sexual attraction to people along the full spectrums of sex, gender, and sexuality.

Today, empirical research conducted with more than 17,000 people in 48 countries supports Kinsey's argument that sexuality exists on a continuum rather than as discrete categories (Epstein et al., 2012). In Canada, we see that discourses based on the heterosexual/homosexual dualism have been replaced, to some extent, by more recognition of the spectrum of sexualities, such as the recognition of **bisexuality** (i.e., attraction to both males and females). The term **pansexuality** has become more common as well, referring to sexual attraction to people along the full spectrums of sex, gender, and sexuality.

Elite discourses of sex, gender, and sexualities have traditionally been based on dualisms—male/female; masculine/feminine; heterosexual/homosexual—and those dualisms have been equated with one another, so that females are presumed to be both feminine and sexually attracted to men and males are presumed to be masculine and sexually attracted to women. Because these dualisms are socially constructed, we might say that they are not "real." But they most certainly *are* real in their consequences. Being identified as male or female affects most aspects of our lives, and individuals who fall outside the elite discourses face stigmatization. Before 1969, people could go to prison as dangerous sex offenders if convicted of having a consensual sexual relationship with someone of the same sex, and from the 1950s to the 1980s, the Canadian government conducted an active campaign to purge homosexuals from public service (Kinsman & Gentile, 2009). Since then, through the efforts of LGBTQ movements, significant changes have come about, one of which is that since 2005, members of the same sex have the right to marry in Canada. Yet in many ways, society continues to be **heteronormative** (i.e., characterized by the view that heterosexuality is the expected or preferred sexual orientation). Consequently, people who fall outside the dualisms are still stigmatized. The situation for LGBTQ youth is especially difficult. LGBTQ youth hear anti-gay slurs an average of 26 times a day, and 26 percent are forced by their parents to leave home. They are often the victims of bullying, which can contribute to higher suicide rates; 30 percent of youth suicides are among LGBTQ youth (PFLAG Canada, n.d.). Many forms of support have emerged in response, including the "It Gets Better" video campaign, gay-straight alliances in schools, and online peer support (such as http://www.youthline.ca).

TIME TO REVIEW

- In what ways is the recognition of only two sexes a social construction?
- How does knowledge of diverse cultures and of Canadian history demonstrate the socially constructed nature of gender?
- What constitutes femininity, masculinity, and hypermasculinity?
- In what ways does knowledge of Sambian society and of Alfred Kinsey's research demonstrate the socially constructed nature of sexualities?
- What are some of the consequences of falling outside the dualisms of sex, gender, or sexualities?

GENDER: THE CONSEQUENCES OF HAVING BEEN BORN FEMALE OR MALE

How would your life be different if you were another sex (see *Sociology in My Life*)? This is a question that David and Myra Sadker (Sadker & Sadker, 1994; Sadker, Sadker, & Zittleman, 2009) asked students over several decades of research. The answers to this question are revealing. They highlight the many ways that our everyday lives are structured on the basis of biological sex; they also underscore the continued presence of traditional discourses that equate sex, gender, and sexualities.

Heteronormative: The view that heterosexuality is the expected or preferred sexual orientation.

YOUR SOCIOLOGICAL TOOLKIT

SOCIOLOGY IN MY LIFE

IMAGINING MY LIFE DIFFERENTLY

Elite discourses of sex, gender, and sexuality have implications for us from the moment of birth or even sooner. Those implications are so far-reaching that they often lie beneath our awareness, and we must make a conscious effort to "see the strange in the familiar" (see Chapter 1).

Think Outside the Box: Imagine that tomorrow morning you woke up as a member of another sex. In what ways would your life be different? In what ways would it remain the same?

SOCIOLOGY IN MY COMMUNITY

BECAUSE I AM A GIRL

Plan International is a humanitarian organization that operates in more than 50 countries to promote children's rights as a way to end child poverty. Their "Because I am a Girl" program emphasizes girls' rights in particular. Globally, girls are twice as likely as boys to be malnourished; more than 60 million girls do not attend primary or secondary school; every two seconds, a girl under the age of 18 is married (Plan International, 2015). The organization highlights gender equality as important for improving children's rights and advancing countries' economic and social development. For instance, each year of female education results in a 10 to 20 percent increase in income. Furthermore, with seven years of formal schooling, females are significantly less likely to marry before the age of 18, they have fewer children, and their children are healthier at birth and in the following years (Plan International, 2015).

In 2011, Plan International conducted a survey of children ages 12 to 17 living in Canada, the United Kingdom, Rwanda, and India. The survey explored the underlying attitudes toward gender that can either reinforce existing gender inequalities or facilitate social change (Plan International, 2015). The results from the Canadian portion of the survey reveal, on the one hand, that children have a strong belief in gender equality. More than 90 percent think that gender equality is beneficial to both boys and girls, that girls should have the same rights and opportunities as boys, and that parents should take equal responsibility for their children. On the other hand, gender inequalities continue to be reinforced. Approximately one-third believe that a woman's most important role is taking care of the household and cooking, and almost half believe that men should be responsible for earning and providing. Because of pressure from peers, media, and family (in that order), those who do not conform to traditional gender ideals are negatively sanctioned. For example, respondents indicate that boys are likely to be made fun of if they are bad at sports (57 percent), wear pink (62 percent), cry (77 percent), or play with dolls (92 percent).

Think Outside the Box: Reflecting back on your own childhood, where did you see pressure to conform to traditional gender ideals? Conversely, where did you encounter messages that promoted gender equality? As you read through the upcoming sections on educational, occupational, economic, and family experiences, you may identify other messages that you, too, have encountered.

The extent to which children and adolescents are able to recognize the implications of gender might be surprising to some people. In the Sadkers' research, many girls found good things to say about being male: getting a better job; earning more money; feeling more secure; being treated with more respect. In the end, most girls said that although it might be interesting to be a boy for a while, they would prefer to be a girl. In contrast, almost all of the boys saw nothing but bad things about being female: PMS; having to do all the cooking; having to worry about their hair; being a bad athlete; having less freedom; dieting; being weaker; being smaller; getting no respect; experiencing sexual harassment. One boy said, "I couldn't stand it if people messed with me the way they do with girls" (Sadker et al., 2009, pp. 35, 88). Both boys *and* girls had to be prodded to come up with a list of advantages to being a girl: not having to pay for dates; shopping; talking on the phone; looking gorgeous (Sadker et al., 2009).

More recently, research finds that although Canadian children recognize gender equality in many ways, traditional views continue as well (see *Sociology in My Community*). When the views of children and adolescents are brought together, we see that from a young age, people believe that the implications of having been born a particular sex extend through all facets of life. Sociological research supports that assumption. Gendered norms result in (1) different educational experiences, (2) different occupational experiences, (3) different economic experiences, and (4) different family experiences.

LO3 DIFFERENT EDUCATIONAL EXPERIENCES

Children spend much of their time in the classroom—approximately 35 hours per week during the school year. So, it is important to explore children's educational experiences and the gender socialization that occurs in their classrooms.

The different educational experiences of females and males begin in the classrooms of young children. Research on the classroom behaviours of preschool teachers during free play finds that they reinforce dualisms of sex and gender, as well as traditional gender roles, in many ways (Granger et al., 2017). Although preschool teachers facilitate gender-neutral activities during free play (e.g., playing with clay), they are most likely to do so when interacting with mixed-sex groups of children. When teachers are interacting with single-sex groups, they may encourage some gender-neutral activities, but gender-specific activities are facilitated as well—feminine activities with girls-only groups (e.g., playing with dolls) and masculine activities with boys-only groups (e.g., building cars out of Lego).

David and Myra Sadker (along with Karen Zittleman) have observed children's classrooms at all ages, from preschool through high school. Over the course of several decades, they found that boys and girls sitting in the same classroom are receiving very different educations. Because of the pragmatic demands of the classroom and gender stereotypes, even the best teachers may inadvertently treat boys and girls differently. Although blatant bias in classroom practices has declined over the decades, subtle differences continue (Sadker et al., 2009). Through these understated practices, boys are drawn to the forefront of the classroom, whereas girls slip quietly into the background. Boys are encouraged to figure out how to solve problems on their own, whereas girls have their problems solved for them (Sadker et al., 2009).

In the classroom, boys are louder and more active (Sadker et al., 2009). Thus, maintaining classroom order means controlling the boys—by interacting with them, asking them questions, and disciplining them more often than girls. While the boys receive all of this attention, the girls quietly do their work. Teachers say that boys "need" more attention (because they are weaker in some subjects) or "demand" more attention (by misbehaving and speaking out of turn). But not *all* boys receive this attention—just the ones who exhibit more traditional forms of masculinity by being active, loud, and assertive.

Overall, what type of attention is it that male and female students receive? There are four forms that teacher feedback on student work can take: (a) *praise*, whereby the teacher highlights an aspect of work that has been done well; (b) *remediation*, when the teacher gives direction that enables a student to solve a problem; (c) *criticism*, a critique about something that has been done wrong; and (d) *acceptance*, a brief acknowledgment (e.g., "Okay"). Boys receive more of every type of response, but especially remediation. When boys are having difficulty with an assignment, teachers are more likely to encourage them to figure it out for themselves) in contrast, when girls are having problems with a question, teachers are more likely to *show* them how to solve it. Of the four types of comments, girls most often receive a brief acknowledgment ("Okay"). When teachers are asked why they give girls brief acknowledgments so often, their responses reflect gender stereotypes; they say they don't want to be too "tough" on a girl, hurt her feelings, or make her cry (Sadker et al., 2009).

Yet despite the greater attention that boys receive, girls are more likely to enjoy school (Hudon, 2017). They are also more likely to excel. Girls achieve higher overall grades and get higher scores on standardized reading tests (Ferguson, 2016; Hudon, 2017). Boys are more likely to be disciplined; both male and female students say that teachers often "pick on" the boys and punish them unfairly. Teachers often subscribe to stereotypes about boys' academic abilities. For example, Heyder and Kessels (2015) had teachers read a vignette about a male or female student and then identify other qualities they believed that student possessed. Overall, teachers who read vignettes about male students described those students as lazy and inattentive—especially when boys were engaged in gender-typical behaviours, and even when the male and female students were described as engaging in identical behaviours.

Females are also more likely to pursue a postsecondary education and to graduate from postsecondary studies (see *Figure 7.2*) (Ferguson, 2016). That pattern is even more pronounced for Indigenous people (and especially younger cohorts), where among those ages 25 to 34, women comprise 68 percent of those with a university degree. By comparison, among non-Indigenous people, that proportion is 59 percent (Ferguson, 2016).

What is it that boys and girls are ultimately learning in the classroom? Within the official curriculum, both are learning math, science, social studies, and other subjects. When it comes to mastering this material, it appears that female students are at an advantage. Besides the official curriculum, students are also exposed to a *hidden curriculum*, whereby they learn what being a male or a female means in our society. By being drawn to the forefront of classroom life and encouraged to solve their own problems, boys develop problem-solving skills and independence. But there is a dark side to these lessons as well in that boys are also learning that no one is going to solve their problems for them, that they are on their own in

FIGURE 7.2

Proportion of Women and Men (Ages 25 to 64) with Postsecondary Credentials

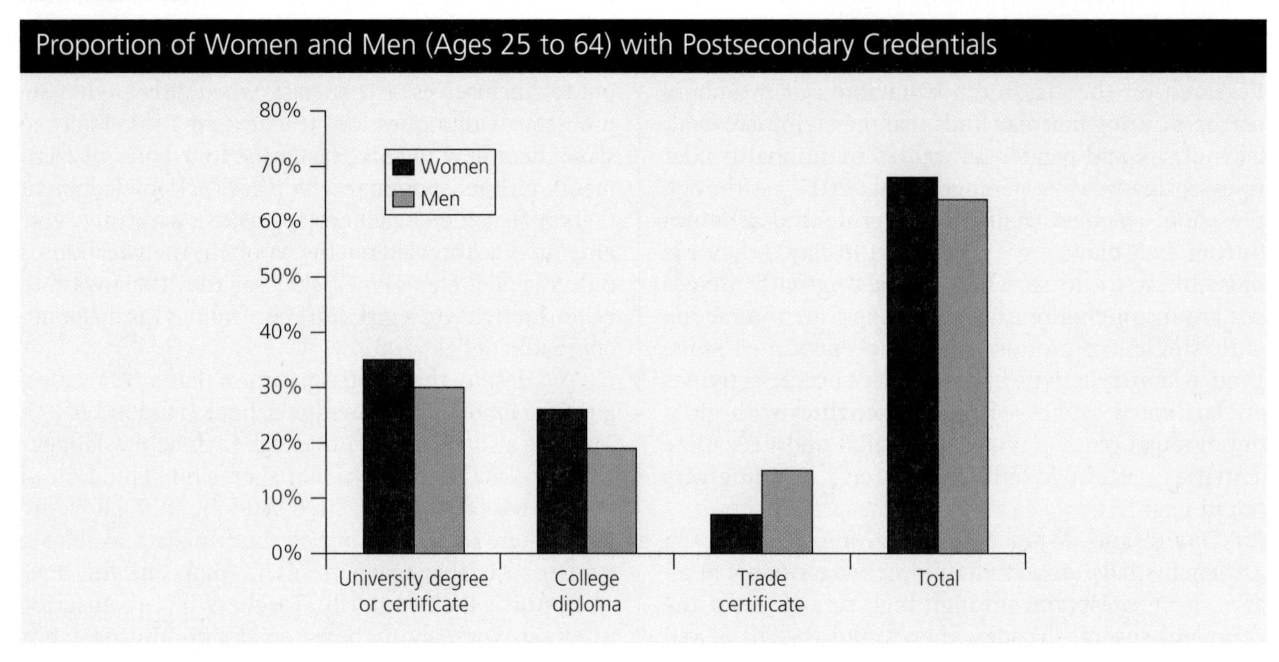

Adapted from: Ferguson, A. (2016). Women and education: Qualifications, skills, and technology. *Women in Canada: A gender-based statistical report.* Ottawa, ON: Statistics Canada. Catalogue No. 89-503-X.

this world, and that they *must* be tough, strong, and independent. Girls are learning passivity, silence, and dependence, but at the same time, they are learning that they can rely on others when they face difficulties in life.

The gendering of education first appears with young children but is not limited to the lives of children and adolescents. The gendering of postsecondary studies is also evident in the areas of study that women and men pursue.

Monkey Business Images/Shutterstock

Subtle differences in the treatment of male and female students begin in early education but continue in the postsecondary environment as well.

In most countries in the world, women are overrepresented in the humanities and social sciences, whereas men are overrepresented in "STEM" programs (i.e., science, technology, engineering, and mathematics) (Ferguson, 2016). In Canada, among younger cohorts (ages 25 to 34), 61 percent of university graduates from STEM programs are male, whereas 66 percent of graduates from non-STEM programs are female (Ferguson, 2016). In recent decades, we have seen some shifts in areas of postsecondary study, primarily in terms of women entering male-dominated areas of study (e.g., law, medicine, science). Despite these shifts, gender segregation in postsecondary education continues to be the norm rather than the exception. In exploring the reasons why, research tends to focus on the underrepresentation of women in STEM programs rather than the underrepresentation of males in the humanities and social sciences. Some research posits that this pattern is due to a lack of female interest in math, which in large part is influenced by gender/math stereotypes harboured by the adults in children's lives (Gunderson et al., 2012). Many parents and teachers continue to perceive their sons or their male students as inherently more logical and skilled at math than their daughters or their female students. These stereotypes are maintained even in the face of contradictory evidence, such as when boys and girls are performing equally well in math or when girls are performing better. Gender/math stereotypes are also maintained in the explanations parents offer for their children's success in math; male success in math is explained in terms of natural mathematical abilities, whereas female success is explained in terms of effort. Over time, girls who interact with adults who hold these stereotypes may show a declining interest in math, whereas boys' interest in math is facilitated. Early research suggested that children's degree of interest in math would then be associated with their mathematical performance. In other words, because girls were less interested in math, they would put less effort into their math classes and thereby attain lower marks in math (Barone, 2011; Gunderson et al., 2012). However, research finds that males with *lower* levels of mathematical ability in secondary school (as measured by standardized tests) are still more likely to enroll in STEM programs in university than females with *higher* levels of ability (Ferguson, 2016).

One analysis of first-year university students found that stereotypes are central to the segregation of males in science programs and females in the social sciences and humanities (Lane, Goh, & Driver-Linn, 2012). Stereotypes can take two forms—explicit and implicit. *Explicit* stereotypes are those that people are consciously aware of holding, whereas *implicit* stereotypes are those that people are not conscious of. Because implicit stereotypes operate at a subconscious level, they remain outside an individual's control and thus may have an even greater impact. Implicit stereotypes are measured by the Implicit Association Test (IAT), where an individual must quickly group words together as they flash on a computer screen; people have much faster reaction times when a series of words reflects a stereotype. Lane and colleagues (2012) found that those students who held implicit stereotypes associating males with science and females with the social sciences and humanities tended to enroll in programs of study accordingly. These researchers went a step further, pointing out that implicit stereotypes also account for gender segregation across the various fields of study that exist within each of the sciences and social sciences/humanities. That is, within the sciences, male and female students tend to be segregated in different fields of study; for example, males are overrepresented in engineering and computer science, and females are overrepresented in biology and nursing. The same is true of the social sciences/humanities; for instance, males are overrepresented in economics, and females are overrepresented in psychology. Lane and colleagues proposed that there is not just a gendered "science/humanities" divide in programs of study but also a "care/technical" divide. Students who hold implicit attitudes associating females with caring and people skills and males with technical prowess are more likely to enroll in fields of study in a way that maintains gender segregation.

Why does segregation in programs of study matter? After all, society needs economists *and* psychologists, engineers, *and* nurses. Gender segregation in programs of study matters because it emerges from and reinforces broader stereotypes—stereotypes that maintain elite discourses of sex, gender, and sexuality and their consequences. Moreover, there are direct implications for areas of study. Some areas of study are more directly "marketable," meaning that employment directly related to one's area of study may be more certain (e.g., an engineering degree compared to an art history degree). Second, occupations related to some areas of study are more highly paid than others (Ferguson, 2016; Moyser, 2017).

TIME TO REVIEW

- How do children say their lives would be different if they woke up as another sex?
- In what ways are girls and boys treated differently in the classroom? What do they learn from the official and hidden curricula?
- How and why are postsecondary studies gendered?

LO4 DIFFERENT OCCUPATIONAL EXPERIENCES

Arising, in part, from different areas of postsecondary study are divergent occupational experiences. In the mid-20th century, the male breadwinner and female homemaker predominated. However, beginning in the 1960s, women began moving into the labour force in large numbers. Several forces contributed to this social change. Broader economic shifts caused inflation to rise more rapidly than people's wages. This meant that it was increasingly difficult for families to survive on only one income. In addition, what was known as the "second wave" of the women's movement emerged. The "first wave" of feminism in the early 20th century focused on women obtaining the right to vote and being legally declared "persons" (rather than the property of their fathers or husbands). The second wave emphasized other aspects of "equality," such as occupational and economic equality. Within this broader context of economic changes and the women's movement, more and more women became breadwinners

FIGURE 7.3

Labour Force Participation by Sex (Ages 25 to 54), 1950, 1983, and 2015

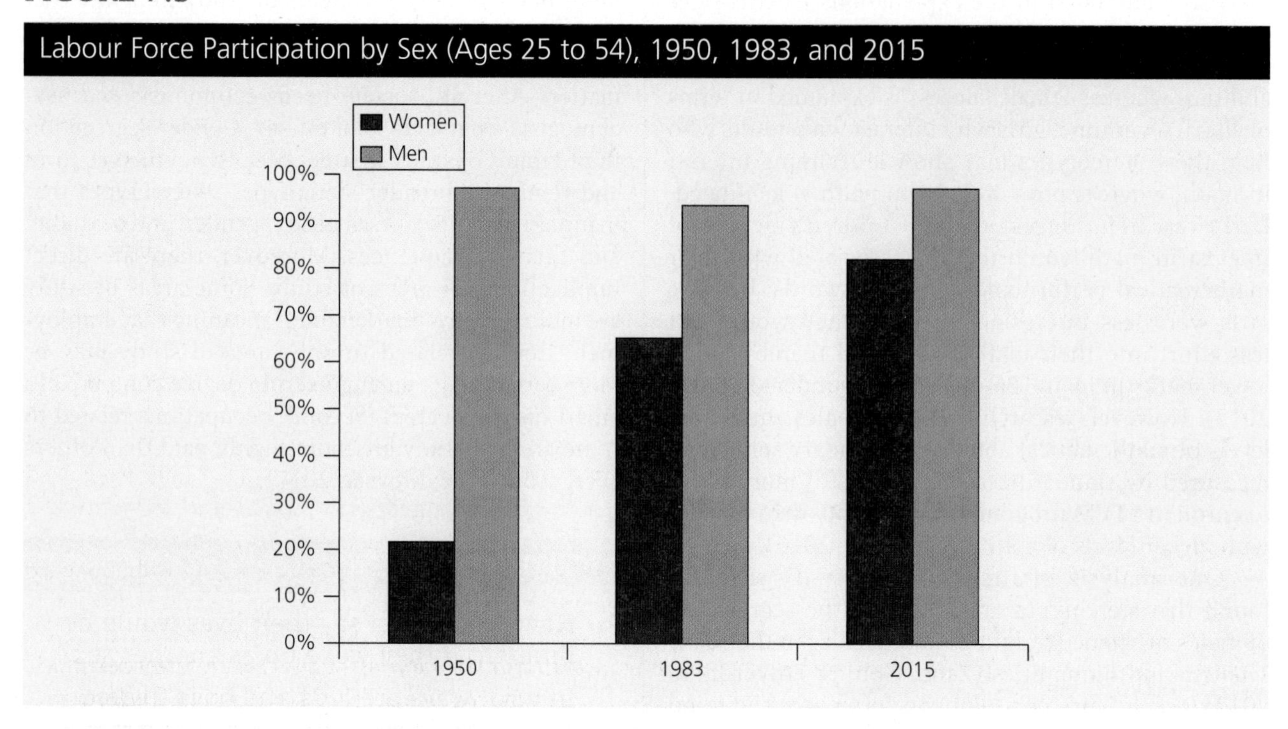

Source: Adapted from Moyser, M. (2017). Women and paid work. *Women in Canada: A gender-based statistical report.* Ottawa, ON: Statistics Canada. Catalogue No. 89-503-X.

as well. By 2014, 82 percent of Canadian women of "prime" working age (i.e., 25 to 54) were participating in the labour force; in contrast, 91 percent of men were labour force participants (see *Figure 7.3*). Although the majority of women are in the labour force, a greater proportion of women than men are employed part-time (18 percent of women, 6 percent of men). This translates into lower pay and no benefits for women (Moyser, 2017).

Uppal and LaRochelle-Côté (2014) analyzed patterns of male and female employment in Canada for those ages 25 to 34. People in this age group have completed any postsecondary education most recently and are embarking on their careers; thus, they are considered predictive of future trends in occupational segregation. Here we see that much like in postsecondary education, women and men are segregated into different occupations. The three most common occupations for female university graduates were elementary or kindergarten teacher, registered nurse, and secondary school teacher (in that order). The three most common occupations for male university graduates were computer programmer or interactive media developer, financial auditor/accountant, and secondary school teacher.

Women show more segregation in their occupational choices overall. When comparing women and men at all levels of education, 41 percent of women are employed in the top three female-dominated industries: health care and social assistance (where 82 percent of workers are female); educational services (where 69 percent of workers are female); and accommodation and food services (where 59 percent of workers are female). In contrast, only 18 percent of men are employed in the top three male-dominated industries: construction (where 88 percent of workers are male); forestry, fishing, mining, oil/gas extraction, and quarrying (where 81 percent of workers are male); and utilities (where 78 percent of workers are male) (Moyser, 2017).

Over the past few decades, there has been some decline in occupational sex segregation, with a growing number of people choosing to enter nontraditional occupations. Between 1991 and 2011, there were significant gains in the number of women entering some traditionally male occupations, including civil engineering and law enforcement (Uppal and LaRochelle-Côté, 2014). In fact, most of these shifts have been the result of women entering male-dominated fields rather than the reverse. In part, this is because occupations in male-dominated fields tend to be higher paid and feature more independence and authority; women entering those occupations have something to gain, whereas men entering female-dominated occupations would have something to lose (Furr, 2002).

Although women have more freedom than men to enter nontraditional careers, they are less likely to rise to the top of their fields and hold positions of authority, a phenomenon known as the **glass ceiling**. In Canada, only 6 percent of employed women serve in management positions (compared to 10 percent of employed men), and women comprise only 19 percent of members on the boards of the largest publicly listed companies (Organisation for Economic Co-operation and Development, n.d.). Women who enter nontraditional careers are also at risk of experiencing workplace harassment, which can range from derogatory comments about their ability based on their gender, to unwanted attempts to establish romantic relationships, to sexual assault. For example, in 2013, two female RCMP officers initiated a class action lawsuit against the RCMP, alleging chronic harassment—sexual propositioning, derogatory comments about ability, differential accommodations to male and female officers, and more. In 2017, a settlement was reached that awarded the more than 1,000 claimants up to $220,000 each (Perkel, 2017).

Although women continue to encounter the glass ceiling in nontraditional careers, the reverse is true for men. Rather than encountering a glass ceiling, they benefit from a **glass escalator**, whereby they are more likely to attain positions of authority or leadership (Moyser, 2017, p. 30).

The occupational segregation of men and women and the differential likelihood of holding positions of authority together account in part for yet another way in which one's life is affected by virtue of having been born female or male—different economic experiences.

LO5 DIFFERENT ECONOMIC EXPERIENCES

When looking at the gendering of economic experiences, what stands out the most is the ratio of female-to-male earnings. Ever since data were first collected on this issue in 1967, women's earnings have been only a fraction of men's. In terms of annual income for full-year, full-time workers, the earnings differential is 78 percent—for every dollar that men earn, women earn 78 cents (Ferguson, 2016). Although the earnings differential has improved over time, women are still earning less money than men, regardless of whether we look at full-time, part-time, permanent, temporary, unionized, or nonunionized work (Ferguson, 2016; Moyser, 2017).

What accounts for this ongoing wage gap? In part, it emerges from sex segregation in areas of postsecondary study and subsequent career choices. Male-dominated areas tend to be associated with higher wages. A greater proportion of women are employed in jobs that are lower paid and lower in status (e.g., clerical, part-time, temporary). They are also less likely to enter supervisory and management positions, especially senior management positions, which receive greater remuneration. In addition, on average, women work fewer hours per day in paid employment than men (Moyser, 2017) and are more likely to have temporary absences from the labour force in response to childbirth and childrearing. However, educational choices and career patterns account for less than half of the earnings differential, which means that much of the gap is unexplained and open to alternative explanations (Frenette & Coulombe, 2007). Some explanations emphasize the devaluation of "women's work," whereby, historically, the types of work that women were restricted to were less respected and thus received lower remuneration. Furthermore, it was presumed that women's incomes were "peripheral" to family life; whereas a man's income had to be sufficient to support a family, a woman's income was thought to be only for the little extras. Those early wages served as the foundation for subsequent wage increases over the decades, and in this way, income differentials between men and women were maintained. Other explanations highlight discrimination within the labour force, where assumptions about the way that family obligations will affect women's job commitment and career patterns influence hiring and promotion practices (Moyser, 2017). And indeed, the different educational, occupational, and economic experiences of women and men are intertwined with their family experiences.

TIME TO REVIEW

- Why did many women begin moving into the labour force in the 1960s?
- What is the nature of occupational sex segregation in society?
- What is the earnings differential or wage gap when comparing women and men, and why does it exist?

LO6 DIFFERENT FAMILY EXPERIENCES

The significance of sex and gender within families begins before people are even born. The question of whether the child

Glass ceiling: Intangible barriers that prevent women from attaining positions of authority or leadership.

Glass escalator: Intangible factors that enable men to attain positions of authority or leadership.

will be a boy or a girl is at the forefront of people's minds, and at birth, the sex of the child is the very first news that parents receive—in fact, more and more expectant parents find the sex of the child to be so important that they request that information while ultrasonography is being performed during pregnancy. Once a child is born, gendered perceptions and treatment begin almost immediately, setting the stage for the gendering that individuals will later experience educationally, occupationally, and economically. Classic studies from the 1960s and 1970s illustrate ways that sex serves as a master status from early infancy. Within 24 hours of birth, parents of newborn girls described them as "delicate" and "weak," whereas parents of boys referred to them as "strong" and "alert" (Rubin, Provenzano, & Lurra, 1974), even though objective measures revealed no significant differences in weight, length, muscle tone, reflexes, or heart rate. In another study, infants were shown an unfamiliar toy while adults observed their reactions. Adults who thought they were observing a boy described his reaction to the strange toy as "pleasure" or "excitement"; in contrast, those who thought they were observing a girl (although they were, in fact, observing the very same infant) identified her reaction as "fearful" (Condrey & Condrey, 1976).

Master statuses not only influence attitudes but also behaviour, such that parents subsequently treat their sons and daughters differently. Goldberg and Lewis (1969) found that when mothers brought their six-month-old infants into a child observation lab, mothers of girls kept their infants closer and spoke with them more often than did mothers of boys. When mothers then brought their children in seven months later, the room was set up in an interesting way. A waist-high barrier divided the room *almost* completely in half; there was a small gap at one end of the barrier that allowed people to move from one side of the room to the other. The toddlers were placed on one side of the barrier and the mothers on the other side; the mothers then waved a toy enthusiastically in order to capture their children's attention. Being separated from their mothers and the toy resulted in many of the toddlers becoming upset. When the little girls started to cry, mothers were likely to pick them up and bring them to the other side. In contrast, the little boys were encouraged to make their way to the gap at the end of the barrier and find their own way to the other side.

Almost half a century later, research continues to find differential treatment of girls and boys by parents. As you will learn in the chapter on socialization, parents interact with their daughters more, offer them more comfort, and assist them in difficult situations (Clearfield & Nelson, 2006). Parents also tolerate more noise, physical activity, and exploration in boys than in girls. For instance, Garner and Grazian (2016) observed families who were spending the day at a local zoo. They found that parents tended to discipline their daughters for talking loudly, jumping up and down, and climbing on fences or large rocks. In contrast, not only were sons not disciplined for these same activities, but parents would even memorialize those moments in photos. Gender socialization occurred in more subtle ways at the zoo as well, such as by gendering the animals. Parents talked about small, quiet, especially cute, or caretaking animals as female and larger, active, assertive animals as males (when, in fact, in many cases, the animals in a specific display were all of the same sex). In the context of families, children are also exposed to gender-stereotyped colours in their clothing and bedroom decor and are provided with gender-stereotyped toys. Thus, patterns found in classrooms (Sadker et al., 2009) are also found in families.

pumpuija/Shutterstock

Is this toy just as likely to be found in a little boy's bedroom as a little girl's bedroom?

Although socialization into traditional gender roles remains common in contemporary society, a growing number of parents are stepping outside of these constraints. Parents who are LGBTQ or gender non-conforming in other ways are especially likely to offer their children a "gender buffet" by offering them a wider range of toys, clothing options, and room decor (Averett, 2016, p. 198). However, they often face considerable resistance from outside the family, in the form of questions, staring, dirty looks, and overt criticism (Averett, 2016). Kathy Witterick and David Stocker experienced this resistance firsthand in 2011, when they announced to friends and family that they would not reveal the sex of their recently-born child, named Storm. Instead, they would offer Storm a gender buffet and allow the child to form an independent gender identity—much as they did with their other children. In the age of social media, their decision quickly became a topic of conversation around the world. Although they encountered a great deal of support, some friends and family members distanced themselves, and strangers heavily criticized them, both online and in person. At the age of five, Storm announced that she identified as female, and would like to be referred to as "she" and "her." One of Storm's siblings identifies as a transgender female, while the other identifies as gender non-binary and prefers to be referred to as "they" or "them" (much like their parents) (Botelho-Urbanski, 2016).

In some cases, even the most supportive parents may face internal struggles when raising a child who is gender non-conforming. Interviews with parents of transgender children reveal that their relational identities as parents are often embedded within elite discourses of sex and gender (Field & Mattson, 2016). When their child was born a specific sex, it created expectations about what the future would hold—parents looked forward to having certain types of relationships with their sons, and other types with their daughters. Thus, when their child identified as transgender, some parents experienced a sense of loss or sadness about that imagined future never coming to fruition. Those feelings were magnified in those cases where their child elected to undergo medical treatment (e.g., hormone therapy) to change their bodies to better correspond to their identities.

Gendered experiences in families begin with childhood socialization and continue through to adulthood, with gendered differences in the household division of labour. Historically, the male breadwinner–female homemaker model meant that tasks associated with paid labour were the realm of men, whereas those associated with unpaid domestic labour were the realm of women. However, as many women moved into the labour force in the 1960s, patterns in domestic labour continued. Although women were employed in the labour force, they continued to carry the bulk of the responsibility for tasks at home. This led Arlie Hochschild and Anne Machung (1989) to conceptualize the *second shift*, wherein women would put in a full day in the workplace and then come home and have to put in another "shift" of domestic labour. Women tended to do routine, indoor tasks (such as laundry, housecleaning, and cooking), whereas men were likely to do less frequent outdoor tasks, such as mowing the lawn and vehicle maintenance. Today, a survey of 19 countries finds that the gender gap in domestic labour has declined over the past several decades but has not disappeared (Altintas & Sullivan, 2016). We can see that trend by looking more closely at Canadian patterns (see *Table 7.1*). In 1971, women were spending two and a half more hours per day than men on housework, but by 2010, that had declined to one extra hour per day (Altintas & Sullivan, 2016).

Younger cohorts are more likely to express egalitarian ideals about domestic labour. Nonetheless, actual practices do not always meet those ideals. Egalitarian practices are more likely when young women have economic power, such that middle-class women are better able to work toward those ideals compared to working-class women (Miller & Carlsen, 2016). Furthermore, even among more egalitarian couples, the gender gap in domestic labour tends to increase with the birth of a couple's first child (Yavorsky, Dush, & Schoppe-Sullivan, 2015).

In an era in which dual-income families are normative, a small proportion draw upon domestic outsourcing to ease the burden of the second shift. The most common forms of domestic outsourcing are

TABLE 7.1

Time Spent on Housework (Minutes/Day), 1971–2010

Year	Women	Men	Gender Gap
1971	194	34	160
1986	147	37	110
1992	149	43	106
1998	137	51	86
2005	118	51	67
2010	119	55	64

Adapted from: Altintas, E., & Sullivan O. (2016). Fifty years of change updated: Cross-national gender convergences in housework. *Demographic Research, 35*(16), 455–470.

eating in restaurants or purchasing takeout meals (an average of four to five times over a two-week period) and taking laundry to a dry cleaner or laundry service (12 percent of families). Only 8 to 10 percent of families make use of hired help (i.e., hiring someone to clean the house or do the yard work) (Craig & Baxter, 2016). Domestic outsourcing reduces the time spent on household labour for both women and men but does not decrease the gender gap. In fact, men are more likely to benefit from hired help, in that it is more common to hire someone to do the yard work, such as mowing the lawn (a traditionally male task), than to clean the house (a traditionally female task) (Craig & Baxter, 2016).

The gendered nature of family experiences in adulthood interacts with occupational and economic experiences. Women with higher incomes tend to assume responsibility for a smaller proportion of household tasks compared to women with lower incomes. For every extra $10,000 per year a woman earns (above the average female income), she does four hours less housework each week (Carlson & Lynch, 2017). In the past, research found that women's household responsibilities had a negative impact on their earnings; because of family responsibilities, women were more likely to choose jobs with fewer hours and/or greater flexibility, both of which typically meant lower earnings (Zhang, 2009). New methodologies suggest that this may not be the case. Carlson and Lynch (2017) find that although women with higher incomes do less housework, the amount of housework women do does not result in lower earnings. However, the time that men spend on household responsibilities is associated with lower earnings. Every 10 hours per week that men spend on household responsibilities *is* associated with an average of $17,000 less in earnings.

Is domestic labour allocated more equally among LGBTQ couples, where elite discourses of sex, gender, and sexuality are already being challenged? In interviews with 30 LGBTQ couples, Kelly and Hauck (2015) found that, in fact, only eight couples said that their household division of labour is egalitarian. But rather than the second shift being allocated on the basis of gender, among these couples, it is determined by a combination of personal preferences, time availability, and income (where the lower income earner tends to bear responsibility for more of the second shift).

To some extent, the gendering of educational, occupational, economic, and family experiences has declined in recent years (see *Sociology in My Life*). However, the process is uneven for different social groups, and some scholars suggest that the trend has "stalled" (Guppy & Luongo, 2015, p. 241). Why do gendered experiences continue to exist?

YOUR SOCIOLOGICAL TOOLKIT

SOCIOLOGY IN MY LIFE

THE IMPACT OF GENDERED NORMS IN MY LIFE

Simply by virtue of having been born a particular sex, our lives are affected in myriad ways, from seemingly insignificant differences, such as the side our shirts button on, to more profound inequalities, such as higher or lower earnings. From the moment we are born, our parents are likely to perceive and then treat us in certain ways. When we enter the school system, that pattern continues, despite the best intentions of teachers. We develop, are reinforced (or punished) for particular interests, and acquire some skills more than others. We are likely to pursue certain postsecondary paths, which then influence the occupations we pursue. In heteronormative families, being male or female leads to distinctive roles within the family, associated with certain responsibilities; this then influences our career trajectories. The occupations we pursue, and our career trajectories and other "unexplained" phenomena (e.g., devaluation or discrimination), then affect our economic experiences.

Think Outside the Box: In what ways have your educational, occupational, economic, and family experiences been influenced by gendered norms and assumptions?

YOUR SOCIOLOGICAL TOOLKIT
SOCIOLOGY IN THEORY

LO7 SOCIOLOGY IN THEORY

The earliest sociological theories—functionalism and conflict theories—addressed the nature of gendered experiences, primarily in the context of families. Over time, other sociological perspectives came to address gender as well—interactionist, feminist, and postmodern.

FUNCTIONALIST THEORIES

Talcott Parsons (1902–1979) is best known for addressing gender role differentiation and the household division of labour from a functionalist perspective (Parsons, 1954; Parsons & Bales, 1955). He described two key functions of the family—the socialization of children and the stabilization of adult personalities—that are important for the well-being of both individuals and society. Gendered task differentiation is one ways these functions are fulfilled.

Writing in the mid-20th century, Parsons (1954) proposed that males are responsible for *instrumental* tasks that connect the family to the outside world (e.g., financial support), whereas females are responsible for the *expressive* tasks necessary for the internal world of the family (e.g., nurturing children). The father is the technical expert and executive; the mother is the expressive leader. As long as these tasks are differentiated by gender, families can ensure that everything that needs to get done will get done; if tasks were not differentiated on this basis, time would be wasted, with each family member trying to figure out what he or she should be doing. Of course, in the 21st century, parents increasingly share instrumental and expressive tasks, and this change has led to corresponding changes in social policy (see *Critical Thinking in Action*).

CONFLICT THEORIES

Early conflict theories traced gender inequality to capitalist economic systems. Friedrich Engels (1884/1972), a colleague of Karl Marx, suggested that the transition from feudalism to capitalism resulted in patriarchy. Just as male workers were subordinated by their employers, women and children were subordinated by adult men; children gained power as they grew up (or at least male children did), but women remained subordinated throughout their lives. Engels contended that female subordination in families would end if women entered paid employment. Today, conflict theories are commonly used

YOUR SOCIOLOGICAL TOOLKIT

CRITICAL THINKING IN ACTION

PARENTAL LEAVE BENEFITS

As women began entering the workforce en masse in the latter half of the 20th century, social policy changed to accommodate the different day-to-day realities of Canadian families. In 1971, women who met eligibility requirements (in terms of the number of paid work hours they had in the past year) were able to claim up to 15 weeks of maternity leave through Unemployment Insurance (now known as Employment Insurance) upon the birth of a child. In recognition of the greater prevalence of shared parenting in families and to encourage such sharing, in 1990, the federal Parental Benefits Program included an additional 10 weeks of parental leave that could be utilized by either parent (or shared). In 2000, there were further changes to the Parental Benefits Program. Fifteen weeks of maternity leave are now followed by 35 weeks of parental leave that can be shared between parents (Government of Canada, 2016).

Even though social policy enables fathers to take parental leave, only a minority actually do so. In 2013, only 12 percent of fathers (outside Quebec) of newborn or newly adopted children intended to take or took parental leave; the average length of leave was 16 weeks. This stands in contrast to 90 percent of mothers, who take an average leave of 32 weeks (Lero, 2015).

Think Outside the Box: Drawing upon what you have learned about elite discourses of sex and gender and the differential educational, occupational, and economic experiences of males and females, what would have to change in society for more fathers to take advantage of the parental leave they are entitled to?

YOUR SOCIOLOGICAL TOOLKIT

SOCIOLOGY IN PRACTICE

SUPPORTING GENDER NONCONFORMITY WITH BILL C-16

Conflict theorists propose that the law emerges not from consensus but from conflict and serves the interests of dominant groups. Thus, emancipating subordinated groups often means advocating for changes in legislation. Due to the efforts of LGBTQ activist groups, in 2017, Bill C-16 (An Act to amend the Canadian Human Rights Act and the Criminal Code) became law, adding legal protections on the basis of gender identity and expression. The attorney general of Canada released a statement saying, "The purpose of this legislation is to ensure that everyone can live according to their gender identity and express their gender as they choose. It will protect people from discrimination, hate propaganda and hate crime" (Heidenreich, 2017).

Think Outside the Box: What other instances are you aware of where marginalized groups were able to successfully advocate for changes in the law?

in analyses of gendered violence, especially within intimate relationships. In the chapter on families, you will learn more about the role that competition for resources and power plays in intimate violence. Arising from their emancipatory interest, conflict theories are also used to analyze social movements and social change regarding sex, gender, and sexualities (see *Sociology in Practice*).

INTERACTIONIST THEORIES

Interactionist theories focus on how we come to *understand* gender and develop our own gender identities. Through our interactions with significant others, our development of a sense of the generalized other, and the power of the looking-glass self, we come to know that we are "female" or "male." Through childhood experiences in our families and our classrooms, we come to understand that males and females are supposed to act in certain ways, develop particular interests, enter specific types of occupations, and hold certain roles within families. On the basis of this knowledge, we then "do" gender in our everyday lives (West & Zimmerman, 1987).

Erving Goffman (1979) conducted a classic analysis of gender differentiation from an interactionist perspective. He explored how gender differentiation is reproduced in social interactions through *gender displays*. Gender displays include everything from putting on makeup and selecting clothes to wear, to the positions in which we place our bodies, to our facial expressions, to the "appropriate" use of separate public restrooms for men and women. Gender displays are based on what Goffman called *codes of gender*—the norms governing acceptable appearances and behaviours for males and females. These codes of gender rest on and reinforce dualisms of sex, gender, and sexualities. They also maintain male dominance and independence and female passivity and subordination. Goffman stated that it was important to draw attention to the nature of these hidden codes so that individuals could make a conscious decision about whether to accept or reject them in their own gender displays.

FEMINIST THEORIES

As you recall from previous chapters, feminist theories are characterized by considerable diversity. We can see an example of the range of feminist theorizing by contrasting two well-known (and somewhat controversial) scholars: one argues that we must embrace gender differences, whereas the other claims that we must seek to create a genderless society. Germaine Greer (2007), a prominent feminist voice for almost half a century, argues that the women's movement has gone astray. She criticizes it for emphasizing "equality," which in practice has led to women trying to become like men. Male characteristics and experiences are perceived as the ideal, and female characteristics and experiences are to be left behind. Instead of equality, she argues that women must attain "liberation," wherein they become free to define themselves and their aspirations from a distinctly female perspective. In contrast, Sheila Jeffreys (2014) argues for moving beyond dualisms of sex and gender. She contends that the notion of "transgender" does not move beyond those dualisms but instead reinforces them and maintains notions of essential differences between the sexes. That is, the need to label individuals who do not conform to the discourses that equate male bodies with masculinity and female bodies with femininity means that those discourses maintain their power in society. Jeffreys calls for a *post-gender* society, in which a person whose body is of a particular sex would be able to adopt any appearance, attitude, behaviour, or characteristic and no longer have a distinctive label attached.

Going beyond these two specific scholars, the range of feminist theorizing is even greater (Nelson, 2010). *Liberal feminist theories* claim that the inequalities in education, occupation, economics, and families are the result of differential opportunities. By reducing forces that restrict opportunities (e.g., stereotyping, discrimination, certain policies, and organizational practices), both women and men will be able to pursue life trajectories that fit their interests and skills as *individuals* rather than as *sexes*, and inequalities will be reduced. *Marxist feminism* ties the oppression of women to capitalism; overthrowing capitalism and eliminating private property would end their subordination and the different educational, occupational, economic, and family experiences that women and men currently have. *Cultural feminism* supports dualistic assumptions about sex and gender and posits that men and women *are* inherently different; women are peaceful, nurturing, and more in touch with nature, whereas men are more aggressive and competitive. Those qualities cannot change—what *can* change is that female abilities and values are given venues for expression, such as through women-centred activities and organizations.

A variety of racially based feminist theories argue that we can't speak of "women" as a general category—that the educational, occupational, economic, and family experiences of women of different races, ethnic groups, and classes have very little in common with one another. Instead, we must recognize **intersectionality**, the way that our individual array of multiple identities (e.g., based on sex, gender, race, and social class) combines to create a distinctive whole (Crenshaw, 1989)—much like the way that multiple roads intersect with each other at a complex freeway interchange. For instance, the everyday experiences of a black, working-class, transgender woman will be very different from those of a white, middle-class, cisgender woman (or even a black, middle-class, transgender woman, for that matter). Structured social inequalities that are based on sex, gender, race, or social class form intersecting systems of oppression—what is known as a **matrix of domination** (Collins & Bilge, 2016).

Ingus Kruklitis/Shutterstock

Much like a complex highway interchange, our individual array of multiple identities intersect to create a cohesive whole.

Postcolonial feminism also recognizes the diverse experiences of different groups of woman, specifically drawing attention to the effects of racism and colonization on women in non-Western cultures. It proposes that the educational, occupational, economic, and family experiences of women living in societies that were colonized are distinct from those of women living in the colonizing cultures. Furthermore, the activities and expressions traditional to women in non-Western cultures, and which might be labelled as oppressive by women in Western cultures (such as wearing a hijab), may be considered by non-Western women to be acts of resistance to colonial discourses (Ali, 2007; Chatterjee, 2016).

Indigenous feminism in Canada, the United States, and Australia points out that colonization is not only a racist project, but also a patriarchal one (Anderson, 2001; Suzack, Huhndorf, Perreault, & Barman, 2011). Gender issues are intertwined with land, treaty, and Indigenous cultural practices. As such the colonialist project required that Indigenous women be disempowered. For Indigenous peoples, colonialism is not relegated to the past, but continues to the present day. Ongoing colonialism is illustrated in cases where governments enact legislation that violates treaty agreements or erodes Indigenous sovereignty in other ways, as well as in the overrepresentation of missing and murdered Indigenous women in Canada. Indigenous feminists are critical of mainstream feminism as a movement for privileged, white women. For example, while "first-wave" feminist efforts achieved voting rights for some groups of women in Canada in 1918, Indigenous women would not have the right to vote for another half century.

Intersectionality: The way in which our individual array of multiple identities (e.g., based on sex, gender, race, and social class) combines to create a distinctive whole.

Matrix of domination: Intersecting systems of oppression in society, such as those based on sex, gender, race, or social class.

Similarly, at the same time as "second-wave" feminism advocated for gender equality, large numbers of Indigenous girls were being psychologically, physically, sexually, and culturally abused in residential schools (which you will learn more about in the chapter on race and ethnicity). For Indigenous feminists, gender equality is intertwined with sovereignty for Indigenous peoples overall.

POSTMODERN THEORIES

Postmodern theories question the very notion of gender itself. In the postmodern world, a cohesive gender "identity" does not exist (Butler, 1990). Gender is not an internal essence that individuals have but rather is a set of repeated behaviours. The only way to understand ourselves is by observing our own actions. In other words, we do not *have* a gender; instead, we *do* gender. This is much like the way very young children believe that *because* they are wearing certain clothes, they are a girl or a boy; if, for example, you put a dress on a little boy, he may think that you are not dressing him *like* a girl but rather are changing him *into* a girl (Kerr & Multon, 2015). The performativity of gender is not a matter of individual choice but rather emerges from elite discourses that construct only certain forms of gender as possible.

How do we explain the different educational, occupational, economic, and family experiences of women and men? Sociological theorizing shows us that there is no single explanation. Functionalist theories emphasize the ways that traditional gender roles are functional for individuals, their families, and society. Conflict theories focus on the forms power takes and how it subordinates women. Interactionist theories say that gendered experiences emerge from our understandings of sex and gender, developed through our interactions with others. Diverse feminist theories explain these differential experiences in a variety of ways, ranging from unequal opportunities, to the devaluation of the female "essence," to drawing attention to the different experiences of diverse groups of women. Postmodern theories deny the possibility of a gender identity and question whether we can even speak of a cohesive category of "gender."

TIME TO REVIEW

- What do classic and contemporary studies tell us about the ways parents perceive and treat their sons and daughters differently?
- In what ways do the family experiences of men and women differ in adulthood?
- How are family experiences intertwined with gendered educational, occupational, and economic experiences?
- How do functionalist, conflict, interactionist, feminist, and postmodern theories address gender and gender inequality?

CHAPTER SUMMARY

LO1 Describe the elite discourses that equate sex, gender, and sexuality.

These discourses are based on dualisms: male/female; masculine/feminine; heterosexual/homosexual. These discourses also equate the three, in that to be male is presumed to be both masculine and attracted to women; similarly, to be female is presumed to be both feminine and attracted to men.

LO2 Explain the ways in which sex, gender, and sexuality are socially constructed.

When we question elite discourses, we see that sex, gender, and sexuality are socially constructed. Cross-cultural research has clearly established that norms governing gender vary across cultures and over time. Even sex is socially constructed; rather than discrete categories of female/male, it is more accurate to speak of a sex spectrum.

LO3 Discuss the different educational experiences of males and females in childhood and in postsecondary studies.

Through subtle and often unintended behaviours in the classroom, boys are drawn to the front, whereas girls (as well as nontraditional boys) fade into the background. Boys learn independence and problem solving, whereas girls learn passivity and silence. Areas of postsecondary studies become gender segregated.

LO4 Describe the occupational sex segregation within the labour force.

Educational segregation contributes to occupational segregation. Females tend to be overrepresented in lower-status, lower-paying, part-time, and temporary work.

LO5 Discuss the ways that economic experiences are gendered and the reasons why.

Men continue to earn more money than women. Explanations include the consequences of educational and occupational segregation, a devaluation of women's work that has historical origins, and discrimination based on assumptions about women's family obligations.

LO6 Identify the gendered nature of family life for children and adults.

Boys and girls continue to be treated differently in families in terms of clothing, toys, room décor, and level of supervision. Among adults, although the gender gap in the household division of labour has declined over the last few decades, it has not disappeared.

LO7 Outline the various sociological theories that address gender.

Functionalist theories address the functional role of gender-differentiated tasks. Conflict theories emphasize the role of power in creating patterns of subordination. Interactionist theories explore the ways we come to understand gender through our interactions with others. Feminist theories explain gender differentiation in variety ways, ranging from unequal opportunities to an emphasis on the diverse experiences of women in different social groups (e.g., race, ethnicity, and social class). Postmodern theories question the very idea of gender.

RECOMMENDED RESOURCES

1. To learn more about the federal government's efforts to purge gays and lesbians from public service, see G. Kinsman and P. Gentile, *The Canadian War on Queers: National Security as Sexual Regulation* (Vancouver, BC: UBC Press, 2009).
2. To learn more about the National Inquiry into Missing and Murdered Indigenous Women and Girls, which was launched in September 2016, see http://www.mmiwg-ffada.ca/.
3. To hear the personal stories of 11 transgender Americans, see the HBO documentary *The Trans List*, directed by Timothy Greenfield-Sanders.

FOR FURTHER REFLECTION

1. What are the implications of different economic and family experiences in adulthood? For instance, why does it matter if a woman earns less money than her male partner? Why does it matter if he is spending more hours per day in paid employment while she is spending more hours per day in the unpaid labour associated with family life?
2. In what ways do the different types of theories that were presented either reflect dualisms of sex, gender, and sexuality or challenge them?
3. Return to the part of the chapter where children talk about how their lives would be different if they woke up as another sex. Were they correct in their assumptions given what research tells us about the differential outcomes for males and females based on sex?

ENDNOTE

1 Retrieved June 17, 2017, from brainquote.com.

CHAPTER

Race and Ethnicity: Defining Ourselves and Others

oneinchpunch/Shutterstock

After Zorro, people spoke Spanish to me for ages. I'm Welsh but that movie instantly gave me a new ethnicity.

(Catherine Zeta-Jones)[1]

LEARNING OBJECTIVES & OUTCOMES

After completing this chapter, students should be able to do the following:

LO1 Compare the concepts of ethnicity, race, racialization, visible minorities, and racialized groups.

LO2 Describe contemporary patterns of ethnicity in Canada.

LO3 List the three objectives of Canada's immigration policy, outline the types of individuals who enter the country on the basis of each of those objectives, and describe contemporary immigration patterns.

LO4 Describe the implications of ethnicity for families and for economic experiences.

LO5 Distinguish between dominant and minority groups and describe the forms of interaction that can take place between them.

LO6 Outline the three components of prejudice and describe the different forms that discrimination can take.

LO7 Discuss theories of prejudice and racialization, including social psychological theories, interactionist theories, conflict theories, and critical race theory.

AF archive/Alamy

Actress Catherine Zeta-Jones.

In 1998, actress Catherine Zeta-Jones starred in the movie The Mask of Zorro. As she played the role of a Spanish woman and has dark eyes, hair, and complexion, people assumed that she was Spanish; in fact, she is Welsh. Her statement on the previous page reflects how we identify ourselves on the basis of ethnicity but at the same time are identified by others; she identifies herself as Welsh, but others identified her as Spanish on the basis of her accent in the movie and aspects of her physical appearance. The ethnicity that is integrated into our self-concepts and the ethnic identities that others may ascribe to us have a variety of implications.

LO1 ETHNICITY, RACE, RACIALIZATION, AND VISIBLE MINORITIES

The term **ethnicity** comes from the Greek word *ethnos*, which refers to "people living and acting together in a manner that we might apply to a 'people' or a 'nation': a collectivity with a 'way of life'" (Jenkins, 2007, para. 1). It includes cultural characteristics such as language, religion, taste in food,

Ethnicity: Cultural characteristics such as language, religion, taste in food, shared descent, cultural traditions, and shared geographic locations.

shared descent, cultural traditions, and shared geographic locations. We can speak of **objective ethnicity** (also known as **ethnic origin**), which is your ancestral background, and **subjective ethnicity** (also known as **ethnic identity**), which is how you personally identify yourself. The two may or may not align (Lee et al., 2016). You may be of Lebanese ancestral descent but identify yourself as "Lebanese," "Lebanese Canadian," or "Canadian." Ethnicity is not fixed but rather is flexible and permeable. Your own ethnic identity may vary across contexts; when you are travelling outside Canada, you may identify yourself as "Canadian"; while at a family gathering, you identify yourself as "Japanese"; and when you are at school, you consider yourself "Japanese Canadian." Furthermore, there are no singular definitions of any particular ethnic group. To be "Polish," do you have to be born in Poland? Do all of your ancestors have to have come from Poland or only some of them (e.g., a grandfather)? Do you have to speak Polish? Do you have to enjoy eating pierogies? Must you include "Polish" as part of your subjective identity?

Objective ethnicity: The ethnic characteristics of your ancestors. Also known as ethnic origin.

Ethnic origin: The ethnic characteristics of your ancestors. Also known as objective ethnicity.

Subjective ethnicity: How you personally identify your ethnicity. Also known as ethnic identity.

Ethnic identity: How you personally identify your ethnicity. Also known as subjective ethnicity.

Race: A socially constructed category used to classify humankind according to such physical characteristics as skin colour, hair texture, and facial features.

Racialization: The process by which racial categories are constructed as different and unequal in ways that have social, economic, and political consequences.

Visible minorities: Persons, other than Aboriginal (i.e., Indigenous) persons, who are non-Caucasian in race or non-white in colour. Also known as racialized groups.

Racialized group: Persons, other than Aboriginal [i.e., Indigenous] persons, who are non-Caucasian in race or non-white in colour. Also known as visible minorities.

The concept of ethnicity is further complicated by its intersection with race. **Race** is "a socially constructed category used to classify humankind according to such physical characteristics as skin colour, hair texture, and facial features" (Galabuzi, 2006, p. 251). Thus, whereas ethnicity is based on cultural characteristics, race is based on physical ones. You may think of "races" as including white and black, or you may have heard people referring to themselves as brown. Historically, the concept of race has been traced by some scholars to the Biblical story of Ham, whose descendants (black Africans) were "condemned to servitude" because of Ham's sins (Arthur, 2007, para. 2). Others trace its origins to Britain's colonization of the Irish, beginning in the 13th century. In either case, the concept's origins are intertwined with power and social inequality in a process known as **racialization**, wherein "racial categories are constructed as different and unequal in ways that have social, economic, and political consequences" (Galabuzi, 2006, p. 251). With the Enlightenment, scientific thought elaborated on racial differences, and this furthered racialization at a global level by justifying the oppressive practices associated with European colonization.

Carolus Linnaeus (1707–1778) developed the first scientific classification of race. He stated that there were four races: Americanus, Europaeus, Asiaticus, and Africanus. Many other racial classification systems followed, some indicating as few as three races and others as many as 30. Although the concept of race is based on "physical characteristics ... that are seen as essential and permanent" (Arthur, 2007, para. 1), there are varying conceptions of how many "races" there are as well as precisely which physical characteristics are associated with particular races. Furthermore, all human beings are far more genetically similar than they are different, sharing the vast majority of their genes. There is no specific gene associated with "race"; there are only small genetic mutations that reflect the geographic mobility of early human beings as they expanded outward from Africa to other environments and climates. The variations in the genetic material of peoples found worldwide are subsets of the original genetic pool found on the African continent (see *Sociology Online*).

Ethnicity and race are intertwined (Arthur, 2007; Jenkins, 2007). Historically, scientific classifications of race sometimes went beyond physical characteristics to include cultural ones. Conversely, in society today, "race" is often integrated into conceptions of "ethnicity," just as when people based their evaluations of Catherine Zeta-Jones's ethnicity in part on her physical appearance (see *Sociology in My Life*). Race is also integrated into the definition of **visible minorities**. Visible minorities are defined by the Employment Equity Act (1995) as "persons, other than Aboriginal [i.e., Indigenous] persons, who are non-Caucasian in race or non-white in colour." Galabuzi (2006) argues for the term "racialized groups" as a replacement. He suggests that "visible minority" implies a permanent status that reinforces essentialist assumptions about race; in contrast, **racialized group** draws attention to the oppressive social and political practices that give rise to inequalities experienced by people of colour.

SOCIOLOGY ONLINE

"A FAMILY TREE FOR HUMANITY": THE GENOGRAPHIC PROJECT

In his TED talk "A Family Tree for Humanity," Dr. Spencer Wells explains how DNA works and discusses the genetic mutations that accompanied the geographic mobility of humans as part of evolution. Highlighting the social construction of race, he points out that all of the mitochondrial diversity in the world today (wherein mitochondrial DNA is passed down from mothers to children of all sexes) can be traced to a single woman (Mitochondrial Eve) approximately 200,000 years ago. Similarly, all of the Y-chromosome diversity (wherein Y-chromosomes are passed from fathers to their male children) can be traced to a single man (Y-Chromosome Adam) approximately 60,000 to 90,000 years ago. You can watch his TED talk at https://www.ted.com/.

Spencer Wells also established The Genographic Project in collaboration with the National Geographic Society. The project uses "cutting edge genetic and computational technologies to analyze historical patterns in DNA ... to better understand our shared genetic heritage" (National Geographic Society, 2017). Much like a crowdsourcing campaign, members of the public can participate by submitting a DNA sample using a kit they can purchase online; in return, they receive information based on the results of the analysis of their own DNA. The money spent on the kit contributes to the National Geographic Society's research fund. You can learn more about The Genographic Project at https://genographic.nationalgeographic.com/.

Canada, like Australia and the United States, is a nation that exists in its current form only because of Indigenous peoples as the original inhabitants of the land, several centuries of immigration, and the protection of refugees. Indigenous cultures have inhabited the land for at least 14,000 years, and oral histories claim "for time immemorial" (Blackstock, 2006–2007). When the first European explorers arrived, the geographically varied land space was already home to several distinct cultural regions. There were hundreds of tribes, languages, and dialects. Complex relationships existed among tribes, involving trade, cooperation, and/or conflict. With colonization, those nations were denied recognition; instead, through settlement by France and Britain and subsequent immigration from those nations and many others, the nation "Canada" was eventually created. With that history, ethnicity and racialization are concepts of particular relevance for Canadian society.

YOUR SOCIOLOGICAL TOOLKIT

SOCIOLOGY IN MY LIFE

MY ETHNICITY

Sometimes the term *ethnic* is mistakenly used to refer only to groups outside the dominant culture. In Canada, people who proclaim that they like eating "ethnic" foods may be thinking of bannock, chicken biryani, empanadas, hummus, and pho rather than roast beef or mashed potatoes. However, everybody has an ethnicity—both in terms of the objective ethnic origins of our ancestors and our subjective ethnic identities.

Think Outside the Box: How would you describe your ethnicity? What specific characteristics are you using to define your ethnicity?

TIME TO REVIEW

- What is ethnicity, and how do objective and subjective ethnicity differ?
- What are the origins of the concept of "race," and in what way is race socially constructed?
- What is the nature of the relationship between the concept of race and racialization?
- Who are visible minorities and racialized groups?

LO2 CONTEMPORARY ETHNIC PATTERNS

Hundreds of years of immigration have made Canada an ethnically diverse nation. People in Canada report more than 200 different ethnic origins (Morency, Caron-Malenfant, & MacIsaac, 2017). Around 4 percent of Canadian residents report an Aboriginal (i.e., Indigenous) identity; of these, 61 percent are First Nations, 32 percent are Métis, and 4 percent are Inuit (Morency et al., 2015). Nineteen percent of the population belong to a racialized group; of these, the majority are South Asian, Chinese, or black (Morency et al., 2017).

Most of the population (61 percent) are *at least* third generation in Canada, meaning that they, their parents, and at least one grandparent were born in Canada. Twenty-one percent of the population are foreign-born, having immigrated from another country. Those countries are increasingly likely to be non-European, with the top three source countries being the Philippines, China, and India (Morency et al., 2017). It is projected that by 2036, between 25 and 30 percent of Canada's population will be foreign-born and between 34 and 40 percent will be members of racialized groups. Almost half of Canadians will either be foreign-born or the first generation in their families to be born in Canada (Morency et al., 2017). Toronto is the city of choice for the largest proportion of immigrants and will continue to be. By 2036, between 77 and 81 percent of Torontonians will either be foreign-born or the first generation in their families to be born in Canada (Morency et al., 2017).

As a result of immigration, more than 200 languages are reported as *mother tongues and/or as languages spoken at home* (see Chapter 3). Due to longer histories of immigration to Canada, the most common mother tongues are English (58 percent of the population) and French (21 percent) (Houle & Corbeil, 2017). Seventeen percent of the Aboriginal (i.e., Indigenous) identity population speak an Indigenous

SOCIOLOGY IN WORDS

"ABORIGINAL" AND "INDIGENOUS"

The Constitution Act (1982) defines "Aboriginal peoples of Canada" as those who are Indian (subsequently referred to as First Nations), Inuit, or Métis. Because the term "Aboriginal" is entrenched in the constitution, many federal government policies and federally funded research (such as through Statistics Canada) continue to use the term "Aboriginal." Nevertheless, the term "Indigenous" is more appropriate, with important social, political, and legal implications. In 2015, Prime Minister Justin Trudeau changed the name of the ministry of Aboriginal Affairs and Northern Development to the Ministry of Indigenous and Northern Affairs. Similarly, on June 21, 2017, he announced that National Aboriginal Day would henceforth be National Indigenous Day. These were important symbolic steps.

In 2007, the *United Nations Declaration on the Rights of Indigenous Peoples* was passed. The declaration entrenches "the rights of Indigenous peoples to live in dignity, to maintain and strengthen their own institutions, cultures and traditions and to pursue their self-determined development, in keeping with their own needs and aspirations" (United Nations, 2007). When the member states of the United Nations voted on this resolution, there were 177 votes in favour and four opposed; those opposed were Canada, Australia, New Zealand, and the United States. Thus, using the term "Indigenous" instead of "Aboriginal" acknowledges Indigenous peoples' fundamental rights, as outlined in the *United Nations Declaration on the Rights of Indigenous Peoples* (Joseph, 2016).

language. They report more than 60 languages across 12 different language families. The most common Indigenous languages are Cree, Inuktitut, and Ojibway (Langlois & Turner, 2014). In the non-Indigenous population, the most commonly reported non-English and non-French mother tongues are Chinese languages (19 percent), Italian (7 percent), and Punjabi (6 percent) (Houle & Corbeil, 2017).

LO3 HISTORICAL IMMIGRATION PATTERNS AND POLICIES

Historically, immigration patterns have varied over time and reflect Canada's immigration policies and practices. The Immigration and Refugee Protection Act (2001) is based on three objectives: reuniting families, contributing to the nation's economic development, and protecting refugees. **Family-class immigrants** have been sponsored by close relatives living in Canada, particularly spouses/partners, dependent children, grandparents, and parents. **Economic immigrants** are selected on the basis of some combination of educational attainment, occupational skills, entrepreneurship, business investment, and ability to contribute to the Canadian economy. **Refugees** are persons who have been forced to flee from persecution. They may meet the criteria of the 1951 Geneva Convention, now institutionalized within international law: "A person must be outside of their country of origin and have a well founded fear of being persecuted for reasons of race, religion, nationality, membership of a particular social group or political opinion" (Canadian Council for Refugees, n.d.-b). Immigrants and people who have been granted refugee status are known as *permanent residents* until such time as they may apply for and successfully attain Canadian citizenship.

The number of immigrants and refugees who have been accepted into Canada has varied over the past 150 years. This reflects "push" factors, which motivate people to leave their countries of origin (e.g., religious persecution), as well as "pull" factors, which include economic prosperity, the need for workers, and immigration policies that draw people to Canada. Before 1906, Canada had no cohesive immigration policy. The government's goal was to increase the nation's population (more specifically, its white, English-speaking population), especially after the US government began expressing an interest in colonizing the Canadian West. Between 1896 and 1905, the government advertised for agricultural immigrants (from the United States, the United Kingdom, and northern Europe) to settle the West. Thus, we see immigration increasing in the first years of the 20th century. Canada implemented its first cohesive immigration policy in 1906 (the Immigration Act). The largest number of immigrants to enter Canada in a single year occurred in 1913, when 400,000 people arrived in Canada (Citizenship and Immigration Canada, 2014).

Since that time, immigration has waxed and waned. It decreases during times of economic decline (e.g., the Great Depression) as well as during wartime (e.g., the First and Second World Wars). As immigration policies changed over the years, certain groups were barred entry; others were accepted as immigrants only after being disqualified for many years. It was only in the 1960s that "nation of origin" was removed from immigration applications. Once it was, all applicants, regardless of their country of origin, were evaluated using the same criteria. This removed an important barrier that had prevented many ethnic groups from immigrating to Canada.

In 1951, the UN adopted the Refugee Convention, which recognized that refugees are different from immigrants and must be protected, in that refugees do not choose to immigrate but rather are forced to flee from their countries of origin. Eighteen years later, Canada signed the convention and implemented its first formal refugee determination system. Since that time, more than 500,000 refugees have settled in Canada. You might be most familiar with Canada's leading role in protecting refugees by the more than 40,000 refugees from Syria who arrived in Canada between November 2015 and January 2017 (Canadian Council for Refugees, n.d.-a). But people who have fled to Canada throughout its history comprise many social groups and countries of origin, from loyalists and pacifists during the American Revolution, to black slaves in the 19th century escaping from the United States using the Underground Railroad, to a range of minority groups (based on religion, ethnicity, sexual orientation, or other factors) fleeing persecution in a variety of countries today.

Because of Indigenous peoples as the original inhabitants of the land, several centuries of immigration, and the protection of refugees, Canadian society today is characterized by tremendous ethnic diversity. Individuals "objectively" come from certain ethnic backgrounds and

Family-class immigrants: Immigrants who are sponsored by close relatives living in Canada.

Economic immigrants: Immigrants selected on the basis of some combination of educational attainment, occupational skills, entrepreneurship, business investment, and ability to contribute to the Canadian economy.

Refugees: Persons who are forced to flee from persecution.

Stacey Newman/Shutterstock

Canada is recognized as a world leader in protecting refugees.

then "subjectively" incorporate specific ethnicities into their self-concepts. Regardless of whether people identify themselves, or are identified by others, as having a particular ethnicity, there are consequences to that identification.

TIME TO REVIEW

- What are the ethnic origins and characteristics of people living in Canada today?
- How and why have immigration patterns varied historically?

LO4 CONSEQUENCES OF ETHNIC IDENTIFICATION

The implications of ethnicity range from the micro to the macro level. Two areas where ethnicity has especially clear implications relate to family and economic experiences.

DIVERSE FAMILY EXPERIENCES

Family life is strongly affected by ethnicity and immigration status.

FAMILY STRUCTURE

The nuclear family predominates in Canada, regardless of ethnic group or immigration status. However, immigrants are four times more likely than non-immigrants to live in extended families, and members of racialized groups are 20 times more likely than non-racialized groups to live in extended families. Also, especially on reserves, Indigenous people are more likely than non-Indigenous people to live in extended family households. The greater prevalence of extended families among Indigenous peoples, immigrants, and members of racialized groups is the result of various factors, which can include traditional cultural norms, financial constraints, and the fact that the family serves as a source of support and protection in a racialized society (Frideres & Gadacz, 2012; Frideres & Madibbo, 2014).

FAMILY INTERDEPENDENCE

Feelings of obligation toward one's family tend to be stronger in individuals from non-European cultures; among those of European background, interdependence of family members is stronger in southern European cultures (Georgas et al., 2006; Vedder et al., 2008). In these families, youth spend more time with adults and therefore under adult supervision. Also, youth see household work as communal—as something expected of family members rather than something that will be financially rewarded (e.g., through a weekly allowance) (Fuligni, Yip, & Tseng, 2002; Kagitcibasi, 2007; Vedder et al., 2008).

Family interdependence is also reflected in the age at which youth move out of the family home. In Canada, home leaving is affected by macro-level economic conditions (e.g., the need for a postsecondary education) and demographic forces (e.g., the average age of the first marriage). But it is also influenced by factors that vary among and within ethnic groups—socioeconomic status, family connectedness, norms that govern the timing of life events, the degree of segregation of particular ethnic groups in urban centres, and the recency of immigration to Canada. For example, a comparison of co-residence patterns in Canadian young adults with varied ethnic origins finds that those with southern European (e.g., Portuguese), Asian (e.g., Chinese), and Latin American (e.g., Puerto Rican) origins were more likely to be living in the parental home than those with other ethnic origins (Jeong, Hamplová, & Le Bourdais, 2014).

Monkey Business Images/Shutterstock

Immigration status is also associated with co-residence. Young adults who were the first generation in their families to be born in Canada were more likely to be co-residing with parents; furthermore, the effects of ethnicity decline the longer a family has been living in Canada (Jeong et al., 2014).

INTERGENERATIONAL RELATIONSHIPS

Parents in some ethnic groups may engage in stricter or more lenient parenting practices than parents in other ethnic groups. This means that the impact of parenting practices on child outcomes may vary across ethnic groups (Ho, Bluestein, & Jenkins, 2008). A large body of research has found that very strict parenting styles are associated with child obedience in the short term but in the long term are associated with rebellion, aggression, lower grades in school, and substance use (Baumrind, 1968, 1991). More recently, researchers have found that this association varies across ethnic groups and is not associated with negative child outcomes in families from many current immigrant cultures, such as Chinese, Indian, Pakistani, and Korean (Ho et al., 2008).

One aspect of intergenerational relationships that is unique to immigrant families is the potential conflict that can arise between parents who attained adulthood in their nation of origin and their children, who may have come to Canada while still quite young or who may have been born in Canada. These youth are **bicultural**: they have been exposed to the family's heritage culture *within* the home, yet they are part of the new, national culture when *outside* the home (see *Sociology on Screen*).

Bicultural youth may respond to the demands of two cultures in a number of ways. One study of 5,000 immigrant youth from 30 ethnic backgrounds now living in 13 different countries found four different adaptation patterns (Berry et al., 2006).

FIGURE 8.1

Bicultural Adaptation Patterns

		Identifies with Heritage Culture	
		Yes	**No**
Identifies with National Culture	**Yes**	Integration Pattern	National Pattern
	No	Ethnic Pattern	Diffuse Pattern

Source: Adapted from J. W. Berry, J. P. Phinney, D. L. Sam, & P. Vedder (2006). *Immigrant youth in cultural transition: Acculturation, identity, and adaptation across national contexts*. Mahwah, NJ: Lawrence Erlbaum Associates.

The first adaptation pattern is the **integration pattern**, where youth identify with both their heritage culture and their new, national culture. The second pattern is the **ethnic pattern**, with youth identifying primarily with their heritage culture. Youth who orient themselves primarily to the new, national culture are following the **national pattern**. Finally, those who are confused about how they should be adapting to their bicultural experiences are following a **diffuse pattern** (see *Figure 8.1*). Adaptation patterns have

Bicultural: Participating in two distinct cultures simultaneously.

Integration pattern: Identifying with both one's heritage culture and one's new, national culture.

Ethnic pattern: Identifying primarily with one's heritage culture.

National pattern: Identifying primarily with one's new, national culture.

Diffuse pattern: Uncertainty about which culture(s) one should or should not identify with.

SOCIOLOGY ON SCREEN

GENERATION ONE

The CBC documentary *Generation One: Living in Two Worlds* looks at the experiences of bicultural youth. It follows journalist Nahlah Ayed, who is the first generation in her family to be born in Canada, as she returns to her high school in Winnipeg, Manitoba, to speak with a younger generation of bicultural youth. She finds that although there have been many changes in Canadian society since she was in high school, the struggles with identity that bicultural youth face are similar to her own at that age.

implications for youth's *psychological adaptation* (their self-esteem, their mental health) and *sociocultural adaptation* (their experiences in school and in the community). Those who follow the integration pattern, identifying with both their heritage culture and their new, national culture, have the most positive adaptation experience overall. Youth who orient themselves primarily to their ethnic culture experience positive psychological adaptation but negative sociocultural adaptation and have negative school experiences and problems in the community. Those who follow the national pattern experience negative psychological and sociocultural adaptation, as do those who follow the diffuse pattern; however, the negative adaptation experiences of the latter are more significant.

A variety of factors influence how strongly the children of immigrants identify with their ethnic origins. Stronger ethnic identities are found among youth who are members of racialized groups, have a greater sense of belonging with their families, speak a heritage language at home, and have a preponderance of co-ethnic friends (Sano, Kaida, & Tenkorang, 2015).

DIVERSE ECONOMIC EXPERIENCES

Economic experiences can vary considerably on the basis of ethnicity. Economic variations become especially evident when we compare the average incomes of Indigenous and non-Indigenous persons and the average incomes of immigrants and Canadian-born.

Income disparity between Indigenous and non-Indigenous persons is considerable. This is accounted for, in part, by differences in employment rates. Among those ages 25 to 54 (considered the prime working ages), the employment rate for Indigenous persons is 69 percent, compared to 82 percent for non-Indigenous persons (Statistics Canada, 2017). However, even among those who are employed, there is an income gap. Indigenous persons who are employed full-time have an average income of $26.00 per hour, compared to $27.41 per hour among their non-Indigenous counterparts (Moyser, 2017). There are, however, significant differences among Indigenous groups, with First Nation persons having the lowest average income and Métis the highest (Statistics Canada, 2015). Indigenous persons are less likely to be employed in the knowledge sector (which tends to have higher wages) and are also less likely to hold senior management positions (Moyser, 2017). However, level of education has the greatest impact on the degree of income disparity between Indigenous and non-Indigenous populations. Approximately half of the Indigenous population has some type of post-secondary credential, compared to almost two-thirds of the non-Indigenous population (Statistics Canada, 2015). With postsecondary credentials, the income disparity declines considerably—and with a university degree virtually disappears (Moyser, 2017; Statistics Canada, 2015).

Analyses of the average incomes of immigrant and Canadian-born populations have found that level of education has less influence on income disparity. At all education levels, immigrants earn less than the Canadian-born. Income disparity is especially marked among those who have immigrated within the past five years, and that disparity has increased over the past several decades. The average earnings of recent immigrants declined by 15 percent between 1985 and 1990 and by another 13 percent between 1990 and 1995. From the late 1990s to the present, their average earnings have remained stable (Hou & Picot, 2016). And this income gap continues even though immigrants in the 21st century have higher levels of education and are more highly skilled than in the past as *economic immigrants* are selected on the basis of their ability to contribute to our knowledge-based Canadian economy (Hou & Picot, 2016). In fact, a larger proportion of the immigrant population than the Canadian-born population has a university degree, and those who immigrate to Canada as children are far more likely to pursue a university education than their Canadian-born counterparts (Hou & Bonikowska, 2016).

So, if immigrants are better educated than ever before, and are in fact better educated than the Canadian-born, why does the income disparity exist, and why has it grown over the past several decades? Several contributing factors have been emphasized that are largely functions of the changing source countries for immigrants (from primarily European to primarily Asian and South Asian): degree of proficiency in one of Canada's two official languages; real or perceived differences in educational systems (the recognition of foreign credentials); a preference among employers for Canadian work experience; and racial discrimination (Frank & Hou, 2017).

Ethnicity has implications for various aspects of daily life, including family structure, family interdependence, intergenerational relationships, and economic experiences. At a more macro level, relationships between groups in society are affected by sociocultural forces related to ethnicity, race, and aspects of immigration.

TIME TO REVIEW

- In what ways are family structure, family interdependence, and intergenerational relationships affected by ethnicity and/or immigration?
- What are the experiences of bicultural youth, what different patterns of adaptation might they use, and what are the implications of those patterns?
- How are economic experiences affected by Indigenous ancestry and immigration status, and what role is played by level of education?

LO5 RELATIONSHIPS BETWEEN GROUPS

In ethnically diverse nations such as Canada, the different ethnic groups interact with one another. Based on a nation's history, such as colonization and historical immigration patterns, power differentials emerge, resulting in dominant groups and minority groups. **Dominant groups** are those that have greater power and privilege. For example, when the British defeated the French on the Plains of Abraham in the 18th century, the British became the dominant group, and the colony was renamed British North America. **Minority groups** are definable groups that are socially disadvantaged and that experience unequal treatment (Wirth, 1945). Note that here "minority" refers to *power*, not to *number*. In other words, a group can be the statistical majority yet still be a minority group because of lesser power. For example, when the French colonized what is now Canada, they became the dominant group and Indigenous peoples became minority groups. Interactions between dominant groups and minority groups can take a number of forms: assimilation, pluralism, and segregation and population transfer.

ASSIMILATION

Assimilation occurs when a minority group is absorbed into the culture of the dominant group. Sometimes assimilation is voluntary, such as following immigration. Other times, it is sought through force, such as in the Canadian government's treatment of Indigenous peoples following colonization.

ASSIMILATION AND IMMIGRATION

Immigration is often associated with voluntary assimilation, where over the course of generations, people increasingly adopt the norms, values, and practices of the dominant culture; they stop speaking the language of their ancestors and give up cultural traditions. It had long been assumed that assimilation was a linear process characterized by upward mobility for each successive generation. More recently, scholars have posited that the linear model is based on immigration patterns from the past—that is, on the experiences of white immigrants from largely European source countries. Source countries for immigration today are such that more and more immigrants, and thus their descendants, are members of racialized groups. For these groups, physical characteristics are an obstacle to full assimilation; to some extent, they will always be perceived as, and will perceive themselves to be, a distinct Other (Hiller & Chow, 2005). As one young woman stated, "It is quite confusing sometimes to be Chinese in a Canadian society, *but also difficult to be Canadian with a Chinese look* [emphasis added]" (p. 94). As a consequence, assimilation is more likely to be segmented than linear; some groups are assimilated to a greater extent than others (Hiller & Chow, 2005).

ASSIMILATION AND COLONIZATION

Colonization involves the expansion of territory through the acquisition of Indigenous populations' lands, as well as exploitation of those peoples. It is associated with involuntary, coercive assimilation by colonial powers. Historically, the Canadian government's policies regarding Indigenous peoples were based on the goal of full assimilation.

When European colonization began in the 15th and 16th centuries, the fur trade established patterns of economic exchange between European traders and Indigenous groups, as well as intimate relationships between European men and Indigenous **femmes du pay** ("country wives") (Goulet and Goulet, 2014). The children born of these intimate relationships were known as *métis*, a French term referring to "mixed blood"; over time, a distinct ethnocultural group emerged, the Métis Nation.

By the late 18th century, agriculture was

Dominant groups: Groups that have institutionalized power and privilege in society.

Minority groups: Definable groups that are socially disadvantaged and face unequal treatment.

Les femmes du pays: The Indigenous "country wives" of European traders.

the principal economic activity of Euro-Canadians. With the decline of the fur trade, affiliations with Indigenous cultures came to be seen as less useful. Although the government of France had initiated a formal Christian conversion policy as far back as 1632, the pragmatic realities of life in the harsh environment and the economic requirements of the fur trade meant that cultural differences were tolerated. As those economic alliances weakened, more attention was paid to implementing the conversion policy. A series of policies followed, intended to convert every facet of Indigenous cultures. The reserve system, established in 1830, often compelled communities to abandon their traditional activities, such as nomadic hunting and gathering. With the Act to Encourage the Gradual Civilization of Indian Tribes in This Province (1857) and the Gradual Enfranchisement Act (1869), the goal became full assimilation and the eradication of every aspect of those cultures (known as **ethnocide**). Traditional ceremonies and celebrations were criminalized—even dancing was outlawed in Indigenous communities for 75 years. The Indian Act (1876) made all Indigenous people wards of the federal government.

It took less than a century for laws and government policies to render Indigenous people almost completely dependent on Europeans. The government policy that had the most devastating effect involved residential schooling.

RESIDENTIAL SCHOOLING

In the government's view, the key to assimilation was changing how Indigenous children were socialized. Schooling was seen as the most effective means to this end. In 1831, the government launched a program to educate and assimilate Indigenous children. **Residential schools** would be funded by the government but operated by various Christian denominations. At first, these *day schools* were located adjacent to reserves, and children lived at home. However, the Davin Report (Davin, 1879) concluded that "the influence of the wigwam is stronger than the influence of the schools" and that assimilation would be better served by removing children from their homes and placing them in boarding schools. Although a few day schools continued to exist, *residential* schools came to predominate.

Ethnocide: The eradication of a culture.

Residential schools: A boarding school funded by the Canadian government used to assimilate Indigenous children.

Because all "Indians" were wards of the government, parents had no choice but to send their children away to these boarding schools. By 1884, boarding schools were mandated for all Indigenous children under 16, and agents from the Department of Indian Affairs had the power to fine, detain, or arrest parents who tried to keep their children at home. In British Columbia, where many Indigenous children were already participating in the public school system, children were removed from those schools and placed in residential schools instead (Barman, 2003). By 1896, there were already 45 residential schools in operation, and a total of 130 schools existed over a period of more than 100 years. Around 150,000 Indigenous children attended residential schools (National Centre for Truth and Reconciliation, 2016).

Until 1951, students in residential schools received only a half-day of academic instruction; the rest of the day was spent in manual labour. Instruction was not only academic (e.g., arithmetic) but also religious and cultural. So even after six or seven years in school, most children remained at a Grade 1, 2, or 3 level (Barman, 2003). Education beyond Grade 8 was prohibited for Indigenous youth. Until the 1950s, most teachers in residential schools had no professional training. Instead, they were members of the religious order that operated the school and were often more interested in religious conversion than in education (Barman, 2003).

Inferior education was just one of the features of the residential school system that created a lasting legacy in Indigenous communities. Psychological, physical, and sexual abuses were common (National Centre for Truth and Reconciliation, 2016). The first allegations of physical and sexual abuse were made in 1880; of the 150,000 children attending the schools, 91,000 reported being physically and/or sexually abused. Psychological abuse was even more common and included the use of insults and derogatory names; as well, students' letters home were censored. Neglect was even more prevalent than abuse. Funding formulas were such that residential schools received only a fraction of the government funding per student enjoyed by public schools; compounding this, many residential schools were being operated for profit. As a result, students were often left hungry, schools were overcrowded, and buildings were unkempt and unsanitary. In the early 20th century, two government reports documented horrendous living conditions that had resulted in student death rates of up to 47 percent in residential schools. Although neglect and abuse were prevalent in many schools, ethnocide occurred in all of them.

All aspects of the students' traditional cultures were forbidden. When students first arrived at the schools, their hair was cut short, their clothing was burned, and their names were changed. They were to speak only English. Some schools used positive reinforcement for the use of English. For instance, students received a bag of buttons each week; each time they were caught speaking their mother tongue, a button was taken away, and at the end of the week, the remaining buttons could

Library and Archives Canada NL-022474

Student Thomas Moore, before and after entering Regina Indian Industrial School, 1897.

be exchanged for a prize. But other schools punished students for language transgressions—having to write lines, having their mouths taped shut, being given the strap, being deprived of food, and even having needles poked through their tongues.

When the required period of schooling ended, former students found themselves stranded between cultures. They had no traditional skills, but the inferior education they had received and the discrimination they faced meant they also had difficulty

SOCIOLOGY IN WORDS

THE VOICES OF RESIDENTIAL SCHOOL STUDENTS

- "I was literally thrown into St. Mary's Residential School at four years of age.... My very first memory of my entry into the school is a painful flashback. For whatever reason, I am thrown into a kneeling position. My head is bashed against a wooden cupboard by the boys' supervisor." (Kelly, 2008, p. 14)
- "A nun shaved my head and stripped me bare in front of all the other boys, followed by months of repeated beatings, whippings, sexual abuse and solitary confinement in a dark, locked closet. Why? Because I was bad and deserved it. That's what they said." (Kakfwi, 2008, para. 4)
- "I was hungry from the day I went into the school until they took me to the hospital two and a half years later. Not just me. Every Indian pupil smelled of hunger." (cited in Barman, 2003, p. 222)
- "The constant message [was] that because you are Native, you are part of a weak and defective race, unworthy of a distinguished place in society.... That to me is not training for success, it is training for self-destruction." (cited in Barman, 2003, p. 229)

integrating into Euro-Canadian society. Having experienced severe neglect, abuse, and ethnocide, many former students developed a condition known as *residential school syndrome* (similar to post-traumatic stress disorder), which was characterized by recurring nightmares, painful memories, and intense feelings of fear or anger (Brasfield, 2001).

In the 1990s, a number of religious authorities formally apologized to the Indigenous people for the role they had played in residential schooling. The federal government issued a formal apology in 2008, followed by a restitution package for former students, a commemoration initiative, $125 million for the Aboriginal Healing Foundation, and the establishment of the Truth and Reconciliation Commission, whose mandate was to further analyze the long-term consequences of residential schooling and gather the stories of survivors. In 2015, the commission released its final report and a list of recommendations for reconciliation in areas such as justice, education, child welfare, and language (Truth and Reconciliation Commission, 2015).

Pluralism: Cultural differences are maintained and celebrated.

PLURALISM

Cultural **pluralism** is characterized by ethnic groups maintaining the traditions of their heritage cultures and by diversity being valued. Switzerland is often considered a model of cultural pluralism: its French, German, Romansh, and Italian populations maintain their cultures and their languages; all four languages are "official" languages of the country. Canada is also characterized by cultural pluralism, which is reflected in its multiculturalism policy (see *Sociology in Practice*).

YOUR SOCIOLOGICAL TOOLKIT

SOCIOLOGY IN PRACTICE

MULTICULTURALISM IN CANADA

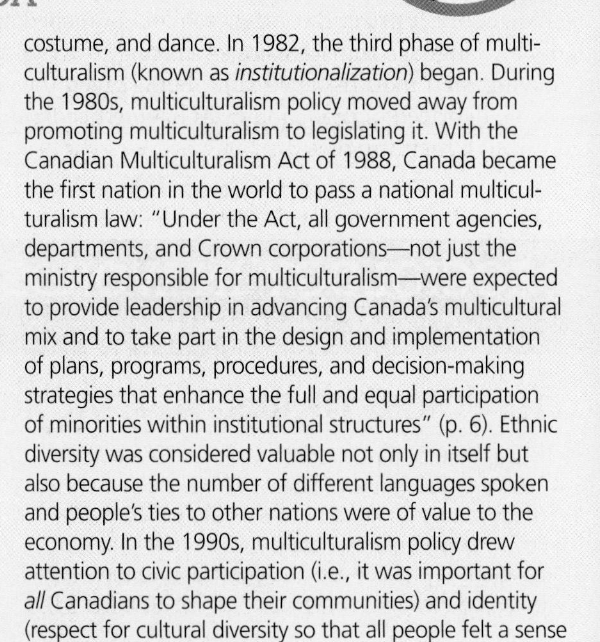

Federal multiculturalism has progressed through three phases of development (Dewing, 2009). During the *incipient stage* (pre-1971), Canada's political, social, and economic institutions were based on a British model. Large-scale immigration following the Second World War, along with the activism of Indigenous people for greater independence and redress of past wrongs, contributed to the movement away from assimilation. Multiculturalism became an official policy in Canada in 1971, and thus began the *formative period* of development (1971–1981). The objectives of the policy were these:

- "to assist cultural groups to retain and foster their identity;
- to assist cultural groups to overcome barriers to their full participation in Canadian society…;
- to promote creative exchanges among all Canadian cultural groups; and
- to assist immigrants in acquiring at least one of the official languages" (p. 4).

This era of multiculturalism had a folkloric orientation, one that emphasized the celebration of the traditional practices often embodied in cultural festivals—food, costume, and dance. In 1982, the third phase of multiculturalism (known as *institutionalization*) began. During the 1980s, multiculturalism policy moved away from promoting multiculturalism to legislating it. With the Canadian Multiculturalism Act of 1988, Canada became the first nation in the world to pass a national multiculturalism law: "Under the Act, all government agencies, departments, and Crown corporations—not just the ministry responsible for multiculturalism—were expected to provide leadership in advancing Canada's multicultural mix and to take part in the design and implementation of plans, programs, procedures, and decision-making strategies that enhance the full and equal participation of minorities within institutional structures" (p. 6). Ethnic diversity was considered valuable not only in itself but also because the number of different languages spoken and people's ties to other nations were of value to the economy. In the 1990s, multiculturalism policy drew attention to civic participation (i.e., it was important for *all* Canadians to shape their communities) and identity (respect for cultural diversity so that all people felt a sense of belonging to Canada).

Think Outside the Box: In your opinion, to what extent have the objectives of this policy been realized?

SEGREGATION AND POPULATION TRANSFER

Under **segregation**, minority groups are separated from the dominant group. Until the Civil Rights Movement of the 1960s, blacks were segregated from whites in the American South in a variety of ways. They were barred from many public places (e.g., restaurants) and had to sit at the back of buses and drink from separate water fountains. Their children were required to attend separate schools, and **anti-miscegenation laws** prohibited interracial marriage. Although many Canadians are unaware of it, the segregation of blacks existed here as well. In 1945, Halifax resident Viola Desmond was arrested for sitting in the "whites only" section of a theatre. Although Canadian provinces enacted legislation banning segregation in the mid-1940s, the underlying attitudes remained for some time. In 1954, two black men were refused service in an Ontario restaurant. An undercover story by the *Toronto Telegram* revealed that although segregation no longer existed in law, it continued unabated in everyday practice (Black History Canada, n.d.).

Population transfer forcibly expels members of certain minority groups from a country or limits them to a particular location. In Canadian history, this has occurred multiple times. One example is the reserve system established for Indigenous peoples that was discussed earlier. As another example, in the mid-18th century, more than 7,000 Acadians (an ethnic group of French descent living in the Maritimes) were expelled by the British, and all of their farms were burned to the ground. They were sent to France, England, and several American states. Thousands later returned to Canada, where they reside today in New Brunswick, Prince Edward Island, and Nova Scotia. Pubnico, Nova Scotia, is the oldest Acadian village in the world still inhabited by Acadians (http://www.pubnico.ca), and its museum is listed on the UNESCO archives portal in recognition of the important historical material it has preserved. During both world wars, members of ethnic groups defined as "enemy aliens" had their property seized and were relocated to internment camps. During the First World War, it was mainly people of Ukrainian descent who were interned; they were used as forced labour—for example, they cleared the forest for what would become Kapuskasing, Ontario, and they built roads through the Rocky Mountains. During the Second World War, it was mainly those of Japanese descent who were placed in internment camps.

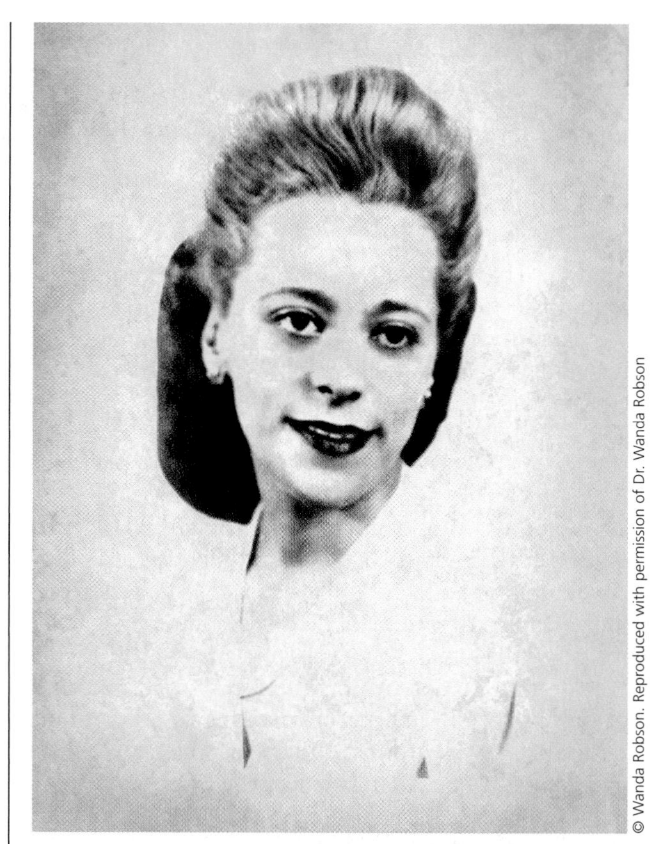

Viola Desmond was arrested in a Nova Scotia theatre for sitting in the "whites only" section.

Forcible assimilation, segregation, and population transfer have their foundations in prejudice and discrimination. Both have long histories in Canada and throughout the world and continue to be problematic in the 21st century.

Segregation: Minority groups are separated from the dominant group.

Anti-miscegenation laws: Laws that prohibit interracial marriages.

Population transfer: A process whereby minority groups are forcibly expelled or are limited to a specific location.

TIME TO REVIEW

- What are the differences between dominant groups and minority groups?
- What forms of interaction can occur between the dominant group and minority groups in society, and what are some examples?
- How has multiculturalism changed in Canadian history?

LO6 PREJUDICE AND DISCRIMINATION

Prejudice is an attitude that is unrelated to reality and is generalized to all members of a certain group. **Racism** is a specific form of prejudice, one based on aspects of physical appearance. Like all attitudes, prejudice has a *cognitive component* and an *affective component*. It is also linked to a third component, the *behavioural component*. These three components correspond to what we *think*, how we *feel*, and how we *act* (Aronson et al., 2017).

THE COGNITIVE COMPONENT

The cognitive component of prejudice reflects *what we think*, with stereotypes as the foundation. Stereotypes are assumptions that members of a specific group are more similar than they actually are; they reflect our image of the typical example of a member of a certain group. Stereotypes can be directed at any type of group—truck drivers, professors, women, ethnic groups, religious groups, and so on. Just as we may overgeneralize by saying that trees are green (when, in fact, some trees have red or purple leaves), we may overgeneralize about the members of a social group; for example, we may think that women are poor drivers when, in fact, male drivers have more car accidents.

Once we hold a specific stereotype, we are more likely to notice and remember information that is consistent with it. In one classic study, participants were presented with photos and labels for people in certain social categories (e.g., a photo of a smiling, grey-haired woman with the label "grandmother"). Then they were given additional information about the person in the photo (e.g., "kind"). At a later point in time, they were asked to recall the information about that person. The researchers found that information was best remembered when it conformed to the stereotype associated with that label; for instance, it was easier to remember descriptions of "kind" when shown the photo of the grandmother than it was to recall "competitive." Furthermore, in trying to recall information about a person in a stereotyped group, we tend to falsely remember information that is consistent with that stereotype; participants in the study would falsely recall "kind" as being part of the description of the grandmother, even if it hadn't been (Brewer, Dull, & Lui, 1981).

Prejudice: An attitude that is unrelated to reality and is generalized to all members of a certain group.

Racism: A specific form of prejudice based on aspects of physical appearance, such as skin colour.

Discrimination: Treating someone unfairly because of his or her group membership.

THE AFFECTIVE COMPONENT

The affective component of prejudice reflects *how we feel*. These are the emotions we attach to the stereotype. We may feel dislike toward a particular group that we stereotype as being untrustworthy or admiration for another group that we stereotype as being hard workers. Sometimes we aren't even aware of the emotions we may be feeling. Another classic study used the galvanic skin response (GSR) to overcome this problem (Poirier & Lott, 1967). GSR devices are attached to the skin using wires and sticky patches. They are then able to measure the electrical conductivity of the skin. Electrical conductivity increases when we are feeling strong emotions. Participants in this study completed a questionnaire that measured their level of ethnocentrism—that is, the tendency to see things only from the point of view of one's own culture—as the standard for the "normal" way of doing things. They were then attached to the GSR device and told to wait for a research assistant to come in and assign them a problem-solving task. Researchers found that participants who were higher in ethnocentrism showed greater GSR when in the presence of a black rather than a white research assistant; participants who were low in ethnocentrism did not show this pattern. In this study, ethnocentrism resulted in specific reactions to racial differences. Ethnocentrism can also contribute to the many forms of individual, institutional, and systemic discrimination discussed later in the chapter. Furthermore, we can see ethnocentrism when someone judges another culture's food as "weird" or deems that people in England drive on the "wrong" side of the road.

It is the emotional component that makes prejudice so resistant to change. It is much easier to correct someone's inaccurate cognitive beliefs (e.g., by presenting that person with accurate information that dispels their beliefs) than it is to change emotions (of which the person may not even be aware).

In addition to what we think and how we feel, prejudice is connected to a behavioural component—*how we act*.

THE BEHAVIOURAL COMPONENT

Prejudice put into action is **discrimination**—treating someone unfairly because of his or her group membership. Discrimination can occur anywhere from the individual level (e.g., not sitting next to someone on the bus because of the colour of her skin) to the institutional level (e.g., laws that treat certain groups unequally).

INDIVIDUAL DISCRIMINATION

Individual discrimination can include avoiding contact with members of certain groups, making offensive jokes, using derogatory names, hurling insults and verbal abuse, using physical violence, and committing hate crimes (see *Sociology in My Life*). **Hate crimes** are criminal offences that are motivated by hate toward an identifiable group, such as groups based on race/ethnicity, religion, sexual orientation, physical or mental disability, or political beliefs. In Canada's Criminal Code, hate crimes include public incitement of hatred, willful promotion of hatred, advocating genocide, and mischief in relation to religious property; other crimes (e.g., assault) are classified as hate crimes if they have been motivated by hatred against an identifiable group. The significance of hate crimes is that they affect not only the individual who has been victimized but also, indirectly, members of an entire community. Hate crimes are underreported in police statistics, in that victims may be hesitant to report their experiences. A victim's decision to report an incident to the police is based on many factors, including the perceived seriousness of the incident, language or cultural barriers, the perceived sensitivity of the police, the presence of specialized hate crimes units, and the accessibility of victim services (Leber, 2017).

Most police-reported hate crimes are based on race/ethnicity (47 percent), followed by religion (34 percent) and sexual orientation (10 percent). Hate crimes based on race/ethnicity are primarily directed at blacks (35 percent), followed by Arabs/West Asians (14 percent) and East or Southeast Asians (8 percent). Hate crimes based on religion are largely directed at members of the Jewish faith (38 percent), followed by Muslims (34 percent) and Catholics (12 percent). Only 38 percent of hate crimes overall are violent; however, most hate crimes based on sexual orientation are violent (59 percent). Hate crimes are most commonly committed by people over the age of 18 (Leber, 2017).

The cognitive and affective components of prejudice do not necessarily correspond to its behavioural component. Individuals may have prejudicial thoughts and feelings yet not engage in any discriminatory acts; conversely, others may engage in discriminatory acts even though they do not have prejudicial thoughts and feelings. Robert Merton (1949) developed a typology that reflects the variety of ways that thoughts/feelings and behaviours may be related; this typology continues to be used today, although its specific labels can vary (see *Figure 8.2*).

FIGURE 8.2

Relationships between Prejudice and Discrimination

		Prejudicial Thoughts	
		Yes	**No**
Discriminatory Actions	**Yes**	Prejudiced Discriminators (*"active bigots"*)	Non-prejudiced Discriminators (*"fair-weather liberals"*)
	No	Prejudiced Non-discriminators (*"timid bigots"*)	Non-prejudiced Non-discriminators (*"all-weather liberals"*)

Source: Adapted from R. K. Merton (1949). Discrimination and the American creed. In R. M. MacIver (Ed.), *Discrimination and national welfare* (pp. 77–145) New York, NY: Harper.

People who have prejudicial thoughts/feelings and then act on them are *prejudiced discriminators* (what Merton called "active bigots"). Those who do not act on their prejudicial thoughts/feelings are *prejudiced non-discriminators* (or "timid bigots"); as prejudice becomes less acceptable in society, those who have prejudices are less likely to engage in overt discrimination. People who do not have prejudicial thoughts/feelings yet still act in discriminatory ways are *non-prejudiced discriminators* (or "fair-weather liberals"). People may engage in discriminatory acts because of group pressure or without realizing they are acting in discriminatory ways. Finally, those who do not have prejudicial thoughts/feelings and who do not act in discriminatory ways are *non-prejudiced non-discriminators* (or "all-weather liberals").

INSTITUTIONAL AND SYSTEMIC DISCRIMINATION

Institutional discrimination and systemic discrimination are embedded in policies and practices. Both can occur within organizations, such as through discriminatory hiring practices. Hiring practices may be intentionally discriminatory, where a business will not hire members of certain ethnic groups. But they may be unintentionally discriminatory as well; for example, for many years, the height restrictions for

Hate crimes: Criminal offences motivated by hate toward an identifiable group.

police officers were indirectly discriminatory against people of Asian descent, who are (on average) slightly shorter than people of British, western European, or northern European descent. Subtle forms of discrimination are also evident in some geographic place names. For many years, the Chinese community expressed concern over the name of a mountain overlooking Canmore, Alberta—"Chinaman's Peak." A series of hearings was held by the Geographical Names Board of Canada and the Alberta Historical Resources Foundation, and in the late 1990s, the peak was renamed "Ha Ling Peak" (http://kananaskis.com). In the same vein, place names using the term "squaw" were eliminated in Alberta and British Columbia in the 1990s.

We have only to look at the news to see instances of discriminatory practices within organizations today: an inquiry finds that on multiple occasions, Saskatoon police officers drove Indigenous individuals to the outskirts of the city to find their way home (even in the middle of winter); police statistics show that members of racialized groups are far more likely to be subjected to random street checks (known as "carding"); the Black Lives Matter movement arises in response to the number of unarmed black men being shot by the police (Black Lives Matter, n.d.; Campbell, 2016; Huncar, 2017).

Institutional and systemic discrimination can occur at the government level as well, as reflected in policies and laws that result in forcible assimilation, segregation, and population transfer. Immigration policy itself can be discriminatory. For example, special immigration policies have sometimes been directed at particular groups. Chinese immigration was encouraged in Canada in the 1880s, when the Canadian Pacific Railway (CPR) was being built; thousands of Chinese men were brought to Canada as labourers. But once the CPR was completed, strong anti-Asian sentiment led the government to restrict further Chinese immigration. A $50 head tax was imposed on Chinese immigrants in 1885; this was increased to $500 in 1903 (equal to two years' wages for Chinese labourers). A total of $23 million was collected by the federal government through the Chinese head tax, at the same time as the government was *spending* more than $10 million to encourage immigration from Europe. Because the head tax did not sufficiently halt Chinese immigration in the eyes of the government, in 1923, the Chinese Exclusion Act was passed, which essentially halted immigration from China until that act was repealed in 1947. As a result of the head tax and the Exclusion Act, many Chinese immigrants (including those who were brought to Canada to work on the CPR) were later unable to bring their wives and children to Canada. This broke up many families and created a Chinese "bachelor community" (Chinese Canadian National Council, 2017).

Authoritarian personality: A personality type that values authority and obedience, is low in tolerance, and is high in stereotypical thinking.

YOUR SOCIOLOGICAL TOOLKIT
SOCIOLOGY IN THEORY

LO7 UNDERSTANDING PREJUDICE AND RACIALIZATION

SOCIAL PSYCHOLOGICAL THEORIES

Social psychological theories focus on the causes of prejudice in individuals and in group interactions. Adorno (1950) suggested that some people have **authoritarian personality**, which value authority and obedience, are low in tolerance, and are high in

YOUR SOCIOLOGICAL TOOLKIT

SOCIOLOGY IN MY LIFE

HAS RACISM "ALL BUT DISAPPEARED"?

Some people describe racism as an artifact of the past and suggest that we have become a tolerant and accepting society. In fact, more than a decade ago, one of your authors saw a textbook that contained the quotation, "Racism has all but disappeared from Canadian society." However, we have only to look at the data on hate crimes to know this is not the case.

Think Outside the Box: Does racism exist at your school? Have you ever personally experienced or observed a behaviour, gesture, facial expression, or comment that you consider to be racist?

stereotypical thinking. People with authoritarian personalities are more likely to have prejudicial thoughts and feelings and to engage in discriminatory behaviour. Other scholars (e.g., Marger, 2003) propose that when experiencing frustration, some people direct their frustration at a **scapegoat**, someone they can blame for their difficulties, such as unemployment.

Other social psychological theories attribute prejudice to interactions between specific groups. For example, one classic study (Sherif et al., 1961) illustrates *realistic conflict theory*, which is the idea that prejudice emerges from competition over scarce resources. At a boys' summer camp, boys were divided into two groups located in separate cabins some distance apart. Each group designed its own flag and chose a name ("Rattlers" and "Eagles"). For the first week, the two groups engaged in a variety of activities together. During the second and third weeks, they were forced to become competitors in a series of games and activities in which the winning team would receive a variety of prizes. It didn't take long for prejudice to appear. Each team started describing the other in derogatory terms (e.g., "bums") and expressed the superiority of their own group. Soon name calling began, and then physical acts—stealing the property of members of the other team and vandalizing the other team's cabin. In fact, the researchers had to intervene to halt the escalating destruction. Conflict between groups set the stage for the emergence of prejudicial thoughts, feelings, and behaviours. Today, we can see this process occurring in the way that anti-immigration sentiment increases during economic downturns.

INTERACTIONIST THEORIES

Interactionist theories attribute prejudice to the processes by which we come to understand different ethnic groups (including our own) and judge them accordingly. Through direct interactions (e.g., with significant others) or indirect ones (e.g., with media), we may develop understandings of certain groups that are based on stereotypes and of our own group as being superior. The labels we then attach to members of specific groups affect how we perceive them and subsequently treat them—that is, we treat them in terms of the generic label rather than as individuals. We can see this in the way that varied ethnic groups are portrayed in the media (see *Critical Thinking in Action*).

Scapegoat: An individual or group that is wrongfully blamed for a personal or social problem.

YOUR SOCIOLOGICAL TOOLKIT

CRITICAL THINKING IN ACTION

FRAMING ETHNICITY

As you learned in the chapter on media, from an interactionist perspective, the media play a key role in *framing* issues, events, and people (Goffman, 1974). The overall way that phenomena are portrayed in the media serves as the lens through which we come to understand those phenomena. Thus, the frames of ethnicity that exist in mainstream media (e.g., network television shows, Hollywood movies, and even animated Disney films) have important implications (Bereska, 2017).

In their analysis of various forms of media, Fleras and Kunz (2001) found that certain frames of ethnicity are pervasive and that they reproduce processes of racialization in society. The first frame of ethnicity is *invisibility*, in that members of racialized groups are largely absent (e.g., think about who anchors the national news broadcasts on television). The second frame of ethnicity is *stereotyping*, in that when racialized groups are shown in the media, they are often presented in ways that support stereotypes (e.g., the basketball player in a television episode may be black). The third frame of ethnicity is *socially problematic*, in that certain racialized groups are portrayed as posing some threat to society (e.g., the news may emphasize that an Iranian man was recently arrested for terrorism, but not a "white person of Irish descent"). The fourth frame of ethnicity is *adornment*, which suggests overidealization (e.g., think of Tonto, the Lone Ranger's trusty sidekick). The final frame of ethnicity is *white-washed*, where the experiences of racialized groups are portrayed as no different from those of dominant, non-racialized groups. This last frame includes television shows and movies in which white actors play non-white characters. For example, Johnny Depp played Tonto in *The Lone Ranger* and Scarlett Johansson played Major Motoko Kusanagi in the Japanese manga adaptation film *Ghost in the Shell*.

Think Outside the Box: What are the implications of these frames of ethnicity, at both the micro level of individual choices and experiences and the macro level of larger social structures and processes?

CONFLICT THEORIES

Conflict theories propose that the structure of society creates prejudice and racialization. For instance, Marxist conflict theories emphasize inequalities in the structure of societies under capitalism. Here, the powerful have a vested interest in maintaining prejudice in society. The economically oppressed will then be too distracted by fighting with one another over scarce resources to join together to fight against their oppressors (Olzak, 2006). Although powerful groups are able to maintain their power, in part by reproducing their ideology in social institutions (e.g., the education system), at other times, they use overt forms of coercion (see *Sociology in My Community*).

Dual/split labour market theory also focuses on the economic sphere. It proposes that members of the dominant group will develop prejudices against minority groups in order to protect their position in the labour market (Bonacich, 1972). The *primary labour market* consists of higher paid, more secure jobs with upward mobility. The *secondary labour market* comprises jobs that are poorly paid and insecure (e.g., part-time, temporary) and that provide little opportunity for advancement—jobs that people in the primary labour market would consider demeaning. Historically, members of minority groups have been overrepresented in the secondary labour market.

CRITICAL RACE THEORY

Critical race theory (CRT) is perhaps the most comprehensive theory of prejudice and racialization. It references the economic, cultural, ideological, political, and psychological spheres. Historically, it was influenced, in part, by the work of sociologist and NAACP founder W.E.B. Du Bois (1868–1963). It was formally developed as a distinct theory in the 1970s and 1980s by a group of activists and legal scholars who were disillusioned with the limited achievements of the Civil Rights Movement of the mid-20th century. Derrick Bell is typically recognized as the intellectual founder of this theory (Crenshaw et al., 1995), which argues that racism is not aberrant but rather is the typical way that society conducts its affairs. Consequently, the "white-over-colour ascendancy" (Delgado & Stefanic, 2012, p. 3) is embedded in the entirety of the social fabric, in every social institution. Racism serves the economic interests of the (white) dominant class but also the interests of (white) working-class people who are not members of racialized groups (in that there are always other groups that face greater subordination than they themselves do). Critical race theory also emphasizes the unique voices of members of racialized groups because of their histories of oppression—voices that are in the best position to contribute to scholarly and activist discourses of racism (Delgado & Stefanic, 2012). Thus,

YOUR SOCIOLOGICAL TOOLKIT

SOCIOLOGY IN MY COMMUNITY

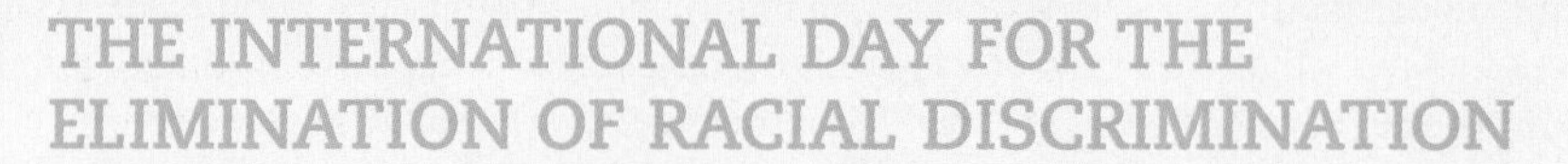

THE INTERNATIONAL DAY FOR THE ELIMINATION OF RACIAL DISCRIMINATION

On March 21, 1960, 69 peaceful demonstrators were killed in South Africa during a protest against apartheid. Since then, the United Nations has declared March 21 to be the International Day for the Elimination of Racial Discrimination. Canada's first campaign was in 1989, and since that time, most of its campaigns have been targeted at youth. In 1996, the Canadian government launched an annual national video competition associated with that day, open to youth ages 10 to 20. Today, the winning videos are available on YouTube and on the Government of Canada website (http://www.cic.gc.ca). Events are held in recognition of this day at universities and colleges across the country as well.

Think Outside the Box: What events are being held this year at your institution to commemorate the International Day for the Elimination of Racial Discrimination? Why are those events important?

most critical race theorists are themselves members of racialized groups.

Scholar and activist Cornel West refers to critical race theory as "the last gasp of emancipatory hope" for racialized groups (West, 1995, p. xii). Identifying himself politically as a non-Marxist socialist, he suggests that an analysis of racism requires the following: (a) an analysis of the metaphors and concepts that have been used in dominant European discourses (and resistance to them); (b) a micro-institutional analysis of the mechanisms that sustain those discourses in the lives of non-Europeans (and resistance to them); and (c) a macro-structural analysis of economic and political oppression (and resistance) (West, 1995; West, n.d.).

TIME TO REVIEW

- What are the three components of prejudice?
- What is discrimination, and at what levels does it occur?
- Do prejudicial thoughts/feelings and discriminatory behaviours necessarily accompany each other?
- In what ways have Canada's immigration policies been discriminatory?
- How do social theorists explain prejudice and racialization?

CHAPTER SUMMARY

LO1 Compare the concepts of ethnicity, race, racialization, visible minorities, and racialized groups.

Ethnicity refers to classifications of self and others based on cultural characteristics, such as shared ancestry, language, and cultural traditions; it has objective and subjective dimensions. Race is a socially constructed category used to classify people according to physical characteristics, such as skin colour. Racialization is the process whereby racial categories are constructed as different and unequal. Visible minorities/racialized groups are those that are non-Caucasian or non-white in skin colour.

LO2 Describe contemporary patterns of ethnicity in Canada.

More than 200 different ethnic origins are reported by people living in Canada. The most frequently reported ethnic origins are those groups that have the longest immigration histories in Canada, such as the English and the French. Nineteen percent of people in Canada are visible minorities and around 4 percent are Indigenous.

LO3 List the three objectives of Canada's immigration policy, outline the types of individuals who enter the country on the basis of each of those objectives, and describe contemporary immigration patterns.

The three objectives of immigration policy are to reunite families, contribute to the nation's economic development, and protect refugees. Immigrants in the *family* class are sponsored by close relatives living in Canada. *Economic immigrants* are selected on the basis of their ability to contribute to the Canadian economy. *Refugees* are persons who have been forced to flee from persecution. More than 20 percent of Canada's population today is foreign-born, with immigrants increasingly coming from non-European countries. Immigration patterns are based on a variety of "push" and "pull" factors. Immigration peaked in 1913, when a larger number of immigrants came to Canada's shores than at any time since.

LO4 Describe the implications of ethnicity for families and for economic experiences.

Ethnicity affects multiple aspects of family life, including family structure, family interdependence, and intergenerational relationships. Youth who have immigrated, or whose parents were immigrants, are bicultural and must adapt to having both a heritage culture and a new, national culture. In the economic realm, Indigenous people have lower incomes than non-Indigenous people; however, this income disparity is reduced with postsecondary education. Immigrants have lower incomes than non-immigrants regardless of level of education; income disparity has actually increased over the past several decades, even though immigrants are more likely to have a university degree than those born in Canada.

LO5 Distinguish between dominant and minority groups and describe the forms of interactions that can take place between them.

Dominant groups and minority groups are differentiated on the basis of power. Interactions between dominant and minority groups can take the form of assimilation, segregation, or population transfer.

LO6 Outline the three components of prejudice and describe the different forms that discrimination can take.

Prejudice is an attitude that has cognitive, affective, and behavioural components. Discrimination can occur at the individual level, with behaviours ranging from offensive jokes to hate crimes. It can also occur at institutional and systemic levels, such as in relation to immigration policies.

LO7 Discuss theories of prejudice and racialization, including social psychological theories, interactionist theories, conflict theories, and critical race theory.

Social psychological theories attribute prejudice to characteristics of individuals (e.g., authoritarian personality, frustration) or to small group interactions (e.g., competitive settings). Conflict theories attribute prejudice and racialization to the structure of society, especially under capitalism. Interactionist theories draw attention to how we come to understand racialized groups, such as through media frames of ethnicity. Critical race theory posits that racism is endemic in the economic, cultural, ideological, political, and psychological spheres.

RECOMMENDED RESOURCES

1. For an analysis of the ways racialized groups are socially excluded in the educational, economic, and political spheres, see G.E. Galabuzi, *Canada's Economic Apartheid: The Socialized Exclusion of Racialized Groups in the New Century* (Toronto, ON: Canadian Scholars' Press, 2006).
2. To learn more about the colonization of Indigenous persons and the path to reconciliation, go to the website for the National Centre for Truth and Reconciliation, which is located at the University of Manitoba (http://umanitoba.ca/centres/nctr/).
3. To learn more about the ways that the media equates Islam with terrorism (when, in fact, domestic, right-wing extremist groups are responsible for more violence), see the Media Education Foundation's documentary *Constructing the Terrorist Threat: Islamophobia, the Media and the War on Terror* (featuring Deepa Kumar) (http://www.mediaed.org).

FOR FURTHER REFLECTION

1. How can prejudice be reduced? Do you think prejudice can be completely eliminated?
2. What are the pros and cons of assimilation?
3. Many instances of institutional or systemic discrimination have occurred in Canadian history. What are the solutions to redressing these past wrongs?

ENDNOTE

[1] Retrieved May 7, 2017, from www.brainyquote.com.

09 CHAPTER

Canadian Families: Past, Present, and Future

iravgustin/Shutterstock

Other things may change us, but we start and end with families.

(Anthony Brandt)[1]

LEARNING OBJECTIVES & OUTCOMES

After completing this chapter, students should be able to do the following:

LO1 Compare varying definitions of family and explain why the way family is defined is important.

LO2 Identify the key trends that indicate changes in Canadian families.

LO3 Distinguish between the main assumptions of the family decline and family pluralism perspectives.

LO4 Outline the difficulties that some families face in Canada today.

LO5 Explain why the fact that some families experience problems is not indicative of a decline of the family as a social institution.

LO6 Explain how each of the following theories contributes to knowledge about families: social exchange, family life course development, functionalist, conflict, feminist, and interactionist.

FAMILIES ARE EVERYWHERE

We are surrounded by families, from our own families to other people's families, families in our neighbourhoods and in our workplaces, fictional families on television and in movies, and even families in the news and online. When you wake up in the morning, it may be in the home of your own family (the one you were raised in and/or the one you have initiated in adulthood). While drinking your morning coffee, you might hear or read about families in the news—a story about a family within which something tragic has occurred, an editorial outlining the projected impacts of a new government policy on families, or a lifestyle story describing affordable back-to-school fashions for children. You might look out your window and see parents loading their children into the car to drive them to school (or perhaps you are doing so yourself). Throughout the day, you may encounter families in a variety of settings—shopping malls, restaurants, movie theatres, neighbourhoods, and the pages of your Facebook friends. Families may affect you even more directly throughout your workday. If you are a teacher, you teach children who are growing up in various types of families and whose family lives influence the classroom; if you are in advertising, you are marketing directly to people whose consumer interests are shaped by their family lives; if you serve in a managerial position in business, your employees are trying to achieve a balance between work and family responsibilities. In the evening, you perhaps return home to your partner and/or children, or to get ready for a date, or perhaps to turn on the television to watch *Fresh Off the Boat*, *Blackish*, or *Modern Family*. Families are *everywhere*.

Personal experience gives us a great deal of knowledge about our own families, and that knowledge serves as a foundation for what we "know" about families more generally (see *Sociology in My Life*). But our own family experiences provide us with a mental snapshot of only one small corner of the social world. Using the lens of sociology to better understand families more generally means delving into patterns and variations that exist in families across cultures, over time, and within a given culture at a particular point in time. To accomplish this, we need to explore virtually every aspect of family life, beginning with attempts to define exactly what constitutes a family.

This chapter introduces you to the sociological study of families. It begins with a review of some of the different ways that "family" has been defined, along with a discussion of corresponding macro- and micro-level issues raised by these particular definitions. In our everyday lives, our own personal definitions of family frame our attitudes toward changing trends in Canadian families, along with the corresponding family-related choices we make.

YOUR SOCIOLOGICAL TOOLKIT

SOCIOLOGY IN MY LIFE

MY FAMILY

The opening quotation in this chapter suggests that families are of the utmost importance in determining who we are, creating the frameworks on which our lives are built. Families are at the core of our socialization experiences throughout our lives. In childhood, our parents and other family members are key socializing agents, providing us with some of the knowledge and life skills we will carry with us throughout our lifetimes. We undergo further socialization in the context of family life if and when we marry or enter a common-law relationship, have children, get divorced, remarry, acquire additional children through remarriage, have our children move out of the family home, and become grandparents. We spend a considerable amount of time and energy interacting with and thinking about our families.

Think Outside the Box: How would you describe your family?

LO1 WHAT IS A FAMILY?

The term "family" is used so regularly that we often take it for granted. Each of us can easily list the individuals whom we consider family, but we may not find it as easy to extrapolate from that list to a more general definition of "family." Definitions vary with the specific context and the specific needs or interests of the groups involved. For instance, federal benefits policy outlines a precise legal definition of family that may differ considerably from how you define family. Various definitions may emphasize structure, process, function, or emotion. But all definitions are both inclusive and exclusive, embracing certain individuals as legitimate family members for the purposes at hand while barring others. In this way, definitions have macro- and micro-level impacts on people's lives.

STRUCTURAL, FUNCTIONAL, AND EMOTIONAL DEFINITIONS

Much of the information describing the *demographic* (i.e., statistical) characteristics of Canadian families is drawn from census data, gathered nationally every five years. The census uses a very precise definition of "family": a married or common-law couple with or without children living in the same dwelling; a lone parent with at least one child living in the same dwelling; or a grandparent living with at least one grandchild (without a parent present) in the same dwelling (Statistics Canada, 2017). Census families are further classified as *intact* (where children are the biological/adopted children of both parents) or *stepfamilies* (where at least one child is from a previous relationship of one of the spouses/partners).

The census definition has changed a great deal over the years, which means that caution must be exercised when comparing data about families over time. For instance, couples living in common-law relationships were not integrated into the definition until 1981, same-sex couples were not included as common-law partners until 2001 or as married spouses until 2006 (after same-sex marriage was legalized), and stepfamilies were not included as a distinct entity until 2011.

The census definition is *structural*—that is, it defines families on the basis of particular statuses (e.g., parent, child) and a specific physical location (the same dwelling). Its precision facilitates social policy and program planning at the community, regional, and national levels, but that precision also makes it restrictive—that is, it does not include people you may have listed in the description of your own family, such as aunts, uncles, cousins, or pets. And most certainly, many would argue that families are about more

wavebreakmedia/Shutterstock

What is a family?

Michael Ochs Archives/Stringer/Getty

What kinds of families do you see every day?

than just location and a narrow range of statuses. Other definitions of family do go beyond structure to emphasize family processes, functions, and emotions.

Murdock (1949) provided an early anthropological definition of family that referred not only to its structure but also to its internal processes and functions. He defined a family as "a social group characterized by common residence, economic cooperation and reproduction. It contains adults of both sexes, at least two of whom maintain a socially approved sexual relationship, and one or more children, own or adopted, of the sexually cohabiting adults" (p. 1). By this definition, children are necessary for a "family," as is a heterosexual relationship that is "socially approved" (e.g., legal marriage).

The Vanier Institute of the Family presents a contemporary definition that emphasizes the internal processes and functions of families—the everyday "doing" of family life. The institute defines a family as follows:

> Any combination of two or more persons bound together over time by ties of mutual consent, birth, and/or adoption or placement and who, together, assume responsibilities for *variant combinations of some* of the following [emphasis added]:
>
> - physical maintenance and care of group members
> - addition of new members through procreation or adoption
> - socialization of children
> - social control of members
> - production, consumption, distribution of goods and services
> - affective nurturance—love (Vanier Institute of the Family, 2017a)*

*Vanier Institute of the Family, Definition of family. Found at: http://www.vanierinstitute.ca/definition_of_family#.U9pahEje56U (accessed December 3, 2016).

This definition provides much looser boundaries around what a family is than does the census definition or Murdock's structural/functional definition of the mid-20th century. A family does not require the presence of children and does not have to be based on a heterosexual relationship; its members do not necessarily live in the same dwelling; and it may engage in a range of functional activities that differ from those engaged in by other families. The Vanier Institute's definition also brings emotions into the picture—"love."

Many of us would give a central place to the emotional dimension of family life—or, at the very least, of what we think a family is *supposed* to include. A large-scale survey conducted in 1989 found that 74 percent of people defined a family as any group whose members love and care for one another (Coontz, 1992, p. 21), and many of you might support that definition today as well. In cultures around the world, individuals who are not related by blood, marriage, or adoption may be brought inside the boundaries of one's family as **fictive kin** (Ahern & Bailey, 1997; Johnson & Barer, 1990), in *families of choice* or what some Indigenous communities refer to as *families of the heart* (Castellano, 2002, p. 23), assuming some of the benefits and/or some of the obligations of family life.

A growing body of research is exploring how even pets are integrated into this conception of family (Irvine & Cilia, 2017; Laurent-Simpson, 2017). Power's (2008) analysis of dog owners found that more than 95 percent viewed their dogs as family members, referring to them as their children, as similar to their children, or as siblings; they also often referred to their families as "packs." This use of language serves "to emphasize the intensive nature of the relationship that people experienced with their dogs, and to highlight the love, and ongoing emotional and time commitment engendered by those relations" (p. 541). Power conceptualizes such families as "more-than-human families" (p. 535). We have only to look at the value of the pet industry to see how important pets are to Canadian families. More than half of Canadians have at least one pet, and that proportion rises to 75 percent among people ages 45 to 54. In 2015, Canadians spent more than $4 billion on their pets—on food, toys, pet services, and clothing (Packaged Facts, 2015).

Fictive kin: Individuals who are not related by blood, marriage, or adoption but who assume some of the benefits and/or some of the obligations of family life.

Defining family on the basis of love offers the most flexibility, but that strength is also a weakness. First, although it captures the emotional dimension of family life, it is only the positive emotions—love and care—that are emphasized. This represents something of an idealized version of families, one that characterizes some families very well but that glosses over the problems (e.g., family violence) experienced by others. Second, by emphasizing only positive emotions, it fails to capture the complexity of emotions within families. Even families characterized by positive emotional bonds overall experience many challenges and conflicts, and at times the members' feelings toward one another can be ambivalent. For instance, you may enjoy travelling to visit relatives each year and yet not truly consider this to be a vacation. As the famous 20th-century comedian George Burns (1896–1996) quipped: "[For some people] happiness is having a large, loving, caring, close-knit family *in another city* [emphasis added]."[2]

Whether we are talking about the structurally defined census family, Murdock's structural/functional family, the Vanier Institute's functional family, or the "emotional" family of the average person, certain individuals will be *included* within the family boundaries and others necessarily *excluded*. The boundaries placed around families by different groups of people in varying contexts have important real-world implications. Definitions of family determine who is included in social policies, who receives workplace or social benefits, who is accepted as a new immigrant, who can be legally married, and how people are treated in their social interactions. At the micro level, the way *you* define family underlies the choices you make for your own life, your judgments about other people's choices, and your attitudes toward changing trends in Canadian families (see *Sociology in My Life*).

TIME TO REVIEW

- How much of a role do families play in our lives?
- What are the similarities and differences between structural, functional, and emotional definitions of family, and why are definitions of family important?

LO2 CHANGING FAMILIES

The past several decades have been characterized by significant changes in family life, reflected in their structure. Declining marriage rates and delayed onset of marriage, more common-law relationships, increases in lone parenthood, fewer children, and the greater prevalence of same-sex couples are some of the more noteworthy changes. These changes in family structure have led some people to become concerned about the future of family life in Canada.

DECLINING MARRIAGE RATES AND DELAYED ONSET OF MARRIAGE

Fewer people are getting married today than half a century ago. The marriage rate declined from 8.5 to 4.4 per 1,000 between 1975 and 2008 (Ambert, 2015; Milan, 2013) (see *Figure 9.1*). This means that in 2008, of every 1,000 people ages 15 and over, only about half as many got married compared to 1975. Statistics Canada stopped releasing data on marriage rates in 2008. Because marriage rates are based on those ages 15 and over, they include the very young (i.e., 15- to 20-year-olds), who are much less likely to get married now compared to the past. Thus, we must consider additional data in order to look at the state of marriage in Canadian society. In fact, other data do suggest that marriage is slightly less common than it used to be. For example, married couples comprised 67 percent of all census families in 2011, a decrease from 70 percent in 2001 (Statistics Canada, 2012).

However, what accounts for the decline is not really that fewer people believe in marriage or that most people won't marry. Today, people tend to marry at a much later age than in the past. In 1973, the average age of first marriage was 25.2 for men and 22.8 for women; by 2008, those ages had risen to 31.1 and 29.1, respectively (Statistics Canada, 2011). Cohabitational (i.e., common-law) relationships have become much more common as well. In an analysis of cohorts born from 1930 to 1979, Wright (2016) found that the younger cohorts were more likely to choose cohabitation (rather than marriage) as their first union. But Wright reported that when you consider marriage and cohabitation together, the proportion of people who are living in a committed, intimate relationship by the age of 35 has remained relatively constant over the decades.

FIGURE 9.1

Marriage Rates, 1975–2008 (per 1,000 population ages 15+)

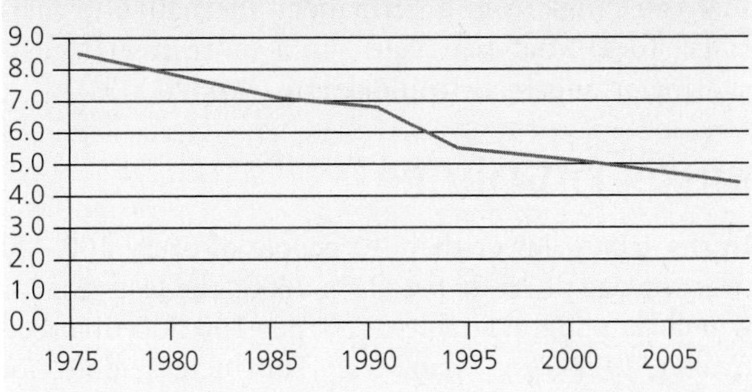

Source: Author drawn. Adapted from: Statistics Canada, CANSIM Table 101-1004, "Crude marriage rates, all marriages, provinces and territories, annual (rates per 1,000 population)"; F. Nault, (1996). Twenty years of marriage. *Health Reports*, 8(2), pp. 39–45 [Table 1: Crude marriage rates, selected countries, 1975, 1980, 1985, 1990, 1994 (Pg. 42)]; A. Milan, (2013). Marital status: Overview, 2011 [Table 1: Marriages and crude marriage rates, Canada, provinces and territories, 1981–2008 (Pg. 9)]. Statistics Canada Catalogue No. 91-209-X.

MORE COMMON-LAW UNIONS

Cohabitational relationships have increased considerably over the last few decades. When common-law unions were first counted in the 1981 census, 6 percent of all census families were common law. This rose to 14 percent in the 2001 census and to almost 17 percent in 2011. Cohabitational relationships are most prevalent in Nunavut, where 33 percent of all census families are common-law couples; they are least prevalent in Ontario (11 percent). Cohabitational unions are most common among individuals ages 25 to 29, but such relationships

YOUR SOCIOLOGICAL TOOLKIT

SOCIOLOGY IN MY LIFE

DEFINING MY FAMILY

The definitions of family presented above are just a few among many specific definitions that exist. They do, though, represent the different types of definitions of families that are often encountered both inside and outside the academic world.

Think Outside the Box: Which definition best corresponds to your earlier description of your own family?

have increased for every age group, including people over 65, indicating the growing acceptability of such relationships in society (Statistics Canada, 2012). Cohabitational relationships may result in marriage; that said, people cohabit in a variety of circumstances that can range from a permanent alternative to marriage, to a "trial marriage," to a more casual cost-sharing arrangement while dating (Wu, 2000).

MORE DIVORCES

In the 1950s, fewer than 40 people of every 100,000 over the age of 15 divorced. In 2008 (the last year for which data are available), 211 per 100,000 divorced (Milan, 2013) (see *Figure 9.2*). This increase does not necessarily mean that significantly more marriages are falling apart. In the past, legislation prevented many couples whose marriages had already "fallen apart" in every meaningful sense from divorcing. Prior to 1968, couples could divorce only if one spouse was able to provide evidence of "fault," such as abuse or adultery; even then, judges had the authority to refuse to grant a divorce. The Divorce Act was changed in 1968 to allow couples to divorce provided that they had been separated for at least three years. Also introduced at that time was *no-fault* divorce, so that evidence of abuse or adultery was no longer necessary; couples could divorce for any reason, such as falling out of love. At the same time, property rights were also changing. In the past, married women's rights to property were limited, so that even if a woman could prove abuse or adultery in court, divorce often meant poverty for herself and her children. With the implementation of new divorce legislation and changing property rights, divorce rates increased, indicating that many couples had already been separated for at least that length of time; now, legislation finally enabled them to legally end their marriages. In 1986, the legislation was changed again, reducing the required period of separation to one year. Again, divorce rates increased. However, since the late 1980s, divorce rates have been declining. Even divorced people continue to value marriage; the vast majority of people who divorce eventually remarry (Ambert, 2009).

In the media, we often hear casual references to half of marriages ending in divorce, but that is not the case. That number is drawn from the United States, when divorces peaked in the 1980s. In Canada, the risk of divorce by the thirtieth anniversary is around 41 percent (Kelly, 2012). However, this number includes divorces that occur in second (or subsequent) marriages as well, when divorce rates are higher (Ambert, 2009).

On remarriage, stepfamilies are often created. The 2011 census was the first to count stepfamilies as distinct entities. Of all families with children, more than 12 percent are stepfamilies. Most of those are *simple stepfamilies*, in which one spouse brings a child into the relationship and no additional children are born. Five percent are *complex stepfamilies*—that is, both spouses bring children from a previous relationship and additional children may or may not be born, or one spouse brings a child from a previous relationship and additional children are born. Stepfamilies must deal with a range of unique issues, such as maintaining relationships with an ex-spouse (as a co-parent of one or more of the children), ambiguity over social roles (e.g., whether a stepparent can legitimately exercise discipline), rivalries between children who may be step- or half-siblings, and more.

FIGURE 9.2

Divorce Rates, 1960–2008 (per 100,000 population ages 15+)

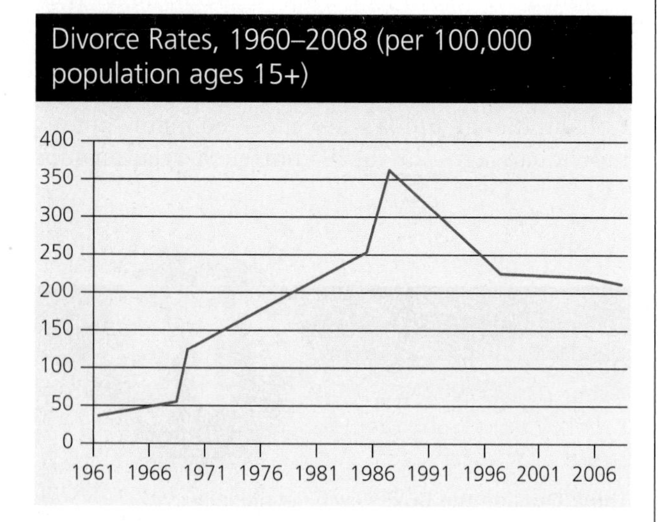

Source: Author drawn. Adapted from: A. M. Ambert, (2009). *Divorce: Facts, causes, and consequences*, 3rd ed. Ottawa, ON: Vanier Institute of the Family [Table 2, Pg. 7]; A. Milan, (2013). Marital status: Overview, 2011 [Table 2: Divorces and crude divorce rates, Canada, provinces and territories, 1981–2008 (Pg. 11)]. Statistics Canada Catalogue No. 91-209-X; Statistics Canada. CANSIM Table 101-6501. Divorces and crude divorce rates, Canada, provinces and territories, annual.

MORE LONE PARENTS

In 1931, 12 percent of children under the age of 24 lived with a lone parent. By 2011, that proportion had increased to 22 percent (Statistics Canada, 2015) (see *Figure 9.3*). Among some groups, that proportion is higher. For instance, 30 percent of Métis children and 37 percent of First Nations children live in lone-parent families (Vanier Institute of the Family, 2017b). This increase is due, in part, to the increase in divorce rates and the dissolution of common-law relationships. Since 2001, the proportion of lone-parent

FIGURE 9.3

Living Arrangements of Children, ages 24 and under, in census families, Canada, 1931 to 2011.

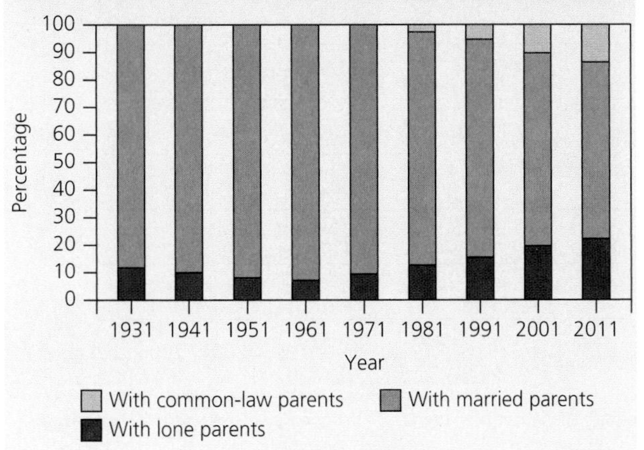

Source: Statistics Canada (2015). Lone-parent families: The new face of an old phenomenon. (Chart 1). *The Daily: Canadian Megatrends*. Catalogue No. 11-630-X2015002. Ottawa, ON: Statistics Canada.

families headed by fathers has increased. However, 80 percent of lone-parent families remain headed by mothers (Statistics Canada, 2015).

MORE SAME-SEX COUPLES

Ontario was the first province to legalize same-sex marriage, in June 2003. Two years later, same-sex marriage was legalized throughout Canada. Although less than 1 percent of married or common-law couples are of the same sex, the number of same-sex couples has increased by more than 42 percent since 2006; this is compared to only a 5 percent increase in the number of opposite-sex couples during the same period. The 2011 census reports that almost 10,000 children under the age of 24 live with two same-sex parents, predominantly female parents (Statistics Canada, 2016a).

FEWER CHILDREN

In 1851, the average woman gave birth to 6.6 children. After that time, birth rates steadily declined, until the post–World War II. This era was known as the baby boom, a time when birth rates increased substantially. In Canada, the **baby boom** occurred between 1946 and 1965 and was a result of several forces. First, the Great Depression of the 1930s caused many women to postpone having children; by 1937, the birth rate had declined to 2.6 children. With strong economic growth during and after the World War II, these women finally began having the children they normally would have had earlier in their lives. Second, during this era, the marriage rate increased, and those who married tended to have more children. Third, people were getting married younger than in previous decades and having their children within the first few years of marriage. Consequently, the baby boom reached a peak in 1959, when the birth rate increased to 3.9 children. By the late 1960s, the boom was over; women were getting married later (in part due to their entry into the labour force) and were postponing parenthood until they were older (in part due to more reliable birth control methods). As a result of these lower fertility rates, by 2011, the average woman was giving birth to 1.6 children (see *Figure 9.4*) (Statistics Canada, 2014). However, birth rates are higher among some immigrant groups and Indigenous peoples (Adserà & Ferrer, 2016; Vanier Institute of the Family, 2017b).

Delayed childbearing can have implications for couples, in that with increased age, women and men are more likely to experience reproductive difficulties. Worldwide, around one in six couples of childbearing age experience infertility (European Society of Human Reproduction and Embryology [ESHRE], 2016). Some may turn to artificial reproductive technologies (known as ART), such as donor insemination, fertility drugs, in vitro fertilization, or surrogate mothers. Around 1 percent of children born in the United States and more than 3 percent of those born in Sweden, Belgium, Czech Republic, Denmark, Estonia, Finland, and Iceland are the result of technologies such as in vitro fertilization. Since 1978 (when the first "test tube" baby was born in England), more than 5 million babies have been born worldwide using these technologies. These technologies provide a wide range of options to alleviate the burden of infertility, but critics point to a number of bioethical issues (Ambert, 2015). First, these technologies are intertwined with social stratification and inequality. Because costs can range up to tens (or even hundreds) of thousands of dollars for many of the technologies, only those who are socioeconomically advantaged are able to resort to them. Second, the broader context of reproductive technologies is such that children are no longer perceived as self-determining human beings but rather as **commodities**—that is, as raw materials to be bought and sold. Children become one more product available for purchase in

Baby boom: The period from 1946 to 1965 during which several demographic forces coalesced, resulting in a larger number of births than would normally be the case.

Commodities: Raw materials that can be bought and sold.

FIGURE 9.4

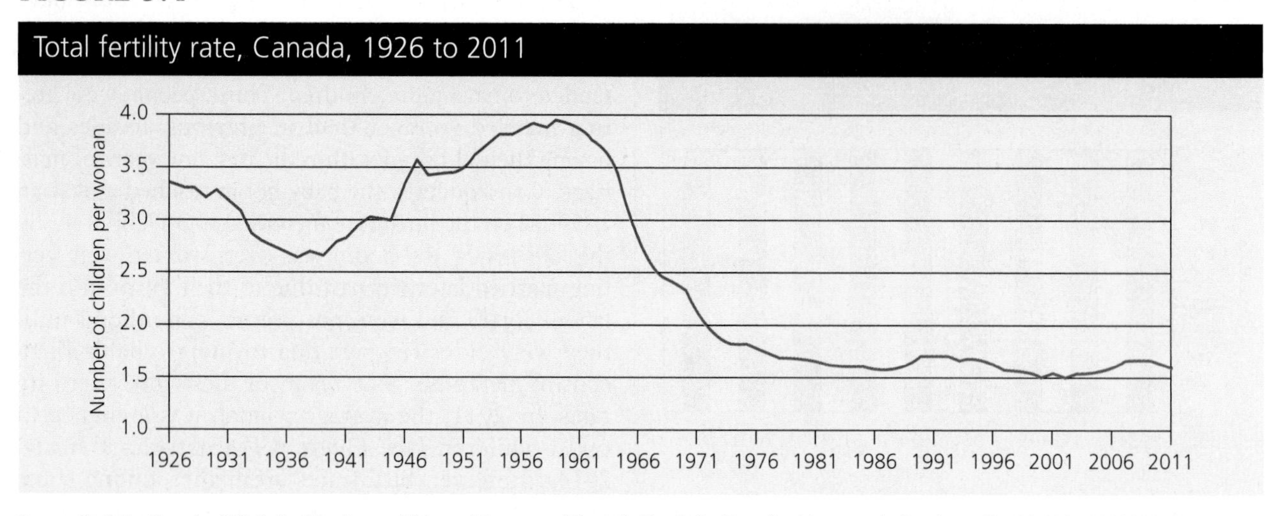

Source: Statistics Canada. (2014). Fertility: Fewer children, older moms. (Chart 1). *The Daily: Canadian Megatrends*. Catalogue No. 11-630-X2014002. Ottawa, ON: Statistics Canada.

a consumerist society, such as a designer handbag or a new car. Third, in cases that involve donor eggs or sperm or a surrogate mother, the resulting children "have needs and rights separate from the wishes of their parents" (Ambert, 2015, p. 239), which opens the door to a variety of legal and human rights debates. Outside of legal debates, additional questions may arise about when it is and is not appropriate to use ART. For example, in 2017, a 64-year-old woman in Spain gave birth to twins after undergoing in vitro fertilization (Associated Press, 2017). Although the twins were described as "perfectly healthy," many people questioned the mother's age, arguing that there was a very good chance that she might not live even to see her children reach adulthood.

Reproductive technologies are becoming more common, even though success rates are not that high, ranging from a low of 25 percent (using frozen embryo transfer) to a high of 48 percent (using egg donation) (ESHRE, 2016). So, in many cases, the decision to delay childbearing for *too* long means that biological children are no longer an option.

Considerable changes have occurred in Canadian families. Since the mid-20th century, large numbers of people have been making very different choices about their family lives. The resulting changes in family structures have led some people to express concern about the future of the family in Canada. But are there other ways to interpret these trends? What do these statistics actually mean?

> There are three kinds of lies: lies, damned lies, and statistics.
>
> (Mark Twain)[3]

Mark Twain is not saying that statistics are fabrications. Rather, he is saying that statistics take on meaning only through interpretation. In other words, the same statistics can be used to support very different and even opposing arguments. Consequently, political, social, and moral arguments that use statistics as a key source of support must be viewed very critically: could the same statistics be interpreted otherwise? On what basis has a particular interpretation been made? One's definition of "family" and the images of family life associated with that definition serve as one's framework for making interpretations. For those who adhere to definitions that stress diversity, choice, and emotional connections, the changes imply greater freedom in society and the removal of constraints that at one time inhibited choice. For those who adhere to definitions that emphasize marriage, the presence of children, and heterosexuality, "family change on the scale that we have seen and are seeing smacks of moral decay" (Lewis, 2003, p. 13) and elicits concern over both what is causing these changes and what the consequences may be: "Are we looking into the abyss where we will no longer care for our kin and learn the habits of industry and respect for others?" (p. 52) Is the family declining? For more than two decades, these questions have been at the heart of the sociology of the family (Ambert, 2015; Powell & Branden, 2007).

LO3 IS "THE FAMILY" DECLINING?

Concerns over family decline are not new. In 1893, Charles Henry Pearson (1893/2003) argued that the increase in non-arranged marriages, the growth of divorce, and declining parental interest in child care had weakened the family, forcing the state to take on a greater role in child care. Public debates over family decline became especially widespread a century later; between 1980 and 1996, Brooks (2002) found a 10-fold increase in the proportion of people who cited family decline as the "most important problem" society faced. In the 21st century, these concerns continue unabated.

Debates over family decline arise from two opposing views: the family decline perspective and the family pluralism perspective (Amato, 2005; Coontz, 1992). The *family decline perspective* is voiced by both some religious conservative groups and some sociologists, the best known of whom is sociologist David Popenoe (1994, 2007). Adherents to this perspective emphasize the disappearance of what they refer to as the "traditional" family—a legally married man and woman, in their first marriage, with children. Increases in divorce, common-law relationships, and same-sex relationships, along with decreases in marriage rates and delayed onset of marriage, are considered indicative of the deterioration of marriage. The reduction in birth rates is interpreted as a "loss of childcenteredness" (Popenoe, 2007, p. 21), which further weakens marriage. The presence of two married, biological parents is said to be the "gold standard for childrearing" (Natelson, 2009); it follows that lone parenthood and stepfamilies are equated with ineffective child socialization. The appropriate type of family is viewed as "not just a private relationship, but a public good" (Hawkins & Van Der Berghe, 2014), in that the supposed consequences of these changes include child poverty, poor school performance, drug use, and criminal behaviour. When the family is perceived as the "bedrock" (Lewis, 2003, p. 9) of society, weaker marriages and the decline of the family necessarily mean that society's well-being is put at risk. Even democracy itself is endangered (Whitehead, 2006).

Proponents of the family decline perspective underscore the harm done by "non-traditional" families. Conversely, those who support the *family pluralism perspective* applaud family diversity (Amato, 2005; Coontz, 1992). They argue that the decline perspective is based on myths and misunderstandings about family life that draw from nostalgia for some golden age in which families were somehow better off than they are today. Supporters of the pluralism perspective contend that the past was not as "golden" as these nostalgic images suggest. Families in all cultures and at all times have faced difficulties—poverty, violence, marital disruption, social disruption, family dissatisfaction, inequality. The common-law couples, single parents, and remarriages that are lamented within the decline perspective have, in fact, always existed in Canadian society; the difference is that in the past, they were normally due not to choice but rather to circumstances outside the individual's control, such as the death of a spouse or the need to provide care for one's aging parents in an era that lacked public social supports (Milan, 2000). The fact that individuals have greater freedom of choice now than in the past means that they have more opportunity to achieve relationship and life satisfaction (Ambert, 2015).

Coontz (1992) cautions against the extremism evident in both perspectives. She argues that the decline and pluralism perspectives both tend to be oversimplified and are based on idealized images. The decline perspective upholds an idyllic image of a better, stronger family from the past (something akin to an image drawn from 1950s television). The pluralism perspective often maintains an idealized image of diverse contemporary families freed from the rigid constraints of the past, offering "soothing words about achieving 'self-actualization' ... [and] divorce [as] a 'growth experience'" (p. 1). The former tends to ignore the family problems and crises of the past; the latter tends to gloss over those of today.

SOCIOLOGY ON SCREEN

THE PERFECT FAMILY DINNER

On YouTube, you can find a 10-minute public service announcement called "1950 Family Date, Dinner in a 1950s Home." It reflects the idealized, nostalgic image of family life that Coontz (1992) suggests underlies the contemporary arguments of proponents of the family decline perspective. This video clip will make some of you laugh, whereas others may find themselves yelling at the screen. Show your own family this clip the next time you are about to sit down for dinner!

Because statistical trends require careful interpretation, the lens through which one views those trends is crucial. What do rising divorce rates and declining marriage rates mean? Through one lens, it means that commitment has become unimportant to people; through another, it can mean that marriage and commitment are *so* important to people that they are unwilling to tolerate the dissatisfying marriages that many people were forced to endure in the past. What about declining birth rates? One lens reveals that people are becoming more selfish and are unwilling to sacrifice their own interests; another reveals that people are taking the time to plan for their children (Hareven, 1994).

So how *are* we to interpret the changes in Canadian families? Ambert (2015) points out that *some* families do experience difficulties, in large part because of structured social inequalities and a lack of sufficient public resources. Nevertheless, she argues that the challenges faced by families should not be conflated with the decline of *the* family as a social institution.

TIME TO REVIEW

- What are some of the most significant trends in family life over the last several decades, and what do these changes mean?
- What are the arguments used on both sides of the family decline debate, and why does Coontz (1992) warn against extremism?

LO4 DIFFICULTIES FACED BY SOME FAMILIES

Greater diversity in family life does reflect more freedom and choice, which we value in society. But at the same time, family diversity cannot simply be equated with positive outcomes. For example, children born into common-law relationships are at more than four times greater risk of experiencing family disruption by the age of 10 than are those born into marital relationships (Ambert, 2015). Divorce does not just bring opportunities for greater life satisfaction; it is also associated with emotional strife and hardship for both adults and children (at least temporarily).

Monogamous: A marriage that includes two spouses.

Polygamous: A marriage that includes three or more spouses simultaneously.

Nuclear: A family structure comprising parents and their children.

Extended: A family structure that includes parents, their children, and additional relatives.

In addition to the challenges posed by greater family diversity, some families face other types of problems. In previous chapters, you learned about many of the difficulties some individuals encounter in Canada today and thus also some families. In the chapter on social inequality, you learned that between 9 and 13 percent of Canadians have low incomes and that some social groups are at greater risk of poverty than others, including lone-parent families, people with disabilities, those who are foreign-born, and Indigenous people. More than 15 percent of Canadian children live in low-income families, with the proportion higher for children in female-headed lone-parent families (45 percent) and in Indigenous families (50 percent of those living off-reserve and 60 percent of those living on reserve) (Macdonald & Wilson, 2016; Statistics Canada, 2016b).

In the chapter on race and ethnicity, you learned about the various challenges faced by members of some ethnic groups, especially those who are foreign-born and those who are racialized. Children of immigrants are bicultural and must find ways to adapt to the often-conflicting norms of the heritage culture they are exposed to at home *and* to the new, national culture outside the home. Some adaptations benefit youth's psychological and/or sociocultural adjustment, whereas others are detrimental to that adjustment (Berry et al., 2006). Furthermore, members of minority groups continue to face discrimination; because it affects individuals, it affects their families (as well as the broader ethnic community). The effects of discrimination on families are especially evident in Indigenous families in that practices and policies associated with colonization have had an impact on families over generations.

INDIGENOUS FAMILIES: PAST AND PRESENT

Worldwide, there are varied family structures and arrangements. In some cultures, marriages are **monogamous** (i.e., an individual has only one spouse at any given time), whereas in others, they are **polygamous** (i.e., an individual has multiple spouses at any given time). Whereas households in some societies are built around **nuclear** families (consisting of those within the marital relationship and their children), others are **extended**, including additional relatives such as siblings and/or grandparents. Structures of power vary as well. Some cultures are

YOUR SOCIOLOGICAL TOOLKIT

CRITICAL THINKING IN ACTION

PATRIARCHY AND PATRILINEALITY TODAY

Because of the changes in gender roles over the past several decades, people often consider patriarchy and patrilineality as characteristic of only the past. But many scholars still consider Canadian society to be patriarchal and patrilineal.

Think Outside the Box: In what ways do you continue to see patriarchy and patrilineality in society today?

patriarchal, in that power is vested in the male head of the household according to social custom, religious doctrine, and the law. Although there is some debate over whether **matriarchal** cultures (wherein power is vested in the female head of the household) have ever existed, women have certainly held more power within some cultures than within others. Some cultures trace family lineage through the father's side of the family (i.e., they are **patrilineal**), whereas others trace ancestry through the mother's side of the family (known as **matrilineal**) or both sides of the family (known as **bilineal**) (see *Critical Thinking in Action*).

Thus, when Europeans first arrived in the land now called Canada, they encountered varied family structures and arrangements in different Indigenous cultures (Castellano, 2002). Some intimate relationships were monogamous, whereas others were polygamous.[4] Some households were nuclear, whereas others were extended. Although Indigenous cultures were not matriarchal, women frequently had greater power than their European counterparts. Some Indigenous cultures were patrilineal, whereas others were matrilineal (Chansonneuve, 2005). Among most Indigenous cultures, the notion of family was (and still is) extensive, based more on relationships between people than on static roles within a structure. Families were created and expanded through affiliations, adoptions, ceremonial practices, marriages that joined bloodlines, and the real or symbolic presence of past and future generations (Perrault & Proulx, 2000). Language reflected the various forms of family ties, so among the Inuit, *qatangutgiit* referred to family relationships based on blood ties, whereas *ilagiit* referred to an "outer" family of extended relationships, and *tuqlluraniq* referred to the ancestor whose spirit was thought to reside in a particular child and after whom that child was named (Chansonneuve, 2005).

The sheer variability in family structures and arrangements in Indigenous cultures was viewed as problematic by European colonizers, for whom the only family form that was legally and religiously sanctioned was monogamous, patriarchal, and patrilineal (Gaffield, 1990, 1992). In Euro-Canadian families, religious doctrine and social norms dictated that the husband/father bore responsibility for his wife and children's salvation. With short lifespans and high death rates, especially for children and women, achieving salvation was seen as an urgent matter. Considering this religious interpretation at the time, along with the view of women and children as property rather than "persons," it should come as no surprise that paternal discipline of both wives and children was quite strict and sometimes even violent. Child abuse and wife abuse would not be criminalized until near the turn of the 20th century, several decades *after* animal abuse was criminalized.

The relative absence of patriarchal authority in many Indigenous cultures, in conjunction with different spiritual belief systems, created different familial contexts. Children were perceived as gifts from the Creator, gifts not only to the parents but also to the entire community; as such, they were the responsibility of everyone in the community. As "gifts," they were

Patriarchal: Power is vested in the male head of household and men in society more generally.

Matriarchal: Power is vested in the female head of household and women in society more generally.

Patrilineal: Lineage is traced through the father's side of the family, especially its male members.

Matrilineal: Lineage is traced through the mother's side of the family, especially its female members.

Bilineal: Lineage is traced through both parents' sides of the family.

to be treated with kindness and affection. Children were socialized through observation, role modelling, natural consequences for misbehaviour, and counselling by elders rather than through discipline informed by physical punishment, fear, or humiliation.

These differences in family life were tolerated during the fur trade era, but as agriculture expanded, economic alliances between Europeans and Indigenous peoples declined in importance, and the government focused increasingly on assimilation. Indigenous children were key to that effort; once they were assimilated, whole Indigenous cultures would follow. Central to this project were the residential schools (discussed in the chapter on race and ethnicity), which tore families apart. Indigenous children were forcibly sent to them, and as a result, multiple generations of children grew up outside any type of family environment. Indeed, tearing families apart was the *purpose* of those schools. Chief Cinderena Williams of the Spallumcheen band (cited in Castellano, 2002, pp. 18–19) explains:

> Later when these children returned home, they were aliens. They did not speak their own language, so they could not communicate with anyone other than their counterparts. Some looked down on their families because of their lack of English, their lifestyle, and some were just plain hostile. They had formed no bonds with their families, and some couldn't survive without the regimentation they had become accustomed to.... Consequently, when these children became parents, and most did at an early age, they had no parenting skills. They did not have the capability to show affection. They sired and bred children but were unable to relate to them on any level.

And then *their* children were taken to residential schools, where they faced the very same experience. As a result, many members of several generations developed residential school syndrome. In the 1960s, child welfare authorities began to step in on a large scale. Sometimes this was because of problems in individual families, such as substance abuse or domestic violence. Other times, "children were taken from parents whose only crime was poverty—and being aboriginal" (Fournier and Crey, 1997, p. 85). This era is known as the *sixties scoop*. For instance, in British Columbia in 1955, only 1 percent of all children in foster care were Indigenous; by 1964, that proportion rose to 34 percent, with almost all of those children having been placed with non-Indigenous families in non-Indigenous communities (Johnston, 1983). Today, although Indigenous children comprise only 7 percent of all children in Canada, they account for 48 percent of those in foster care (Vanier Institute of the Family, 2017b). Many of the challenges facing Indigenous people in the present day have their roots in colonial practices: poverty, family disruption, illness, violence, disability, poverty, and suicide (Chartrand & McCay, 2006). According to many scholars and community activists, reducing the problems faced by some Indigenous communities must begin with strengthening families (Sinclair, 2016).

FAMILY VIOLENCE

Although families in certain social groups can face very distinctive problems, other problems can affect families of all socioeconomic statuses and ethnic backgrounds—for example, family violence. Family violence can be psychological, physical, sexual, or financial and can take different forms, including

SOCIOLOGY ON SCREEN

(DIS)PLACED: INDIGENOUS YOUTH AND THE CHILD WELFARE SYSTEM

In the documentary *(Dis)Placed: Indigenous Youth and the Child Welfare System*, director Melisa Brittain and First Nations advocate Cindy Blackstock point out that just as the residential schooling policy of the past forcibly removed Indigenous children from their homes and families, so too does the child welfare system of the present day. In the film, Indigenous youth who have spent time in the child welfare system discuss their experiences in foster care, their strategies of resistance to assimilation, and the implications from the micro level of their own lives to the macro level of Indigenous cultures and Canadian society as a whole.

spousal/partner abuse, child abuse, or elder abuse. The prevalence of family violence is unclear because it is significantly underreported and takes place behind closed doors. In the 2014 General Social Survey, 4 percent of adults with a current or former spouse or common-law partner reported having been physically or sexually assaulted within the previous five years. Men were just as likely as women to report being abused, but a greater proportion of women experienced more severe forms of abuse, such as being beaten, threatened with a weapon, or sexually assaulted. Seventy percent of victims (more men than women) said they did not report the incident to the police (Burczycka, 2016).

The General Social Survey found that intimate violence occurred in dating relationships as well. Of those who had dated within the past five years, 7 percent said that a dating partner had tried to limit their contact with family or friends, called them derogatory names, or threatened to harm them or someone close to them. Another 4 percent reported physical violence, and 1 percent experienced sexual violence within a dating relationship (Burczycka, 2016).

Data on child abuse are often gathered from police reports. In 2014, more than 50,000 cases of physical assault and sexual offences against children came to the attention of authorities. In almost one-third of cases, it was by a family member, most often a parent; the younger the child, the more likely the abuse was perpetrated by a parent. However, child abuse at the hands of a family member is most likely during adolescence, between the ages 12 and 17. The rate of victimization by family violence is higher for girls (274 per 100,000 population) than for boys (190 per 100,000 population), and girls are four times as likely to be sexually abused compared to boys (Ibrahim & Karam, 2016). There appears to be a relationship between child abuse and intimate partner violence in later life, in that a greater proportion of people who have been abused by an intimate partner report abuse during childhood compared to people who have not been abused by an intimate partner (Burczycka, 2016).

The prevalence of senior abuse is also difficult to ascertain. In 2014, more than 9,000 cases of violence against persons ages 65 and over were reported to the police. Of these, 34 percent were at the hands of a family member, making the rate of family violence against seniors 59.6 per 100,000 population (more for women than for men). The perpetrators are most often a spouse or an adult child; women are more likely to be assaulted by a spouse, whereas men are more likely to be assaulted by an adult child (Ibrahim, 2016).

LO5 IS THE FAMILY IN DECLINE?

In Canadian society, *some* families experience significant difficulties, be it because of poverty, cultural destruction, or violence. But this does not mean that the family as a social institution is declining. Rather, it is more indicative of an absence of social supports for the diverse needs of families in a changing society. This problem is worsened by governments' emphasis on quick fixes to garner votes in the next election rather than on family support policies that would take longer (in some cases, even a generation) to have beneficial effects (Ambert, 2015).

TIME TO REVIEW

- What types of difficulties are faced by some families in Canada today, and what are their relationships to socioeconomic status and ethnicity?
- In what ways did the positions of women and children in Indigenous and Euro-Canadian families differ historically?
- How did government policies, such as residential schooling, affect Indigenous individuals, families, and communities?
- What are the patterns of family violence in Canada today?
- Why should the problems faced by some families not be considered indicative of the decline of the family as a social institution?

YOUR SOCIOLOGICAL TOOLKIT
SOCIOLOGY IN THEORY

LO6 SOCIOLOGY IN THEORY

The study of families has always been more empirical than theoretical, focusing on narrow, specific topics (e.g., marital and life satisfaction within arranged marriages; factors influencing the decision not to have children) (Powell & Brandon, 2007; Turner, 2005). Although empirical research normally has some type of theoretical foundation, sometimes that foundation is not explicitly stated. Furthermore, Taylor and Bagdi (2005) find that the two most common theories applied in family studies—social exchange theory and family life course development theory—lie outside the core theoretical frameworks described in Chapter 1. Both emphasize the micro level more than the macro level.

SOCIAL EXCHANGE THEORY

Social exchange theory is "among the most prevalent conceptual frameworks for examining and understanding ... relationship dynamics" (Paat, 2013, p. 938). It is most closely associated with *social psychology*, which studies individual thoughts, feelings, and behaviours in social situations. This area of study straddles the line between sociology and psychology and is practised by both sociologists and psychologists. This theory begins with the assumption that society is composed of individuals who are motivated by self-interest. Thus, in our social interactions, we make choices based on a rational calculation of the costs and benefits of those interactions.

According to Nye (1979), every relationship is an exchange between people that carries with it both benefits and costs; that is, in any relationship, we do some "giving" and we do some "getting." The resources exchanged can be tangible, such as financial support, or intangible, such as loyalty and affection. Ultimately, individuals wish to pursue or maintain relationships in which a **profit** is derived—the positive benefits outweigh the costs of being in that relationship. However, costs and benefits are relative rather than absolute. First, there is the **comparison level**, where we ask ourselves how much we are putting into and getting out of the relationship compared to other people in similar relationships. Second, there is the **comparison level for alternatives**, where we compare our relationship to possible alternatives ("Could I find a better partner?"). We also seek some level of **equity** in our relationships, such that the contributions made by each party are viewed as being fair.

Profit: The benefits of being in a particular relationship outweigh the costs.

Comparison level: A comparison of the costs and benefits of a particular relationship compared to other people who are in similar types of relationships.

Comparison level for alternatives: A comparison of our relationship to alternative possibilities for our lives.

Equity: The contributions each party is making in a relationship are perceived as "fair."

As the most common theory used in the study of families, social exchange theory has been applied to a range of topics, beginning with dating and the mate selection process (Paat, 2013). Principles of exchange come into play even in deciding whom to date. Dating apps or online dating sites make the exchange explicit, where dating profiles offer the resources the individual has (such as physical appearance) and the resources sought in a dating partner (such as age or hobbies). Equity becomes more important as dating relationships progress and is associated with satisfaction within relationships and the likelihood of relationships lasting. The role of equity continues to gain in importance with marriage, where perceptions of fairness are based on relationship outcomes meeting or exceeding a person's expectations (Paat, 2013).

Previti and Amato (2003) evaluated the tenets of exchange theory in a 17-year longitudinal study of married couples. They found that marital cohesiveness depended more on the *rewards* associated with the relationship (e.g., love, respect, friendship, good communication) than on perceptions of *alternatives* or on *barriers* to divorce (the costs associated with divorcing, such as loss of contact with children, financial strain, and religious views). They concluded that barriers to divorce keep unhappy couples together only for a little bit longer. Some research analyzes the role of specific types of resources in determining the likelihood of divorce. As discussed in another chapter, on average, women continue to have lower incomes than men. This means that in many heterosexual marriages, women have lower incomes than their husbands, which reduces the range of alternatives for women and thereby creates an obstacle to divorce. Although higher levels of education and income tend to create more satisfying marriages overall (and thereby reduce the likelihood of divorce), women with more education and higher incomes are more likely than other women to leave dissatisfying marriages, especially in cases of domestic violence (Kreager et al., 2013).

Parent–child relationships are characterized by exchange as well, especially once children reach adulthood (Paat, 2013). You might consider your own situation or that of many of your classmates. As an adult, living with parents means sacrificing some of your freedom, privacy, and independence. Yet if you are a full-time postsecondary student, you might consider that sacrifice to be "fair" because of the financial benefits you derive from not having to pay the costs of living independently (e.g., rent or a mortgage, groceries, utilities). Living in the family home as an adult often involves negotiations about exchange as well. For instance, the adult child may not have to pay rent but may have to adhere to parental rules (e.g., music volume; overnight partners), purchase the groceries, or take care of the yardwork.

FAMILY LIFE COURSE DEVELOPMENT THEORY

This framework has as its core assumption the notion that families transition through a series of qualitatively different "stages" over time. As families transition from

YOUR SOCIOLOGICAL TOOLKIT

SOCIOLOGY IN MY COMMUNITY

STRENGTHENING NEWCOMER FAMILIES

For recent immigrants to Canada, the challenges faced in the transition to parenthood are magnified by the complexities of adapting to life in a new culture. The Global Gathering Place in Saskatoon offers a wide range of programs and services for recent immigrants. As part of their ESTEEM program (Enhancing Skills To Enrich Eager Minds), *BrightStart!* uses weekly songs, presentations, and structured play to help immigrant mothers with young children increase language skills, expand parenting skills, and develop tools to enhance their children's development. Similar programs can be found in communities across the country.

Think Outside the Box: Why might a group setting, such as in BrightStart!, be especially beneficial for young mothers who are new to Canada?

one stage to the next, family structures, roles, and relationships change. The transition to parenthood is the stage of family development that has received the most academic attention. As anyone who has made this transition can likely attest, bringing one's first baby home is accompanied by a considerable amount of stress, caused by everything from a lack of sleep to changes in roles; in fact, research has found that this is one of the most stressful family transitions. New parenthood takes a particular toll on the relationship between spouses or partners, causing a significant decline in feelings of "love," as well as increases in conflict and feelings of ambivalence about the relationship. This has been found with both biological and adoptive parents and with heterosexual, gay, and lesbian parents (Goldberg, Smith, & Kashy, 2010). However, the magnitude of this impact varies with the psychological and social resources the parents bring to their new roles (see *Sociology in My Community*).

Not only can the transition to parenthood affect the quality of the relationship between the parents, it can also have a negative impact on psychological well-being. Women who have had an unwanted birth (i.e., who did not plan to have children) or a mistimed birth (i.e., who wanted a child, but at some time in the future) are more likely to experience depression 5 to 13 years later compared to women who have had wanted and appropriately timed births (Rackin & Brasher, 2016).

So far, we have seen that sociological knowledge about families is often derived from perspectives outside the core theoretical perspectives in sociology. However, although the core theoretical perspectives are not applied as widely, we can see families being addressed within functionalist, conflict, feminist, and interactionist theories.

Design Pics/Thinkstock

Becoming a new parent is one of the most stressful family transitions.

FUNCTIONALIST THEORIES

In another chapter, you learned about Parsons's theorizing about the functionality of traditional gender roles (Parsons, 1954; Parsons and Bales, 1955). Making males responsible for instrumental tasks and females responsible for expressive tasks ensured that the family (a cornerstone of society, from the functionalist perspective) kept running smoothly. Of course, in the 21st century, parents increasingly share instrumental and expressive tasks, and this has necessitated changes in social policy, such as policies governing parental leave.

Functionalist theorizing about families precedes the work of Parsons. Émile Durkheim questioned how modernization was affecting families and how changes in families were affecting the social order. He addressed issues such as the liberalization of divorce, the effective socialization of children, and the household division of labour (Lamanna, 2002)—issues also highlighted in contemporary debates about family decline. However, Durkheim did not consider the family to be in trouble due to modernization. In response to a colleague who decried a decline in parenting and the weakening of the family, Durkheim argued that the family "is not appreciably worse than it was; it is [just] different" (in Lamanna, 2002, p. 1). Anne-Marie Ambert (2015) concurs, pointing out that families today serve some additional functions to those of the past, such as policing children's use of media, as well as integrating or coordinating the various other sources of socialization that children face (such as at school, in extracurricular activities, and with peers).

The functionalist perspective is also evident in current debates about family decline, when family is defined in terms of its internal processes and functions, such as the socialization of children and affective nurturance (Murdock, 1949; Vanier Institute of the Family, 2017a). Functionalist assumptions can be applied to a number of areas within the study of families. In this regard, there is a sizeable body of research on gender role differentiation and the household division of labour (White, Klein, & Martin, 2015).

CONFLICT THEORIES

In another chapter, you learned that Engels (1884/1972) proposed that the transition from feudalism to capitalism had resulted in patriarchy. Male workers were subordinated by their employers, and women and children were subordinated by adult men. Engels claimed that female subordination in families would end if women entered paid employment. Shifting attention to inequalities within groups, conflict theories propose that resources are distributed unequally *within* families; thus, conflict emerges as family members compete over those resources.

Conflict is viewed as an inherent (and normal) part of family relationships, which are characterized by everyday disagreements. For instance, siblings often have conflicts over valuable resources (e.g., the gaming console, parental attention). Conflicts between full siblings (who share two parents) are more common than between half-siblings (in stepfamilies). Research suggests that this is because competition over parental attention is a primary source of sibling conflict, and full siblings must compete over attention from two shared parents (rather than just one). Despite the higher levels of conflict, relationships between full siblings tend to be closer than between half-siblings (Tanskanen et al., 2016).

Monkey Business Images/Shutterstock

According to conflict theories, some degree of conflict is characteristic of all relationships, including within the family.

Some conflict theories suggest that family conflict is distinctive because of the uniquely emotional nature of resources within families. Other conflict theories, however, suggest that family conflict is a microcosm of societal conflict, a reflection of broader social inequalities (White Klein, & Martin, 2015). In a classic analysis of wife abuse in the United States, Straus (1994) found some support for this latter view. Straus found that the prevalence of wife assault varied across states, based on both gender inequality (e.g., differences in the average income of men and women) and social disorganization (e.g., high divorce rates, low levels of religious affiliation). Today, we see additional support in the fact that Indigenous women are much more likely to be victims of domestic violence than non-Indigenous women (Burczycka, 2016). Family violence is one of the topics to which conflict theories are most often applied. Feminist theories have also addressed family violence, among a range of other topics.

FEMINIST THEORIES

Families are central to feminist theorizing (Allen, 2016; Fox, 2015). Families are highlighted as playing a pivotal role in the gendering of people's experiences at the micro level and in the reproduction of the gendered structure of society at the macro level. Feminist theories are critical of mainstream theories for reinforcing romantic images of family life. Instead, feminist theories have been central to "problematizing assumptions of equality, fairness, and well-being in marriage in family relationships, particularly as they disadvantage women" (Allen, 2016, p. 208). Feminist theories were the first to draw attention to household responsibilities (like laundry and child care) as being "work" rather than "leisure," women's ambivalent

YOUR SOCIOLOGICAL TOOLKIT

SOCIOLOGY IN PRACTICE

PARENTING AFTER SEPARATION

Parental separation or divorce carries with it significant psychological, social, and practical consequences for children. Research shows that how parents carry on their roles *as parents* during and after separation is central to the magnitude of the effects on children and how long those effects last. In regions across North America, Parenting After Separation (PAS) courses or workshops have been developed to address these issues. PAS courses provide information on legal issues, child development, research on the effects of divorce on children, conflict resolution skills, and how to develop effective co-parenting plans. In most regions, PAS courses are free of charge, and any parent who has recently separated may voluntarily enroll. Some Canadian provinces and U.S. states go a step further by mandating that parents must take a PAS course prior to filing a divorce application.

Think Outside the Box: From a symbolic interactionist perspective, why are PAS courses beneficial?

feelings toward motherhood, and the second shift (whereby women tend to bear the brunt of household responsibilities even when employed full-time) (Allen, 2016; Fox, 2015).

Feminist theories were also the first to challenge heteronormativity and point out that there is no single, monolithic "family" but rather a plurality of family forms (Allen, 2016; Eichler, 1988, 1997; Fox, 2015). Today, that view is extended even further, "incorporating intersectional and international perspectives on how race, class, sexual orientation, nation, and other structures of social hierarchy differentially stratify and challenge gendered experiences in families" (Allen, 2016, p. 208).

Even when feminist theories are not explicitly applied, the knowledge we have about families owes a great debt to feminist scholars and activists. Although feminist scholars were the first to emphasize the importance of analyzing the nature and implications of the gendered division of labour within families, now sociologists of all theoretical orientations explore this area of study. And because feminist scholars pointed to the power of gender in all aspects of our lives, gender is now integrated into virtually every topic area in the study of families, from mate selection to parenting to aging families.

INTERACTIONIST THEORIES

Interactionist theories suggest that as the most "significant" of *significant others*, families shape our understandings of the world and our place in it. Similarly, our understandings of the world come into play in our everyday lives as family members. In a classic interactionist analysis of marriage, Jessie Bernard (1972) pointed out that husbands and wives often have very different perceptions of their marriage, such that one can refer to "his marriage" and "her marriage." For example, the husband may indicate that they rarely have disagreements, whereas the wife may say they often have disagreements; he may say he engages in childcare activities on a daily basis, whereas she says he does so only a few times a week.

When two people have differing perceptions of the same issue, there can be significant consequences. Research with divorced mothers and fathers shows that they often have different perceptions of both fathers' parenting skills and mothers' willingness to accommodate changes to visitation schedules. When perceptions vary on these issues, parents are less able to establish effective co-parenting styles, and conflicts

...honestly I just feel like we don't communicate like we used to!

between them increase—to the detriment of the children involved (Madden-Derdich & Leonard, 2002) (see *Sociology in Practice*).

People's subjective perceptions and understandings also play a role in intimate violence. Some victims of dating violence or domestic violence don't identify themselves as having been abused because they define "abuse" as something more than the slapping and pushing that they may have experienced. Similarly, perpetrators often don't identify themselves as "batterers" because they have hit their partner only a few times or have perpetrated violence against only one partner throughout their lives (Goodrum, Umberson, & Anderson, 2001).

As the quotation at the start of the chapter pointed out, "we start and end with families." But precisely which family each of us "starts" and "ends" with can vary—from the specific family structure defined by the census, to the functional family described by the Vanier Institute, to the relationships established on the basis of love that are described in emotional definitions of family, to the fictive kin or families of the heart that are a part of many people's lives. Even though some families experience more challenges than others, families remain central to contemporary social life, and sociology enables us to better understand various aspects of families—in the past, the present, and the future.

TIME TO REVIEW

- Why has the study of families been described as an empirically driven enterprise?
- What are the two most frequently used theories in empirical research on families? What are their core assumptions, and what family-related topic areas have been studied?
- Which of the core theoretical frameworks in sociology have been recognized as some of the main intellectual traditions in the study of families? In what areas have those theories contributed to our knowledge about families?

CHAPTER SUMMARY

LO1 Compare varying definitions of family and explain why the way family is defined is important.

There are structural, functional, and emotional definitions. Structural definitions emphasize family statuses, whereas functional definitions focus on the everyday "doing" of family life, and emotional definitions draw attention to affection. The definition used has implications at the macro level *and* the micro level.

LO2 Identify the key trends that indicate changes in Canadian families.

Marriage rates have declined, cohabitation has increased, divorce has increased, same-sex relationships have increased, and people have had fewer children.

LO3 Distinguish between the main assumptions of the family decline and family pluralism perspectives.

The family decline perspective claims that recent changes in families are indicative of family crisis or decline. By contrast, the family pluralism perspective suggests that changes in families are indicative of fewer constraints and greater freedom than in the past.

LO4 Outline the difficulties that some families face in Canada today.

Many children live in low-income families, which affects various aspects of their lives. Families of certain ethnic backgrounds face particular challenges in terms of economic conditions and racialization. The effects of systemic/institutionalized discrimination are especially evident when considering Indigenous families, not just in the past but in the present day. The problem of family violence is not limited to any social group.

LO5 Explain why the fact that some families experience problems is not indicative of a decline of the family as a social institution.

The problems experienced by some families are indicative of a lack of societal supports for the diverse needs of families in a changing society. Government policies emphasize short-term issues rather than long-term outcomes.

LO6 Explain how each of the following theories contributes to knowledge about families: social exchange, family life course development, functionalist, conflict, feminist, and interactionist.

Social exchange theory claims that relationships are based on an exchange of resources and associated with costs and benefits. Family life course development theory suggests that families progress through qualitatively different stages associated with changes in family structures, roles, and interactions. Functionalist theories explore how families are best able to fulfill their functions, such as child socialization. Conflict theories state that even within families, there is competition over scarce resources that can be associated with power differentials. Feminist theories are of a wide range, but the relationship between families and gender is central to all of them. Interactionist theories draw attention to the fact that families shape our understandings of the world and ourselves and that our understandings of the world come into play within our everyday lives as family members.

RECOMMENDED RESOURCES

1. For a broad introduction to the sociology of families, see M. Ward & M. Belanger, *The Family Dynamic: A Canadian Perspective* (6th ed.) (Toronto, ON: Nelson, 2015).
2. In media debates about children being raised by same-sex parents, the voices of children themselves are often absent. To hear some of their voices, see director Maya Newell's award-winning Australian documentary film *Gaybe Baby* (http://thegaybyproject.com).
3. To learn more about how to educate children about the value in family diversity, see the short educational film *Our Family: A Film About Family Diversity* (a joint production of *Our Family Coalition* and *Not in Our School*). The film is available at no cost on YouTube.

FOR FURTHER REFLECTION

1. Where would you situate yourself in the family decline debate?
2. Consider an issue you consider central in your own family. Which of the theories addressed in this chapter do you think could best address that issue? Which of the theories do you think would be the least useful in exploring that issue?

ENDNOTES

1 Retrieved April 14, 2017, from "ThinkExist.com Quotations" (thinkexist.com).

2 Retrieved April 22, 2017, from "The Quotations Page" (thequotationspage.com).

3 Retrieved April 23, 2017, from "The Quotations Page" (thequotationspage.com).

4 Some family historians (Bourgeault, 1991) suggest that polygamous marriages did not exist in Indigenous cultures until after colonization, when intense competition in the fur trade, along with the central role of women in trade relationships, required some men to take on multiple wives for pragmatic economic reasons.

10 CHAPTER

Learning What Is "True": Religion, Science, and Education

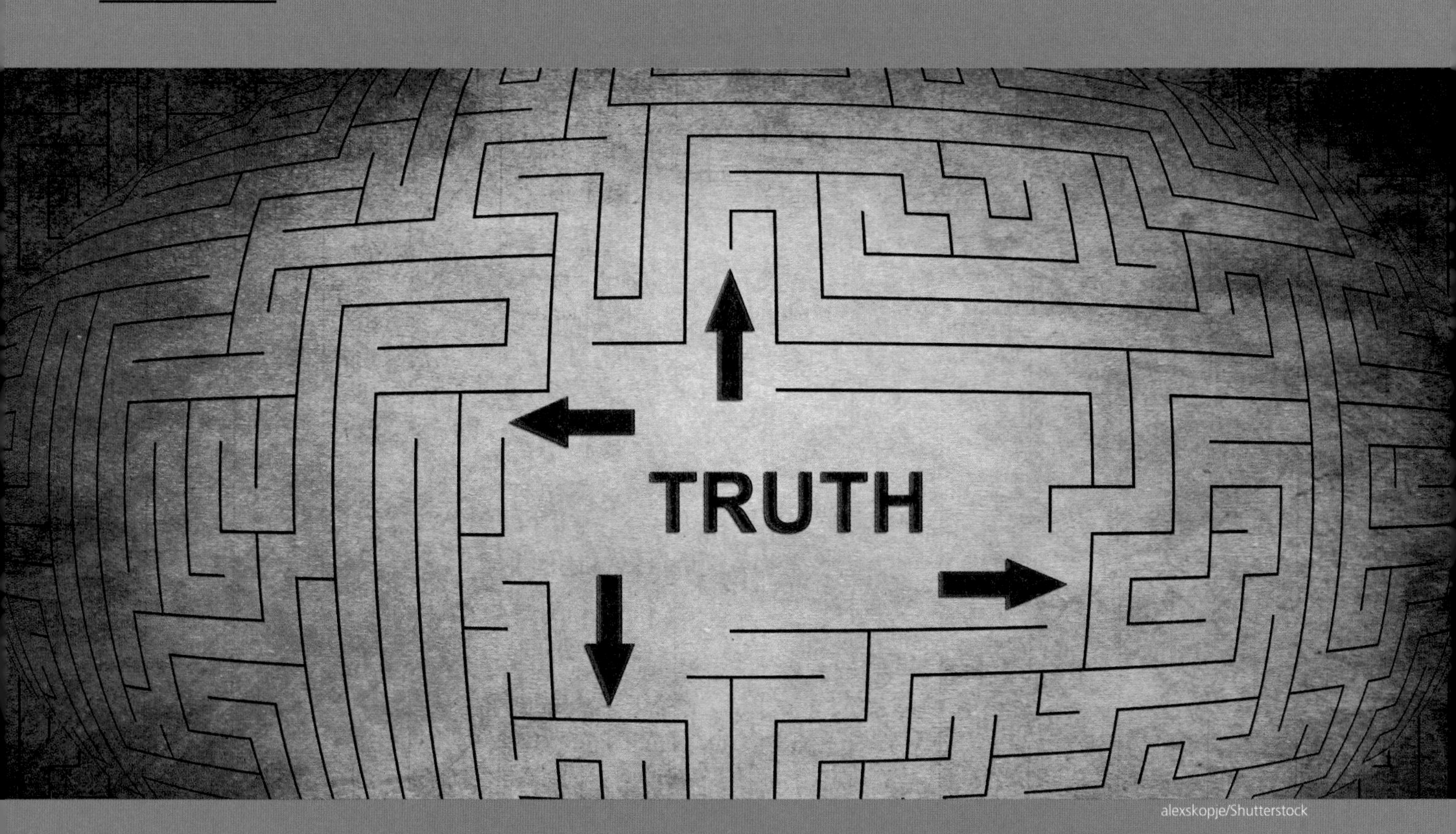

alexskopje/Shutterstock

Facts are the enemy of truth.

(Miguel de Cervantes Saavedra)[1]

LEARNING OBJECTIVES & OUTCOMES

After completing this chapter, students should be able to do the following:

LO1 Explain what belief systems are and identify their components.

LO2 Describe religious patterns in Canada and identify the implications of religiosity for individuals and for society.

LO3 Compare key sociological theories of religion.

LO4 Identify the different ways that sociologists perceive the nature of scientific "truth" and explain the role of postmodern and feminist perspectives in the sociological study of science.

LO5 Compare theoretical views of the role of education in modern society within contemporary debates about education.

At first glance, the above quotation, from the novel *Don Quixote*, appears contradictory. After all, aren't "truth" and "fact" one in the same? As the main character in the novel discovers, the two are not necessarily related. In Don Quixote's imagined world, he lives a life of chivalry—his "truth" is that a neighbouring girl is his love, a nearby innkeeper is the lord of a castle, windmills are evil beasts to be destroyed, and he is the knight in shining armour dedicated to saving the world. Even if not based upon facts, what Don Quixote believes to be true is the foundation for his everyday life. Eventually, "facts" come to light that begin to challenge his beliefs, and he discovers that this world was only imaginary; this new "truth," based on fact, is his demise, sending him into a deep depression from which he never recovers.

How does each of us come to know truth and fact? Three of society's institutions are central. *Religion* has served as a purveyor of truth for thousands of years; for most of human history, its claims have been granted the greatest legitimacy. Religion continues to play a significant role today. However, after the Enlightenment, *science* became the institution whose claims to truth were the most legitimatized; we often believe what scientists tell us simply because they are viewed as authorities. Finally, the *education* system presents us with various facts and teaches us what is true; throughout its history, it has embodied both religion and science. But facts and truth are not static—they are dynamic and therefore subject to change. For instance, before Copernicus and Galileo, the accepted truth was that the Earth is the centre of the universe. The work of those two astronomers presented new facts and eventually changed what was accepted as truth; nevertheless, at the time, Galileo was convicted as a heretic for proclaiming this truth.

LO1 BELIEF SYSTEMS

To accept something as true, regardless of whether it is *actually* true or not, is to have a belief. When **beliefs** are interconnected in a systematic fashion and shared among groups of people, they are called **belief systems** (Stebbins, 1996). The different religions of the world, disciplines of science, and even ideologies of political parties are belief systems. Belief systems have three different components (Ben-Yehuda, 1990) (see *Figure 10.1*). First, they include *claims about the*

Belief: Something one accepts as true, regardless of whether it is true or not.

Belief system: A set of interconnected beliefs that are shared among groups of people.

FIGURE 10.1

Belief Systems

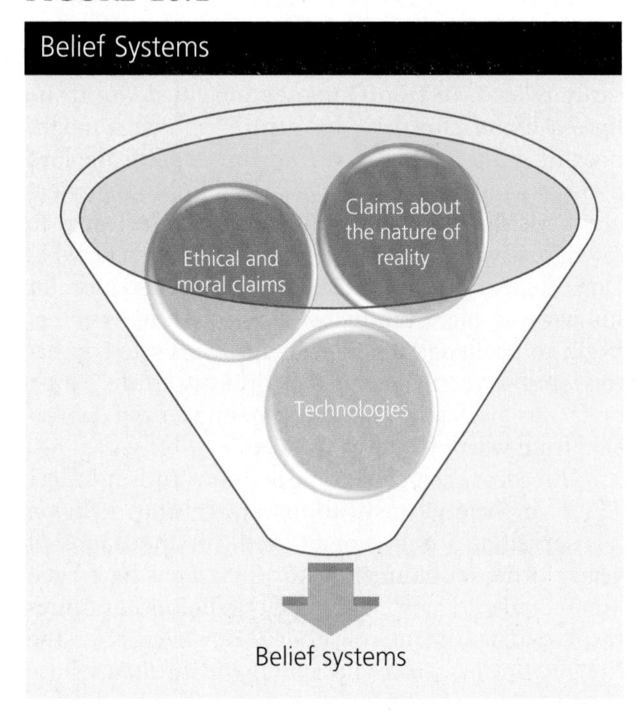

nature of reality. Thus, Buddhism tells us that reincarnation is real, chemistry tells us that combining hydrogen and oxygen (in specific amounts) creates water, and social conservative political parties tell us that the family is declining.

Second, belief systems include *ethical and moral claims*. Most of the world's major religions explicitly tell us that the right thing to do is to treat others the way we would like them to treat us. The ethical and moral claims in political ideologies are also typically explicit, such as statements about controversial issues (e.g., gay–straight alliances in schools) that are found in political parties' election platforms. In science, ethical and moral claims are less explicit but present nonetheless. Such claims are reflected, in part, in what scientists choose to study; thus, research on gene editing contains an implicit claim that gene editing is acceptable.

Religion: A united system of beliefs and practices related to sacred things.

Finally, belief systems are enacted using *technologies* (or techniques) to obtain or use the knowledge. Prayer, meditation, and religious rituals are techniques used in religion; techniques in science include the research methods described earlier in the textbook, as well as methodologies specific to certain scientific disciplines (e.g., astronomers measure radio waves to determine what is happening with stars). The techniques associated with politics are reflected in government policies (e.g., spending money on infrastructure is a means to stimulate the economy).

RELIGION

Religion is one of those terms that we implicitly understand but find difficult to define. Just as we recognize varying definitions of "family," there are varying definitions of religion. Durkheim (1915/1965) provides us with a sociological definition that is still commonly used today: "a united system of beliefs and practices related to sacred things" (p. 47). Religion plays a part in many people's lives today, although to a greater degree in some people's lives than in others (see *Sociology in My Life*).

YOUR SOCIOLOGICAL TOOLKIT

SOCIOLOGY IN MY LIFE

RELIGION IN MY LIFE

Religion is not unidimensional but rather multidimensional. Thus, in examining the role of religion in people's lives, it is important to consider religious affiliation, religious participation, and religious attendance.

Think Outside the Box: Consider the extent to which religion plays a role in your own life: Do you believe in a supreme being or a higher power? Do you identify yourself with a specific religion? Do you participate in private religious activities, such as prayer or spiritually oriented meditation? Have you engaged in, or do you expect to engage in, religious rituals as part of certain rights of passage (e.g., have a marriage ceremony conducted by a religious figure)? Do you attend religious services regularly?

LO2 RELIGIOUS PATTERNS

There are at least 22 major world religions (e.g., Christianity, Islam, Buddhism), subdivided into hundreds of large religious groups and an even greater number of smaller groups. The largest religious groups in the world, based on proportion of the population, are Christianity (31 percent), Islam (21 percent), and Hinduism (15 percent). Projections are that by 2060, Islam will grow to 31 percent of the global population, whereas Christianity will remain relatively stable (Pew Research Center, 2017).

In many ways, Canadian society, as well as the rest of the world, is becoming more **secular** (i.e., not governed by religion). In 2011, 24 percent of Canadians reported that they had no religious affiliation—an increase from 17 percent in 2001 (Statistics Canada, 2014). Nevertheless, religion continues to play a significant role in many people's lives. In Canada, **religious affiliation** (i.e., identifying with a particular religion) declined from 88 percent to 76 percent between 1985 and 2011 (Statistics Canada, 2014). Reflecting Canada's Eurocentric immigration patterns, the predominant religious affiliation is Catholicism (39 percent of those with a religious affiliation), followed by various forms of Protestantism (20 percent) (see *Figure 10.2*). But as immigration patterns increasingly include people from non-European countries, a variety of Eastern religions have become more prevalent. Seven percent of people in Canada are now affiliated with Islam, Hinduism, Sikhism, and Buddhism, and it is projected that by 2031, 14 percent of people in Canada will be affiliated with a non-Christian religion (Malenfant Lebel, & Martel, 2010).

Just as religious affiliation has declined in recent decades, so has **religious attendance** (i.e., attendance at organized religious services, such as church services). Regular attendance has declined in North America by more than 20 percent since 1986. Similar decreases are evident in other predominantly Christian nations as well, such as Australia, New Zealand, and many European countries. Research on religious attendance is lacking in countries that are not predominantly Christian, so it is unclear what the trends in those nations may be (Brenner, 2016; Eagle, 2011). But it is important to note that people who do not attend organized religious rituals may still engage in private rituals, such as prayer and reading sacred texts, and religious beliefs may still be important to them (Clark & Schellenberg, 2006) (see *Sociology in My Community*).

Sociologists combine religious affiliation, attendance, participation in private religious activities, and the importance of religion into a single measure, called **religiosity**. Religiosity tends to be higher among immigrants than among Canadian-born people, especially those from South and Southeast Asia, the Caribbean, and South America. Also, religiosity tends to be higher among older age groups than among younger ones (Clark & Schellenberg, 2006). Religiosity has implications from the micro to the macro level.

Secular: The state of not being governed by religion.

Religious affiliation: The identification with a particular religion.

Religious attendance: Attendance at organized religious services.

Religiosity: A combined measure of religious affiliation, attendance, and participation.

FIGURE 10.2

Religious Affiliation, Canada (2011)

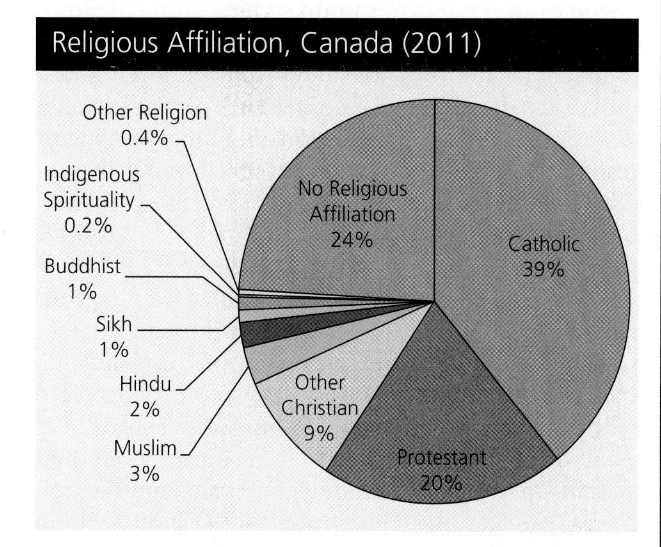

Source: Author drawn. Adapted from: Statistics Canada (2014). 2011 National Household Survey. NHS Profile. Statistics Canada Catalogue No. 99-010-X201132.

TIME TO REVIEW

- What are beliefs and belief systems?
- What role do religion, science, and education play in teaching us the "truth"?
- How many religions are there in the world, and which are the largest?
- What are the patterns of religious affiliation, religious attendance, private religious participation, and religiosity in Canada?

YOUR SOCIOLOGICAL TOOLKIT

SOCIOLOGY IN MY COMMUNITY

RELIGION IN THE LIVES OF CANADIANS

Reginald Bibby has studied religious patterns in Canada over several decades and is also a practitioner of public sociology. In 2004, he brought the results of sociological research into the "real world" of Canada's Christian churches in his book *Restless Churches: How Canada's Churches Can Contribute to the Emerging Religious Renaissance*. Directing his work at an audience involved in ministry, he presents data on religious beliefs, affiliation, and attendance. He critiques media stories that equate declines in religious affiliation and attendance with a decrease in religious beliefs and points out that most Canadians are not abandoning religion. Bibby makes suggestions for what churches can do to remain contemporary—for example, by attracting and keeping youth interest. He states: "What I am attempting to do is to present the key findings with clarity, reflect on some of the major implications, acknowledge a number of significant hurdles that have to be cleared, and spell out some of the tangible responses that groups need to consider" (p. ix).

Think Outside the Box: Reginald Bibby brings sociological research to people involved in the ministry and provides practical suggestions for making Christian churches more contemporary and relevant. What other fields of work would benefit from greater sociological knowledge?

IMPLICATIONS OF RELIGION

IMPLICATIONS FOR INDIVIDUALS

At the micro level, religion has an impact on various aspects of people's lives. Research has found that among adolescents, varied aspects of religiosity may have different effects. In a study of Ontario students in Grades 11 and 12, Good and Willoughby (2014) found that personal beliefs were important. Youth with strong religious beliefs had lower levels of depression and social anxiety and higher levels of self-esteem and life satisfaction. They also suffered less stress from daily hassles and experienced more positive relationships with parents and a stronger academic orientation. Religious attendance has a positive impact on youth as well, contributing to lower levels of substance use (Goldstein et al., 2013; Rawana & Ames, 2012).

Social capital: Resources in the form of accumulated social networks.

Bridging capital: Resources accumulated within groups that can be used outside those groups.

Bonding capital: Resources in the form of community ties and identity.

Among adults, religiosity is also associated with better physical health, lower levels of depression and anxiety, and lower levels of substance use (Bailey et al., 2015; Schieman, 2008). Religion provides people with a community and a sense of belonging. Among those who attend religious services regularly, 22 percent say that the people, the community, and the fellowship are the main things that religious involvement adds to their lives (Bibby, 2006). Religious involvement provides *social capital* (Bramadat, 2005; Putnam, 2000). **Social capital** refers to resources we accumulate from our social networks. Just as a screwdriver enables us to assemble the toys we bought our children and a university degree provides us with a higher income, our relationships with other people provide us with resources we can use in various aspects of our lives—they provide us with knowledge, skills, understandings of the world and ourselves, and a network of support.

One form of social capital is **bridging capital**, where the resources we accumulate through interactions with our religious group can be used outside the religious realm, just as religious attendance provides people with intangible resources that steer them away from substance use. Another form is **bonding capital**—a sense of community and belonging, as well as a social identity (Putnam, 2000). That bonding can have both positive and negative consequences for society.

IMPLICATIONS FOR SOCIETY

Bramadat (2005) refers to **positive bonding capital** and **negative bonding capital**. The group cohesiveness, solidarity, and social identity that religion provides can bring benefits to society in some situations while causing social harms in other circumstances. Religiosity can be beneficial for society. For example, among university students, religiosity is associated with higher levels of interaction with peers across racial groups, which is important for erasing the boundaries between social groups that can lead to prejudice and contribute to social inequality (Park & Bowman, 2015).

Furthermore, some research finds that Canadians with religious affiliations are more philanthropic than those without such affiliations, donating more money to social causes and volunteering more of their time (Berger, 2006). Berger finds that feelings of communal responsibility and reciprocity underlie this pattern, feelings that are stronger in those with religious affiliations. On the other hand, some research calls these findings into question. Is it religious belief itself that contributes to philanthropic behaviour or rather the bonding capital that arises from any type of structured group membership? Recent research investigates this question by comparing members of religious groups, members of secular groups (such as sports teams or book clubs), and people who do not belong to structured groups (Galen, Sharp, & McNulty, 2015). The results indicate that religious belief, in itself, has little to no effect on philanthropic behaviour. Instead, members of both religious and secular groups donated more time and money to charitable causes than did people who were not members of structured groups.

Just as religious *individuals* may donate their own money or time to social causes, religious *groups* take on social causes, both historically and in the present. During the Victorian era in Canada, the theology of the Social Gospel (which applied Protestant ideals to solving social problems) gave rise to the **child-savers movement**, which dedicated itself to the betterment of children's social conditions (Jordan, 1998; Platt, 1977; Valverde, 1991). The child-savers movement spearheaded several new pieces of legislation. Child labour laws placed restrictions on the employment of children (e.g., minimum age, hours worked). Compulsory schooling laws required children to attend school for a certain number of days each year until they reached a particular age. Criminal laws prohibited abuse and neglect.

Today, religious groups often engage in charitable work. They bring humanitarian aid following natural disasters; offer hot meals to the homeless; operate food bank pickup locations in the basements of churches, temples, mosques, and synagogues; and raise funds for various charities.

Shutterstock.com

Charitable work is an important aspect of many religious groups, as when Muslims give gifts to the less fortunate during Ramadan.

Unfortunately, not all religious bonding capital serves positive ends; negative bonding capital contributes to social inequality, religious conflict, acts of violence, and war. When a cohesive group sees itself as "part of a purely embattled minority" (Bramadat, 2005), an "us versus them" mentality is created. Members of such groups perceive their belief system and associated way of living as the only moral path—their ways are "right," and everyone else's ways are "wrong" (Rhodes, 2012).

Some groups may isolate themselves from the larger society, creating a separate existence based on their own religious principles. In other cases, members of such groups or the group as a whole may try to create large-scale change to either spread their belief system or punish those with different belief systems (Bramadat, 2005). The consequences can be far-reaching. They include 500 years of war between the Christian and Islamic churches during the Crusades (from the 11th through the 16th centuries); the European "witchcraze," when between 40,000 and 100,000 people were persecuted as witches from the 14th through the 17th centuries (Barstow, 1994; Quaife, 1987); the colonization of Indigenous groups worldwide and Canadian residential schooling; the murder of doctors who perform abortions by anti-abortion extremists; and terrorist acts (such as those undertaken or inspired by ISIS/ISIL).

Positive bonding capital: Community ties and sources of identity that benefit the wider society.

Negative bonding capital: Community ties and sources of identity that harm the wider society.

Child-savers movement: A movement dedicated to the betterment of social conditions involving children.

The only Universal Truths that all religions agree upon

TIME TO REVIEW

- What are the implications of religiosity in the everyday lives of adults and adolescents?
- What is social capital, and what types of social capital emerge from belonging to a religious group?
- What are some positive and negative outcomes of religious bonding capital?

YOUR SOCIOLOGICAL TOOLKIT
SOCIOLOGY IN THEORY

LO3 SOCIOLOGY IN THEORY: RELIGION

When sociologists study religion, they do not try to validate or to disprove particular belief systems. Rather, they analyze "how individuals, social institutions, and cultures construe God or the sacred ... how these ideas penetrate public culture and individual lives, and ... the implications of those interpretations for individual, institutional, and societal processes" (Dillon, 2007, para. 6). *Substantive* approaches focus on the meanings that are contained within specific doctrines and how those meanings are understood by people in their everyday lives. *Functional* approaches emphasize the social aspects of religion, the functions it serves, and its implications for individuals and for society.

Collective conscience: The unified body of cultural knowledge that is transmitted in group religious rituals.

Collective effervescence: A euphoria that enables people to transcend the challenges of everyday life—to a degree not possible when alone—that emerges from group religious rituals.

The sociological study of religion is as old as the discipline of sociology itself. Durkheim (1915/1965), a functionalist, suggested that religion plays an important role in creating and maintaining social solidarity. He stated that even in premodern societies, large numbers of people would gather to participate in religious rituals. These collective rituals would transmit the accumulated wisdom of the culture to participants—a unified body of knowledge known as the **collective conscience**. In their group worship of sacred objects and ideals, people would also be caught up in a **collective effervescence**, an excitement or euphoria that enabled them to transcend the challenges of every day to a degree not possible when alone. Both the collective conscience and collective effervescence serve important functions: they strengthen social bonds and thereby maintain the social order. In preindustrial societies, social order is maintained through mechanical solidarity, or bonding based on sameness; in this context, religion plays a central role. Durkheim suggested that with industrialization and the ensuing organic solidarity, other institutions would increasingly take over some of the functions that were traditionally fulfilled by religion. For example, the school system now plays a greater role in socializing children to treat others with kindness and respect. Contemporary functionalists continue to focus on the role religion plays in social integration. They also study the impact of religion on individual behaviours and outcomes, such as those related to physical and mental health, substance use, and philanthropic behaviours (as described earlier). Finally, they analyze some of the *dysfunctions* of religion, such as residential schooling, war, and acts of violence.

From a functionalist perspective, when people gather for religious rituals, they develop a collective conscience and get caught up in collective effervescence.

Karl Marx (1844/1970) described religion as the *opium of the people*. The oppressed proletariat escapes from the ugliness of their lives into religion. This provides them with temporary relief from life's difficulties but also prevents them from seeing the structured inequality within which they live. Consequently, it precludes them from rising up and overthrowing their oppressors. Contemporary conflict theorists continue to look at the ways religion can serve as an agent of social control, creating, maintaining, and justifying inequality. For example, the conflict perspective gives rise to analyses of inequalities that exist within religion, such as in religions that restrict the participation of women as religious leaders. At a more macro level, the perspective also draws attention to the role of religion in perpetuating societal inequalities, such as the doctrine that rationalized the colonization of the world's non-Christians and the religious interpretations that are often drawn upon in opposition to same-sex marriage.

Perhaps the best-known sociological analysis of religion comes from Max Weber, who analyzed the relationship between religion and social change, studying Protestantism, Confucianism, Hinduism, Buddhism, and ancient Judaism. His book, *The Protestant Ethic and the Spirit of Capitalism* (1904/1958), has been ranked as the fourth most influential sociology book of the 20th century (Drysdale, 2007). In that book, he analyzes the foundational role that Protestant doctrine played in establishing early capitalism. Unlike Marx, who suggested that changing economic structures create subsequent changes in thought, Weber argued that changes in thought—the way people understand themselves and the world around them—precede structural changes.

Catholicism had emphasized the abandonment of worldly lives; people had to have a vocation in order to survive, but their attention should be focused on their faith. In contrast, Protestant doctrine established that participating in worldly economic activities was a morally worthy vocation. Each of us has been placed on the Earth for a specific purpose, whether it is religious leadership, carpentry, or farming. Working hard at that vocation is fulfilling your life's purpose. Protestant doctrine also emphasized predestination, the belief that what would happen to your soul in the afterlife was predetermined. Because there was no certain way to know what that future would be, people experienced anxiety. However, achieving economic success in one's vocation could be taken as a small sign of your soul's predestined path, thereby reducing some of your anxiety. Thus, the accumulation of wealth was a sign of salvation to come, and the accumulation of wealth is the foundation of capitalism. In this regard, Weber's work was the underpinning of the future interactionist perspective. Contemporary interactionists study the ways that the social interactions, rituals, and symbols that comprise religious belief and practice contribute to people's understandings of life and society and to the development of their identities.

Feminist perspectives focus on various aspects of religion, but with a shared emphasis on the absence or the oppression of women. Feminist research on religion is intimately intertwined with forms of feminist religious and spiritual practice. *Revisionists* suggest that if the doctrines of the world's major religions are interpreted "correctly," the true message is one of equality. *Reformists* draw attention to the sexist language and rituals that have become a part of some religions; they emphasize the importance of removing those aspects of religious practice and integrating more female imagery and symbols. *Revolutionaries* look at how removing some of the traditional boundaries of certain religions, and integrating some images and rituals from outside those traditional boundaries, can serve positive ends for women in society. Finally, *rejectionists* perceive inherent sexism in the world's major religions and call for abandoning those religions while adopting female-centred spirituality, such as Goddess Worship (Neitz, 2014; Paludi & Ellens, 2016; Stuckey, 1998).

Postmodern perspectives highlight the plurality of all religions and spiritualities. There is no singular "Hinduism" or "Judaism" that we can speak of but rather a multiplicity of different forms. For example, the "Islam" of ISIS/ISIL-inspired extremists is not the same "Islam" as that adhered to by most people who consider themselves Muslim, yet this is arguably the strongest image of the Muslim faith that is perpetuated by the media. Even within the multiplicity of different forms of particular religions, each individual has his or her own experience and perceptions of that religion and/or spiritual pursuit. In terms of religious practice, postmodern perspectives are associated with individually focused religious and spiritual practice, such as "New Age" spirituality and "spiritual seeking," which draw upon bits and pieces of a variety of world religions (especially Eastern religions, such as Hinduism or Buddhism) and other non-religious spiritual pursuits (e.g., astrology, crystals, yoga).

TIME TO REVIEW

- What is the difference between substantive and functional approaches to the sociological study of religion?
- How is religion studied within functionalist, conflict, interactionist, feminist, and postmodern perspectives?

LO4 THE TRANSITION TO SCIENTIFIC "TRUTH"

Although religion continues to play a role in the "truth" of most people's lives, since the Renaissance and the scientific revolution, **scientism**—"a worldview that uses the insights of natural science to inform people's way of living, their purpose in life, and the choices they make" (Walach & Reich, 2005, p. 425)—has increasingly characterized society. **Science** is an institution that provides "a way to understand the natural makeup of the world by means of rational methods of inquiry" (Walach & Reich, 2005, p. 425). The truths provided by science are often granted the greatest legitimacy in society—if science tells us something, we presume it must be true.

Robert Merton (1973) is often credited as the founder of the sociology of science (or scientific knowledge). In the present day, the study of science is highly interdisciplinary, studied by sociologists, historians, feminists, and philosophers. These scholars tend to identify themselves in an interdisciplinary way rather than associate themselves with any single discipline (Varcoe, 2007). Contemporary social studies of science share the basic assumption that science is intertwined with social structures and processes and is therefore a social endeavour (Hird, 2012). Outside of that shared assumption, there are a myriad of ways in which science is studied. One way of looking at the diversity in social studies of science is to explore perceptions of scientific truth.

Scientism: A worldview that uses the insights of natural science to inform people's ways of living, their purpose in life, and the choices they make.

Science: An institution that provides a way to understand the natural makeup of the world by means of rational methods of inquiry.

Norm of communism: The notion that scientific knowledge is to be freely shared with others.

Norm of universalism: The notion that scientific knowledge is free of social biases.

Norm of disinterestedness: The notion that scientists do their work solely for the purposes of discovering truth.

Norm of organized skepticism: The notion that scientific claims should be subjected to rigorous scrutiny.

What is the nature of scientific truth? Sociologists do not agree on the answer to that question. One approach proposes that scientific knowledge is a distinct form of knowledge that provides an objective truth. The other approach suggests that scientific truths are no different from any other types of truths. All forms of knowledge are socially constructed, emerging from a complex web of social structures, processes, and interactions. We examine these two approaches in the following sections.

SCIENTIFIC KNOWLEDGE AS OBJECTIVE TRUTH

Sociologists who perceive scientific knowledge as objective and distinct from other forms of knowledge focus their analyses on particular aspects of science. They study "the institutional norms that regulate the activity of the community of scientists; competition; the reward structure of science operating through 'recognition' (citation processes, Nobel prizes, peer review); and similar topics" (Varcoe, 2007, para. 2).

Merton (1973) describes the *normative structure of science*, a set of norms that are embedded in the institution of science itself and that make science a self-governing institution based on objectivity. The first norm is the **norm of communism**, the notion that scientific knowledge is to be freely shared with others. The second is the **norm of universalism**—scientific knowledge is to be free of any social biases, such as racism. The third is the **norm of disinterestedness**, whereby scientists do their work for the purposes of discovering truth rather than for any personal gains. The final norm is the **norm of organized skepticism**, the idea that scientific claims should be subjected to rigorous scrutiny before they are accepted. It is because of these four norms that scientific knowledge is considered to be a distinct form of knowledge. Merton recognized that the norms of science could be perverted in some societies, such as Nazi Germany, and acknowledged that some individual scientists might violate these norms. But when the institution of science was in a fit state, objective truths were uncovered.

SCIENTIFIC KNOWLEDGE AS CONSTRUCTED

Those who perceive scientific knowledge as similar to other forms of knowledge focus their analyses on how scientific knowledge emerges, is accepted, and is affected by social and political forces. Thomas Kuhn (1962) placed science in an historical context and analyzed the processes by which scientific knowledge develops and comes to be accepted as truth. He suggested that the history of science is one of *scientific revolutions* rather than a gradual accumulation

YOUR SOCIOLOGICAL TOOLKIT

CRITICAL THINKING IN ACTION

SHIFTING PARADIGMS

Kuhn (1962) posited that paradigm shifts are restricted to the natural sciences, where there is an ongoing search for the most accurate explanations of physical phenomena. In the social sciences and humanities, he argued, multiple paradigms coexist, each offering a different lens through which to view a social phenomenon. In fact, the importance of looking at a social phenomenon using a variety of different paradigms is inherent in the social sciences as the means of developing the most comprehensive understanding of phenomena. Nevertheless, the concept of paradigm shifts has expanded beyond Kuhn's restrictive view and is now used to refer to changing views in the social sciences as well. In the chapter on socialization, you learned about one of these paradigm shifts. Historically, the developing self was contextualized in debates over nature (i.e., biological factors, such as genetics) *or* nurture (i.e., environmental influences). Now the two are no longer considered mutually exclusive. A child's genotype can affect temperament to impact the type of parenting received, and some reactions from early caregivers are now believed to change how genes are expressed in offspring via epigenetic processes (Avinun & Knafu-Noam, 2015; Waddington, 1942). Thus, socialization itself is now viewed as being influenced by a complex interplay between genetic preconditions and environmental factors.

Think Outside the Box: In what other ways have we seen paradigms, in whatever form, shifting?

of knowledge. Certain **paradigms** (i.e., conceptual frameworks) characterize particular sciences; these paradigms govern how reality is understood. Most scientists operate within those paradigms for extended periods of time, building knowledge within them and refining that knowledge when necessary. But once in a while, a **paradigm shift** occurs—anomalies accumulate, a scientist proposes a different way of understanding the object of study, and this changes the scientific discipline forever (see *Critical Thinking in Action*). However, this shift is often resisted. This is what happened when Galileo reiterated Copernicus's claim that the planets in the solar system revolve around the sun and was subsequently imprisoned.

Other analysts draw attention to the fact that scientific knowledge is "dependent on the social frameworks in which it is produced" (Eriksson, 2007, para. 7). Some scholars emphasize the ways that social and political influences shape the topics scientists study and thus the scientific truths that are created. For example, under Prime Minister Stephen Harper (2006–2015), the federal Conservative Party (with a strong pro–oil sands platform) drastically reduced funding for research on climate change and prevented government scientists from speaking to the media (even though their research is funded by Canadian taxpayers). During Donald Trump's first week in office as president of the United States, similar measures were taken against scientists working for the Environmental Protection Agency (Learn, 2017).

Also, social and political forces can shape scientific knowledge outside the ideologies of specific political parties. The success of the Human Genome Project, which completed a first map of the human genome in the early 21st century, opened up a new world of genetic research. But scientific, social, and ethical concerns have emerged regarding the potential of that research to violate human rights if used in the wrong way. Consequently, some national governments have passed laws to control potential harms—for example, by prohibiting human cloning. Also, various international organizations have established broader frameworks to guide genetic research.

Sociologists who study the social construction of scientific truths also draw attention to the impact of funding structures, such as those associated with the corporatization of science (Bereska, 2018). Over the past few decades, the proportion of research funded by private enterprises and conducted in commercial

Paradigm: A conceptual framework or model for organizing information.

Paradigm shift: Movement away from a particular conceptual framework.

research centres has grown; this is especially the case with biomedical research. This has significant implications for the development of scientific knowledge. First, the contracts between the corporations and the scientists often give all publication rights to the corporate sponsor. The latter has the right to decide which research results will or will not be submitted for publication, and this has a direct impact on the body of scientific knowledge in the area. Second, and even more significantly, research that is sponsored by private enterprises is more likely to have positive findings than research that is publicly funded through research grants. For instance, pharmaceutical research that is conducted by industry-funded scientists is more likely to conclude that a new drug is effective than publicly funded research on the very same drug (Born, 2004; Caulfield, 2004). In other words, the scientific "truths" uncovered within certain funding structures can be very different from those obtained within other types of funding structures.

Analyses of the processes whereby scientific knowledge develops, and of the social, political, and economic forces that can shape that knowledge, draw attention to the fact that scientific truths are socially constructed rather than objective realities (see *Sociology in Practice*). At a theoretical level, postmodern and feminist approaches play key roles within this perspective.

YOUR SOCIOLOGICAL TOOLKIT
SOCIOLOGY IN THEORY

POSTMODERN THEORIES

Foucault (1980) explained that "knowledge" is not an independent, objective entity; rather, it is deeply intertwined with power. When particular truths emerge from positions of power in the social structure, those claims come to be recognized as legitimate knowledge. Thus, when Galileo's scientific claims contradicted those of the Christian Church, Galileo was persecuted because the church had the ultimate institutionalized power in society at the time. But during the Enlightenment, as science came to hold more institutionalized power, its knowledge became more legitimized. In science today, power continues to be intertwined with knowledge; this is evident in the tangible economic power that governments

YOUR SOCIOLOGICAL TOOLKIT

SOCIOLOGY IN PRACTICE

INDIGENOUS SCIENCE

What is recognized as legitimate knowledge (and thereby the "truth") emerges from social, economic, and political forces. In other words, knowledge is socially constructed. With colonization, Indigenous knowledge—passed down over many generations through oral tradition—was devalued and, in fact, suppressed by colonialist authorities via various social policies (such as residential schooling). Reconciliation requires that the legitimacy of Indigenous knowledge and wisdom be recognized. On April 22, 2017 (Earth Day), approximately 1,500 Indigenous scientists joined non-Indigenous scientists the world over in the March for Science, intended as support for climate change research and a protest against President Donald Trump's anti–climate change (and anti-science) agenda. For Indigenous participants and allies, the event was also a statement that "Indigenous knowledge is just as important as Western science" (Fontaine, 2017) and, in fact, *is* science (Snively & Williams, 2016). Scholars point out that Indigenous knowledge and Western science are not mutually exclusive but rather complementary. With Indigenous knowledge closely tied to the environment and long-past events, bringing the two together is important in solving some of the most important problems of our time, such as relationships between groups of people, global sustainability, and the equitable management of resources (McCallum, 2012; Snively & Williams, 2016). In fact, a growing body of research is drawing upon both Indigenous and Western science to further the development of knowledge about diverse topics such as prehistoric patterns of human migration and geological events (e.g., earthquakes) (Mortillaro, 2016). There are also calls to integrate Indigenous knowledge into the K–12 science curriculum (McCallum, 2012).

Think Outside the Box: In addition to modifying the school science curriculum, what other changes might be necessary for the legitimacy of Indigenous knowledge to be recognized?

Everett Historical/Shutterstock

The institutionalized power of the Christian Church prior to the Enlightenment meant that Galileo was punished for his scientific claims.

and corporations have to control research funds. In this case, power affects not only what is accepted as knowledge but also what gets *produced* as knowledge in the first place.

FEMINIST THEORIES

Over the past two decades, feminist researchers have devoted a considerable amount of time to analyses of science, lending an explicit social justice dimension to the discussion. Given the diversity of feminist perspectives, there is substantial diversity in the analyses of science emerging from those perspectives. Broadly, these researchers have emphasized (1) women in science, (2) tying science to social and political action, and (3) proposing "new" ways of practising science.

The position of women in science—in particular, their underrepresentation—has been the subject of considerable work (Eriksson, 2007; Kerr, 2003). Feminist scholars address the underrepresentation of women as scientists and the challenges that female scientists have faced in a male-dominated profession. They also highlight the absence of women from the knowledge that science produces. For example, medical research has traditionally studied male research subjects and then presented the findings as applicable to all people—males become the generic "human," and it is presumed that female bodies work in the same fashion. Consequently, there is a relative lack of knowledge regarding how various diseases may vary in men and women (e.g., the most common symptoms of heart attacks) and how pharmaceuticals may affect them differently (e.g., varying side effects).

In the social sciences, an **androcentric** (or male) **bias** has also long been present. In courses in child development or the sociology of youth, you may learn about Kohlberg's (1958; 1981) theory of moral development, a series of stages through which individuals progress as they develop moral reasoning. That theory was first constructed on the basis of his analysis of males. In response to the absence of the female experience in Kohlberg's theory, one of his students, Carol Gilligan (1984), developed a theory on the development of moral reasoning in females. Similarly, Erikson's (1968) theory of identity formation in youth is based on the male experience, such that in his book, he has only one chapter on identity formation in females. He has a "theory of identity formation" and then a "theory of *female* identity formation," thus making the male experience the normative one.

For these feminist scholars, making science "better" means removing the obstacles women may face in becoming scientists, as well as the androcentric biases that have long pervaded scientific research. For other feminist scholars (Longino, 1990; Nelson, 1990), improving science means tying it to social and political action. Although the traditional model of science dictates that science should be value-free, these scholars point out that knowledge and values are tightly intertwined, that values *should* underlie scientific practice, and that scientists *should* allow their own political affiliations or social movement memberships to guide their research.

Finally, some feminist scholars present a vision of a "new" way of practising science. For instance, Harding (1991) applies *feminist standpoint theory* to the realm of science. She argues that women occupy a distinctive location in society (i.e., a "standpoint") as a marginalized and oppressed group. Because of their distinctive location, women see and understand the world in a different way than men do—women's unique "standpoint" is not only structural but also intellectual. Harding claims that science emerging from the standpoint of women (or other oppressed and marginalized groups) would create a superior body of scientific knowledge. Coming from more of a postmodern foundation, Haraway (1991) suggests that "women" are not a single cohesive group and do not reflect a unified standpoint. Instead, each woman has multiple standpoints based on all of the different aspects of her life (e.g., female, Indigenous, mother, scientist, Catholic). Given their various achieved and ascribed statuses, women's perspectives are constantly shifting and may even conflict with one another at times. Constructing "better" scientific knowledge means having as diverse a group of scientists as possible, who hold various statuses and have developed different standpoints accordingly.

Androcentric bias: A tendency to favour males.

TIME TO REVIEW

- What is science?
- What are the two different perspectives on the nature of scientific "truth"?
- What are the components of the normative structure of science, according to Merton?
- According to Kuhn, how does scientific knowledge develop?
- What are some examples of social and political influences on scientific knowledge?
- What impact does the corporatization of science have on scientific knowledge?
- In what ways do postmodern and feminist perspectives draw attention to the social construction of scientific knowledge?

LO5 RELIGION AND SCIENCE

Religion and science both offer us "truths" about the world around us and about ourselves. Four types of relationships between religious knowledge and scientific knowledge have been postulated (Barbour, cited in Campbell, 2005). Some scholars view the relationship as one of *independence*, with no common ground between the two bodies of knowledge. Others claim that the relationship between religious and scientific knowledge is based on *conflict*, wherein accepting one of those bodies of knowledge necessarily means rejecting the other. In contrast, because both religion and science are interested in questions of meaning and existence, some academics suggest that a meaningful *dialogue* is possible. Finally, some scholars take it a step further and address the *integration* that they believe is possible between the two bodies of knowledge. Dialogue and integration are reflected in the academic journal *Zygon: Journal of Religion and Science*: "Zygon's hypothesis is that, when long-evolved religious wisdom is yoked with significant, recent scientific discoveries about the world and human nature, there results credible expression of basic meaning, values, and moral convictions that provides valid and effective guidance for enhancing human life" (http://www.zygonjournal.org).

In people's lives, both religion and science play important roles. A survey of more than 400 undergraduate students found that 88 percent think that a person can be both religious and scientific—that one does not necessarily exclude the other. Three-quarters of them say that science influences their own daily lives, whereas almost half indicate that religion affects their daily lives. However, the power of science in contemporary society is reflected in their views as well; 84 percent state that science will hold a more important role in future world affairs than at the present time; only 17 percent say the same of religion (Campbell, 2005).

RELIGION, SCIENCE, AND EDUCATION

The interplay between religious and scientific belief systems is especially evident in the education system. At a time when a growing array of faith-based educational opportunities are available for children in separate and private schools, the presence of religious belief systems in publicly funded educational spaces is a matter of considerable debate. In the United States, recent controversy centres on whether to include "intelligent design" in science classes as a balance to the theory of evolution. In some school districts, science teachers have had to present the theory of evolution as "just a theory" that has not been proven beyond doubt, with intelligent design as a theory of equal validity. Court cases have resulted in many states, and judges have often ruled that intelligent design is not a scientific theory but rather a religious ideology with no place in science classes.

Although the intelligent design–evolution debate does not permeate our educational system in the same way that it does in the United States, discussion and debate about religious belief systems in publicly funded education are evident in other ways. In December 2010, a parent in Morinville, Alberta, filed a complaint with the school board because she had no choice but to send her daughter to a faith-based school; for historical reasons, the public school system in Morinville was Catholic (it was the only place in Alberta where the public schools were faith-based). Although she had the right to exempt her children from religious instruction classes, she argued that the religious belief system permeated the entire school day, not just the classes in religious instruction.

© Harris, C., shrn31, Cartoonstock.com

The initial complaint eventually transpired into a push for a secular option by a group of parents. The rights of the parent delegation met much opposition, and the desire to maintain Catholic hegemony continued for several years, with the board of trustees voting down recommendations for a secular option and instead advocating for Catholic school exemption and Catholic faith only for board trustee membership (Buckreus, 2016). Eventually, largely due to shifting demographics (e.g., immigrants, Indigenous peoples from the Alexander First Nation, families of military personnel stationed in Namao, Alberta) and growing parental advocacy, the Catholic school status was changed from public to separate and one school was converted to non-Catholic public status in September 2012 (Buckreus, 2016).

TIME TO REVIEW

- What types of relationships between religious and scientific belief systems have been proposed?
- How do undergraduate students perceive religious knowledge and scientific knowledge, according to Campbell?
- What are some examples of the interplay of religion and science in contemporary schools in the United States and Canada?

THE ROLE OF EDUCATION IN MODERN SOCIETY

Education is a major agent of socialization and a formal institution that systematically instills much of the knowledge that individuals require in order to function as productive adults. Sociologists are interested in what is taught, who decides what is taught, how schools teach, what goes on during interactions in the classroom, and what the overall functions are of education for individuals, groups, and society. They also examine the relationships between education and other social institutions—family, politics, and so on—and how sociocultural forces, such as religious beliefs, scientific views, and cultural values, influence educational outcomes and personal development (Kibera & Kimokoti, 2007). In this section, we explore theoretical views concerning the functions of schooling that continue to spark current debates about the educational system, including the benefits and drawbacks of public versus private schooling, the costs of obtaining an education (see *Sociology in Practice*), and the ways in which education is socially stratified in Canada.

Education:
A formal institution that systematically instills much of the knowledge that is needed to function as productive adults in society.

YOUR SOCIOLOGICAL TOOLKIT

SOCIOLOGY IN PRACTICE

EDUCATION IN CANADA

There is no one unified system of education in Canada. Instead, Canada's Constitution Act, 1867, grants educational jurisdiction to each of the provinces and territories to develop and deliver education from the elementary through the postsecondary levels. Each province and territory has one or two educational departments, most of these led by a provincial cabinet minister. Public education is provided to all Canadians for free, funded by provincial and territorial governments and sometimes also by funds raised through local taxes (Council of Ministers of Education, Canada, 2017). Although public education is "free" to all Canadians, there are many hidden costs of sending children to school, including the purchase of school clothes (e.g., indoor and outdoor shoes) and school supplies, mandatory fees associated with student supervision (i.e., lunch hour), payments associated with school activities (e.g., field trips, clubs, sports), and costs incurred through various fundraisers (e.g., hot-lunch programs, book sales). In addition to public schooling, parents can choose from a range of alternative schooling options for their children using a range of funding and policy models: mainstream public schools, charter schools, faith-based schools, private schools, single-sex schools, home schooling, and more.

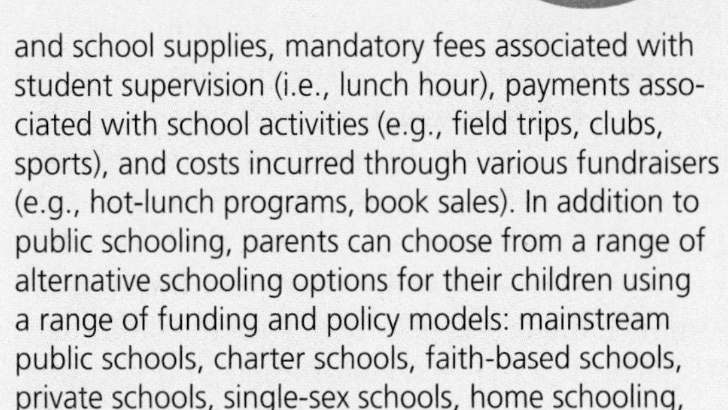

Think Outside the Box: In what ways might the hidden costs of education impact upon Canadian families who are low-income earners?

YOUR SOCIOLOGICAL TOOLKIT
SOCIOLOGY IN THEORY

SOCIOLOGY IN THEORY: EDUCATION

Education is a complex field of study. It includes a vast range of processes and functions beyond the basic three Rs associated with Reading, Writing, and Arithmetic (i.e., *functional literacy*). It occurs at different stages of people's lives, from the earliest preschool years to postsecondary schooling in adulthood.

Because of the complexity of this area of study, sociologists often specialize in particular areas. Some focus on what is taught in schools, others on gendered school experiences, and still others on differential outcomes for particular groups. As a result of this complexity, divergent viewpoints emerge with respect to describing the overall functions of education for individuals and society.

FUNCTIONALIST PERSPECTIVES

Functionalist perspectives focus on how educational practices help promote stability and order in society by training members to obey the law, respect one another, and work productively. Durkheim (1956) emphasized the importance of education for instilling cultural values and norms that help maintain moral order in society: "Education is the influence exercised by adult generations on those not yet ready for social life. Its objective is to arouse and develop in the child certain physical, intellectual, and moral states that will be demanded of him by society as a whole and in the milieu for which he is destined."

Similarly, Parsons (1959) explained how schools transition individuals from informal, person-centred roles in their families to more formal roles required by a highly competitive, achievement-oriented work domain (Wotherspoon, 1998). For example, in preschool and kindergarten, a teacher (usually a woman) provides a lot of nurturing and encouragement, similar to that experienced in the home. Children are allotted free time to play with toys and make crafts and often sit together in unstructured groups, such as while listening to a story. As children progress through the grades, more emphasis is placed on structure and rules. Students sit in rows at desks and learn to be on time and to respect the rights of other students and school property, as well as to follow the teacher's directions; free time is limited to short periods of recess. Students are increasingly assessed and compared on measures of individual achievement through assignments and exams. Over time, the knowledge and skills taught become more specialized. Class time becomes segregated into distinct required subjects, such as math and science, and eventually includes optional programs of study, such as Spanish, Indigenous studies, and drama.

THE MANIFEST AND LATENT FUNCTIONS OF EDUCATION

In Chapter 1, you learned the distinction between the *manifest* (i.e., intended) functions of social institutions and their *latent* (i.e., unintended or hidden) functions. Functionalists analyze these different functions within the education system (Merton, 1957). Manifest functions are formally documented in provincial school acts, incorporated into assessment practices by teachers, and communicated to parents via student report cards. Four main manifest functions of education are summarized as follows:

1. *Skill and knowledge development*. At each grade level, students are taught a standardized curriculum relevant to their age and/or existing level of knowledge and skills. For example, a student in Grade 1 would be expected to be able to sort objects and demonstrate an understanding of repeating patterns as part of early math skills.
2. *Historical and cultural transmission*. Schools play a central role in passing on historical knowledge and teaching cultural values and norms. For example, high school graduates in Alberta are expected to be well versed in the history and geography of Canada; understand Canada's political, social, and economic systems; and show respect for Canada's cultural diversity (Alberta Education, 2016).
3. *Social development*. The education system helps socialize members of society so that they can get along with one another in a variety of contexts. Teachers provide opportunities for children to play, cooperate, and share with one another and, conversely, enact consequences for behaviour considered to be unacceptable. As children progress through school, social skills are taught more formally in health and life skills courses. In Grade 9, for example, students learn how to refine personal goals relevant to career paths and to develop strategies for risk and stress management (Alberta Education, 2017).
4. *Social control*. Students learn the importance of respecting authority figures and following rules. This begins in early childhood education and is reflected in various practices, such as raising your hand before speaking, waiting in a line to exit and enter the classroom, sitting quietly at a workstation for a given period of time, keeping a workspace organized, and completing projects in the time allotted.

Rawpixel.com/Shutterstock

Social control is one of the main functions of education.

"No response. We'll have to use the corporate logo flashcards again."

© Goddard, Clive, cgon580, Cartoonstock.com

The expectation is that most students will achieve particular normative learning outcomes as well as some more specialized forms of knowledge that will enable them to contribute to society as citizens and employees. For example, after a basic education to the end of Grade 12, students in Alberta are able to read, write, and speak clearly; use math; understand the scientific method; and describe the history and geography of Canada. In addition, they are able to work independently, manage time, and demonstrate important social characteristics such as fairness and respect for others (Alberta Education, 2016).

The education system also has latent functions. Because of changing patterns of parental employment, they now provide primary daycare functions, such as lunch-hour supervision and after-school care. Schools also serve a latent matchmaking function: students often develop their first serious crush on a classmate or begin to date fellow students. Clearly, schools help develop important friendships and social networks, which can provide future benefits, such as business contacts and perhaps, eventually, spouses.

CRITICAL PERSPECTIVES

Functionalist views emphasize the many benefits of education for producing skilled employees. For their part, conflict and feminist views highlight how the education system reproduces the existing social order and poses disadvantages for particular groups.

THE SOCIAL REPRODUCTION OF CLASS

Because of hidden school costs (see *Sociology in Practice*), the school experience can be quite different for children of different social classes. But according to conflict perspectives, the education system does more than just treat the social classes differently; it actually maintains and reproduces class differences and social inequality (Gintis and Bowles, 1980). As noted in the chapter on gender, although women now constitute the majority of postsecondary students, jobs in which women are overrepresented tend to be lower paying and of lower status. Similarly, more Indigenous people are obtaining high school and postsecondary educations than in the past, but non-Indigenous people are still more likely to graduate from high school and pursue a postsecondary education. Members of the lower classes are also underrepresented among high school and postsecondary graduates. These inequalities are often discussed by critical theorists as resulting from education-based practices known as the hidden curriculum, streaming, and credentialism.

Hidden Curriculum. Conflict perspectives are concerned not only with *whose* values and norms are transmitted but also with *how* learning takes place and the environment in which it takes place, something that Philip W. Jackson (1968) originally termed the *hidden curriculum* in his book, *Life in Classrooms*. The **hidden curriculum** refers to the process whereby students inadvertently learn, through participation in the school system, a subtle agenda of norms, values, and expectations that fall outside the formal curriculum. Much of the knowledge learned via the hidden curriculum resembles indicators of social control, such as raising your hand before answering a question and sitting quietly at a desk for long periods of time. But the hidden curriculum also includes more subtle lessons and messages learned during

Hidden curriculum: The process by which a subtle agenda of norms, values, and expectations that fall outside the formal curriculum is learned inadvertently through participation in the school system.

SOCIOLOGY IN MUSIC

EDUCATION AS CONTROL

In 1979, Pink Floyd released its album *The Wall*, which would go on to become one of the top-selling albums of all time. The song "Another Brick in the Wall" critiques the British educational system as an oppressive regime designed to create obedient automatons rather than critical thinkers. In the 1982 musical film based on the album, this view of the education system is reflected with the imagery of students being processed through a meat grinder, until some become aware of their oppression and rise up to destroy their school. Concerned about the potential effects of the song and film on youth audiences, the South African government banned the song in 1980 after it became the anthem for a national strike involving students protesting the social stratification of education based on race (Sievert, 2010).

the educational process as a function of teaching methods and the interactions among and between teachers and students. You may recall from the chapter on gender that the hidden curriculum conveys important messages about gender that have a lasting impact on people's lives.

Streaming. School systems also aid in social reproduction through an educational policy called **streaming** in Canada (or *tracking* in the United States and more broadly known throughout the world as "student selection"), which places students in specific programs and levels of curriculum based on perceived individual levels of achievement. In elementary school, streaming is generally used to identify children with learning or behavioural challenges, who may require specialized assistance (Curtis, Livingstone, & Smaller, 1992). In high school, this practice is used mainly to sort students into an advanced upper tier bound for university and a lower tier geared more toward vocational training (Davis & Guppy, 2006; Taylor & Krahn, 2009). Your own high school may have required students to select an "academic" or "applied" route for core classes based on some combination of previous grades, teacher assessments, advice of counsellors, and/or parental input. Tracking occurs in all 35 Organisation for Economic Co-operation and Development (OECD)[2] countries at a median age of 15 but may start as early as age 10 (e.g., Austria, German) (OECD, 2012). Although this practice is designed to help facilitate career goals given the different interests and skill sets of students, it is linked to socioeconomic status. Children of higher-income families are disproportionately represented among those in the higher academic streams (Hamlin & Cameron, 2015).

Streaming: A process whereby students are placed into specific programs and levels of curriculum based on perceived levels of achievement.

Streaming may be influenced in part by processes and practices that inadvertently include components of *cultural capital*, a mechanism whereby higher classes exclude the lower classes. Bourdieu and Passeron (1964, 1970) explained how initial differences in cultural capital are legitimized in the school system in ways that contribute to social reproduction (Izquierdo & Mínguez, 2003). Because the school is viewed as a neutral forum, students in the lower classes come to accept status symbols associated with high culture (e.g., theatre, ballet), even though these are not cultural elements they are likely to experience for themselves (Feinberg & Soltis, 2009).

Students from lower classes are also socialized within their families in ways that may further differentiate them from those in the higher classes within the educational system. For example, Lareau (2011) has found that middle-class parents take a *concerted cultivation* approach to parenting: they impress on their children the value of education, enroll them in structured after-school activities that enhance problem solving and critical thinking, and take a proactive role in identifying resources when their children are having problems in school. Lower-class parents are less able to instill the value of education in their children (because they tend to have lower levels of education themselves). Because of restricted resources (e.g., money, time), they are less likely to place their children in structured activities that facilitate learning; instead, their children spend their free time playing with friends in the neighbourhood—a *natural growth*

SOCIOLOGY IN WORDS

PETITION FOR AN INCLUSIVE CURRICULUM

In April of 2017, a petition was developed and circulated by Robert Green, a history teacher and chair of the Committee for the Enhancement of the Curriculum of History in Quebec. The committee, consisting of parents and educators, seeks changes to the educational curriculum in Quebec on the grounds that the recently revised curriculum fails to appropriately represent Indigenous peoples, Anglophones, and minorities. Three excerpts are provided below.

PETITION FOR AN INCLUSIVE HISTORY CURRICULUM

Quebec's Secondary III & IV History Curriculum: In Need of Change

What We Are Asking For

- First and foremost, we want a curriculum whose content acknowledges the complexity and diversity of Quebec society and challenges students to develop critical thinking skills in examining historical events. A curriculum that seeks to indoctrinate students with a simplistic ideologically driven narrative is an insult to the intelligence of students and a disservice to society as a whole. To be clear, we are not asking to replace one narrow ideological vision of history with another. This is not about replacing a sovereignist narrative with a federalist one or a conservative narrative with a liberal one. Conservative nationalist perspectives have a place in the telling of Quebec's history. But they, like other important currents of thought, should be presented as that, perspectives, not the defining narrative.
- We want a curriculum that addresses Indigenous History as noted in items 62, 63 and 64 of the Calls to Action made by the Truth and Reconciliation Commission (TRC). The current reform has ignored these recommendations. We also want a curriculum that reflects the current scholarship on Indigenous history which reveals the active role of Indigenous people in shaping North American history in every historical period, rather than portraying them merely as hapless and passive victims of colonization. Achieving these goals will require extensive consultation with Indigenous communities and scholars at every step of the curriculum development process.
- We want a curriculum that acknowledges the struggles and positive contributions of Quebec's various ethnic minority and local communities. Students need to learn about the over 4,000 Black and Indigenous people enslaved in Quebec during the French regime, about the struggles against discrimination faced by Jewish, Italian and Greek immigrants during the early waves of immigration, about the more recent efforts to welcome refugees fleeing war and oppression in places like Vietnam, Lebanon, Chile, Haiti or Syria. The history of Quebec's Black community also needs to be integrated into the curriculum rather than leaving it to be taught at the discretion of individual teachers. The current curriculum has completely omitted the historical contributions of its minority communities. No community that has contributed to the development of Quebec society should be rendered invisible or demonized.

Source: "For an Inclusive History Curriculum," https://www.change.org/p/ministre-de-l-éducation-du-loisir-et-du-sport-pour-un-programme-d-histoire-inclusif-for-an-inclusive-history-curriculum.

approach to parenting. The latter approach to parenting enables children to develop greater independence and the ability to entertain themselves, but the former approach facilitates better performance in school. Furthermore, written and spoken assessments as well as intelligence quotient (IQ) tests that are used in school to gauge ability use language that is more familiar to children from the upper classes, providing them with a distinct advantage.

From a critical perspective, streaming promotes social reproduction because those in the middle and upper classes are more likely to end up in the upper tracks en route to university, whereas the lower classes are disproportionately streamed into lower educational tiers (Oakes, 2005). Contemporary debates centre on whether streaming diverts lower-class students from the university track and into lower-status and lower-paying jobs or whether it helps them develop the skills they need to become productive workers. Shavit and Müller's (2000) comparative research on tracking found that vocational secondary education in a number of countries served as both a diversion and a safety net. That is, tracking into vocational routes helped produce more skilled rather than unskilled workers, but it also led to jobs of lower status compared to students with academic-based educations. So, tracking helps lower-class students obtain jobs, albeit less desirable ones. Recent research on a number of countries (e.g., Austria, Canada, Czech Republic, and Sweden, among others) highlights inequities for economically disadvantaged students and recommends less early streaming (e.g., by eliminating the lowest tracks and by postponing it until later years) and more flexibility so that students can change tracks (OECD, 2012).

Private schools accept fees, usually in the form of an annual tuition, and are run by private individuals or corporations. They are most likely to be attended by individuals from the upper strata of society. There are about 1,935 private schools in Canada, attended by 368,717 students (Our Kids, 2017). They vary considerably depending on the location, size, student-to-teacher ratio, and costs. The most expensive private school in Canada is Appleby College, a liberal arts school for Grades 7 to 12 in Oakville, Ontario, with tuition fees ranging from $33,510 to $65,980 (Our Kids, 2017). In contrast, **public schools** are funded through provincial and local governments. Most students attend public schools (see *Sociology in My Community*).

Private schools: Schools operated by private individuals or corporations, for which parents pay an annual tuition.

Public schools: Schools funded through provincial and local governments.

Credentialism: The reliance on increasingly higher educational qualifications as necessary minimal requirements for employment.

Credentialism. Finally, social stratification is fostered in the educational system through a process called **credentialism**. This refers to the reliance on increasingly higher educational qualifications as the minimal requirements for employment. For example, a Ph.D. is now usually required for permanent employment as a university professor, whereas four decades ago, a master's degree was sufficient. Functionalists argue that higher educational attainment is necessary due to technological advancements in society and to ensure that specialized occupations are filled by the most qualified people. Conflict theorists refute this claim, pointing out that skills can often be learned on the job and that those with higher levels of education are not always more productive (Collins, 1977). Critical views also point out how increased education in industrial societies has moved well beyond the technical needs of the workforce, such that there is a surplus of over-educated unemployed individuals (Feinberg & Soltis, 2009; Livingstone, 1998). There are even many forms of employment that yield incomes that may be considered questionable in terms of their comparable worth or value to society. Is a hockey player who earns several million dollars in a season more valuable to society than a daycare worker who earns only about $15 an hour? Which position is more vital?

YOUR SOCIOLOGICAL TOOLKIT

SOCIOLOGY IN MY COMMUNITY

PEOPLE FOR EDUCATION

People for Education is a charitable organization that acts as an advocate for public education in Ontario. The organization conducts independent research on publicly funded schools, organizes educational conferences, and makes policy recommendations in an effort to improve public education. One current area of focus is Indigenous education and building better relationships with Indigenous peoples. In addition to reports and other efforts to increase Indigenous educational opportunities, People for Education's website brings together a wealth of Indigenous educational materials for all grade levels, including resources aimed at non-Indigenous Canadians to help them learn more about Indigenous issues. For more information, visit http://www.peopleforeducation.ca.

Think Outside the Box: Consider the core subjects, such as math, science, and humanities, as well as the typical extracurricular activities offered in schools, such as physical education. What is one additional skill you feel should be developed into a course to help students become active members of society? Explain why this skill is important.

Conflict theorists claim that credentialism reproduces inequality because it is linked to class privilege, which is why people with higher education attainment end up in better-paying jobs (Bills, 2004). In other words, as educational requirements increase in relation to specific occupations, so do the odds that those positions will be disproportionately filled by members of society who came from privileged families who could afford to send them to the best schools and universities. Combine credentialism with government cutbacks and increases to tuition and you can begin to appreciate how those in the upper echelons of society have a tremendous advantage over those in the lower classes when it comes to completing a postsecondary education.

INTERACTIONIST VIEWS

To understand how educational practices influence individuals, it is necessary to understand how teachers perceive their students, how teachers act and react in relation to the meanings they ascribe to the actions and words of pupils, and, in turn, how students interpret their instructors, the curriculum, and the behaviour of fellow students. Power differentials between students and teachers can play an important role in how meanings are constructed in classroom settings. The teacher is the authority figure who can make and enforce rules, whereas a student is in a position of deference to the teacher, who at any given time may label a student's behaviour appropriate or inappropriate.

Because of the generalized other and the looking-glass self, how one is labelled by others has important implications for future behaviours and one's self-esteem. One potential outcome of labelling in the educational system is the development of self-fulfilling prophecies. A **self-fulfilling prophecy** is an originally false belief that becomes true simply because it is perceived as such. For example, suppose a student often disrupts others and fails to finish his assignments. The teacher, believing that he has an attention-deficit/hyperactivity disorder (ADHD), moves the student to a table separated from the rest of the class designated for extra help. Because the boy has now been moved into the "special" section, other students become more tolerant and accepting of his infractions because he probably "can't help himself." The student continues to fidget and not complete his work because he now realizes that the teacher will perceive him as unable to finish it himself and eventually help him finish his work—a self-fulfilling prophecy.

Are students always streamed appropriately based on their true abilities and according to objective, fair, and equitable criteria? Webb et al. (2005) suggest that many children (especially boys) who are actually gifted with high IQs are misdiagnosed as having ADHD. Because they are not being intellectually challenged in school and subsequently become restless, teachers (and, later, parents and physicians) *incorrectly* label their misbehaviour in the classroom as indicative of an inability to maintain focus.

A classic study by Rosenthal and Jacobson (1968) illustrates the role of the self-fulfilling prophecy in classrooms. In this study, teachers were informed that a special intelligence test would not only measure IQ but also identify which students would make the most significant progress over the academic year; these children were labelled "academic bloomers." The test really did nothing more than measure IQ, and the "academic bloomers" were actually selected at random. However, a second intelligence test given at the end of the year revealed that those students who had been randomly identified as "academic bloomers" showed an increase in IQ of approximately 12 points. Once the students were falsely labelled as "academic bloomers," the teachers began to perceive and treat them as children who would make significant progress. Subsequently, these students began to perceive themselves in that way, and their academic behaviours changed to enable them to meet those expectations.

POSTMODERN PERSPECTIVES

Postmodern perspectives discount traditional theories of education that

Self-fulfilling prophecy: An originally false belief that becomes true simply because it is perceived as such.

make general assumptions about educational practices and processes and, instead, try to locate educational issues in the contexts and tensions in which they occur. For example, in *Postmodernism and Education*, Usher and Edwards (1994) note how the experiential learning practices that emerged in the 1980s can be seen in many different ways: as opportunities for trying out innovative practices (e.g., learning contracts); as spaces for understanding the values and struggles of marginalized groups; or as new middle-class movements that broke down some of the barriers of social and cultural reproduction. Similarly, whereas various theorists might argue for or against a particular form of testing, postmodern approaches advocate the use of a variety of methods to assess student achievement and the selection of methods that work best for individual outcomes (Ballentine, 2001).

TIME TO REVIEW

- What does a functionalist perspective on education focus on?
- What are the four main manifest functions of education?
- What does a critical perspective on education highlight?
- In what ways is social reproduction fostered by the hidden curriculum, streaming, and credentialism?
- What is a self-fulfilling prophecy, and how might a teacher create one?
- What view of education is held by postmodernists?

CHAPTER SUMMARY

LO1 Explain what belief systems are and identify their components.

Belief systems are sets of interconnected beliefs that are shared among groups of people. They consist of claims about the nature of reality, ethical/moral claims, and technologies.

LO2 Describe religious patterns in Canada and identify the implications of religiosity for individuals and for society.

The largest religious group in the world is Christianity, followed by Islam. In Canada, Catholicism is the most common religious affiliation; with recent immigration patterns, a variety of Eastern religions are becoming more predominant. Religious affiliation and attendance have declined since 1986, but religion continues to play a role in most Canadians' lives. Religiosity has positive implications for individuals in terms of physical and mental health, social capital, and performance in school. At a societal level, religiosity can be associated with positive or negative outcomes.

LO3 Compare key sociological theories of religion.

Substantive approaches focus on the meanings contained within specific doctrines and how those meanings are understood by people in their everyday lives. *Functional* approaches emphasize the social aspects of religion, the functions it serves, and its implications for individuals and for society. Sociological theorizing about religion is as old as the discipline of sociology itself. Durkheim addressed the role of religion in maintaining social solidarity, Marx spoke of religion as an obstacle to proletarian revolution, and Weber explored the role of Protestantism in establishing early capitalism. Diverse feminist perspectives share a foundation in analyzing the oppression of women in religion, and postmodern perspectives draw attention to the multiplicity of individual religious experiences.

LO4 Identify the different ways that sociologists perceive the nature of scientific "truth" and explain the role of postmodern and feminist perspectives in the sociological study of science.

Some sociologists perceive scientific knowledge as a distinct form of knowledge based on objective truth based on the normative structure of science. Others perceive it as socially constructed, emerging from social and political influences, as well as the influence of funding structures. Foucault proposed that claims that emerge from positions of institutionalized power come to be accepted as "legitimate" knowledge; that is the position of science today. Feminist perspectives analyze the position of women in science, the need to tie science with social and political action, and "new" ways of practising science.

LO5 Compare theoretical views of the role of education in modern society within contemporary debates about education.

Functionalist views identify ways in which schools teach members of society to become law-abiding, productive members of the workforce. Critical perspectives point out ways in which educational practices and processes serve to perpetuate inequality and reproduce the existing social order through the hidden curriculum, streaming, and credentialism. Interactionists are interested in how educational practices such as labelling influence individuals based on teacher expectations. Postmodernists emphasize the need to locate educational practices and processes in the modern contexts and conflicts within which they occur.

RECOMMENDED RESOURCES

1. For an overview of the religious patterns of Canadians, as well as what those patterns may mean, see R. Bibby, *Beyond the Gods and Back* (Lethbridge, AB: Project Canada Books, 2011).
2. Robert Merton is often credited as the founder of the sociology of science. His groundbreaking book (1973) is *The Sociology of Science* (Chicago, IL: University of Chicago Press, 1973).
3. Non-Indigenous (settler) peoples are invited to learn more about Indigenous issues (e.g., terminology, treaties, and residential schools) by visiting the website Groundwork for Change at http://www.groundworkforchange.org.

FOR FURTHER REFLECTION

1. Some scientists may engage in scientific misconduct, such as forging data. How might this practice be connected to the corporatization of science?
2. Do you think a person can be both religious and scientific? In what ways might such a person reconcile those two belief systems?
3. Do you have any siblings? In what ways do you think the educational experience of a younger sibling is affected by that child having an older brother or sister?

ENDNOTES

1 Retrieved June 2, 2017, from Goodreads.com (*www.goodreads.com*).

2 The OECD is a group of 35 countries committed to working together for the benefit of economic prosperity.

11 CHAPTER

Social Control, Deviance, and Crime

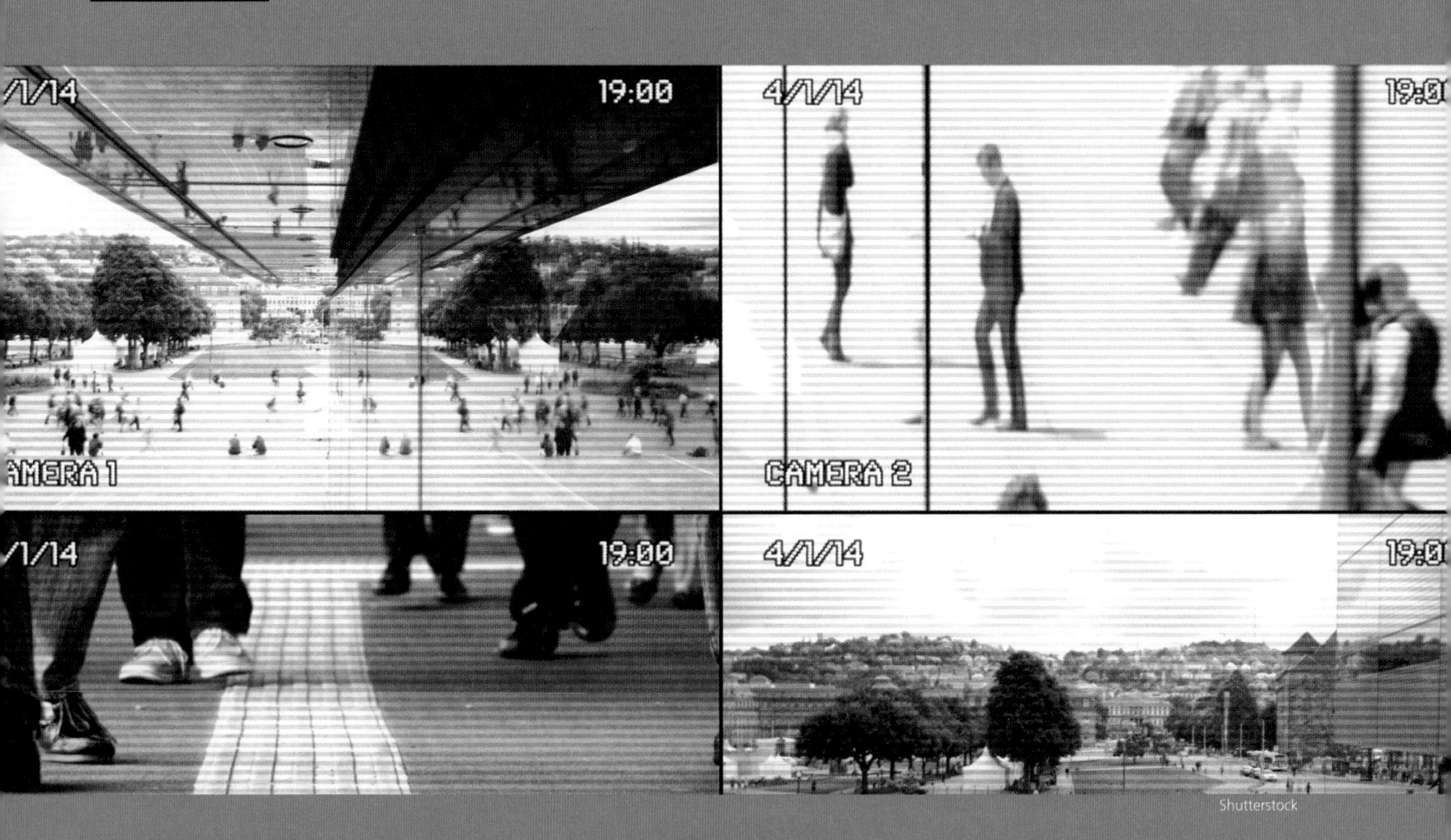

Shutterstock

All societies have ways of keeping deviants under control.... The ancient Greeks killed them; nineteenth-century societies hid them in their closets and attics, and twentieth-century societies rationalized this solution by building large institutions in which they were hidden.

(Newman, 2008, p. xi)

LEARNING OBJECTIVES & OUTCOMES

After completing this chapter, students should be able to do the following:

LO1 Define social control, identify its relationship to deviance, and differentiate among its varying types.

LO2 Compare the different criteria that are highlighted as the foundation for determining deviance and explain the view that deviance is socially constructed.

LO3 Explain the relationship between the concepts of deviance and crime.

LO4 Outline the contrasting views of how laws are created, identify the legal meaning of a crime, and differentiate among crime classifications.

LO5 Describe the criminal justice system and the rationale for punishment as the primary means for controlling crime.

LO6 Discuss critiques of traditional forms of punishment and explain how restorative justice differs from retributive forms of punishment.

LO7 Identify and describe the theories used to explain the causes of deviance and those that explain our perceptions of and reactions to particular behaviours and characteristics.

LO1 SOCIAL CONTROL

We all know that "some people" are subjected to measures of **social control**, actions that are intended to prevent, correct, punish, or cure behaviours or characteristics perceived as unacceptable—those that are labelled **deviant**. But how many of us recognize that *we* are those people who are socially controlled (see *Sociology in My Life*)? And how many of us recognize that at the same time we are also the ones who are *doing* the controlling?

Once a person, behaviour, or characteristic is viewed as unacceptable, measures of social control kick in (Becker, 1963; Bereska, 2018; Edwards, 1988). Sometimes measures of social control are formal, implemented through an "official" mechanism that carries some institutionalized authority—such as a workplace dress code dictating that you must conceal your tattoos or piercings or the police arresting and charging you with a crime. Other times, we are subjected to informal measures of social control in everyday social interaction—bullied for being a "geek" or stared at because of your physical appearance. Some forms of control are intended to punish or cure (and may be formal or informal) *after* a deviant behaviour or characteristic has been detected. Examples include receiving a speeding ticket or being teased about your weight. Other forms of control are intended to prevent deviance from occurring in the first place—for example, educational programs in schools that teach children about the dangers of smoking (to prevent substance use) or community programs that provide leisure activities for inner-city youth (to prevent criminal activity). Sometimes we even exert measures of social control upon ourselves, such as by going on a diet to lose weight or studying harder for a final exam to avoid failing a class.

Thus, social control is not just targeted at "some people." We are all subjected to measures of control every single day. Furthermore, sometimes *we* are the ones who stare at, tease, or bully others; *we* are the parents disciplining our children for breaking the house rules; *we* are the people who avoid making eye contact with a homeless person; *we* are the people who enter professions that formally exert measures of social control (as teachers, police officers, employees in the university's registrar's office, or group home workers).

Social control: Actions intended to prevent, correct, punish, or cure people, behaviours, and characteristics that are perceived as unacceptable.

Deviant: A person, behaviour, or characteristic perceived as unacceptable.

YOUR SOCIOLOGICAL TOOLKIT

SOCIOLOGY IN MY LIFE

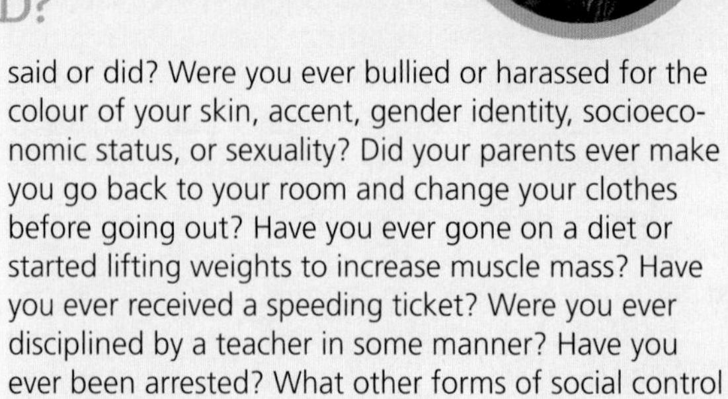

ARE YOU SOCIALLY CONTROLLED?

There are myriad forms of social control, ranging from informal to formal, from retroactive to preventive, from controls directed at us to controls we impart upon ourselves. Considering how many varied measures of social control we are subjected to reveals how all of us are, at some points, viewed as deviant in our lives—or at least *potentially* deviant.

Think Outside the Box: Have you ever received a dirty look from someone because of something you said or did? Were you ever bullied or harassed for the colour of your skin, accent, gender identity, socioeconomic status, or sexuality? Did your parents ever make you go back to your room and change your clothes before going out? Have you ever gone on a diet or started lifting weights to increase muscle mass? Have you ever received a speeding ticket? Were you ever disciplined by a teacher in some manner? Have you ever been arrested? What other forms of social control have you experienced in your life?

LO2 WHAT IS DEVIANCE?

At its most general level, deviance refers to those people, behaviours, or characteristics that are viewed as unacceptable. But why are some perceived as unacceptable, whereas others are not? What do being too thin, committing a crime, being gender non-conforming, and speeding have in common?

Perhaps what they have in common is that they violate norms. In fact, you will often see "deviance" defined as a behaviour that violates society's norms. This is even the definition of deviance you will find in the dictionary (Merriam-Webster, 2017). But from a sociological perspective, deviance is far more complex than this definition suggests. Norms are not universal and unchanging but rather are socially constructed. Societies evolve and change over time, which means that norms change over time as well. Furthermore, society is composed of countless different social groups. Which group's specific expectations for behaviour are the ones being used as the standards for judgment in society more generally?

Thus, within academia, there is some disagreement over the definition of deviance. Some scholars put forward "objective" definitions that highlight a specific quality that inherently makes certain acts deviant and in need of social control (Bereska, 2018; Sacco, 1992). At the same time, these scholars often dispute precisely what that quality is. Are behaviours that are statistically uncommon the ones in need of control (e.g., being very thin, having purple hair)? Or is it those that cause harm that are unacceptable (e.g., criminal activity, cyberbullying)? Might it be behaviours and characteristics that "most Canadians" disapprove of (e.g., racism)? Maybe it is those that violate norms, as the dictionary suggests (e.g., closing the elevator door when someone is rushing to get on). Each of these four qualities has served as the definition of deviance for some scholars.

But even "objective" criteria can be called into question because there are times when a behaviour fits one of these criteria (e.g., is statistically rare) yet is not considered unacceptable or subjected to measures of social control (e.g., unusual sports prowess, such as embodied in NHL star Connor McDavid). Conversely, alcohol consumption is statistically *common* among high school students (Boak et al., 2015) but is still considered to be unacceptable by many parents (who punish their underage children for coming home drunk from a party) and by the state (in that the law prohibits the sale of alcohol to people under a certain age).

Because of the shortcomings in defining deviance on the basis of a single objective quality, many deviance scholars today propose a "subjective" definition instead, one that draws attention to the social processes that teach us how to label acts as good/bad, right/wrong, and normal/abnormal (Bereska, 2018; Sacco, 1992). This view emphasizes the subjective manner in which deviance is socially constructed and how it is influenced by the structure of power in society. For instance, although alcohol consumption is considered acceptable now (among adults), the sale of alcohol was considered criminal during a period of national prohibition from 1918 to 1919. And today, you might argue that the legalized substance of alcohol causes more harm to society than do the illicit drugs that are prohibited by law. In the chapter on health and illness,

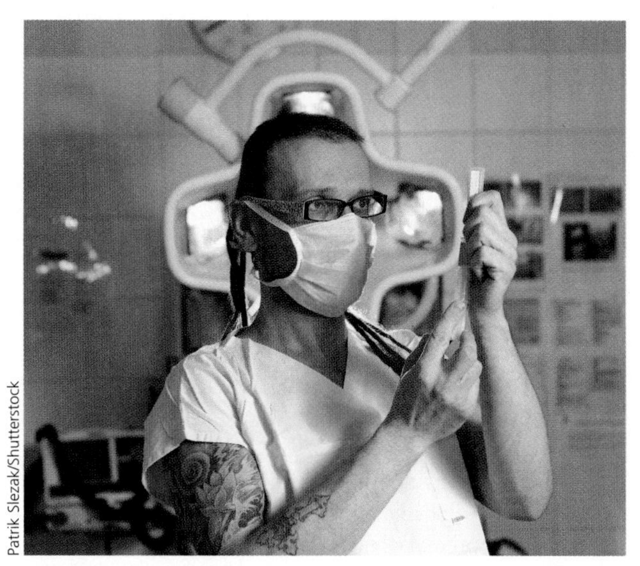
Patrik Slezak/Shutterstock

Most of us would agree that medical malpractice is deviant. In contrast, there would likely be disagreement over whether it is acceptable for medical staff to sport tattoos and dreadlocks.

you will see that alcohol misuse is one of the top three leading actual causes of illness and death worldwide.

From this perspective, deviance is defined as "people, behaviours, and characteristics that society's dominant moral codes deem to be unacceptable and in need of control" (Bereska, 2018, p. 14). So, then, why are you given a ticket for speeding? Because legislators have determined that speeding is unacceptable, and law enforcement agencies are tasked with enforcing that view. Why are individuals who date others of the same sex too frequently victimized by hate crimes? Because they are perceived by some as stepping outside the dualisms equating sex, gender, and sexuality that have historically dominated Euro-Canadian discourses. In some cases, there will be agreement in society that a specific act is unacceptable (e.g., murder). In other cases, there will be less agreement or even considerable dispute (e.g., body modification).

Deviance scholars study a wide range of behaviours and characteristics (Bereska, 2018): cyberdeviance (e.g., cyberbullying, digital piracy); body modification (e.g., tattoos); the sex industry (e.g., pornography, exotic dancing); bodies deemed to be "too fat" or "too thin"; substance use; mental illness; alternative religious groups; criminal activity; and more.

LO3 DEVIANCE AND CRIME

Criminal behaviours are often viewed as acts that most of us would agree are unacceptable. Furthermore, they are subjected to the most formal, institutionalized measures of social control in contemporary society—those stemming from the criminal justice system. Scholars who focus their analyses on crime are known as **criminologists**. Because there has always been widespread concern about crime in society, **criminology** has become a significant area of study within the sociology of deviance.

TIME TO REVIEW

- What is social control, and what relationship does it have with deviance?
- What forms does social control take?
- What are the various "objective" criteria that some scholars use to define deviance?
- How do other scholars define deviance subjectively (rather than objectively)?
- What topics are studied by deviance scholars, and why has a distinct area of study evolved to study criminal forms of deviance in particular?

LO4 CRIME

Which behaviours, exactly, are considered criminal? They are those that are deemed by legislators as so unacceptable that they must be embodied in government legislation. At that point, a behaviour is labelled a crime; in other words, a **crime** is any behaviour that violates criminal law. Which acts receive this label is not static but varies over time. For example, in the chapter on sex, gender, and sexuality, you learned that in Canada before 1969, having a (consensual) sexual relationship with someone of the same sex was considered criminal. As a result of LGBTQ activism, that behaviour is no longer labelled a "crime."

Although we might initially assume that there is considerable agreement that criminal activity is unacceptable, there is some question of how much consensus is really involved in determining which behaviours are legislated against. In fact, there are several different perspectives on the nature of the law (Linden, 2016; Siegel & McCormick, 2016). The *consensual view* of law is that the

Criminologists: Researchers who specialize in the study of criminal behaviour.

Criminology: The academic discipline that focuses on the study of crime and those labelled as criminals.

Crime: Any behaviour that violates criminal law.

behaviours legislated against in criminal law are those that most people agree should be legislated against; furthermore, it is presumed that the ensuing measures of social control are then equally applied to everyone. However, other scholars argue that "law creation is a political activity, wherein the [behaviours] that are embodied in law do not necessarily reflect the view of the majority of citizens" (Bereska, 2018, p. 12). The *conflict view* argues that the ruling class creates and uses the law as a tool for oppressing powerless groups in society and serving its own interests. The *interactionist view* proposes that legislation emerges from interactions between special interest groups who have identified a social problem and powerful groups they approach to resolve that problem (the government). Finally, others view the law as a "balance" that has been struck among the opinions of special interest groups, the attitudes of the majority, and the interests of the powerful. Whatever the process of law creation, in Canada, we can find the outcome of that process in the Criminal Code of Canada (1985), which lists crimes and their corresponding penalties.

According to Canadian legislation, a criminal offence has occurred when a criminal act has taken place and there was corresponding *intent* to commit the act (Verdun-Jones, 2015). Intent here refers to "blameworthy" in the sense that a "reasonable" person would understand the outcome of those actions. For instance, an adult may deliberately take and keep someone's unattended purse, including the money it contains. In contrast, there would not be intent if the person took the purse in order to return it to the owner. Criminal laws apply equally to everyone, independent of ascribed or achieved characteristics, such as ethnicity or social status. Hence, all who commit the same act of theft and who have the capacity to do so with intent are subject to arrest and, if convicted, will face similar consequences for this violation against society. However, research has found that although the law may be intended to apply to everyone, in practice, the *application* of the law is not always neutral. Members of some social groups (especially racialized groups) are more likely than others to be monitored by law enforcement, arrested, charged, found guilty, and sentenced to imprisonment (Becker, 1963; Chan & Chunn, 2014). We see this today in the overrepresentation of Indigenous people in the Canadian criminal justice system.

TYPES OF CRIMES AND LAWS

In Canada, there are several different types of laws; criminal law is only one of them. As one of Britain's former colonies, our legal system has its roots in early English "common law." The common-law system was developed by judges, based on decisions from individual court cases that set "precedents" such that future cases of that nature were to be treated in a similar fashion. Since its origins, common law has continuously evolved as sociocultural circumstances have broadened (Siegel & McCormick, 2016). In Canada, there are two main types of law: private law and public law. *Private law* concerns relationships between individuals, often in the form of contracts and agreements (e.g., marriage, property, and wills), whereas *public law* concerns relationships between the individual and society (e.g., constitutional law, criminal law, and taxation law) (see *Figure 11.1*).

When there is an issue involving private law (i.e., wrongs against a person), the offending party pays for damages or otherwise compensates for the wrongdoing (Vago & Nelson, 2014). For example, traffic laws pertaining to speed limits are developed at the provincial and municipal levels under private law, and offenders pay fines, receive demerit points, and/or pay compensation to victims. In contrast, issues under public law are considered wrongs against the state. For example, by trafficking an illegal substance, a drug dealer is considered to be causing harm to society as a whole; consequently, under public law, court cases are not between a victim (e.g., the person who became ill from the drugs he or she purchased) and the accused but rather between the Crown and the accused. When wrongs are against the state, the penalties are more severe (such as imprisonment). The public law in Canada, which includes the Criminal Code, the Youth Criminal Justice Act, and the Controlled Substances Act, is the area of law that criminologists focus their attention on. All of these acts are located on the federal government's "Justice Laws Website" (http://www.laws-lois.justice.gc.ca).

TIME TO REVIEW

- What is the formal definition of "crime," and how is this similar to and different from the concept of deviance?
- In practice, are laws applied equally to everyone?
- Are the crimes studied by sociologists primarily part of private or public law?
- What does intent refer to?

FIGURE 11.1

Types of Law

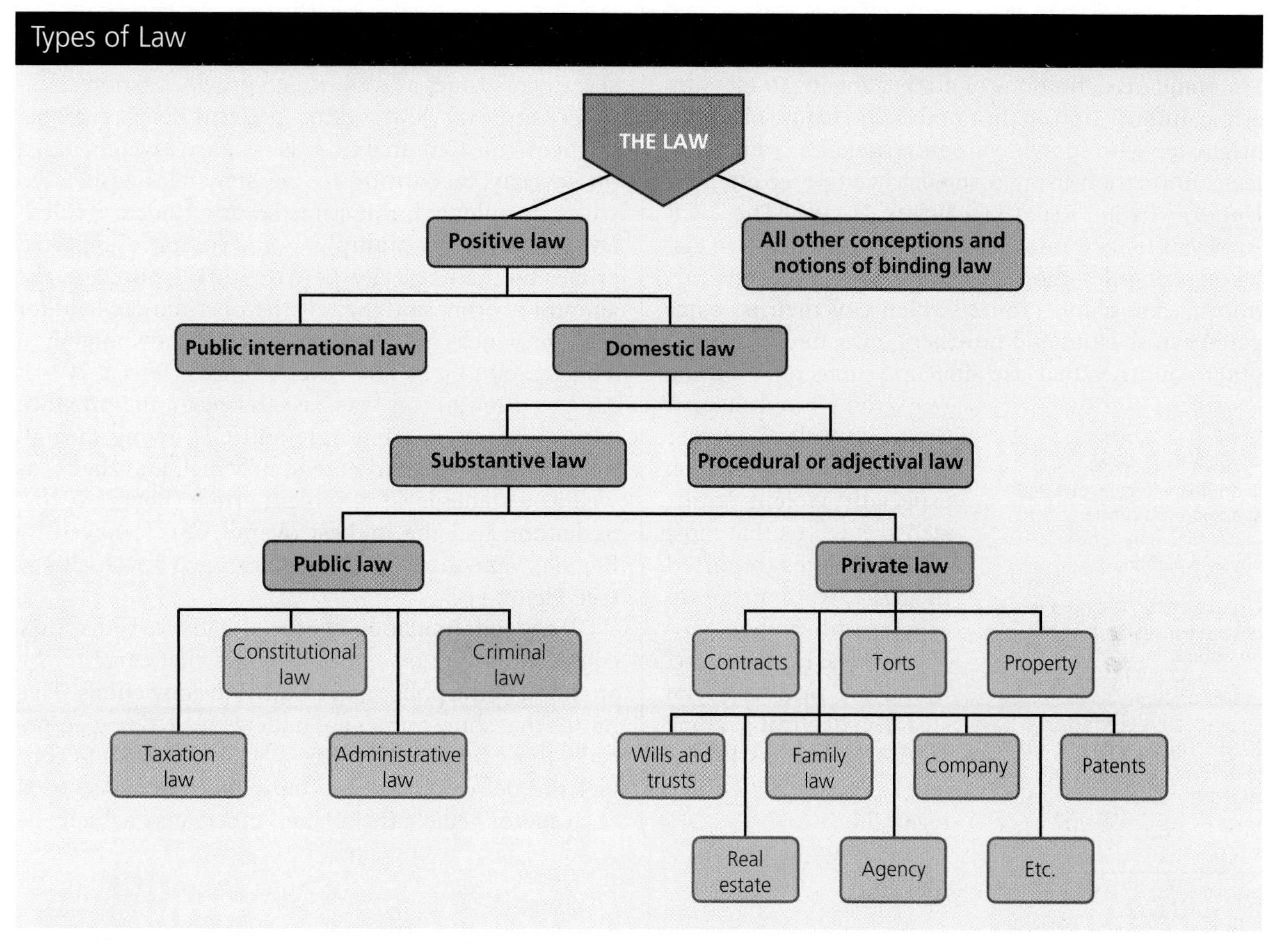

Source: Figure 2.7 "The Law" from *The Canadian Legal System, Fifth Edition*, by Gerald L. Gall (2004 edition 0-459-24128-1 (HC); 0-459-24153-2 (PB)), Chapter 2 The Divisions of Law, Pg. 29. Adapted by permission of Thomson Reuters Canada Limited.

CRIME CLASSIFICATIONS AND STATISTICS

Crimes are often categorized on the basis of their *perceived seriousness*. **Summary conviction offences** are perceived as causing the least harm; they include acts such as theft under $5,000, unauthorized use of a computer, and taking a motor vehicle without consent. The maximum punishment for summary offences is a fine of not more than $5,000, a jail sentence not exceeding six months, or both (Criminal Code, 1985). **Indictable conviction offences** are those that are viewed as causing the most harm; examples include trafficking in persons, terrorist activity, and murder. They correspond to more severe penalties, such as a lengthy prison term (Criminal Code, 1985). Some offences, such as assault or sexual assault, range in the level of seriousness depending on a number of factors (e.g., whether or not a weapon was used, whether there was a threat to a third party, and the amount of harm incurred by the victim) (Criminal Code, 1985); they are referred to as *hybrid offences* because they can be prosecuted as summary or indictable convictions (Jourard, 2017).

Crimes are also treated somewhat differently within the legal system depending on the *intended victim of harm*. **Violent crimes** are offences committed against a person, such as assault, sexual assault, manslaughter, and homicide.

Summary conviction offences: Less serious criminal offences that are punishable by a maximum of six months in prison and/or a fine of not more than $5,000.

Indictable conviction offences: More serious criminal offences than summary offences with penalties that vary but could result in life imprisonment.

Violent crimes: Criminal offences that involve physical harm to another person.

Property crimes are "economic" offences committed against property enacted to bring about financial gain, such as identity theft, credit card theft, or break and enter (Siegel & McCormick, 2016).

Standard definitions of crime allow us to measure crime. Information on the number and nature of crimes originates with individual police agencies, which collect information using a standardized procedure, the *Uniform Crime Reporting Survey (UCR)*. The UCR surveys are forwarded annually to Statistics Canada, which compiles the data into statistics that give us information about crimes, which can then be compared across cities and provinces, over time, and with other countries that use similar systems of recording (e.g., the United States). For example, despite media attention on crime, especially violent crime, statistics tell us that most of the crimes reported in 2014 were property crimes rather than violent crimes. Furthermore, the crime rate has been steadily declining since 1991 and is at its lowest level since 1972 (see *Figure 11.2*).

Property crimes: Economic offences directed at someone's property rather than someone's physical person.

Crime rate: The number of criminal incidents reported to the police divided by the population.

Crime severity index (CSI): The volume of crimes multiplied by their severity.

Besides the **crime rate** (the number of criminal incidents reported to the police divided by the population), the crime severity index (CSI) is also calculated. The **crime severity index (CSI)** takes into account the severity of crimes as well, which provides a more comprehensive overview of crime patterns. Every criminal offence in the Criminal Code is assigned a weight based on severity (according to the sentences associated with that offence); the crime severity index is calculated each year by multiplying the volume of reported crimes by their severity. Between 2013 and 2014, the amount of crime and the severity of crime declined for most provinces and territories, largely attributable to a decrease in break and enter offences (Boyce, 2015). An exception to this was Saskatchewan, the province with the highest crime rate and CSI owing to high numbers of break and enters, mischief, and thefts, as well as a stable level of violent crime (Boyce, 2015). Saskatoon had the highest overall CSI, followed by Regina, Vancouver, and Thunder Bay (Boyce, 2015) (see *Figure 11.3*).

The main limitation of official statistics is that they contain information only on crimes that came to the attention of the police and resulted in convictions. This means that some crimes are underestimated (e.g., especially those involving victims who are reluctant to contact the police), some are more accurately recorded (e.g., motor vehicle thefts), and others may actually be

FIGURE 11.2

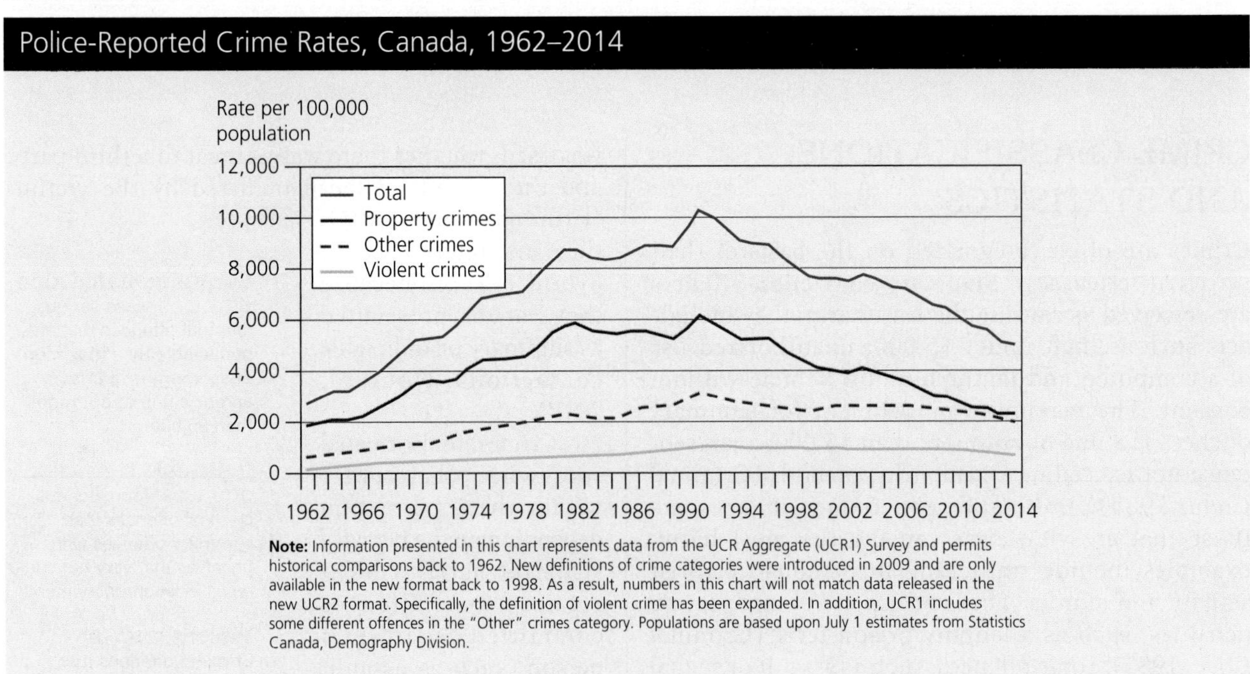

Source: J. Boyce, (2015, July 22). Police-reported crime statistics in Canada, 2014. [Chart 2: Police-reported crime rates, Canada, 1962–2014, Pg. 5]. *Juristat.* Catalogue No. 85-002-X. Ottawa, ON: Statistics Canada.

FIGURE 11.3

Police-Reported Crime Severity Index, by Census Metropolitan Area, 2014

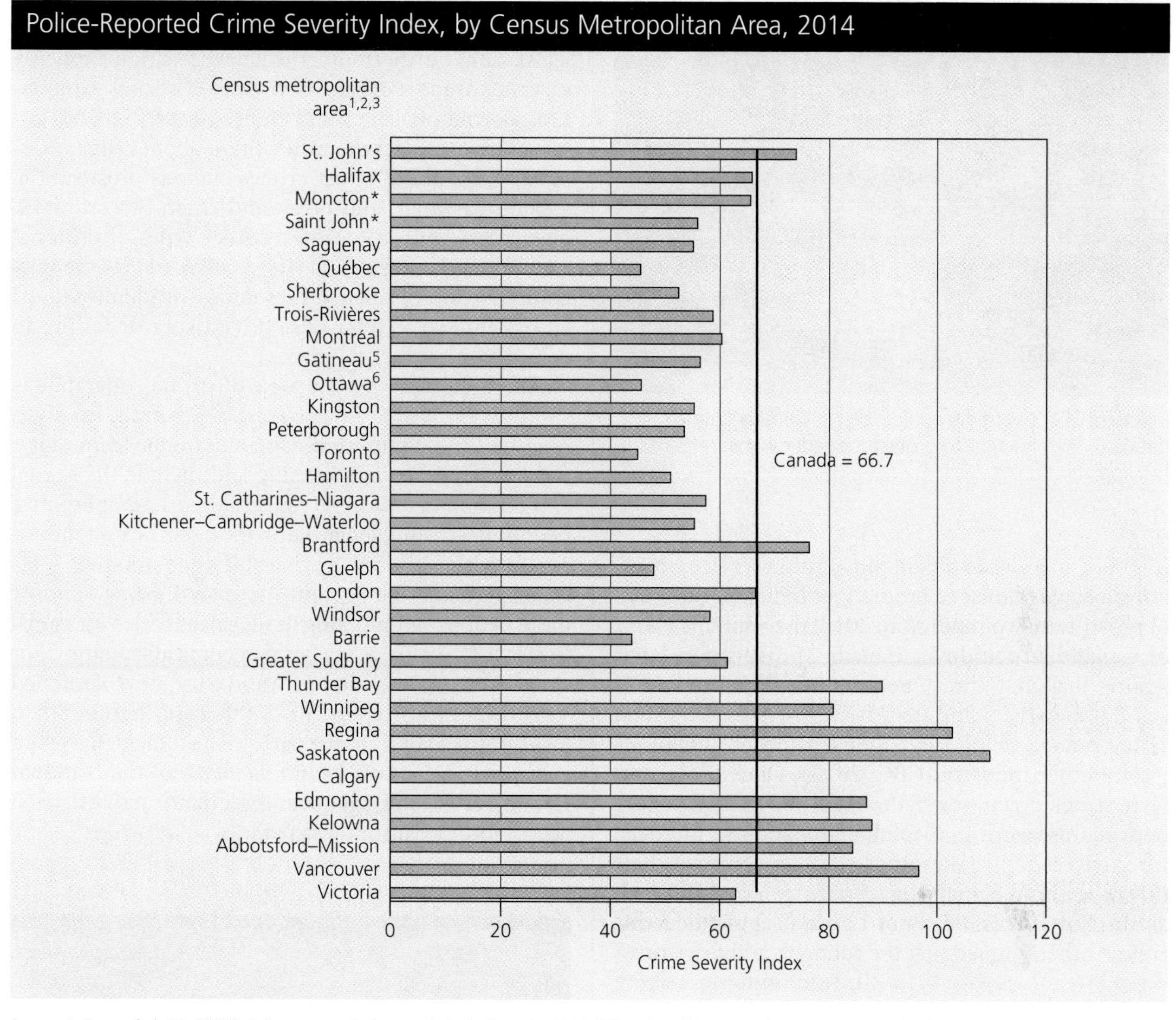

Source: J. Boyce, (July 22, 2015). Police-reported crime statistics in Canada, 2014. [Chart 8: Police-reported Crime Severity Index, by census metropolitan area, 2014, Pg. 5.] *Juristat*. Catalogue No. 85-002-X. Ottawa, ON: Statistics Canada.

*over*represented (e.g., crimes deemed a priority by individual police agencies). To help gain a broader perspective, official statistics are sometimes supplemented by data obtained from victimization surveys. The General Social Survey (GSS), which is conducted regularly in Canada, includes questions on whether respondents have been victimized by a criminal act in the past 12 months and whether they reported the incident to the police. The 2014 GSS reported that about one in every five Canadians age 15 and over had been a victim of a criminal incident within the previous year. Yet just under one-third of these incidents were reported to the police (Perreault, 2015).

Some crimes are classified as "victimless." **Victimless crimes** involve consensual relations in the exchange of illegal goods or services; they include drug use, prostitution, and online gambling. These are sometimes referred to as "crimes involving morality" or "crimes against public order" (Winterdyk, 2016). High levels of debate often surround victimless crimes. We see this quite clearly when looking at the debates over the decriminalization of prostitution.

Prior to 2013, in Canada, the act of prostitution (exchanging money for some type of sexual behaviour) was not illegal. However, it was difficult to engage in prostitution without violating a criminal law related to prostitution, such as communicating

Victimless crimes: Criminal offences that involve consensual relations in the exchange of illegal goods or services.

The Canadian Press/William Campbell

In June 2014, sex trade workers across Canada held a national day of action to protest the federal government's new prostitution law.

in public in order to obtain prostitution services, operating a bawdy house (a brothel), or living off the avails of prostitution (pimping). In 2013, the Supreme Court of Canada struck down Canada's prostitution laws, stating that they threatened the health and safety of sex trade workers and that the workers were entitled to the same level of occupational safety as employees in any other industry (CBC, 2013). Once these laws were struck down, sex trade workers were able to hire bodyguards, work in a common location (a brothel), hire drivers, and take other steps to improve their safety. Although many sex trade workers, as well as the Sex Professionals of Canada, applauded this ruling, others argued that the ruling would drive prostitution indoors, where police officers and social workers would have more difficulty identifying those who might be in need of help (Bereska, 2018). The Supreme Court gave the federal government one year to develop a new prostitution law if it so chose. In 2014, the government did introduce new legislation, emphasizing the criminalization of "johns" (the customers) and pimps. Many sex trade workers, and the Sex Professionals of Canada, were outraged, arguing that the new legislation did not follow the intent of the Supreme Court's ruling—that, in fact, they would now be at even greater risk of violence than under previous legislation. Furthermore, the new legislation explicitly casts sex trade workers as victims of sexual exploitation, devoid of agency and choice (Davies, 2015).

White-collar crime: Criminal offences involving the misappropriation of financial resources.

Corporate crime: Criminal offences carried out by organizations or by knowledgeable employees in the course of their employment.

Cybercrime: Criminal acts committed using computer technology.

Organized crime: Two or more persons consorting together on a continual basis to participate in illegal activities, either directly or indirectly, for gain.

Many people, when they think about crime, most often think about street crimes such as prostitution, assault, car theft, and break and enter. But criminologists draw our attention to other types of criminal activities as well, such as **white-collar crime** (the misappropriation of financial resources, or identity theft) and **corporate crime** (false advertising or failing to comply with safety standards).

Perhaps the newest area of crime, one that is rapidly evolving, is **cybercrime**, which involves criminal acts committed using computer technology. Cybercrimes are wide-ranging and include the sexual exploitation of children (e.g., child pornography sites; pedophiles using social networking sites to communicate with children); cyberbullying; stalking; sales scams; identity theft; and **organized crime** (two or more people participating in illegal activities for gain). In May of 2017, a massive cyberattack using ransomware with the name "WannaCry" was launched worldwide, with reports of 75,000 cases in more than 99 countries (BBC News, 2017) The attack encrypted computer user files, including those of the National Health Service in England and Scotland, and restricted access until a ransom was paid.

Nicescene/Shutterstock

In 2017, more than 75,000 people worldwide woke up to this ransomware message on their computers.

TIME TO REVIEW

- What are the three main types of crime by offence seriousness?
- In what ways do violent and property crimes differ?
- Why are certain crimes considered victimless, what are some examples of victimless crimes, and what is the nature of debate surrounding prostitution laws?

LO5 CONTROLLING CRIME: THE CRIMINAL JUSTICE SYSTEM

In Canada, individuals who have engaged in deviant behaviours that have been criminalized are labelled "criminal" and subjected to social control measures through the criminal justice system. The **criminal justice system** comprises the police, courts, and prisons, which are responsible for apprehending, prosecuting, and punishing those deemed offenders. The process begins with the commission of an act, which, if reported to the police, may result in an arrest. Law enforcement in Canada operates at various levels, from national (the RCMP) to provincial (e.g., Ontario Provincial Police, la Sûreté du Québec) and municipal (e.g., the Toronto Police Service).

After initial contact with the police, who may then lay a charge (through a Crown attorney), someone accused of a crime comes into contact with the courts, which hear the case and treat the individual using principles of fairness and justice. The court system comprises various courts (e.g., provincial courts, federal courts) that have different areas of authority. Most cases involve summary conviction offences and are dealt with in the provincial and territorial courts. After being convicted, offenders may end up at the end point of the criminal justice system, "corrections," where they serve time in a provincial or federal prison. Most convicted offenders end up as the responsibility of provincial correctional organizations, such as the Corrections Division of Manitoba Justice or the Ministry of Community Safety and Correctional Services for Ontario. Only those who are sentenced to two or more years in prison become a federal responsibility under Correctional Service Canada.

PUNISHMENT AS SOCIAL CONTROL

A principal means for controlling behaviour is punishment. Although punishment in the form of penalties such as paying a fine or spending time in prison is sometimes viewed as a form of **retribution** (a morally justified consequence, as in an "eye for an eye"), from the perspective of criminal law, the main purpose of punishment is to deter people from committing crimes.

CRIMINAL DETERRENCE

Deterrence theory rests on the assumption that punishment can be used to prevent crime. Deterrence can operate on a specific and general level such that an offender is deterred from repeating the act in the future as a result of receiving the punishment (*specific deterrence*), whereas others in society also come to avoid the act by witnessing the consequences for the offender (*general deterrence*). Deterrence theory originated with the

Criminal justice system: The social institution responsible for the apprehension, prosecution, and punishment of criminal offenders.

Retribution: A morally justified consequence.

SOCIOLOGY ONLINE

CRIMINAL JUSTICE IN CANADA

A diagram outlining Canada's court system along with a description of how the various courts are organized can be found on Canada's Department of Justice website (http://www.justice.gc.ca). Other organizations associated with criminal justice in Canada include the following, among others:

- Correctional Service Canada, http://www.csc-scc.gc.ca
- Royal Canadian Mounted Police, http://www.rcmp-grc.gc.ca
- Parole Board of Canada, https://www.canada.ca/en/parole-board.html
- John Howard Society of Canada, http://johnhoward.ca

classical school of criminology, a perspective from the late 18th and early 19th centuries attributed to Jeremy Bentham (1748–1832) and Cesare Beccaria (1738–1794). This school of thought rests on the premise that people are rational and that crime, therefore, is the end result of a decision-making process wherein the individual decides that the benefits of committing the act outweigh the perceived costs. Social order can be achieved through deterrence if rules (laws) with appropriate punishments are put into writing and enforced by the state (Tierney, 2009). According to Beccaria (1764/1963), for punishment to be effective in preventing crime, it must be prompt, severe, and certain:

1. *Promptness*. The punishment should occur very close in time to when the actual event happened in order to establish an association between the act and its consequence.
2. *Severity*. The punishment must be severe enough to outweigh the benefits but not so severe that it constitutes torture.
3. *Certainty*. There must a high probability that an offender will be caught and that the punishment will be carried out.

One difficulty faced by the criminal justice system today is that punishment often does not meet the three criteria simultaneously and thus cannot effectively deter future crime. Also, critics of deterrence theory call into question the very notion of deterrence itself. They suggest that offenders' actions are often not the result of rational decision making and point out that countries with very harsh penalties, such as the death sentence, or high rates of incarceration have not managed to reduce crime rates.

PROTECTING SOCIETY AND REHABILITATING OFFENDERS

Besides deterrence, punishment that involves incarceration—especially a lengthy jail sentence—generally serves as a means for *protecting society* from an offender who might otherwise continue to do harm. Incarceration is also an opportunity for *rehabilitating an offender*, which involves helping the offender become law abiding, perhaps by providing resources to help him or her overcome addictions or develop anger management skills. According to the Corrections and Conditional Release Act (1992), the purpose of Correctional Service Canada is to contribute to the maintenance of a just, peaceful, and safe society by

> (a) carrying out sentences imposed by courts through the safe and humane custody and supervision of offenders; and
>
> (b) assisting in the rehabilitation of offenders and their reintegration into the community as law-abiding citizens through the provision of programs in penitentiaries and in the community. (p. 5)

TIME TO REVIEW

- Which social institutions comprise the criminal justice system?
- What is the main purpose behind the punishment of known offenders?
- What three components of punishment need to be present in order for it to be effective in deterring crime?

LO6 ALTERNATIVE MEASURES OF CRIMINAL CONTROL

Most societies, including Canada, have relied largely on punishment (or *retribution*) to deal with offenders and to protect society from further harm. Sociologists question whether the extensive use of punishment is effective for rehabilitating offenders or deterring future crime and whether it is the best overall use of societal

SOCIOLOGY ON SCREEN

PRISON AS DETERRENCE: INCARCERATING US

The United States has the largest prison population in the world, with more than 2 million people incarcerated. In *Incarcerating US* (2016), filmmaker Regan Hines argues that this state of affairs is the outcome of the decades-long "war on drugs"—an ineffectual campaign resulting in excessive punishments, racial discrimination, and innumerable costs to families, communities, and taxpayers. The film gives us important insight into the question, "What is the purpose of prison?" (https://incarceratingus.com)

resources (see *Sociology in Practice*). Some have even joined **abolitionism**, a movement calling for a complete overhaul or dismantling of the criminal justice system.

Tierney (2009, pp. 2–3) notes that abolitionists claim that imprisonment

- is a punitive response that deflects attention away from the social circumstances and experiences that lead to offending in the first place;
- is the culmination of social control and judicial processes that discriminate on the bases of class and "race." The criminal justice system concentrates on the crimes of the powerless rather than the crimes of the powerful;
- does not provide an appropriate setting for rehabilitation, or as abolitionists put it, dispute settlement and the integration of the offender into society. On the contrary, imprisonment exacerbates social exclusion and reduces the likelihood of successful reintegration into society. This is reflected in high rates of recidivism;
- may remove an individual from society and thus the opportunity to offend, but only in terms of the "outside world." A great deal of offending—for example, violence and illicit drug use—occurs in prisons;
- places the offender into a brutal and brutalizing enclosed society, one in which there are countless opportunities to learn new criminal skills and join new criminal networks; and
- increases, rather than reduces, feelings of anger, resentment, humiliation, frustration, and alienation.*

Recognizing the limitations of a criminal justice system focused mainly on retribution,

Abolitionism: A movement calling for the dismantling of the criminal justice system.

Ombudsperson: An independent body with authority to conduct thorough, impartial, independent investigations and to make recommendations to government organizations with respect to the problems of citizens.

*J. Tierney, *Key Perspectives in Criminology*, Berkshire, UK: Open University Press McGraw-Hill Education, Pg. 2–3, 2009. Reproduced with the kind permission of Open University Press. All rights reserved.

YOUR SOCIOLOGICAL TOOLKIT

SOCIOLOGY IN PRACTICE

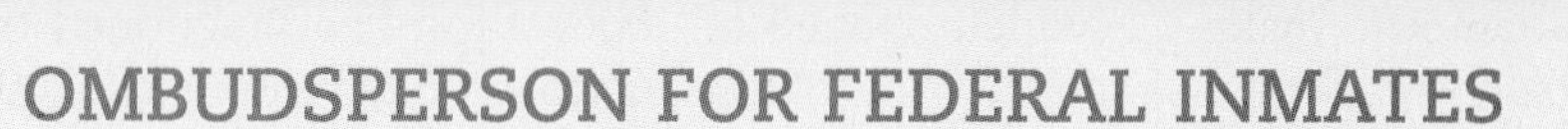

OMBUDSPERSON FOR FEDERAL INMATES

The Office of the Correctional Investigator (OCI), currently under the direction of Dr. Ivan Zinger, serves as an ombudsperson for federal inmates. An **ombudsperson** is an independent body with authority to conduct thorough, impartial, independent investigations and to make recommendations to government organizations with respect to the problems of citizens. The OCI provides oversight of Correctional Service Canada to ensure that federally sentenced offenders experience "safe, lawful and human corrections" by providing "accessible, impartial and timely investigation of individual and systemic concerns" (Office of the Correctional Investigator, 2017b). The OCI investigates complaints made by federal offenders (about issues involving themselves or made on behalf of other offenders) or complaints initiated by family members on behalf of inmates. The OCI also prioritizes a variety of issues, including access to physical and mental care, deaths in custody, conditions of confinement, Indigenous issues, safe and timely reintegration, and federally sentenced women (Office of the Correctional Investigator, 2017b). Finally, the OCI writes reports on its findings that include recommendations for acts that need to be taken to improve corrections in Canada.

A report sent to parliament on February 15, 2017, details the death of Matthew Ryan Hines, who, at age 33, died while in federal custody at New Brunswick's Dorchester Penitentiary following a series of incidents involving force (e.g., being taken to the ground and pepper sprayed). The report outlines various areas of non-compliance by Correctional Service Canada, including "inappropriate use of inflammatory spray" and "failure to provide emergency health care" (Office of the Correctional Investigator, 2017a). The OCI concludes that Matthew Hines's death was preventable and lists 10 major findings, such as "multiple uses of unnecessary and inappropriate force contributing to ensuing medical emergency and death" and "questions about quality, timeliness and adequacy of health care response" (Office of the Correctional Investigator, 2017a).

Think Outside the Box: Why is it important for an independent authority to provide oversight for Correctional Service Canada?

Source: Office of the Correctional Investigator (2013b). Annual report of the Office of the Correctional Investigator, 2011–2012, Pg. 30, 32. Ottawa, ON: Her Majesty the Queen in Right of Canada. Found at: http://www.oci-bec.gc.ca/cnt/rpt/annrpt/annrpt20112012-eng.aspx.

SOCIOLOGY ON SCREEN

RESTORATIVE JUSTICE: HOME FIRE

Home Fire (2014) is a candid documentary on family violence and restorative justice. Viewers learn about colonization, historical trauma, grassroots healing programs, and the benefits of involving community members in a process of justice from elders, community leaders, and individuals working in the criminal justice system (National Film Board of Canada, 2017). This film, by Greg Miller, is available from the National Film Board of Canada.

critical and feminist criminologists have developed alternative frameworks to the "war on crime." For example, *peacemaking criminology* is a non-violent movement and approach to crime that centres on transforming individuals and society in order to reduce the suffering and social injustices that result from structural inequalities based on class, race, and gender (Braswell, Fuller, & Lozoff, 2001; Pepinsky & Quinney, 2001).

In addition, many criminologists now support **restorative justice**, an approach based on informal processes that emphasize healing and the reparation of harm that offenders have caused victims and community members rather than focusing on punishing the offender (Elliot, 2011; Woolford, 2009). In this approach, the offender is required to assume responsibility for his or her actions and to attempt to make some kind of restitution to the victim (such as a formal apology). Restorative justice also emphasizes the need to involve all of the stakeholders in the process of justice (victims, offenders, and other members of the community). Finally, restorative justice rests on the premise of rebuilding relationships (Zehr, 2002). Restorative justice practices have taken a number of forms, including victim–offender reconciliation programs, victim–offender mediation, community justice circles, and reparative probation programs (Winterdyk, 2016). Prior to colonization, Indigenous peoples regularly practised restorative justice, and more recently, attempts have been made to reimplement restorative justice programs in various communities. For example, the Tsuu T'ina Peacemaker Court in Alberta (established in 2000), the Cree-speaking and Dene-speaking courts in Saskatchewan (introduced in 2001 and 2006 respectively), the Gladue Court in Ontario (which commenced in 2001 and was expanded to three courts in 2007), and the First Nations Court in British Columbia (which opened in 2006) all utilize sanctioned traditional forms of dispute resolution (Whonnock, 2008).

Restorative justice: An approach to justice emphasizing healing and reparation of harm.

Okimaw Ohci Healing Lodge, Maple Creek, Saskatchewan.

TIME TO REVIEW

- On what bases do abolitionists call for the overhauling of the criminal justice system?
- What is peacemaking criminology?
- What are the premises on which restorative justice rests?

YOUR SOCIOLOGICAL TOOLKIT
SOCIOLOGY IN THEORY

LO7 EXPLAINING DEVIANCE AND SOCIAL CONTROL

A variety of theories are used to analyze criminalized and non-criminalized forms of deviance. Like the study of families, wherein some theorizing is done from within the core theoretical perspectives in sociology (e.g., functionalist theories), but other theorizing arises from outside those boundaries (e.g., social exchange theories), the same is true for the study of deviance. Although functionalist, conflict, interactionist, feminist, and postmodern theories are applied, so are theories specific to the study of deviance (e.g., neutralization theory). Some theories focus on the causes of deviant behaviours; these theories are *positivist* (see Chapter 1). Other theories emphasize social construction—how we come to perceive behaviours or characteristics in a given way and then exert certain forms of social control over them. These are *interpretive* and *critical* theories (see Chapter 1).

EXPLAINING DEVIANCE

FUNCTIONALIST THEORIES OF DEVIANCE

Functionalist theories propose that the social structure causes deviance. Durkheim indicated that deviance emerges from *anomie* (see Chapter 1). When society changes too rapidly (such as during the process of industrialization or when a large-scale natural disaster occurs), people become unsure of precisely what is expected of them, and feelings of *normlessness* emerge. In a context of normlessness, people begin to engage in excessive levels of deviant behaviour, including the commission of crimes. But Durkheim suggested that only *excessive* levels of deviance are harmful to society, when they disrupt the smooth running of the social order. Less than excessive levels of deviance can actually *contribute* to the maintenance of the social order. For instance, seeing someone being punished for a transgression reminds us of the rules; this resembles the concept of general deterrence, discussed earlier in the chapter.

In another chapter, you learned about Robert Merton as the founder of the "sociology of science." But what Merton (1938, 1968) is best known for is his theory of deviance, known as *classic strain theory*. This theory dominated the study of deviance for several decades and is recognized by some as one of the most significant sociological theories of all time (Featherstone & Deflam, 2003).

Like Durkheim, Merton connected deviance to the social structure. He explained that an individual's location within the social structure—for example, in terms of socioeconomic status—contributes to deviance. People who occupy certain locations face more constraints than those located in other parts. These constraints, which can lead to deviance, arise from institutionalized goals and legitimate means. The **institutionalized goals** of society today include wealth, power, and prestige. From early childhood, we are socialized to aspire to earn a lot of money, be leaders rather than followers, and attain respect. We are taught that the **legitimate means** for attaining those goals include getting a good education, working hard, and investing money wisely. However, Merton pointed out that society is structured in a way that some people, such as children growing up in inner-city neighbourhoods, have less access to those legitimate means. Regardless of their lack of legitimate means, most people will still dream of achieving institutionalized goals; hence, a "gap" exists between the goals and the means for obtaining them, which creates a sense of "strain." People respond to this "gap" in different ways; that is, they engage in different *modes of adaptation*.

Most people continue to aspire to conventional goals and do their best to pursue the legitimate means of achieving them (e.g., getting a university degree). Merton labelled this mode of adaptation *conformity*, and the associated behaviour is considered acceptable.

Others respond to the gap by accepting the goals of wealth, power, and prestige but rejecting the legitimate means of obtaining them. Using *innovation*, they find alternative means—for instance, obtaining wealth through credit card fraud, becoming powerful through gang membership, or gaining prestige by using performance-enhancing drugs to become a star athlete. Some people engage in *ritualism*, giving up on the institutionalized goals but continuing to engage in the means, such as by reliably working at their low-paid jobs until retirement even though they will never earn enough money to obtain a mortgage for a home. Others may adapt to the discrepancy between means and goals by rejecting the institutionalized goals *and* the legitimate means, perhaps escaping into substance abuse or not even bothering to look for work anymore—a mode of adaptation called *retreatism*. Finally, some people engage in *rebellion*, rejecting the current goals and means but living according to an alternative set of goals and means. For instance, in the 1960s, some hippies created alternative lifestyles for themselves in communes, pursuing peace and love and sharing material goods. In the present day, extremist groups (such as the Aryan Nations and ISIL/ISIS) reflect rebellion in their use of violence to create a world that corresponds to their ideological visions.

For several decades, Merton's theory was primarily applied in explanations of criminal activity, such as property crimes, illegal drug use, white-collar crimes, and corporate crimes. Today, it is also applied to non-criminal behaviours, such as people's pursuit of fame and

Institutionalized goals: The goals that we are supposed to aspire to in contemporary society.

Legitimate means: The socially accepted ways of attaining wealth, power, and prestige.

An Vino/Shutterstock

During the countercultural era of the 1960s, peace, love, and music were at the core of the hippies' "rebellion."

celebrity, as well as anti-ethnic and anti-immigrant prejudice (Hövermann et al., 2015; Parnaby & Sacco, 2004).

In Merton's description of the structural constraints that lead some people into deviance and Durkheim's suggestion that excessive levels of deviance emerge in contexts of anomie, we see the foundational assumptions of functionalism at work. That is, something in the *social structure*, rather than in the individual, causes varied forms of deviance.

LEARNING THEORIES

Learning theories lie outside the four core theoretical perspectives in sociology but are important to the study of deviance. These theories propose that deviant behaviours emerge through processes of learning—that is, some people "learn" to act in deviant ways, whereas others do not (Bereska, 2018). Thus, *social learning theory* states that deviant behaviours occur when individuals are rewarded for those acts; are not punished for those acts; or, through imitation and modelling, see others being rewarded for similar acts. Social learning theory has been applied to behaviours ranging from criminal activity, to youth drug use, to cyberbullying (Li et al., 2016; Norman & Ford, 2015).

Techniques: The skills needed to engage in either deviant or conforming behaviour.

Motives: The reasons for engaging in either deviant or conforming behaviour.

Techniques of neutralization: Rationalizations that allow us to justify our behaviour to others and to ourselves.

Edwin Sutherland's (1947) *differential association theory*, one of the most influential theories in the study of deviance, posits that we learn deviant (and conforming) behaviour through interactions within small, intimate groups that are important to us (e.g., friends, family). Here we learn both **techniques** (skills) and **motives** (reasons) to engage in certain behaviours. If we learn more "deviant" techniques and motives (how to smoke, roll a joint, or hotwire a car and why we might enjoy smoking, doing drugs, or stealing a car) than "conforming" techniques and motives (how to do well in school and why it is important to do well in school), then we are more likely to engage in deviant behaviour. Today, the theory is applied to varied behaviours, including terrorism, youth drug use, online hate groups, and criminal activity (Armstrong & Matusitz, 2013; Gray et al., 2015; Hawdon, 2012; Janssen et al., 2016).

A learning theory of deviance that is especially popular today is Sykes and Matza's (1957) *neutralization theory*. This theory proposes that we learn **techniques of neutralization**—that is, rationalizations that allow us to justify our deviant acts to others and to ourselves. With the *denial of injury*, we can claim that we really aren't hurting anyone, as in the case of perpetrators of supposed "victimless crimes." *Denial of the victim* involves the claim that the person on the receiving end of our behaviour deserved what he or she got. For instance, someone who shoplifts may claim that stores jack up their prices anyway.

With *denial of responsibility*, the transgressor argues that he or she isn't *really* responsible for what happened. Instead, that person shifts the blame onto someone or something else, such as a parent (e.g., for being absent) or the community (e.g., for being "boring"). *Condemning the condemners* involves the transgressor arguing that the person or group that is condemning him or her is hypocritical and guilty of its own misdeeds. For example, cyclists who use performance-enhancing drugs claim that everyone uses substances to enhance performance, whether it is drinking a cup of coffee before an exam to increase alertness, taking aspirin to get rid of a headache at work, or having a beer to facilitate social interaction with new acquaintances (Sefina, 2012). Finally, in an *appeal to higher loyalties*, transgressors claim that they engaged in deviance for a good reason. For instance, environmental activists who are arrested for vandalizing company property in the oil sands may claim that their actions were necessary to draw attention to how oil companies are destroying the environment.

SOCIAL CONTROL THEORIES

Like learning theories, *social control theories* also fall outside the core theoretical perspectives in sociology but are central to studying deviance. It is important to note that social control *theories* are distinct from the *measures* of social control that are directed at unacceptable behaviours or characteristics. Social control theories draw attention to the factors that restrain most of us from unacceptable acts (Bereska, 2018). Hirschi's (1969) early social control theory rested on the premise that *social bonds* prevent most people from engaging in deviance. Social bonds are connections people have to conventional society. Emotional *attachment* to others (e.g., parents) holds us back from deviant behaviour. *Commitment* to the conventional world (e.g., a job, a scholarship, or home ownership) constitutes an "investment"—people simply have too much to lose by engaging in deviance. People who are high in *involvement* are so busy carrying out conventional activities (e.g., studying and working part time) that they don't have time to engage in deviance as well. Finally, *belief* in the norms and values of the conforming world (such as respect for the law) restrains people from deviance—put simply, they see behaving as the right thing to do. Several studies have found that people who have these social bonds are less likely to be criminally active or engage in other unacceptable acts and have better attitudes toward the police (Salvatore & Taniguchi, 2012; Wu, Yuning, & Cao, 2015).

Travis Hirschi is now also associated with a second theory—initially called the *general theory of crime* and now more commonly known as *self-control theory* (Gottfredson & Hirschi, 1990; Grasmick et al., 1993). Self-control theory rests on the assumption that self-control develops in early childhood (through socialization by parents) and restrains most of us from deviance. It follows that the failure to develop adequate self-control leads to deviance. Low levels of self-control are associated with a variety of risky behaviours, such as substance use and risky driving behaviours (such as texting while driving) (Koeppel et al., 2015; Quisenberry, 2015).

TIME TO REVIEW

- What are the basic assumptions of functionalist, learning, and social control theories of deviance?
- How is deviance explained by Durkheim and within classic strain theory?
- How is deviance explained by differential association theory and neutralization theory?
- How is deviance explained by social bonds theory and self-control theory?

EXPLAINING OUR PERCEPTIONS OF, AND REACTIONS TO, BEHAVIOURS AND CHARACTERISTICS

INTERPRETIVE THEORIES

Interpretive theories have a foundation in the interactionist perspective. From this perspective, through our interactions with *significant others* and the *generalized other*, as well as the influence of the *looking-glass self*, we develop understandings of what acts are acceptable or unacceptable; we also come to understand ourselves in this context and choose our actions on that basis. Although some of those understandings will be shared with other people, our interactions are not identical to anybody else's, and as such, different understandings may develop as well. Thus, you might understand facial piercing to be deviant, whereas someone else does not.

Edwin Lemert's (1951) *labelling theory* emerges from this interactionist foundation. Lemert states that we all engage in acts of **primary deviance**—minor acts that are done rarely or infrequently (e.g., drinking alcohol to excess). Because infrequent transgressions are likely to go undetected, people are able to maintain a non-deviant self-image. However, with more frequent acts of deviance, the chances of detection are greater. Lemert argues that getting *caught* at deviance is the impetus for a chain of events that change how people are treated and how they come to understand and identify themselves. For example, getting caught drinking alcohol at work may lead an employer to label an employee a "problem drinker" or "alcoholic." Because of that label, people start to treat that person differently; a person who is labelled a problem drinker at work may be reprimanded by the boss, avoided by co-workers, or required to seek treatment. Perceived as deviant, the legitimate world starts to reject him or her, and only similar others in the deviant world, such as one's fellow patrons of the familiar bar, continue to accept him or her. Also, the deviant comes to view himself or herself differently as a result of the label, increasingly accepts the label, and builds a lifestyle and an identity around it—this is known as **secondary deviance**. A person who has been labelled a "problem drinker" may drink even more to cope with deteriorating relationships at work and/or at home because he or she has internalized that label and is acting in accordance with its role.

Primary deviance: The little acts of deviance that many of us engage in occasionally.

Secondary deviance: Chronic deviance as a lifestyle.

YOUR SOCIOLOGICAL TOOLKIT

SOCIOLOGY IN MY COMMUNITY

YOUTH CONFRONTING THE STIGMA OF MENTAL ILLNESS

Mental illness (which is discussed in the chapter on health and illness) affects the majority of Canadians, either directly (through the experience of mental illness) or indirectly (through having a relationship with someone who has a mental illness). Nevertheless, mental illness continues to be stigmatized in society, characterized by damaging media portrayals and overwhelmingly negative public attitudes (Goodwin & Tajjudin, 2016; Mental Health Commission of Canada, 2016; Parrott & Parrott, 2015). The organization *Jack.org* (https://www.jack.org) is "the only national network of young leaders transforming the way we think about mental health." They use peer-to-peer engagement to provide information on mental illness, as well as its stigmatization. Resources are available to assist youth on high school and university campuses to set up their own Jack.org chapters; currently, there are more than 100 chapters across Canada. The organization makes available toolkits, TEDx talks, funding opportunities, and guest speakers for local chapters and holds an annual cycling event to raise funds (Jack Ride). As an organization "designed for young people by young people," its goal is to "end the stigma of mental illness in our generation."

Think Outside the Box: Does your campus have a Jack.org chapter? What other resources are available on your campus to resist the stigmatization of mental illness and facilitate positive mental health?

Goffman (1963) spoke of a similar process, whereby people who engage in certain acts or who have particular characteristics face **stigmatization** in society; that is, they become treated as "outsiders" once they are labelled as such. Those individuals may respond to stigmatization in a number of ways, ranging from trying to hide that stigmatized characteristic to developing a lifestyle around it and publicly embracing it. Thus, the person who often drinks to excess may try to prevent detection by using mouthwash or drinking vodka out of a water bottle, or alternatively may be known to friends as throwing the best parties because of a well-stocked bar.

The process described in labelling theory and Goffman's notion of stigmatization are similar in that they propose that once our deviance has been detected, people begin to treat us differently, with implications for how we feel about ourselves and the choices we make for future actions. Although this process was initially applied to studies of criminal activity, it is now used to understand diverse groups of people who are negatively labelled or stigmatized: ex-cons trying to enter the labour force; people with financial problems; mothers of school shooters; those involved in criminal activity; and members of certain religious groups (Halushka, 2015; Keene, Cowan, & Castro-Baker, 2015; Melendez, Lichenstein, & Dolliver., 2016; Moore, Stuewig, & Tangney, 2016; Sohrabi & Farquharson, 2016) (see *Sociology in My Community*).

Stigmatization: The process by which individuals are excluded because of particular behaviours/characteristics.

Interpretive theories involving processes such as labelling and stigmatization, then, explain how we come to understand certain behaviours, characteristics, and people (including ourselves) as deviant, as well as how we learn to respond accordingly. Critical theories explain why some people's understandings of deviance have more of an influence in society overall, are accepted by larger numbers of people, and end up reflected in society's institutions (e.g., the criminal justice system, the education system, the mass media) (Bereska, 2018) (see *Critical Thinking in Action*).

CRITICAL THEORIES

Conflict theories propose that structures of power determine which behaviours or characteristics are defined and treated as deviant. Although the various conflict theories describe that structure of power in distinct ways (see Chapter 1), they all agree that holding power enables groups to define their own behaviours as "normal" while defining the behaviours of others as

YOUR SOCIOLOGICAL TOOLKIT

CRITICAL THINKING IN ACTION

DEVIANCE AND SOCIAL CONTROL ON YOUR CAMPUS

DeiMosz/Shutterstock.com

As you have learned in this chapter, social control is not just directed at "some people"; it is directed at each one of us, for a variety of reasons. Simply by walking across your campus, you can see messages about the actions that are considered acceptable or unacceptable and forms of social control. As you walk across campus looking for "the strange in the familiar" (see Chapter 1), look closely at the following: the posters located on bulletin boards; the physical structure of campus buildings (e.g., the behaviours that are expected, condoned, frowned upon, or prohibited in particular locations); the university's policies and regulations; and the social interactions of people (e.g., in classrooms, hallways, library, cafeteria, fitness centre, pubs).

Think Outside the Box: What behaviours or characteristics are socially constructed as acceptable or unacceptable on your campus? What formal and informal measures of social control are directed at those deemed to be unacceptable? Are those behaviours rare? Do they cause harm? Do "most people" on campus disapprove of those actions? Do they violate norms (and if so, whose norms)? Who has the power to claim that those behaviours are unacceptable?

"deviant" and in need of social control. The powerful then also have the means to enforce those measures of social control, whether in creating criminal laws, legislating physical appearance (as with Bill 62 on the wearing of conspicuous religious attire, which you learned about in Chapter 3), police "carding" of black high school students in Toronto, or viewing members of racialized groups as "police property" (Hayle, Wortley, & Tanner, 2016; Reiner, 2013).

From a *postmodern perspective*, Foucault (1995) focused his attention, in part, on the internalization of social control. He focused on why we often don't have to be controlled by others but actually control our own behaviours through **self-surveillance**. We live in a society where we are constantly monitored, or at least feel that we are being monitored, through surveillance cameras, photo radar, bureaucratic mechanisms that influence everything from who is/is not allowed to drive to what class you must take as a prerequisite for another course, and strangers judging our physical appearance when we walk down the street. Because of this perception of ongoing monitoring, we eventually monitor our own behaviours—we weigh ourselves once a week or slow down when we see the speed limit sign on a given street. Self-surveillance has been studied with a wide range of topics, including distinguishing between responsible gambling and problem gambling in our lives or the caution that gender non-conforming individuals must use in choosing a public restroom (Bender-Baird, 2016; Miller et al., 2015).

Feminist theories draw attention to facets of deviance such as the differential standards that women and men face in determining what is considered deviant and the varying experiences they have of being socially typed as deviant and subjected to measures of social control. For instance, they point out that what are considered acceptable

Self-surveillance: Monitoring our own behaviours in order to prevent being considered deviant.

ArtOfPhotos/Shutterstock

Foucault proposes that we don't always need other people to monitor us for transgressions because we often monitor ourselves.

behaviours/characteristics in society are gendered. A male who wishes to be a daycare worker is more likely to be considered deviant than a woman with that same wish, whereas a woman who wants to work on an oil rig is more likely to be socially typed as deviant than a male in that position (Bereska, 2018). For example, some scholars have explored how societal views of prostitution emerge from larger discourses about women's sexuality, others draw attention to how the experiences of women who commit crimes are influenced by gender, and yet others have analyzed how norms governing motherhood are created, reinforced, and interpreted in specific situations (Clevenger, 2016; Shdaimah & Leon, 2016). As with other critical theories, feminist perspectives on deviance emphasize the broader social processes that result in certain perceptions of and reactions to deviance carrying more weight in society as a whole.

TIME TO REVIEW

- What is the role of interpretive and critical theories in those approaches to deviance that emphasize its socially constructed nature?
- What are the basic interactionist assumptions regarding deviance, and how are those reflected in Lemert's labelling theory and Goffman's notion of stigmatization?
- What aspects of deviance do conflict theories, Foucault's work, and feminist theories focus on?

CHAPTER SUMMARY

LO1 Define social control, identify its relationship to deviance, and differentiate among its varying types.

Social control refers to measures intended to prevent, punish, or cure unacceptable (i.e., deviant) behaviours and characteristics. Social control can stem from organizations (formally) or from the actions of individuals in everyday interactions (informally). Some measures are directed at deviance that has already occurred, whereas others prevent deviance from occurring in the first place. Some forms are directed at others, whereas other forms we direct at ourselves.

LO2 Compare the different criteria that are highlighted as the foundation for determining deviance and explain the view that deviance is socially constructed.

Some scholars highlight "objective" characteristics, such as rarity, harm, normative violation, or a negative reaction by "most people" in society. Others view deviance as socially constructed and intertwined with structures of power.

LO3 Explain the relationship between the concepts of deviance and crime.

Deviance is an umbrella term referring to behaviours or characteristics that are deemed unacceptable and in need of social control. Crime is one specific form—behaviours that are considered so unacceptable they are legislated against and subjected to control via the criminal justice system. Scholars who focus on criminalized behaviours are known as criminologists.

LO4 Outline the contrasting views of how laws are created, identify the legal meaning of a crime, and differentiate among crime classifications.

There are different views on the process of law creation: consensual, conflict, interactionist, and balanced. Crime refers to violations of criminal law, which is a form of public (rather than private) law. Crimes are categorized as summary versus indictable, victimless, white-collar, corporate, and cybercrime.

LO5 Describe the criminal justice system and the rationale for punishment as the primary means for controlling crime.

The criminal justice system consists of police, courts, and prisons, which control criminal behaviour through punishment that is designed to prevent (or deter) criminal activity, rehabilitate offenders, and protect society.

LO6 Discuss critiques of traditional forms of punishment and explain how restorative justice differs from retributive forms of punishment.

Abolitionists call for the overhaul of the criminal justice system, whereas others point to the covert and subtle racism that pervades it. Restorative justice seeks to heal and repair harm caused by an offender. This approach requires that an offender take responsibility for the resolution process, which includes relationships among victims, offenders, and the wider community.

LO7 Identify and describe the theories used to explain the causes of deviance and those that explain our perceptions of and reactions to particular behaviours and characteristics.

Positivist theories explain the causes of deviance: functionalist theories include Durkheim's theory of anomie and classical strain theory; learning theories include social learning theory, differential association theory, and neutralization theory; social control theories include social bond theory and self-control theory. Interpretive and critical theories explain how we come to perceive (and react to) behaviours in certain ways: interpretive theories include Lemert's labelling theory and Goffman's notion of stigmatization. Critical theories (including conflict, postmodern theories, and feminist theories) explain why some people's views influence society more than others.

RECOMMENDED RESOURCES

1. To gain a better understanding of the origins of the sociological study of deviance, we recommend a classic book by H. Becker (Ed.), *The Other Side: Perspectives on Deviance* (New York, NY: Free Press, 1964).
2. To view a short Statistics Canada (2016) video that explains the crime severity index, visit: *Measuring crime in Canada: A detailed look at the Crime Severity Index* at http://www.statcan.gc.ca.
3. The Centre for Justice and Reconciliation offers an online tutorial that teaches you about restorative justice (e.g., more on what it is; its values, programs, conceptual issues, implementation issues, and benefits); see http://restorativejustice.org.

FOR FURTHER REFLECTION

1. Why do media portrayals of crime contradict the actual patterns of crime, which show that crime is at its lowest point since 1972?
2. Considering what you have learned in the other chapters in this book thus far (e.g. media; sex, gender, and sexualities; race and ethnicity), where have you seen certain behaviours and characteristics identified as being deviant and then subjected to formal or informal measures of social control?

12 CHAPTER

Health and Illness: Is It "Lifestyle" or Something More?

Lyubov Kobyakova/Shutterstock

Every human being is the author of his [or her] own health or disease.

(Prince Gautama Siddharta, 563–483 BCE, founder of Buddhism)[1]

LEARNING OBJECTIVES & OUTCOMES

After completing this chapter, students should be able to do the following:

LO1 Outline the development of the sociology of health and illness and describe its focus.

LO2 Describe the four phases in the epidemiological transition.

LO3 Identify the top causes of death in Canada today and explain what the "actual" causes are.

LO4 Describe patterns of tobacco use, alcohol misuse, diet, and physical inactivity and describe their roles in morbidity and mortality.

LO5 Outline the "fundamental" causes of illness and describe how health and illness are affected by socioeconomic status and ethnicity.

LO6 Describe the evolution and objectives of the Canadian healthcare system and identify the challenges it faces in contemporary society.

LO7 Explore how functionalists, interactionists, conflict theorists, feminist theorists, and postmodernists address health and illness.

What is "health," and how do we attain it? Precisely what constitutes **health** can be a matter of discussion and debate, but many organizations define it as "a state of complete physical, mental and social well-being and not merely the absence of disease or infirmity" (World Health Organization, 1948, p. 100). The opening quotation suggests that health and illness are the result of individual choices made at the micro level. In this case, we might consider the extent to which an individual engages in health-promoting behaviours such as eating a nutritious diet and exercising or, conversely, engages in unhealthy lifestyle behaviours such as smoking, drinking to excess, and consuming a diet high in processed foods. Although these behaviours do play a role in health and illness, sociology also draws our attention to the macro level, the social context in which each "author" lives. Health and illness are about something *more* than just lifestyle; they emerge from broader sociocultural forces.

LO1 THE SOCIOLOGY OF HEALTH AND ILLNESS

Medical sociologists are one of the largest groups of sociologists in the world. They are found both within academia (e.g., sociology departments, medical schools, nursing schools, schools of public health) and outside academia in government agencies and research organizations. The sociology of health and illness emerged in the post–World War II, largely as an applied field advocating public health and formulating health policies (Cockerham, 2007). Weeks (2016) points to four important changes in medicine in the 1950s and 1960s that contributed to the rapid development of medical sociology. First, as degenerative diseases such as heart disease replaced infectious diseases as the primary causes of death, the role of social patterns and lifestyles became more obvious. Second, preventive medicine and public health efforts drew attention to significant factors such as poverty and malnutrition. Third, modern psychiatry emphasized the role of the social environment in psychological healing. Finally, medicine became more bureaucratic and administrative (in the regulation and delivery of medical care). Research funds were made widely available to study the "social causes and consequences of health and illness" (Cockerham, 2007, para. 1), and the sociology of health and illness developed rapidly.

Today, the sociology of health and illness focuses on a variety of specific topics, from the everyday experiences of

Health: A state of complete physical, mental, and social well-being and not merely the absence of disease or infirmity.

people with illnesses and healthcare providers to the healthcare system itself (Strohschein & Weitz, 2014). This chapter explores historical changes in patterns of health and illness; contemporary patterns of mortality and morbidity; the lifestyle factors that are the leading "actual" causes of illness and death; the sociocultural forces that are the "fundamental" causes of health and illness; Canada's healthcare system; and the forms of sociological theorizing that dominate this field of study.

PATTERNS OF HEALTH AND ILLNESS

Patterns of health and illness have changed considerably over time, along a specific trajectory labelled the **epidemiological transition** (Budrys, 2017; Strohschein & Weitz, 2014). Until very recently in human history, **morbidity** (the prevalence and patterns of disease in a population) and **mortality** (the incidence and patterns of death in a population) were concentrated in the young and were primarily the result of infectious and parasitic diseases. It was only in the latter half of the 20th century, in the developed world, that morbidity and mortality became concentrated in the older population, primarily due to degenerative diseases.

LO2 HISTORICAL PATTERNS

There have been four phases in the epidemiological transition (see *Figure 12.1*). The first was characterized by famine, as well as infectious and parasitic diseases (Budrys, 2017). For most of human history, life expectancy was between 20 and 30 years. In the premodern world, one-third of infants did not survive to their first birthday, half of all deaths occurred in children under 5, and less than half of people lived to 25 (Weeks, 2016). In the Middle Ages, infectious diseases were rampant, and a series of epidemics swept through Europe. For example, in just four years (1347–1351), as much as half of Europe's population (at least 25 million people) died of bubonic plague, transmitted by bacteria spread by fleas carried on rats. Several factors contributed to these epidemics (Strohschein & Weitz, 2014). In Europe's cities, the streets were a breeding ground for bacteria and parasites found in human waste, which people tossed from their windows to the gutters below. The crowded living conditions of the poor facilitated rapid transmission of infections. And growing trade relationships with the Middle East brought new diseases to Europe, for which Europeans had no preexisting immunity.

Epidemiological transition: Historical changes in patterns of morbidity and mortality, from a predominance of infectious and parasitic diseases to degenerative diseases.

Morbidity: The prevalence and patterns of disease in a population.

Mortality: The incidence and patterns of death in a population.

The second phase of the epidemiological transition featured a decline in epidemics (Budrys, 2017) owing to improvements in agriculture and nutrition (making people better able to resist disease), changes in warfare that moved battles (and related diseases) away from cities, and lower birth rates (improving women's health) (Strohschein & Weitz, 2014). By the early 1800s, life expectancy had increased to around 40 years. More than 25 percent of deaths were still in children under the age of 5, but two-thirds of people were then surviving to the age of 25 and 29 percent even to the age of 65 (Weeks, 2016). Although epidemics had declined, infectious diseases remained the primary cause of death, their transmission facilitated by industrialization and urbanization. Infectious disease remained the leading cause of death into the early 20th century. People died of smallpox, measles, mumps, whooping cough, and more—in 1918, an influenza pandemic killed between 30,000 and 50,000 people in Canada and between 20 million and 100 million people worldwide (Historica Canada, n.d.-b).

In the third phase of the epidemiological transition, infectious and parasitic diseases declined even further, and degenerative diseases (e.g., heart disease, diabetes) became the primary causes of morbidity and mortality (Budrys, 2017). Improvements in agriculture

FIGURE 12.1

The Epidemiological Transition

Famine, infectious and parasitic diseases → Epidemics of infectious and parasitic diseases → Decline in epidemics, increase in degenerative diseases → Degenerative diseases and *new* infectious diseases

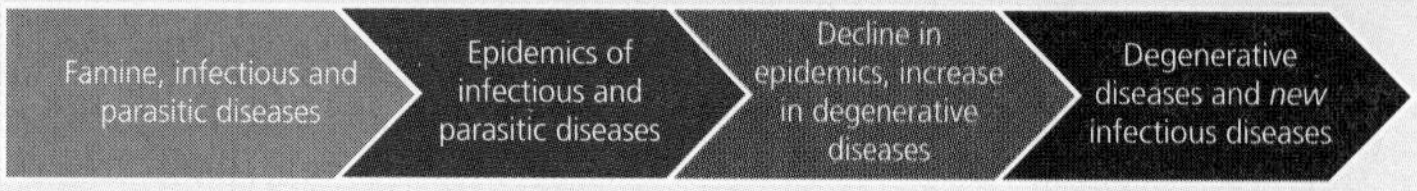

Source: Author drawn. Adapted (text only): G. Budrys, *Unequal health: How inequality contributes to health or illness*. New York: Rowman & Littlefield, 2017.

and nutrition, developments in public health, and medical interventions (in that order) were responsible for the decline in infectious and parasitic diseases (Decady, 2016; Markle & McCrea, 2008).

Subsequently, life expectancy increased rapidly. In the 21st century, 91 percent of Canadians live to 65, and 90 percent of deaths are in people over 65. Less than 1 percent of deaths are in children under 5, in part due to childhood vaccinations that reduce the prevalence of many childhood infectious diseases and virtually eliminate others.

However, in the 1990s, one scientist made a claim linking childhood vaccinations with autism. Although his research was subsequently found to be fraudulent, it received widespread media attention. The proportion of parents who were vaccinating their children declined (Picard, 2011), and, as a result, many infectious diseases are resurging. For instance, in 2010, California faced its worst outbreak of whooping cough in more than 60 years, with more than 9,000 cases and 10 deaths, leading the state to legislate mandatory whooping cough vaccinations for children (Johnson, 2011). In 2017, clusters of mumps plagued Alberta and Ontario, whereas measles were identified in several communities in Nova Scotia (Mehta, 2017). The resurgence of previously controlled infectious diseases not only characterizes Canada but the United States and many European countries as well (Chai, 2017).

In the late 20th and early 21st centuries, the fourth phase of the epidemiological transition has emerged, during which an increase in degenerative diseases has been accompanied by the emergence of *new* infectious diseases (Budrys, 2017), such as Ebola, HIV-AIDS, severe acute respiratory syndrome (SARS), the H1N1 variant of the swine flu, and Middle East respiratory syndrome (MERS). The new infectious diseases that are now appearing are, in large part, the result of a variety of social forces (Budrys, 2017; Strohschein & Weitz, 2014). The overuse of antibiotics in medicine and livestock production has created strains of drug-resistant bacteria that medical science is unable to treat. In many parts of the world, urban development has disturbed ecosystems, bringing unknown bacteria and viruses to the surface. Rapid population growth in many places in Africa, Asia, and Latin America has created crowded living conditions that facilitate the swift transmission of infections. The transmission of new infectious diseases is also facilitated by global travel (see *Sociology on Screen*).

LO3 CONTEMPORARY PATTERNS OF MORTALITY IN CANADA

Contemporary patterns of mortality in Canada reflect the epidemiological transition in that seven of the top 10 causes of death in 2013 were degenerative diseases (see *Figure 12.2*). The top three causes of death (cancer, heart disease, and stroke) account for more than half of all deaths, and the top 10 causes are responsible for 75 percent (Statistics Canada, 2017e). There are some variations in the leading causes of death based on sex and age (Statistics Canada, 2017f).

For both men and women, the two leading causes of death are cancer and heart disease. The third leading cause of death for women is stroke, but for men, it is accidents. Men are also three times as likely to die as a result of suicide and twice as likely due to liver disease (often caused by alcohol misuse).

Degenerative diseases are less common in younger age groups than in older ones. Accidents and suicide are two of the top three causes of death in those ages 1 to 44, accounting for more than half of all deaths in people ages 1 to 24 and more than one-third in

SOCIOLOGY ON SCREEN

PREVENTING NEW GLOBAL PANDEMICS

The PBS documentary *Spillover—Zika, Ebola, and Beyond* (2016) draws attention to the fourth stage of the epidemiological transition, when new infectious and parasitic diseases emerge. Zika in Brazil, Ebola in Africa, and MERS in the Middle East are only a few of the disease outbreaks the media has covered in recent years. All of these "new" diseases originated in other animals and have since been transmitted to humans. The film looks at the process of animal-to-human transmission, the social factors that underlie it, and what scientists and governments are doing to prevent a global pandemic. You can find out more about the film at http//www.pbs.org.

FIGURE 12.2

Top 10 Causes of Death, Canada (2013)

1. Malignant neoplasms (cancer)
2. Diseases of the heart (heart disease)
3. Cerebrovascular diseases (stroke)
4. Chronic lower respiratory diseases
5. Accidents (unintentional injuries)
6. Diabetes mellitus
7. Influenza, pneumonia
8. Alzheimer's diseases
9. Intentional self-harm (suicide)
10. Kidney disease

Source: Adapted from Statistics Canada. (2017e). *Leading causes of death, total population, by age group and sex, Canada, annual*. CANSIM Table 102-0561. Ottawa, ON: Statistics Canada.

those ages 25 to 44. These patterns shift in older age groups, with cancer and heart disease moving to the top in those 45 and older. When we look at some of the variations in the leading causes of death for people of different ages and for women and men, we begin to discern the social contexts of morbidity and mortality.

Two of the three leading causes of death among 1- to 44-year-olds—accidents and suicide—are, to a large extent, preventable. But so are the degenerative causes among those in older age groups. Leading causes of death are listed in official records using standardized terms from the World Health Organization's *International Classification of Diseases (ICD)*, such as "malignant neoplasms (cancer)" and "cerebrovascular diseases (stroke)" (Statistics Canada, 2017e). But what are the *actual* causes of death? What causes strokes, respiratory diseases, or heart disease? Research into this question has found that the top three *actual* causes of death are tobacco use, a poor diet combined with physical inactivity, and alcohol misuse (Lim et al., 2012; World Health Organization, 2017a, 2017f). In Canada, the regions that have the lowest life expectancies also have the highest rates

Jack Dagley Photography/Shutterstock.com

Accidents are the leading cause of death in Canadians ages 1 to 44.

of smoking, heavy drinking, and obesity (which is frequently associated with a poor diet or physical inactivity) (Greenberg & Normandin, 2011). Thus, it appears that Prince Gautama Siddharta, quoted at the beginning of this chapter, is partly correct—to some extent, we are the authors of our own health and disease. Still, a sociological perspective shows us that those behaviours that may initially appear to be a matter of individual choice actually arise from broader sociocultural forces.

TIME TO REVIEW

- What is the sociology of health and illness, and what are its origins?
- What are the four phases in the epidemiological transition, and what factors are responsible for it?
- What are the leading causes of death in Canada?
- What are the top three "actual" causes of death, and what does this tell us about the role of individual health behaviours?

LO4 THE "ACTUAL" CAUSES OF ILLNESS: THE ROLE OF LIFESTYLE

TOBACCO USE

Tobacco use is the leading cause of preventable death in the world, killing half of its users and resulting in more than 7 million deaths per year—one death every six seconds (World Health Organization, 2017a). Tobacco caused 100 million deaths in the 20th century, and if smoking trends continue, one billion people will die of tobacco-related illnesses before the end of the 21st century (World Health Organization, 2017e).

Worldwide, roughly 22 percent of people over the age of 15 years old smoke (World Health Organization, 2017e). Tobacco use is increasing globally, primarily due to smoking patterns in low- and middle-income countries, where the vast majority of the world's smokers live (World Health Organization, 2015). Tobacco use is declining in upper-middle- and high-income countries (such as Canada) due to education and changing governmental regulations and varies on the basis of gender and age (World Health Organization, 2017c). In Canada, among those over the age of 15, more males (16 percent) than females (10 percent) smoke; this is the lowest proportion of smokers ever recorded in Canada (Health Canada, 2017). Tobacco use is highest in people ages 20 to 24, but most people who smoke begin as teenagers; only a small proportion of people begin smoking after the age of 20. Thus, the best predictor of future smoking patterns in society is the current smoking patterns of youth. Among 18- and 19-year-olds, 18 percent of males and 11 percent of females smoke, and the numbers are even lower for younger teens (Health Canada, 2017). Should the trends among those currently under the age of 20 persist, tobacco use will continue its decline, and tobacco-related illnesses and death will decrease as well.

A number of macro-level factors contribute to youth smoking—cultural norms, the availability of tobacco products, tobacco control policies, and the promotion of cigarettes by tobacco companies. Advertising has been of special concern because it has its greatest impact on youth; around one-third of smoking initiation in youth is the result of advertising (World Health Organization, 2013). However, recent research suggests that images of smoking in movies have an even greater impact on youth. Research done in more than a dozen countries shows that tobacco images in movies are associated with attitudes toward smoking, intention to smoke, and smoking initiation in youth. In fact, youth who view the greatest number of tobacco images in movies are four times more likely to smoke than youth who view the fewest (Millett & Glantz, 2010). As restrictions on tobacco advertising have become more stringent in many countries, images of smoking have become more prevalent in films—especially those with youth ratings (G, PG, PG-13). In 2015, almost half of Hollywood films rated PG-13 included images of smoking, most often by the lead characters (Polansky et al., 2016). The World Health Organization, national governmental bodies, and local groups are pressuring movie studios to reduce tobacco images in movies and movie ratings boards to assign an "R" (restricted adult) rating to all movies that have images of tobacco use (see *Sociology in My Community*).

Our attention was first drawn to the social contexts of health and illness by the variations in the leading causes of mortality, based on gender and age. Now we have seen that gender and age are also important in patterns of tobacco use and that the movie industry is a powerful force in the initiation of youth smoking. The social contexts of "lifestyle" factors associated with health and illness are also important for understanding patterns of alcohol use and misuse.

YOUR SOCIOLOGICAL TOOLKIT

SOCIOLOGY IN MY COMMUNITY

THE THUMBS UP! THUMBS DOWN! PROJECT

Maksim Toome/Shutterstock

Smoking in youth-rated movies has a significant impact on youth attitudes toward smoking and smoking behaviours—especially when the lead characters are smoking.

Images of tobacco in Hollywood films impact youth in particular. Interestingly, youth are playing a central role in drawing attention to the issue, contributing to academic research, and mobilizing change. The *Thumbs Up! Thumbs Down! Project*, which is physically based in California, monitors tobacco images in films grossing at least $1 million each week, and youth volunteers (ages 14 to 22) are trained to gather the data. They record information on the number of tobacco images, the use of tobacco by lead actors, the contexts and implications of tobacco use, the messages conveyed by the tobacco images (e.g., sexy, rebellion, loser), and more. Since its inception, more than 1,000 youth volunteers have contributed to the project, gathering data on more than 2,000 films. The data are analyzed at the Center for Tobacco Control Research and Education at the University of California (San Francisco) (https://tobacco.ucsf.edu). The project's website (http://scenesmoking.org) contains a database of all of the movies ever reviewed and information on the previous week's top 10 movies (which are rated using a pink, light grey, dark grey, or black lung). In 2016, 18 youth-rated Hollywood movies were given a lung rating of dark grey or black (the worst ratings), including *X-Men: Apocalypse, Miss Peregrine's Home for Peculiar Children*, and *Fantastic Beasts and Where to Find Them*.

Think Outside the Box: Why do you think images of smoking have a greater impact than tobacco advertising on youth?

ALCOHOL USE AND MISUSE

Alcohol is directly related to more than 3.3 million deaths worldwide per year (World Health Organization, 2017a), but the harms caused by alcohol misuse vary across nations. The Global Information System on Alcohol and Health (GISAH) evaluates the drinking patterns in different countries on the basis of several factors, such as the proportion of the population that drinks daily, the number of drinks consumed per occasion, and the proportion of drinking occasions that involve drunkenness. Nations receive a score on a scale of 1 through 5, where 1 indicates the least risky and 5 the riskiest drinking patterns. Two countries—the Russian Federation and Ukraine—receive a score of 5. In contrast, Canada receives a score of 2 (World Health Organization, 2014). Countries with high levels of alcohol use, combined with poor public health resources, experience more morbidity and mortality.

Worldwide, 62 percent of adults have not consumed alcohol within the previous 12 months, mainly for religious and cultural reasons (World Health Organization, 2014). In Canada, the situation is very different. The *Canadian Tobacco, Alcohol and Drugs Survey* (CTADS) is a biennial survey of more than 15,000 Canadians over the age of 15. In 2015, the CTADS found that 91 percent have consumed alcohol at some point in their lives and 77 percent in the past year (Health Canada, 2017).

There are significant variations in alcohol use based on both gender and age. Men are more likely than women to drink, with 81 percent of men and 73 percent of women having consumed alcohol within the past year. Male and female drinking patterns vary as well. Men drink more frequently and are more likely to engage in high-risk drinking. Among those who have consumed alcohol within the past week, 40 percent of men and 30 percent of women exceeded low-risk drinking guidelines (Health Canada, 2017).

There are also age variations in alcohol use. People over 25 are more likely to have consumed alcohol in their lifetimes (93 percent) than either 20- to 24-year

FIGURE 12.3

Alcohol Use by Age (2015)

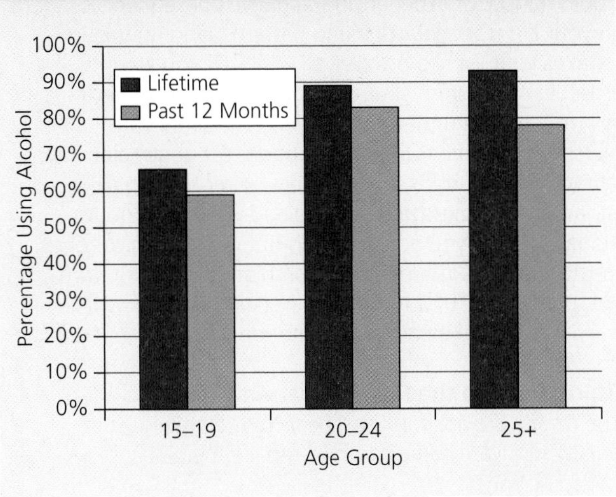

Source: Adapted from Health Canada. (2017). *Canadian Tobacco, Alcohol and Drugs Survey (CTADS)*. [Table 1]. Retrieved from http://www.canada.ca.

olds (89 percent) or 15- to 19-year-olds (66 percent) (see *Figure 12.3*) (Health Canada, 2017). Still, alcohol plays a prominent role in the lives of youth, wherein more than half of those in Grade 12 have used alcohol within the past month (Boak et al., 2015). Younger age groups tend to engage in higher-risk drinking patterns, with the highest rates among 20- to 24-year-olds, where more than half of those who have consumed alcohol within the past week exceeded low-risk drinking guidelines (see *Sociology in My Life*) (Health Canada, 2017).

Despite the role that alcohol misuse plays in morbidity and mortality on a global level, the World Health Organization (2010) finds that governments are less willing to develop reduction strategies for alcohol than for tobacco use. Governments derive economic benefits from tobacco and alcohol sales and production. Also, alcohol holds a central place in the economies of many nations and has for centuries. In the early 1800s in Canada, taxes on alcohol producers generated more than half of all government funds in some regions (Heron, 2003). The economic power of the alcohol industry has only increased since then. In the fiscal year ending March 2016, provincial and territorial governments generated more than $11.5 billion in alcohol-related revenues, including "sin taxes" on consumers and revenues from liquor licences and permits (Statistics Canada, 2017g). Alcohol's role as an economic powerhouse is also evident in sales by retail outlets and distributors. During that same year, retail sales of alcohol in Canada totalled more than $22 billion. The physical amount of alcohol sold, as measured in "litres of absolute alcohol," is staggering. "Litres of absolute alcohol" is a calculation that standardizes the amount of pure alcohol sold (accounting for differences in the alcohol content of beer, wine, and spirits); this enables one litre of any type of alcohol to be equated with one litre of any other type of alcohol. In that same fiscal year, more than 246 million litres of absolute alcohol were sold in Canada (Statistics Canada, 2017h)—equivalent to 8.2 litres per person (ages 15 and over). Governments, when they craft policies for alcohol, try to strike a balance between long-term health and shorter-term economic development.

YOUR SOCIOLOGICAL TOOLKIT

SOCIOLOGY IN MY LIFE

HOW DOES ALCOHOL AFFECT YOUR LIFE?

To many people, university life and alcohol-fuelled parties appear to go hand in hand, a perception reflected in the media. From the classic frat-party film *Animal House* (1978), to college party drinking games on Pinterest, to a list of "6 Frat Movies That Will Make You Drink! Freshman!" found on the movie review site screenjunkies.com, we are bombarded by messages suggesting that being a university student means consuming alcohol. And indeed, alcohol use is common on university campuses. Ever since research was first conducted on the issue in the early 1990s, a consistent 35 to 40 percent of students have engaged in binge drinking within the previous few weeks—a larger proportion than their same-age peers who are not in university (Byrd, 2016; Johnston et al., 2016). The harms that arise from the misuse of alcohol are greatest among youth. Almost 10 percent of all deaths in people ages 15 to 29 have alcohol-related causes, and in the

continued

United States alone, almost 2,000 youth ages 18 to 24 die in alcohol-related accidents each year, and more than 600,000 are assaulted by someone who has been consuming alcohol; this is on top of the 25 percent of university students who say they have experienced negative academic consequences arising from alcohol consumption (e.g., missing a class, doing poorly on an exam or assignment) (National Institute on Alcohol Abuse and Alcoholism, 2017; World Health Organization, 2015). Given these consequences, the role of alcohol in university culture is important to consider.

To what extent, and in what ways, is your life affected by alcohol consumption? The website for the Centre for Addiction and Mental Health's Alcohol Help Center (http://camh.alcoholhelpcenter.net) includes a Check Your Drinking (CYD) Survey. This survey asks questions about your frequency of drinking, amount of alcohol consumed, and consequences you may have experienced. Your results are placed in the context of your gender and age group as a whole and provide you with a wide range of information: how much money you have spent on alcohol in the past year; how many calories you are consuming from alcohol; your chances of experiencing negative consequences in your life from your drinking patterns; and how long it takes your liver to process one drink. If you are interested in monitoring your alcohol consumption, there is a free program that enables you to identify your personal triggers, track consumption, set goals, plan ahead for high-risk situations, receive motivational emails or text messages, and upload your own motivational video. If you personally do not consume alcohol, you may find it interesting to complete the survey from the perspective of a few "hypothetical" persons with varying levels of alcohol consumption.

Think Outside the Box: In what ways might the results provided in the Check Your Drinking survey motivate some youth to reduce their alcohol consumption?

Again, the patterns of alcohol consumption across age groups, in males compared to females, and within university culture indicate the importance of broader sociocultural forces. The same is true of diet and physical activity.

POOR DIET AND PHYSICAL INACTIVITY

Some people use tobacco or consume alcohol, whereas others do not. But everybody eats and engages in some level of physical activity. Precisely *what* you eat and *how much* physical activity you engage in have a significant impact on health and illness. Globally, low consumption of fruits and vegetables is associated with 1.7 million deaths per year, and physical inactivity accounts for another 1.6 million deaths (World Health Organization, 2017f). Although a poor diet and physical inactivity may be associated with being overweight for some people (which may also contribute to morbidity), they impact patterns of illness in people of all weights. When we narrow our focus to Canada, we see the magnitude of these problems.

EATING HABITS

The 2004 *Canadian Community Health Survey* was the first national survey of eating habits conducted since the 1970s. More than a decade later, it remains the most comprehensive survey of its kind to date (with more than 35,000 participants) (Garriguet, 2007). Half of adults were not eating enough fruits and vegetables, nor were 60 to 70 percent of children between 4 and 13. A significant proportion of Canadians were not consuming sufficient amounts of dairy, grains, or protein either. One food group that all Canadians were consuming more than enough of was the "other" category—soft drinks, salad dressings, sugars/syrups/preserves, beer, and fats (in that rank order). In fact, these "other" low-nutrient, high-calorie foods comprise approximately one-quarter of all calories consumed.

More recent data on fruit and vegetable consumption suggest that Canadians' eating patterns have not improved. In 2015, less than one-third of both adults (ages 18 and over) and adolescents (ages 12 to 17) ate the recommended five or more servings of fruits and vegetables per day (Statistics Canada, 2017d).

PHYSICAL INACTIVITY

If the eating habits of Canadians leave something to be desired, levels of physical activity are even worse. The World Health Organization (2017b) provides the following guidelines for physical activity: adults should engage in *at least* 150 minutes of moderate physical activity or 75 minutes of vigorous activity weekly and children *at least* 60 minutes daily. Strength training is an essential component of that weekly activity for both children and adults, and senior citizens should also integrate flexibility and balance training. Self-report data show that worldwide, 25 percent of adults and 80 percent of adolescents do not meet these minimum requirements, with inactivity being a greater problem in higher-income countries (such as Canada) than lower-income countries (World Health Organization, 2017b).

Although most research on physical activity is based on people's self-reports, some research today has people wear accelerometers, which measure exactly how much movement occurs. Perhaps not surprisingly, people aren't getting as much exercise as they report. Comparisons of self-report data with direct measurement reveal differences of up to 30 minutes per day (totalling more than three hours per week) (Garriguet, Tremblay, & Colley, 2015). Thus, although Canadian self-report data indicate that half of adults and two-thirds of adolescents meet the minimum requirements for physical activity (Statistics Canada, 2015), accelerometer data reveal that this is not the case. In fact, only 18 percent of adults engage in the recommended level of activity. The most active age group is 18- to 39-year-olds (21 percent of whom engage in the recommended level of activity) (Statistics Canada, 2017c).

An even smaller proportion of children meet the recommendations. Only 12 percent of children ages 5 to 11 engage in the recommended amount of physical activity, and that proportion declines to only 4 percent during adolescence; the least physically active age/sex group is adolescent girls (Statistics Canada, 2017c). Children's physical inactivity is of particular concern because of the short- and long-term health implications. One response has been the establishment of the Quality Daily Physical Education (QDPE) program—a set of guidelines for high-quality physical education in schools. Standards include a minimum of 30 minutes of varied physical activity daily, qualified teachers, and an emphasis on fun. Although the QDPE recommendations have been in place since 1988, few schools are complying with them (Physical and Health Education Canada, 2017). Given that children have become less physically active over time (even when their schools do have fitness programs), it is clear that once again sociocultural forces are playing a role in children's patterns of physical activity and inactivity, with negative health outcomes, such as weight problems.

YOUR SOCIOLOGICAL TOOLKIT

SOCIOLOGY IN PRACTICE

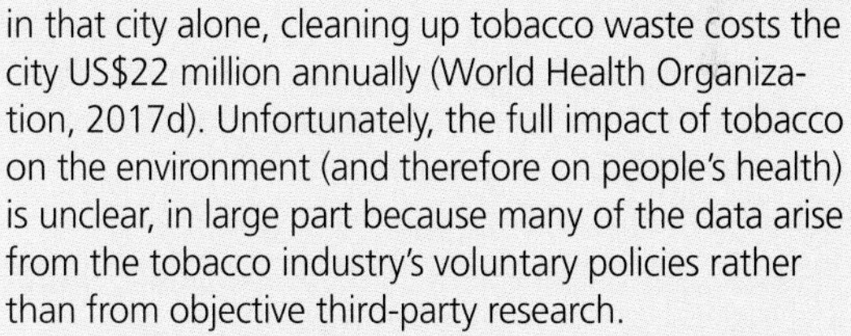

TOBACCO AND THE ENVIRONMENT

The health risks arising from tobacco are not limited to people's exposure to first- or second-hand smoke. Human health is affected by the full life cycle of tobacco products via their impact on the environment (see *Figure 12.4*). From the health problems experienced by tobacco farmers and their families (primarily in low-income countries), to pollution arising from the transportation and distribution of tobacco products, to the toxic chemicals released into the environment by the disposal of used cigarettes, human health and the environment as a whole suffer significant harms (World Health Organization, 2017d). Post-consumer tobacco litter is the largest component of litter globally, creating 340 to 680 million kilograms of waste annually and releasing more than 7,000 toxic chemicals into the air, ground, and water supply. One in three cigarettes is tossed directly into the environment (rather than into a garbage can), and cigarette butts or packaging constitute 30 to 40 percent of the waste collected during neighbourhood or coastal clean-up days (e.g., "Clean Up in the Park"). One study done in San Francisco estimates that in that city alone, cleaning up tobacco waste costs the city US$22 million annually (World Health Organization, 2017d). Unfortunately, the full impact of tobacco on the environment (and therefore on people's health) is unclear, in large part because many of the data arise from the tobacco industry's voluntary policies rather than from objective third-party research.

One of the strategies recommended by the World Health Organization to address tobacco's environmental impact is for nations to implement Extended Producer Responsibility (EPR) and Product Stewardship programs for tobacco companies. Under EPR programs, tobacco companies would be liable for verified environmental damage (e.g., deforestation); be responsible for economic expenses associated with recollection, recycling, or disposal of products; carry physical responsibility for the product's full life cycle; and be required to provide accurate data on the environmental risks associated with the product (World Health Organization, 2017d). Many countries have already implemented EPR programs for a variety of

continued

FIGURE 12.4

Life Cycle of Tobacco—from Cultivation to Consumer Waste

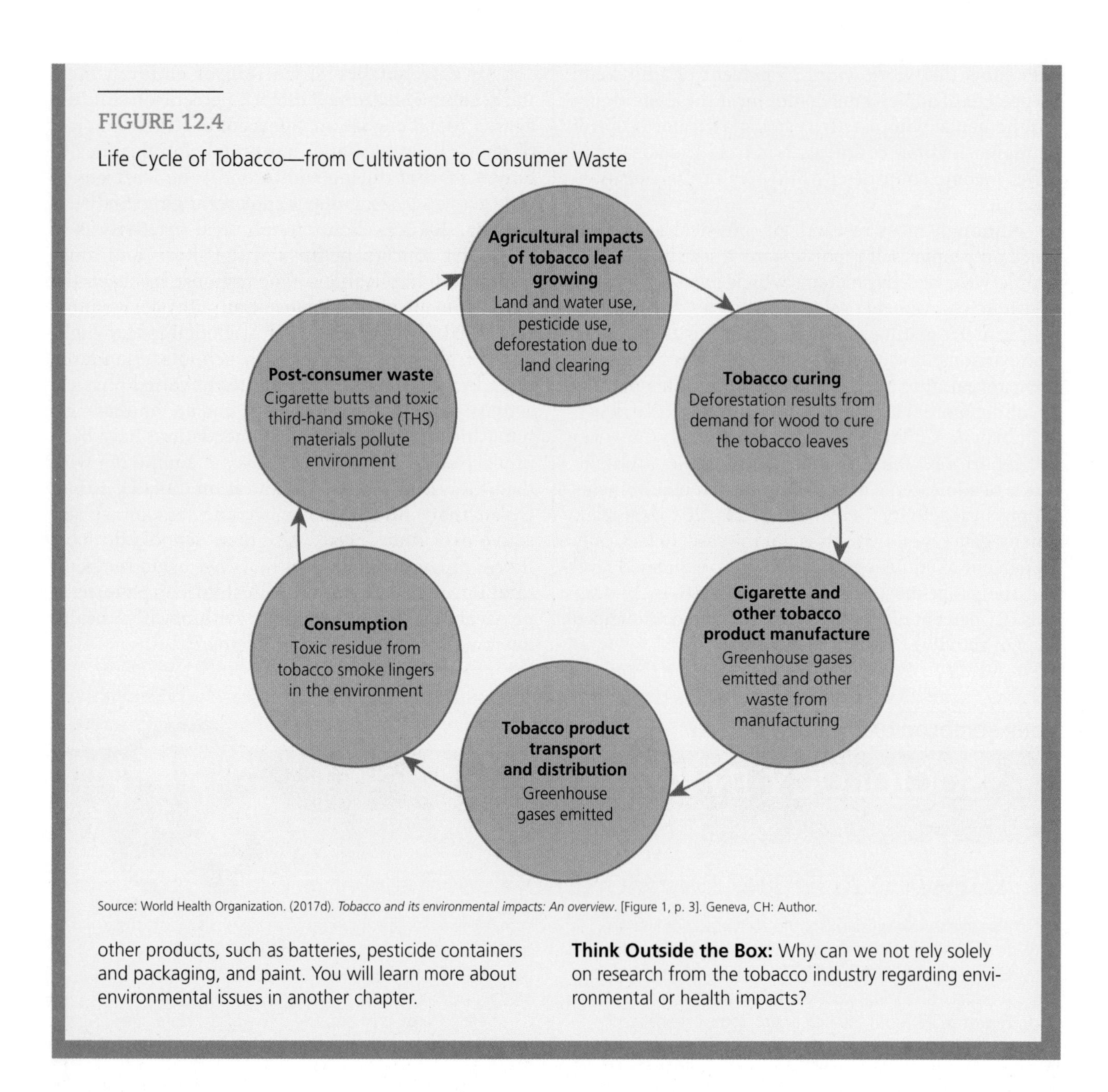

Source: World Health Organization. (2017d). *Tobacco and its environmental impacts: An overview*. [Figure 1, p. 3]. Geneva, CH: Author.

other products, such as batteries, pesticide containers and packaging, and paint. You will learn more about environmental issues in another chapter.

Think Outside the Box: Why can we not rely solely on research from the tobacco industry regarding environmental or health impacts?

SUMMARY

The top three "actual" causes of death are tobacco use, poor diet and inactivity, and alcohol use. Globally, these patterns of behaviour are having a growing impact on patterns of morbidity and mortality. Because of this, the World Health Organization and its member states have developed global strategies to reduce these behaviours and their impact (see *Sociology in Practice*).

Behaviours related to smoking, drinking, diet, and physical activity are significant for national and global patterns of morbidity and mortality. Initially, these choices appear as micro-level behaviours. However, if "lifestyles" were purely a matter of individual choice, then related behaviours would be randomly distributed across social groups and we would not see the gender and age patterns mentioned earlier (Strohschein & Weitz, 2014). These patterns tell us that something more than lifestyle is at play. When we shift our focus to an even more macro level, we find "fundamental" causes of health and illness—and we learn that their foundations are rooted in social inequality.

TIME TO REVIEW

- What are the patterns of tobacco use?
- Why do youth start smoking, and what role do the media play in smoking initiation?
- What are the patterns of alcohol use, and how prevalent are high-risk drinking patterns?
- Why may governments be reluctant to implement alcohol reduction strategies?
- To what extent do people eat well and engage in physical activity?

LO5 THE "FUNDAMENTAL" CAUSES OF HEALTH AND ILLNESS: SOCIAL INEQUALITY

We have already demonstrated that sociocultural forces impact our experiences of health and illness by influencing lifestyle behaviours. Sociocultural forces are intertwined with stratification in society, and in this regard, two of the most significant "fundamental" causes of health and illness are socioeconomic status and ethnicity (Raphael, 2016).

SOCIOECONOMIC STATUS

The single most important determinant of health globally is socioeconomic status: a higher position in the social structure is associated with better health (Beckfield, Olafsdottir, & Bakhtiari, 2013; Strohschein & Weitz, 2014). Canadians with lower incomes have shorter life expectancies and poorer health overall (Auger & Alix, 2016; Canadian Institute for Health Information [CIHI], 2016a). Furthermore, health inequalities based on socioeconomic status have not improved over the past decade. In fact, health inequalities have increased for some indicators (e.g., self-rated mental health, hospitalization for chronic obstructive pulmonary disease) (CIHI, 2016a). One Norwegian study found that a lower socioeconomic status has a cumulative negative effect on health over the lifespan and may carry its greatest effects when poverty is experienced during childhood (Claussen, Davey Smith, & Thelle, 2003).

Socioeconomic status is associated with access to material resources, such as adequate housing, safe neighbourhoods, healthy food, clean water, clean air, educational opportunities, and control over one's work. A lack of some material resources (e.g., clean water and healthy food) can have a direct impact on health and illness. A lack of material resources can also indirectly affect health and illness through other factors, such as chronic stress. Stress causes physiological changes in the body, such as an increase in heart rate and blood pressure and the release of the hormone cortisol. These physiological changes can be functional when we are facing an immediate threat (e.g., being chased by a bear) or a short-term stressor (e.g., having to stay awake to complete a term paper). When stress is long term, such as ongoing job insecurity, these physiological changes are dysfunctional and contribute to high blood pressure, heart disease, and digestive diseases (Strohschein & Weitz, 2014).

Beyond stress and job insecurity, *control of destiny* (having control over one's life) is an important contributor to health and illness (Marmot, 2005). People of lower socioeconomic status have a feeling of less control over their lives, and this may reduce the impetus to engage in healthier behaviours (Bolaria & Bolaria, 2009). Furthermore, smoking can give the false impression of easing stress, and the effects of alcohol can provide a temporary escape. Even physical activity can be a challenge (World Health Organization, 2017b). Low socioeconomic status means that people probably cannot afford gym memberships. That leaves the option of exercising at home. However, going for a 30-minute walk around the neighbourhood may not be possible if that neighbourhood is unsafe due to crime rates or environmental conditions (e.g., pollution), and even working out inside one's home may be difficult if one lives in overcrowded conditions. Low socioeconomic status may also mean working at more than one job, leaving little leisure time for physical activity.

Eating an adequately nutritious diet is also more challenging for low-income individuals (Statistics Canada, 2017d). Processed, high-calorie, low-nutrient foods are often much cheaper than healthy fare. An analysis of food costs in 10 high-income countries (including Canada) found that a nutritious diet costs approximately $550 more per person in one year, or $1.50 more per meal; for a family of four, this would total $2,000 per year (Rao et al., 2013).

Also, people may have limited access to healthy foods. Large supermarkets provide a wider range of nutritious foods, and at lower prices, than do convenience stores; having access to supermarkets is associated with better eating habits. People living in lower-income neighbourhoods are less likely to have a supermarket within a reasonable distance for walking or easy public transit (Hilmers, Hilmers, & Dave, 2012; Ni Mhurchu et al., 2013), and low-income individuals are less likely to own vehicles (Ghirardelli, Quinn, & Foerster, 2010). This trend has grown in recent years as supermarket ownership has become more concentrated. Five supermarket chains control 70 percent of the Canadian market (Sturgeon, 2014). Over time, these chains have closed many of their smaller urban locations in favour of larger superstores in suburban areas, where large parcels of open land are available.

Because of the higher costs of a healthy diet and the difficulty some social groups have accessing healthy foods, *food insecurity* is an issue for many Canadians and has significant health implications (McIntyre & Anderson, 2016; Tarasuk, 2016). According to Statistics Canada (2015), more than 1 million households experience food insecurity. Lone-parent households are especially at risk, wherein 23 percent are food insecure (compared to 8 percent in Canada overall).

Food insecurity varies across Canada, with the highest levels in the three territories: Nunavut, Northwest Territories, and Yukon (Statistics Canada, 2015). The situation is the worst in Nunavut, where 37 percent of households experience moderate to severe food insecurity and two-thirds of children under the age of 18 live in food-insecure households (Le Vallée et al., 2017). There, the lack of highways and railways means that consumer goods must be flown in. Electricity costs are higher for refrigeration. A monopoly by a single food supplier means a lack of competition in the marketplace. All of this has resulted in astronomical food prices. After a scathing report by the United Nations, in 2011, the federal government implemented the Nutrition North Canada (NNC) program, which gives subsidies to Northern retailers so that food prices can be controlled. As a result of this program, prices on "eligible" foods have been reduced by an average of 15 percent. However, in a territory where the minimum wage is only $13 per hour and the unemployment rate is more than 15 percent, grocery shopping continues to be a challenge: 1.36 litres of apple juice (with an average price of $2.21 in the rest of Canada) costs $8.95; 1 kg of celery is $12.44 (compared to $3.38); and 1 kg of carrots is $6.90 (versus $2.25) (Nunavut Bureau of Statistics, 2016).

Social selection hypothesis: The suggestion that people with mental disorders may drift into lower levels of socioeconomic status or be prevented from rising out of lower levels of status.

Social causation hypothesis: The suggestion that the stresses associated with having a lower socioeconomic status contribute to the development of mental disorders.

In addition to all of this, socioeconomic status has an impact on the extent to which people engage in lifestyle behaviours related to tobacco, alcohol, physical activity, and diet. Importantly, even when lifestyle factors are controlled for, socioeconomic status continues to have an effect on morbidity and mortality. Not only is physical health influenced by socioeconomic status, but so is mental health.

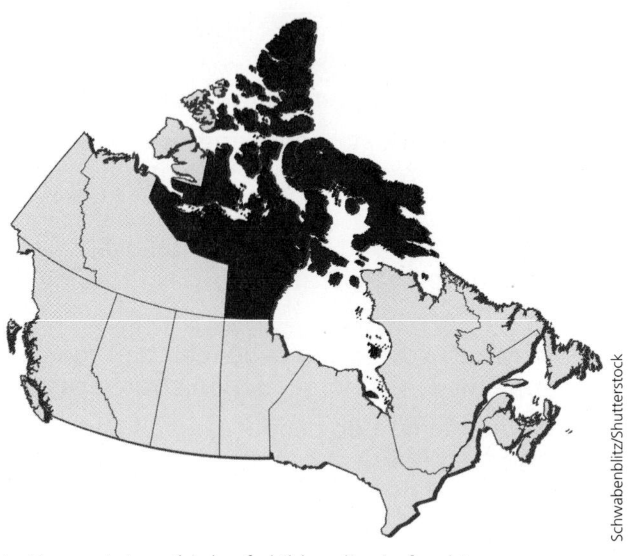
Schwabenblitz/Shutterstock

In Nunavut, two-thirds of children live in food-insecure households.

SOCIOECONOMIC STATUS AND MENTAL HEALTH

Most Canadians are affected by mental illness. One-fifth of the population will experience a mental disorder, and 80 percent personally know someone who has a mental disorder. Depression is projected to be the second leading disease burden by 2020 (behind heart disease) (World Health Organization, 2016).

Mental illness is both a contributor to and an outcome of lower socioeconomic status (World Health Organization, 2016). The **social selection hypothesis** proposes that if people's mental disorders are not effectively treated, they may experience functional difficulties in school or work that cause them to "drift" into a lower socioeconomic status or prevent them from rising into a higher status position. The **social causation hypothesis** posits that a lack of material resources creates stress, which contributes to the development of mental disorders. Research lends greater support to the social causation hypothesis, especially for depression and anxiety (Eaton, 2001; World Health Organization, 2016).

Besides socioeconomic status, several other social factors are associated with poor mental health. These include rapid social change, low levels of education, stressful work conditions, gender discrimination, and human rights violations (World Health Organization, 2016).

ETHNIC INEQUALITY AND HEALTH

Socioeconomic status is one of the two primary *fundamental* causes of health and illness. Ethnicity is the other. The relationship between ethnic inequality and health is especially evident in health patterns for Indigenous populations and for recent immigrants to Canada.

INDIGENOUS HEALTH: THE LEGACY OF COLONIZATION

On average, Indigenous populations face higher morbidity and mortality than non-Indigenous populations; this is the case not only for Indigenous populations in Canada but also in the United States, Australia, and New Zealand (Reading & Halseth, 2013). In Canada, Indigenous populations are more likely to experience degenerative diseases such as diabetes, heart problems, cancer, and emphysema (Gionet & Roshanafshar, 2013). They are also more likely to die from accidents, and their life expectancies are an average of five years less for men and seven years less for women. There are variations in morbidity and mortality among Indigenous groups (First Nations, Inuit, or Métis), on- or off-reserve, and rural/remote versus more urban place of residence (Reading & Halseth, 2013).

Some of the factors affecting Indigenous health are related to socioeconomic status—income inequality, low-quality employment, and lower levels of education (Reading & Halseth, 2013). But colonization has had an impact on the health of Indigenous people that goes well beyond socioeconomic status to deeper issues arising from colonization, coercive cultural change, and altered relationships with the land (Chandler & Dunlop, 2015; Reading, 2015). In Indigenous populations, *control of destiny* is affected not only by lower levels of socioeconomic status but also by a long history of laws and federal policies that have imposed control over treaty status, marriage and divorce, education, place of residence, medical treatment, housing, and more (see *Sociology in the News*).

Inadequate housing on many reserves and in some rural/remote areas (where almost half of the Indigenous population lives) creates health hazards

SOCIOLOGY IN THE NEWS

FROM THE DAVIS INLET TO NATUASHISH

Until 1967, the Innu in Labrador lived nomadic lives. In 1967, the federal government relocated them to a permanent settlement in order to better provide services for them. Told that they would be given comfortable homes and schools and access to healthcare, they were relocated to a distant island off the coast, where their way of life completely changed.

The government did not keep its promises. Instead, the Innu were left to endure overcrowded living spaces that lacked running water, reliable heating, and flushable toilets (White, 2017). Substance use was rampant, family violence increased, and the suicide rate was the highest in the world. The situation came to a head in 1993, when a videotape surfaced of three teenagers sniffing gasoline and screaming to a tribal police officer that they wanted to die. Subsequently, the federal government agreed to relocate the Innu back onto the mainland. This finally occurred in 2002, when the community of Natuashish was formed. The Labrador Innu Healing Strategy was also formed to help resolve the community's social problems.

However, critics point out that to this day, many social problems persist. Within just a period of a few months in 2017, two youth committed suicide (in a population of only 936 people). Although the community voted to ban alcohol back in 2008, recently RCMP officers reduced the frequency of baggage checks with people coming into the community (via ferry in the summer and by air in the winter). As a result, bootleggers are bringing alcohol into the community (charging $300 for a single bottle), and alcohol abuse is increasing (White, 2017). One community leader says that bootleggers and drug dealers are "... killing our youth and killing our culture and killing everything we hold precious." Community leaders say that a combination of factors are necessary for healing, including cooperation from law enforcement in preventing bootlegging, more resources to treat addiction and give young people hope, reduced isolation, and cultural reclamation.

related to water quality, indoor pollution from wood- and coal-burning stoves, toxins from lead paint and mould, and overcrowding. Many of these regions are also sites for resource extraction and hydroelectric development. One result has been the destruction of the land surrounding some Indigenous communities, which limits traditional diets and raises concerns about environmental toxins. The transition from traditional diets has had a significant impact on health, especially in terms of heart disease and diabetes. In part, this reflects the trend toward packaged and processed foods across the developed world. In addition, as a result of resource extraction and hydroelectric development, environmental toxins have made their way into the fatty tissues of fish and game, making them unsafe for consumption. As a result, some communities have had to abandon their traditional hunting and fishing activities (Reading & Halseth, 2013; Teegee, 2015).

Many Indigenous communities also face greater food insecurity because of lower socioeconomic status and/or remote locations. Food insecurity affects 8 percent of Canadian households overall (Statistics Canada, 2015) but is more pervasive among Indigenous populations (18 percent). In Nunavut, twice as many Inuit as non-Inuit live in food-insecure households (Le Vallée et al., 2017).

IMMIGRATION AND HEALTH

Socioeconomic status alone does not explain patterns of morbidity and mortality by ethnicity. Recent immigrants are actually *healthier* than people who are Canadian-born; this is known as the **healthy immigrant effect** (Vang et al., 2015). Immigration policy prioritizes those who have higher levels of occupational skills and education, which means that immigrants tend to be located at higher levels of the social structure in their countries of origin and therefore experience the health benefits of those social positions.

However, the healthy immigrant effect quickly dissipates, especially for women and racialized groups. Within four years, their health patterns become similar to those who are Canadian-born. Despite the higher statuses they may have occupied in their countries of origin, as well as their higher levels of education, people who are foreign-born have lower occupational statuses and lower incomes than people who are Canadian-born. Even when controlling for socioeconomic status, declines in health status persist. Difficulties with English- or French-language proficiency, higher levels of discrimination, social isolation, and higher levels of stress are associated with poorer health (Vang et al., 2015).

Healthy immigrant effect: Recent immigrants tend to have better health than people who are Canadian-born.

SUMMARY

Across social groups, socioeconomic status is the primary *fundamental* cause of health and illness because it affects access to material resources such as adequate housing, safe neighbourhoods, healthy food, clean water, clean air, educational opportunities, and control over one's work. Socioeconomic status also has an impact on lifestyle behaviours and control of destiny. Thus, people of lower socioeconomic status are of poorer health, have higher mortality rates, and have lower life expectancies than people of higher socioeconomic status. Ethnic inequality is another important fundamental cause of health and illness. Although it interacts with socioeconomic inequality, there are dimensions of ethnic inequality that go beyond socioeconomic status; we see this especially clearly when looking at the health of Indigenous populations in Canada, as well as recent immigrants to Canada.

TIME TO REVIEW

- What are the sociocultural forces that influence health and illness, and what are two of the "fundamental" causes of health and illness?
- In what ways does socioeconomic status influence health and illness?
- How does socioeconomic status affect lifestyle behaviours?
- How does the health of Indigenous and the health of non-Indigenous populations in Canada compare, and why do these disparities exist?
- How do patterns of health and illness for recent immigrants compare to the Canadian-born, and how do patterns for immigrants to Canada change over time?

LO6 HEALTHCARE

The prevention and treatment of illness and injury exist in the broader context of healthcare *systems*. In Canada, the first systems of medicine were those of Indigenous cultures, each of which had its own

Granger Historical Picture Archive/Alamy

In New France, some medical care was provided by barbers, who were also trained as surgeons.

definition of what constituted health and illness, as well as its own medical treatments. Depending on the specific culture, medical care was provided by shamans, medicine men, or other members of the community, such as the *Midewiwin* of the Ojibway. Many of the plants that were used to treat illness have since been found, by modern science, to have treatment properties. For instance, the Iroquois introduced early European explorers to the bark of the white cedar (now known to be high in vitamin C) to prevent scurvy, which was one of the greatest health dangers explorers faced during long periods at sea (Historica Canada, n.d.-a).

Early settlers in New France received medical treatment at the hands of apothecaries, who acted as general practitioners, and barber-surgeons—barbers who were also trained in some forms of surgery, most commonly the amputation of limbs. By the early 19th century, Euro-Canadians were receiving treatment from a wide variety of practitioners—lay healers who had no formalized training, homeopaths, midwives, and, for the wealthy, physicians trained in the United States or Great Britain—as well as through products sold by travelling salespeople (Clarke, 2016).

Canada's first medical school was established in 1832, and after the implementation of the Ontario Medical Act (1869), a number of privately owned medical schools opened that would later become affiliated with various universities. Although medical schools flourished in the late 19th century, it wasn't until 1912 (with the Canada Medical Act) that licensing procedures and criteria were standardized in Canada.

Until the 1950s, Canadians had to pay for medical services. Demands for universal medical insurance were made as early as 1919, by William Lyon Mackenzie King and various organized labour groups. However, the first publicly funded medical insurance did not come until 1957, with the Hospital Insurance and Diagnostic Services Act. This act provided for medically necessary care and services in hospital settings; half of the funding for this came from the federal government and half from the provincial governments. In 1961, the Royal Commission on Health Services was formed. This led to the Medical Care Act (1966), which created Canada's system of universal medical insurance, more commonly known as "medicare." It had four objectives: (a) *universality*, that is, equal access to medical care for all residents of Canada regardless of income, age, social group, or previous health conditions; (b) *portability* across provinces; (c) *comprehensive coverage* of all necessary medical services; and (d) *administration* that would be nonprofit. In 1984, a fifth objective was added, that of *accessibility*—medicare would involve the redistribution of income from richer to poorer provinces.

THE HEALTHCARE SYSTEM TODAY

Because of medicare, Canadians have more access to medical services than in the past. Still, there are questions about the extent to which the objectives of medicare have been achieved. Canada has lower physician-to-population ratios than most other member countries of the Organisation for Economic Co-operation and Development (OECD). In 2015, we had 2.5 physicians per 1,000 population; only three member countries had lower physician-to-population ratios (Korea, Poland, and Mexico) (OECD, 2017). The shortage of family and general practitioners in particular has resulted in widespread concern over the "doctor shortage"; more and more Canadians have to use walk-in medical clinics, where wait times are long and staff turnover is high. Besides problems of access, some medical services require out-of-pocket expenditures (e.g., dental care, prescription medications), which not all Canadians can afford.

The healthcare system today is in a state of transition. At a time when concerns are growing about out-of-pocket medical expenditures, a shortage of physicians, and long wait times in the nation's emergency rooms, governments are expressing concerns about the rapidly rising costs of healthcare. In attempts to control costs and improve healthcare delivery, alternative models are being explored, including changes in federal contributions to healthcare and the possibility of a parallel private (patient-funded) healthcare system.

THE RISING COSTS OF HEALTHCARE

In 2016, the OECD nation that spent the most per person on healthcare was the United States, at US$8,985. Canada was in the top 20 percent of nations in per capita healthcare spending (US$4,378), in the same bracket as other nations with publicly funded healthcare systems (OECD, 2017).

Total healthcare expenditures in Canada in 2016 were $228 billion, or 11 percent of GDP. Since 2010, healthcare spending has not kept pace with inflation, and with population growth, per capita spending has actually declined by about 0.1 percent annually. The largest component of health-care spending is hospitals, which account for almost 30 percent of total healthcare expenditures. This is followed by drugs (16 percent of spending) and physicians' services (15 percent of spending) (CIHI, 2016b).

Population pyramid: A horizontal bar chart that shows how many people are in the various age groups, divided by sex.

THE AGING POPULATION

One explanation offered for the rising costs of health-care is the aging of the population. As more people in a population come from older age groups, healthcare utilization increases. In 1966, people over 65 were less than 8 percent of the population; because of the aging of the *baby boom* cohort (see the chapter on families), by 2016, they were more than 16 percent of the population. The average age in 1956 was 29.8 years; by 2016, it was 41.0 years (Statistics Canada, 2017b). You can see the age-by-sex structure of the population by looking at a **population pyramid**, a horizontal bar chart that shows how many people in a population are members of particular age groups (see *Figure 12.5*). Comparing population pyramids in 1871 (indicated by the red outline) and 2016, you can see

FIGURE 12.5

Age Pyramid of Canada in 1871 and 2016: 150 Years of Demographic History

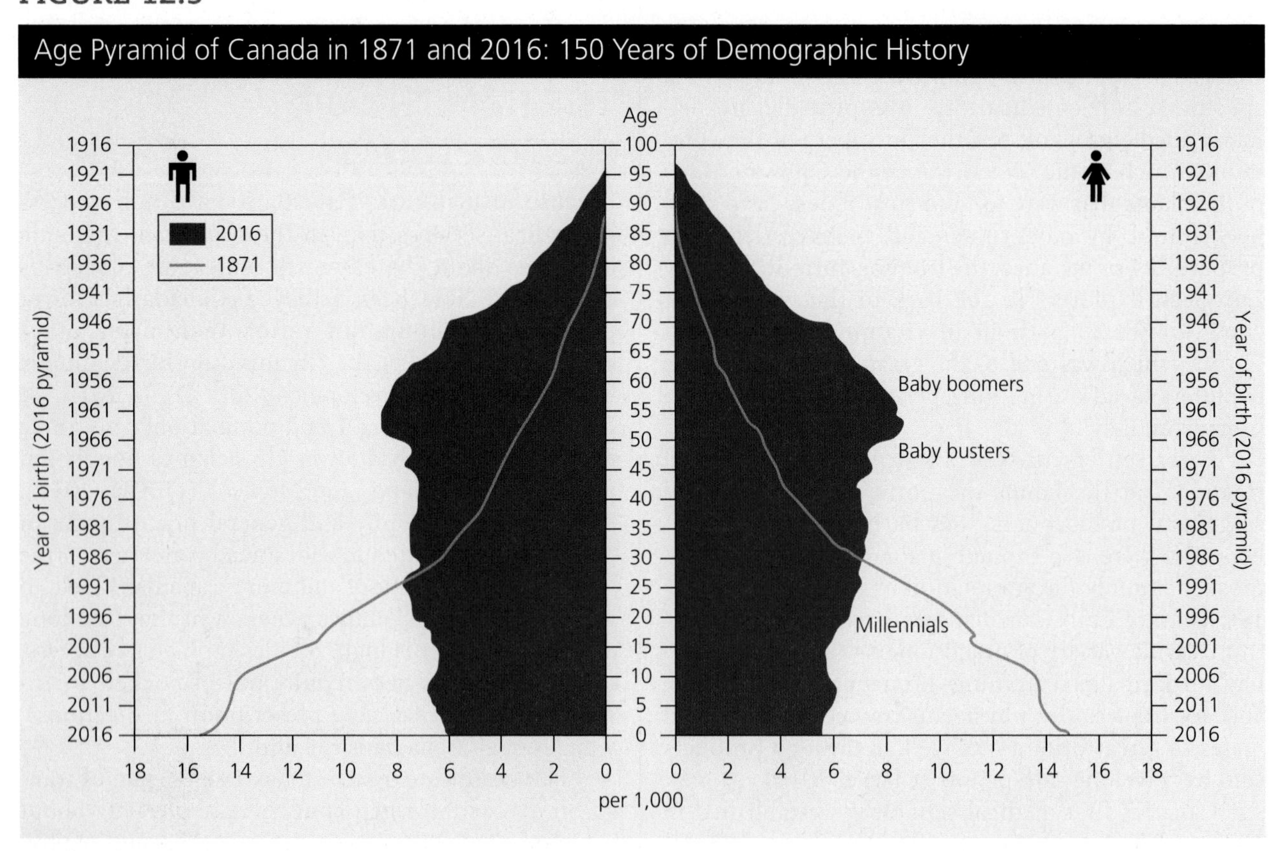

Source: Statistics Canada. (2017a). Age and sex, and type of dwelling data: Key results from the 2016 Census. *The Daily*. [Infographic 1: Age pyramid of Canada in 1871 and 2016: 150 years of demographic history.] Catalogue No. 11-001-X. Ottawa, ON: Statistics Canada. http://www.statcan.gc.ca/daily-quotidien/170503/g-a001-eng.htm

FIGURE 12.6

Annual per Capita Healthcare Spending for Seniors

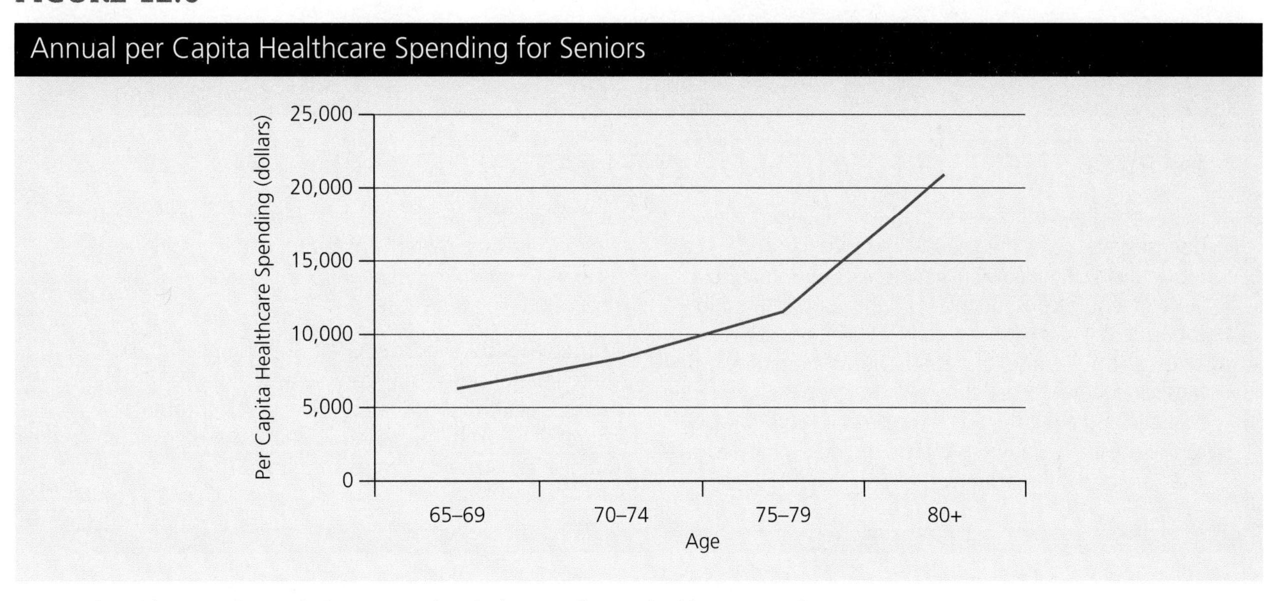

Source: Adapted from Canadian Medical Association. (2016). The state of seniors' healthcare in Canada. Ottawa, ON: CMA.

how significantly the population has changed. In 1871, there was a large proportion of the very young and smaller proportions of older age groups. In 2016, the structure of the Canadian population is quite different. The bulge in the pyramid indicates baby boomers, who were between 51 and 70 years old in 2016 (Statistics Canada, 2017a).

IMPLICATIONS OF THE AGING POPULATION

As people age, they are more likely to develop chronic health conditions; between 75 and 80 percent of seniors have at least one chronic health condition (Canadian Medical Association, 2016). Thus, as people age, healthcare costs tend to increase (see *Figure 12.6*). The annual per capita healthcare spending associated with those ages 65 to 69 is approximately $6,000, and it rises to more than $20,000 for seniors over the age of 80 (Canadian Medical Association, 2016). But it is not age itself that determines healthcare utilization; rather, it is the presence of multiple chronic conditions. The CIHI (2011) has found that, controlling for chronic health conditions, older seniors (those ages 85 and over) do *not* use more healthcare services than younger seniors (those ages 65 to 84). Seniors with three or more chronic health conditions made three times more visits to health professionals than those with only one or two conditions. People with multiple health conditions make up only 24 percent of the seniors population but account for 40 percent of healthcare use in that age group.

Chronic health conditions are not an inevitable part of aging; they are closely linked to lifestyle behaviours (which are intertwined with social factors, such as socioeconomic status) (see *Critical Thinking in Action*). Ramage-Morin and Shields (2010) analyzed eight different lifestyle behaviours among people ages 45 to 64 and 65 and over: smoking, weight, physical activity, diet, sleep, oral health, stress, and social participation. Each behaviour was individually associated with health; the greater the number of positive behaviours, the better the resulting health. Although advancing age is associated with poorer health overall, seniors who reported five or more positive behaviours were actually in better health than 45- to 64-years-olds who reported two or fewer positive behaviours.

TIME TO REVIEW

- How has the healthcare system changed in Canadian history?
- What are the five objectives of medicare?
- What challenges are being faced within the healthcare system today?
- In what ways does Canada's aging population affect larger patterns of health and illness and patterns of healthcare utilization?

YOUR SOCIOLOGICAL TOOLKIT

CRITICAL THINKING IN ACTION

IMPROVING THE HEALTH OF THE NATION

In this chapter, you have learned that degenerative diseases are the leading causes of morbidity and mortality in Canada. Many of these diseases are, to a large extent, a consequence of behaviours related to tobacco use, alcohol consumption, diet, and physical activity. Furthermore, those behaviours are influenced by sociocultural forces; they vary on the basis of gender and age and are affected by the broader cultural environment (such as advertising and images in movies). They are also influenced by the "fundamental" causes of health and illness—socioeconomic status and ethnic inequality. Thus, patterns of health and illness reflect a complex interplay between multiple factors at the micro and macro levels.

Think Outside the Box: Given the complexity of these relationships, how can we best improve the nation's health? What factors are most important to address? What solutions would make the biggest difference for the widest range of people?

YOUR SOCIOLOGICAL TOOLKIT
SOCIOLOGY IN THEORY

LO7 SOCIOLOGY IN THEORY

The sociology of health and illness began primarily as an applied, non-theoretical field of study, exploring patterns of morbidity and mortality, personal and social determinants of health, and the structure and functioning of the healthcare system. However, sociological theorizing about health and illness has expanded since the mid-20th century. As the functionalist perspective dominated the discipline of sociology in the mid-20th century, the first theorizing about health and illness was also functionalist.

FUNCTIONALIST PERSPECTIVES: THE SICK ROLE

Talcott Parsons was one of the preeminent sociologists of the mid-20th century. When he theorized about the *sick role*, he added legitimacy to the new field of medical sociology (Parsons, 1951). Parsons described sickness as dysfunctional for society. When people are sick, they are unable to fulfill their roles as students, employees, or parents. Instead, they adopt the sick role, a temporary role associated with certain rights and responsibilities. There are four components of the sick role. First, the sick person is granted a temporary exemption from his or her normal social duties. It is acceptable to miss an exam or a day of work, although some official documentation may be required to legitimize the absence. Second, the sick person is not considered to be responsible for his or her condition but rather is given sympathy. Third, it is the sick person's responsibility to try to get well; failure to do so results in the sick role no longer being considered legitimate. Finally, it is the sick person's responsibility to seek competent technical help and cooperate with the physician's directions.

Subsequent research has found that the components of the sick role do not always apply. For instance, the extent to which someone is exempted from normal social roles varies with the nature and severity of the illness (De Maio, 2010; Perry, 2011). In your workplace, a cold may not be considered a legitimate excuse for missing a day of work, whereas a chronic health problem (e.g., diabetes) may result in an ongoing level of exemption. Sometimes individuals *are* blamed for their illnesses. For example, Perry (2011) found that people who are diagnosed with more severe mental disorders have larger, more functional support networks than those diagnosed with milder mental disorders. Because the symptoms of the latter are less overt, other people may wonder why the individual cannot simply "snap out of it"; he or she is assigned responsibility for the lack of well-being. Finally, even when able to legitimately occupy a sick role, some individuals face constraints. Those of lower socioeconomic status may not be able to afford to lose the wages associated with missing one or more days of work. Lone parents bear the full brunt of child care, and if they do not have other resources to draw upon (e.g., family or friends), they must continue with the daily responsibilities of parenting, regardless of illness.

Beginning in the 1960s, functionalist perspectives began to lose their dominance as the interactionist, conflict, feminist, and postmodern perspectives took their place.

INTERACTIONIST PERSPECTIVES: THE CULTURAL MEANINGS OF HEALTH AND ILLNESS

Whereas demographers analyze *patterns* of health and illness, sociologists who apply interactionist theories focus on the *experience and meanings* of health or illness. In a classic study, Schneider and Conrad (1983) distinguished between *sickness* and *illness*. Sickness is a pathology of the body, whereas illness is the meaning attached to that physical experience. Schneider and Conrad interviewed people who had been diagnosed with epilepsy, which is a "sickness" of particular etiology. They found that something as seemingly straightforward as following physicians' instructions is actually embedded in a complex system of meaning and understanding; this is the individual's experience of "illness." Using medication is not simply a matter of following physicians' instructions; it emerges from the interaction between physicians' instructions and one's own relationships, beliefs, and experiences. Thus, the manner in which people with epilepsy use their medication is based on factors such as the meaning that seizures have for the individual, perceptions of the side effects of the medication, the desire to prevent others from becoming aware of the epilepsy, and the need to prevent seizures in some social situations more than others.

Sense of self lies at the core of people's experiences with illness. People with the same illness may adopt very different identities. Ethnographies of children with leukemia reveal that some adopt a resistant identity, seeing themselves as they have always been (e.g., an athletic teen) and talking about cancer as a "fight" that they will win (Rindstedt, 2016, p. 281). Others adopt a distinctive patient identity, following the instructions of medical staff to the letter but immersed in sadness about being separated from friends and their previous lives (Rindstedt, 2016). An individual's illness identity can have implications for recovery. For example, among young people with eating disorders, those who adopt a positively valued illness identity resist treatment, whereas those who develop a recovery identity—especially a socially based recovery identity with others who have the same disorder—are more likely to comply with treatment (MacNamara & Parsons, 2016).

CONFLICT PERSPECTIVES: THE CONSEQUENCES OF POWER AND INEQUALITY

The interactionist perspective emphasizes the subjective meanings of health and illness at the micro level; conflict theories focus on the macro level. They analyze topics such as the role of inequality in patterns of health and illness and problems with the healthcare system. Because of social inequality and relations of power, different groups have varying levels of access to both health-promoting resources and sickness-causing factors. We saw this earlier in the chapter in the context of patterns of morbidity and mortality among people of low versus high socioeconomic status, Indigenous people, and recent and longer-term immigrants.

Engels (1845/1985) was the first conflict theorist to address sociocultural influences on health and illness. He argued that with capitalism, large numbers of people left rural agricultural life for wage labour in urban areas. But the bourgeois owners of the means of production were guided by their own profit motives. To make the largest profits possible, they underpaid their workers, who had no choice but to live and work in unhealthy conditions. This set the stage for the emergence and transmission of infectious diseases.

Navarro (1976) indicates that there is an inherent contradiction between the profit motive of capitalism and the health needs of people. The corporate need for profit that results in people having to live or work in unhealthy conditions has continued beyond Engels's time into the 21st century, during which multinational corporations are moving their production facilities to low-income countries that often have lower occupational health and safety standards.

Besides analyzing the social determinants of health and illness, conflict theorists critique the healthcare system itself, such as the state's power to legitimize some forms of healthcare (e.g., a visit to a physician) over others (e.g., a visit to a holistic health practitioner) and the power of the corporate elite in the healthcare system. In a capitalist system, health becomes a commodity, and the pursuit of health occurs via gym memberships, athletic shoes, vitamins and supplements, meditation classes, and audio recordings to help you quit smoking. Health is about convincing people to engage in health-promoting behaviours (using the right products) rather than about changing the structural conditions that contribute to health and illness in the first place. The capitalist motive is even evident in fundraising efforts, in what is called "cause marketing" or "social marketing" (Firestone et al., 2017). When

AFP/Getty Images

A lack of occupational safety standards led to the collapse of Rana Plaza (in Bangladesh), which housed garment factories that supply several multinational corporations, including Joe Fresh and Walmart; more than 1,000 people were killed.

one purchases a particular product within a certain period of time—a shade of lipstick, a specially marked case of beer, a cup of Tim Hortons coffee, a McDonald's Big Mac, or even a certain model of car—*a portion* of the proceeds will go to support a particular cause, such as breast cancer or autism.

FEMINIST PERSPECTIVES: WOMEN'S HEALTH AND ILLNESS

Feminist analyses of health and illness are diverse and address topics ranging from the micro level to the macro level. For example, at the micro level, feminist scholars analyze the "moral boundary work" (Pryma, 2017, p. 66) that women with chronic pain engage in when trying to manage their interactions in the healthcare system (Kempner, 2014). Historically, women's physical symptoms were often dismissed as the result of stress or anxiety rather than physical illness. Scholars point out that this tendency continues to this day. Women face "barriers to credibility as their symptoms are read through gendered and moral discourses that cast women as hypochondriacs, and weaker, less rational, more emotional, and more likely to complain than men" (Pryma, 2017, p. 66). Women with chronic pain must use various techniques in order to be perceived as credible by not only medical professionals but also friends and family members. For instance, they try to strike a careful balance in the way they style their hair and makeup prior to a visit to a physician. If they looked too put together, doctors would assume that their physical health was fine (Kempner, 2014; Pryma, 2017).

At a more macro level, some feminist analyses of health and illness have focused attention on the processes by which certain characteristics and conditions come to be perceived as indicative of health or illness in the first place. In this regard, they have analyzed the medicalization of women's lives. Medicalization refers to the ways that certain characteristics or conditions are "defined in medical language, understood through the adoption of a medical framework, or 'treated' with medical intervention" (Conrad, 2007, p. 5). Beginning during the second wave of the women's movement in the 1960s, feminist researchers and activists pointed to the ways that women's lives were increasingly being medicalized. For most of human history, issues related to pregnancy and childbirth were handled by other women, such as midwives. But in the more medicalized environment of the 20th century, both became conditions that required a physician's care. Even the normal functioning of the female body (e.g., PMS, menopause) became a condition to be monitored and treated by medical professionals (McHugh & Chrisler, 2015).

POSTMODERN PERSPECTIVES: KNOWLEDGE, POWER, AND DISCOURSE

Postmodern approaches also address the medicalization of society, in terms of the relationship between knowledge and power (Foucault, 1965, 1966). Those claims to truth that emerge from institutionalized positions of power become legitimized and accepted as "truth." As medical science became increasingly intertwined with rational-bureaucratic healthcare systems in the 20th century, physicians' claims about health and illness gained supremacy over those of other types of health practitioners, such as midwives (Frailing & Harper, 2010). Once medical discourses become increasingly legitimized, more aspects of people's lives are subjected to the medical gaze and monitored by the medical profession—and its closely affiliated partner, the pharmaceutical industry (McHugh & Chrisler, 2015). And because medical discourses are elite discourses, we perceive them as the only possible means of understanding the world.

In a classic study, Fox (1993) applied Foucauldian assumptions to an analysis of communications between physicians and patients during post-surgical ward rounds. Fox notes that the way surgeons structure postoperative communications ensures that medical discourses remain privileged. Physicians begin these communications while patients are still recovering from sedation or are under the influence of high doses of pain medication, which immediately limits the extent to which patients can participate in the communication. The structure of post-surgical discourses involves a transition from communicating about the patient's physiology, to the conditions of the wound (where healing of the wound is presented as a sign of "successful" surgery), to aspects of recovery/discharge. When patients try to disrupt this linear transition (e.g., they ask about being discharged while the physician is still addressing the condition of the wound), physicians quickly use medical discourses to bring the communication back on track.

Medical discourses are also privileged via communications among medical staff located in different positions within the healthcare hierarchy. Interviews with healthcare assistants (HCAs) working with dementia patients reveal the way that "biomedical discourses … position them as less knowledgeable or expert relative to nurses and other health-care professionals" (Scales et al., 2017, p. 233). Despite being the ones who spend the most time in direct contact with patients, nurses and physicians disparage them, dismiss their opinions, and exclude them from providing input into patient care plans. One HCA talks about being explicitly told, "'… you're just a shit shoveller'" (p. 232). Thus, the nature of communication between doctors and patients, or between doctors/nurses and HCAs, at the micro level helps reinforce the power of medical discourses in society at the macro level.

TIME TO REVIEW

- In what way did Talcott Parsons first theorize health and illness?
- What are some of the ways that interactionists have explored the experience of health and illness?
- What aspects of health and illness are emphasized by conflict theorists, and what are some examples?
- What are some of the ways that feminist perspectives inform research about health and illness?
- What do postmodern analyses of medical communications tell us?

CHAPTER SUMMARY

LO1 Outline the development of the sociology of health and illness and describe its focus.

The sociology of health and illness emerged in the post–World War II. This field of study, found both inside and outside academia, analyzes the social causes and consequences of health and illness.

LO2 Describe the four phases in the epidemiological transition.

The epidemiological transition refers to changes in morbidity and mortality, from a predominance of infectious diseases to a predominance of degenerative diseases. The first phase is characterized by famine as well as epidemics of infectious and parasitic diseases. The second phase features a decline in these epidemics due to changing social conditions. In the third phase, infectious and parasitic diseases decline even further, and degenerative diseases predominate. In the late 20th and early 21st centuries, the fourth phase of the epidemiological transition has emerged, where an increase in degenerative diseases is accompanied by the emergence of *new* infectious diseases.

LO3 Identify the top causes of death in Canada today and explain what the "actual" causes of death are.

The top three causes of death are cancer, heart disease, and stroke. The top causes of death vary for women and men and for people of different ages. The *actual* causes of death are tobacco use, poor diet combined with physical inactivity, and alcohol misuse.

LO4 Describe the patterns of tobacco use, alcohol misuse, diet, and physical inactivity and describe their roles in morbidity and mortality.

Although only a minority of Canadians smoke, most consume alcohol. Patterns of both vary on the basis of sex and age. Many Canadians do not consume enough of any food group except for "other" (soft drinks, sugars, fats). Few adults and even fewer children engage in the minimum amount of recommended physical activity. Tobacco use killed more than 100 million people in the 20th century and now causes approximately 7 million deaths per year globally. Alcohol misuse contributes to 3.3 million deaths per year. Improving diet through greater consumption of fruits and vegetables and increasing physical activity could also save millions of lives each year.

LO5 Outline the "fundamental" causes of illness and describe how health and illness are affected by socioeconomic status and ethnicity.

The "fundamental" causes of health and illness lie in structures of social inequality. The two most significant fundamental causes are socioeconomic status and ethnic inequality. Morbidity and mortality are higher in groups of lower socioeconomic status. Socioeconomic status also explains some of the variations in patterns of health and illness in Indigenous populations and in recent immigrants; however, other dimensions of ethnic inequality play important roles as well. The legacy of colonization has affected the health of Indigenous populations in numerous ways. New immigrants are healthier than the Canadian-born, but within a few years, this changes; discrimination and stress play significant roles.

LO6 Describe the evolution and objectives of the Canadian healthcare system and identify the challenges it faces in contemporary society.

Healthcare systems have changed over time, from the systems of healthcare that existed in Indigenous cultures to the rational-bureaucratic system of today. Medicare was implemented in 1972 and has five objectives: universality, portability, not-for-profit administration, comprehensive coverage, and accessibility. Governments face the challenge of controlling the rapidly rising costs of healthcare (due, in part, to an aging population) while maintaining a high quality of care.

LO7 Explore how functionalists, interactionists, conflict theorists, feminist theorists, and postmodernists address health and illness.

Parsons was the first to theorize about health and illness, in terms of the sick role. Interactionist perspectives emphasize not the patterns of health and illness but rather the experiences of health and illness, such as changing conceptions of self. Conflict theorists devote much of their attention to the inequalities that underlie social determinants of health, as well as the inherent contradiction between the profit motive and providing for the health of the population in capitalist societies. Feminist theorizing about health and illness is diverse, ranging from analyzing the credibility work that women with chronic pain must engage in to be taken seriously by health professionals to the (over)medicalization of women's lives. Postmodern theories, informed by Foucauldian notions of knowledge, power, surveillance, and discourse, also address medicalization.

RECOMMENDED RESOURCES

1. For an overview of theories of health and illness, see F. De Maio, *Health and Social Theory*, Themes in Social Theory Series (Series Editor: R. Stones) (New York, NY: Palgrave Macmillan, 2010).
2. To see the low-risk drinking guidelines adopted in Canada and elsewhere, see the website for the Canadian Centre on Substance Use and Addiction (http://www.ccsa.ca) or the Centre for Addiction and Mental Health (http://www.camh.ca).

FOR FURTHER REFLECTION

1. How has your own experience of health and illness been affected by lifestyle behaviours, socioeconomic status, ethnicity, and the structure and functioning of the healthcare system? What changes would be necessary at each of these levels for your health to improve?
2. Think about your favourite television shows and movies. How prevalent are various behaviours related to tobacco use, alcohol consumption, diet, or physical activity? In addition to *prevalence*, what are the *messages* being conveyed about those behaviours?

ENDNOTE

1 Retrieved June 3, 2017, from www.thinkexist.com.

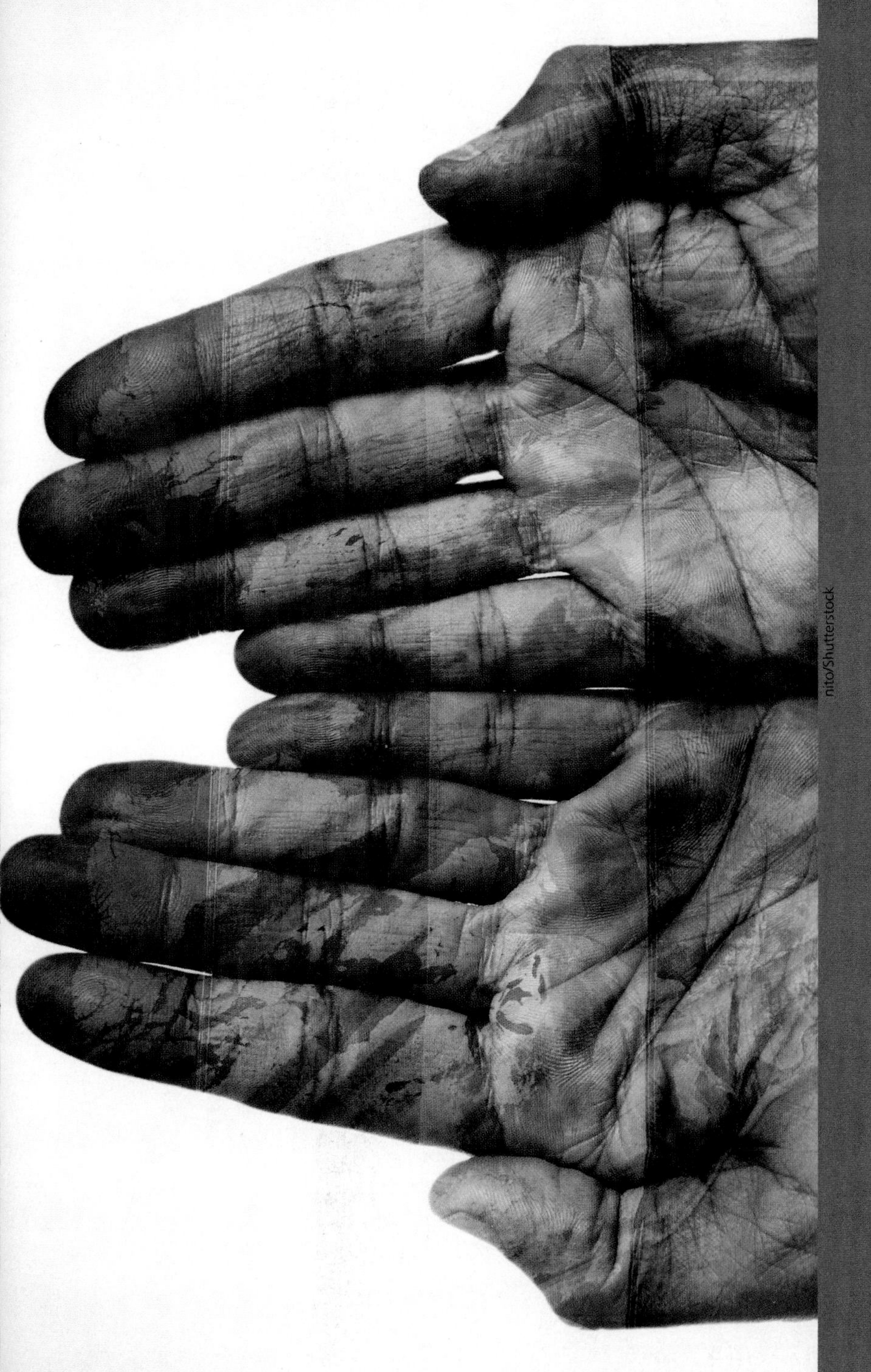
nito/Shutterstock

04 PART

Our Changing World

13 CHAPTER

Social Change: Collective Behaviour and Social Movements

Rena Schild/Shutterstock

Never doubt that a small group of thoughtful, committed citizens can change the world. Indeed, it is the only thing that ever has.

(Margaret Mead)[1]

LEARNING OBJECTIVES & OUTCOMES

After completing this chapter, students should be able to do the following:

LO1 Define collective behaviour, identify its central features, and differentiate it from conventional behaviour.

LO2 Identify the different types of crowds and explain which ones contribute to collective behaviour.

LO3 Explain how sociological theories (i.e., social contagion, convergence, and emergent norm) contribute to our understanding of collective behaviour.

LO4 Describe fads, rumours, urban legends, moral panic, and disasters as dispersed forms of collective behaviour.

LO5 Explain how social movements are both similar to and different from collective behaviour and discuss the relevance of claims making for movement organizations.

LO6 Differentiate between alternative, redemptive, reform, and revolutionary social movements.

LO7 Compare theoretical views on the development of social movements.

SOCIAL CHANGE AND SOCIAL PROGRESS

From what you've learned so far, it may be difficult to believe that Canada is "the True North strong and free" given at least 200 years of history involving the exploitation of particular social groups (e.g., the treatment of Indigenous peoples and reliance on child labour). It wasn't until the late 1800s, when the Social Gospel (a Protestant branch that applied Christian principles to social problems) was increasingly adopted by the middle classes, that groups such as the Victorian child-savers' movement started rallying for change (Valverde, 1991). By the 20th century, various groups were making strides in their efforts toward the legal protection of their own rights and those of vulnerable others (human rights, Indigenous peoples' rights, workers' rights, women's rights, minority rights, LGBTQ rights, animal rights, political rights, religious rights, and environmental rights). The pursuit of these goals has entailed efforts to change people's views and value systems through education (awareness campaigns), widespread action (organized protests, unions, social movements), and even acts of violence (terrorism).

As we saw in the early wave of the Arab Spring, protests and revolution brought an end to autocratic rule (e.g., in 2011, the leaders of Tunisia, Egypt, and Libya were all ousted from leadership) and facilitated positive outcomes (e.g., the right to hold elections, human rights, and monetary compensation such as increased wages). The outcomes stemmed from precipitating events led by "committed citizens" as suggested by cultural anthropologist Margaret Mead (1901–1978) in this chapter's epigraph. Robert E. Park (1864–1944), an American sociologist who initiated the field of study called *collective behaviour*, believed that the actions of crowds were essential to social change. In this chapter, we examine how various forms of collective behaviour and social movements develop and promote change. *Figure 13.1* summarizes some important events in Canadian history that had their origins in collective behaviour and social movements.

LO1 DEFINING COLLECTIVE BEHAVIOUR

Collective behaviour is not synonymous with all group behaviour. **Collective behaviour** refers to group behaviour that is relatively spontaneous, unstructured, and unconventional in nature (Goode, 1992). It is spontaneous and unstructured in the sense that it is unplanned and does not take a specific form. It is unconventional in that it generally lies outside

Collective behaviour: Group behaviour that is relatively spontaneous, unstructured, and unconventional in nature.

FIGURE 13.1

Historical Events with Origins in Collective Behaviour

- Nationally, certain women gained the right to vote as early as 1917 with the inclusion of most British subjects by 1918.
- Canada supports *the Universal Declaration of Human Rights* (1947/1948).
- Non-enfranchised Indigenous peoples (i.e., with Indian Status) are given the right to vote in 1960.
- The Canadian Civil Liberties Association is formed in 1964.
- The Canadian Charter of Rights and Freedoms is enacted in 1982.
- Canada adopts the United Nations Convention on the Rights of the Child in 1989.
- Same-sex marriage is legalized via the Civil Marriage Act in 2005.
- Bill C-16 protecting gender identity and expression passed in 2017.

what is considered normative. For example, people rioting in the street after a popular sporting event such as the Stanley Cup playoffs could be yelling, drinking, smashing windows of nearby businesses, climbing light posts, and even lighting cars on fire. That is not to say that all collective behaviour is entirely random and destructive—just that compared to conventional behaviour, it is *less* predictable and *less* institutionalized. Let's begin with a look at the behaviour of crowds.

LO2 COLLECTIVE BEHAVIOUR IN LOCALIZED CROWDS

Crowd: A temporary gathering of people who are in the same place at the same time.

Casual crowd: A gathering of people who by proximity alone happen to be in the same location at the same time.

Conventional crowd: A group of people who have gathered in the same place at the same time because of a common shared interest or objective.

CASUAL, CONVENTIONAL, EXPRESSIVE, AND ACTING CROWDS

A **crowd** is a temporary gathering of people in the same place at the same time (McPhail, 1991). Herbert Blumer (1969) distinguished four main types of crowds: casual, conventional, expressive, and acting. A **casual crowd** is a gathering of people who by proximity alone happen to be in the same location at the same time. For example, several individual families might be in the same park on the same day at the same time; some might be having lunch, others might be playing games, and others might be taking a walk. Since casual crowds do not originate for any intended larger purpose or shared interest, they are not a focal point for collective behaviour. That is, people who are part of a casual crowd are most likely to engage in rule-abiding individual (and even parallel) forms of conventional behaviour.

A **conventional crowd** is a group of people who have gathered in the same place at the same time because of a shared interest or objective. For example, as a conventional crowd, you and your classmates are currently attending a scheduled sociology lecture. Similarly, people in a movie theatre constitute a conventional crowd with a specific shared objective. A conventional crowd's behaviour tends to be planned, structured, predictable, and controlled by social norms. For example, people sit quietly in a theatre in seats, facing forward, in order to watch the show. They also put their cellphones on silent mode, and when they eat and drink, it is only products purchased at the theatre concession. Like casual crowds, conventional crowds generally do not lead to collective behaviour.

Tom Szczerbowski/Stringer/Getty Images

Saskatchewan Roughrider fans wear melonheads to support their team.

An **expressive crowd** is a gathering of people who share a common interest and are gathered at the same event at the same time for an explicit participatory purpose (see *Sociology in My Life*). Whereas the conventional crowd is attending a movie in order to watch the show, the expressive crowd has gathered because as a group it can respond or react emotionally in particular ways (e.g., by shouting or cheering to indicate encouragement). Fans at a hockey game engage in a variety of collective behaviours: they wear jerseys to denote their favourite players/teams, they paint their faces, and they participate in spontaneous "waves."

Finally, an **acting crowd** consists of people gathered at the same place at the same time who engage in overt collective behaviour in pursuit of a common goal. For example, in 1990 in Oka, Quebec, the Mohawk on nearby reserves conducted a highly publicized protest to halt the town's plans to expand a private golf course onto what they considered a sacred burial ground. During the "Oka Crisis," Mohawk supporters marched through the town protesting the golf course expansion and publicly declaring Mohawk ownership of the property. In the ensuing 78-day dispute, the group set up barricades that restricted access to roadways, confronted Quebec's provincial police, and stood up against members of the RCMP and the Canadian Armed Forces before finally negotiating an agreement to stand down (Alfred, 1995; Ciaccia, 2000; Swain, 2010). In an earlier failed attempt to mitigate the crisis, Quebec's Native affairs minister, John Ciaccia, wrote a letter to the mayor and councillors in which he pointed out the stakes involved and requested a suspension of the golf course plans. Ciaccia (2000) argued that historical land claims, cultural context, and community relations went well "beyond the strict legality of the situation as interpreted by our tribunals, which base themselves on laws put into place by our society, laws which do not necessarily answer to the claims of Native people" (p. 59). The Oka Crisis underscored the importance of recognizing Mohawk land claims and their fight to retain traditions they had been following since 1770.

Expressive crowd: A gathering of people Who share a common interest and are gathered At the same event at the same time with an Explicit participatory purpose.

Acting crowd: A group of people gathered at the same place at the same time who engage in overt collective behaviour in pursuit of a common goal.

YOUR SOCIOLOGICAL TOOLKIT

SOCIOLOGY IN MY LIFE

FAN BEHAVIOUR

Think about the last time you were part of a crowd attending some kind of entertainment event (e.g., a sporting event or a concert). Consider the norms governing the behaviour of attendees. Likely, fans were expected to sit in their designated seats and could purchase food, drinks, and memorabilia from the established vendors, but they were not allowed onto the stage where the performance was taking place. These are examples of conventional forms of behaviour. Also think about any unconventional behaviour displays you witnessed or any audience actions that were particular to this event.

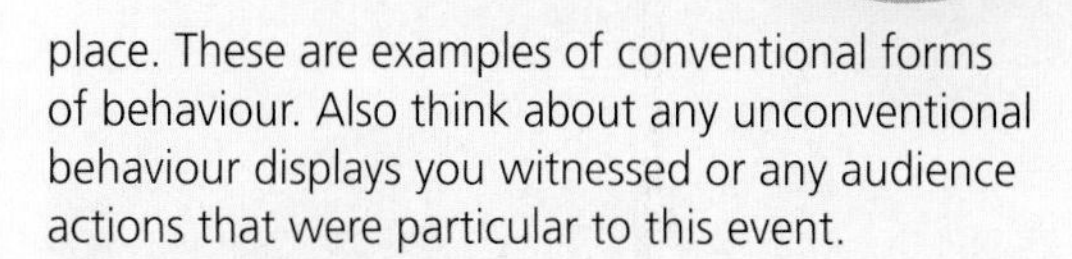

Think Outside the Box: Would you classify these latter behaviours as forms of collective behaviour? Why or why not?

TIME TO REVIEW

- In what ways has collective behaviour led to social progress in Canadian society?
- What is the main difference between a casual crowd and a conventional crowd?
- In which two types of crowds is collective behaviour most likely to occur?
- What is the main difference between an expressive crowd and an acting crowd?

YOUR SOCIOLOGICAL TOOLKIT
SOCIOLOGY IN THEORY

LO3 EXPLAINING COLLECTIVE BEHAVIOUR IN CROWDS

CONTAGION THEORY

An early explanation for crowd behaviour was that of French social psychologist Gustave Le Bon (1841–1931), who wrote extensively about characteristics that increased the likelihood of social action by groups. In his most influential work, *The Crowd* (1895/2006), he described how people lose their individuality in crowds as they are transformed into a "collective mind" that leads them to think and behave in ways quite unlike how they would otherwise behave as individuals. According to Le Bon, this transformation into a collective mind occurs as a function of *anonymity, contagion*, and *suggestibility*. Because people in crowds cannot readily be singled out for individual actions, they are free from social constraints and therefore are more likely to act on desires that might otherwise be held in check. This kind of anonymity was later described by Festinger, Pepitone, and Newcomb (1952) as "deindividuation," or the loss of self-awareness that occurs in groups. Le Bon noted that crowds are easily swayed into action by others (i.e., they are suggestible)—something akin to mass hypnosis (i.e., contagion). The high level of surveillance in modern society is reducing anonymity in crowds, and it facilitated 887 charges being laid over a period of three years following the 2011 Vancouver hockey riots (Crawford, 2015). Likely as a result of surveillance and the ensuing criminal liability, there have been no further hockey incidents of this magnitude in Canada.

Photography by Michael Caswell - Vancouver, BC (www.sceneinthedark.com)

Contagion theory helps explain the impulsive behaviour displayed by crowds.

Herbert Blumer (1900–1987) elaborated on Le Bon's ideas by clarifying how the collective transformation to social action takes place. According to Blumer (1939, 1969), a crowd engages in collective behaviour when the individuals who comprise it communicate their "restlessness" to one another. This generates social unrest that is likely to result in one of three forms of collective behaviour. First, it can lead to *milling*, wherein "individuals move around amongst one another in aimless and random fashion." Although harmless, milling increases emotions (excitability) and makes the members of the crowd "more sensitive and responsive to one another" and less responsive to "objects and events that would ordinarily concern them" (1969, p. 75). In addition, crowds may engage in *collective excitement*, or "a more intense form of milling," which is accompanied by an emotional enthusiasm that is obvious to others. You see this in crowds that linger after a football or hockey game to extend a winning celebration in honour of their favourite team by shouting victory cheers at strangers. In this state, people are "more likely to be carried away by impulses and feelings," prompting behaviours "which previously they would not likely have thought of, much less dared to undertake" (p. 76). Finally, crowds may partake in *social contagion*, which is the "rapid, unwitting, and nonrational dissemination of a mood, impulse, or form of conduct" (p. 76). Riots following sports games are a prime example of this.

CONVERGENCE THEORY

Contagion theory suggests that anyone who happens to be in a crowd is likely to get caught up in the action; by contrast, *convergence theory* posits that people in crowds come together in a particular location specifically in order to behave in accordance with their *prior predispositions*. In other words, like-minded individuals "converge" on a place, where collective behaviour then ensues. In this sense, crowd behaviour is not irrational, as suggested by contagion theorists; instead, it is the natural outcome of existing psychological impulses. From this we can infer that "*certain kinds of people* have the propensity to engage in *certain kinds of behaviour*"

(Goode, 1992, p. 59, emphasis in original). This view, which suggests that the blame lies within individual actors, reflects preconceived ideas about groups that are well known for engaging in violent collective acts (neo-Nazi groups and Islamic extremist groups such as ISIL). It fails to account for group influences, just as contagion theory cannot account for individual differences. A more middle-of-the-road approach is offered by emergent norm theory.

EMERGENT NORM THEORY

Turner and Killian (1987) contend that collective behaviour is both rational and diverse and that various courses of action are available to members of a group. A particular course of action results from new norms being established as meaning is constructed by a group in a particular situation. Thus, collective behaviour in crowds is the end result of norms being developed that redefine "right" and "wrong" in response to unique situational events (Turner & Killian, 1987).

For example, imagine you head for your class tomorrow as per your usual schedule. Normally, your instructor is already in the classroom setting up her laptop for a PowerPoint lecture when her students arrive. But this time, when you reach your class, the door is locked and the students are gathered in the hallway. Due to the uncertainty of the present situation (your instructor appears to be absent and the door is locked), the student crowd is likely to start offering up ideas about what is taking place (perhaps the instructor is ill or has gone to find security to open the locked door). People who have never spoken to each other in or out of class may now converse as they attempt to figure out what is going on. Eventually, they discuss what they should do next: should everyone wait or leave? How long should everyone wait? As suggestibility increases, new norms may be established. The crowd may determine that it is appropriate to wait 10 more minutes and then leave. In this type of ambiguous situation, the crowd also comes up with *justifications* for the emergent norms that are now being established. Some students may say they think there is an existing rule that says you have to wait for only a maximum of 10 minutes; others may suggest that the instructor wouldn't want them to waste their time standing in the hallway for an entire period.

Justification, which is the end stage of this process, involves redefining the situation to resolve the original uncertainty (i.e., that no one knows whether the instructor will arrive). The collective behaviour may not be uniform—some students may leave early, others may choose to wait a little longer, a few may act in some other fashion during the established 10-minute wait period (will check the instructor's office). Emergent norm theory, then, explicates a process whereby collective behaviour results from the sharing of information in groups, which helps establish situation-appropriate forms of social action.

TIME TO REVIEW

- According to contagion theory, what promotes the development of a collective mind?
- What does convergence theory point to as the main contributor to collective behaviour?
- According to emergent norm theory, how is situational ambiguity resolved?

LO4 DISPERSED FORMS OF COLLECTIVE BEHAVIOUR

Recall that crowds are considered to be localized when people are gathered in one place at the same time. Fairly large numbers of people can also be engaged in similar behaviours or be invoked by similar causes *while not in the general proximity of one another*. For example, men dispersed across Canada who have never been in contact with one another sport beards, whereas women wear jeggings in accordance with the latest styles in fashion. Canadians also participate in local events such as Canada Day breakfasts or Pride parades (refer to *Sociology in My Community*) that may take place in different cities on the same day.

FADS AND FASHION

Fads are temporary but highly popular social patterns such as activities, events, hobbies, or types of collectables that make up a current trend but eventually disappear when interest wanes (e.g., Beanie Babies, Silly Bandz). Fashion also includes popular social patterns but is longer lived and more likely to be closely associated with identity. For example, some people wear a particular brand of perfume or cologne as their personal scent for decades. Drake is so attached to Drakkar Noir by Guy Laroche that he named his old Twitter account after it (i.e., @Drakkardnoir) and recently had the men's fragrance bottle tattooed on his arm (Khal, 2017).

Fashion typically involves clothing lines that represent an entire fashion

Fads: Temporary but highly popular social patterns such as activities, events, music genres, or hobbies.

Fashion: Long-lasting popular social patterns that typically involve clothing lines and accessories.

YOUR SOCIOLOGICAL TOOLKIT

SOCIOLOGY IN MY COMMUNITY

PRIDE PARADES

John Lehmann/The Globe and Mail/The Canadian Press

Pride Parade attendees supporting the LGBTQ community.

A dispersed form of collective behaviour can be found in the actions of tens of thousands of people who take part in an annual Pride parade held in cities throughout Canada, usually during the month of June. Partakers dress in colourful clothes and either walk the parade route or cheer on the procession from sidelines waving pride flags. Attendees also take part in a host of other organized events that celebrate the culture and pride of the LGBTQ community, such as organized festivals, exhibits, drag shows, documentary screenings, information sessions, and faith-based gatherings.

Think Outside the Box: Which type or types of crowds discussed earlier in the chapter do attendees at a Pride parade best exemplify? Be sure to explain your answer.

industry of designers and brand labels. Although particular hair or clothing styles change over time, the category remains part of fashion (e.g., hair styles of the 1960s versus hair styles of the 1990s). In contrast, fads generally pertain to particular products (Shopkins, Pokémon Go) or activities (planking, ALS ice bucket challenge) that are often popularized through social media. Fads and fashion are forms of collective behaviour because they impact a large scattering of people who end up buying similar products, wearing similar styles, and acting in similar ways.

Rumours: Unsubstantiated stories about people or events.

Dieter Hawlan/Shutterstock

Although the Paleo Diet fad has prompted debates over diets high in animal protein, current research points to health benefits, including lowered inflammation and fat mass (e.g., Mellberg et al., 2014; Whalen et al., 2016).

RUMOURS, GOSSIP, AND URBAN LEGENDS

Rumours are unsubstantiated stories about people or events. In 2010, a rumour circulated that Canadian folk music artist Gordon Lightfoot had died. The rumour spread worldwide, beginning with a posting on Twitter by "someone in Ottawa." It was eventually proven to be false (at which point, it stopped being a rumour), but not before one of Lightfoot's close friends heard about it and passed the message on to friends in the music industry, who sent out various versions of the story via social media (Nurwisah, 2010). Luckily, Lightfoot was able to reach the media and his five children to quickly dispel the rumour. He displayed a sense of humour about the whole episode even after hearing about his own supposed death on the radio while driving to his Toronto office following a dental appointment. He noted that although he was "shocked of course," it was also "the best day for airplay that [he'd] had in weeks" (CTV News, 2010). A recent study by Lee and

Oh (2017) on the spreading of rumours via Twitter showed that people are more likely to perceive rumours to be true and to share them if they have already been retweeted multiple times. The number of retweets serves as a "normative cue" that others are sharing stories because they believe in them (Lee & Oh, 2017).

Rumours often accompany ambiguous situations as people try to make sense of what is going on and how they should proceed. *Why are all the tenants gathered outside my apartment building—is there a fire in the building?* Rumours are common in advance of major events and generally involve categories of people. For example, the mass media may circulate rumours about hockey teams that may be involved in upcoming trades. Similarly, the mass media sometimes inform us that certain groups, such as teachers or nurses, are soon to go on strike due to failed contract negotiations. According to Goode (1992), rumours exist in all societies and are good examples of collective behaviour in that they result from social interaction, they "fill in the gaps" with spontaneous bits of information, and their content can be unconventional.

The spread of rumours generally follows a predictable pattern: information tends to get modified and lost over time and from person to person as the story is retold. Rumours are highly inaccurate—as much as 70 percent of the original details have been lost by the time a rumour has been retold five or six times (Allport & Postman, 1947). Allport and Postman (1947) note that information loss and distortion occur largely as a result of three common practices. First, information during rumour transmission gets *levelled*—that is, a lot of the original details get omitted or lost. Also, information becomes *sharpened* to the viewpoint of the particular teller—that is, only the most interesting or salient details are most likely to be retained. Finally, a type of *assimilation occurs*—the storyteller focuses on a particular theme or part of the rumour and may even embellish on it by adding details so that the story better fits the storyteller's personal viewpoint.

Gossip is unsubstantiated or substantiated stories about specific individuals. Although it was dubbed a rumour by the mass media, the alleged death of Gordon Lightfoot was more accurately gossip because it pertained to a specific person. Celebrity gossip websites such as TMZ attest to the vast popularity of this form of collective behaviour. Gossip is unconventional (i.e., it's generally not considered appropriate to tell hurtful, private, or personal stories about other people); it is spontaneous (a celebrity can be engaged in any multitude of behaviours at the moment when a photographer strikes); and it may or may not be verifiable. We may never find out whether Jay Z actually cheated on Beyoncé with fashion designer Rachel Roy or whether Beyoncé called him out on it in her *Lemonade* album lyrics, but we can substantiate that her sister Solange once attacked Jay Z in an elevator for his flirtatious behaviour involving Rachel Roy (Roschke, 2016).

Urban legends are unsubstantiated stories that persist over time and contain an underlying message or moral. Jan Harold Brunvand defines urban legends as "believed oral narratives" that are passed on from person to person, somewhat like folklore (Brunvand, 2003). Although urban legends are purportedly about specific people and events, references to them tend to be general or abstract (a hitchhiker, a babysitter, a motorist, and a fast-food restaurant), and the details change from place to place and over time, much as with rumours. Also, urban legends contain a moral, such as "Keep a close watch on your children" or "Do not trust strangers." Urban legends span a variety of topics, from contaminated food, to cruelty toward animals, to natural disasters, and many are about death, murders, accidents, or ghosts (Brunvand, 2014b). How legends first get picked up is unknown, but they tend to circulate among "relatively sophisticated, educated, urbanized modern people" (Brunvand, 2014a). This may be in part because the source of an urban legend is believed to be an actual credible person who is a FOAF, or a "friend of a friend"—an "unnamed, elusive, but somehow readily trusted anonymous individual" (Brunvand, 2003, p. 51).

WIDESPREAD PANIC AND MORAL PANIC

A shared fear related to a threat such as a terrorist attack or a pandemic can sometimes produce collective action in the form of a **widespread panic** during which a large number of people try to flee an area, believing that they have little time left before meeting some horrible fate. A famous example of a large-scale panic originated with a radio broadcast on October 30, 1938. At a time when radio was known for its factual content, listeners heard what came across as news reports of a Martian invasion with references to actual buildings, streets, and towns. The broadcast was in fact a theatre adaptation of H.G. Wells's *War of the Worlds*, in which Martians invade New England, but many listeners tuned in a few minutes after the broadcast started and missed the opening disclaimer (Miller, 2000).

Gossip: Unsubstantiated or substantiated stories about specific individuals.

Urban legends: Abstract unsubstantiated stories containing an underlying message or moral that persists over time.

Widespread panic: A generalized belief regarding impending danger that can lead a large number of people to flee an area or engage in other protective measures.

SOCIOLOGY ONLINE

NICOTINE AND TIM HORTONS COFFEE: DEBUNKING URBAN LEGENDS

Did you ever hear a story or receive an email warning that bears a resemblance to an urban legend? Did you believe it? Our students often mention an urban legend involving the Tim Hortons franchise. The story usually centres on the notion of people getting addicted to Tim Hortons coffee because one of its "secret" ingredients is nicotine. Another variation is that the nicotine is in the paper cups; thus, the addiction includes other customers, such as tea drinkers. Are the many people who "roll up the rim to win" with their teeth exposing themselves to even greater doses? For a comprehensive Internet resource dedicated to exposing the truth or, in most cases, false facts on trending rumours and urban legends, including the untrue story about Tim Hortons described above, we recommend David Mikkelson's site Snopes.com.

Although the print media later exaggerated the public reaction (widespread stampedes, personal injuries), a significant number of listeners *did* believe the broadcast was factual and acted on that belief (by trying to contact police, hospitals, family members, and so on) (Miller, 2000). Few people today worry about Martian attacks; however, many are concerned about the health and safety issues associated with possible influenza pandemics (and, more recently, Zika virus spread through a mosquito bite).

Stanley Cohen (1972) used the term **moral panic** to describe the irrational but widespread worry that certain *groups* represent a terrible threat to the social order. A moral panic "is a scare about a threat or supposed threat from deviants or 'folk devils,' a category of people who, presumably, engage in evil practices and are blamed for menacing a society's culture, way of life, and central values" (Goode & Ben-Yehuda, 2009, p. 2). Three sources contribute to the development of moral panics (Zajdow, 2008). First, there is the particular group whose behaviour is causing the moral panic (i.e., the folk devils). Cohen (2002) notes that youth are a recurring target of blame for society's moral decay, especially in relation to the taking or selling of banned drugs. For example, shortly after three young Canadians died from taking ecstasy, a moral panic spread in the Toronto area regarding the risks associated with drug-plagued "rave communities" and "rave dance parties" (Hier, 2002). As another example, ongoing terrorist attacks by Muslim extremist groups such as ISIL increase public fear and provoke a situation whereby many citizens who also happen to be Muslim end up being unfairly viewed and treated as part of the ensuing moral panic.

Moral panic: Irrational but widespread worry that certain groups present an enormous threat to the social order of society.

Moral entrepreneurs: A person who brings perceived morally damaging behaviour to the attention of others.

The second element in the seeding of moral panics is **moral entrepreneurs**—that is, people who deem it important to bring the morally damaging behaviour to the attention of others. Moral entrepreneurs might be concerned parents, citizens, or others who try to advocate for measures to alleviate what they perceive as a social problem. Moral entrepreneurs, for example, write letters to politicians or newspaper editors to detail their views and to elicit support. In the cases just mentioned, moral entrepreneurs tried to get raves banned from city-owned property (Hier, 2002), and, more recently, moral entrepreneurs are vocal in their support for American President Trump's attempts to implement a travel ban on Muslim majority countries (BBC News, 2017).

The third element is the mass media, which help spread the panic by making a particular version of the story widely available. Hier (2002) reported that there were 192 stories in Toronto newspapers on raves over a four-month period. News sites and social media alike are filled with stories of terrorism that emphasize particular themes and interpretations. For example, in cases of religious extremism directed against the West, the concept of "jihad" is often associated with violence and depicted as meaning "holy war." The term actually means "striving," including "personal striving to have the ideals of Islam become a way of life," with a focus on "improving the religious condition of the

YOUR SOCIOLOGICAL TOOLKIT

SOCIOLOGY IN PRACTICE

CHIROPRACTIC FOLK DEVILS

Chiropractors are health care professionals who are musculoskeletal experts who assess and treat disorders of the muscular, skeletal, and nervous systems (Canadian Chiropractic Association, 2017). On September 12, 1996, an Ontario woman named Lana Dale Lewis died of a stroke at the age of 45. Her family and various moral entrepreneurs were convinced that the cause originated in a chiropractic manipulation she had received for migraines. The ensuing moral panic surrounding the use of chiropractic services lasted from 1996 to 2005 and was fuelled by media coverage, which occurred daily throughout the 22-month investigation into her death (Villanueva-Russell, 2009). The inquest into Lewis's death by a coroner's jury eventually rendered a verdict of "death by means of an accident" (Laeeque & Boon, 2004). Nonetheless, the media were successful in creating a moral panic, and anti-chiropractic messages began appearing in magazines and on websites (e.g., Chirowatch.com). The end result was a widespread but largely unfounded fear relative to statistical realities that damaged the reputation of the chiropractic profession (Villanueva-Russell, 2009). Moral panic over chiropractors led to reforms in Canadian health insurance systems. After 30 years of coverage, in 2004, Ontario "delisted" chiropractic services from its health insurance plan; the other provinces followed suit. This meant that people who utilized chiropractic services now had to pay for the treatment themselves (Deloitte, 2004). Chiropractic services are still delisted in most provinces; however, health plans provided by employers and private health care providers typically cover at least some of the costs associated with chiropractic use in Canada today (Healthquotes.ca, 2015).

Think Outside the Box: Can you think of an example of a fad or event that was highly sensationalized in the media at some point in history as a threat to morality?

community of believers" (not violence) for the majority of Muslims (Lutz & Lutz, 2013). A final distinguishing feature of a moral panic is that the "scare" is disproportionate to the actual threat. The assumption that all young people who attend raves are drug prone is not supported by verifiable empirical data. Similarly, the vast majority of followers of Islam do not support the use of violence "either between Sunni and Shia or against Christians or Jews," and most Muslim groups, including fundamentalists, "do not subscribe to [holy war] views of Jihad ... and do not participate in the violence" (Lutz & Lutz, 2013, p. 76). See *Sociology in Practice* for an additional example of moral panic involving the chiropractic profession.

DISASTERS

A final situation in which we find dispersed forms of collective behaviour is in the wake of disasters. A **disaster** has been defined as "a relatively sudden, unscheduled, one-time event that causes a great deal of property or ecological damage, or large-scale loss of life, and substantial disruption or stress among residents in the stricken area" (Goode, 1992, p. 219). As recent events around the globe have taught us, naturally occurring climate-based disasters such as earthquakes, floods, tsunamis, cyclones, tornadoes, and heat waves have resulted in large numbers of deaths and even more cases of injury. In 2016, floods in China left millions of people homeless (and hundreds dead), earthquakes killed more than 200 people in Italy and more than 300 in Ecuador, and Hurricane Matthew wreaked havoc in the Caribbean and United States (Phillips, 2016). Canada has also seen its share of hurricanes, earthquakes, floods, volcanic eruptions, storm surges, landslides, forest fires, and tsunamis (Natural Resources Canada, 2009). The worst hurricane in Atlantic history struck the coast of Newfoundland in 1775 and killed more than 4,000 people (Stokes Sullivan, 2010). And, most recently, the damages stemming from the wildfires that spanned more than 500,000 hectares and destroyed more than 2400 structures in Fort McMurray, Alberta, in 2016 are believed to exceed 9 billion (Globe Staff and the Canadian Press, 2017).

Disaster: A relatively sudden, unscheduled, one-time event that causes a great deal of property or ecological damage, or large-scale loss of life, and substantial disruption or stress among residents in the stricken area.

Disasters can also be caused by humans (plane crashes, train derailments, sinking ships, bridge failures), power struggles (war, terrorism), and technological advances (industrial explosions, oil spills, mining accidents, engineering failures). An example of this would be the 2013 collapse of Rana Plaza in Savar, Bangladesh, due to structural inadequacies. Two of the worst industrial disasters occurred in the 1980s. In one of these, in Bhopal, India, in 1984, a poisonous leak from a Union Carbide pesticide factory resulted in as many as 4,000 fatalities and 50,000 injuries. Then in Chernobyl, Ukraine, in 1986, an explosion in a nuclear reactor killed 56 people and contributed to 4,000 subsequent cancer cases (Lepisto, 2009). Examples of a few of Canada's pipeline disasters include a Plains Midstream spill of 4.5 million litres of oil near Little Buffalo, Alberta, in 2011; a Pace Oil and Gas line leak of 3.5 million litres of water-oil emulsion near Rainbow Lake, Alberta, in 2012; an Apache Canada pipeline leak of 15 million litres of toxic water contaminated with salt in 2013; and a 5 million–litre bitumen, sand, and water spill near Fort McMurray (The Canadian Press, 2016). Although not all spills are of such magnitude, research on pipelines regulated in Alberta shows that there were 28,666 crude oil spills between 1975 and 2012, averaging two spills a day (Kheraj, 2015). "When it comes to oil spills, the question is never if but when and how bad" (Eaves, 2011).

The interest here for sociologists lies not so much in distinguishing among types of disasters or in uncovering how a natural or a human-made disaster occurred but in identifying commonalities. These include social, political, and economic factors that predispose certain groups to disproportionately higher disaster risks and that affect how resources are deployed throughout and in the aftermath of such crises. Sociologists are also interested in how disasters affect individuals and their broader social structures. In *Everything in Its Path*, sociologist Kai Erikson (1976/2012) described how massive flooding in Buffalo Creek, West Virginia, created "collective trauma" in survivors, whose close ties to one another and to their community were destroyed. One's identity is in part created by and invested in the wider social structure that includes one's family, friends, and neighbours; it also entails shared understandings about how that community exists (people exchange meals, look after one another's children and property, and develop an affinity toward local attractions). The loss of all of this at once deeply impacts individuals in a manner that is not readily recreated following a disaster.

Social movements: Organized efforts by a substantial number of people to change or to resist change in some major aspect or aspects of society.

Bloomberg/Getty Images

Fort McMurray wildfire, 2016

This sense of "communality" helps explain the seemingly irrational behaviour of people who choose not to leave a disaster site even when remaining poses additional hardships (such as living in close proximity to a contaminated water supply or a flood danger zone). Erikson (1994) draws an analogy between the trauma experienced by disaster survivors and the long-term suffering experienced by people who live in poverty, both of whom lack important ties to the existing social structure.

TIME TO REVIEW

- Are fads considered to be forms of collective behaviour? Why or why not?
- In what ways does information get lost and distorted during the rumour process?
- How do urban legends differ from rumours?
- What does widespread panic entail?
- What three sources contribute to moral panic?
- Why might people choose to stay on living in a disaster site even when remaining poses additional risk of hardships?

LO5 SOCIAL MOVEMENTS

Recall at the start of the chapter that we discussed the importance of collective behaviour and social movements for facilitating social change. **Social movements** are "organized efforts by a substantial number of people to change or to resist change, in some major aspect or aspects of society" (Goode, 1992, p. 28). For example, early Canadian social movements advocated for civil liberties (freedom of speech, the right to own property) and human rights (workers' rights, women's rights). Current movements such as "Idle No More" and "gay–straight alliances" continue to advocate for rights (the right to Indigenous self-government, the right to be socially accepted). Charles Tilly and Sidney Tarrow (2015) define a social movement as "a sustained campaign of claim making, using repeated performances that advertise the claim, based on organizations, networks, traditions and solidarities that sustain these activities" (p. 11). Some but not all movements are forms of "contentious politics"—"contentious in the sense that social movements involve the collective making of claims that, if realized, would conflict with someone else's interests, political in the sense that governments of one sort or another figure somehow in the claims making, whether as claimants, objects of claims, allies of the objects, or monitors of the contention" (McAdam, Tarrow, & Tilly, 2001, cited in Tilley & Wood, 2013, pp. 3–4). In many cases, social movements are created by the masses in order to resolve large-scale issues, such as income inequality and human rights violations, that are not being adequately dealt with via existing political structures. The revolt in Tunisia, for example, was primarily led by unemployed college graduates who had openly critiqued the existing regime over social media for more than a decade (Castells, 2015).

Social movements share some of the characteristics of earlier-mentioned forms of collective behaviour, including their *unconventional nature*—that is, both tend to go against established cultural values and practices. Riots, protests, and various forms of civil disobedience, including strikes and acts of violence, may be carried out during the history of the movement. Thus, social movements also share with collective behaviour a reliance on social action stemming from group efforts. Social movements, however, also possess a number of features that disqualify them as collective behaviour. Specifically, although collective behaviour is relatively spontaneous and unstructured, social movements involve prior *organization* and *planning*. This was evident in the way social media was utilized during the early stages of the Arab Spring, as one Egyptian activist tweeted, "We use Facebook to schedule the protests, Twitter to coordinate, and YouTube to tell the world" (Tilly & Wood, 2013, p. 97). Social movements also often have identifiable leaders (Martin Luther King, Jr., is generally acknowledged to have been the leader of the American Civil Rights Movement), and they conduct public campaigns and recruiting drives on behalf of the movement. However, unlike political leaders, leaders of social movements are not elected, they do not operate within a rigid set of rules and processes (as in the case of political institutions), and they may advocate various, divergent perspectives at the same time within the same movement, as in the case of different feminisms in the women's movement (West, 2013). Also, collective behaviour tends to be fairly short-lived—a post-game riot plays itself out after a few hours, gossip about your professor may last only a few days, a fad typically runs its course over a season—whereas social movements can endure for many years. For example, the environmental movement has been active since the 1960s and continues to develop momentum today (see Chapter 14). *Table 13.1* provides a summary of the main similarities and differences.

TABLE 13.1

Differentiating between Collective Behaviour and Social Movements

Collective Behaviour and Social Movements	Collective Behaviour	Social Movements
Involves the behaviour of a fairly large number of individuals	Spontaneous	Prior planning
Unconventional in nature	Unstructured	Organized
Based on social action	Short-lived	Enduring
	No identifiable leaders	Identifiable leaders
	No basis in claims	Claims/claims making
	Not goal-oriented	Goal driven

CLAIMS AND CLAIMS MAKING

The concepts of "claims making" and "change" are central for understanding social movements and for differentiating between them. Every social movement rests on some kind of claim. Here, a **claim** is a statement about some phenomenon that is

Claim: A statement about the nature of some phenomenon that is constructed as a social problem.

constructed as a social problem. Social movements engage in **claims making**, declaring that a particular condition is unjust and identifying the measures it considers necessary to correct the injustice. For example, the lesbian, gay, bisexual, transgender, and queer/questioning social movement claimed that LGBTQ couples were being treated unjustly in Canada because they lacked rights that married couples have (such as property and parenting rights). Citizens, LGBTQ community members, and organizations such as Canadians for Equal Marriage and Egale Canada advocated for legalized same-sex marriages as a solution; by 2005, they had won their battle throughout Canada. Uprisings as part of the Arab Spring and Winter have roots in claims of government corruption, widespread poverty, high levels of unemployment, human rights violations, and political repression.

DIMENSIONS OF SOCIAL CHANGE

Social movements differ from one another in terms of their underlying claims and the changes they are proposing. They vary with regard to the type and degree of change they are seeking, the intended beneficiaries of that change, and the means utilized to bring it about. First, in terms of the *type of change*, social movements seek to either promote or prevent change from occurring. More progressive movements challenge existing norms and values by presenting new ideas and advocating their acceptance; more conservative movements challenge new ideas to prevent change from occurring so as to maintain the status quo. Also, social movements are distinguished by the *degree of change* they seek: some call for limited change, such as an adjustment to an existing policy; others call for sweeping change. Similarly, social movements may direct their efforts at *particular recipients* (Indigenous youth, working Canadians, impaired drivers, seniors) or may seek to change the views of all Canadians (to promote green living or healthy lifestyles). Finally, social movements differ greatly with respect to the *means utilized*—for example, they can be confrontational or not, peaceful or not.

Claims making: A process whereby a social movement declares that a particular condition is unjust and identifies measures needed to resolve the unfairness.

Social movement organization (SMO): A complex or formal organization that identifies its goals with the preferences of a social movement or a countermovement and attempts to implement those goals.

Alternative social movements: Social movements that seek limited societal change for a specific group or narrow segment of society.

Social movements also vary in size and geographic scope, from local grassroots movements to country-wide or even international movements. For instance, women's movements of various sizes emerged in 32 different countries over a 100-year period beginning in the mid-1800s (Staggenborg, 1998). The actual "work" of social movements is typically carried out by social movement organizations. A **social movement organization (SMO)** is "a complex, or formal, organization which identifies its goals with the preferences of a social movement or a countermovement and attempts to implement those goals" (McCarthy & Zald, 1977, p. 1218). For example, the environmental movement in Canada is associated with several major Canadian environmental organizations, such as Greenpeace Canada and the Suzuki Foundation.

LO6 TYPES OF SOCIAL MOVEMENTS

Based on the degree of change sought and the intended recipients of the change, four main types of social movements can be identified: alternative, redemptive, reformative, and revolutionary (see *Figure 13.2*).

Alternative social movements seek limited societal change for a specific group or narrow segment of society. Thus, there are social movements that promote alternative media (the Association of Alternative

FIGURE 13.2

Typology of Social Movements

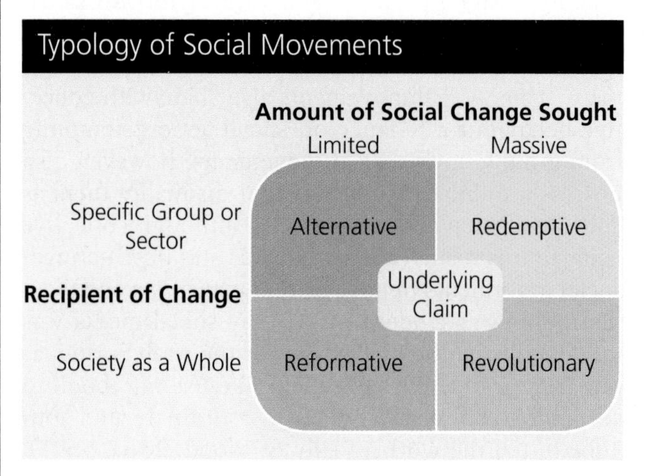

Source: D. F. Aberle, *The Peyote religion among the Navaho*, Chicago: Aldine, 1966, Pg. 315.

Newsmedia and Media Alliance) for people who are interested in non–mainstream perspectives. Similarly, there are alternative religious movements (Wicca, Integral Yoga), alternative educational movements (Canadian homeschooling), and alternative political movements (the Pirate Party of Canada, the Rhinoceros Party). A newer social movement is targeting distracted drivers and has the support of many grassroots organizations, including People Against Distracted Driving (PADD) and Stop Texting and Driving Distracted (STANDD).

Redemptive social movements seek large-scale change for a specific group in society. Often their goal is to change the entire way of life for a particular group. Mothers Against Drunk Drivers Canada (MADD Canada) seeks to stop impaired driving and to support victims of impaired driving. The Animal Liberation Front seeks to accord animals the same treatment as humans (by prohibiting the consumption of animals, the use of leather or fur for clothing, and the use of animals in medical experiments).

Reformative social movements seek to get everyone in society to adopt a new viewpoint or a particular position on an issue. For example, the Civil Rights Movement in the 1950s and 1960s included a series of reformative movements seeking equality under the law and an end to discrimination based on race. The second wave of the women's movement (1960–1985) sought to empower women in public and private spheres (e.g., equal education and the right to abortion), whereas the LGBTQ movements today continue to strive for acceptance and social equality. Slow Food in Canada is a newer reformative movement that encourages people to strike a balance between food enjoyment and agricultural biodiversity while discouraging the consumption of fast foods.

Finally, there are **revolutionary social movements**, which seek large-scale change that affects everyone in society. At the extreme, such a movement might overthrow an existing political system to pave the way for a new one with a different ideology. The Russian Revolution of 1917 included various forms of collective behaviour, such as riots, strikes, mass demonstrations, and open warfare (during the Russian Civil War that immediately followed). Its two pivotal events were the February Revolution, which removed Tsar Nicholas II from power, and the October Revolution, which established the Soviet Union in place of the temporary government. Radical Islamic fundamentalist movements such as al-Qaeda and the Islamic State group (also known as ISIL and ISIS) are more current illustrations of enduring movements seeking large-scale changes to existing belief systems. The first wave of the Arab Spring revolutions in the Middle East (2010–2012) demonstrated just how quickly civil movements can organize to achieve their goals, especially when communication is facilitated by social media (Twitter, Facebook, the Internet). The second wave, dubbed the "Arab Winter" (mid-2012–present), has illustrated that not all revolutions are successful and that civil unrest also opens the door to militant terrorist organizations (e.g., al-Qaeda insurgency in Yemen, ISIS in northern and western Iraq and Syria) (Fisk et al., 2016). Finally, as in the case of the Idle No More movement led by Indigenous peoples, discussed in the *Critical Thinking in Action* box, a revolution can sometimes even be peaceful in nature.

AFP/Getty Images

Euromaidan began with public protests in Ukraine.

Redemptive social movements: Social movements that seek large-scale change for a specific group.

Reformative social movements: Social movements that seek limited societal change for everyone in society.

Revolutionary social movements: Social movements that seek large-scale change that affects everyone in society.

TIME TO REVIEW

- How are social movements different from other forms of collective behaviour?
- What does claims making entail?
- What are the four dimensions of change that help differentiate among social movements?
- Which type of social movement seeks massive change for a narrow segment of society?

YOUR SOCIOLOGICAL TOOLKIT

CRITICAL THINKING IN ACTION

IDLE NO MORE: A PEACEFUL REVOLUTION OR A RESISTANCE MOVEMENT?

THE CANADIAN PRESS IMAGES/Graham Hughes

Does a revolution have to be synonymous with the use of force, violence, and war? The contemporary Idle No More movement asks people to join in a "peaceful revolution" aimed at protecting Indigenous rights and the environment (lakes, forests, wildlife). That movement can also be considered a form of "resistance" in that many of its efforts are directed at resisting the government's attempts at reforms that undermine the movement's aims. Idle No More's founding activists (Nina Wilson, Sylvia McAdam, Jessica Gordon, Sheelah McLean) held a "teach-in" in Saskatoon to make people aware of federal legislation that would pose risks to environmental waterways and threaten **Indigenous sovereignty**. In this context, sovereignty refers to "the right to self-government ... which Aboriginal people neither surrendered nor lost by way of conquest" (LaForme, 1991, p. 253). When European settlers came upon lands in what are now the provinces and territories of Canada, they made various treaties with the existing occupants regarding how the nations would coexist. As explained in Idle No More's manifesto:

> The Treaties are nation to nation agreements between First Nations and the British Crown who are sovereign nations. The Treaties are agreements that cannot be altered or broken by one side of the two Nations. The spirit and intent of the Treaty agreements meant that First Nations peoples would share the land, but retain their inherent rights to lands and resources. (Idle No More, n.d.)

In a speech at the ABO Aboriginal Law Program, Justice Harry LaForme noted that although Indigenous people in Canada were supposed to be treated "as partners, as invested nations," they have instead been marginalized, managed, and defined as "wards of the state" (Taddese, 2013).

Think Outside the Box: Can you provide an example of a historical event, policy, or act that lends support to LaForme's claims?

Source: Idle No More. (n.d.). The Manifesto. Found at: http://www.idlenomore.ca/manifesto

YOUR SOCIOLOGICAL TOOLKIT
SOCIOLOGY IN THEORY

LO7 VALUE-ADDED THEORY

Indigenous sovereignty: The right of Indigenous peoples to self-government.

In explaining social movements, it is important to consider historical conditions and events because social movements often arise in response to existing social conditions, especially those that cause strain. In his *value-added theory*, Neil Smelser (1962, pp. 15–18)* discussed six factors that facilitate social action:

1. *Structural conduciveness*—the broad social conditions that are necessary for collective behaviour to take place (e.g., economic pressure, political corruption).

* Neil J. Smelser, *Theory of Collective Behaviour*, The Free Press, Copyright © 1962 by Neil J. Smelser.

2. *Structural strain*—underlying problems that have resulted from or that have not been adequately addressed by the current system (gender inequality, racism, pay inequities, environmental degradation, widespread unemployment, etc.).
3. *The growth and spread of a generalized belief*—the widespread awareness that a particular issue is a social problem and that steps should and can be taken to change it. The Internet is especially helpful in spreading claims and outlining the impetus for change underlying modern social movements. As a function of the high rate of social media diffusion and the Internet's capacity to act as an independent source of media, Castells (2015) explains how protesters in Tunisia were able to keep "up demands for full democratization of the country throughout 2011 in spite of the persistent police repression and continuing presence of politicians from the old regime in the provincial government and in the high levels of administration" (p. 29).
4. *Precipitating factors*—events or behaviours that serve as "triggers" or breaking points. The Arab Spring can be traced to a precipitating event wherein a poor street vendor named Tarek el-Tayeb Mohamed Bouazizi set himself on fire in protest after he was unable to obtain a permit to sell fruits and vegetables to help support his family (Fisk et al., 2016).
5. *Mobilization of participation for action*—the gathering of potential participants. This often requires inspirational leaders who spread the message and encourage others to get directly involved in the solution. In the case of Bouazizi, initially a teacher noted that "the unions got involved, teachers, lawyers, doctors, all sections of civil society, and set up a Popular Resistance Committee to back the people of Sidi Bouzid, but with no support from the outside" (Fisk et al., 2016). Outside support was soon to follow once the news broke on Facebook and Twitter.
6. *The operation of social control*—in the absence of strong forms of direct control by police or the military, people are no longer restrained from carrying out collective efforts (as was the case in Tunisia once the ousted President Ben Ali fled to Saudi Arabia).

According to Smelser (1962), each factor, in its corresponding order, must be present to promote the next step or stage in the development of collective behaviour; if one or more of these precipitating factors is absent, collective action is unlikely to occur.

Critiques of value-added theories (e.g., see McAdam, 1982) point out that they fail to address the broader political context in which many social movements arise. "Collective behaviour is more likely to be perceived as deviant behaviour than political action" (Buechler, 2010, p. 51). Also, these theories imply that only people who are deprived in some way will participate in them. A value-added approach, then, fails to explain how a movement gathers diverse supporters who come to collectively believe in a cause (McAdam, 1982).

RESOURCE MOBILIZATION THEORY

Structural strains, including relative deprivation, are present in most societies; it follows that resource mobilization is an important factor in the development of social movements (e.g., McCarthy & Zald, 1977). The assumption underlying resource mobilization theory is that social movements develop as a function of how resources are brought together and utilized by leaders. According to Edwards and McCarthy (2004), this includes how leaders organize *moral resources* (the legitimacy of the claim), *cultural resources* (such as strategic know-how), *social-organizational resources* (the development of networks), *human resources* (experienced activists and people with the skills to further organizational goals), and various *material resources* (finances, office space). Whether or not social movements develop in particular places at particular times, then, is largely a function of how well leaders develop and channel various resources. Beyond resource mobilization itself, which Carroll (2016) suggests is more on the "supply side" of collective action, there must also be an opportunity to act – on the "demand side." At various points in history, there are ways claims can be advanced (e.g., via petitions and protests) and structures that may be more or less conducive to the enactment of claims (e.g., political forces can serve as agents of repression or facilitation) (Carroll, 2016).

Social movements are far more organized, institutionalized, and enduring than other forms of collective behaviour. This is important because it implies that members of social movement organizations are "rational actors" who come together to further their collective interests (Buechler, 2010) rather than people who get out of hand when they become part of a group (as would be implied by contagion theory, for example). Building on the more rational and organized approaches, *political process theory* emphasizes the importance of *cycles of contention* (wherein there is large-scale unrest) and of *political opportunities* to pave the way for protest movements (see Tarrow, 1998; Tilly & Tarrow, 2015). In *Power in Movement* (1998), Tarrow explained that *political opportunities* are situational features that enable movement development through access (e.g., elections), shifting alignments (e.g., changes in what a particular political party supports or does not support), divided elites, influential allies, and repression or facilitation by the state (pp. 77–80).

More recent approaches combine the assumptions of resource mobilization theory and political process theory into a synthesized model of "political entities aiming to create social change" (Staggenborg, 2008, p. 18). According to this combined approach (see Benford & Snow, 2000), a social movement (often with the aid of leaders and an organization) interprets a particular issue as a form of social injustice, calls attention to that issue in particular ways (known as framing and discussed later on) to develop a constructed meaning that resonates with the collectivity, and inspires them to mobilize for action (Staggenborg, 2008).

NEW SOCIAL MOVEMENT THEORY

A final approach, *new social movement theory*, focuses solely on social movements that have arisen in post-industrial or advanced societies, largely since the 1960s. According to this theory, post-industrial movements tend to emphasize human rights (women's rights, LGBTQ rights) and global issues (global warming, poverty, peace) rather than economic issues, as was the case with earlier labour and worker movements. An important contribution of the new social movement theory has been the notion of a collective identity. A **collective identity** is a shared sense of belonging or "we-ness" that binds individuals in a social movement; it serves as the "animating spirit" that propels them to take action on behalf of that social movement (Snow, 2001).

FRAMES AND FRAME ALIGNMENT

Collective identity develops from the meanings people come to share regarding a social movement's purpose, claims, activities, and leadership. Framing processes help transition individual views into shared ones that become part of the collective identity (Snow, 2007). To explain how objects and events come to have meaning for particular individuals, Goffman (1974) introduced the idea of "frames" as cognitive structures that allow people to take notice of objects and events in the wider world in the context of their own life experiences. "Frame alignment" processes entail attempts by social movement organizations to present their claims and directives in a manner that "fits" individuals' existing ideas and values (Snow et al., 1986). There are four main processes here: "frame bridging," which involves linking ideologically compatible individuals; "frame amplification," which involves the "idealization, embellishment, clarification, or invigoration of existing values or beliefs"; "frame extension," which moves interests beyond the primary focus to other areas of interest to potential members; and "frame transformation," which includes attempts to bring about complete changes in ideology (Benford & Snow, 2000, pp. 624–625).

Collective identity: A shared sense of belonging that binds individuals in a social movement and propels them to take action on behalf of that social movement.

The Idle No More movement is an exemplary model for all of these processes. On its website you find statements of support from individuals, groups, and organizations (Canadian artists, the Canadian Nurses Association, the Green Party of Canada, the federal NDP, Greenpeace)—this demonstrates bridging. Amplification is evident in the many events that first brought public attention to the cause in 2012 (press releases, protests, and especially Attawapiskat's Chief Theresa Spence's six-week hunger strike). It is also evident in the movement's ongoing efforts to draw attention to its cause (teach-ins, healing walks, conference talks). Frame extension includes calls for action beyond treaty rights and environmental protection (such as calls to resist the use of violence against women and for an inquiry into cases of murdered or missing Indigenous women). Frame transformation can be inferred from the many resources the movement has provided to educate prospective supporters and to dispel commonly held myths about treaties, land rights, and Indigenous sovereignty.

The construction of a social identity is paramount to both the existence and the endurance of a social movement (Gamson, 1991). Hund and Benford (2010) summarize the distinction between old and new social movements by noting that "class consciousness" has, for all intents and purposes, been replaced by "collective identity" "as the factor that accounts for mobilization and individual attachments to new social movements" (p. 437). Current research is now aimed at developing our understanding of how collective identities develop, how tensions develop among multiple identities, and how collective identities translate into various forms of action (della Porta & Diani, 2008). The environmental movement, which is the focus of the next chapter, is both an old and a new social movement, one that currently includes a growing collective identity bound in environmental awareness and a global call to action.

CHAPTER SUMMARY

LO1 Define collective behaviour, identify its central features, and differentiate it from conventional behaviour.

Collective behaviour refers to group behaviour that is relatively spontaneous, unstructured, and unconventional relative to conventional behaviour, which is planned, structured, and normative in nature.

LO2 Identify the different types of crowds and explain which ones contribute to collective behaviour.

A crowd is a temporary gathering of people who are in the same place at the same time (i.e., a crowd is localized, whereas other groups are more dispersed). Casual crowds share only proximity, conventional crowds share an interest, expressive crowds share an interest and are participatory, and acting crowds engage in the pursuit of a common goal. Both expressive and acting crowds facilitate collective behaviour.

LO3 Explain how sociological theories (i.e., social contagion, convergence, and emergent norm) contribute to our understanding of collective behaviour.

Contagion theory suggests that people are transformed in a group much as if through hypnosis, and this causes them to behave in irrational ways; convergence theory claims that like-minded people come together to behave in accordance with predisposition; and emergent norm theory suggests that crowds are more likely to consist of rational people.

LO4 Describe fads, rumours, urban legends, moral panic, and disasters as dispersed forms of collective behaviour.

Dispersed crowds engage in similar behaviours while not in the same general proximity. Fads are popular social patterns, rumours are unsubstantiated stories about people and events, gossip pertains to unsubstantiated and substantiated stories about specific individuals, and urban legends are unsubstantiated stories that persist over time. Widespread panic refers to shared fear, whereas moral panic describes irrational but widespread worry that certain groups pose a threat to the social order. Disasters are relatively sudden events that cause damage and disruption but often bring together collective relief efforts.

LO5 Explain how social movements are both similar to and different from collective behaviour and discuss the relevance of claims making for movement organizations.

Social movements and collective behaviour both include unconventional forms of group-based action. However, collective behaviour is spontaneous and unstructured, whereas social movements involve prior organization and planning. Social movements rest on the premise of claims making, which identifies a perceived social problem that the movement wishes to remedy, for example, by changing norms or resisting new ones, by seeking limited or massive changes, or through changes that affect only a small group versus the entire society.

LO6 Differentiate between alternative, redemptive, reform, and revolutionary social movements.

Alternative social movements seek limited societal change for a specific group. Redemptive social movements seek massive (or large-scale) changes for a specific group. Reformative social movements seek limited societal change, but the recipient of the change is everyone in society. Revolutionary social movements seek massive changes that affect everyone.

LO7 Compare theoretical views on the development of social movements.

In identifying factors that promote social action, value-added theory identifies the importance of structural conduciveness, structural strain, generalized beliefs, precipitating factors, mobilization for action, and a lack of social control; resource mobilization theory emphasizes resources over other structural factors; and new social movement theory emphasizes the formation of a collective identity.

RECOMMENDED RESOURCES

1. For an overview of the history and development of the Idle No More movement, see K. Coates, *#IDLENOMORE and the Remaking of Canada* (Regina, SK: University of Regina Press, 2015) or visit http://www.idlenomore.ca.
2. For an in-depth look at the emergence of historical and current social movements, refer to C. Tilly & S. Tarrow, *Contentious Politics* (2nd ed.) (New York, NY: Oxford University Press, 2015).
3. Canadian filmmaker Alanis Obomsawin spent the full 78 days on-site capturing the Oka Crisis in its entirety in the award-winning 1993 National Film Board documentary *Kanehsatake: 270 Years of Resistance*.
4. For a detailed overview of revolutionary movements (particularly of the 20th and 21st centuries), we recommend J. Defronzo, *Revolutions and Revolutionary Movements*, 5th ed. (Boulder, CO: Westview Press, 2014).

FOR FURTHER REFLECTION

1. List five current fads. How are these fads similar to and different from ones you participated in when you were younger? What are some factors that contribute to the end of a fad's popularity?
2. Think about the last time you heard a rumour or participated in spreading one. In what ways might a rumour be considered a functional form of collective behaviour?
3. Note that the Idle No More movement continues to host events that raise awareness and build support for its cause in various communities in the absence of identifiable leadership. In what ways might the development of a collective identity eliminate the need for a directive leader?

ENDNOTE

1 Retrieved June 15, 2017, from www.quotationspage.com.

CHAPTER 14

"Going Green": Environmental Sociology

ParabolStudio/Shutterstock

When we try to pick out anything by itself, we find it hitched to everything else in the universe.

(John Muir)[1]

LEARNING OBJECTIVES & OUTCOMES

After completing this chapter, students should be able to do the following:

LO1 Explain how social factors pose environmental challenges.

LO2 Provide an overview of the growing awareness of environmental issues.

LO3 Explain how the human exemptionalism and new ecological paradigms further our understanding of environmental issues.

LO4 Compare the assumptions underlying functionalist and critical approaches to the environment.

LO5 Demonstrate an understanding of strategies for making better environmental choices.

When you think of economic prosperity, what comes to mind? Are you able to readily conjure up items you could buy or activities you could do while "living the good life," such as purchasing a nice home complete with a multitude of electronic devices and a few new vehicles or travelling to exotic places for holidays? Indeed, very few of us think of the downside of economic prosperity in terms of fossil fuel consumption, the excessive use of water, the creation of pollution, and waste disposal. Until fairly recently, sociologists mainly viewed economic prosperity and technological advancement in terms of societal development toward improved living standards, better health, higher educational attainment, more global business opportunities, and greater social mobility. Less thought was given to the lasting negative implications for the environment in the form of resource depletion, land degradation, and climate change. Indigenous peoples and early environmentalists such as John Muir understood our connectedness with nature and called for environmental protection long before the formalization of environmental sociology (see *Sociology in Practice* to learn about a successful conservation effort spearheaded by Indigenous peoples).

Today, *environmental sociologists* study the interrelationships between societal issues and environmental concerns, including the impact of the human activity on the environment, and they make recommendations for preserving the planet. In this chapter, we explore social factors that pose environmental challenges, examine global environmental issues, look at the social construction of environmental issues, and discuss strategies for making better environmental choices.

LO1 SOCIAL FACTORS POSING ENVIRONMENTAL CHALLENGES

HUMAN OVERPOPULATION

Social factors begin with people. Researchers predict a global population of 9.7 billion by 2050 (Schlosser et al., 2014). This figure raises a central question that scientists, theorists, and **demographers** (people who study changes that affect human populations) are now trying to answer: *Exactly how many people can this planet sustain?* The concept of the "ecological footprint" was developed by Wackernagel and Rees (1996) as a means to gauge

Demography: The study of human populations.

the growing human population's needs relative to the planet's capacity to support those needs. An **ecological footprint** is the total area of land and water ecosystems a human population needs in order to produce the resources it consumes and to assimilate the wastes that the population generates, wherever on the Earth the land and water are located (Rees, 2013, p. 230).

According to the Global Footprint Network (2017b), the impact of human consumption is already greater than the Earth can sustain, largely due to overfishing, overharvesting, and the high emission of carbon dioxide. The Earth is beyond its carrying capacity (i.e., we use more resources and generate more waste than what can be regenerated), and humanity now needs 1.6 planets to sustain itself—a phenomenon called **ecological overshoot** (Catton, 1980). The World Wildlife Fund's (2012) *Living Planet Report* predicts that humanity will need two planets by 2030. Overshoot does not mean a sudden and dramatic end to life as we know it but rather the gradual degradation of ecological assets (fishing grounds, grazing lands, forests). Every country affects the ecological footprint by consuming renewable resources and generating waste. From an ecological standpoint, among the "worst" offenders are high-income countries, whose consumption footprints are well above the global average (Ewing et al., 2010). Canada has a high consumption footprint (8.8 global hectares per capita) but an even higher biocapacity (16.2 global hectares per capita), unlike the United States, which has a high rate of consumption (8.6) and a low biocapacity (3.8) (Global Footprint Network, 2017a, 2017c). Refer to *Figure 14.1* to see which countries have footprints that exceed their biocapacity and refer to *Sociology in My Life* to estimate your own personal carbon contributions.

Ecological footprint: An estimate for gauging the total area of land and water ecosystems a human population needs in order to produce the resources it consumes and to assimilate its wastes.

Ecological overshoot: Growth beyond the Earth's carrying capacity.

YOUR SOCIOLOGICAL TOOLKIT

SOCIOLOGY IN PRACTICE

WORLD WILDLIFE FUND CANADA'S CONSERVATION FIRST PRINCIPLE

World Wildlife Fund Canada (WWF-Canada) is a conservationist organization working to protect wildlife and to promote the sustainable use of resources along with the reduction of waste. A founding *Conservation First Principle* is that "there should be no new or expanded large-scale industrial development in Canada until a network of protected areas is reserved which adequately represents the natural region(s) affected by that development" (WWF-Canada, 2017b). In accordance with this principle, WWF-Canada assisted Indigenous groups with proposals that eventually led to the suspension of industrial activity in the Mackenzie River Basin area, enabling local groups to come up with permanent plans for establishing protected areas. Now deemed the biggest "conservation success" in Canada's history, more than 10 million hectares of wilderness are permanently protected (WWF-Canada, 2017a). The Mackenzie River Basin extends all the way from the Mackenzie River and Rocky Mountains in the west to the Canadian Shield in the east and includes boreal forest, alpine, and arctic tundra. The basin covers about 1.8 million square kilometres, comprising 20 percent of Canada's landmass, and includes nine lakes of over 1,000 square kilometres (e.g., Great Bear Lake, Great Slave Lake, and Lake Athabasca) (Mackenzie River Basin Board, 2003).

Gunter Marx/Alamy

The Mackenzie River Basin area.

FIGURE 14.1

The Ecological Wealth of Nations

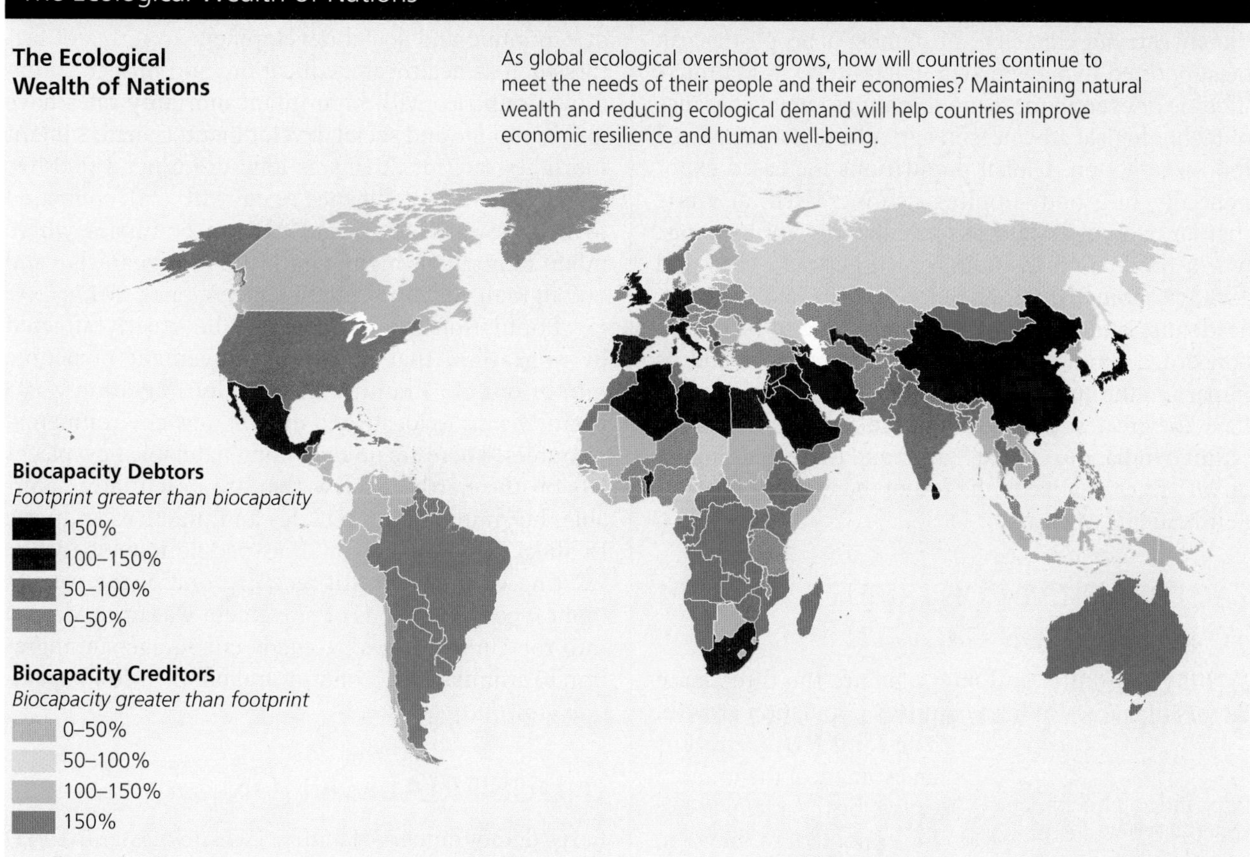

Source: Global Footprint Network, 2017. National Footprint Accounts, 2012 Edition. Found at: http://www.footprintnetwork.org.

Early demographer and political economist Thomas Robert Malthus (1766–1834), in *An Essay on the Principles of Population* (1798/1998), wrote about factors that limit population overgrowth; these included epidemics and famines. Malthus predicted that in the absence of certain "population checks," exponential population growth would exceed *the planet's* capacity in terms of food supply. **Population checks** include factors that help limit population growth, such as events

Carbon footprint: A method for identifying and keeping track of behaviours that negatively impact the environment through greenhouse gas production.

YOUR SOCIOLOGICAL TOOLKIT

SOCIOLOGY IN MY LIFE

HOW BIG IS YOUR ENVIRONMENTAL FOOTPRINT?

The notion of a **carbon footprint** was developed largely as a method for identifying and keeping track of human behaviours that negatively impact the environment through greenhouse gas production. You can calculate your own environmental footprint using one of the calculators provided at various sites online (e.g., refer to http://www.footprintnetwork.org/resources/footprint-calculator).

Think Outside the Box: Of the various potential contributors to your footprint (e.g., type of foods eaten on a weekly basis, mode of transportation), in which areas are you least environmentally responsible? Are these factors or conditions you can readily change? Why or why not?

that lead to deaths, including war or disease, and factors that prevent births, such as birth control and the postponement of childbearing.

The world's population did not grow beyond its **human carrying capacity** (the number of people that can be supported in a given area indefinitely) in Malthus's lifetime or even in more modern times, largely because of technological advances in agriculture that increased food production. Global populations increased exponentially, but food supplies also increased, at a rate that far exceeded Malthus's calculations; for example, wheat production in India tripled between 1965 and 1980 (Robbins Hintz, & Moore, 2010). Nonetheless, academics and scientists today continue to be deeply concerned about sustained population growth and its impact on the environment, especially in countries that have the greatest proportion of the world's inhabitants (China, India, the United States) and those with higher growth rates relative to the rest of the world (Lebanon, South Sudan, Malawi).

FACTORS THAT CONTRIBUTE TO POPULATION GROWTH

Fertility, *mortality*, and *migration* are the three main factors that account for a country's population growth. The **total fertility rate** is an estimate of the number of live births a female can be expected to have in her lifetime (Statistics Canada, 2015). Canada's total fertility rate for 2016 was 1.6 (Central Intelligence Agency, 2017c). This is low, and it indicates that women today are having very few children. In Canada, there are also fewer women in their childbearing years relative to older age groups (i.e., Canada has an aging population). The highest birth rate in the world is in Niger, where the total fertility rate is 6.6 and the median age is 18.3 (compared to 42.0 in Canada) (Central Intelligence Agency, 2017b, 2017c).

Mortality is influenced by factors that promote longevity (access to clean water, proper nutrition, and healthcare) as well as factors that reduce life expectancy (diseases or widespread unrest, as in the case of civil war). The **infant mortality rate** is the best measure of a country's level of economic and social development in terms of factors such as healthcare, education, and proper sanitation. Countries with high infant mortality rates have low economic and social development. Canada's infant mortality rate for 2016 was low, at 4.6 per 1,000 live births (Central Intelligence Agency, 2017a), compared to many South Asian and African countries where infant mortality is high (e.g., 112.8 in Afghanistan and 100 in Mali) (Central Intelligence Agency, 2017a).

Population growth can also be greatly affected by **migration**, that is, by the movement of people into or out of a country. Historically, migration was a useful means to locate and inhabit new environmental resources. There are no remaining habitable new places left on the Earth and few that are potentially habitable, but immigration policies and practices continue to affect population growth as people move between existing countries (until recently, one of the world's highest concentrations of movement was from Mexico into the United States). Canada encourages immigration to stimulate its economy and offset its *low population growth rate*.

Population checks: Factors that limit population growth.

Human carrying capacity: The number of people that can be supported in a given area indefinitely.

Total fertility rate: The number of live births a female can be expected to have in her lifetime.

Infant mortality rate: The incidence of deaths among infants under one year of age per 1,000 live births in a given population.

Migration: The movement of people into or out of a country.

Demographic transition theory: As a result of modernization, societies eventually progress from being characterized by high fertility and mortality rates to being characterized by low fertility and mortality rates.

INDUSTRIALIZATION

Early demographers (Landry, 1934; Notestein, 1945) introduced the notion of a demographic transition, which later became known as **demographic transition theory**. This theory explains changes in populations as countries progress from premodern societies with high birth and death rates to modern ones characterized by low birth and death rates (Kirk, 1996), as shown in *Figure 14.2*.

Largely due to the Industrial Revolution (which began in Europe in the late 1700s, spread to North America in the 1800s, and is still advancing throughout the world), countries experienced tremendous economic growth and innovation in many sectors (e.g., textile manufacturing, iron production, steam power). These innovations led to other massive societal changes, such as the growth of cities, the development of an industrial workforce, the reliance on child labour, and the accumulation of capital; all of these furthered economic development cycles (e.g., the introduction of new industries, such as steel and petroleum) and spawned subsequent changes in cultural values and practices (e.g., healthcare, family planning). Although economic growth and social development vary considerably from country to country, fertility and mortality trends are strikingly close to what is predicted by demographic transition theory.

FIGURE 14.2

The Demographic Transition Model of Development

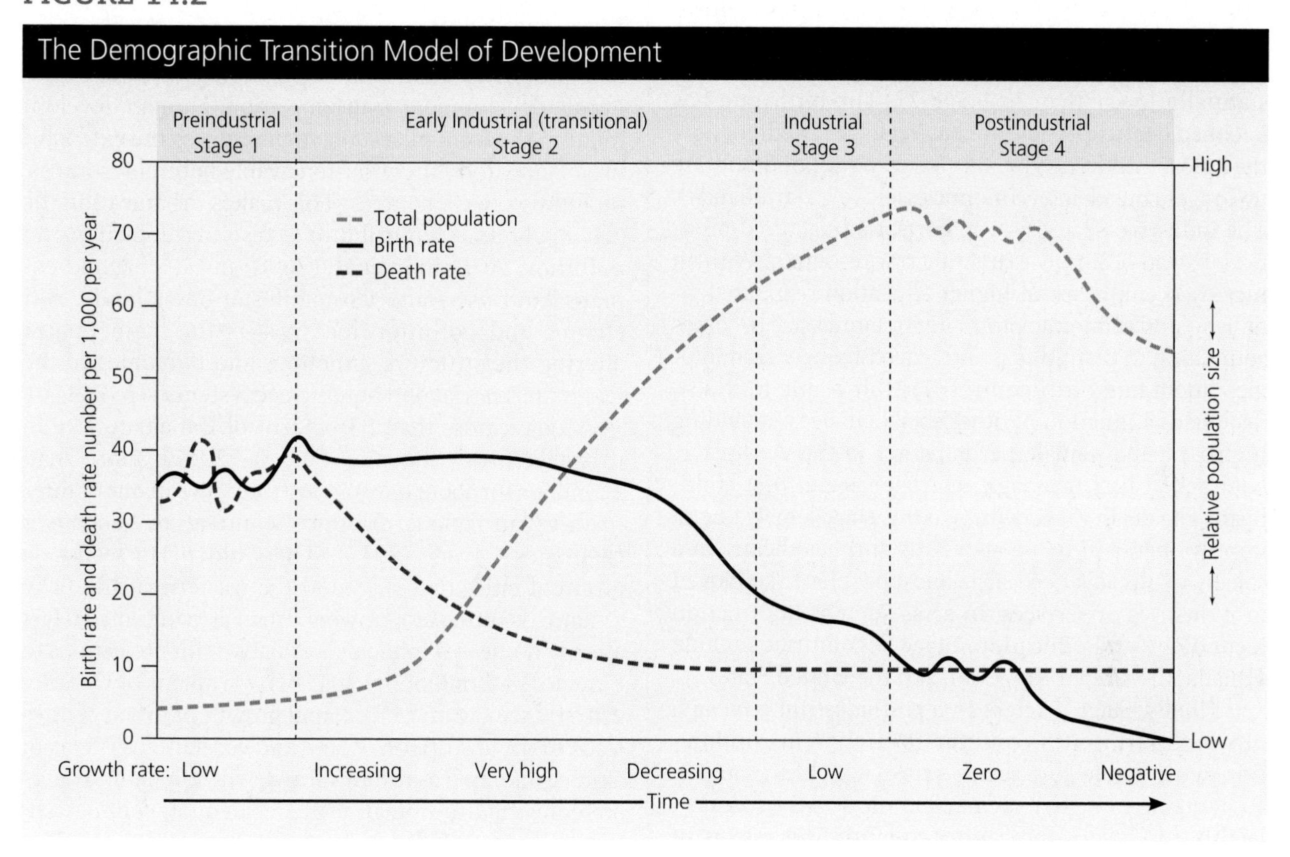

Source: From DRAPER/REED. *Our Environment*, 4E. © 2009 Nelson Education Ltd. Reproduced by permission. www.cengage.com/permissions

In Stage 1 of the demographic transition, we find *preindustrial societies* (those with entirely agriculture-based economies), in which fertility rates are high in order to offset correspondingly high infant mortality rates. High birth rates reflect a lack of family planning (e.g., the absence of contraception) in conjunction with a need to supply labour for agricultural subsistence; a need to repopulate, given low life expectancy; and a need to care for the elderly in the absence of social safety nets. Mortality is high for various reasons, such as inadequate healthcare, lack of sanitation, deficient education, and famine, drought, and disease. Stage 1, then, is characterized by high and highly fluctuating birth and death rates, resulting in very little overall population growth. All countries in existence today have progressed past this stage; however, there are still agriculture-based villages within countries (e.g., Peru, Brazil), and some countries retain many preindustrial qualities such as limited education and poor healthcare, especially for women (e.g., Afghanistan). In addition, some preindustrial societies (e.g., early Polynesian societies) collapsed altogether before reaching the second stage after a period of population growth that too quickly depleted the natural environment (Diamond, 2000)—a small-scale version of the fate described by Malthus.

Stage 2 societies are characterized by *early industrialization*. In these, the beginnings of industrialization are reflected in improved crop cultivation, education, and healthcare. Population growth continues with the introduction of more machinery, innovations such as fertilizers and pesticides, and the widespread extraction of resources, such as fossil fuels. Early industrialization is marked by population growth as a result of high birth rates alongside corresponding *lowered* death rates. Stage 2 developing countries can be found in East and Southeast Asia (Afghanistan, Bangladesh, Jordan) but especially in Africa, where we find countries with some of the highest overall growth rates in the world (Zimbabwe, Malawi, Niger). Other countries (Mexico, Brazil, India, Turkey) have advanced economies with modest birth rates that straddle the line between Stage 2 and Stage 3.

Stage 3 refers to *advanced (or mature) industrialization*. This corresponds to a *declining birth rate* coupled with an already reduced death rate, which results in only a slight increase in population growth (i.e., substantially lower than in Stage 2). The birth rate has declined because people are having fewer children, now that most children now survive to adulthood and are no longer considered economic assets (e.g., farmhands). The industrial sector now exports manufactured products instead of simply extracting raw resources. With an increased emphasis on higher education (e.g., credentialism) and economic productivity, family size becomes something to plan; this is influenced by new technologies, including birth control. The birth rate may also decline as a function of other social changes, including higher rates of female participation in the workplace, later age at first marriage, and later age at first childbirth. The death rate declines in this stage largely due to improvements in living standards and healthcare. In a society in this advanced stage, most people are employed in industries or services, in areas such as information technology and education. Stage 3 countries include Canada, the United Kingdom, and the United States.

Finally, Stage 4 refers to *a postindustrial economy*, in which birth rates continue to decline in conjunction with stable low death rates, which are largely attributable to higher socioeconomic status or wealth, health, education, and gender equality. This results in *zero* population growth or even a declining population. Postindustrial societies tend to be service based; much of the working population is employed in areas such as finance, healthcare, or sales rather than in industry. Countries that have completed the demographic transition to Stage 4 include Italy, Germany, Belgium, and Sweden.

Urban sprawl:
A process by which rapid urban growth necessitates the conversion of natural land for human-made uses.

URBAN SPRAWL

URBANIZATION

A logical consequence of population growth and economic development is urbanization. Human development in the form of *urbanization* requires the extensive use of land and other non-renewable natural resources, including energy sources. This makes urbanization the principal human contributor to resource depletion and pollution. As Grimm et al. (2008) put it, "beyond climate, land use—and its manifestation as land-cover change and pollution loading—is the major factor altering the structure, function, and dynamics of the Earth's terrestrial and aquatic ecosystems" (p. 264).

Today, more than 83 percent of Canadians live in urban centres (Statistics Canada, 2017); more than 12 million, or about one in every three, live in one of three main urban regions: Toronto, Montréal, or Vancouver (Statistics Canada, 2017). The Golden Horseshoe, a group of cities that surround the western end of Lake Ontario, is the fastest growing urban area in Canada. It is already home to 9 million Canadians, with projections to grow to 13.5 million by 2041 (Government of Ontario, 2016a) (see *Figure 14.3*). Rapid growth of urban centres leads to the absorption of land and coastal ecosystems in a process known as **urban sprawl**, wherein natural lands are converted to human uses (residential, commercial, transportation). Urban centres and the areas surrounding them become the main hubs for activities that contribute to global pollution (Wali, Evrendilek, & Fennessy, 2010).

OVERCONSUMPTION OF RESOURCES

In countries that have reached advanced stages of industrial development, much of the population is concentrated in and around large urban centres,

SOCIOLOGY ONLINE

DESMOG CANADA

Desmog Canada is a nonprofit society that provides an online news forum on issues dealing with energy and the environment. Here you can learn more about how major developments in the oil and gas industry negatively impact Canada's environment and can share your views and opinions. You can also find out about new directions in the energy sector. For example, Saskatchewan is the first province to sign an agreement for the development of geothermal power. Geothermal power is a renewable and zero-emission process whereby water heated by the Earth's core is used to activate a generator that produces electricity (SaskPower, 2017). See https://www.desmog.ca.

FIGURE 14.3

Map of the Golden Horseshoe

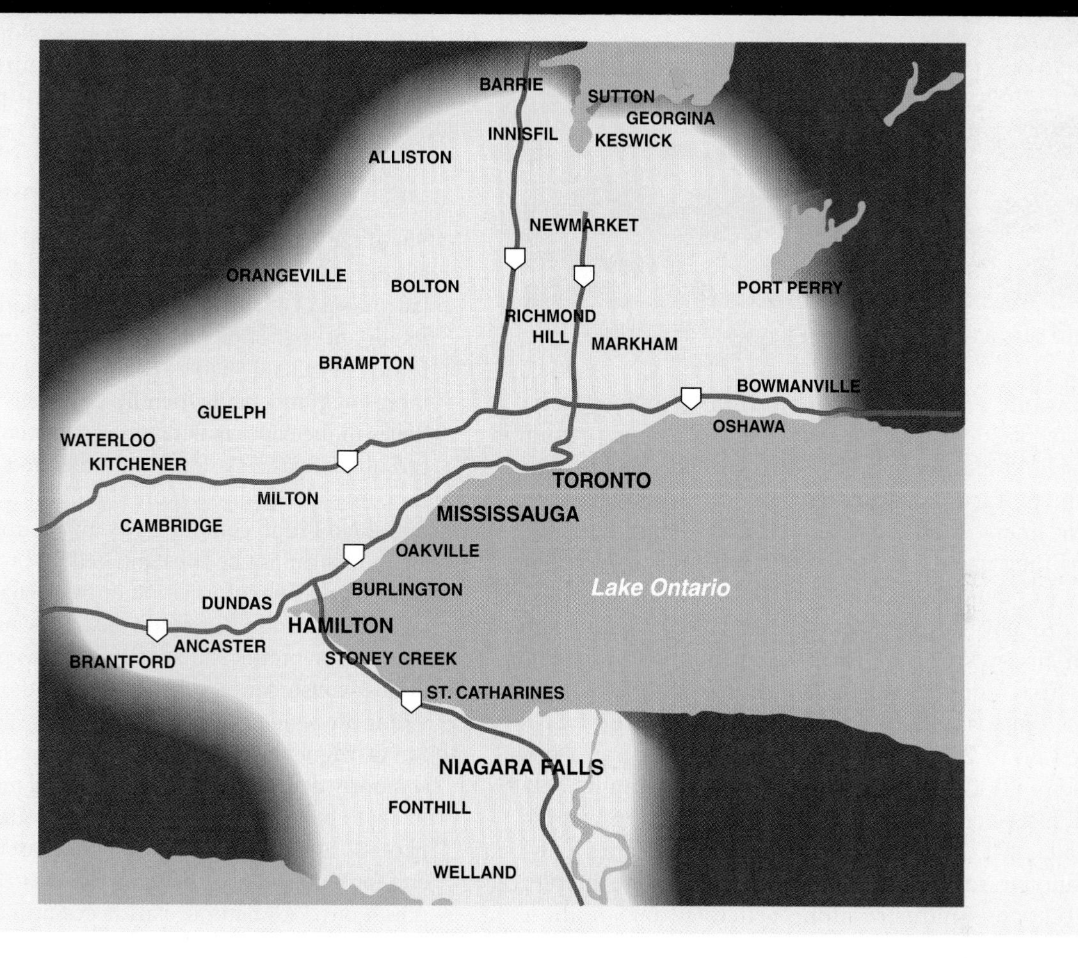

where inhabitants exhibit excessively high levels of consumption, a phenomenon known as *overconsumption*. **Consumption** refers to the general use of natural resources as people go about their daily lives; **overconsumption** refers to the use of resources at a rate that exceeds **sustainability** (i.e., the use of natural resources at a rate on par with natural replenishment). There are vast differences in the rates of consumption between developed and developing countries. For example, the average North American consumes the equivalent of about 90 kilograms of resources per day eating, drinking, driving, and in relation to housing relative to the average African, who consumes only about 10 kilograms per day (Sustainable Europe Research Institute, Friends of the Earth Austria, and Friends of the Earth Europe, 2009). This means that North Americans contribute considerably more to the emissions that produce air pollution and global climate change.

DISPOSABLE SOCIETIES

When was the last time you ordered takeout food? Did you purchase your last new cellphone because you lost the old one or it no longer worked, or did you simply decide one day to "upgrade" in order to keep up with the latest trend? Advanced industrial societies are distinguished by an overabundance of material culture, especially in the form of technologies (televisions, computers, cellphones, etc.) that are used for only a short time and then thrown away; this has contributed to the creation of

Consumption: The general use of natural resources.

Overconsumption: Use of natural resources at a rate on par with natural replenishment.

Sustainability: Use of natural resources at a rate on par with natural replenishment.

moodboard/Thinkstock

Landfill sites are heavily relied on for waste disposal.

disposable societies. From electronics to food containers, plastic packaging, bags, and storage wrap, from household cleaning and dusting products to hygiene products, razor blades, and baby products (diapers, bottle liners, food, and wipes), Canadians purchase items they use for only a short time and then throw away. Residential solid waste makes up about one-third of the total waste disposal in Canada, and the rest comes from non-residential (non-hazardous) waste from industrial, commercial, and institutional sectors (Statistics Canada, 2012). Canada's residential solid waste added up to 25,871,310 tonnes or 777 kilograms per person in 2008, most of which was picked up by collection services and sent on to landfill sites (Statistics Canada, 2012). During the same year, industries' contribution to solid waste was considerable. For example, the oil sands industry alone generated 645 million tonnes from surface mining and another 547 million tonnes through sand tailing (Statistics Canada, 2012).

GREENWASHING

Marketers have tried to address society's growing awareness of the need to reduce consumption by claiming that their products are *environmentally friendly* or *organic*. This is meant to entice you to keep consuming at your usual rate, guilt-free, by purchasing "green" brands. "Environmentally friendly" is generally taken to mean that a product or service was developed with minimal harm to the environment; "organic" usually means that the item was produced without chemicals such as pesticides or hormones. In 2007, an Ottawa-based environmental marketing firm examined 2,739 "green" products in Canada and the United States and found that the vast majority (98 percent) failed to live up to their green claims, committing at least one of the "seven sins of greenwashing" (Sadler, 2010). **Greenwashing** refers to the "misleading of consumers regarding the environmental practices of a company or the environmental benefits of a product or service" (TerraChoice, 2009, p. 1).

Disposable societies: Societies characterized by an excess of manufactured products that are used for only a short period of time and then disposed of.

Greenwashing: Misleading consumers regarding the environmental practices of a company or the environmental benefits of a product or service.

These are the "seven sins of greenwashing":

1. **Sin of the Hidden Tradeoff**, committed by suggesting a product is "green" based on an unreasonably narrow set of attributes, without attention to other important environmental issues. For example, paper from a sustainably harvested forest is not necessarily more environmentally friendly. Other environmental issues in the paper-making process, including energy, greenhouse gas emissions, and water and air pollution, may be equally or more significant.
2. **Sin of No Proof**, committed by an environmental claim that cannot be substantiated by easily accessible supporting information or by a reliable third-party certification. Common examples are facial or toilet tissue products that claim various percentages of post-consumer recycled content without providing any evidence.
3. **Sin of Vagueness**, committed by every claim that is so poorly defined or broad that its real meaning is likely to be misunderstood by the consumer. "All-natural" is an example. Arsenic, uranium, mercury, and formaldehyde are all naturally occurring, and poisonous. "All natural" isn't necessarily "green."
4. **Sin of Irrelevance**, committed by making an environmental claim that may be truthful but is unimportant or unhelpful for consumers seeking environmentally preferable products. "CFC-free" is a common example, since it is a frequent claim despite the fact that CFCs are banned by law.

TerraChoice, The Sins of Greenwashing and Family Edition 2010: A Report on Environmental Claims Made In the North American Consumer Market. © [2014] UL LLC. Reprinted with permission.

5. **Sin of Lesser of Two Evils**, committed by claims that may be true within the product category, but that risk distracting the consumer from the greater environmental impacts of the category as a whole. Organic cigarettes are an example of this category, as are fuel-efficient sport-utility vehicles.
6. **Sin of Fibbing**, the least frequent Sin, is committed by making environmental claims that are simply false. The most common examples were products falsely claiming to be Energy Star certified or registered.
7. **Sin of Worshipping False Labels** is committed by a product that, through either words or images, gives the impression of third-party endorsement where no such endorsement actually exists. (TerraChoice, 2010, p. 10)*

*TerraChoice, *The Sins of Greenwashing and Family Edition 2010: A Report on Environmental Claims Made In the North American Consumer Market.*

The same firm conducted follow-up studies on products in 24 stores in North America in 2009 and 2010 and found that although green offerings had increased by 73 percent (to 4,744 products), misrepresentation of environmentally friendly practices had declined only slightly (95 percent of the products still included some form of greenwashing). This indicated a persistent use of greenwashing techniques. Interestingly, Rona, Canada's largest hardware distributor and retailer, was identified as a leader in legitimate green retailing (TerraChoice, 2010). To familiarize yourself with eco-labels that refer to good environmental products and practices, refer to *Table 14.1*.

TABLE 14.1

A Sample of Eco-Label Names

GENERAL INFORMATION PROCESS			CERTIFICATION OR LABELLING			
Eco-Label Name and Website	**Year Founded**	**Product Categories**	**Life Cycle-Based***	**Third-Party Certified**	**Publicly Available Standard**	**Transparent Standard Development Process**
EcoCert www .ecocert.com	2000	Organic ingredients	Single issue (organic certification)	√	√	√
EcoLogo www. ecologo.org	1988	Health and beauty products, cleaning products, home products, office products, electronics, building/construction products	√	√	√	√
Energy Star www.energystar. gov	1992	Home products, building and construction products, electronics	Single issue (energy efficiency)		√	√
EPEAT www. epeat.net	2005	Electronics	√		√	√
Green Seal www. greenseal.org	1989	Cleaning products, office products, building/construction products	√	√	√	√
WaterSense www.epa.gov/ WaterSense	2006	Home products, building/construction products	Single issue (saving water)	√	√	√

*Life cycle-based eco-labels consider the environmental impacts from all phases of a product's life including the raw materials, the manufacturing process, the product itself, its distribution and use, and its ultimate disposal (or recycling/reuse).

Source: TerraChoice, *The Sins of Greenwashing and Family Edition 2010: A Report on Environmental Claims Made In the North American Consumer Market.*

TIME TO REVIEW

- What are the four main social contributors to environmental problems?
- What factors contribute most to population growth?
- What kind of rate is a good indicator of a country's economic and social development?
- How does urban sprawl pose implications for the natural environment?
- What are some of the common forms that greenwashing takes?

LO2 GROWING AWARENESS OF ENVIRONMENTAL ISSUES

Sociological interest in the environment can be largely traced back to the 1960s and 1970s, when it was becoming evident that social and economic factors posed challenges for the natural environment. During those decades, scientists, conservationists, and early environmental sociologists focused largely on air and water pollution, waste management, urban improvement, and wildlife conservation (Dunlap, Michelson, & Stalkers, 2002). The *Sierra Club* (a grassroots environmental organization founded by American conservationist John Muir) became active in Canada in 1963; *World Wildlife Fund Canada* was founded in 1967; and the first *Earth Day* was held in the United States on April 22, 1970 (this event is now celebrated annually by more than a billion people, including Canadians). *Greenpeace*, an international organization dedicated to increasing awareness of environmental issues through direct action and government lobbying, set out on its first anti-nuclear voyage in 1971 from Vancouver. The Canadian government established the *Department of the Environment* in 1971; the United Nations launched the *United Nations Environment Programme* in 1972.

Steve Byland/Shutterstock

Hundreds of species of boreal birds can be found in the boreal forest of northern Canada. The Rusty Blackbird breeds in the boreal forest, but due to deforestation and habitat loss, it has declined by about 90 percent since 1970 and is now considered a species at risk (Wildlife Conservation Society Canada, 2017).

THE FIRST WAVE OF ENVIRONMENTALISM

The first wave of environmentalism in the 1960s and 1970s highlighted the negative implications of industrialization and population growth by drawing people's attention to various forms of pollution, resource depletion, and environmental disasters in the form of oil spills and energy shortages. Pesticides, for example, had been developed to control organisms that interfere with agriculture. Although some of the early forms were biodegradable (i.e., they contained compounds that would eventually break down), most of the more effective "second-generation" pesticides were non-biodegradable and contained damaging toxic substances. Dichlorodiphenyltrichloroethane (DDT) was one such chemical; it was first developed to be a "miracle-compound: highly toxic to insects, virtually insoluble in water, and of low toxicity to mammals," but after many years of use, its environmental and human risks became more readily apparent, and it was reframed as one of the "dirty dozen" of "persistent organic pollutants." That is the common term for chemicals that stay "intact in the environment for long periods, become widely distributed geographically, accumulate in the fatty tissue of living organisms, and are toxic to humans and wildlife" (Wali et al., 2010, p. 245).

Similar lessons were learned about many highly convenient but ozone-depleting substances, including chlorofluorocarbons (CFCs), which are commonly associated with aerosol sprays (cooking spray, hair sprays, cleaning products) but are also part of blowing agents for plastic foam packaging and are most often used as cooling agents in refrigerators and air conditioners. Consider how many refrigerators there are just in Canada! When CFCs are released into the air, as happens when products containing them are disposed of, they can persist long enough to be broken down in a chemical reaction that contributes to ozone depletion (Draper, 1998).

Many of the early efforts to manage environmental issues (especially air pollution) were "band-aid solutions" that focused mainly on technological innovations, such as the use of pumps rather than aerosol sprays and specialized filters on power plants, as well as auto engine modifications to reduce harmful emissions. But these supposed solutions actually created other environmental problems (such as the need to dispose of hazardous waste) or failed to address the broader issue of energy reform (i.e., the need to discontinue the use of CFC as a coolant, to construct fewer power plants, and to drive less, especially in urban areas). In more cases than not, increased production continues to override the benefits of emission efficiency measures (Cheremisinoff, 1992).

THE SECOND WAVE OF ENVIRONMENTALISM

In the 1980s, it became clear that human consumption and development—including industries such as forestry, mining, fisheries, and transportation—were contributing to new and potentially greater environmental threats in the form of ozone depletion, acid rain, and global warming. In 1985, an "ozone hole" was discovered in the Antarctic, and representatives from various countries gathered at the Vienna *Convention for the Protection of the Ozone Layer* to discuss research on ozone depletion as a worldwide environmental issue. Note that the ozone hole wasn't a hole in the literal sense; rather, it was socially constructed as such when ozone depletion above the Antarctic turned out to be far greater than what scientists had predicted. An international agreement was reached in 1987 called the *Montreal Protocol on Substances That Deplete the Ozone Layer*, which called for the phasing out of production of most of the known ozone-depleting compounds (CFCs, halons, methyl chloroform). The agreement was signed by 24 countries responsible for more than 80 percent of the world's consumption (Hernan, 2010; United Nations Environment Programme, 2000).

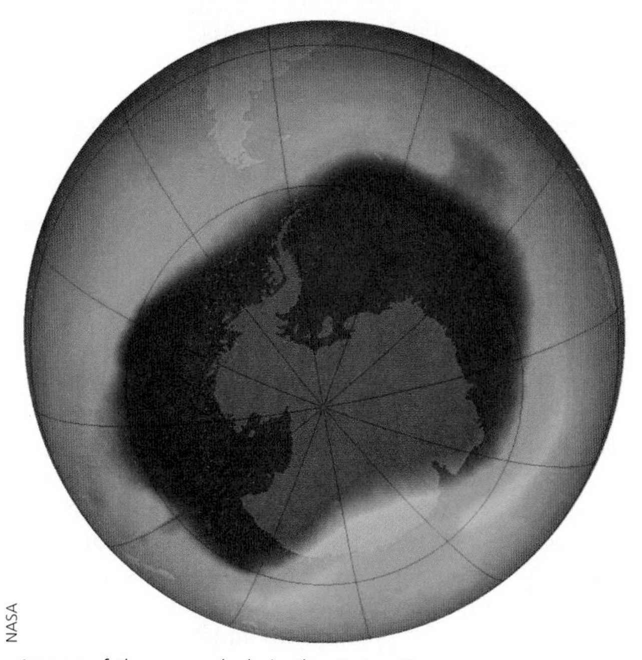
NASA

Image of the ozone hole in the Antarctic.

Scientists and environmentalists were now also teaching the public about acid rain as a major contributor to air, land, and water pollution. **Acid rain** refers to the dilute sulphuric and nitric acids that, many believe, are created when fossil fuels such as coal and oil are burned in power stations, smelters, and motor vehicles. Those acids then fall over areas long distances downwind of their possible sources (Park, 1992, p. 1). It was first believed that these pollutants would reach the Earth's surface only if they mixed with water—hence the term "acid rain." But those acids were later discovered in hail and snow and even in dry forms, such as dust. Increased acidity damages aquatic ecosystems—for example, it is highly toxic to fish and other forms of biological life found in lakes. It also affects soils, and this in turn affects plant life. And it is considered a contributor to forest degradation. Acid rain also contributes to air pollution and to health problems associated with inhaling acid aerosols, besides reducing air quality more generally (Environment Canada, 1998; Houle, 2004; Kahan, 1986; Kahaner, 1988; Leaf, 1990; Raloff, 1988; Schindler, 1988).

Global warming (or climate change) refers to the heating of the Earth's atmosphere and is often explained using the analogy of how warming occurs in a greenhouse. A greenhouse traps warmer air inside it; in roughly the same way, air pollutants such as carbon dioxide form a covering above the Earth's surface, thus trapping heat. This heating is intensified by ozone depletion because solar energy (in the form of ultraviolet rays) now enters the atmosphere in even higher concentrations but is less readily transmitted back out, having been trapped by pollution-based gases in the lower part of the stratosphere. The result is an increase in the Earth's temperature, long-term changes to weather patterns, and increased sea levels. If current trends continue, the world's surface temperature is predicted to rise more than 3 degrees this century (United Nations, 2017) (see *Critical Thinking in Action* for more information on the outcomes of climate change).

Since the 1990s, more and more people are

Acid rain: The dilute sulphuric and nitric acids created when fossil fuels are burned.

Global warming: An increase in the temperature of the Earth's atmosphere.

CRITICAL THINKING IN ACTION

INTERGOVERNMENTAL PANEL ON CLIMATE CHANGE

The Intergovernmental Panel on Climate Change (IPCC), established by the United Nations Environment Programme and the World Meteorological Organization, is a collective and consensus-reaching scientific body for assessing research on climate change. IPCC's major function is to "provide policymakers with regular assessments of the scientific basis of climate change, its impacts and future risks, and options for adaptation and mitigation" (IPCC, 2017). The IPCC notes that global warming is most apparent over the past 50 years, has negatively impacted ecological systems, and, in the absence of mitigating factors, will continue to do so. Some of the especially salient negative implications include an increased risk of extinction among certain plant and animal species and an increased vulnerability of many regions to extreme weather conditions such as heat waves and floods.

A recent review of the evidence on climate change indicates that we are now undergoing a large-scale "climate-driven redistribution of species" wherein various marine, terrestrial, and freshwater species are relocating to environments that most closely approximate the ones they have lost to climate changes (e.g., those preferring cooler temperatures are moving to higher elevations on land or deeper depths to reach colder waters below sea). These shifts have positive and negative implications for all species (including humans) as new interactions in ecosystem feedbacks develop, whereas other necessary interactions are interrupted (Pecl et al., 2017). Humans are likely to be especially impacted by shifts that affect food supplies (e.g., fish, crops) and increase the propensity for diseases (e.g., mosquitoes carrying malaria and dengue) (Pecl et al., 2017).

Think Outside the Box: In what ways does industry contribute to climate change? How do industry practices pose challenges for individuals who are trying to live "greener" lives?

"It's just their little way of saying, 'Sorry we wrecked the planet.'"

realizing that environmental problems such as water pollution, deforestation, overcultivation, soil degradation, and loss of habitat are threatening the survival of life on the Earth. For example, although this planet has substantial water reserves, most of that water is ocean salt water; less than 3 percent by volume is fresh water (Wali et al., 2010). Moreover, much of the fresh water is hidden away in frozen glaciers, leaving more than 1.1 billion people worldwide without access to fresh water and twice that many facing insecurity intermittently (World Wildlife Fund, 2017). Agriculture also faces a severe shortage of fresh water, and access to safe drinking water will be an even greater issue for at least two-thirds of the world's population by 2025 if the current trends in population growth, urbanization, and consumption continue (United Nations, 2009).

In addition to all of this, the endless search for energy sources and minerals has led to competition and even war within and between countries for nonrenewable resources. This has implications in terms of depletion and degradation; furthermore, resource extraction processes are highly polluting in themselves (atmospheric pollution, toxic waste) (Wali et al., 2010).

The shortage of crude oil, for example, has led to the search for alternative energy sources. A leading alternative to oil today comes from Alberta in the form of *bituminous sands*, more often referred to as "oil sands" (because oil is extracted from the soil) or "tar sands" (because of their resemblance to tar-covered sand). The process for extracting oil from bituminous sands generates much more greenhouse gases than conventional oil extraction.

The consequences of oil spills, chemical leaks, and hazardous waste disposal can be even more serious. This has led to the study of "risk societies" and of "megahazards," defined as disasters that are the end result of human actions. The term **environmental refugee** (or *climate refugee*) is now widely used to describe the forced migration that results from life-endangering natural and human-made environmental change (Boano, Zetter, & Morris, 2008). The label applies as readily to survivors of floods and hurricanes as it does to those affected by exposure to industrial disasters such as poisonous gases and radiation leaks. More than 19.3 million people in 100 countries were displaced in 2014 as a result of disasters. Asia was the hardest hit, with most displacement in China, India, and the Philippines largely attributable to weather-related disasters including floods, earthquakes, and volcanic eruptions (Internal Displacement Monitoring Centre, 2015).

TIME TO REVIEW

- What issues were focal concerns of the first wave of environmentalists?
- What issues and concerns distinguish the second wave of environmentalism from the first?

YOUR SOCIOLOGICAL TOOLKIT
SOCIOLOGY IN THEORY

ENVIRONMENTAL SOCIOLOGY

Environmental sociology as a subdiscipline of sociology tends to be more empirical than theory driven. This is in part because environmental sociology originated as an approach to the study of environmental issues rather than of the relationships between society and the natural environment (Dunlap & Catton, 1979). Classical sociology began as a study of such things as population growth, urbanization, and capitalist expansion. For example, Karl Marx emphasized economics and productivity; Herbert Spencer spoke of consumption in terms of survival of the fittest; and human ecology perspectives (Park and Burgess) explained the growth of cities (Buttel & Humphrey, 2002).

LO3 HUMAN EXEMPTIONALISM AND NEW ECOLOGICAL PARADIGMS

Early environmental sociologists pointed out that theoretical debate is lacking because the physical environment is largely viewed as separate and distinct from human society. Society's impact on the natural environment has sometimes been viewed as "inconsequential" (Petty et al., 2007). William R. Catton and Riley Dunlap (1978) contended that most early sociological theories tended to be human centred, or based in **anthropocentrism**—a view of the world that places humans above all other forms of life in terms of value and importance. This framing notion is best captured by what Catton and Dunlap (1978) called the *Human Exceptionalism Paradigm*, now more commonly called the **Human Exemptionalism Paradigm (HEP)**, which refers to the tendency to consider humans as unique from other organisms in the natural world because of their capacity to reason and develop culture.

In relation to environmental issues, HEP

Environmental refugee: A person who is forced to flee his or her country as a result of environmental displacement resulting from life-endangering natural and human-made environmental change.

Anthropocentrism: A world view that considers humans to be the most important form of life.

Human Exemptionalism Paradigm (HEP): The view of humans as unique from other organisms in the natural world because of their capacity to reason and develop culture.

"THERE'S NINETY-NINE ZILLION OF US, AND THEY THINK THEY'RE RUNNING THINGS."

assumes that humans have the ability to overcome problems through technological innovation. Unfortunately, this kind of thinking perpetuates the propensity to believe that humans are somehow exempt from environmental constraints. Williams (2007) argues that even if we reject the assertion that we are independent of the natural environment, we persist in believing that we have features, such as the ability to reason, that make us "exceptional." Because of this, we end up "taking the world for granted"—that is, we assume that we can always come up with technological solutions and that people will readily follow through on those solutions. In reality, however, both assumptions probably amount to little more than wishful thinking. After all, you might realize you are harming the environment in various ways, but how willing are you to change and how much are you willing to forgo indefinitely in order to preserve the environment for future generations? To learn about events designed to raise public awareness about environmental and social justice issues, see *Sociology in My Community*.

New Ecological Paradigm (NEP): The view of humans as possessing a superior capacity to reason and adapt to social/cultural conditions while also recognizing the interdependence between humans and the natural environment.

Catton and Dunlap also identified a competing environmental paradigm that developed as a critique of HEP and its early failure to study human–environment interrelations, called the *New Ecological Paradigm*. The **New Ecological Paradigm (NEP)** highlights the superior capacity of humans to reason and adapt to social/cultural conditions while also recognizing the interdependence between humans and the natural environment. This paradigm does not assume that technology can solve all problems because it recognizes that there is a feedback loop with nature whereby human actions can have unintended consequences and that the natural environment consists of limited resources (Catton & Dunlap, 1980).

Overall, the HEP is especially useful for identifying why environmental concerns were lacking in sociology: the focus was on humans as separate and distinct from the environment. The NEP was instrumental in pointing out that the environment had been left out by the classical theorists and that it was important to consider the interrelationships between society and the finite natural environment.

YOUR SOCIOLOGICAL TOOLKIT

SOCIOLOGY IN MY COMMUNITY

BE THE CHANGE FILM SERIES

Once a month, the Blue Mountain Watershed Trust Foundation and Elephant Thoughts host *Be The Change Film Series* in Collingwood, Ontario, where community members can view documentaries and learn more about environmental and social justice issues such as overfishing, sustainability, and overreliance on oil. Recent films shown that serve as excellent resources include the following:

- *Koneline* (2016) is an art film about the beauty of British Columbia set in the Tahltan First Nation of northern British Columbia. Visit https://www.canadawildproductions.com.
- *After the Last River* (2015) traces the struggles of the poverty-stricken community of Attawapiskat in the wake of a resource-rich mine on its territory. Visit http://www.afterthelastrivermovie.com.
- *Occupy Love* (2014) explores activist movements against corporate greed and discusses evolving social change based on more sustainable alternative economic systems. Visit http://occupylove.org.
- *Misconception* (2014) is a portrait of three lives deeply affected by their countries' family planning policies. Visit https://www.participantmedia.com.

Think Outside the Box: Are there any public awareness campaigns or events in your community that help people learn about environmental or social justice issues? If so, describe them. If not, can you describe a movie you have seen that helped you learn more about an environmental issue?

LO4 FUNCTIONALIST PERSPECTIVES: ECOLOGICAL MODERNIZATION

Functionalist approaches to the study of the environment emerged in the 1980s. They were based on an assumption that humans, industry, and the environment can coexist provided that everyone (politicians, industry management, environmentalists) works together to protect the environment for the collective good of society. This movement, collectively known as *ecological modernization*, encompasses many global efforts to promote greening practices, including energy reforms, energy-efficiency regulations, sustainability efforts, the phasing out of hazardous chemicals, improved methods for dealing with waste, and new forms of environmental governance. For example, functionalists advocate for alternative and more efficient fuel sources, such as solar and wind energy in developed countries and bioenergy (burning plants and agricultural waste) in developing countries, to help reduce oil and coal consumption.

CRITICAL PERSPECTIVES: THE TREADMILL OF PRODUCTION

Whereas functionalists focus on the interconnectedness of people and the environment and the need for everyone to work toward energy-efficient alternatives, critical theorists point to important ways in which societal and environmental dynamics differ. Thus, American sociologist Schnaiberg (1980) notes that "whereas the ecosystem reaches a steady-state by permitting the growth of just enough species and populations to offset the surplus [energy], societies tend to use the surplus to *accumulate* still more surplus in future periods" (p. 19, emphasis in original). Schnaiberg describes the incessant need to increase production and profit as a treadmill of production. In accordance with a Marxist paradigm, the **treadmill of production** places the economy at the heart of decision making. Schnaiberg's model also identifies two environmental concerns that became apparent in the second half of the 20th century with the growth of modern factories:

1. *High extraction of natural resources.* Modern factories required substantial capital, which was invested in machinery, which largely replaced workers and necessitated the use of greater and greater amounts of raw materials, such as land (*resource depletion*).
2. *High accumulation of waste.* Modern factories utilize "energy/chemical intensive technologies to transform raw materials into finished products" en masse, which has contributed to the creation of *more and more pollution and waste* (Schnaiberg, Pellow, & Weinberg, 2002, p. 2).

Besides all of this, Gould, Pellow, and Schnaiberg (2008) identify five shared pillars of modern industry: economic expansion; increased consumption; a propensity to solve social and ecological problems by speeding up the treadmill; economic expansion via large firms; and alliances among capital, labour, and governments. These pillars help us better understand the changing relations among capitalists, workers, and the state; in part, they also explain how practices that damage the environment come to be constructed as "proeconomic" measures that are readily condoned by capitalists, individuals, and the state. For example, setting aside the profits incurred by capitalists, workers perceive that economic expansion will benefit them through enhanced employment opportunities that could help reduce poverty, and governments perceive that they will gain tax revenues that can be redistributed into education or housing.

Foster, Clark, and York (2010) point out how "ironically, most analyses of the environmental problem today are concerned less with saving the planet or life or humanity than saving capitalism" (p. 7). Thus, conflict theories now emphasize a treadmill of *accumulation* over one of production and equate "sustainable capitalism" with "ecological denial." This is because capitalism requires greater and greater economic expansion, which corresponds to ever-heightening worker exploitation and environmental degradation, irrespective of efforts to manage these. Given the speed at which irreversible climate change is occurring, modern conflict theorists suggest that the only solution is an ecological revolution that will replace capitalism with socialism (Foster, 2009; Foster et al., 2010).

It is becoming overwhelmingly apparent that those who have the fewest resources (the poor, minority groups) are likely to suffer the greatest negative environmental impacts (exposure to environmental hazards, and so on). *Ecofeminism* is a social movement that links women with nature (oppression against women with the domination of nature). From this perspective, patriarchal society rests on four pillars of injustice: racism, sexism, class exploitation, and environmental destruction (Davies, 1988; Harris, 2017; Plant, 1989).

Treadmill of production: A theoretical model that explains environmental issues as resulting from an incessant need to increase production and profit.

SOCIOLOGY ON SCREEN

TIPPING POINT: THE AGE OF THE OIL SANDS

Tipping Point: The Age of the Oil Sands (2011), directed by Tom Radford and Niobe Thompson of Clearwater Media in association with CBC TV, aired on CBC News Network in January 2011. The film describes the early health and environmental concerns of residents of Fort Chipewyan, Alberta, regarding high rates of rare forms of cancer and suspected pollution in the Athabasca River. The documentary highlights the struggle for environmental justice as government and industry officials maintain that the oil sands do not contribute to pollution. The "tipping point" is a culmination of media attention involving James Cameron, who, after visiting the oil sands and meeting with the premier of Alberta, expressed his concerns alongside Indigenous peoples, and the new research confirming the presence of toxic pollution. The sponsor-paid congratulatory message to James Cameron shown in the ad on the next page was used to further awareness of the environmental issues posed by the oil sands.

Environmental justice is a movement aimed at environmental security and the equitable treatment of all people in relation to environmental impacts. This is primarily an effort to expose environmental issues as abuses disproportionately incurred by the disadvantaged and to advocate for environmental policies and regulations crafted with the input of those most affected.

Corporate Ethics International

In Canada, environmental justice spans a range of current issues involving land claims, health risks, and environmental politics (see, Agyeman et al., 2009). A study by University of Alberta biologists and ecologists concluded that "contrary to claims made by industry and government in the popular press," the oil sands project is responsible for 13 toxic elements currently polluting the Athabasca River, all of which are "priority pollutants" that warrant federal government follow-up (Dearing, 2010). The Athabasca River is a primary food source for many Indigenous peoples (e.g., those living in Fort McKay and Fort Chipewyan). The Indigenous Environmental Network's Canadian Indigenous Tar Sands Campaign seeks to halt further oil sands expansion (Indigenous Environmental Network, 2017).

TIME TO REVIEW

- Why were environmental concerns largely ignored by early sociologists?
- How does the new ecological paradigm differ from the Human Exemptionalism Paradigm?
- Why might a functionalist perspective believe that sustainable development is a foreseeable possibility in advanced societies?
- What two postindustrial changes are emphasized by the treadmill of production model?
- What does environmental justice refer to?

LO5 STRATEGIES FOR BETTER ENVIRONMENTAL CHOICES

LIVING GREEN: CHANGING THE BEHAVIOUR OF INDIVIDUALS

We are not advocating that you take extreme measures such as chaining yourself to a tree in order to save the forest, but we hope you will consider modifying a few of your daily activities in order to reduce consumption and waste. The first step to living green is acknowledging behaviours that represent consumption (driving, eating primarily animal-based products and processed foods, regularly purchasing consumer products, and using large amounts of energy) and then changing some of your unnecessary or particularly wasteful habits. Here are four suggestions for becoming "less consumptive":

1. *Change your eating habits.* Try to eat less meat, eat organically, eat sustainable seafood, and consume more local produce. Also try to be less wasteful with food (e.g., buy less, take it out of plastic packaging, and wash it just before you consume it so that it stays fresh longer). Close to half of all of the food that is produced is thrown away, and much of this ends up in the landfill, a high contributor to greenhouse gas emissions (David Suzuki Foundation, 2017b).
2. *Change your energy habits.* Walk, ride a bike, or take the LRT/bus more often. Commute with others when you have to drive a vehicle. Consider buying a small hybrid car rather than a large truck or SUV. Turn off lights, computers, and the television when you leave a room at home. Don't stand in front of the fridge with the door open! Take more showers than baths and use less water by getting out of the shower sooner. Wear your clothes several times before washing them.
3. *Change your waste habits.* You can divert most of your garbage from the landfill by sorting your trash into organics (compostable food items), recyclable materials (plastics, Styrofoam, glass), and waste. Donate used household items and clothing to charitable organizations or join an "upcycling" group on Facebook to pass on items to others in need of them. Resist the urge to upgrade your TV monitor. As O'Sullivan (2008) notes, very little electronic waste is recycled and disposal is problematic because TV and computer monitors contain lead.
4. *Change your purchasing habits.* Household cleaners (toilet bowl cleaners, oven cleaners, glass cleaners, laundry detergents), cosmetic products, sunscreens, and personal hygiene products such as shampoo and toothpaste can all be replaced with greener alternatives (products that are non-toxic, biodegradable, and even all-natural in some cases) that limit your exposure to toxins and help save the planet. For examples and recipes on "green" cleaning and body products, see http://www.davidsuzuki.org.

SUSTAINABLE DEVELOPMENT: CHANGING PRACTICES IN GROUPS AND ORGANIZATIONS

The term **sustainable development** has been used for some time now and is generally taken to mean development "which meets the needs and aspirations of the present generation without compromising the ability of future generations to meet their own needs" (World Commission on Environment and Development, 1987, p. 5). This seems straightforward, but when we consider more closely what "the needs of the present" might entail and whose needs should take priority, competing interests render actual sustainability difficult to achieve. For example, economic objectives might centre on the need to produce efficient food supplies, social concerns might centre on reduced health risks to humans and the humane treatment of animals, and environmental concerns might centre on mitigating climate change. What this generally boils down to in the way of developing effective environmental policies and action plans is a determination of how much emphasis should be placed on current economic priorities over various social and environmental ones.

Also, sustainable development can only be achieved once other conditions are in place in the economy, in society, and in the environment. Some examples: A healthy economy has multiple buyers and sellers and the absence of corruption. A healthy society has a base level of subsistence, protection, and participation alongside strong educational and healthcare systems, as well as a large middle class (little disparity between those with and

Sustainable development: Development that meets the needs of the present without compromising the ability of future generations to meet their own needs.

those without resources). A healthy environment has a generous supply of contained fossil fuels, minerals, and other resources (not ones that are extracted and used to deplete the Earth in greater and greater concentrations) (Hitchcock & Willard, 2009).

Assuming that the necessary factors are in place to begin with or could feasibly be put in place, society as a whole needs to adopt sustainable practices everywhere—in homes, in schools, in government, and in business. In *The Business Guide to Sustainability*,* Hitchcock and Willard (2009, pp. 21–22) show us what a sustainable pizza operation might entail:

- **Materials:** All your produce, pizza boxes, cleaning products, and so on, come from sustainable/green/socially responsible sources. (You could buy organic tomatoes from farmers who provide good working conditions and wages for their migrant workers. Your pizza boxes could be made from 100 percent recycled paper or pulp from certified forests. Cleaning products would be environmentally benign.)
- **Energy:** All your energy for cooking, transportation, and space heat came from renewable resources. (You could buy "green power"' from your utility and your delivery vehicles could run on biodiesel.)
- **Process:** Your cooking and other processes are as efficient as possible. (You could even use non-disposable tableware and capture the waste heat from your ovens.)
- **Product design:** Your main product is biodegradable, even edible, so it is quite benign. (Do the ingredients come from local and sustainable or organic sources? You could vary the menu to take advantage of seasonal availability. What about the packaging? Could you invent a reusable pizza box?)
- **Waste:** All your waste products can either be reused, recycled, or composted. (You could choose biodegradable serving items, eliminating plastic drink covers or polystyrene cups.)
- **Industry influence:** You apply your leadership and buying power to drive the rest of the industry towards sustainability. (To have an adequate and affordable supply of organic produce, you might help set up a cooperative.)
- **Community contribution:** You have a program to help solve a pressing social problem that relates in some way to your business. You might work on migrant labour issues and/or hunger, for example. If you serve beer, then drunk driving might [be] an issue to address.

*Source: *The Business Guide to Sustainability: Practical Strategies and Tools for Organizations,* Hitchcock & Willard, Copyright (c) 2009 AXIS Performance Advisors, Inc., p. 21–22. Reproduced by permission of Taylor & Francis Books UK.

Finally, sustainable development encompasses more than a consideration of what is important now along with a consideration of how green practices can be implemented in the future (recycling, the use of biodegradable products). It also entails looking at how practices can be modified to correct for problems that have already occurred (waste cleanup), and it necessitates a look *toward the future*. Increasingly, governments are developing regulatory controls for dealing with yesterday's waste and managing today's emissions. However, corporate and government initiatives that deal with the future tend to be lacking (Hart, 1999). An example of this is Canada's federal lighting efficiency standard requiring Canadians to purchase energy-efficient bulbs (replacing banned incandescent energy-wasteful ones). The standard came into effect in 2014 without an accompanying plan for the safe disposal of these new, highly toxic (mercury-containing) bulbs, which should not be thrown into the trash (Government of Canada, 2014), even though half of Canadians improperly dispose of the bulbs by doing so (Dewis, 2014). Because of these issues with florescent bulbs, more people are now switching to non-toxic, energy-saving LED bulbs. These bulbs also provide a light quality more similar to incandescent bulbs.

A GLOBAL CALL TO ACTION: BRINGING EVERYONE ON BOARD

At the United Nations Sustainable Development Summit held on September 25, 2015, more than 150 world leaders agreed to adopt an *agenda for sustainable development* to be achieved by 2030 (United Nations Development Programme, 2017b). The 193 sovereign states that make up the United Nations (and are equally represented in the United Nations General Assembly, including Canada) agreed to adopt the *2030 Agenda for Sustainable Development*, including 17 interconnected goals that focus on collective efforts to protect the environment, end poverty, and ensure peace and prosperity for all of the Earth's inhabitants. The *17 Sustainable Development Goals* include no poverty; zero hunger; good health and well-being; quality education; gender equality; clean water and sanitation; affordable and clean energy; decent work and economic growth; industry, innovation, and infrastructure; reduced inequalities; sustainable cities and communities; responsible consumption and production; climate action; life below water; life on land; peace, justice, and strong institutions; and partnerships for the goals (United Nations Development Programme, 2017a).

Refer to *Figure 14.4* to learn more about the Sustainable Development Goals and how they align with some of the targets for 2030.

FIGURE 14.4

Sustainable Development Goals and Targets for 2030

Goal 1: No poverty	• Reduce at least by half the proportion of men, women, and children of all ages living in poverty in all its dimensions according to national definitions • Implement nationally appropriate social protection systems and measures for all, including floors, and achieve substantial coverage of the poor and vulnerable
Goal 2: Zero hunger	• End hunger and ensure access by all people, in particular the poor and people in vulnerable situations, including infants, to safe, nutritious, and sufficient food all year round • End all forms of malnutrition, including achieving, by 2025, the internationally agreed targets on stunting and wasting in children under 5 years of age, and address the nutritional needs of adolescent girls, pregnant and lactating women, and older persons
Goal 3: Good health and well-being	• Reduce the global maternal mortality ratio to less than 70 per 100,000 live births • End preventable deaths of newborns and children under 5 years of age, with all countries aiming to reduce neonatal mortality to at least as low as 12 per 1,000 live births and under-5 mortality to at least as low as 25 per 1,000 live births • End the epidemics of AIDS, tuberculosis, malaria, and neglected tropical diseases and combat hepatitis, water-borne diseases, and other communicable diseases
Goal 4: Quality education	• Ensure that all girls and boys complete free, equitable, and quality primary and secondary education eading to relevant and Goal-4 effective learning outcomes • Ensure that all girls and boys have access to quality early childhood development, care, and preprimary education so that they are ready for primary education
Goal 5: Gender equality	• End all forms of discrimination against all women and girls everywhere • Eliminate all forms of violence against all women and girls in the public and private spheres, including trafficking and sexual and other types of exploitation • Eliminate all harmful practices, such as child, early, and forced marriage and female genital mutilation
Goal 6: Clean water and sanitation	• Achieve universal and equitable access to safe and affordable drinking water for all • Improve water quality by reducing pollution, eliminating dumping and minimizing release of hazardous chemicals and materials, halving the proportion of untreated wastewater, and substantially increasing recycling and safe reuse globally
Goal 7: Affordable and clean energy	• Ensure universal access to affordable, reliable, and modern energy services • Increase substantially the share of renewable energy in the global energy mix • Double the global rate of improvement in energy efficiency
Goal 8: Decent work and economic growth	• Sustain per capita economic growth in accordance with national circumstances and, in particular, at least 7 percent gross domestic product growth per annum in the least developed countries • Achieve higher levels of economic productivity through diversification, technological upgrading, and innovation, including through a focus on high-value-added and labour-intensive sectors
Goal 9: Industry, innovation, and infrastructure	• Develop quality, reliable, sustainable, and resilient infrastructure, including regional and transborder infrastructure, to support economic development and human well-being, with a focus on affordable and equitable access for all • Promote inclusive and sustainable industrialization and significantly raise industry's share of employment and gross domestic product, in line with national circumstances, and double its share in least developed countries

(Continues)

Sustainable Development Goals and Targets for 2030 (Continued)

Goal 10: Reduced inequalities	• Progressively achieve and sustain income growth of the bottom 40 percent of the population at a rate higher than the national average • Empower and promote the social, economic, and political inclusion of all, irrespective of age, sex, disability, race, ethnicity, origin, religion, or economic or other status
Goal 11: Sustainable cities and communities	• Ensure access for all to adequate, safe, and affordable housing and basic services and upgrade slums • Provide access to safe, affordable, accessible, and sustainable transport systems for all, improving road safety, notably by expanding public transport, with special attention to the needs of those in vulnerable situations, women, children, persons with disabilities, and older persons
Goal 12: Responsible consumption and production	• Implement the 10-year framework of programs on sustainable consumption and production, all countries taking action, with developed countries taking the lead, taking into account the development and capabilities of developing countries • Achieve the sustainable management and efficient use of natural resources
Goal 13: Climate action	• Strengthen resilience and adaptive capacity to climate-related hazards and natural disasters in all countries • Integrate climate change measures into national policies, strategies, and planning • Improve education, awareness raising, and human and institutional capacity on climate change mitigation, adaptation, impact reduction, and early warning
Goal 14: Life below water	• Prevent and significantly reduce marine pollution of all kinds, in particular from land-based activities, including marine debris and nutrient pollution • Sustainably manage and protect marine and coastal ecosystems to avoid significant adverse impacts, including by strengthening their resilience, and take action for their restoration in order to achieve healthy and productive oceans
Goal 15: Life on land	• Ensure the conservation, restoration, and sustainable use of terrestrial and inland freshwater ecosystems and their services, in particular forests, wetlands, mountains, and drylands, in line with obligations under international agreements • Promote the implementation of sustainable management of all types of forests, halt deforestation, restore degraded forests, and substantially increase afforestation and reforestation globally
Goal 16: Peace, justice, and strong institutions	• Significantly reduce all forms of violence and related death rates everywhere • End abuse, exploitation, trafficking, and all forms of violence against and torture of children
Goal 17: Partnerships for the goals	• Strengthen domestic resource mobilization, including through international support to developing countries, to improve domestic capacity for tax and other revenue collection • Promote the development, transfer, dissemination, and diffusion of environmentally sound technologies to developing countries on favourable terms, including on concessional and preferential terms, as mutually agreed

Source: United Nations (UN), Sustainable Development Goals, 2017. Found at http://www.undp.org/content/undp/en/home/sustainable-development-goals.html

Many communities, schools, and businesses are already taking the lead in pursuing global challenges. Toyota Motor Corporation, for example, achieved zero waste across all of its European manufacturing plants back in 2006 (Hitchcock & Willard, 2009). Carbon footprint–neutral programs exist in all of the offices that work on behalf of the David Suzuki Foundation. Suzuki, a Canadian zoologist, environmentalist, and activist, is well known for his advocacy for nature and for his willingness to challenge governments and industries over practices they support that pose environmental concerns. As part of a Declaration of Interdependence, Suzuki and his wife (and others) wrote for the UN Earth Summit in 1992 this reminder, which nicely brings this chapter to close: "When we compromise the air, the water, the soil and the variety of life, we steal from the endless future to serve the fleeting present" (David Suzuki Foundation, 2017a).

TIME TO REVIEW

- What are some individual-level strategies that reflect better environmental choices?
- Why is sustainable development so difficult to achieve?
- What are the sustainable development goals, and who agreed to adopt them?

CHAPTER SUMMARY

LO1 Explain how social factors pose environmental challenges.

Human overpopulation, industrialization, urban sprawl, and overconsumption all result in practices (extraction of minerals, agricultural production, pollution, etc.) that deplete and degrade the natural environment (soil, air, water, wildlife, and fossil fuels).

LO2 Provide an overview of the growing awareness of environmental issues.

Since the early 1960s, scientists, naturalists, and sociologists have helped us better understand the interconnectedness of human actions and environmental concerns. The first wave of environmentalism highlighted the negative implications of industrialization (e.g., forms of pollution and the use of pesticides), whereas the second wave taught us more about ozone depletion, acid rain, and climate change. With increased competition and the extraction of scarce resources, we can continue to expect environmental degradation and the threat of even greater dangers associated with hazardous waste and accidents such as oil spills.

LO3 Explain how the human exemptionalism and new ecological paradigms further our understanding of environmental issues.

The human exemptionalism paradigm identifies the anthropocentrism of early sociology with its view that humans are unique and hold a place above other forms of life. In contrast, the new ecological paradigm helps us realize the interdependence between humans and the natural environment.

LO4 Compare the assumptions underlying functionalist and critical approaches to the environment.

Functionalist approaches assume that pro-environmental changes will result from similar views regarding the need to make the world a better place, whereas critical approaches maintain that divergent societal and environmental interests in the capitalist pursuit of profit will continue to pose ever-greater environmental threats.

LO5 Demonstrate an understanding of strategies for making better environmental choices.

Strategies for making better environmental choices at the level of individuals include practices that reflect greener living (e.g., conservation of energy and water), whereas strategies at a more macro level include efforts to achieve sustainable development and meet global challenges (to mitigate climate change, reduce waste, and preserve natural habitats and wildlife, etc.).

RECOMMENDED RESOURCES

1. For a resource on environmental science and climate change, we recommend J. Withgott, M. Laposata, and B. Murck, *Environment: The science behind the stories* (3rd ed.) (Toronto, ON: Pearson, 2017).
2. Environment Canada, established in 1971, is a federal department dedicated to environmental enhancement, preservation, conservation, and protection. Much of Environment Canada's budget is allocated to science and technology (e.g., climate monitoring networks, water survey offices) in an effort to improve our understanding of ecosystems (e.g., wetlands, forests, the Arctic) and risk assessment (e.g., changes in air quality, weather hazards). See http://www.ec.gc.ca.
3. For a historical overview of the environmental movement and a call to action, you can view David Suzuki's talk *For Thought: Hope for the Planet* published March 10, 2016, at https://www.youtube.com.
4. For information on the difficulties of transitioning people away from overreliance on meat, we recommend P. Pohjolainen, M. Vinnari, and P. Jokinen, "Consumers' perceived barriers to a plant-based diet," *British Food Journal*117 (2015): 1150–1167.

FOR FURTHER REFLECTION

1. Which is more important: protecting the environment or feeding everyone who currently exists on the Earth? Defend your answer.
2. Are environmental problems mainly the end result of population overgrowth or structural inequality? Explain your answer.
3. Is sustainable development achievable in postindustrial societies? Why or why not?

ENDNOTE

1 Opening quotation retrieved March 27, 2017, from www.brainyquote.com.

15 CHAPTER

Globalization: The Interconnected World

Toria/Shutterstock

The speed of light does not merely transform the world. It becomes the world. Globalization is the speed of light.

(French writer Paul Virilio)[1]

LEARNING OBJECTIVES & OUTCOMES

After completing this chapter, students should be able to do the following:

LO1 Define "globalization" and differentiate it from "globality."

LO2 Describe historical precursors to globalization.

LO3 Explain how changes after the Second World War precipitated modern globalization.

LO4 Describe the technological, economic, political, cultural, and social characteristics of globalization.

LO5 Outline the vision of globalization, including its proposed world benefits.

LO6 Describe the dark side of globalization highlighted by various social organizations.

LO7 Describe global justice movements, including their affiliated activities.

LO8 Explain how different theories contribute to our understanding of global inequality.

In the 21st century, the term "globalization" is common. We read about it in the news, hear it mentioned on television, and listen to our employers or coworkers discussing it. Each of us is a cog in the wheel of globalization, which affects almost every aspect of our lives, and we in turn affect globalization every single day. Indeed, globalization has become the world.

LO1 DEFINING GLOBALIZATION

Globalization has been defined in various ways. Formal definitions typically resemble the following: it is "a set of [uneven] *social processes* that appear to transform our present social condition of conventional nationality into one of globality" (Steger, 2017, p. 12). In contrast, **globality** is "a *social condition* characterized by tight global economic, political, cultural and environmental interconnections and flows that make most of the current borders and boundaries irrelevant" (Steger, 2017, p. 10). That is, globalization is a *process*, whereas globality is a *condition*.

Globalization: A set of (uneven) social processes that appear to transform our present social condition of conventional nationality into one of globality.

Globality: A social condition characterized by tight global economic, political, cultural, and environmental interconnections and flows that make most current borders and boundaries irrelevant.

A better understanding of what globalization entails comes from an exploration of its origins, its essential characteristics, its achievements, and its shortcomings. All of these issues will be addressed

in this chapter. As you continue reading, you will see that globalization is closely intertwined with the topics we have discussed throughout this book. Globalization is a part of media, culture, social structure, socialization and the self, gender, ethnicity, families, deviance, religion, science, education, health, social movements, and the environment. And perhaps most importantly, it is connected to myriad forms of social inequality that have been discussed throughout this textbook.

THE EMERGENCE OF GLOBALIZATION

LO2 THE FOUNDATIONS OF GLOBALIZATION

Globalization is based on "the exchange of goods, the development of trade routes, the migration of peoples, and the spread of information" (Hebron & Stack, 2016, p. 2). This is a dynamic that has existed for thousands of years, from the migration of ancient peoples, to the explorations of Marco Polo (1254–1324) that resulted in trade relationships between Europe and the Far East (see *Figure 15.1*), to the international trade of today.

Technological developments in the latter half of the 19th century laid the foundation for modern globalization (Steger, 2017). The invention of the steamship increased the speed and decreased the costs of transporting goods and people. It also led to the laying of the first transatlantic telegraph cable, which increased the speed of international communication.

Decolonization: The process whereby colonial empires are dismantled and former colonies are granted political and economic independence.

LO3 GLOBALIZATION AFTER THE SECOND WORLD WAR

The linking together of people separated by geography and politics accelerated during and after the Second World War. First, the colonial empires were dismantled, a process known as **decolonization**. Those empires, including the English, the French, and the Dutch, granted independence to their colonies throughout the world. This resulted in 88 new countries that had their own governments and controlled their own economic activities. Second, a variety of transnational political and financial institutions were created to address the war's consequences as well as the social, economic, and political forces that had caused it. For example, the United Nations was formed to address issues of human rights, international peace and security, and international economic and political cooperation. The United Nations (UN) has a number of subsidiary organizations, including the World Health Organization (WHO), the United Nations Educational, Scientific, and Cultural Organization (UNESCO), and the International Court of Justice, an international court that tries cases of war crimes and crimes against humanity.

FIGURE 15.1

Early Trade Routes

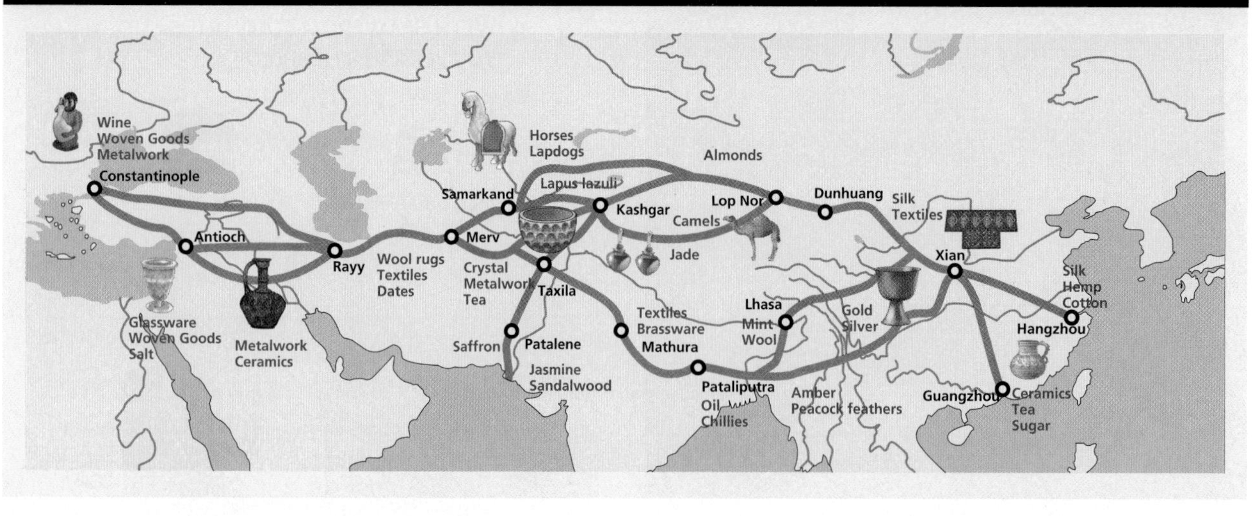

Source: Courtesy of the Penn Museum.

When we think of globalization, the first institutions that usually come to mind are the transnational financial ones that were founded near the end of Second World War: the International Monetary Fund (IMF), the World Bank, and the General Agreement on Tariffs and Trade (GATT), which later became the World Trade Organization (WTO) (see *Figure 15.2*). These institutions were formed, in part, to facilitate the reconstruction of Europe and Japan after the war. They were also formed to assist in the postwar economic recovery of countries around the world. A hard economic lesson had been learned after First World War. At that time, countries sought economic recovery by strengthening their economic borders, engaging in competitive currency devaluation to gain export advantages, and imposing high **tariffs** (fees levied by a government on imported goods). Each nation focused on its own market, with devastating results. This practice contributed to the stock market crash of October 1929, which caused the Great Depression of the 1930s.

It was thought that **neoliberalism** would help avoid a similar outcome after Second World War. That economic doctrine emphasizes freedom for market forces, unimpeded by governments. Government interference in the free market leads to political corruption, ineffective government, and social stagnation. Prosperity and democracy will flourish through measures such as privatization, deregulation, tax cuts, controls on organized labour, decreased government spending (especially on social programs), expansion of international markets, and the downsizing of governments. Neoliberalism values individualism over collective well-being, its assumption being that through free market competition, a social process similar to Darwin's biological process of *natural selection*

Tariffs: Fees imposed by a government on imported goods.

Neoliberalism: An economic philosophy claiming that when market forces are unimpeded by government, prosperity and democracy will flourish.

FIGURE 15.2

The International Monetary Fund, World Bank, and World Trade Organization

In the 21st century, the most significant transnational economic institutions are the International Monetary Fund, the World Bank, and the World Trade Organization.

International Monetary Fund (IMF)

The IMF provides short-term lending to governments and collects data on the world economy. It has 186 member-states and a 24-member board of executive directors. Voting power is based on the size of each member-state's economy. The United States, with the world's largest economy, has the most voting power on the board—in fact, it has veto power. The IMF provides three categories of loans. Standby loans are for short-term financial crises, extended loans are for longer-term financial problems, and concessional loans are part of a poverty reduction strategy available to the poorest countries of the world. Being granted a loan from the IMF is a necessary precursor to being considered for a loan from the World Bank (International Monetary Fund, 2017).

World Bank

The World Bank is an international bank that provides low-interest or interest-free loans, as well as technical assistance for development projects (infrastructure, agriculture, private enterprise development, and social programs) in low- and middle-income countries. As with the IMF, voting power is based on the size of a member-state's economy, with the United States having the most influence. The World Bank has two components. The International Bank for Reconstruction and Development (IBRD) offers loans of 15 to 20 years to creditworthy developing nations. Its second component, the International Development Association (IDA), provides interest-free loans of 35 to 40 years to the poorest countries. In fiscal year 2016, the IBRD granted $29.7 billion and the IDA $16.1 billion in loans for 275 projects or operations in various countries in Africa, Asia, Europe, Latin America, the Caribbean, and the Middle East (World Bank, 2016).

World Trade Organization (WTO)

The World Trade Organization, which has 164 member-states, "ensure(s) that trade flows as smoothly, predictably and freely as possible" (World Trade Organization, 2017). In part, its member-states agree to extend their best tariff rates to other member states, to treat foreign goods equally with domestic goods, and to engage in trade fairly. Negotiations take place through rounds of talks involving the member-states as a whole. In order to give smaller, less powerful nations equal participation, decisions are made through consensus rather than a majority vote. Because of the consensus model, negotiations often extend for years, as seen in the softwood lumber disputes between Canada and the United States that have been ongoing (off and on) since 1982.

© imagebroker/Alamy

The destruction of the Berlin Wall in 1989 marked both the collapse of the Soviet Union and maturation of the concept of globalization.

will prevail. The "fittest" will rise to the top, and the weakest—those of least use to society—will sink to the bottom. People become poor and marginalized because they are weak (Steger, 2017). Taken to its extreme, in the words of Scrooge, "If they would die ... they had better do it and decrease the surplus population."

Decolonization and the founding of transnational institutions marked the beginning of modern globalization. But globalization came fully into its own with the collapse of the Soviet Union in 1989, which erased one the world's last important boundaries—the one between East and West, between capitalism and communism. It suddenly became much easier to imagine a world without borders, with free-flowing goods, information, and people, a world characterized by globality (Eitzen & Zinn, 2012; Steger, 2017).

TIME TO REVIEW

- What is globalization, and how is it related to globality?
- What are the historical foundations of globalization?
- Why did globalization expand during and after World War II?
- What are the IMF, the World Bank, and the WTO?
- Why did the collapse of the Soviet Union cause globalization to enter its mature form?

LO4 CHARACTERISTICS OF GLOBALIZATION

In the 21st century, globalization is characterized by "the Internet, instantaneous 24-hour news stations, interconnected financial markets, the spread of communications and transportation systems, unprecedented integration of economic activities, and the rise of increasingly important non-state, transnational actors" (Hebron & Stack, 2016, p. 2). Globalization has a range of technological, economic, political, and cultural dimensions.

TECHNOLOGICAL DIMENSION

Technology facilitates all other dimensions of globalization. This includes traditional technologies, such as container ships, and newer technologies, such as communications satellites and the Internet. The economic, political, and cultural dimensions of globalization are enabled by technology, such as by transporting goods across the globe and communicating with people on the other side of the world in real time; those same dimensions influence technological development. Each of these dimensions has various positive and negative impacts, which will be addressed at a later point in this chapter.

ECONOMIC DIMENSION

Informed by neoliberalism, the economic dimension of globalization is reflected in the transnational financial institutions already described and in expanded markets, flexible production and assembly, and the concentration of economic power (Eitzen & Zinn, 2012; Steger, 2017). In Canadian history, we saw the early expansion of markets in the transition to industrialization. At that time, Canadians who were involved in farming and lumber were encouraged to expand their economic activities. First, they started to produce more agricultural products and lumber than they needed for their own survival, in order to supply the growing urban populations of Canada, the United States, and Western Europe. In the 21st century, with globalization, markets have continued to expand more than anyone would have ever imagined a century ago.

As markets expand globally, so does production. Flexible production makes use of various nations' physical and human resources. Assembly lines for products are no longer local but global, with manufacturers creating products using the resources of a variety of nations. Consider the global assembly line involved in manufacturing the iPhone: "The blueprint, crystal, specialized parts and processors from the US, display panels, chipsets, and memory from Japan, Korea, and Taiwan, gyroscope from Europe and rare earth minerals from Mongolia all come together [i.e., are combined into the finished product] in China, the world's factory" (Finances Online, n.d.). On the global assembly line, manufacturing jobs are moved into low-wage countries. Also, more service jobs are being outsourced to different parts of the world. For instance, if you purchase a new printer and need to phone the help line, you may be connected to a call centre in Edmonton, Houston, Mexico City, Mumbai, or any of a number of other cities around the world. Cities, regions, and nations bid to attract these exported or outsourced jobs by offering advantages to corporations that can be detrimental to workers and communities.

Economic globalization has also meant a concentration of economic power. Since the 1980s, widespread corporate restructuring and mergers have created larger, economically more powerful corporations, such as the media giants described in the chapter on media. The 200 largest transnational corporations "account for half of the world's industrial output" and none "maintain headquarters outside North America, Mexico, Europe, China, Japan, and South Korea" (Steger, 2017, p. 53). Transnational corporations have greater wealth than many nations. In 2015, Apple had a market value of more than $700 billion, compared to the GDPs of Austria ($373 billion), South Africa ($317 billion), Colombia ($274 billion), and Finland ($231 billion) (see *Figure 15.3*).

POLITICAL DIMENSION

The economic dimension of globalization is intertwined with its political dimension (see *Sociology on Screen*). For instance, the International Development Association (IDA), which is part of the World Bank, had its origins in Cold War political and military tensions between the Soviet Union and the United States in the latter half of the 20th century. During the Cold War, the United States feared that the world's poorest nations would approach (or be approached by) the Soviet Union and thereby contribute to its expanding power. So, the United States provided 42 percent of the IDA's initial funding to assist in the development of these nations and prevent them from becoming part of the Soviet empire (Lee, 2007).

With globalization, the power of nation-states has declined. The power of national governments has transferred "upward" to international organizations such as the United Nations (Steger, 2017). It is also being transferred "downward" (Steger, 2017). In some cases, this downward transfer is to regional trading blocs such as the North American Free Trade Agreement (NAFTA), the European Union (EU), and regional trade alliances. In other cases, power is transferred downward to *global cities,* those that play key roles in the global economic system independent of their nation-states. Cities such as

FIGURE 15.3

Apple's Market Value Compared to Select Countries' Gross Domestic Products (GDPs) (2015)

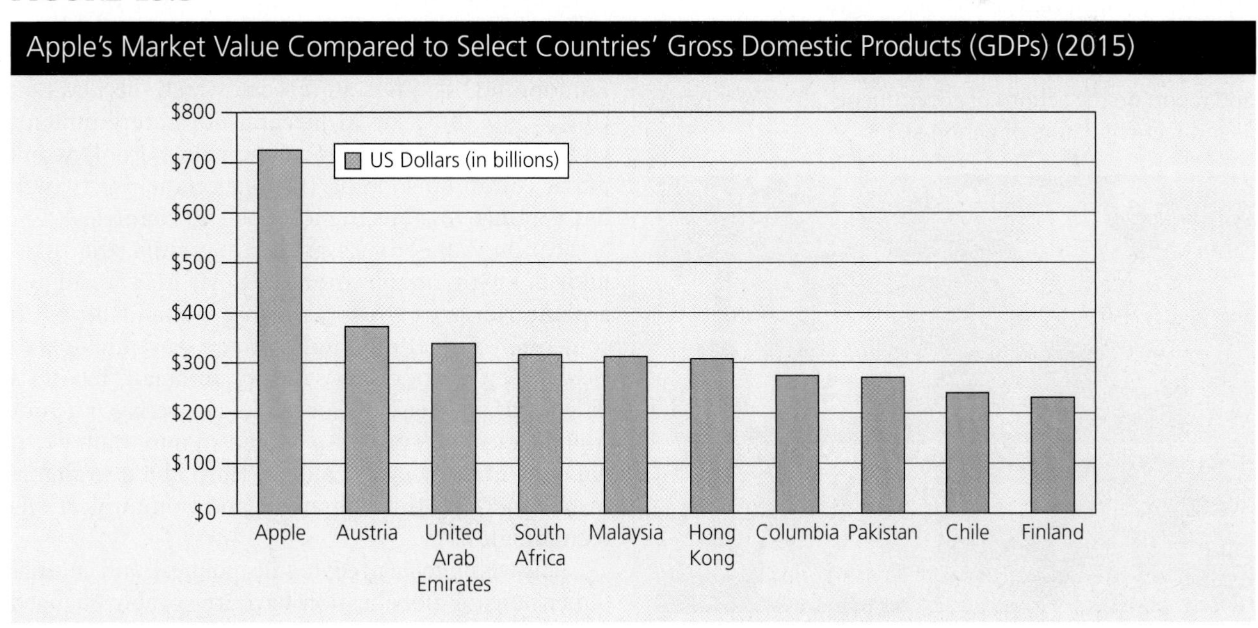

Source: Adapted from Steger, M. B. (2017). *Globalization: A very short introduction* (4th ed.). (Figure E: Transnational corporations versus countries: A comparison, p. 55.) Oxford, UK: Oxford University Press.

SOCIOLOGY ON SCREEN

MONEY, POWER, AND WALL STREET

In a four-hour special investigation on the PBS news series *Frontline*, "Money, Power, and Wall Street" explores the uneasy relationship between the U.S. government administration and the global banking industry headquartered on Wall Street. Preventing and resolving financial crisis mean that government leaders often have to make difficult decisions—such as offering banks financial bailouts in the aftermath of the global economic crisis in 2008. But what are the human consequences? For more information, including an interactive website, see http://www.pbs.org/frontline.

New York, Tokyo, London, and Toronto have a strong influence on world affairs and house many of the head offices of transnational corporations. Cities from around the world also join together in networks with similar interests and problems. For example, ICLEI (Local Governments for Sustainability; formerly the International Council for Local Environmental Initiatives) is a coalition of more than 1,500 local and regional governments with a shared interest in becoming "sustainable, low-carbon, resilient, ecomobile, biodiverse, resource-efficient and productive, healthy and happy, with a green economy and smart infrastructure" (ICLEI, n.d.). It includes 31 local governments in Canada—not just cities that you might expect (e.g., Toronto, Vancouver) but also smaller cities (e.g., Red Deer) and municipal districts (e.g., Town of the Blue Mountains). The power of nation-states is also being transferred downward to global civil society (Steger, 2017). Citizens who participate in groups such as Amnesty International and Human Rights Watch monitor and report on the actions of governments, thereby serving as indirect regulators of nation-states.

Syda Productions/Shutterstock

When you travel to other countries, you take Canadian culture with you and bring home bits of the cultures you have experienced in your travels.

CULTURAL DIMENSION

The cultural dimension of globalization involves areas as diverse as tourism, the media, communications, global consumption culture, transnational migration, and identities. People may migrate to other nations either temporarily, as students or foreign workers, or permanently, as residents. As discussed in the chapter on race and ethnicity, when people immigrate to another country, they adopt some aspects of that country's culture while also contributing aspects of their cultures of origin. But cultural products and ideas can be conveyed transnationally even without physical migration, through the Internet, electronic communications, and the marketing of consumer products. Whether you live in Canada or in countless other countries in the world, on any given day you may be able to eat poutine, chicken vindaloo, or sushi. You can purchase blue jeans, a sari, or even an Edmonton Oilers jersey. You can watch the news on CBC, CNN, BBC, or Al Jazeera. For entertainment, you can watch a Beyoncé music video, a Bollywood movie, or an episode of *The Voice* franchise (which has national versions in more than 50 countries). For a vacation, Vancouver's great restaurants, the pyramids of Egypt, or an ecotour in Costa Rica are all just a plane ride away. After forming a friendship with someone you met on a holiday, you can quickly and easily keep in touch by sending an email, having a video chat on FaceTime, or posting a message on your friend's Facebook page. And when an important event happens in the world, you can learn about it almost instantaneously through media and communications technologies.

The technological, economic, political, and cultural dimensions of globalization have irrevocably changed how the world's people live their daily lives. Whether those changes are for the better or the worse is a matter of discussion and debate (see *Sociology in My Life*).

YOUR SOCIOLOGICAL TOOLKIT

SOCIOLOGY IN MY LIFE

WHAT ROLE DO YOU PLAY IN GLOBALIZATION?

Consider how various dimensions of globalization have permeated the products and activities that make up your day. Think about the food you buy in the grocery store (e.g., bananas) or the restaurants you frequent (e.g., McDonald's, Indian, and/or Japanese). Where do you shop (e.g., Canadian Tire or Walmart)? Look at the tags on your clothing or the boxes your television, laptop, and mobile device came in to see where they were manufactured. Make note of the websites you visit or the movies, TV shows, and YouTube videos you watch. How do you learn about world events? You can even go online and try to trace the goods you consume, such as the ownership structure of the companies, who is involved in the production of those goods, and under what type of conditions. In all likelihood, a consideration of your daily life will reflect the global assembly line, expanding markets, the concentration of economic power in transnational corporations, and the centrality of technology.

Think Outside the Box: Who do you think benefits from the way that globalization permeates your life, and how do they benefit? Who might be harmed? You may find that your answers are reinforced as you progress through the next part of the chapter.

TIME TO REVIEW

- What is the role of technology in globalization?
- What is the nature of expanding markets, the global assembly line, and the concentration of corporate power?
- How does globalization transfer power away from nation-states?
- What are some examples of the cultural dimension of globalization?

THE VISION OF GLOBALIZATION AND ITS REALITY: THE GOOD, THE BAD, AND THE UGLY

LO5 THE GOOD

The vision of the neoliberal forces underlying globalization is that it will improve the lives of the world's people (Hebron & Stack, 2016). Better living conditions will emerge through the globalization of production; the global assembly line that brings employment to the developing world will help develop those nations' economies.

Communication technologies, such as the Internet, increase people's knowledge of the world and of their own society. People become aware of the different possible ways of living and being in the world and they hold their politicians to greater accountability. Proponents of globalization point to the central role that communication technologies played during the Arab Spring (beginning in 2011), Euromaidan (in 2014), and the Dakota Access Pipeline protests (in 2016). Cellphones, Facebook, and the Internet were used to instantaneously coordinate protesters' activities and allowed them to send photos, videos, and information to one another and to the rest of the world (Hebron & Stack, 2016). Their photos, videos, and audio served two functions. First, the rest of the world was made aware of the activities of the protesters and the responses of the government in real time, as they were happening. Various organizations and governments were then able to respond. When protesters in Libya sent out images of government forces shooting peaceful protesters, the UN held an emergency meeting of its members that led to an arms embargo, a travel ban for the Libyan leader and his relatives, and the freezing of his family's international bank accounts. The images and audio served a second function as well. As the government of Tunisia fell, and then Egypt's, and then those of other nations, these forms of communication demonstrated to citizens in surrounding nations that change is possible—that the demands of ordinary people can change the country they live in. Finally, the greater level of knowledge that develops through globalization increases understanding of other people, cultures, and important social issues. With knowledge and understanding, conflicts between groups should decline, and informed citizens are in a better position to resolve social problems.

Many people acknowledge that transnational institutions such as the IMF have helped maintain financial stability and supported development (Steger, 2017). Legrain (2002) draws attention to the successes of globalization during the latter half of the 20th century. Between 1950 and 2000, per capita income quadrupled. In the 1970s and 1980s, those developing nations that had opened themselves up to international trade saw their economies expand by 4.5 percent per year. In contrast, the economies of those developing countries that did not open up to trade grew by less than 1 percent per year. Finally, each percentage point increase in a nation's GDP is associated with a similar increase in the standard of living: "The process of economic cooperation and integration has helped a number of countries benefit from high rates of economic growth and employment creation, to absorb many of the rural poor into the modern urban economy, to advance their developmental goals, and to foster innovation in product development and the circulation of ideas" (International Labour Organization, 2008, p. 5).

But the experiences of globalization are diverse. Some people benefit, whereas others are harmed, and measures are necessary to ensure that the benefits of globalization are shared by all. The most important question to ask is *who benefits* from globalization and who does not (Eitzen & Zinn, 2012).

LO6 THE BAD AND THE UGLY

> Globalization, as defined by rich people like us, is a very nice thing.... You are talking about the Internet, you are talking about cellphones, you are talking about computers. This doesn't affect two-thirds of the world's people.... If you're totally illiterate and living on one dollar a day, the benefits of globalization never come to you.
>
> (Jimmy Carter, former American president and recipient of the 2002 Nobel Peace Prize)[2]

SOCIAL INEQUALITY

As Jimmy Carter points out, those who live in extreme poverty do not benefit from globalization in the same way as those who live in wealth. We may not view ourselves as "rich people like us," but compared to many people in the world, we are wealthy. In 2013, 767 million people in the world lived below the international "extreme" poverty line of US$1.90 per day, which means they can only purchase the same goods (e.g., food, shelter, clothing) that someone living in the United States would be able to buy with $1.90 (United Nations, 2017). Most of these are working poor—that is, they are employed, but their wages are less than that amount. Every year, 7 million children die before their first birthday because of a lack of healthcare, nutrition, sanitation, and access to basic childhood vaccinations. Almost 900 million people don't have enough food to eat, 780 million lack access to safe drinking water, and, lacking electricity, 2.6 billion are forced to burn wood, coal, or dung in their homes (leading to 1.5 million deaths per year) (United Nations, 2013). Almost three-quarters of the world's population controls only 3 percent of global wealth, whereas the wealthiest 0.7 percent of the population controls 45 percent of global wealth (Credit Suisse Research Institute, 2015).

ECONOMIC CONSEQUENCES

EXPLOITATION AND WORKING CONDITIONS IN THE DEVELOPING WORLD

Globalization's economic dimensions have had negative consequences for many people in the world. Critics suggest that globalization is fundamentally based on wealthy corporations and nations exploiting the people of the developing world. Flexible production exports jobs to countries where the wages are lower and where there are fewer regulations governing working conditions. Corporations are able to pay employees low wages and make them work long hours in poor conditions; this enhances corporate profits and lowers prices for consumers living in the developed world.

The exploitation of workers in developing nations is illustrated by the state of child labour. The International Labour Organization (2017a) reports that there are an estimated 165 million child labourers in the world, with the vast majority in Asia and sub-Saharan Africa. Of those 165 million children, 85 million are involved in hazardous work where their health, and even their lives, are in danger. They are found in virtually every industry, ranging from agriculture (e.g., harvesting cut flowers in Colombia and bananas in Ecuador), to manufacturing (e.g., surgical instruments in Pakistan and footwear in the Philippines), to resource extraction (e.g., diamond mines in Côte d'Ivoire), to hotels, restaurants, and domestic services. An estimated 5 million are involved in forced or bonded labour, such as slavery and the international sex trade. Trade policies, the race to the bottom, and

AP Photo/Hoshang Hashimi/The Canadian Press

There are 165 million child labourers in the world, including this child, who works in a brick factory.

structural adjustment programs are obstacles to efforts to end child labour.

It is not just in the developing world that globalization is negatively affecting wages and working conditions. A *race to the bottom* results in lower wages, declining working conditions, and job insecurity in the developing and developed worlds (Eitzen & Zinn, 2012; Hebron & Stack, 2016).

THE RACE TO THE BOTTOM

The globalization of production, combined with the economic power of transnational corporate giants, means that corporations' threats to move their operations to other countries wield considerable influence. This creates job insecurity for workers who are employed with a specific company or in a particular industry, who must live in constant fear of losing their jobs (see *Sociology in Practice*).

In the world market, corporations can shop for the best deal. Different nations compete to become the location for a company's operations, undercutting one another in terms of employee wages and benefits, tax breaks, and social and environmental regulations. After NAFTA was implemented in 1994, companies began exporting jobs from Canada and the United States to Mexico, with weak labour laws and few environmental restrictions. Critics suggest that only the wealthy in Mexico benefited. In the 10 years following NAFTA, real manufacturing wages in Mexico declined because of corporate pressure to restrict increases in the minimum wage. Countries such as Canada and the United States lost manufacturing jobs when cheaper production environments became available; since 2004, countries such as Mexico are experiencing the same thing.

YOUR SOCIOLOGICAL TOOLKIT

SOCIOLOGY IN PRACTICE

THE INTERNATIONAL LABOUR ORGANIZATION'S (ILO) FLAGSHIP PROGRAMMES

The International Labour Organization (ILO) is a tripartite agency of the UN that gives equal voice to workers, employers, and governments in shaping policies and programs related to labour standards. The ILO's "vision is based on the premise that lasting peace can only be established if it is based on social justice" (http://www.ilo.org). Its objectives are to (1) promote rights at work, (2) enhance social protection, (3) encourage decent employment opportunities, and (4) strengthen dialogue on work-related issues.

The ILO is built around five flagship programmes (International Labour Organization, 2017b). The *Better Work* program focuses on improving the working conditions in the global footwear and garment industries, which often have a high proportion of female and child labourers. Their program *Social Protection*

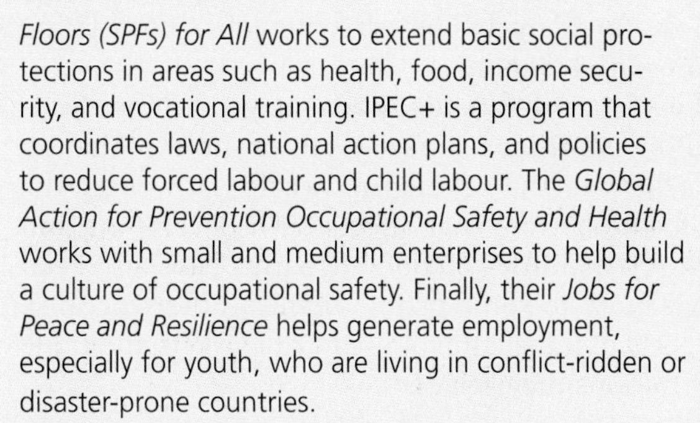

Floors (SPFs) for All works to extend basic social protections in areas such as health, food, income security, and vocational training. IPEC+ is a program that coordinates laws, national action plans, and policies to reduce forced labour and child labour. The *Global Action for Prevention Occupational Safety and Health* works with small and medium enterprises to help build a culture of occupational safety. Finally, their *Jobs for Peace and Resilience* helps generate employment, especially for youth, who are living in conflict-ridden or disaster-prone countries.

Think Outside the Box: Which of these flagship programmes do you think might have the biggest impact on the largest number of people in the long term?

Corporations that moved production to Mexico in the past are now moving that production to countries where production is even cheaper, such as China, and the impact of the race to bottom continues to be felt across North America to the present day (Faux, 2013; Steger, 2017).

Corporate decisions to move production facilities are made in a broader context. Both consumers and big-box retailers (e.g., Walmart, Best Buy) are demanding lower-priced products. There are two ways to reduce the prices of products: reduce either production costs or the company's profit. A decline in company profit has larger implications for the company, so the path to reducing prices is typically controlling production costs.

Production facilities that are closed down in one country are not always moved to another. Transnational corporate giants have money vested in a range of goods or services throughout the world. Sometimes a business operation is shut down as part of a corporation's broader business plan. For example, in 2006, the Canadian government approved the purchase of Canadian mining company Inco by Vale, a Brazilian company and the second-largest mining company in the world. One of Inco's assets was a nickel smelter and refinery in Thompson, Manitoba. In 2010, Export Development Canada granted Vale a $1 billion loan for its proposal to increase employment. Demonstrating that job insecurity exists even in a context of economic success, only six weeks later, Vale announced that it would be closing the Thompson mine by 2015, despite the company's record-setting profits of $17.3 billion in 2010 and its intention to invest $10 billion in activities in other parts of the country. The life of the mine was later extended, with the mine itself closing operations in October 2017 and the smelter and refinery at the end of 2018. This constitutes a loss of approximately 600 jobs (and largely higher-paying jobs), devastating Thompson's economy.

People are differentially advantaged, or disadvantaged, by globalization as a result of the exploitation of workers in the developing world, as well as the race to the bottom that affects both developing and developed countries. Economic harms have also been caused more to some people than to others because of aspects of transnational financial markets and trade organizations themselves.

INSTITUTIONAL CONCERNS

The IMF and the World Bank both have a mandate to facilitate development and ease financial crisis. Critics, though, argue that in practice, developing countries are not always helped. A key criticism of these organizations is that they are not held accountable to the people they are supposed to be helping. Instead, their accountability is to the wealthy, powerful nations that steer their activities—especially the United States (where their offices are located). The poorest nations have no input into the composition of the 24-member board of executive directors of the IMF and therefore no direct influence on the IMF's policies and programs. The United States, Japan, Germany, France, the United Kingdom, China, Russia, and Saudi Arabia each appoint one director to the board. The remaining directors are voted upon, and because voting power is based on the size of each member-state's economy, the United States controls 17 percent of the vote, and European nations as a whole control another one-third of the vote. The EU gets to appoint the IMF's managing director, and the United States gets to appoint the first deputy managing director. A similar process is involved with the board of executive directors of the World Bank, except that it is the United States that appoints the president of the World Bank (who is also the head of the board). Because the poorest nations have no input into the board of either organization, they have no institutional influence on the policies, programs, or reforms it adopts (Steger, 2017).

"Sorry lads.I'm closing this workshop down,and relocating in the far east."

Another criticism of the IMF and World Bank has to do with the structural adjustment programs they implemented in the 1980s. These programs were collectively known as the **Washington Consensus** because they were supported by the IMF, the World Bank, and the U.S. Treasury Department, all of which are located in Washington, DC. Structural adjustment programs were developed as a result of the worsening debt crisis of the 1980s. Loans would be granted to developing nations only if they reduced government spending and liberalized their trade policies. Government expenditures were to be controlled by reducing spending on social programs. That is, in nations that often had limited social programs in the first place, governments were supposed to spend even *less* on health, education, and housing (Hebron & Stack, 2016; Shah, 2013; Steger, 2017). It is the most vulnerable groups that have been the most negatively affected by structural adjustment programs. "Feeding programs and medical clinics closed, food subsidies and housing assistance ended, and the cost of living climbed precipitously. Many developing nations perceived a new colonialism, with poor nations suffering for the sake of profits and bank balance sheets in rich nations" (Lee, 2007, para. 12).

Developing nations that receive funding are not allowed to subsidize agriculture (either with the funding or with any other monies the government may have). However, countries such as Canada and the United States continue to offer extensive subsidies to their farmers. Developed nations spend, in total, hundreds of billions of dollars each year in agricultural subsidies. Because of these subsidies, agricultural commodities from these nations can be sold at lower prices. This drives down agricultural prices worldwide. The unsubsidized farmers in developing nations aren't able to compete, and as a result, the livelihoods of the two-thirds of the world's people who depend on agriculture are threatened or destroyed (Hebron & Stack, 2016; Steger, 2017). One consequence is that people are forced to migrate to urban areas to find work, often in other countries. Women from developing nations leave their own children in the care of others while they migrate to Canada, the United States, France, and the United Kingdom to work as nannies and housekeepers for others. Also, corporations recruit women and men as temporary foreign workers in a variety of industries, from food services to the oil and construction industries (Wang & Zong, 2014).

For some people, globalization has had negative economic consequences, which are transformed into social consequences such as unemployment and separated families. But for people in many countries, the cultural dimension of globalization has had even more of an impact than the economic dimension.

CULTURAL CONSEQUENCES

The cultural dimensions of globalization are diverse, and so are the consequences. Small, local enterprises that reflect aspects of culture—food, clothing, folk art—are unable to compete with multinational corporations and go out of business. Meanwhile, more and more people buy blue jeans at Walmart and eat lunch at McDonald's. The homogenization of culture is also reflected in the loss of languages. In the 1500s, more than 14,000 distinct languages were spoken in the world; in the late 20th century, fewer than 7,000. It is estimated that by the end of the 21st century, between 50 and 90 percent of the languages that currently exist will be extinct (Steger, 2017). English has become more dominant in the world. It is the first language for 350 million people and a second language for another 400 million. More than 80 percent of content on the Internet is English (Steger, 2017).

Concerns about cultural homogenization abound. But some people argue that it isn't just *homogenization* that is occurring; it is *Americanization*. The United States exerts considerable control over the global economy; it is also central to global culture. The United States is home to most of the top 100 brand names in the world. And although Bollywood releases more movies each year, Hollywood movies are the only ones to have penetrated every market in the world. The biggest-grossing films and the top-rated TV shows in every country are American (Hebron & Stack, 2016).

Others contend that global culture does not necessarily mean the destruction of local culture or cultural diversity (Hebron & Stack, 2016). They draw attention to the blending of the global and the local—**glocalization**. A popular restaurant cuisine is "fusion" cuisine, combining the tastes of two cultures—Cuban–Chinese, Asian–Italian, and so on. When Walt Disney expanded outside the United States, the company first went to France and established Euro-Disney. It was almost a colossal failure, in part because Disney did not take the local culture into consideration. For example, its alcohol-free policy was problematic for people living in a culture where the moderate consumption of wine is integrated into daily

Washington Consensus: The structural adjustment programs supported by the IMF, the World Bank, and the U.S. Treasury Department.

Glocalization: The blending of the global and the local.

life. Learning from its mistakes, when the company expanded into Hong Kong, it integrated Chinese food and music (Hebron & Stack, 2016).

Although the economic and cultural consequences of globalization that disadvantage some people in the world are the most emphasized, there are myriad other potentially negative consequences of globalization as well. These include increased conflict, terrorism, organized crime networks, environmental destruction, and even epidemics and pandemics (Eitzen & Zinn, 2012; Hebron & Stack, 2016; Steger, 2017).

Proponents of globalization suggest that the knowledge it brings to people promotes understanding and tolerance and thereby reduces conflict between different cultures and different groups. But others argue that conflict actually becomes more pronounced with globalization. The European colonial empires brought together disparate groups of people within borders drawn by the colonizers themselves. This created politically cohesive colonial states, but there was no pre-existing cultural cohesiveness. Thus, in post-colonial societies, people are more likely to define themselves in terms of their religion and ethnicity rather than their nation. This has actually increased hostility between the different ethnic and religious groups that were forcibly brought together within the borders of nation-states. This sets the stage for many conflicts today, such as those between Sunni and Shia Muslims in some countries in the Middle East. More broadly, the perceived Americanization of the world and the exploitation of lower-income nations by higher-income nations have also increased the hostility that some non-Western groups feel for the Western world overall and the rise of global terrorist networks such as ISIS/ISIL (Hebron & Stack, 2016).

McDonald's is McDonald's? At this McDonald's in Japan, menu items include Juicy Chicken Akatougarashi, Teriyaki Mac Burger, and Shrimp Filet-O.

Organized crime networks also benefit from globalization. Just as the ease of transportation of goods and people facilitates legitimate business, it facilitates illegitimate business—flows of drugs, weapons, money, slaves, and criminals. Communications technologies are sites for organized crime as well. As people, companies, and governments carry out more and more of their business in electronic environments, they are being criminally victimized in those environments (Gachúz, 2016).

Globalization even affects people's health, not just through environmental destruction or unhealthy working conditions, but also as a result of human migration. Pandemics have always followed the movements of people. As trade routes between Europe and the Far East were established hundreds of years ago, it wasn't only silks and spices that began to flow across borders. It was through these trade routes that the bubonic plague was introduced to Europe (Hebron & Stack, 2016), killing up to 50 percent of the European population between 1347 and 1351 (Strohschein & Weitz, 2014).

A few hundred years later, European colonization introduced various diseases to Indigenous people in the Americas (e.g., smallpox, influenza). It is estimated that up to 100 million Indigenous people in the Americas died as a result of epidemics over a period of 100 years; this has been referred to as *the Great Dying* (Marks, 2012). And the influenza pandemic of 1918 (see the chapter on health) was the result of soldiers returning home from the battlefields of Europe at the end of the First World War (Hebron & Stack, 2016).

In modern society, the ease and speed of human migration have contributed to a number of health scares. In 2003, the WHO declared a pandemic of severe acute respiratory syndrome (SARS). It began in China in 2002, and in February 2003, Chinese health officials notified the WHO that it had an outbreak of this new disease, with 305 cases. When a Chinese professor travelled to Hong Kong, the global spread of SARS began. Hospitals were closed to visitors, schools were closed, and thousands of people were quarantined. Before the pandemic ended, more than 8,000 cases of SARS had been confirmed, with more than 700 deaths worldwide (including 43 in Canada) (World Health Organization, 2017). The responses of governments and health organizations were evaluated after the pandemic, and policies and practices were reformed and changed. These changes facilitated a

YOUR SOCIOLOGICAL TOOLKIT

SOCIOLOGY IN MY COMMUNITY

GLOBAL CITIZENSHP

Global Citizen is a grassroots "network of Global Citizens speaking out and taking action to solve the world's biggest challenges." Although it partners with several non-governmental organizations and corporate affiliates (e.g., UNICEF, MSNBC, Bill & Melinda Gates Foundation), it relies on the advocacy of individual people around the world. Using social media outreach, it calls upon members of the public to email, post, and tweet world leaders about global policy issues. On their website, you can find information, stories of the organization's successes, and current campaigns related to their core areas: girls and women; health; education; finance and innovation; food and hunger; water and sanitation; environment; and citizenship.

On the eve of each G20 summit, Global Citizen hosts a festival attended by members, celebrities, leaders, activists, and musical artists and calls upon its members to message world leaders, asking them to attend as well. At the 2017 Global Citizen Festival (in Hamburg, Germany), Prime Minister Justin Trudeau, Argentinean President Mauricio Macri, and Norway's Prime Minister Erna Solberg joined musical artists from around the world, including Demi Lovato, Pharrell Williams, Andreas Bourani, Shakira, and Sido. In Justin Trudeau's speech, he called upon the leaders of (and citizens in) other G20 countries to increase their efforts on environmental issues, and in Prime Minister Erna Solberg's speech, she announced an $85 million program for women's rights and girls' education. Since the organization went digital in 2012, almost one million "actions" by members (i.e., emails, tweets, posts) have helped achieve $700 million dollars in commitments from governments and private organizations to help solve global problems. To obtain more information or sign up to become a Global Citizen yourself, you can go to their website (https://www.globalcitizen.org) or find them on Facebook or Twitter.

Think Outside the Box: What role do you think recruiting celebrities and musical artists plays in global justice movements?

more effective response to the world's next pandemic, the H1N1 virus in 2009, and to the Ebola outbreak in 2017.

Globalization has benefited the world's people in many ways. But its impacts are not uniform. Various aspects of globalization have had negative consequences for large numbers of people. In response, global justice movements have emerged.

LO7 GLOBAL JUSTICE MOVEMENTS

Global justice movements share a resistance to neoliberalism and its effects. Beyond that, however, they differ greatly. They include labour groups, leftist activists, agricultural workers, religious groups, feminist groups, environmental organizations, anarchist groups, and more. Although global justice movements have existed for several decades, they came to widespread public awareness during the WTO summit in Seattle in 1999 (Steger, 2017). Between 40,000 and 50,000 activists descended on Seattle, and as skirmishes between activists and the police gained in magnitude, the event came to be known as the Battle of Seattle. Groups such as these were initially labelled the "anti-globalization movement." However, they are not opposed to globalization in its entirety but only to certain aspects of it. Furthermore, they actually participate in globalization as well. They organize transnational networks, and they use the communication technologies of globalization to organize activities that occur simultaneously in countries around the world. So, they are now more accurately described as "global justice movements" rather than "anti-globalization movements" (see *Sociology in My Community*).

Global justice movements participate in various activities: they organize protests at meetings of the World Bank, IMF, and WTO; they operate their own summits to counter the meetings of transnational institutions; they develop campaigns related to specific issues, such as the Alberta oil sands, debt relief for developing nations, and working conditions; and they create infrastructures such as the World Social Forum and the Independent Media Center (Indymedia). The World Social Forum is an annual meeting, first held in 2001, that acts as a countersummit to the World Economic Forum. The World Social Forum, attended by more than 100,000 people each year, "is an open meeting place where social movements, networks, NGOs and other civil society organizations opposed to neo-liberalism and a world dominated by capital or by any form of imperialism come together to pursue their thinking, to debate ideas democratically, for formulate proposals [*sic*], share their experiences freely and network for effective action" (World Social Forum, 2016). Regional social forums have emerged in a number of countries in the world as well. Indymedia is a collective of independent, alternative media organizations and journalists that provide non-corporate news coverage of events throughout the world. Anyone can upload photos, videos, or audio to the site (https://www.indymedia.org).

TIME TO REVIEW

- In what ways do communication technologies enhance people's knowledge?
- How has globalization improved the economies of some developing nations?
- In what way does social inequality determine the effects of globalization?
- How does the economic dimension of globalization contribute to the exploitation of workers in the developing world and to the race to the bottom in both the developing and developed worlds?
- Why have the IMF and the World Bank been criticized for their structures and some of their programs?
- What is the nature of the debate over the homogenization of cultures versus glocalization?
- How does globalization contribute to conflicts, terrorism, pandemics, and crime?
- What are global justice movements?

YOUR SOCIOLOGICAL TOOLKIT
SOCIOLOGY IN THEORY

LO8 SOCIOLOGY IN THEORY

Globalization is connected to a wide range of topics—socialization and the self, social inequality, families, gender, race and ethnicity, media, religion, education, science, crime, the environment, social movements, and health. The theories that can be applied to globalization are just as wide ranging. Many of the theories that have been presented in this book are applicable to particular aspects of globalization. Besides those particular theories, there are an almost countless number of what one might call "mini-theories" related to several of the specific topics addressed in this chapter, such as cultural homogenization, glocalization, Americanization, transnational capitalism, and the transfer of nation-state power "upward" and "downward" (and the list could go on) (Ritzer & Stepnisky, 2017). In fact, the lines between empirical and theoretical research can become quite blurred in that some authors refer to many of the ideas presented in this chapter as "theories" rather than "concepts" (e.g., glocalization). But when trying to explain the global inequality that has emerged over time and that in some cases has been heightened as a result of globalization, three classic theories are of particular relevance: modernization theory, dependency theory, and world systems theory. Those theories emphasize the economic sphere. More recently, post-colonial and feminist theories have argued that the social inequalities associated with globalization include, but extend beyond, the economic sphere.

MODERNIZATION THEORY

The origins of modernization theory go back more than 200 years, when it was first argued that economic growth and technological innovation would yield moral and social progress. In the post–Second World War era, modernization theory created a foundation for globalization. During the Cold War, the United States and the Soviet Union each argued that developing nations would be best served on their path to modernization by adopting the superpower's ideology (capitalism or communism) (Nikolayevna, 2013).

Drawing from functionalist assumptions, the postwar version of modernization placed the responsibility for underdevelopment on the underdeveloped nations themselves. They lacked the capital to invest in modern industrial and agricultural practices. They also remained too tied to traditional, irrational values and therefore lacked the rational values necessary to create a drive toward achievement, investment, and education (Inkeles & Smith, 1976; Lerner, 1958). By providing these nations with capital (e.g., through foreign aid and loans from transnational financial institutions) and instilling them with Western values, wealthy "modernized" nations could help underdeveloped countries down a path to modernization; this was the solution to global inequality. Critics of modernization quickly emerged, pointing out that underdevelopment is actually *created* by developed nations (Frank, 1966). This critique was embedded in dependency theory and more recently in world systems theory, both of which draw upon conflict theory—especially Marxism.

DEPENDENCY THEORY

Dependency theory posits that the nations that were first to industrialize exploited other countries for their natural resources, such as oil, gold, and coffee. Relationships of exploitation turned these latter countries, however rich they were, into the mines or plantations of the developed world. Whichever resource was the most valued by colonizers and by the industrialized world as a whole was increasingly emphasized in the nation's economic production. As a result of domination and exploitation, these nations did not have the opportunity to develop their own independent economies (Frank, 1966; Furtado, 1984). After decolonization, countries may have gained political independence, but because of the pattern of economic exploitation, they have remained economically dependent on the developed world (Eitzen & Zinn, 2012; Kalaska & Wites, 2015).

WORLD SYSTEMS THEORY

World systems theory (Wallerstein, 2000) also describes hierarchical relationships between nations. *Core nations* are those that first industrialized; in many cases, they are also the countries that headed colonial empires. Core nations are wealthy and powerful within the world system. *Semi-peripheral nations* are those that became economically dependent on the core nations because of trade relationships. Next are the *peripheral* Eastern European nations, whose economies are even less developed. Finally, there is the *external area*, which historically has had limited or non-existent economic relationships with the core nations; however, this has changed with globalization, and these are the countries that are most vulnerable to exploitation. For both dependency theory and world systems theory, globalization is a problem. But there are varying points of view on what the solution is. Some adherents of these views suggest that countries within the semi-periphery, periphery, and external areas would benefit from separating from the global economy and developing their own cooperative economic relationships with one another. Other adherents of these views argue that the solution to exploitative relations and global inequality lies in creating new transnational financial and political institutions or reforming the existing ones (Jacobs & Van Rossem, 2016; Ritzer & Stepnisky, 2017).

POST-COLONIAL THEORIES

Post-colonial theories focus on the impact of colonization and decolonization on the economic, cultural, political, and linguistic spheres. They suggest that current global social inequalities are not limited to this historical period but rather are extensions of Western thought that portray West and East (or global North and global South) as opposites. These portrayals can be found in art, literature, film, government publications, and academic texts—with the West (or global North) depicted as advanced and the East (or global South) as backwards (Routledge, 2011). Post-colonial theorists argue that transnational corporations and the global businesses that comprise the global assembly line are responsible for new forms of colonialism; by bringing business and employment to areas of the developing world, they have the power to shape local practices (Munck, 2016; Parekh & Wilcox, 2014; Ritzer & Stepnisky, 2017).

FEMINIST THEORIES

Feminist theories about globalization are diverse, but with several commonalities (Parekh & Wilcox, 2014). First, feminist theories draw attention to the gender inequalities associated with globalization (e.g., the gendered nature of work in electronics factories). Second, they emphasize the importance of resisting the subordination of women within the global economy. Third, they argue for the value of feminist methodologies: (a) recognizing that the experiences of women vary based on ethnicity, socioeconomic status, industry of employment, age, ability or disability, marital status, parenthood, and more; (b) focusing on the local conditions that affect the experiences of women in those locales; and (c) developing self-reflective critiques that will allow women to speak out.

A range of feminist theories have emerged from these commonalities. For example, *post-colonial* and *Third World* feminisms claim that we can only understand local practices that affect women in the larger context of histories of colonialism. *Ethics of care* feminism focuses on the "care work" that women do within the global economy (e.g., as nannies) and on their daughters, who are left behind and must assume household duties. *Transnational* feminism acknowledges the inequalities many women face that are associated with globalization but also emphasizes a positive outcome of globalization—it has given women, worldwide, "feminist solidarity across national borders" and "new political spaces that enable feminist resistance" (Parekh & Wilcox, 2014, para. 32).

As proposed by Paul Virilio, quoted at the beginning of this chapter, globalization has not just transformed the world — it has *become* the world. Through its technological, economic, political, and cultural dimensions, it affects the lives of everyone. The importance of the sociological imagination is perhaps most evident when we consider the implications of globalization. Who benefits from globalization? Who is harmed by it, and in what ways? And how do we maximize the benefits while minimizing the harms for people who are living in both the developed and the developing nations of the world? These questions can be answered only by using the sociological imagination, tracing the complex links between the micro level of individual choices and experiences and the macro level of larger global forces (see *Critical Thinking in Action*).

TIME TO REVIEW

- In what way does modernization theory blame underdeveloped nations for their own lack of development?
- According to dependency theory, why do developing nations remain dependent on the developed world?
- According to world systems theory, what are the relationships between core, semi-peripheral, peripheral, and external nations?
- What are the main assumptions of post-colonial theories?
- What are commonalities shared by feminist theories of globalization, and what are some examples of those theories?

YOUR SOCIOLOGICAL TOOLKIT

CRITICAL THINKING IN ACTION

THE 2030 AGENDA FOR SUSTAINABLE DEVELOPMENT

In 2000, the member-states of the UN adopted a set of millennium development goals (MDGs) to reduce global inequalities and enhance development by 2015. Some of the targets were reached ahead of schedule; for example, the number of people living in extreme poverty was halved by 2010. Significant progress was made on other goals (e.g., by 2011, child mortality for those under the age of 5 was reduced by 17,000 children per day). Little progress was made on other targets (e.g., G20 nations reducing their national trade restrictions). In 2012, the UN appointed a 27-member panel to develop recommendations for post-2015, to build on the successes of the MDGs and also ameliorate the barriers to continued progress (e.g., social inequality *within* developing nations). After consulting with 5,000 civil society organizations, 50 CEOs of major corporations, and thousands of ordinary global citizens (see http://www.theworldwewant.org), the *2030 Agenda for Sustainable Development* was ratified in 2015. It lists 17 "sustainable development goals" (SDGs) and 165 specific targets associated with those goals: no poverty; zero hunger; good health and well-being; quality education; gender equality; clean water and sanitation; affordable and clean energy; decent work and economic growth; industry, innovation, and infrastructure; reduced inequalities; sustainable cities and countries; responsible consumption and production; climate action; life below water; life on land; peace, justice, and strong institutions; and partnerships for the goals. You can learn more about the SDGs and associated targets and find updates on progress toward those targets at https://sustainabledevelopment.un.org.

Think Outside the Box: What kind of world do you want, and how do we create it? Given what you have learned about social inequality throughout this book, which of these universal goals do you think should be prioritized, and why? What are some of the barriers that might be faced? What changes are needed economically, politically, and culturally? What are some of the steps that can be taken to achieve those goals? What specific steps can you take to contribute to progress on these goals?

CHAPTER SUMMARY

LO1 Define "globalization" and differentiate it from "globality."

"Globalization" is the process whereby "globality"—the tight global economic, political, cultural, and environmental interconnections and flows that make most of the current borders and boundaries irrelevant—is achieved. More informally, globalization is sometimes referred to as the greater interconnectedness of the world's people.

LO2 Describe historical precursors to globalization.

The dynamic that underlies globalization is thousands of years old, involving the migration of people, the exchange of goods, the creation of trade routes, and the sharing of information. In the late 19th century, the invention of the steamship and the laying of the first transatlantic telegraph line lowered the cost and increased the speed of transportation and communication.

LO3 Explain how changes after the Second World War precipitated modern globalization.

Several changes following the Second World War heralded modern globalization: the dissolution of colonial empires; the formation of transnational political and financial institutions such as the UN, the IMF, the World Bank, and the WTO; and the collapse of the Soviet Union.

LO4 Describe the technological, economic, political, cultural, and social characteristics of globalization.

Technology facilitates all other dimensions of globalization. Information storage and retrieval, transportation, communication, and production have been transformed. The economic dimension includes expanding markets, flexible production, the global assembly line, and corporate restructuring that has resulted in a concentration of economic power. The political dimension of globalization involves the declining power of nation-states, shifting their power "upward" to transnational bodies and "downward" to regional trade bodies, global cities, and civil society.

LO5 Outline the vision of globalization, including its proposed world benefits.

Proponents of globalization suggest that its technological, economic, political, and cultural dimensions have the potential to improve living conditions through the globalization of production, spread democracy, and increase knowledge and understanding, thereby decreasing conflict.

LO6 Describe the dark side of globalization highlighted by various social organizations.

Global social inequality has increased in many ways. Workers in developing nations are frequently exploited and subjected to poor working conditions. The "race to the bottom" lowers wages and increases job insecurity in both developing and developed nations. Transnational organizations such as the IMF are criticized for being governed by the interests of wealthy, powerful nations. A trend toward homogenization and uniformity of culture occurs, at the expense of local cultures, although others argue that global and local cultures are often combined.

LO7 Describe global justice movements, including their affiliated activities.

Global justice movements have a unifying interest in resisting neoliberalism and its effects. They are opposed to certain aspects of globalization, yet they also participate in it. They organize protests at meetings of transnational financial institutions; host counter-summits; develop campaigns around specific issues, such as child labour; and develop infrastructures such as the World Social Forum and Indymedia.

LO8 Explain how different theories contribute to our understanding of global inequality.

Modernization theory attributes underdevelopment to characteristics of the underdeveloped nations themselves. Dependency theory suggests that the countries first to industrialize exploited the resources of other nations, turning them into their own personal mines or plantations. World systems theory describes a hierarchical relationship between core, semi-peripheral, peripheral, and external countries, where the latter three are all economically dependent on the core. Post-colonial theories focus on the effects of colonization and decolonization on people and communities. Feminist theories draw attention to gender equalities in the global economy, work to end the subordination of women in that economy, and emphasize the importance of using feminist methodologies.

RECOMMENDED RESOURCES

1. The 17 sustainable development goals that comprise the *2030 Agenda for Sustainable Development* guide policy development in member nations. But achieving those goals depends on each one of us. To learn more about what you can do, use the free tools and resources at http://17goals.org.
2. George Ritzer uses the fast-food restaurant as a metaphor for the way that rationality, efficiency, and uniformity have come to characterize the globalizing world in *The McDonaldization of Society* (Thousand Oaks, CA: Sage Publications, 2013).
3. Human Rights Watch is a nonprofit organization that investigates human rights conditions across the globe, releasing more than 100 reports (including hidden video footage) on human rights abuses in 90 countries. To learn about current human rights conditions, see https://www.hrw.org.

FOR FURTHER REFLECTION

1. In your opinion, in what ways has Canadian culture been "Americanized," and in what ways is it characterized by glocalization?
2. What image of global justice movements is portrayed in the media? What impact might these portrayals have on the efforts of global justice groups?

ENDNOTES

1 Retrieved June 14, 2017, from thinkexist.com.
2 Retrieved February 17, 2011, from brainyquote.com.

Glossary

A

abolitionism A movement calling for the dismantling of the criminal justice system. p. 231

achieved status A social position obtained through personal actions. p. 81

acid rain The dilute sulphuric and nitric acids created when fossil fuels are burned. p. 297

acting crowd A group of people gathered at the same place at the same time who engage in overt collective behaviour in pursuit of a common goal. p. 269

agency People's capacity to make choices, which then have an impact on other people and on the society in which they live. p. 4

agents of socialization The groups, social institutions, and/or social settings that have the greatest amount of influence on the developing self. p. 75

alienation The detachment that exists between the worker and his or her labour as perpetuated under capitalism. p. 105

alternative social movements Social movements that seek limited societal change for a specific group or narrow segment of society. p. 278

androcentric Male-centred, failing to account for women's experiences. p. 14

androcentric bias A tendency to favour males. p. 209

anomie A feeling of normlessness. p. 10

anthropocentrism A worldview that considers humans to be the most important form of life. p. 299

anticipatory socialization The process by which individuals learn about the roles associated with a particular status before taking on that status. p. 80

anti-miscegenation laws Laws that prohibit interracial marriages. p. 169

ascribed status A social position conferred at birth. p. 81

augmented reality (AR) An enhanced version of reality created by the use of technology to overlay digital information on an image of something being viewed through a device (such as a smartphone camera). p. 116

authoritarian personality A personality type that values authority and obedience, is low in tolerance, and is high in steretypical thinking. p. 172

auxiliary traits Characteristics presumed to accompany a specific master status. p. 68

B

baby boom The period from 1946 to 1965 during which several demographic forces coalesced, resulting in a larger number of births than would normally be the case. p. 185

behaviourism A school of thought that denies free will, emphasizes observable phenomena, and claims that all behaviour is learned from the environment. p. 69

belief Something one accepts as true, regardless of whether it is true or not. p. 199

belief system A set of interconnected beliefs that are shared among groups of people. p. 199

bicultural Participating in two distinct cultures simultaneously. p. 163

bilineal Lineage is traced through both parents' sides of the family. p. 189

bio-ecological theory of human development A theory that views human development as a dynamic process of reciprocal interaction in which individuals play an important role in shaping the environment in which they develop. p. 69

biological determinism The belief that human behaviour is controlled by genetics. p. 68

bisexuality Sexual attraction to both males and females. p. 140

bitcoins A form of digital currency mined on the Internet and later exchanged for goods and services. p. 114

bonding capital Resources in the form of community ties and identity. p. 202

bourgeoisie In Marxist conflict theory, the owners of the means of production. p. 11

bridging capital Resources accumulated within groups that can be used outside those groups. p. 202

bureaucracy A formal organization model consisting of an explicit chain of authority and a set of procedures and protocols that guide the relationships and processes that exist within it. p. 83

C

carbon footprint A method for identifying and keeping track of behaviours that negatively impact the environment through greenhouse gas production. p. 289

caste system A hierarchical system of stratification based on inherited social standing. p. 91

casual crowd A gathering of people who by proximity alone happen to be in the same location at the same time. p. 268

child-savers movement A movement dedicated to the betterment of social conditions involving children. p. 203

cisgender Individuals whose gender identity or expression corresponds to their birth sex, based on elite, dualistic discourses. p. 137

claim A statement about the nature of some phenomenon that is constructed as a social problem. p. 277

claims making A process whereby a social movement declares that a particular condition is unjust and identifies measures needed to resolve the unfairness. p. 278

class system A hierarchical system of stratification based on achieved *and* ascribed economic measures such as annual income or the possession of resources. p. 91

collective behaviour Group behaviour that is relatively spontaneous, unstructured, and unconventional in nature. p. 267

collective conscience The unified body of cultural knowledge that is transmitted in group religious rituals. p. 204

collective effervescence A euphoria that enables people to transcend the challenges of everyday life—to a degree not possible when alone—that emerges from group religious rituals. p. 204

collective identity A shared sense of belonging that binds individuals in a social movement and propels them to take action on behalf of that social movement. p. 282

commodities Raw materials that can be bought and sold. p. 186

comparison level A comparison of the costs and benefits of a particular relationship compared to other people who are in similar types of relationships. p. 192

comparison level for alternatives A comparison of our relationship to alternative possibilities for our lives. p. 192

concept An abstract idea expressed as a word or phrase. p. 24

conformity A form of social influence in which individuals change their behaviour in order to adhere to group norms. p. 83

conglomerate A corporation made up of several different widely diversified companies. p. 119

consumption The general use of natural resources. p. 293

content analysis A secondary analysis technique used to systematically examine messages contained in text or portrayed in images. p. 38

control group Participants in an experiment who are not exposed to the independent variable. p. 34

conventional crowd A group of people who have gathered in the same place at the same time because of a common shared interest or objective. p. 268

convergent design Employs at least one qualitative and one quantitative method at the same time in order to compare different perspectives as part of the overall data integration. p. 42

corporate crime Criminal offences carried out by organizations or by knowledgeable employees in the course of their employment. p. 228

cost of living A measure of the average price for essential goods and services in a given area, including transportation. p. 95

counterculture A type of subculture that strongly opposes central aspects of mainstream culture. p. 58

credentialism The reliance on increasingly higher educational qualifications as necessary minimal requirements for employment. p. 216

crime Any behaviour that violates criminal law. p. 223

crime rate The number of criminal incidents reported to the police divided by the population. p. 226

crime severity index (CSI) The volume of crimes multiplied by their severity. p. 226

criminal justice system The social institution responsible for the apprehension, prosecution, and punishment of criminal offenders. p. 229

criminologists Researchers who specialize in the study of criminal behaviour. p. 223

criminology The academic discipline that focuses on the study of crime and those labelled as criminals. p. 223

critical An approach to theorizing that explores the role power plays in social processes and emphasizes the importance of knowledge being tied to emancipation. p. 9

crowd A temporary gathering of people who are in the same place at the same time. p. 268

cultural relativism An ability to understand another culture on its own terms sympathetically enough so that the culture appears to be a coherent and meaningful design for living. p. 57

cultural universals Common practices shared by all societies. p. 47

culture The sum total of the social environment in which we are raised and continue to be socialized throughout our lives. p. 47

culture shock A sense of disorientation and confusion that results when placed in unfamiliar surroundings where aspects of the material and nonmaterial culture are new or unknown. p. 48

cybercrime Criminal acts committed using computer technology. p. 228

D

data analysis Compilation of observations into a format that helps us learn more about the research problem. p. 28

debriefing The later disclosure of all relevant details in cases where research participants cannot be told all of the information ahead of time. p. 31

decolonization The process whereby colonial empires are dismantled and former colonies are granted political and economic independence. p. 310

deductive reasoning A theory-driven approach that typically concludes with generalizations based on research findings. p. 24

demographic transition theory As a result of modernization, societies eventually progress from being characterized by high fertility and mortality rates to being characterized by low fertility and mortality rates. p. 290

demography The study of human populations. p. 287

dependent variable The outcome or variable that is measured in an experiment. p. 34

descriptive research Describes features and characteristics of a group, event, activity, or situation. p. 26

deviant A person, behaviour, or characteristic perceived as unacceptable. p. 221

differences in sexual development (DSD) A term used in place of *intersexed*, referring to physical sex characteristics that fall outside the boundaries of the male/female dualism. p. 136

diffuse pattern Uncertainty about which culture(s) one should or should not identify with. p. 163

disaster A relatively sudden, unscheduled, one-time event that causes a great deal of property or ecological damage, or large-scale loss of life, and substantial disruption or stress among residents in the stricken area. p. 275

discourse analysis The use of multiple methods to critically examine the ways in which language is used to convey social constructions and social relations. p. 39

discourses Ways of understanding a particular subject or social phenomenon. p. 15

discrimination Treating someone unfairly because of his or her group membership. p. 170

disorders of sexual development (DSD) A term used in place of *intersexed*, referring to physical sex characteristics that fall outside the boundaries of the male/female dualism. p. 136

disposable societies Societies characterized by an excess of manufactured products that are used for only a short period of time and then disposed of. p. 294

dominant groups Groups that have institutionalized power and privilege in society. p. 165

dualism A contrast between two opposing categories. p. 135

dysfunctional One of society's structures no longer fulfills its function effectively. p. 10

E

ecological footprint An estimate for gauging the total area of land and water ecosystems a human population needs in order to produce the resources it consumes and to assimilate its wastes. p. 288

ecological overshoot Growth beyond the Earth's carrying capacity. p. 288

economic immigrants Immigrants selected on the basis of some combination of educational attainment, occupational skills, entrepreneurship, business investment, and ability to contribute to the Canadian economy. p. 161

education A formal institution that systematically instills much of the knowledge that is needed to function as productive adults in society. p. 211

emblems Gestures with direct verbal equivalents. p. 54

empirical methods Data collection that produces verifiable findings and is carried out using systematic procedures. p. 9

empowerment research Examines social settings and conditions to identify key issues and involves stakeholders for the purpose of improvement. p. 26

environmental refugee A person who is forced to flee his or her country as a result of environmental displacement resulting from life-endangering natural and human-made environmental change. p. 299

epidemiological transition Historical changes in patterns of morbidity and mortality, from a predominance of infectious and parasitic diseases to degenerative diseases. p. 242

equity The contributions each party is making in a relationship are perceived as "fair." p. 192

ethnic identity How you personally identify your ethnicity. Also known as *subjective ethnicity*. p. 158

ethnic origin The ethnic characteristics of your ancestors. Also known as *objective ethnicity*. p. 158

ethnic pattern Identifying primarily with one's heritage culture. p. 175

ethnicity Cultural characteristics such as language, religion, taste in food, shared descent, cultural traditions, and shared geographic locations. p. 157

ethnocentrism The tendency to believe that one's cultural beliefs and practices are superior and should be used as the standard to which other cultures are compared. p. 58

ethnocide The eradication of a culture. p. 166

ethnography Fieldwork designed to describe everyday behaviour in natural settings. p. 39

evaluation research Assesses the need for or effectiveness of a social program. p. 26

experiment A deductive research method for testing a hypothesis through the use of a carefully controlled environment and random assignment to conditions. p. 34

explanatory research Clarifies aspects of a particular social phenomenon. p. 26

exploratory research Explores an area of interest that very little is known about. p. 25

expressive crowd A gathering of people who share a common interest and are gathered at the same event at the same time with an explicit participatory purpose. p. 269

extended A family structure that includes parents, their children, and additional relatives. p. 188

F

fads Temporary but highly popular social patterns such as activities, events, music genres, or hobbies. p. 271

family-class immigrants Immigrants who are sponsored by close relatives living in Canada. p. 161

fashion Long-lasting popular social patterns that typically involve clothing lines and accessories. p. 271

femininity The behavioural, cultural, or psychological traits associated with being female, within a certain culture, at a given point in history. p. 136

feminism The system of ideas and political practices based on the principle that women are human beings equal to men. p. 13

fictive kin Individuals who are not related by blood, marriage, or adoption but who assume some of the benefits and/or some of the obligations of family life. p. 182

financial wealth Corresponds to economic assets derived from income, real estate, savings, stocks, bonds, income-generating investments, and other sources of revenue or capital. p. 93

folkways Informal norms based on accepted traditions. p. 52

G

gender The behavioural, cultural, or psychological traits associated with a particular sex, within a certain culture, at a given point in history. p. 136

gender non-conforming Individuals whose gender identity or expression falls outside elite, dualistic discourses. May also be referred to as gender variant, gender creative, gender non-binary, or gender fluid. p. 138

general in the particular The broader social patterns that are reflected in the actions of individuals. p. 4

generalized other An overall sense of people's expectations. p. 12

glass ceiling Intangible barriers that prevent women from attaining positions of authority or leadership. p. 147

glass escalator Intangible factors that enable men to attain positions of authority or leadership. p. 147

global warming An increase in the temperature of the Earth's atmosphere. p. 297

globality A social condition characterized by tight global economic, political, cultural, and environmental interconnections and flows that make most current borders and boundaries irrelevant. p. 309

globalization A set of [uneven] social processes that appear to transform our present social condition of conventional nationality into one of globality. p. 309

glocalization The blending of the global and the local. p. 319

gossip Unsubstantiated or substantiated stories about specific individuals. p. 273

greenwashing Misleading consumers regarding the environmental practices of a company or the environmental benefits of a product or service. p. 294

gross domestic product (GDP) An overall indicator of a country's economic productivity based on goods and services as measured by household consumption, government spending, and investments. p. 103

grounded theory A systematic strategy for moving from specific observations to general conclusions about discourses, actions, interactions, and practices. p. 32

groupthink A process in which members of a group favour consensus over rational decision making, producing poor and even disastrous outcomes. p. 83

H

hate crimes Criminal offences motivated by hate toward an identifiable group. p. 171

health A state of complete physical, mental, and social well-being and not merely the absence of disease or infirmity. p. 241

healthy immigrant effect Recent immigrants tend to have better health than people who are Canadian-born. p. 254

heteronormative The view that heterosexuality is the expected or preferred sexual orientation. p. 141

heterosexuality Sexual attraction to members of the "opposite sex." p. 136

hidden curriculum The process by which a subtle agenda of norms, values, and expectations that fall outside the formal curriculum is learned inadvertently through participation in the school system. p. 213

high culture Activities shared by the social elite. p. 60

historical analysis The examination and interpretation of historical forms of data. p. 39

homelessness A state in which a person is unable to secure a permanent residence. p. 106

homosexuality Sexual attraction to members of the "same sex." p. 136

human carrying capacity The number of people that can be supported in a given area indefinitely. p. 290

Human Exemptionalism Paradigm (HEP) The view of humans as unique from other organisms in the natural world because of their capacity to reason and develop culture. p. 299

hypermasculinity Traditional masculinity in an extreme and exaggerated form. p. 139

hypothesis A testable research statement that includes at least two variables. p. 28

I

ideal culture Cultural values a majority of people identify with in a given society. p. 57

ideal type An analytical construct that clearly depicts all of the main features of some social phenomenon but is not an entity that can be found in reality. p. 84

ideology A set of ideas that support the needs and views of a particular group. p. 61

independent variable The presumed cause or variable that is manipulated in an experiment. p. 34

indictable conviction offences More serious criminal offences than summary offences with penalties that vary but could result in life imprisonment. p. 225

inductive reasoning A data-driven approach that begins with observations and ends in theory construction. p. 25

infant mortality rate The incidence of deaths among infants under one year of age per 1,000 live births in a given population. p. 290

institutionalized goals The goals that we are *supposed* to aspire to in contemporary society. p. 233

integration pattern Identifying with both one's heritage culture and one's new, national culture. p. 163

intergenerational mobility Changes in the social class of children relative to their parents. p. 92

interpersonal trust A perception that another person can be relied upon and has your best interests at heart. p. 76

interpretive An approach to theorizing that focuses on the ways people come to understand themselves, others, and the world around them. p. 9

intersectionality The way in which our individual array of multiple identities (e.g., based on sex, gender, race, and social class) combines to create a distinctive whole. p.153

intersexed A person whose physical sex characteristics fall outside the boundaries of the male/female dualism. p. 136

interview A verbal question-and-answer technique used for obtaining information on a topic of interest. p. 36

intragenerational mobility Changes in social class that occur within a person's lifetime. p. 92

L

language A shared system of communication that includes spoken, written, and signed forms of speech as well as nonverbal gestures used to convey meaning. p. 49

latent function An unintended function of one of society's structures. p. 10

legitimate means The socially accepted ways of attaining wealth, power, and prestige. p. 233

les femmes du pays The Indigenous "country wives" of European traders. p. 165

life chances The opportunities an individual has in life based on various factors, including stratification, inequality, race, ethnicity, and gender. p. 5

looking-glass self The sense of ourselves that we develop based on our perceptions of how others view us. p. 73

low-income cutoff An annual family income value in dollars below which a family is worse off than average due to the high proportion of income allocated to food, clothing, and shelter. p. 97

M

macro level The level of broader social forces. p. 4

manifest function An intended function of one of society's structures. p. 10

masculinity The behavioural, cultural, or psychological traits associated with being male, within a certain culture, at a given point in history. p. 136

master status The most influential status in an individual's status set. p. 81

material culture Tangible or physical items that people have created for use and give meaning to in a given culture. p. 48

matriarchal Power is vested in the female head of household and women in society more generally. p. 189

matrilineal Lineage is traced through the mother's side of the family, especially its female members. p. 189

matrix of domination Intersecting systems of oppression in society, such as those based on sex, gender, race, or social class. p. 153

media Communications that target large audiences in print or in electronic format using audio and/or images. p. 79

media literacy The ability to recognize, critically assess, and make informed choices about the messages contained in mass media forms. p. 128

meritocracy A condition of advancement based on worth. p. 105

micro level The level of individual experiences and choices. p. 4

migration The movement of people into or out of a country. p. 290

minority groups Definable groups that are socially disadvantaged and face unequal treatment. p. 165

monogamous A marriage that includes two spouses. p. 188

monopoly A company that has exclusive control over a particular product or service. p. 119

moral entrepreneur A person who brings perceived morally damaging behaviour to the attention of others. p. 274

moral panic Irrational but widespread worry that certain groups present an enormous threat to the social order of society. p. 274

morbidity The prevalence and patterns of disease in a population. p. 242

mores Institutionalized norms embedded in laws used to help maintain social control. p. 53

mortality The incidence and patterns of death in a population. p. 242

mother tongue The first language learned at home in childhood that is still understood by an individual. p. 50

motives The reasons for engaging in either deviant or conforming behaviour. p. 234

N

national pattern Identifying primarily with one's new, national culture. p. 163

negative bonding capital Community ties and sources of identity that harm the wider society. p. 203

neoliberalism An economic philosophy claiming that when market forces are unimpeded by government, prosperity and democracy will flourish. p. 311

net neutrality A principle of equality and detachment with respect to how information on the Internet is treated by network providers. p. 117

net worth Total assets calculated by subtracting all existing financial liabilities from assets. p. 95

New Ecological Paradigm (NEP) The view of humans as possessing a superior capacity to reason and adapt to social/cultural conditions while also recognizing the interdependence between humans and the natural environment. p. 300

nonmaterial culture Intangibles produced by intellectual or spiritual development; also, the use of artifacts in a given culture. p. 48

norm of communism The notion that scientific knowledge is to be freely shared with others. p. 206

norm of disinterestedness The notion that scientists do their work solely for the purposes of discovering truth. p. 206

norm of organized skepticism The notion that scientific claims should be subjected to rigorous scrutiny. p. 206

norm of universalism The notion that scientific knowledge is free of social biases. p. 206

normative Behaviours, appearances, and thoughts that correspond to society's norms. p. 4

norms Society's expectations for how we are supposed to act, think, and look. p. 4

nuclear A family structure comprising parents and their children. p. 188

O

objective ethnicity The ethnic characteristics of your ancestors. Also known as *ethnic origin*. p. 158

ombudsperson An independent body with the authority to conduct thorough, impartial, independent investigations and to make recommendations to government organizations with respect to the problems of citizens. p. 231

operationalization The process whereby variables are defined in a precise manner that is measurable. p. 27

organized crime Two or more persons consorting together on a continual basis to participate in illegal activities, either directly or indirectly, for gain. p. 228

overconsumption Use of natural resources at a rate on par with natural replenishment. p. 293

P

pansexuality Sexual attraction to people along the full spectrums of sex, gender, and sexuality. p. 140

paradigm A conceptual framework or model for organizing information. p. 207

paradigm shift Movement away from a particular conceptual framework. p. 207

participant observation A naturalistic method for collecting systematic data while taking part in a social group or process. p. 40

participatory action research A field method involving stakeholders as co-researchers in a collaborative process designed to improve outcomes. p. 27

patriarchal Power is vested in the male head of household and men in society more generally. p. 189

patriarchy Legal and/or social power that is vested in males. p. 13

patrilineal Lineage is traced through the father's side of the family, especially its male members. p. 189

personal identity The portion of an individual's sense of self that renders him or her unique from others. p. 68

personal–social identity continuum The range of traits you possess that emphasize the manner in which you see yourself as a unique individual on one end and those that underscore your membership in a group on the other end. p. 67

pluralism Cultural differences are maintained and celebrated. p. 168

polygamous A marriage that includes three or more spouses simultaneously. p. 188

popular culture Well-liked everyday practices and products. p. 60

population checks Factors that limit population growth. p. 289

population pyramid A horizontal bar chart that shows how many people are in the various age groups, divided by sex. p. 256

population transfer A process whereby minority groups are forcibly expelled or are limited to a specific location. p. 169

positive bonding capital Community ties and sources of identity that benefit the wider society. p. 203

positivist An approach to theorizing that emphasizes explanation and prediction. p. 9

praxis The responsibility that scholars have to provide subordinated and marginalized groups in society with the knowledge they need to be able to end their powerlessness. p. 12

prejudice An attitude that is unrelated to reality and is generalized to all members of a certain group. p. 170

prescriptive norms Rules concerning behaviours we are expected to perform. p. 53

primary deviance The little acts of deviance that many of us engage in occasionally. p. 235

private schools Schools operated by private individuals or corporations for which parents pay an annual tuition. p. 216

profit The benefits of being in a particular relationship outweigh the costs. p. 192

proletariat In Marxist conflict theory, the people who work for the owners of the means of production. p. 11

property crimes Economic offences directed at someone's property rather than someone's physical person. p. 226

proscriptive norms Rules concerning behaviours we are expected to refrain from doing. p. 53

public schools Schools funded through provincial and local governments. p. 216

Q

qualitative methods Methods most often employed to better understand social phenomena using inductive reasoning and non-numerical data. p. 32

quantitative methods Methods usually employed to test hypotheses based on deductive reasoning and numerical data. p. 32

R

race A socially constructed category used to classify humankind according to such physical characteristics as skin colour, hair texture, and facial features. p. 158

racialization The process by which racial categories are constructed as different and unequal in ways that have social, economic, and political consequences. p. 158

racialized group Persons, other than Aboriginal [i.e., Indigenous] persons, who are non-Caucasian in race or non-white in colour. Also known as *visible minorities*. p. 158

racism A specific form of prejudice based on aspects of physical appearance, such as skin colour. p. 170

real culture Practices engaged in by the majority of people in a given society. p. 57

recession A general economic decline that persists for two or more three-month periods. p. 103

recidivism Committing further crimes after having been convicted of a crime. p. 74

redemptive social movements Social movements that seek large-scale change for a specific group. p. 279

reformative social movements Social movements that seek limited societal change for everyone in society. p. 279

refugees Persons who are forced to flee from persecution. p. 161

reliability There is consistency in the measure for a variable of interest. p. 28

religion A united system of beliefs and practices related to sacred things. p. 200

religiosity A combined measure of religious affiliation, attendance, and participation. p. 201

religious affiliation The identification with a particular religion. p. 201

religious attendance Attendance at organized religious services. p. 201

representative sample A group that closely approximates the population of interest. p. 36

research design A detailed outline of all of the proposed components of a study. p. 28

residential schools A boarding school funded by the Canadian government used to assimilate Indigenous children. p. 166

resocialization A process that involves radically altering one's identity by giving up an existing status in exchange for a new one. p. 85

respondents Persons who consent to provide survey answers. p. 35

restorative justice An approach to justice emphasizing healing and reparation of harm. p. 232

retribution A morally justified consequence. p. 229

revolutionary social movements Social movements that seek large-scale change that affects everyone in society. p. 279

rigour Trustworthiness of a qualitative research process and the data collected. p. 33

role The behavioural component of a given status. p. 80

role conflict A situation in which incompatible role demands exist between two or more commonly held statuses. p. 82

role strain A situation in which incompatible role demands exist within a single status. p. 82

rumours Unsubstantiated stories about people or events. p. 272

S

Sapir–Whorf hypothesis The assertion that language helps shape reality for those experiencing it. p. 51

scapegoat An individual or group that is wrongfully blamed for a personal or social problem. p. 173

science An institution that provides a way to understand the natural makeup of the world by means of rational methods of inquiry. p. 206

scientism A worldview that uses the insights of natural science to inform people's ways of living, their purpose in life, and the choices they make. p. 206

secondary analysis of existing data A research method used to examine information on a topic of interest that was collected or created by someone other than the researcher for an unrelated purpose. p. 38

secondary deviance Chronic deviance as a lifestyle. p. 235

secular The state of not being governed by religion. p. 201

segregation Minority groups are separated from the dominant group. p. 169

self-concept An individual's sense of who he or she is based on perceived similarities to and differences from others. p. 68

self-esteem An evaluation of one's own self-worth. p. 75

self-fulfilling prophecy An originally false belief that becomes true simply because it is perceived as such. p. 217

self-surveillance Monitoring our own behaviours in order to prevent being considered deviant. p. 237

sex Biological characteristics that include sex chromosomes, primary sex characteristics, and secondary sex characteristics. p. 135

significant others People who are important to us. p. 12

single-case design Case study research that focuses on only one person, organization, event, or program as the unit of analysis, as emphasized by the research objectives. p. 42

social capital Resources in the form of accumulated social networks. p. 202

social causation hypothesis The suggestion that the stresses associated with having a lower socioeconomic status contribute to the development of mental disorders. p. 252

social class Shared membership in a group based on economic standing. p. 91

social comparison Refers to how individuals evaluate themselves in terms of appearance, merit, and abilities based on how they compare to others. p. 77

social control Actions intended to prevent, correct, punish, or cure people, behaviours, or characteristics that are perceived as unacceptable. p. 221

social facilitation The tendency for people to do better on simple tasks, but worse on complex tasks, when they are in the presence of others and their individual performance can be evaluated. p. 82

social facts Observable social phenomena external to individuals that exercise power over them. p. 56

social group Two or more people who share relevant cultural elements and interact with regular frequency. p. 82

social identity The portion of an individual's sense of self derived from membership in social groups. p. 68

social inequality An unequal distribution of resources. p. 89

social institutions Relatively permanent societal structures that govern the behaviour of groups and promote social order. p. 83

social loafing The tendency to put in minimal effort on simple group tasks when individual performance cannot be evaluated. p. 82

social mobility Movement that occurs within and between social classes in a stratification system. p. 91

social movement organization (SMO) A complex or formal organization that identifies its goals with the preferences of a social movement or a countermovement and attempts to implement those goals. p. 278

social movements Organized efforts by a substantial number of people to change or to resist change in some major aspect or aspects of society. p. 276

social network An interrelated system of social relationships of varying purpose, relevance, intimacy, and importance. p. 82

social safety net Services and programs designed to lessen financial burdens experienced by low-income groups. p. 104

social selection hypothesis The suggestion that people with mental disorders may drift into lower levels of socioeconomic status or be prevented from rising out of lower levels of status. p. 252

social stratification Socially sanctioned patterns (or classes) of social inequality that exist in society and that are based on distinguishable attributes such as race, age, gender, income, or occupation. p. 89

social structure The framework of cultural elements and social patterns in which social interactions take place. p. 80

socialization The lifelong process through which people learn about themselves and their various roles in society and in relation to one another. p. 68

sociobiology The belief that social behaviour evolved from the need to reproduce and survive. p. 68

socioeconomic status Social standing based on a combined measure of education, income, and occupation. p. 92

sociological imagination The ability to perceive the interconnections between individual experiences and larger sociocultural forces. p. 6

sociology The systematic study of society using the sociological imagination. p. 6

status A recognized social position that exists independently of any given individual who may occupy it. p. 80

status set The sum total of all of the statuses held by a person at a given time. p. 81

status symbols Material indicators of wealth and prestige. p. 60

stereotype An overgeneralization about a group, often based on faulty assumptions. p. 123

stigmatization The process by which individuals are excluded because of particular behaviours/characteristics. p. 236

strange in the familiar Instead of assuming that people's actions are determined solely by personal choice, looking for the ways that society shapes those choices. p. 4

streaming A process whereby students are placed into specific programs and levels of curriculum based on perceived levels of achievement. p. 214

subculture A group that can be differentiated from mainstream culture by its divergent traits involving language, norms, beliefs, and/or values. p. 58

subjective ethnicity How you personally identify your ethnicity. Also known as *ethnic identity*. p. 158

summary conviction offences Less serious criminal offences that are punishable by a maximum of six months in prison and/or a fine of not more than $5,000. p. 225

survey A method of gathering opinions using a questionnaire. p. 35

sustainability Use of natural resources at a rate on par with natural replenishment. p. 293

sustainable development Development that meets the needs of the present without compromising the ability of future generations to meet their own needs. p. 303

symbol An object, image, or event used to represent a particular concept. p. 59

systematic observation A naturalistic but nonparticipatory method for collecting data on a social group or process. p. 40

T

taboos Mores that are considered wrong in and of themselves. p. 53

tariffs Fees imposed by a government on imported goods. p. 311

techniques The skills needed to engage in either deviant or conforming behaviour. p. 234

techniques of neutralization Rationalizations that allow us to justify our behaviour to others and to ourselves. p. 234

theory A set of propositions intended to explain a fact or a phenomenon. p. 9

total fertility rate The number of live births a female can be expected to have in her lifetime. p. 290

total institution An isolated social system in which certain individuals are housed, looked after, and socialized apart from the wider society. p. 85

transgender Individuals whose gender identity or expression corresponds to that of another sex. p. 138

treadmill of production A theoretical model that explains environmental issues as resulting from an incessant need to increase production and profit. p. 301

triangulation The use of multiple data-gathering techniques within the same study. p. 33

two-spirited In Indigenous cultures, individuals who have both male and female spirits. p. 137

U

urban legends Abstract unsubstantiated stories containing an underlying message or moral that persists over time. p. 273

urban sprawl A process by which rapid urban growth necessitates the conversion of natural land for human-made uses. p. 292

V

validity A measure is a good indicator of the intended concept. p. 28

values Collectively shared criteria by which we determine whether something is right or wrong. p. 10

variable A categorical concept for properties of people or entities that can differ and change. p. 24

victimless crimes Criminal offences that involve consensual relations in the exchange of illegal goods or services. p. 227

violent crimes Criminal offences that involve physical harm to another person. p. 225

visible minorities Persons, other than Aboriginal [i.e., Indigenous] persons, who are non-Caucasian in race or non-white in colour. Also known as *racialized groups*. p. 158

W

Washington Consensus The structural adjustment programs supported by the IMF, the World Bank, and the United States Treasury Department. p. 319

white-collar crime Criminal offences involving the misappropriation of financial resources. p. 228

widespread panic A generalized belief regarding impending danger that can lead a large number of people to flee an area or engage in other protective measures. p. 273

References

CHAPTER 1

Arum, R., & Roksa, J. (2010). *Academically adrift: Limited learning on college campuses*. Chicago, IL: University of Chicago Press.

Ashley, D., & Orenstein, D. M. (2001). *Sociological theory: Classical statements* (5th ed.). Boston, MA: Allyn & Bacon.

Association of Universities and Colleges of Canada. (2009, October 22). *Media release: University enrolment up across Canada*. Retrieved from http://www.aucc.ca

Bengston, V. L., Acock, A. C., Allen, K. R., Dilworth-Anderson, P., & Klein, D. M. (2005). Theory and theorizing in family research: Puzzle-building and puzzle solving. In V. L. Bengston, A. C. Acock, K. R. Allen, P. Dilworth-Anderson, & D. M. Klein (Eds.), *Sourcebook of family theory and research* (pp. 3–33). Thousand Oaks, CA: Sage Publications.

Berger, P. (1963). *Invitation to sociology: A humanistic perspective*. New York, NY: Anchor.

Blumer, H. (1969). *Symbolic interactionism: Perspective and method*. Englewood Cliffs, NJ: Prentice-Hall.

Clawson, D., Zussman, R., Misra, J., Stokes, R., Anderton, D. L., & Burawoy, M. (Eds.). (2007). *Public sociology: Fifteen eminent sociologists debate politics & the profession in the twenty-first century*. Berkeley, CA: University of California Press.

Delanty, G. (2005). *Social science: Philosophical and methodological foundations* (2nd ed.). Buckingham, UK: Open University Press.

Delanty, G. (2007). Sociology. In G. Ritzer (Ed.), *Blackwell encyclopedia of sociology*. Retrieved from http://www.blackwellreference.com

DeMello, M. (2016). Memories on the skin: A brief cultural history of tattooing. In D. Davidson (Ed.), *The tattoo project: Commemorative tattoos, visual culture, and the digital archive* (pp. 21–29). Toronto, ON: Canadian Scholars' Press.

Downes, D., Rock, P., & McLaughlin, E. (2016). *Understanding deviance* (7th ed.). New York, NY: Oxford University Press.

Durkheim, E. (1933). *The division of labour in society*. New York, NY: Free Press.

Durkheim, E. (1951). *Suicide*. New York, NY: Free Press.

Engels, F. (1972). *The origin of the family, private property and the state*. New York, NY: Pathfinder. (Original work published 1884)

Fitzpatrick, M. (2013, April 25). Harper on terror arrests: Not a time for 'sociology.' CBC News. Retrieved from http://www.cbc.ca/news

Fletcher, R. (1971). *The making of sociology: A study of sociological theory. Volume 1*. London, UK: Thomas Nelson and Sons Ltd.

Foucault, M. (1978). *The history of sexuality, volume I: An introduction*. New York, NY: Vintage Books.

Foucault, M. (1980). *Power/knowledge: Selected interviews and other writings 1972–1977* (1st American ed.). (C. Gordon, L. Marshall, J. Mepham, & K. Super, Trans.). New York, NY: Pantheon Books.

Foucault, M. (1995). *Discipline and punish: The birth of the prison* (2nd ed.). (A. Sheridan, Trans.). New York, NY: Vintage Books. (Original work published 1977)

Foundation for Critical Thinking. (2015). *Defining critical thinking*. Retrieved from http://www.criticalthinking.org

Gerwing, J., McConnell, D., Stearns, D., & Adair, S. (2007). Critical thinking for civic thinking in science. *Academic Exchange Quarterly, 11*(3), 160–164.

Jones, R. A. (1986). *Émile Durkheim: An introduction to four major works*. Beverly Hills, CA: Sage Publications.

Kaye, J., & Béland, D. (2014, August 22). Stephen Harper's dangerous refusal to 'commit sociology.' CBC News. Retrieved from http://www.cbc.ca/news

Lengermann, P., & Niebrugge, G. (2007a). Feminism. In G. Ritzer (Ed.), *Blackwell encyclopedia of sociology*. Retrieved from http:// www.blackwellreference.com

Lengermann, P., & Niebrugge, G. (2007b). *Women founders: Sociology and social theory 1830–1930* (2nd ed.). Long Grove, IL: Waveland Press.

Martineau, H. (2004). *Illustrations of political economy*. Guelph, ON: Broadview Press. (Original work published 1932)

Massengill, R. P. (2011). Sociological writing as higher-level thinking: Assignments that cultivate the sociological imagination. *Teaching Sociology, 39*(4), 371–381.

Mead, G. H. (1934). *Mind, self and society*. Chicago, IL: University of Chicago Press.

Merton, R. K. (1938). Social structure and anomie. *American Sociological Review, 3,* 672–682.

Merton, R. K. (1968). *Social theory and social structure*. New York, NY: Free Press.

Merton, R. K. (1973). *The sociology of science: Theoretical and empirical investigations*. Chicago, IL: University of Chicago Press.

Mills, C. W. (2000). The promise. In C. W. Mills, *The sociological imagination* (40th anniversary ed., pp. 3–24). New York, NY: Oxford University Press. (Original work published 1959)

Musambira, G. W., Raymond, L., & Hastings, S. O. (2016). A comparison of college students' perceptions of older and younger tattooed women. *Journal of Women and Aging, 28*(1), 9–23.

Parsons, T., & Bales, R. F. (1955). *Family: Socialization and interaction process*. Glencoe, IL: The Free Press.

Rickles, M. L., Schneider, R. Z., Slusser, S. R., Williams, D. M., & Zipp, J. F. (2013). Assessing change in student critical thinking for introduction to sociology classes. *Teaching Sociology, 41*(3), 271–281.

Ritzer, G., & Stepnisky, J. (2014). *Sociological theory* (9th ed.). New York, NY: McGraw-Hill.

Rosenau, P. M. (1992). *Postmodernism and the social sciences.* Princeton, NJ: Princeton University Press.

Smith, D. (1987). *The everyday world as problematic: A feminist sociology.* Boston, MA: Northeastern University Press.

Smith, D. E. (2005). *Institutional ethnography: A sociology for people.* Lanham, MD: AltaMira Press.

Statistics Canada. (2016). *Postsecondary enrolments by registration status, Pan-Canadian Standard Classification of Education (PCSCE), classification of instructional program, primary grouping (CIP_PG), sex and student status, annual (number).* (CANSIM Table 477-0019). Ottawa, ON: Author.

Straightedge Worldwide. (2017). *Tattoo gallery.* Retrieved from http://www.straightedgeworldwide.com/tattoos/

Taylor, C. (1985). *Human agency and language: Philosophical papers 1.* New York, NY: Cambridge University Press.

Timming, A. R. (2015). Visible tattoos in the service sector: A new challenge to recruitment and selection. *Work, Employment and Society, 29*(1), 60–78.

Urry, J. (2000). *Science beyond societies.* London, UK: Routledge.

Weber, M. (1978). *Economy and society.* Berkeley, CA: University of California Press.

Weiss, D. (1995). Ibn Khaldun on economic transformation. *International Journal of Middle Eastern Studies, 27,* 29–37.

White, J. M., Klein, D. M., & Martin, T. F. (2015). *Family theories: An introduction* (4th ed.). Thousand Oaks, CA: Sage Publications.

CHAPTER 2

Adler, E. S., & Clark, R. A. (2003). *How it's done: An invitation to social research* (2nd ed.). Toronto, ON: Thomson Nelson Learning.

Atkinson-Sheppard, S. (2016). The gangs of Bangladesh: Exploring organized crime, street gangs and 'illicit child labours' in Dhaka. *Criminology & Criminal Justice, 16*(2), 233–249.

Baumrind, D. (1964). Some thoughts on ethics of research after reading Milgram's behavioral study of obedience. *American Psychologist, 19,* 421–423.

Bazeley, P., & Jackson, K. (2013). *Qualitative data analysis with NVivo* (2nd ed.). Thousand Oaks, CA: Sage Publications.

Boyd, A. D., Jardine, C. G., & Driedger, S. M. (2009). Canadian media representations of mad cow disease. *Journal of Toxicology and Environmental Health: Part A: Current Issues, 72*(17–18), 1096–1105.

Bryant, J. A., Sanders-Jackson, A., & Smallwood, A. M. K. (2006). IMing, text messaging, and adolescent social networks. *Journal of Computer-Mediated Communication, 11*(2), 577–592.

Canadian Institutes of Health Research, Natural Sciences and Engineering Research Council of Canada, & Social Sciences and Humanities Research Council of Canada. (2014, December). *Tri-Council Policy Statement: Ethical conduct for research involving humans.* Retrieved from http://www.pre.ethics.gc.ca

Chilisa, B. (2012). *Indigenous research methodologies.* Thousand Oaks, CA: Sage Publications.

Creswell, J. W. (2014). *Research design: Qualitative, quantitative and mixed methods approaches* (4th ed.). Thousand Oaks, CA: Sage Publications.

Creswell, J. W., & Clark, V. L. (2011). *Designing and conducting mixed methods research* (2nd ed.). Thousand Oaks, CA: Sage Publications.

Deters, F. G., & Mehl, M. R. (2012). Does posting Facebook status updates increase or decrease loneliness? An online social networking experiment. *Social Psychology and Personality Science, 4*(5), 579–586.

Diener, E., Ng, W., Harter, J., & Arora, R. (2010). Wealth and happiness across the world: Material prosperity predicts life evaluation, whereas psychosocial prosperity predicts positive feeling. *Journal of Personality and Social Psychology, 99*(1), 52–61.

Döring, N., Reif, A., & Poeschl, S. (2015). How stereotypical are selfies? A content analysis and comparison with magazine adverts. *Computers in Human Behavior, 55,* 955–962.

Driedger, S. M., Jardine, C. G., Boyd, A. D., & Mistry, B. (2009). Do the first 10 days equal a year? Comparing two Canadian public health risk events using the national media. *Health Risk & Society, 11*(1), 39–53.

Employment and Social Development Canada. (2013). *Summative evaluation of the Aboriginal Skills and Employment Partnership Program: Final report.* Ottawa, ON: Strategic Policy and Research Branch. Retrieved from http://www.esdc.gc.ca

Eyde, L. D. (2000). Other responsibilities to participants. In B. D. Sales & S. Folkman (Eds.), *Ethics in research with human participants* (pp. 61–73). Washington, DC: American Psychological Association.

Gegeo, D. W., & Watson-Gegeo, K. A. (2001). "How we know": Kwara'ae rural villagers doing indigenous epistemology. *Contemporary Pacific, 13*(1), 55–88.

Goffman, E. (1979). *Gender advertisements.* New York, NY: Harper & Row.

Government of Canada. (2016). *ESDC Aboriginal programs. Aboriginal skills and employment training strategy.* Ottawa, ON: Author. Retrieved from https://www.canada.ca

Greenwood, D. J., & Levin, M. (2007). *Introduction to action research: Social research for social change* (2nd ed.). Thousand Oaks, CA: Sage Publications.

Haney, C., Banks, C., & Zimbardo, P. (1973). Interpersonal dynamics in a simulated prison. *International Journal of Criminology and Penology, 1,* 69–97.

Howell, A. J., & Symbaluk, D. G. (2001). Published student ratings: Reconciling the views of students and faculty. *Journal of Educational Psychology, 93,* 790–796.

Human Resources and Skills Development Canada. (2009). *Formative evaluation of the Aboriginal Skills and Employment Partnership Program: Final report.* Ottawa, ON: Strategic Policy and Research Branch. Retrieved from http://files.eric.ed.gov

Humphreys, L. (1975). *Tearoom trade: Impersonal sex in public places.* Chicago, IL: Aldine.

Karesa, S., & McBride, D. (2016). A sign of the changing times? Perceptions of Canadian psychologists on assisted death. *Canadian Psychology, 57*(3), 188–192.

Lagnado, L. M., & Dekel, S. C. (1991). *Children of the flames: Dr. Josef Mengele and the untold story of the twins of Auschwitz.* New York, NY: William Morrow and Company.

Lee, H. Y., Koopmeiners, J. S., McHugh, J., Raveis, V. H., & Ahluwalia, J. S. (2016). mHealth pilot study: Text messaging intervention to promote HPV vaccination. *American Journal of Health Behavior, 40*(1), 67–76.

Liamputtong, P. (2013). *Qualitative research methods* (4th ed.). Toronto, ON: Oxford University Press.

Lune, H., & Berg, B. L. (2017). *Qualitative research methods for the social sciences* (9th ed.). New York, NY: Pearson Education.

MacDonald, C. (2012). Understanding participatory action research: A qualitative research methodology option. *Canadian Journal of Action Research, 13*(2), 34–50.

McNiff, J. (2017). *Action research: All you need to know.* Thousand Oaks, CA: Sage Publications.

Milgram, S. (1963). Behavioral study of obedience. *Journal of Abnormal and Social Psychology, 67*(4), 371–378.

Mutsaers, B., Jones, G., Rutkowski, N., Tomei, C., Séguin-Leclair, C., Petricone-Westwood, D., ... Lebel, S. (2016). When fear of cancer recurrence becomes a clinical issue: A qualitative analysis of features associated with clinical fear of cancer recurrence. *Support Care Cancer, 24*, 4207–4218.

National Institutes of Health. (2017). *Regulations and ethical guidelines: Directives for human experimentation.* Bethesda, MD: Office of Human Subjects Research. Retrieved from http://www.recerca.uab.es

Owen, C., & Charles, N. (2016). Implementation of a text-messaging intervention for adolescents who self-harm (Teen TEXT): A feasibility study using normalization process theory. *Child and Adolescent Psychiatry and Mental Health, 10*, 14.

Pedersen, S., Grønhøj, A., & Thøgersen. J. (2016). Texting your way to healthier eating? Effects of participating in a feedback intervention using text messaging on adolescents' fruit and vegetable intake. *Health Education Research, 31*(2), 171–184.

Penrod, J., Loeb, S. J., Ladonne, R. A., & Martin, L. M. (2016). Empowering change agents in hierarchical organizations: Participatory action research in prisons. *Research in Nursing & Health, 39*, 142–153.

Plester, B., Wood, C., & Bell, V. (2008). Txt msg n school literacy: Does texting and knowledge of text abbreviations adversely affect children's literacy attainment? *Literacy, 42*(3), 137–144.

Scott, G., & Garner, R. (2013). *Doing qualitative research: Designs, methods, and techniques.* Upper Saddle River, NJ: Pearson Education.

Selenger, D. (1997). *Participatory action research and social change.* New York, NY: Cornell University.

Sieber, J. E. (1992). *Planning ethically responsible research.* Newbury Park, CA: Sage Publications.

Statistics Canada. (2016). *Population by sex and age group.* (CANSIM Table 051-0001). Ottawa, ON: Author.

Statistics Canada. (2017a, May 3). Age and sex and type of dwelling data: Key results from the 2016 Census. *The Daily.* (Catalogue No. 11-001-X). Ottawa, ON: Author.

Statistics Canada. (2017b). *About us.* Ottawa, ON: Statistics Canada.

Symbaluk, D., Heth, C. D., Cameron, J., & Pierce, W. D. (1997). Social modeling, monetary incentives, and pain endurance: The role of self-efficacy and pain perception. *Personality and Social Psychology Bulletin, 23*(3), 258–269.

Symbaluk, D. G. (2014). *Research methods: Exploring the social world.* Whitby, ON: McGraw-Hill Ryerson.

Tifferet, S., & Vilnai-Yavetz, I. (2014). Gender differences in Facebook self-presentation: An international randomized study. *Computers in Human Behavior, 35*, 388–399.

Tobin, G. A., & Begley, C. M. (2004). Methodological rigour within a qualitative framework. *Journal of Advanced Nursing, 48*(4), 388–396.

Traffic Injury Research Foundation. (2017, March 2). *National action plan outlines the road ahead in fight against distracted driving.* Ottawa, ON: Author. Retrieved from http://tirf.ca

van Dijk, C. N., van Wittloostuijn, M., Vasić, N., Avrutin, S., & Blom, E. (2016). The influence of texting language on grammar and executive function in primary school children. *PLoS One, 11*(3), e0152409.

Varnhagen, C. K., McFall, G. P., Pugh, N., Routledge, L., Sumida-MacDonald, H., & Kwong, T. E. (2010). Lol: New language and spelling in instant messaging. *Reading and Writing, 23*(6), 719–733.

Watson, L., Lavack, A. M., Rudin-Brown, C., Burns, P., & Mintz, J. H. (2010). Message content in Canadian automotive advertising: A role for regulation? *Canadian Public Policy, 36* (April Special Issue), S49–S67.

Webb, E. J., Campbell, D. T., Schwartz, R. D., & Sechrest, L. (2000). *Unobtrusive measures* (rev. ed.). Thousand Oaks, CA: Sage Publications.

Wilson, D. W., Thomas, R., Burns, K. K., Hewitt, J. A., Osei-Waree, J., & Robertson, S. (2012). Canadian rural-urban differences in end-of-life care setting transitions. *Global Journal of Health Services, 4*(5), 1–13. Retrieved from http://dx.doi.org

Wood, C., Kemp, N., & Plester, B. (2014). *Text messaging and literacy: The evidence.* New York, NY: Routledge.

CHAPTER 3

Adam, M. (2008). *Unlikely utopia: The surprising triumph of Canadian pluralism.* Toronto, ON: Penguin Canada.

Adorno, T. W. (1991). *The culture industry: Selected essays on mass culture.* Edited with an introduction by J. M. Bernstein. New York, NY: Routledge.

Baddorf, Z. (2010, August 13). *Children too hungry to return to civilian life.* Inter Press Service News Agency. Retrieved from http://www.ipsnews.net

Besner, L. (2016). In their own words: The fight to preserve the Cree language. *The Walrus, 13*(2), 34–37.

Boas, F. (1911/1976). *Handbook of American Indian languages.* St. Clair Shores, MI: Scholarly Press.

Bourdieu, P. (1973). Cultural reproduction and social reproduction. In R. Brown (Ed.), *Knowledge, education, and social change: Papers in the sociology of education* (pp. 71–112). Tavistock, UK: Tavistock Publications.

Bryson, B. (1990). *The mother tongue: English and how it got that way.* New York, NY: HarperCollins.

Canadian Multiculturalism Act (R.S.C., 1985, c. 24 [4th Supp.]). Retrieved from the Justice Laws website: http://laws-lois.justice.gc.ca/eng/acts/C-18.7/

Carroll, J. B. (Ed.). (1956). *Language, thought, and reality: Selected writings of Benjamin Lee Whorf.* Cambridge, MA: Massachusetts Institute of Technology.

CBC Radio. (2010, September 24). *The Current. Pt. 3: Sudan soldiers*. Retrieved from http://www.cbc.ca

Child Soldiers International. (2016). *Where are there child soldiers?* London, UK: The author. Retrieved from https://www.child-soldiers.org

Danesi, M. (2008). *Popular culture: Introductory perspectives*. Lanham, MD: Rowman & Littlefield.

Dollinger, S. (editor-in-chief), Laurel, J. B., & Fee, M. (Eds.). (2013). *DCHP-1 Online: A dictionary of Canadianisms on historical principles online*. Based on Avis et al. (1967). Retrieved from http://dchp.ca

Durkheim, E. (1933). *The division of labour in society* (George Simpson, Trans.). New York, NY: Macmillan. (Original work published 1893)

Durkheim, E. (1938). *The rules of sociological method* (S. A. Solovay and J. H. Mueller, Trans.). Edited with an introduction by G. E. G. Catlin. Chicago, IL: University of Chicago Press. (Original work published 1895)

Ferguson, W., & Ferguson, I. (2001). *How to be a Canadian (even if you already are one)*. Vancouver, BC: Douglas & McIntyre.

Fiske, J. (2010). *Understanding popular culture* (2nd ed.). New York, NY: Routledge.

Gannon, M. (2008). *Paradoxes of culture and globalization*. Thousand Oaks, CA: Sage Publications.

Goldthorpe, J. H., Lockwood, D., Bechhofer, F., & Platt, J. (1969). *The affluent worker in the class structure*. Cambridge, UK: Cambridge University Press.

Government of Canada. (2016). *Coping with culture shock*. Ottawa, ON: Author. Retrieved from https://travel.gc.ca

Gregoire, J. (2017, March 20). Ethnic foods and flavours. *Canadian Food Business*. Retrieved from http://canadianfoodbusiness.com

Lavenda, R. H., Schultz, E. A., & Zutter, C. (2016). *Anthropology: What does it mean to be human?* (Canadian edition). Don Mills, ON: Oxford University Press.

Murdock, G. P. (1945). The common denominator of culture. In Ralph Linton (Ed.), *The science of man in the world crisis* (pp. 123–142). New York, NY: Columbia University Press.

Norris, M. J. (2014). *Aboriginal languages in Canada: Emerging trends and perspectives on second language acquisition*. Ottawa, ON: Statistics Canada. Retrieved from http://www.statcan.gc.ca

Ogburn, W. F. (1922). *Social change with respect to culture and original nature*. New York, NY: The Viking Press.

Osman, H., El Zein, L., & Wick, L. (2009, November 2). Cultural beliefs that may discourage breastfeeding among Lebanese women: A qualitative analysis. *International Breastfeeding Journal*. Retrieved from http://www.internationalbreastfeedingjournal.com

Parsons, T. (1951). *The social system*. London: Routledge and Kegan Paul.

Peterson, R. A. (1992). Understanding audience segmentation: From elite and mass to omnivore and univore. *Poetics, 21*, 243–258.

Ricks, D. A. (1999). *Blunders in international business* (3rd ed.). Malden, MA: Blackwell Publishing.

Siegel, L. J., Brown, G. P., & Hoffman, R. (2006). *Criminology: The core*. Toronto, ON: Nelson Education.

Statistics Canada. (2015a). *Mother tongue of a person. Definitions, data sources and methods*. Retrieved from http://www.statcan.gc.ca

Statistics Canada. (2015b). *Linguistic characteristics of Canadians*. (Catalogue No. 98-314-XWE2011001). Ottawa, ON: Author.

Statistics Canada. (2016). *Population by mother tongue and age groups (total), 2011 counts, for Canada, provinces and territories*. (Catalogue No. 98-314-XWE2011002). Ottawa, ON: Author.

Storey, J. (2009). *Cultural theory and popular culture: An introduction* (5th ed.). Edinburgh Gate, Harlow, UK: Pearson Education.

Sumara, D., Davis, B., & Laidlaw, L. (2001). Canadian identity and curriculum theory: An ecological postmodern perspective. *Canadian Journal of Education, 26*(2), 144–163.

Supply and Services Canada. (1991). *Citizens' forum on Canada's future: A report to the people and government of Canada*. Ottawa, ON: Author.

Swidler, A. (1986). Culture in action: Symbols and strategies. *American Sociological Review, 51*, 273–286.

Texin, T. (2011). *Marketing translation mistakes*. Retrieved from http://www.i18nguy.com

Williams, R. (1976). *Keywords: A vocabulary of culture and society*. New York, NY: Oxford University Press.

CHAPTER 4

Angus, V. D. (2007). Play stage. In G. Ritzer (Ed.), *Blackwell encyclopedia of sociology*. Retrieved from http://www.blackwellreference.com

Aronson, E., Wilson, T. D., Fehr, B., & Akert, R. M. (2017). *Social psychology* (6th Can. ed.). Toronto, ON: Pearson Education Canada.

Asch, S. E. (1956). Studies of independence and conformity: A minority of one against a unanimous majority. *Psychological Monographs, 70*(9) (Whole No. 416).

Avinun, R., & Knafo-Noam, A. (2015). Socialization, genetics, and their interplay in development. In J. E. Grusec & P. D. Hastings (Eds.), *Handbook of socialization: Theory and research* (2nd ed., pp. 347–371). New York, NY: Guilford Press.

Bailey, J. M., Gaulin, S., Agyei, Y., & Gladue, B. A. (1994). Effects of gender and sexual orientation on evolutionarily relevant aspects of human mating psychology. *Journal of Personality and Social Psychology, 66*, 1081–1093.

Bandura, A. (1962). Social learning through imitation. In M. R. Jones (Ed.), *Nebraska symposium on motivation* (pp. 211–269). Lincoln, NE: University of Nebraska Press.

Bandura, A., & Walters, R. H. (1959). *Adolescent aggression*. New York, NY: Ronald Press.

Beitchman, J. H. Mik, H. M., Ehtesham, S., Douglas, L., & Kennedy, J. L. (2004). MAO and persistent, pervasive childhood aggression. *Molecular Psychiatry, 9*, 546–547.

Bereska, T. M. (2018). *Deviance, conformity, and social control in Canada* (5th ed.). Toronto, ON: Pearson Education Canada.

Blumer, H. (1969). *Symbolic interactionism: Perspective and method*. Englewood Cliffs, NJ: Prentice-Hall.

Boyd, D. *It's complicated: The social lives of networked teens*. London, UK: Yale University Press.

Bronfenbrenner, U. (2001). The bioecological theory of human development. In N. J. Smelser and P. B. Baltes (Eds.), *International encyclopedia of the behavioral and social sciences* (Vol. 10, pp. 6963–6970). Oxford, UK: Elsevier Science.

Bronfenbrenner, U. (Ed.). (2005). *Making human beings human: Bioecological perspectives on human development*. Thousand Oaks, CA: Sage Publications.

Bullying Canada. (2017). *What is bullying?* Fredericton, NB: Author. Retrieved from http://bullyingcanada.ca

Canadian Child Welfare Research Portal. (2017). Centre for Research on Children and Families. Montréal, QC: McGill University. Retrieved from http://cwrp.ca/

Canadian Internet Registration Authority. (2016). *Fact book 2016*. Retrieved from https://cira.ca/factbook

Charmaz, K. (2007). Self. In G. Ritzer (Ed.), *Blackwell encyclopedia of sociology*. Retrieved from http://www.blackwellreference.com

Clearfield, M. W., & Nelson, N. M. (2006). Sex differences in mother's speech and play behavior with 6-, 9-, and 14-month-old infants. *Sex Roles, 54*(1–2), 127–137.

Cooley, C. H. (1902). *Human nature and the social order*. New York, NY: Scribner.

Craig, W., & McCuaig Edge, M. (2012). Bullying and fighting. In *The health of Canada's young people: A mental health focus–bullying and fighting*. Retrieved from https://www.canada.ca

Crozier, M. (1964). *The bureaucratic phenomenon*. London, UK: Tavistock Publications.

Dabbs, J. M., Jr., Carr, T. S., Frady, R. L., & Riad, J. K. (1995). Testosterone, crime, and misbehavior among 692 male prison inmates. *Personality and Individual Differences, 18*, 627–633.

Deshotels, T. H., Tinney, M., & Forsyth, C. J. (2012). McSexy: Exotic dancing and institutional power. *Deviant Behavior, 33*(2), 140–148.

Dixit, R. (2015, November 15). Wildlife to sanctuary. *The Week*. Retrieved from http://www.theweek.in/theweek.html

Duff, K. J., & Peace, K. A. (2013). *Think social psychology: Canadian edition*. Don Mills, ON: Pearson Education Canada.

Dunn, J. (2007). Siblings and socialization. In J. E. Grusec & P. D. Hastings (Eds.), *Handbook of socialization: Theory and research* (pp. 309–327). New York, NY: The Guilford Press.

Edwards, A. (2012, September 10). Missing Indian girl who disappeared 38 years ago returns home after living in Myanmar jungle for decades. *Mail Online*. Retrieved from http://www.dailymail.co.uk

Festinger, L. (1954). A theory of social comparison processes. *Human Relations, 7*(2), 117–140.

FRP Canada. (2017). *Downloadable parenting resources*. Ottawa, ON: Canadian Association of Family Resource Programs. Retrieved from http://www.parentsmatter.ca

Gage, M. G., & Christensen, D. H. (2001). Parental role socialization and the transition to parenthood. *Family Relations, 40*, 332–337.

Gamble, W. C., & Yu, J. J. (2008). Adolescent siblings' looking glass self-orientations: Patterns of liabilities and associations with parenting. *Journal of Youth and Adolescence, 37*, 860–874.

Goffman, E. (1961). *Asylums: Essays on the social situation of patients and other inmates*. Garden City, NY: Doubleday Anchor.

Grusec, J. E., & Davidov, M. (2007). Socialization in the family: The role of parents. In J. E. Grusec & P. D. Hastings (Eds.), *Handbook of socialization: Theory and research* (pp. 284–308). New York, NY: The Guilford Press.

Hartner, S. (1999). Symbolic interactionism revisited: Potential liabilities for the self constructed in the crucible of interpersonal relationships. *Merrill-Palmer Quarterly, 45*, 677–703.

Hartner, S., & Whitesell, N. R. (2003). Beyond the debate: Why some adolescents report stable self-worth over time and situation, whereas others report changes in self-worth. *Journal of Personality, 71*, 1027–1058.

Hughes, E. C. (1945). Dilemmas and contradictions of status. *American Journal of Sociology, 50*, 353–359.

Janis, I. L. (1972). *Victims of groupthink*. Boston, MA: Houghton Mifflin.

Jhally, S. (Producer), & Earp, J. (Director). (2013). *Tough guise 2: Violence, manhood and American culture*. San Francisco, CA: Kanopy Streaming.

Jones, A., Sinha, V., & Trocmé, N. (2015). Children and youth in out-of-home care in the Canadian provinces. *CWRP Information Sheet #167E*. Montréal, QC: Centre for Research on Children and Families, McGill University.

Kuczynski, L. (2003). Beyond bidirectionality: Bilateral conceptual frameworks for understanding dynamics in parent–child relationships. In L. Kuczynski (Ed.), *Handbook of dynamics in parent-child relations* (pp. 1–24). Thousand Oaks, CA: Sage Publications.

Kuczynski, L., & Parkin, C. M. (2007). Agency and bidirectionality in socialization: Interactions, transactions, and relational dialectics. In J. E. Grusec & P. D. Hastings (Eds.), *Handbook of socialization: Theory and research* (pp. 259–283). New York, NY: The Guilford Press.

Li, J., & Craig, W. (2015, November 15). *Young Canadians' experiences with electronic bullying*. Ottawa, ON: MediaSmarts. Retrieved from http://mediasmarts.ca

Machalek, R. (2007). Biosocial theories. In G. Ritzer (Ed.), *Blackwell encyclopedia of sociology*. Retrieved from http://www.blackwellreference.com

Maruna, S., LeBel, T. P., Mitchell, N., & Naples, M. (2004). Pygmalion in the reintegration process: Desistance from crime through the looking glass. *Psychology, Crime, and Law, 10*(3), 271–281.

McDonald's Restaurants of Canada Limited. (2017). *Our history*. Retrieved from http://www.mcdonalds.ca

Mead, G. H. (1934). *Mind, self and society*. Chicago, IL: University of Chicago Press.

Minaker, J. (2012). Mothering in the context of contradiction. In G. Wong (Ed.), *Moms gone mad: Madness, oppression and resistance* (pp. 124–140). Toronto, ON: Demeter Press.

Murray, J. L., Linden, R., & Kendall, D. (2017). *Sociology in our times*. (7th Can. ed.). Toronto, ON: Nelson Education.

O'Brien, J. (2011). Who am I? Developing character. In J. O'Brien (Ed.), *The production of reality: Essays and readings on social interaction* (pp. 108–119). Thousand Oaks, CA: Pine Forge Press.

Raine, A. (1993). *The psychopathy of crime: Criminal behaviour as a clinical disorder*. San Diego, CA: Academic Press.

Rathus, S. A. (2014). *Childhood & adolescence: Voyages in development* (5th ed.). Belmont, CA: Brooks/Cole.

Rathus, S. A. (2018). *CDEV2: Child and adolescent development*. Toronto, ON: Cengage.

Ritzer, G. (2015). *The McDonaldization of society* (8th ed.). Thousand Oaks, CA: Sage Publications.

Salmivalli, C., & Peets, K. (2009). Bullies, victims, and bully-victim relationships in middle school and adolescence. In K. H. Rubin, W. M. Bukowski, & B. Laursen (Eds.), *Handbook of peer interactions, relationships and groups* (pp. 322–340). New York, NY: Guilford.

Schieman, S. (2007). Self-concept. In G. Ritzer (Ed.), *Blackwell encyclopedia of sociology*. Retrieved from http://www.blackwellreference.com

Segal, N. L. (2012). *Born together—reared apart: The landmark Minnesota Twin Study.* Cambridge, MA: Harvard University Press.

Shaffer, D. R., & Kipp, K. (2013). *Developmental psychology: Childhood and adolescence* (9th ed). Belmont, CA: Wadsworth.

Sinha, V., Trocmé, N., Fallon, B., MacLaurin, B., Fast, E., Thomas Prokop, S., et al (2011). *Kiskisik Awasisak: Remember the children. Understanding the overrepresentation of First Nations children in the child welfare system.* Ontario: Assembly of First Nations.

Skinner, B. F. (1938). *The behaviour of organisms: An experimental analysis*. New York, NY: Appleton-Century-Crofts.

Swenson, D. (2004). *A neo-functionalist synthesis of theories in family*. New York, NY: Mellen Press.

Tajfel, H., & Turner, J. C. (1986). The social identity theory of intergroup behaviour. In S. Worchel & W. G. Austin (Eds.), *The psychology of intergroup relations* (2nd ed., pp. 7–24). Chicago, IL: Nelson-Hall.

Turner, R. H. (1962). Role taking: Process versus conformity. In A. M. Rose (Ed.), *Human behaviour and social processes: An interactionist approach* (pp. 20–40). Boston, MA: Houghton Mifflin.

Waddington, C. H. (1942). The epigenotype. *Endeavor, 1*, 18–20.

Wasson, L. (2007). Primary socialization. In G. Ritzer (Ed.), *Blackwell encyclopedia of sociology*. Retrieved from http://www.blackwellreference.com

Watson, J. B., (1924). *Behaviorism*. New York, NY: The People's Institute.

Weber, M. (1903–1917/1949). In E. Shils & H. Finch (Eds.), *The methodology of the social sciences*. New York, NY: The Free Press.

Wentzel, K. R., & Looney, L. (2007). Socialization in school settings. In J. E. Grusec & P. D. Hastings (Eds.), *Handbook of socialization: Theory and research* (pp. 382–403). New York, NY: The Guilford Press.

Wilson, E. O. (1975). *Sociobiology.* Cambridge, MA: Harvard University Press.

Yeung, K., & Martin, J. L. (2003). The looking glass self: An empirical test and elaboration. *Social Forces, 81*(3), 843–879.

Young, N. (2012). *The virtual self: How our digital lives are altering the world around us*. Toronto, ON: McClelland & Stewart.

Zajonc, R. B. (1965). Social facilitation. *Science, 149*, 269–274.

Zastrow, C. H., & Kirst-Ashman, K. K. (2016). *Understanding human behaviour and the social environment* (10th ed.). Belmont, CA: Brooks/Cole.

CHAPTER 5

Anand, M. (1935). *Untouchable*. New York, NY: Penguin Putnam.

Basa, E. (2016, February 18). *Forget the American dream—Canada is the true place of opportunity.* Toronto, ON: Narcity Media. Retrieved from https://www.narcity.com

Bill C-545. (2010, June 16 First Reading). An act to eliminate poverty in Canada. Retrieved from http://www2.parl.gc.ca

Brym, R. J. (2016). *New society* (8th ed.). Toronto, ON: Nelson Education.

Canada Revenue Agency. (2017). *Line 255 - Northern residents deductions*. Retrieved from http://www.cra-arc.gc.ca

Canada Without Poverty. (2015). *Human rights and poverty reduction strategies: A guide to international human rights law and its domestic application in poverty reduction strategies*. Ottawa, ON: Author. Retrieved from http://www.cwp-csp.ca

Canada Without Poverty. (2017). *Just the facts*. Ottawa, ON: Author. Retrieved from http://www.cwp-csp.ca

Canadian Council for Refugees. (2016). *Migrant workers: Precarious and unsupported*. Retrieved from http://ccrweb.ca

Canadian Homelessness Research Network. (2012). *Canadian definition of homelessness*. Retrieved from http://www.homelesshub.ca

Canadian Mental Health Association. (2003, April). *Housing and homelessness: Backgrounder*. Retrieved from http://www.cmha.citizens

Canadian Museum of History. (2017a). *Slavery*. Gatineau, QC: The Virtual Museum. Retrieved from http://www.historymuseum.ca

Canadian Museum of History. (2017b). *The abolition of slavery*. Gatineau, QC: The Virtual Museum. Retrieved from http://www.historymuseum.ca

CBC News. (2010, April 15). *Canada escaped worst of recession: StatsCan*. Retrieved from http://www.cbc.ca

Chen, W. H., Ostrovsky, Y., & Piraino, P. (2016, June 17). *Economic Insights. Intergenerational income mobility: New evidence from Canada*. (Catalogue No. 11-626-X – No. 059). Ottawa, ON: Statistics Canada.

Coser, L. A. (1977). *Masters of sociological thought: Ideas in historical and social context* (2nd ed.). Toronto, ON: Harcourt Brace Jovanovich.

Cowling, M., Elton, G. R., Kedourie, E., Pocock, J. G. A., & Ullman, W. (Eds.). (1970). *Cambridge studies in the history and theory of politics: Critique of Hegel's "Philosophy of Right" by Karl Marx* (Annette Jolin and Joseph O'Malley, Trans.). Cambridge, UK: Cambridge University Press.

Davis, K., & Moore, W. (1945). Some principles of social stratification. *American Sociological Review, 7*(April), 242–249.

Deveau, D. (2013, January 29). When does a university degree really pay off? *Financial Post*. Retrieved from http://business.financialpost.com

Dirks, N. (2001). *Castes of mind: Colonialism and the making of modern India*. Princeton, NJ: Princeton University Press.

Echenberg, H., & Jensen, H. (2009). Parliamentary Information and Research Service. Retrieved from http://lop.parl.ca

Fantauzzi, J. (2016, December). *Predatory lending: A survey of high interest alternative financial service users*. Ottawa, ON: Canadian Centre for Policy Alternatives. Retrieved from https://www.policyalternatives.ca

Federation of Canadian Municipalities. (2010). *Mending Canada's frayed social safety net: The role of municipal governments: Quality of life in Canadian communities: Theme report #6*. Ottawa, ON: Author. Retrieved from http://www.fcm .ca

Flanagan, G. (2015, April 20). *From gap to chasm: Alberta's increasing income inequality.* Edmonton, AB: Parkland Institute. Retrieved from http://www.parklandinstitute.ca

Frenette, M. (2014). *The long-term labour market premiums associated with a terminal high school diploma.* (Catalogue No. 11F0019M – No. 354). Ottawa, ON: Statistics Canada.

Gaetz, S., Dej, E., Ritcher, T., & Redman, M. (2016). *The state of homelessness in Canada.* COH Research Paper #12. Toronto, ON: Canadian Observatory on Homelessness Press.

Gans, H. J. (1971). The uses of poverty: The poor pay all. *Social Policy, 2*(2), 20–24.

Gilbert, D. (2015). *The American class structure in an age of growing inequality* (9th ed.). Thousand Oaks, CA: Sage Publications.

Global Slavery Index. (2016). *Findings.* Dalkeith, AU: Walk Free Foundation. Retrieved from http://www.globalslaveryindex.org

Government of Canada. (2017a). *Current and forthcoming minimum hourly wage rates for experienced adult workers in Canada.* Ottawa, ON: Author. Retrieved from http://srv116.services.gc.ca

Government of Canada. (2017b). *Guide IMM 5482 – Instruction to fill the Financial Evaluation form (IMM 1283) Federal Income Table, 2017. Table 3: Low Income Cut-Off (LICO).* Retrieved from http://www.cic.gc.ca

Harris, M. (2013, June 13). Majority of Canadian millionaires are self-made and almost half of them are immigrants, poll shows. *National Post.* Retrieved from http://news.nationalpost.com

Hay, D. I. (2009). *Poverty reduction policies and programs in Canada.* Canadian Council on Social Development. Retrieved from http://cwp-csp.ca

Health Canada. (2017). Drinking water and waste water. In *First Nation and Inuit health.* Ottawa, ON: Author. Retrieved from http://www.hc-sc.gc.ca

Helm-Hayes, R., & Miller, M. (1998). *The vertical mosaic revisited.* Toronto, ON: University of Toronto Press.

Hodson, R., & Sullivan, T. A. (2012). *The social organization of work* (5th ed.). Belmont, CA: Wadsworthhod.

Indigenous and Northern Affairs Canada. (2017). *Water in First Nation communities.* Ottawa, ON: Author. Retrieved from http://www.aadnc-aandc.gc.ca

Jaffrelot, C. (2005). *Dr. Ambedkar and untouchability: Fighting the Indian caste system.* New York, NY: Columbia University Press.

Kerbo, H. R. (2012). *Social stratification and inequality: Class conflict in historical, comparative, and global perspective* (8th ed.). New York, NY: McGraw-Hill.

Klasing, M. (June 7, 2016). *Make it safe: Canada's obligation to end the First Nations water crisis.* New York, NY: Human Rights Watch. Retrieved from https://www.hrw.org

Laboucane, R. (2010). Canada's Aboriginal education crisis. *The Aboriginal Multi-Media Society, 28*(7). Retrieved from http://www.ammsa.com

Lammam, C., & MacIntyre, H. (2016, January 25). *An introduction to the state of poverty in Canada.* Vancouver, BC: Fraser Institute. Retrieved from https://www.fraserinstitute.org

Lenski, G. (1966). *Power and privilege.* New York, NY: McGraw-Hill.

Luce, E. (2007). *In spite of the gods: The rise of modern India.* New York, NY: Anchor Books.

Macdonald, D., & Friendly, M. (2016, December). *A growing concern: 2016 child care fees in Canada's big cities.* Ottawa, ON: Canadian Centre for Policy Alternatives. Retrieved from https://www.policyalternatives.ca

Macdonald, D., & Wilson, D. (2016, May). *Shameful neglect: Indigenous child poverty in Canada.* Ottawa, ON: Canadian Centre for Policy Alternatives. Retrieved from https://www.policyalternatives.ca

MacKenzie, H. (2017, January). *Throwing money at the problem: Ten years of executive compensation.* Ottawa, ON: Canadian Centre for Policy Alternatives. Retrieved from https://www.policyalternatives.ca

Maclean's. (2013, June 28). 99 reasons why it's better to be Canadian. *Maclean's.* Retrieved from http://www2.macleans.ca

Marger, M. N. (2014). *Social inequality: Patterns and processes* (6th ed.). New York, NY: McGraw-Hill.

Marx, K., & Engels, F. (1848/2010). *Manifesto of the Communist Party.* Charleston, SC: CreateSpace.

McClearn, M. (2017, February 21). Unsafe to drink. *The Globe and Mail.* Retrieved from http://www.theglobeandmail.com

Mills, C. W. (1956). *White collar.* New York, NY: Oxford University Press.

Nickalls, J. (1831). *British statutes, relating to the Province of Upper Canada, together with ordinances of the late Province of Quebec, proclamations of Lord Dorchester and Gov. Simcoe* (Revision by James Nickalls). Kingston, Upper Canada: Hugh C. Thomson and James MacFarlane.

Norman, S. (2013, December 15). Federal minister says child poverty not Ottawa's problem: James Moore says child poverty falls under provincial jurisdiction. *News 1130.* Retrieved from http://www.news1130.com

O'Hanlon, R. (2017). Caste and its histories in colonial India: A reappraisal. *Modern Asian Studies, 51*(2), 432–461.

Organisation for Economic Co-operation and Development. (2016). *Canada is adjusting to the end of the commodities boom, but new policies are needed to boost productivity and reduce financial stability risks.* Retrieved from http://www.oecd.org

Oxfam Canada. (2017, January 16). *An economy for the 99%. Oxfam Briefing Paper.* Ottawa, ON: Author. Retrieved from https://www.oxfam.ca

Phipps, S. (2003, June). *The impact of poverty on health.* Canadian Population Health Initiative Collected Papers. Ottawa, ON: Canadian Institute for Health Information. Retrieved from http://dsp-psd.pwgsc.gc.ca

Porter, J. (1965). *The vertical mosaic: An analysis of social class and power in Canada.* Toronto, ON: University of Toronto Press.

Province of Ontario. (2017). *Poverty reduction in Ontario.* Ottawa, ON: Author. Retrieved from https://www.ontario.ca

Rai, M. (2009, March 18). Caste system in India. Interview for *The MacMillan Report*, hosted by Marilyn Wilkes. New Haven, CT: The Whitney and Betty MacMillan Center for International and Area Studies at Yale. Retrieved from http://www.yale.edu

RCMP. (2014). *Human trafficking in Canada: A threat assessment.* Ottawa, ON: Author. Retrieved from http://www.rcmp-grc.gc.ca

Ritzer, G. (1992). *Sociological theory* (3rd ed.). New York, NY: McGraw-Hill.

Ritzer, G., & Stepnisky, J. (2014). *Sociological theory* (9th ed.). New York, NY: McGraw-Hill.

Simeone, T. (2010). *Safe drinking water in First Nation communities: Library of Parliament background paper*. Ottawa, ON: Library of Parliament Research Publications. Retrieved from http://www.parl.gc.ca

Smith-Carrier, T., & Lawlor, A. (2017). Realising our (neoliberal) potential? A critical discourse analysis of the poverty reduction strategy in Ontario, Canada. *Critical Social Policy, 37*(1), 105–127.

Statistics Canada. (2015a, July 8). *Low income lines, 2013-2014*. Income Research Paper Series. (Catalogue No. 75F0002M – No. 001). Ottawa, ON: Author.

Statistics Canada. (2015b). *Low income lines, 2013-2014: Update*. Ottawa, ON: Author.

Statistics Canada. (2016a, July 8). Canadian Income Survey, 2014. *The Daily*. (Catalogue No. 11-001-X). Ottawa, ON: Author.

Statistics Canada. (2016b). *Low income statistics by age, sex and economic family type, Canada, provinces and selected metropolitan areas (CMAs) (annual)*. (CANSIM Table 206-0041). Ottawa, ON: Author.

Statistics Canada. (2016c). *Median total income, by family type, by province and territory (all census families)*. (CANSIM Table 111-0009). Ottawa, ON: Author.

Statistics Canada. (2016d). *Table 3: Persons in low income (after-tax low income measure)*. (CANSIM Table 206-0041). Ottawa, ON: Author.

Statistics Canada. (2016e). *Upper income limit, income share and after-tax income by economic family type and income decile, Canada and provinces (annual)*. (CANSIM Table 206-0031). Ottawa, ON: Author.

Statistics Canada. (2017a, May 3). Age and sex, and type of dwelling data: Key results from the 2016 Census. *The Daily*. (Catalogue No. 11-001-X). Ottawa, ON: Author.

Statistics Canada. (2017b). *People employed, by educational attainment*. (CANSIM Table 282-0004. Catalogue No. 89F0133XIE). Ottawa, ON: Author.

UN Department of Economic and Social Affairs, Secretariat of the Permanent Forum on Indigenous Issues. (2009, December). *The state of the world's indigenous peoples*. New York, NY: United Nations.

Uppal, S., & LaRochelle-Côté, S. (2015). *Changes in debt and assets of Canadian families*. (Catalogue No. 75-00-X). Ottawa, ON: Statistics Canada.

Wanner, R. A. (2004). Social mobility in Canada: Concepts, patterns, and trends. In J. Curtis, E. Grabb, and N. Guppy (Eds.), *Social inequality in Canada: Patterns, problems, and policies*. (4th ed.). Toronto, ON: Pearson Education Canada.

Weber, M. (1904/1958). *The Protestant ethic and the spirit of capitalism* (T. Parsons, Trans.). New York, NY: Scribner.

CHAPTER 6

Agility PR Solutions. (2016). *Top 10 Canadian magazines by circulation*. Ottawa, ON: Innodata. Retrieved from https://www.agilitypr.com

Ahonen, T. (2008). *Mobile as 7th of the mass media*. Retrieved from http://mobile7th.futuretext.com

Ahonen, T. (2009). *Mobile phones: The next 4 billion with Tomi Ahonen*. FORAtvSERIES: PICNIC Festival 2009. Retrieved from http://fora.tv

Ahonen, T. (2013, May 31). *Location is the speedbump on mobile highway – understanding how futile 'location' is the driver of any mobile service concept. Augmented reality*. Retrieved from http://communities-dominate.blogs.com.

Ahonen, T. (2017a, March 2). *Augmented reality reached 3 billion dollars in annual revenues, powered by Pokémon Go*. Retrieved from http://communities-dominate.blogs.com.

Ahonen, T. (2017b, February 9). *Most successful launch in history. Fastest ever to 1 billion. Fastest EVER. Mobile is the magical money-making machine. I am talking about Pokémon Go of course*. Retrieved from http://communities-dominate.blogs.com.

Ahonen, T. (2017c). *Tomi Ahonen almanac 2017* (E-book). Retrieved from http://www.tomiahonen.com

Anderson, C. A., Berkowitz, L., Donnerstein, E., Huesmann, L. R., Johnson, J. D., Linz, D., ... Wartella, E. (2003). The influence of media violence on youth. *Psychological Sciences in the Public Interest, 4*(3), 81–110.

Anderson, R., & Gray, J. (Eds.). (2008). *Battleground: The media* (Vol. 2). Westport, CT: Greenwood Press.

APA Task Force on Violent Media. (2015). *Technical report on the review of the violent video game literature*. Retrieved from http://www.apa.org

Bandura, A. (1965). Influence of model's reinforcement contingencies on the acquisition of imitative responses. *Journal of Personality and Social Psychology, 1*(6), 589–595.

Bandura, A. (1978). Social learning theory of aggression. *Journal of Communication, 28*(3), 12–29.

Bandura, A., Ross, D., & Ross, S. A. (1961). Transmission of aggression through imitation of aggressive models. *Journal of Abnormal and Social Psychology, 63*, 575–582.

Bandura, A., Ross, D., & Ross, S. A. (1963). Imitation of film-mediated aggressive models. *Journal of Abnormal and Social Psychology, 66*, 3–11.

Briscoe, J. (2016). *Top 10 best-selling magazines in the world*. Retrieved from http://gazettereview.com

Broadcasting Act (S.C. 1991, c. 11). Retrieved from the Justice Laws website: http://laws-lois.justice.gc.ca

Burgess, J., & Green, J. (2009). *YOUTUBE: Online video and participatory culture*. Digital Media and Society Series. Cambridge, UK: Polity.

Burgess, M. C. R., Dill, K. E., & Wright, B. A. (2009). You're my bitch: Crude and degrading treatment of women in hardcore rap through the eyes of the predominantly White target audience. In J. H. Urlich and B. T. Cosell (Eds.), *Handbook of gender roles: Conflicts, attitudes and behaviors* (pp. 55–74). Hauppauge, NY: NovaScience Publishers.

Canadian Broadcasting Standards Council. (2017). *History of AGVOT and rating classifications in Canada*. Ottawa, ON: Author. Retrieved from http://www.cbsc.ca

Canadian Internet Registration Authority. (2016). *The CIRA factbook 2016*. Retrieved from http://www.cira.ca

Canadian Radio-television and Telecommunications Commission (CRTC). (2016). *Ownership chart. Quebecor profile*. Retrieved from http://www.crtc.gc.ca

Canadian Radio-television and Telecommunications Commission (CRTC). (2017). *About us*. Retrieved from http://crtc.gc.ca

Clark, A. M., & Clark, M. T. G. (2016). Pokémon Go and research: Qualitative mixed methods research, and the supercomplexity of interventions. *International Journal of Qualitative Methods*, Jan–Dec, 1–3.

Cohen, B. (1963). *The press and foreign policy*. Princeton, NJ: Princeton University Press.

Desmond, R., & Carveth, R. (2007). The effect of advertising on children and adolescents: A meta-analysis. In R. W. Preiss, B. M. Galue, N. Burrell, M. Allen, & J. Bryant (Eds.), *Mass media effects research: Advanced through meta-analysis* (pp. 169–179). Mahwah, NJ: Lawrence Erlbaum.

Dill-Shackleford, K. E. (2016). *How fantasy becomes reality: Information & entertainment media in everyday life*. New York, NY: Oxford University Press.

Dinozzi, R. (Producer). (1997). *Killing screens: Media & the culture of violence* (Documentary film). Northampton, MA: Media Education Foundation.

Dudley, W. (Ed.). (1999). *Media violence: Opposing viewpoints*. San Diego, CA: Greenhaven Press.

Ellis-Petersen, H. (2017, January 3). Record sales: Vinyl hits 25-year high. *The Guardian*. Retrieved from https://www.theguardian.com

Encyclopaedia Britannica. (2017). *Sumerian writing*. Retrieved from http://www.britannica.com

Entman, R. M. (1991). Framing U.S. coverage of international news: Contrasts in narratives of the KAL and Iran Air incidents. *Journal of Communication, 41*(4), 6–27.

Fairness and Accuracy in Reporting (FAIR). (2017). *What's FAIR?* New York, NY: Author. Retrieved from http://fair.org

Filmmakers Magazine. (2017). James Cameron biography. *Filmmakers Magazine*. Retrieved from http://www.filmmakers.com

Gerbner, G., Gross, L., Morgan, M., Signorielli, N., & Shanahan, J. (2002). Growing up with television: Cultivation processes. In J. Bryant & D. Zillman (Eds.), *Media effects: Advances in theory and research* (2nd ed., pp. 43–67). Mahway, NJ: Lawrence Erlbaum.

Goffman, E. (1974). *Frame analysis*. Philadelphia, PA: University of Pennsylvania Press.

Gordon, M. (2014, February 19). *FCC won't appeal ruling on Internet neutrality*. Retrieved from http://hosted.ap.org

Government of Canada. (2016, April 25). *CRTC releases 2015 financial results for Canadian radio stations*. Ottawa, ON: Author. Retrieved from http://news.gc.ca

Grossman, E., & Degaetano, G. (1999). *Stop teaching our kids to kill: A call to action against TV, movie, and video game violence*. New York, NY: Crown Publishers.

Grubb, J. (2016, July 19). *Sensor Tower: Pokémon Go has already passed 30M downloads and $35M in revenue*. San Francisco, CA: VentureBeat. Retrieved from venturebeat.com

Hall, S. (2009). The work of representation. In Stuart Hall (Ed.), *Representation: Cultural representations and signifying practices* (pp. 1–11). Thousand Oaks, CA: Sage Publications.

Hammond Museum of Radio. (2004). *Early broadcasting*. Retrieved from http://www.hammondmuseumofradio.org

Hanson, R. (2017). *Mass communication: Living in a mediated world*. Thousand Oaks, CA: Sage Publications.

Herman, E. S., & Chomsky, N. (1988). *Manufacturing consent: The political economy of the mass media*. New York, NY: Pantheon Books.

Insights West. (2016). *Canadian Social Media Monitor 2016*. Retrieved from http://www.insightswest.com

Jackson, E. (2017). Television cord cutting hits record level in 2016 for Canada's big providers: Report. *Financial Post*. Retrieved from http://business.financialpost.com

Kharpal, A. (2017, May 31). *Bitcoin could hit $100,000 in 10 years, says the analyst who correctly called its $2,000 price*. Retrieved from http://www.cnbc.com

Library and Archives Canada. (2014, March 28). *The virtual gramophone: Early Canadian sound recordings* (Audio podcast). Retrieved from http://www.bac-lac.gc.ca

Lenhart, A., Kahne, J., Middaugh, E., MacGill, A., Evans, C., & Vitak, J. (2008). *Teens, video games and civics. Internet & technology*. Washington, DC: Pew Research Centre. Retrieved from http://www.pewresearch.org

Livesey, B. (2016, July 6). The Irvings' media monopoly and its consequences. Special report: House of Irving. *National Observer*. Retrieved from http://www.nationalobserver.com

Macnamara, J. R. (2006). *Media and male identity: The making and remaking of men*. New York, NY: Palgrave Macmillan.

Maloney, V. (2014, February 6). *Magazine subscriptions and single-copy sales down: AAM report*. Retrieved from http://mediaincanada.com

Mann, G., Venturini, F., Murdoch, R., Mishra, B., Moorby, G., & Carlier, B. (2015). *Digital video and the connected consumer*. New York, NY: Accenture. Retrieved from https://www.accenture.com

Marketing Charts. (2016, June 21). *Global newspaper circulation and advertising trends in 2015*. Gulport, FL: Watershed Publishing. Retrieved from http://www.marketingcharts.com

McCann, L. D. (2012). Halifax. *The Canadian encyclopedia*. Toronto, ON: Historica Canada. Retrieved from http://www.thecanadianencyclopedia.ca

McDonald, H. (2017, March 6). *Big three record labels*. Retrieved from https://www.thebalance.com

McLuhan, M. (1964). *Understanding media: The extensions of man* (1st ed.). New York, NY: McGraw-Hill; reissued by MIT Press, 1994, with an introduction by Lewis H. Lapham.

Media Smarts. (2017). *Key concepts for media literacy. Media literacy fundamentals*. Retrieved from http://mediasmarts.ca

Merriam-Webster. (2017). Augmented reality. In *Merriam-Webster's Online Dictionary*. Retrieved from http://www.merriam-webster.com

Motion Picture Association of America. (2017, March 22). 2016 Theatrical market statistics report. In *Research and Reports*. Retrieved from http://www.mpaa.org

Mrug, S., Madan, A., Cook, E. W., & Wright, R. A. (2015). Emotional and physiological desensitization to real-life and movie violence. *Journal of Youth and Adolescence, 44*, 1092–1108.

Newspapers Canada. (2015). *Circulation report: Daily newspapers 2015*. Retrieved from https://nmc-mic.ca

Nielsen Company. (2017). *Nielsen Music year-end report (Canada 2016)*. Retrieved from http://www.nielsen.com

Nordal, G. (2010). A message from our president. *Nelson's Author Team: Newsletter, 3*(Summer).

Perrin, A. (2016, September 1). *Book reading 2016. Internet and technology.* Washington, DC: Pew Research Center. Retrieved from http://www.pewinternet.org

Phoenix Strategic Perspectives, Inc. (2016). *Final report: Survey of Canadians on privacy-related issues.* Ottawa, ON: Author. Retrieved from https://www.priv.gc.ca/en/opc-actions-and-decisions/research/explore-privacy-research/2016/por_2016_12/

Potter, W. J. (2014). The frontiers of media violence research. In D. A. Gentile (Ed.), *Media violence and children: A complete guide for parents and professionals* (pp. 432–459). Santa Barbara, CA: Praeger.

Province of Nova Scotia. (2017). *Halifax Gazette–Canada's first newspaper*. Halifax, NS: Government of Nova Scotia. Retrieved from http://www.novascotia.ca

Silverblatt, R. (2004). Media as social institution. *American Behavioral Scientist, 48*(1), 35–41.

Soroka, S. (2002). *Agenda-setting dynamics in Canada.* Vancouver, BC: UBC Press.

Statista. (2017). *Television in Canada - Statistics and facts.* Retrieved from https://www.statista.com

Stern, S. R. (2004). All I really needed to know (about beauty) I learned by kindergarten: A cultivation analysis. In R. Ann Lind (Ed.), *Race/gender/media: Considering diversity across audiences, content, and producers* (pp. 22–29). Boston, MA: Pearson Education.

Straubhaar, J., LaRose, R., & Davenport, L. (2014). *Media now: Understanding media, culture, and technology* (8th ed.). Boston, MA: Wadsworth.

Taintor, C. (2004). Chronology: Technology and the music industry (Television series episode). *Frontline.* Retrieved from http://www.pbs.org

Taylor, L. D., & Huesmann, L. R. (2014). Answering the attacks on the media violence consensus. In D. A. Gentile (Ed.), *Media violence and children: A complete guide for parents and professionals* (pp. 354–379). Santa Barbara, CA: Praeger.

Thinktv. (2016a). *Reach and time spent: Major media comparison – Canada (2015-2016 broadcast year).* Retrieved from http://thinktv.ca

Thinktv. (2016b). *Screen time: TV, video and social (full year 2015 – 2016).* Retrieved from http://thinktv.ca

Trend, D. (2007). *The myth of violence: A critical introduction.* Malden, MA: Blackwell Publishing.

Turkle, S. (2011). *Alone together: Why we expect more from technology and less from each other.* New York, NY: Basic Books.

University of Oxford. (2017). Titanic aftermath. In *Wireless world: Marconi & the making of radio.* Oxford, UK: Author. Retrieved from http://www.mhs.ox.ac.uk

Walt Disney Company. (2017). *Our businesses.* Retrieved from https://thewaltdisneycompany.com

Wanta, W., & Ghanem, S. (2007). Effects of agenda setting. In R. W. Preiss, B. M. Galue, N. Burrell, M. Allen, and J. Bryant (Eds.), *Mass media effects research: Advanced through meta-analysis* (pp. 37–51). Mahwah, NJ: Lawrence Erlbaum.

Yu, B. (2014, April 1). *Cable monopoly's gain is community media's loss. Extra!* New York, NY: Fairness & Accuracy in Reporting.

CHAPTER 7

Ainsworth, C. (2015). Sex redefined: The idea of two sexes is simplistic: Biologists now think there is a wider spectrum. *Nature, 518*(7539), 288–291.

Altinatas, E., & Sullivan, O. (2016). Fifty years of change update: Cross-national gender convergences in housework. *Demographic Research, 35*(16), 455–470.

Arboleda, V. A., Sandberg, D. E., & Vilain, E. (2014). DSDs: Genetics, underlying pathologies, and psychosexual differentiation. *Nature Reviews Endocrinology, 10*(10), 603–615.

Barone, C. (2011). Some things never change: Gender segregation in higher education across eight nations and three decades. *Sociology of Education, 84*(2), 157–176.

Bem, S. L. (1974). The measurement of psychological androgyny. *Journal of Consulting and Clinical Psychology, 42,* 155–162.

Bill C-16: An Act to amend the Canadian Human Rights Act and the Criminal Code. (2017). Third reading June 15, 2017, 42nd Parliament, 1st session. Retrieved from http://www.parl.gc.ca/

Butler, J. (1990). *Gender trouble: Feminism and the subversion of identity.* New York, NY: Routledge.

Carlson, D. L., & Lynch, J. L. (2017). Purchases, penalties, and power: The relationship between earnings and housework. *Journal of Marriage and Family, 79,* 199–224.

Clearfield, M. W., & Nelson, N. M. (2006). Sex differences in mothers' speech and play behavior with 6-, 9-, and 14-month-old infants. *Sex Roles, 54*(1–2), 127–137.

Collins, P. H., & Bilge, S. (2016). *Intersectionality.* Cambridge, UK: Polity Press.

Condrey, J., & Condrey, S. (1976). Sex differences: A study of the eye of the beholder. *Child Development, 47,* 812–819.

Craig, L., & Baxter, J. (2016). Domestic outsourcing, housework shares and subjective time pressure: Gender differences in the correlates of hiring help. *Social Indicators Research, 125,* 271–288.

Crenshaw, K. (1989). Demarginalizing the intersection of race and sex: A black feminist critique of antidiscrimination doctrine, feminist theory and antiracist politics. *University of Chicago Legal Forum, 140,* 139–167.

David, D. S., & Brannon, R. (1976). *The forty-nine percent majority: The male sex role.* Reading, MA: Addison-Wesley.

Drucker, D. J. (2010). Male sexuality and Alfred Kinsey's 0-6 scale: Toward "a sound understanding of the realities of sex." *Journal of Homosexuality, 57,* 1105–1123.

Engels, F. (1884/1972). *The origin of the family, private property and the state.* New York, NY: Pathfinder.

Epstein, R., McKinney, P., Fox, S., & Garcia, C. (2012). Support for fluid-continuum model of sexual orientation: A large-scale Internet study. *Journal of Homosexuality, 59,* 1356–1381.

Ferguson, S. J. (2016). Women and education: Qualifications, skills, and technology. *Women in Canada: A gender-based statistical report.* (Catalogue No. 89-503-X). Ottawa, ON. Statistics Canada.

Foucault, M. (1980). *Power/knowledge: Selected interviews and other writings 1972–1977* (1st American ed.) (C. Gordon, L. Marshall, J. Mepham, & K. Super, Trans.). New York, NY: Pantheon Books.

Frenette, M., & Coulombe, S. (2007). *Has higher education among young women substantially reduced the gender gap in employment and earnings?* (Catalogue No. 11F0019, No. 301). Ottawa, ON: Statistics Canada.

Furr, S. R. (2002). Men and women in cross-gender careers. In L. Diamant and J. A. Lee (Eds.), *The psychology of sex, gender, and jobs* (pp. 47–68). Westport, CA: Praeger.

Garner, B., & Grazian, D. (2016). Naturalizing gender through childhood socialization messages in a zoo. *Social Psychology Quarterly, 79*(3), 181–198.

Goffman, E. (1979). *Gender advertisements*. New York, NY: Harper & Row.

Goldberg, S., & Lewis, M. (1969). Play behavior in the year-old infant: Early sex differences. *Child Development, 40,* 21–32.

Government of Canada. (2016). *EI maternity and parental benefits*. Retrieved from http://www.canada.ca/

Granger, K. L., Hanish, L. D., Kornienko, O., & Bradley, R. H. (2017). Preschool teachers' facilitation of gender-typed and gender-neutral activities during free play. *Sex Roles, 76,* 498–510.

Greer, G. (2007). *The whole woman*. London, UK: Black Swan.

Gunderson, E. A., Ramirez, G., Levine, S. C., & Beilock, S. L. (2012). The role of parents and teachers in the development of gender-related math attitudes. *Sex Roles, 66,* 153–166.

Guppy, N., & Luongo, N. (2015). The rise and stall of Canada's gender equity revolution. *Canadian Review of Sociology, 52*(3), 241–265.

Heidenreich, P. (2017, June 15). Senate passes Bill C-16 which defends transgender rights. *Global News*. Retrieved from http://www.globalnews.ca/

Herdt, T. (1984). Ritualized homosexuality in the male cults of Melanesia, 1862–1982: An introduction. In G. Herdt (Ed.), *Ritualized homosexuality in Melanesia* (pp. 1–81). Berkeley, CA: University of California Press.

Heyder, A., & Kessels, U. (2015). Do teachers equate male and masculine with lower academic achievement? How students' gender enactment triggers gender stereotypes at school. *Social Psychology of Education, 18,* 467–485.

Hochschild, A. R., & Machung, A. (1989). *The second shift*. New York, NY: Avon.

Hudon, T. (2017). Women and education: Qualifications, skills, and technology. *Women in Canada: A gender-based statistical report*. (Catalogue No. 89-503-X). Ottawa, ON. Statistics Canada.

Intersex Society of North America. (2008). *What is intersex?* Retrieved from http://www.isna.org

Jeffreys, S. (2014). *Gender hurts: A feminist analysis of the politics of transgenderism*. New York, NY: Routledge.

Jhally, S. (Producer), & Earp, J. (Director). *Tough guise 2: Violence, manhood and American culture* [Documentary film]. San Francisco, CA: Kanopy Streaming.

Kelly, M., & Hauck, E. (2015). Doing housework, redoing gender: Queer couples negotiate the household division of labor. *Journal of GLBT Family Studies, 11,* 438–464.

Kerr, B., & Multon, K. (2015). The development of gender identity, gender roles, and gender relations in gifted students. *Journal of Counseling and Development, 93*(2), 183–191.

Kinsey, A. C., Pomeroy, W. B., & Martin, C. E. (1948). *Sexual behavior in the human male*. Philadelphia, PA: Saunders.

Kinsman, G., & Gentile, P. (2009). *The Canadian war on queers: National security as sexual regulation*. Vancouver, BC: UBC Press.

Koyama, E., & Weasel, L. (2003). From social construction to social justice: Transforming how we teach about intersexuality. In *Teaching intersex issues* (2nd ed., pp. 2–9). Portland, OR: Intersex Initiative Portland.

Lane, K. A., Goh, J. X., & Driver-Linn, E. (2012). Implicit science stereotypes mediate the relationship between gender and academic participation. *Sex Roles, 66,* 220–234.

Lasch, C. (1977). *Haven in a heartless world*. New York, NY: Basic Books.

Lero, D. S. (2015). *Current statistics on paternity leave and fathers' use of parental leave and income support in Canada and Quebec*. Centre for Families, Work and Well-Being. Retrieved from http://www.worklifecanada.ca/

Miller, A. J., & Carlson, D. L. (2016). Great expectations? Working- and middle-class cohabitors' expected and actual division of labour. *Journal of Marriage and Family, 78,* 346–363.

Moyser, M. (2017). Women and paid work. *Women in Canada: A gender-based statistical report*. (Catalogue No. 89-503-X). Ottawa, ON: Statistics Canada.

Nanda, S. (2000). *Gender diversity: Cross-cultural variations*. Long Grover, IL: Waveland Press.

NativeOUT. (n.d.). *Two-spirit terms in tribal language*. Retrieved from http://www.nativeout.com

Nelson, A. (2010). *Gender in Canada* (4th ed.). Toronto, ON: Pearson Education Canada.

Organisation for Economic Co-operation and Development. (n.d.). *Employment*. Retrieved from http://stats.oecd.org/

Parsons, T. (1954). *Essays in sociological theory*. Glencoe, IL: The Free Press.

Parsons, T., & Bales, R. F. (1955). *Family: Socialization and interaction process*. Glencoe, IL: The Free Press.

Perkel, C. (2017). *Landmark deal in RCMP sexual harassment class action wins court approval*. Retrieved from http://www.cbc.ca/news

PFLAG Canada. (n.d.). *Home page*. Retrieved from http://www.pflagcanada.ca

Plan International. (2015). *Because I am a Girl: About the program*. Retrieved from http://www.plancanada.ca

Roscoe, W. (1998). *Changing ones: Third and fourth genders in native North America*. New York, NY: St. Martin's Press.

Rubin, J. Z., Provenzano, F. J., & Lurra, Z. (1974). The eye of the beholder. *American Journal of Orthopsychiatry, 44,* 512–519.

Sadker, D., & Sadker, M. (1994). *Failing at fairness: How America's schools cheat girls*. New York, NY: Scribner.

Sadker, D., Sadker, M., & Zittleman, K. R. (2009). *Still failing at fairness: How gender bias cheats girls and boys in school and what we can do about it*. New York, NY: Scribner.

Uppal, S., & LaRochelle-Côté, S. (2014, April). Changes in the occupational profile of young men and women in Canada. *Insights on Canadian society*. (Catalogue No. 75-006-X). Ottawa, ON: Statistics Canada.

West, C., & Zimmerman, D. (1987). Doing gender. *Gender and Society, 1,* 125–151.

Yavorsky, J. E., Dush, C. M. K., & Schoppe-Sullivan, S. J. (2015). The production of inequality: The gender division of labor across the transition to parenthood. *Journal of Marriage and Family, 77,* 667–679.

Zhang, X. (2009, March). *Earnings of women with and without children.* (Catalogue No. 75-001-X). Ottawa, ON: Statistics Canada.

CHAPTER 8

Adorno, T. (1950). *The authoritarian personality.* New York, NY: Harper.

Aronson, E., Wilson, T. D., Fehr, B., & Akert, R. M. (2017). *Social psychology* (6th Can. ed.). Toronto, ON: Pearson Education Canada.

Arthur, M. L. (2007). Race. In G. Ritzer (Ed.), *Blackwell encyclopedia of sociology.* Retrieved from http://www.blackwellreference.com

Barman, J. (2003). Schooled for inequality: The education of British Columbia Aboriginal children. In N. Janovicek and J. Parr (Eds.), *Histories of Canadian children and youth* (pp. 212–235). Toronto, ON: Oxford University Press.

Baumrind, D. (1968). Authoritative vs. authoritarian parental control. *Adolescence, 3,* 255–272.

Baumrind, D. (1991). The influence of parenting style on adolescent competence and substance use. *Journal of Early Adolescence, 11,* 56–95.

Bereska, T. M. (2018). *Deviance, conformity, and social control in Canada* (5th ed.). Toronto, ON: Pearson Education Canada.

Berry, J. W., Phinney, J. P., Sam, D. L., & Vedder, P. (2006). *Immigrant youth in cultural transition: Acculturation, identity, and adaptation across national contexts.* Mahwah, NJ: Lawrence Erlbaum.

Black History Canada. (n.d.). *Timeline.* Retrieved from http://www.blackhistorycanada.ca

Black Lives Matter. (n.d.). *Home.* Retrieved from http://www.blacklivesmatter.com

Blackstock, C. (2006–2007). Building on the multi-generational strength of First Nations communities. *Transitions, 36*(4), 7–10.

Bonacich, E. (1972). A theory of ethnic antagonism: The split labor market. *American Sociological Review, 37,* 547–559.

Brasfield, C. (2001). Residential school syndrome. *British Columbia Medical Journal, 43*(2), 78–81.

Brewer, M. B., Dull, V., & Lui, L. (1981). Perceptions of the elderly: Stereotypes as prototypes. *Journal of Personality and Social Psychology, 41,* 656–670.

Campbell, M. (2016). New light on Saskatoon starlight tours, *Maclean's.* Retrieved from http://www.macleans.com

Canadian Council for Refugees. (n.d.-a). *Home.* Retrieved from http://www.ccrweb.ca

Canadian Council for Refugees. (n.d.-b). *#Welcome Refugees: Key figures.* Retrieved from http://www.ccrweb.ca

Chinese Canadian National Council. (2017). *Chinese Head Tax and Exclusion Act redress backgrounder.* Retrieved from http://www.ccnc.ca

Citizenship and Immigration Canada. (2014). *Facts and figures: Immigration overview, permanent residents 2014.* Ottawa, ON: Author.

Constitution Act. (1982, c. 11). Schedule B to the Canada Act 1982 (UK). Retrieved from http://laws-lois.justice.gc.ca/

Crenshaw, K., Gotanda, N., Peller, G., & Thomas, K. (Eds.). (1995). *Critical race theory: The key writings that informed the movement.* New York, NY: New Press.

Davin, N. F. (1879). *Report on industrial schools for Indians and half breeds.* Retrieved from http://www.canadianshakespeares.ca

Delgado, R., & Stefanic, J. (2012). *Critical race theory: An introduction* (2nd ed.). New York, NY: New York University Press.

Dewing, M. (2009). *Canadian multiculturalism.* Ottawa, ON: Parliamentary Information and Research Service.

Employment Equity Act. (1995, c. C-44). Retrieved from http://laws-lois.justice.gc.ca/

Fleras, A., & Kunz, J. L. (2001). *Media and minorities: Repressing diversity in multicultural Canada.* Toronto, ON: Thompson Educational Publishing.

Frank, K., & Hou, F. (2017). *Over-education and life satisfaction among immigrant and non-immigrant workers in Canada.* (Catalogue No. 11F0019M—No. 373). Ottawa, ON: Statistics Canada.

Frideres, J. S., & Gadacz, P. R. (2012). *Aboriginal peoples in Canada* (9th ed.). Toronto, ON: Pearson Education Canada.

Frideres, J. S., & Madibbo, A. (2014). Immigrant, visible minority, and Aboriginal families in the twenty-first century. In D. Cheal and P. Albanese (Eds.), *Canada's families today: New perspectives* (3rd ed.). Toronto, ON: Oxford University Press.

Fuligni, A., Yip, T., & Tseng, V. (2002). Impact of family obligation on daily activities and psychological well-being of Chinese-American adolescents. *Child Development, 73,* 302–314.

Galabuzi, G. E. (2006). *Canada's economic apartheid: The social exclusion of racialized groups in the new century.* Toronto, ON: Canadian Scholars' Press.

Georgas, J., Berry, J. W., VandeVijver, F., Kagitcibasi, C., & Poortinga, Y. (Eds.). (2006). *Families across cultures: A 30 nation psychological study.* Cambridge, UK: Cambridge University Press.

Goffman, E. (1974). *Frame analysis.* Philadelphia, PA: University of Pennsylvania Press.

Goulet, G., & Goulet, T. (2014). *Country wives.* Retrieved from http://bcmetis.com

Hiller, H. H., & Chow, V. (2005). Ethnic identity and assimilation among second-generation Chinese youth. *Sociological Studies of Children and Youth, 10,* 75–99.

Ho, C., Bluestein, D. N., & Jenkins, J. M. (2008). Cultural differences between parenting and children's behaviour. *Developmental Psychology, 44*(2), 507–522.

Hou, F., & Bonikowska, A. (2016). *Educational and labour market outcomes of childhood immigrants by admission class.* (Catalogue No. 11F0019M—No. 377). Ottawa, ON: Statistics Canada.

Hou, F., & Picot, G. (2016). *Changing immigrant characteristics and entry earnings.* (Catalogue No. 11F0019M—No. 374). Ottawa, ON: Statistics Canada.

Houle, R., & Corbeil, J. P. (2017). *Language projection for Canada, 2011-2036.* (Catalogue No. 657-X2017001). Ottawa, ON: Statistics Canada.

Huncar, A. (2017). Indigenous women nearly 10 times more likely to be street-checked by Edmonton police, new data shows. CBC News. Retrieved from http://www.cbc.ca/news/

Immigration and Refugee Protection Act. (2001, c. 27). Retrieved from http://laws-lois.justice.gc.ca/

Jenkins, R. (2007). Ethnicity. In G. Ritzer (Ed.), *Blackwell encyclopedia of sociology*. Retrieved from http://www.blackwellreference.com

Jeong, Y. J., Hamplová, D., & Le Bourdais, C. (2014). Diversity of young adults living arrangements: The role of ethnicity and immigration. *Journal of Ethnic and Migration Studies, 40*(7), 1116–1135.

Joseph, B. (2016). Opinion: Indigenous or Aboriginal? Which is correct? CBC News. Retrieved from http://www.cbc.ca/news/

Kagitcibasi, C. (2007). *Family, self, and human development across cultures: Theory and applications*. Mahwah, NJ: Lawrence Erlbaum Publishers.

Kakfwi, S. (2008, June 12). I accept the Prime Minister's apology. *The Globe and Mail*. Retrieved from http://www.globeandmail.com

Kelly, F. (2008). Confession of a born again Pagan. In M. B. Castellano, L. Archibald, & M. DeGagné (Eds.), *From truth to reconciliation: Transforming the legacy of residential schools* (pp. 11–42). Ottawa, ON: The Aboriginal Healing Foundation.

Langlois, S., & Turner, A. (2014). *Aboriginal languages and selected vitality indicators in 2011*. (Catalogue No. 89-655-X—No. 001). Ottawa, ON: Statistics Canada.

Leber, B. (2017). Police-reported hate crime in Canada, 2015. *Juristat*. (Catalogue No. 85-002-X). Ottawa, ON: Statistics Canada.

Marger, M. N. (2003). *Race and ethnic relations: American and global perspectives* (6th ed.). Belmont, CA: Wadsworth/Thomson Learning.

Merton, R. K. (1949). Discrimination and the American creed. In R. M. MacIver (Ed.), *Discrimination and national welfare* (pp. 77–145). New York, NY: Harper.

Morency, J., Caron-Malenfant, E. C., Couloumbe, S., & Langlois, S. (2015). *Projections of the Aboriginal population and household in Canada, 2011 to 2036*. (Catalogue No. 91-552-X). Ottawa, ON: Statistics Canada.

Morency, J., Caron-Malenfant, E. C., & MacIsaac, S. (2017). *Immigration and diversity: Population projections for Canada and its regions, 2011-2036*. (Catalogue No. 91-551-X). Ottawa, ON: Statistics Canada.

Moyser, M. (2017). *Aboriginal people living off-reserve and the labour market: Estimates from the Labour Force Survey, 2007-2015*. (Catalogue No. 71-588-X). Ottawa, ON: Statistics Canada.

National Centre for Truth and Reconciliation. (2016). *Residential school overview*. Retrieved from http://umanitoba.ca/centres/nctr/

National Geographic Society. (2017). *The Genographic Project*. Retrieved from https://genographic.nationalgeographic.com/

Olzak, S. (2006). *The global dynamics of race and ethnic mobilization*. Stanford, CA: Stanford University Press.

Poirier, G. W., & Lott, A. J. (1967). Galvanic skin response and prejudice. *Journal of Personality and Social Psychology, 5*(3), 253–259.

Sano, Y., Kaida, L., & Tenkorang, E. Y. (2015). Racial variations in ethnic identity among the children of immigrants in Canada. *Canadian Ethnic Studies, 47*(3), 49–68.

Sherif, M. O., Harvey, O. J., White, B. J., Hood, W. R., & Sherif, W. (1961). *Intergroup conflict and cooperation: The robbers' cave experiment*. Norman, OK: University of Oklahoma Press.

Statistics Canada. (2015). *Aboriginal statistics at a glance*. (Catalogue No. 89-645-X2015001). Ottawa, ON: Author.

Statistics Canada. (2017). *Labour Force Survey (LFS), by Aboriginal group, sex, and age, Canada, selected provinces and regions*. (CANSIM Table 282-0026). Ottawa, ON: Author.

Truth and Reconciliation Commission. (2015). *Truth and Reconciliation Commission of Canada: Calls to action*. Winnipeg, MB: Author.

United Nations. (2007). General Assembly Resolution 61/295. *United Nations Declaration on the Rights of Indigenous Peoples*. (A/RES/61/295). Retrieved from http://undocs.org

Vedder, P., Berry, J., Sabatier, C., & Sam, D. (2008). The intergenerational transmission of values in national and immigrant families: The role of Zeitgeist. *Journal of Youth and Adolescence, 38*, 642–653.

West, C. (1995). Foreword. In K. Crenshaw, N. Gotanda, G. Peller, & K. Thomas (Eds.), *Critical race theory: The key writings that informed the movement* (p. xii). New York, NY: New Press.

West, C. (n.d.). *Toward a socialist theory of racism*. Retrieved from http://www.chicagodsa.org

Wirth, L. (1945). The problem of minority groups. In R. Linton (Ed.), *The science of man in the world crisis*. New York, NY: Columbia University Press.

CHAPTER 9

Adserà, A., & Ferrer, A. (2016). The fertility of married immigrant women to Canada. *International Migration Review, 50*(2), 475–505.

Ahern, S., & Bailey, K. G. (1997). *Family-by-choice: Creating family in a world of strangers*. Minneapolis, MN: Fairview Press.

Allen, K. R. (2016). Feminist theory in family studies: History, reflection, and critique. *Journal of Family Theory and Review, 8*, 207–224.

Amato, P. R. (2005). Family change: Decline or resilience? In V. L. Bengston, A. C. Acock, K. R. Allen, P. Dilworth-Anderson, & D. M. Klein (Eds.), *Sourcebook of family theory and research* (pp. 112–114). Thousand Oaks, CA: Sage Publications.

Ambert, A. M. (2009). *Divorce: Facts, causes, and consequences* (3rd ed.). Ottawa, ON: Vanier Institute of the Family.

Ambert, A. M. (2015). *Changing families: Relationships in context* (3rd Canadian edition). Toronto, ON: Pearson Education Canada.

Associated Press. (2017, February 16). 64-year-old woman gives birth to 'perfectly healthy' twins. *Global News*. Retrieved from http://www.globalnews.ca

Bernard, J. (1972). *The future of marriage*. New York, NY: Bantam.

Berry, J. W., Phinney, J. P., Sam, D. L., & Vedder, P. (2006). *Immigrant youth in cultural transition: Acculturation, identity, and adaptation across national contexts*. Mahwah, NJ: Lawrence Erlbaum.

Bourgeault, R. G. (1991). Race, class and gender: Colonial domination of Indian women. In Vorst J. (Ed.), *Race, class, gender: Bonds and barriers*. Toronto, ON: Garamond/Society for Socialist Studies.

Brooks, C. (2002). Religious influence and the politics of family decline concern: Trends, sources, and U.S. political behavior. *American Sociological Review, 67,* 191–211.

Burczycka, M. (2016). "Section 1: Trends in self-reported spousal violence in Canada, 2014." In *Family violence in Canada: A statistical profile* (pp. 3–20). (Catalogue No. 85-002-X). Ottawa, ON: Statistics Canada.

Castellano, M. B. (2002). Aboriginal family trends: Extended families, nuclear families, families of the heart. *Contemporary Family Trends.* (Occasional Paper). The Vanier Institute of the Family. Retrieved from http://www.vanierinstitute.ca

Chansonneuve, D. (2005). *Reclaiming connections: Understanding residential school trauma among Aboriginal people.* Ottawa, ON: Aboriginal Healing Foundation.

Chartrand, L. N., & McCay, C. (2006). *A review of research on criminal victimization and First Nations, Métis, and Inuit peoples, 1990 to 2001.* Ottawa, ON: Department of Justice.

Coontz, S. (1992). *The way we never were: American families and the nostalgia trap.* New York, NY: Basic Books.

Eichler, M. (1988). *Families in Canada today: Recent changes and their policy consequences* (2nd ed.). Toronto, ON: Gage.

Eichler, M. (1997). *Family shifts: Families, policies and gender equality.* Toronto, ON: Oxford University Press.

Engels, F. (1884/1972). *The origin of the family, private property and the state.* New York, NY: Pathfinder.

European Society of Human Reproduction and Embryology (ESHRE). (2016). *ART fact sheet.* Retrieved from http://www.eshre.eu

Fournier, S., & Crey, E. (1997). *Stolen from our embrace: The abduction of First Nations children and the restoration of Aboriginal communities.* Vancouver, BC: Douglas and McIntyre.

Fox, B. (2015). Feminism on family sociology: Interpreting trends in family life. *Canadian Review of Sociology, 52*(2), 204–211.

Gaffield, C. (1990). The social and economic origins of contemporary families. In M. Baker (Ed.), *Families: Changing trends in Canada* (2nd ed., pp. 23–40). Toronto, ON: McGraw-Hill.

Gaffield, C. (1992). Canadian families in cultural context: Hypotheses from the mid-nineteenth century. In B. Bradbury (Ed.), *Canadian family history: Selected readings* (pp. 135–157). Toronto, ON: Copp Clark.

Goldberg, A. E., Smith, J. Z., & Kashy, D. A. (2010). Preadoptive factors predicting lesbian, gay, and heterosexual couples' relationship quality across the transition to parenthood. *Journal of Family Psychology, 24*(3), 221–232.

Goodrum, S., Umberson, D., & Anderson, K. L. (2001). The batterer's view of the self and others. *Sociological Inquiry, 71*(2), 221–240.

Hareven, T. K. (1994). Continuity and change in American family life. In A. S. Skolnick & J. H. Skolnick (Eds.), *Family in transition* (8th ed., pp. 40–47). New York, NY: HarperCollins.

Hawkins, A. J., & Van Der Berghe, B. (2014). *Facilitating forever.* Charlottesville, VA: National Marriage Project.

Ibrahim, D. (2016). "Police-reported family violence against seniors." In *Family violence in Canada: A statistical profile* (pp. 27–28). (Catalogue No. 85-002-X). Ottawa, ON: Statistics Canada.

Ibrahim, D., & Karam, M. (2016). "Section 4: Police-reported family violence against children and youth." In *Family violence in Canada: A statistical profile* (pp. 25–26). (Catalogue No. 85-002-X). Ottawa, ON: Statistics Canada.

Irvine, L., & Cilia, L. (2017). More-than-human families: Pets, people, and practices in multispecies households. *Sociology Compass, 11*(2), 1–13.

Johnson, C. L., & Barer, B. M. (1990). Families and networks among older inner-city Blacks. *Gerontologist, 30,* 726–733.

Johnston, P. (1983). *Native children and the child welfare system.* Toronto, ON: Canadian Council on Social Development and James Lorimer & Company.

Kelly, M. B. (2012). Divorce cases in civil court, 2010/2011. *Juristat.* (Catalogue No. 85-002-X). Ottawa, ON: Statistics Canada.

Kreager, D. A., Felson, R. B., Warner, C., & Wenger, M. R. (2013). Women's education, marital violence, and divorce: A social exchange perspective. *Journal of Marriage and Family, 75,* 565–581.

Lamanna, M. A. (2002). Émile Durkheim on the family. Thousand Oaks, CA: Sage.

Laurent-Simpson, A. (2017). "Phil's calling Grandma…": The role of external support in human-companion animal identity pairings. *Symbolic Interaction, 40*(2), 212–228.

Lewis, J. (2003). *Should we worry about family change? The 2001 Joanne Goodman Lectures.* Toronto, ON: University of Toronto Press.

Macdonald, D., & Wilson, D. (2016, May). *Shameful neglect: Indigenous child poverty in Canada.* Ottawa, ON: Canadian Centre for Policy Alternatives. Retrieved from https://www.policyalternatives.ca

Madden-Derdich, D. A., & Leonard, S. A. (2002). Shared experiences, unique realities: Formerly married mothers' and fathers' perceptions of parenting and custody after divorce. *Family Relations, 51,* 7–45.

Milan, A. (2000, Spring). One hundred years of families. *Canadian Social Trends,* 2–12. (Catalogue No. 11-008). Ottawa, ON: Statistics Canada.

Milan, A. (2013). *Marital status: Overview, 2011.* (Catalogue No. 91-209-X). Ottawa, ON: Statistics Canada.

Murdock, G. P. (1949). *Social structure.* New York, NY: Macmillan.

Natelson, R. (2009, March 19). *Traditional marriage is better: David Popenoe.* Retrieved from http://electriccityweblog.com

Nault, F. (1996). Twenty years of marriages. *Health Reports, 8*(2), 39–47. (Catalogue No. 82-003-XIE). Ottawa, ON: Statistics Canada.

Nye, F. I. (1979). Choice, exchange, and the family. In W. Burr, R. Hill, F. I. Nye, & I. Reiss (Eds.), *Contemporary theories about the family* (pp. 1–41). New York, NY: The Free Press.

Paat, Y. F. (2013). Relationship dynamics and healthy exchange across the family life cycle: Implications for practice. *Journal of Human Behavior in the Social Environment, 23,* 938–953.

Packaged Facts. (2015). *Canada's pet market outlook* (2nd ed.). Rockville, MD: Author.

Parsons, T. (1954). *Essays in sociological theory.* Glencoe, IL: The Free Press.

Parsons, T., & Bales, R. F. (1955). *Family: Socialization and interaction process.* Glencoe, IL: The Free Press.

Pearson, C. H. (1893/2003). Charles Henry Pearson on the decline of the family. *Population and Development Review, 29*(2), 299–304.

Perrault, S., & Proulx, J. (2000). Introduction. In J. Proulx & S. Perrault (Eds.), *No place for violence: Canadian Aboriginal alternatives*. Halifax, NS: Ferwood/RESOLVE.

Popenoe, D. (1994). Housing, suburbia, and family decline: A cross-national perspective. *Research in Community Sociology, 4*, 211–227.

Popenoe, D. (2007). *The state of our unions, 2007: The social health of marriage in America. The National Marriage Project.* Piscataway, NJ: Rutgers, State University of New Jersey.

Powell, J., & Branden, K. (2007). Family, sociology of. In G. Ritzer (Ed.), *Blackwell encyclopedia of sociology.* Retrieved from http://www.blackwellreferenceonline.com

Power, E. (2008). Furry families: Making a human-dog family through home. *Social and Cultural Geography, 9*(5), 535–555.

Previti, D., & Amato, P. R. (2003). Why stay married? Rewards, barriers, and marital stability. *Journal of Marriage and Family, 65*, 561–573.

Rackin, H. M., & Brasher, M. S. (2016). Is baby a blessing? Wantedness, age of first birth, and later-life depression. *Journal of Marriage and Family, 78*, 1269–1284.

Sinclair, R. (2016). The Indigenous child removal system in Canada: An examination of legal decision-making and racial bias. *First Peoples Child and Family Review, 11*(2), 8–18.

Statistics Canada. (2011). *Marriages, divorces and demography division (population estimates)*. Ottawa, ON: Author.

Statistics Canada. (2012). *Portrait of families and living arrangements in Canada: Families, households and marital status, 2011 census of population.* (Catalogue No. 98-312-X2011001). Ottawa, ON: Author.

Statistics Canada. (2014). Fertility: Fewer children, older moms. *The Daily: Canadian Megatrends*. (Catalogue No. 11-630-X2014002). Ottawa, ON: Author.

Statistics Canada. (2015). Lone-parent families: The new face of an old phenomenon. *The Daily: Canadian Megatrends*. (Catalogue No. 11-630-X2015002). Ottawa, ON: Author.

Statistics Canada. (2016a). Same-sex couples and sexual orientation... by the numbers. *The Daily: By the Numbers*. Ottawa, ON: Author.

Statistics Canada. (2016b). *Table 3: Persons in low income (after-tax low income measure)*. (CANSIM Table 206-0041). Ottawa, ON: Author.

Statistics Canada. (2017). Census family. In *Dictionary, census of population, 2016*. Retrieved from http://www.statcan.gc.ca

Straus, M. A. (1994). State to state differences in social inequality and social bonds in relation to assaults on wives in the United States. *Journal of Comparative Family Studies, 25*, 7–24.

Tanskanen, A. O., Danielsbacka, M., Jokela, M., David-Barrett, T., & Rotkirch, A. (2016). Diluted competition? Conflicts between full- and half-siblings in two adult generations. *Frontiers in Sociology, 1*(6), 1–12.

Taylor, A. C., & Bagdi, A. B. (2005). The lack of explicit theory in family research: A case study analysis of the *Journal of Marriage and the Family*, 1990–1999. In V. L. Bengston, A. C. Acock, K. R. Allen, P. Dilworth-Anderson, & D. M. Klein (Eds.), *Sourcebook of family theory and research* (pp. 22–25). Thousand Oaks, CA: Sage Publications.

Turner, J. H. (2005). Is a scientific theory of the family desirable? In V. L. Bengston, A. C. Acock, K. R. Allen, P. Dilworth-Anderson, & D. M. Klein (Eds.), *Sourcebook of family theory and research* (pp. 26–29). Thousand Oaks, CA: Sage Publications.

Vanier Institute of the Family. (2017a). *Definition of family*. Retrieved from http://www.vifamily.ca

Vanier Institute of the Family. (2017b). *Indigenous families in Canada*. Retrieved from http://www.vifamily.ca

White, J. M., Klein, D. M., & Martin, T. F. (2015). *Family theories: An introduction* (4th ed.). Thousand Oaks, CA: Sage Publications.

Whitehead, J. W. (2006). *Without the family, there is no freedom*. Retrieved from http://www.familyaction.org

Wright, L. (2016). Type and timing of first union formation in Quebec and the rest of Canada: Continuity and change across 1930-1979 cohorts. *Canadian Studies in Population, 43*(3–4), 234–248.

Wu, Z. (2000). *Cohabitation: An alternative form of family living*. Toronto, ON: Oxford University Press.

CHAPTER 10

Alberta Education. (2016). *Guide to education: ECS to grade 12 (2016–2017)*. (The) Crown in Right of Alberta, as represented by the Minister of Education. Retrieved from http://www.education.alberta.ca

Alberta Education. (2017). *Grade 9 at a glance*. (The) Crown in Right of Alberta, as represented by the Minister of Education. Retrieved from http://www.education.alberta.ca

Avinun, R., & Knafo-Noam, A. (2015). Socialization, genetics, and their interplay in development. In J. E. Grusec & P. D. Hastings (Eds.), *Handbook of socialization: Theory and research* (2nd ed., pp. 347–371). New York, NY: Guilford Press.

Bailey, Z. D., Slopen, N., Albert, M., & Williams, D. R. (2015). Multidimensional religious involvement and tobacco smoking patterns over 9–10 years: A prospective study of middle-aged adults in the United States. *Social Science and Medicine, 138*, 128–135.

Ballentine, J. H. (2001). *The sociology of education: A systematic analysis* (5th ed.). Englewood Cliffs, NJ: Prentice Hall.

Barstow, A. L. (1994). *Witchcraze*. San Francisco, CA: Pandora.

Ben-Yehuda, N. (1990). *The politics and morality of deviance: Moral panics, drug abuse, deviant science, and reversed stigmatization*. Albany, NY: State University of New York Press.

Bereska, T. M. (2018). *Deviance, conformity, and social control in Canada* (5th ed.). Toronto, ON: Pearson Education Canada.

Berger, I. E. (2006). The influence of religion on philanthropy in Canada. *Voluntas, 17*, 115–132.

Bibby, R. W. (2004). *Restless churches: How Canadian churches can contribute to the emerging religious renaissance*. Toronto, ON: Novalis.

Bibby, R. W. (2006). *Why bother with organized religion? The views of insiders, marginals, and outsiders*. Paper presented at the Annual Meeting of the Pacific Sociological Association, Hollywood, CA, April 2006.

Bills, D. B. (2004). *The sociology of education and work*. Malden, MA: Blackwell Publishing.

Born, L. (2004). Fast-tracking the plague: Drugging America to death. *International Socialist Review, 33*. Retrieved from http://www.isreview.org

Bourdieu, P., & Passeron, J. C. (1964). *Les héritiers*. Paris, France: Les Éditions de Minuit.

Bourdieu, P., & Passeron, J. C. (1970). *La reproduction: Éléments pour une théorie du système d'enseignement*. Paris, France: Les Editions de Minuit.

Bramadat, P. A. (2005). Religion, social capital, and "the day that changed the world." *Journal of International Migration and Integration, 6*(2), 201–217.

Brenner, P. S. (2016). Cross-national trends in religious service attendance. *Public Opinion Quarterly, 80*(2), 563–583.

Buckreus, K. (2016). Catholic vs. secular public schooling: Shifting hegemony in Morinville, Alberta. *Journal of Integrated Studies, 8*(1). Retrieved from http://jis.athabascau.ca

Campbell, R. A. (2005). Students' views on the relationship between religion and science: Analysis of results from a comparative survey. *Canadian Review of Sociology and Anthropology, 42*(3), 249–265.

Caulfield, T. (2004). The commercialisation of medical and scientific reporting. *PLoS Medicine, 1*(3), 178–179.

Clark, W., & Schellenberg, G. (2006, Summer). Who's religious? *Canadian Social Trends*, 2–9. (Catalogue No. 11-008). Ottawa, ON: Statistics Canada.

Collins, R. (1977). Some comparative principles of educational stratification. *Harvard Educational Review, 47*(1), 1–27.

Council of Ministers of Education, Canada. (2017). *Education in Canada: An overview.* Toronto, ON: Author. Retrieved from http://www.cmec.ca

Curtis, B., Livingstone, D. W., & Smaller, H. (1992). *Stacking the deck: The streaming of working-class kids in Ontario schools*. Montréal, QC: La maîtresse d'école.

Davis, S., & Guppy, N. (2006). *The schooled society.* Don Mills, ON: Oxford University Press.

Dillon, M. (2007). Religion, sociology of. In G. Ritzer (Ed.), *Blackwell encyclopedia of sociology*. Retrieved from http://www.blackwellreference.com

Drysdale, D. (2007). Weber, Max (1864–1920). In G. Ritzer (Ed.), *Blackwell encyclopedia of sociology*. Retrieved from http://www.blackwellreference.com

Durkheim, E. (1965). *Elementary forms of religious life* (J. W. Swain, Trans.). New York, NY: Free Press. (Original work published 1915)

Durkheim, E. (1956). *Education and sociology* (S. Fox, Trans.). New York, NY: Free Press.

Eagle, D. (2011). Changing patterns of attendance at religious services in Canada, 1986–2008. *Journal for the Scientific Study of Religion, 50*(1), 187–200.

Erikson, E. H. (1968). *Identity: Youth and crisis*. New York, NY: Norton.

Eriksson, L. (2007). Science, social construction of. In G. Ritzer (Ed.), *Blackwell encyclopedia of sociology.* Retrieved from http://www.blackwellreference.com

Feinberg, W., & Soltis, J. F. (2009). *School and society* (5th ed.). New York, NY: Teachers College Press.

Fontaine, T. (2017). 'Let our Indigenous voices be heard': Indigenous scientists join March for Science. CBC News. Retrieved from http://www.cbc.ca/news

Foucault, M. (1980). *Power/knowledge: Selected interviews and other writings 1972-1977* (1st American ed.) (C. Gordon, L. Marshall, J. Mepham, & K. Super, Trans.). New York, NY: Pantheon Books.

Galen, L. W., Sharp, M., & McNulty, A. (2015). Non-religious group factors versus religious belief in the prediction of prosociality. *Social Indicators Research, 122*, 411–432.

Gilligan, C. (1984). *In a different voice*. Cambridge, MA: Harvard University Press.

Gintis, H., & Bowles, S. (1980). Contradiction and reproduction in educational theory. In L. Barton, R. Meighan, & S. Walker (Eds.), *Schooling, ideology and the curriculum* (pp. 51–65). London, UK: Falmer Press.

Goldstein, A. L., Wall, A. M., Wekerle, C., & Krank, M. (2013). The impact of perceived reinforcement from alcohol and involvement in leisure activities on adolescent alcohol use. *Journal of Children and Adolescent Substance Abuse, 22*, 340–363.

Good, M., & Willoughby, T. (2014). Institutional and personal spirituality/religiosity and psychosocial adjustment in adolescence: Concurrent and longitudinal associations. *Journal of Youth and Adolescence, 43*, 757–774.

Hamlin, D., & Cameron, D. (2015, April 13). *Applied or academic high impact decisions for Ontario students*. Toronto, ON: People for Education. Retrieved from http://www.peopleforeducation.ca

Haraway, D. J. (1991). *Simians, cyborgs and women: The reinvention of nature*. New York, NY: Routledge.

Harding, S. (1991). *Whose science? Whose knowledge? Thinking from women's lives*. Ithaca, NY: Cornell University Press.

Hird, M. J. (2012). *Sociology of science: A critical Canadian introduction*. Toronto, ON: Oxford University Press.

Izquierdo, H. M., & Mínguez, A. M. (2003). Sociological theory of education in the dialectical perspective. In C. A. Torres & A. Antikainen (Eds.), *The international handbook on the sociology of education* (pp. 21–41). Lanham, MD: Rowman & Littlefield.

Jackson, P. W. (1968). *Life in classrooms*. New York, NY: Holt, Rinehart & Winston.

Jordan, T. E. (1998). Victorian child savers and their culture: A thematic evaluation. In *Mellon studies in sociology* (Vol. 19). Lewiston, NY: Edwin Mellon Press.

Kerr, C. (2003). Phony research earns 1-year suspension. *Canadian Medical Association Journal, 168*(8), 1032.

Kibera, L. W., & Kimokoti, A. (2007). *Fundamentals of sociology of education: With reference to Africa*. Nairobi, Kenya: University of Nairobi Press.

Kohlberg, L. (1958). *The development of modes of moral thinking and choice in the years 10 to 16* (Doctoral dissertation). Chicago, IL: University of Chicago.

Kohlberg, L. (1981). *Essays on moral development, Volume 1: The philosophy of moral development*. New York, NY: Holt, Rinehart and Winston.

Kuhn, T. (1962). *The structure of scientific revolutions*. Chicago, IL: University of Chicago Press.

Lareau, A. (2011). *Unequal childhood: Class, race and family life*. Berkeley, CA: University of California Press.

Learn, J. R. (2017). Canadian scientists explain exactly how their government silenced science. *Smithsonian Magazine*. Retrieved from http://www.smithsonianmag.com

Livingstone, D. W. (1998). *The education-jobs gap: Underemployment or economic democracy.* Boulder, CO: Westview Press.

Longino, H. (1990). *Science as social knowledge.* Princeton, NJ: Princeton University Press.

Malenfant, E., Lebel, A., & Martel, L. (2010). *Projections of the diversity of the Canadian population, 2006–2031.* (Catalogue No. 91-551-X). Ottawa, ON: Statistics Canada.

Marx, K. (1844/1970). *Introduction to a contribution to the critique of Hegel's philosophy of right.* Cambridge, UK: Cambridge University Press.

McCallum, D. (2012). *7 reasons to integrate Indigenous knowledge into science curriculum.* Retrieved from http://www.ictinc.ca

Merton, R. K. (1957). *Social theory and social structure.* Glencoe, IL: Free Press.

Merton, R. K. (1973). *The sociology of science: Theoretical and empirical investigations.* Chicago, IL: University of Chicago Press.

Mortillaro, N. (2016). How science and First Nations oral traditions are converging. CBC News. Retrieved from http://www.cbc.ca/news

Neitz, M. J. (2014). Becoming visible: Religion and gender in society. *Sociology of Religion, 75*(4), 511–523.

Nelson, H. L. (1990). *Who knows: From Quine to a feminist empiricism.* Philadelphia, PA: Temple University Press.

Oakes, J. (2005). *Keeping track: How schools structure inequality.* New Haven, CT: Yale University Press.

Organisation for Economic Co-operation and Development (OECD). (2012). *Equity and quality in education: Supporting disadvantaged students and schools.* Paris, France: OECD Publishing. Retrieved from https://www.oecd.org

Our Kids. (2017). *School tuition and costs. Private schools.* Retrieved from http://www.ourkids.net

Paludi, M. A., & Ellens, J. H. (2016). *Feminism and religion: How faiths view women and their rights.* Santa Barbara, CA: Praeger Press.

Park, J. J., & Bowman, N. A. (2015). Religion as bridging or bonding social capital: Race, religion, and cross-racial interaction for college students. *Sociology of Education, 88*(1), 20–37.

Parsons, T. (1959). The school class as a social system: Some of its functions in American society. *Harvard Educational Review, 29*(4), 297–318.

Pew Research Center. (2017). *The changing global religious landscape.* Washington, DC: Author.

Platt, A. M. (1977). *The child savers: The invention of delinquency.* Chicago, IL: University of Chicago Press.

Putnam, R. (2000). *Bowling alone: The collapse and revival of American community.* New York, NY: Simon & Schuster.

Quaife, G. R. (1987). *Godly zeal and furious rage: The witch craze in early modern Europe.* New York, NY: St. Martin's Press.

Rawana, J. S., & Ames, M. E. (2012). Protective predictors of alcohol use trajectories among Canadian Aboriginal youth. *Journal of Youth and Adolescence, 41,* 229–243.

Rhodes, J. (2012). The ties that divide: Bonding social capital, religious friendship networks, and political tolerance among evangelicals. *Sociological Inquiry, 82*(2), 163–186.

Rosenthal, R., & Jackson, L. (1968). *Pygmalion in the classroom.* New York, NY: Holt, Rinehart & Winston.

Schieman, S. (2008). The education-contingent association between religiosity and health: The differential effects of self-esteem and the sense of mastery. *Journal for the Scientific Study of Religion, 47*(4), 710–724.

Shavit, Y., & Müller, W. (2000). Vocational secondary education, tracking, and social stratification. In M. T. Hallinan (Ed.), *Handbook of the sociology of education* (pp. 437–474). New York, NY: Kluwer Academic/Plenum.

Sievert, W. (2010, January 14). Another brick in the wall. *Mises Daily.* Retrieved from http://www.mises.org. (Originally published as "Song that's driving teachers up the wall" in *Libertarian Review, 1980, 9*(9), 42–43.)

Snively, G., & Williams, W. L. (2016). *Knowing home: Braiding Indigenous science with Western science.* Victoria, BC: BC Faculty Pressbooks.

Statistics Canada. (2014). *2011 National household survey.* (Catalogue No. 99-010-X201132). Ottawa, ON: Author.

Stebbins, R. A. (1996). *Tolerable differences: Living with deviance.* Toronto, ON: McGraw-Hill Ryerson.

Stuckey, J. H. (1998). *Feminist spirituality: An introduction to feminist theology in Judaism, Christianity, Islam, and feminist Goddess Worship.* York, ON: CFR.

Taylor, A., & Krahn, H. (2009). Streaming in/for the new economy. In C. Levine-Rasky (Ed.), *Canadian perspectives on the sociology of education* (pp. 103–124). Don Mills, ON: Oxford University Press.

Usher, R., & Edwards, R. (1994). *Postmodernism and education: Different voices, different worlds.* New York, NY: Routledge.

Valverde, M. (1991). *The age of light, soap, and water: Moral reform in English Canada, 1885-1925.* Toronto, ON: McClelland & Stewart.

Varcoe, I. (2007). Science. In G. Ritzer (Ed.), *Blackwell encyclopedia of sociology.* Retrieved from http://www.blackwellreference.com

Waddington, C. H. (1942). The epigenotype. *Endeavor, 1,* 18–20.

Walach, H., & Reich, K. H. (2005). Reconnecting science and spirituality: Toward overcoming a taboo. *Zygon, 40*(2), 423–441.

Webb, J. T., Amend, E. R., Webb, N. E., Goerss, J., Beljan, P., & Olenchak, F. R. (2005). *Misdiagnosis and dual diagnosis of gifted children and adults: ADHD, bipolar, OCD, Asperger's, depression, and other disorders.* Scottsdale, AZ: Great Potential Press.

Weber, M. (1958). *The Protestant ethic and the spirit of capitalism* (T. Parsons, Trans.). New York, NY: Scribner. (Original work published 1904)

Wotherspoon, T. (1998). *The sociology of education in Canada: Critical perspectives.* Toronto, ON: Oxford University Press.

CHAPTER 11

Armstrong, T., & Matusitz, J. (2013). Hezbollah as a group phenomenon: Differential association theory. *Journal of Human Behavior in the Social Environment, 23*(4), 475–484.

BBC News. (2017, May 13). *Massive ransomware infection hits computers in 99 countries.* Retrieved from http://www.bbc.com

Beccaria, C. (1963). *On crimes and punishments* (Introduction by H. Paolucci, Trans.). New York, NY: Macmillan. (Original work published 1764)

Becker, H. (1963). *Outsiders: Studies in the sociology of deviance.* New York, NY: Free Press.

Bender-Baird, K. (2016). Peeing under surveillance: Bathrooms, gender policing, and hate violence. *Gender, Place, and Culture, 23*(7), 983–988.

Bereska, T. M. (2018). *Deviance, conformity, and social control in Canada* (5th ed.). Toronto, ON: Pearson Education Canada.

Boak, A., Hamilton, H. A., Adlaf, E. M., & Mann, R. E. (2015). *Drug use among Ontario students, 1977-2015: Detailed OSDUHS findings.* (CAMH Research Documents Series No. 41). Toronto, ON: CAMH.

Boyce, J. (2015, July 22). Police-reported crime statistics in Canada, 2014. *Juristat.* (Catalogue No. 85-002-X). Ottawa, ON: Statistics Canada.

Braswell, M., Fuller J., & Lozoff, B. (2001). *Corrections, peacemaking, and restorative justice: Transforming individuals and institutions.* Cincinnati, OH: Anderson Publishing.

CBC. (2013, December 20). *Supreme Court strikes down Canada's prostitution laws.* Retrieved from www.cbc.ca

Chan, W., & Chunn, D. (2014). *Racialization, crime, and criminal justice in Canada.* Toronto, ON: University of Toronto Press.

Clevenger, S. (2016). Mothers of sexual assault victims: How women "do mother" after their child has been sexually assaulted. *Feminist Criminology, 11*(3), 227–252.

Corrections and Conditional Release Act (S.C. 1992, c. 20). Retrieved from the Justice Laws website: http://www.laws-lois.justice.gc.ca

Criminal Code (R.S.C., 1985, c. C-46). Retrieved from the Justice Laws website: http://www.laws-lois.justice.gc.ca

Davies, J. M. (2015). The criminalization of sexual commerce in Canada: Context and concepts for critical analysis. *Canadian Journal of Human Sexuality, 24*(2), 78–91.

Edwards, A. R. (1988). *Regulation and repression: The study of social control.* Sydney, Australia: Allen & Unwin.

Elliot, E. M. (2011). *Security, with care: Restorative justice and healthy societies.* Halifax, NS: Fernwood.

Featherstone, R., & Deflam, M. (2003). Anomie and strain: Context and consequences of Merton's two theories. *Sociological Inquiry, 73*(4), 471–489.

Foucault, M. (1995). *Discipline and punish: The birth of the prison* (2nd ed.) (A. Sheridan, Trans.). New York, NY: Vintage Books.

Goffman, E. (1963). *Stigma: Notes on the management of spoiled identity.* Englewood Cliffs, NJ: Prentice Hall.

Goodwin, J., & Tajjudin, I. (2016). "What do you think I am? Crazy?": The Joker and stigmatizing representations of mental ill-health. *Journal of Popular Culture, 49*(2), 385–402.

Gottfredson, M. R., & Hirschi, T. (1990). *A general theory of crime.* Stanford, CT: Stanford University Press.

Grasmick, H. G., Tittle, C. R., Bursik, R. J., & Arneklev, B. J. (1993). Testing the core empirical implications of Gottfredson and Hirschi's general theory of crime. *Journal of Research in Crime and Delinquency, 30*(1), 47–54.

Gray, A. C., Durkin, K. F., Call, J. T., Evans, H. J., & Melton, W. (2015). Differential association and marijuana use in a juvenile drug court sample. *Applied Psychology in Criminal Justice, 11*(1), 1–8.

Halushka, J. (2015). Work wisdom: Teaching former prisoners how to negotiate workplace interactions and perform a rehabilitated self. *Ethnography, 17*(1), 72–91.

Hawdon, J. (2012). Applying differential association theory to online hate groups: A theoretical statement. *Research on Finnish Society, 5,* 39–47.

Hayle, S., Wortley, S., & Tanner, J. (2016). Race, street life, and policing: Implications for racial profiling. *Canadian Journal of Criminology and Criminal Justice, 58*(3), 322–353.

Hirschi, T. C. (1969). *Causes of delinquency.* Berkeley, CA: University of California Press.

Hövermann, A., Groβ, E. M., Zick, A., & Messner, S. F. (2015). Understanding the devaluation of vulnerable groups: A novel application of Institutional Anomie Theory. *Social Science Research, 52,* 408–421.

Jack.org. (2017). *Home page.* Retrieved from www.jack.org

Janssen, H. J., Eichelsheim, V. I., Deković, M., & Bruinsma, G. J. N. (2016). How is parenting related to adolescent delinquency? A between- and within-person analysis of the mediating role of self-control, delinquent attitudes, peer delinquency, and time spent in criminogenic settings. *European Journal of Criminology, 13*(2), 169–194.

Jourard, R. (2017). *Summary conviction or indictable?* Toronto, ON: Ron Jourard Professional Corp. Retrieved from http://www.defencelaw.com

Keene, D. E., Cowan, S. K., & Castro-Baker, A. (2015). "When you're in a crisis like that, you don't want people to know": Mortgage strain, stigma, and mental health. *American Journal of Public Health, 105*(5), 1008–1012.

Koeppel, M. D. H., Bouffard, L. A., & Koeppel-Ullrich, E. R. H. (2015). Sexual orientation and substance use: The moderation of parental attachment. *Deviant Behavior, 36*(8), 657–673.

Lemert, E. M. (1951). *Social pathology: A systematic approach to the study of sociopathic behavior.* New York, NY: McGraw-Hill.

Li, C. K. W., Holt, T. J., Bossler, A. M., & May, D. C. (2016). Examining the mediating effects of social learning on the low Self-Control—Cyberbullying relationship in a youth sample. *Deviant Behavior, 37*(2), 1–13.

Linden, R. (2016). *Criminology: A Canadian perspective* (8th ed.). Toronto, ON: Nelson Education.

Melendez, M. S., Lichtenstein, B., & Dolliver, M. J. (2016). Mothers of mass murderers: Exploring blame for the mothers of school shooters through an application of courtesy stigma to the Columbine and Newton tragedies. *Deviant Behavior, 37*(5), 525–536.

Mental Health Commission of Canada. (2016). *Mental health matters.* Retrieved from http://www.mentalhealthcommission.ca

Merriam-Webster. (2017). Deviant. In *Merriam-Webster's Online Dictionary.* Retrieved from http://www.merriam-webster.com

Merton, R. K. (1938). Social structure and anomie. *American Sociological Review, 3,* 672–682.

Merton, R. K. (1968). *Social theory and social structure.* New York, NY: Free Press.

Miller, H. E., Thomas, S. L., Smith, K. M., & Robinson, P. (2015). Surveillance, responsibility, and control: An analysis of government and industry discourses about "problem" and "responsible" gambling. *Addiction Research and Theory, 24*(2), 163–176.

Moore, K. E., Stuewig, J. B., & Tangney, J. P. (2016). The effect of stigma on criminal offenders' functioning: A longitudinal mediation model. *Deviant Behavior, 37*(2), 196–218.

National Film Board of Canada. (2017). *Home Fire. Synopsis.* Retrieved from https://www.nfb.ca

Newman, G. (2008). *Comparative deviance: Perception and law in six cultures.* New Brunswick, NJ: Transaction Publishers.

Norman, L. B., & Ford, J. A. (2015). Adolescent ecstasy use: A test of social bonds and social learning theory. *Deviant Behavior, 36*(7), 527–538.

Office of the Correctional Investigator. (2017a, February 15). *Fatal response: An investigation into the preventable death of Matthew Ryan Hines - Final report.* Retrieved from www.oci-bec.gc.ca

Office of the Correctional Investigator. (2017b). *Home page.* Retrieved from www.oci-bec.gc.ca

Parnaby, P. R., & Sacco, V. F. (2004). Fame and strain: The contributions of Mertonian deviance theory to an understanding of the relationship between celebrity and deviant behavior. *Deviant Behavior, 25*(1), 1–26.

Parrott, S., & Parrott, C. T. (2015). Law and disorder: The portrayal of mental illness in U.S. crime dramas. *Journal of Broadcasting and Electronic Media, 59*(4), 640–657.

Pepinsky, H. E., & Quinney, R. (Eds.). (2001). *Criminology as peacemaking.* Bloomington, IN: Indiana University Press.

Perreault, S. (2015). Criminal victimization in Canada, 2014. *Juristat.* (Catalogue No. 85-002-X). Ottawa, ON: Statistics Canada.

Quisenberry, P. (2015). Texting and driving: Can it be explained by the general theory of crime? *American Journal of Criminal Justice, 40*(2), 303–316.

Reiner, R. (2013). Who governs? Democracy, plutocracy, science and prophecy in policing. *Criminology and Criminal Justice, 13*(2), 161–180.

Sacco, V. F. (1992). *Deviance, conformity and control in Canadian society.* Scarborough, ON: Prentice Hall.

Salvatore, C., & Taniguchi, T. A. (2012). Do social bonds matter for emerging adults? *Deviant Behavior, 33*(9), 738–756.

Sefina, O. (2012). Bike racing, neutralization and the social construction of performance-enhancing drugs. *Contemporary Drug Problems, 39,* 213–245.

Shdaimah, C. S., & Leon, C. (2015). "First and foremost, they're survivors": Selective manipulation, resilience, and assertion among prostituted women. *Feminist Criminology, 10*(4), 326–347.

Siegel, L. J., & McCormick, C. (2016). *Criminology in Canada: Theories, patterns, and typologies* (8th ed.). Toronto, ON: Nelson Education.

Sohrabi, H., & Farquharson, K. (2016). Social integration of Australian Muslims: A dramaturgical perspective. *Journal of Sociology, 52*(2), 387–402.

Sutherland, E. H. (1947). *Principles of criminology.* Philadelphia, PA: J. B. Lippincott.

Sykes, G., & Matza, D. (1957). Techniques of neutralization: A theory of delinquency. *American Sociological Review, 22,* 664–670.

Tierney, J. (2009). *Key perspectives in criminology.* Berkshire, UK: Open University Press McGraw-Hill Education.

Vago, S., & Nelson, A. (2014). *Law and society* (4th Can ed.). Toronto, ON: Pearson Education Canada.

Verdun-Jones, S. (2015). *Criminal law in Canada: Cases, questions, and the code* (6th ed.). Toronto, ON: Nelson Education.

Whonnock, K. (2008). *Aboriginal courts in Canada: Fact sheet.* Retrieved from http://www.scowinstitute.ca

Winterdyk, A. (2016). *Canadian criminology* (3rd ed.). Don Mills, ON: Oxford University Press.

Woolford, A. (2009). *The politics of restorative justice: A critical introduction.* Winnipeg, MB: Fernwood Publishing.

Wu, Y., Lake, R., & Cao, L. (2015). Race, social bonds, and juvenile attitudes toward the police. *Justice Quarterly, 32*(3), 445–470.

Zehr, H. (2002). *The little book of restorative justice.* Intercourse, PA: Good Books.

CHAPTER 12

Auger, N., & Alix, C. (2016). Income, income distribution, and health in Canada. In D. Raphael (Ed.), *Social determinants of health: Canadian perspectives* (pp. 90–109). Toronto, ON: Canadian Scholars Press Inc.

Beckfield, J., Olafsdottir, S., & Bakhtiari, E. (2013). Health inequalities in global context. *American Behavioral Scientist, 57*(8), 1014–1039.

Boak, A., Hamilton, H. A., Adlaf, E. M., & Mann, R. E. (2015). *Drug use among Ontario students, 1977-2015: Detailed OSDUHS findings.* (CAMH Research Documents Series No. 41). Toronto, ON: CAMH.

Bolaria, B. S., & Bolaria, R. (2009). Personal and structural determinants of health and illness: Lifestyles and life chances. In B. S. Bolaria and H. D. Dickinson (Eds.), *Health, illness, and health care in Canada* (4th ed.) (pp. 506–519). Toronto, ON: Nelson.

Budrys, G. (2017). *Unequal health: How inequality contributes to health or illness* (3rd ed.). New York, NY: Rowman & Littlefield.

Byrd, K. M. (2016). Binge drinking in and out of college: An examination of social control and differential association on binge drinking behaviors between college students and their non-college peers. *Sociological Spectrum, 36*(4), 191–207.

Canadian Medical Association. (2016). *The state of seniors' health care in Canada.* Ottawa, ON: Author.

Chai, C. (2017, April 4). Are measles outbreaks here to stay? Here's what Canada's top doctor thinks. *Global News.* Retrieved from http://www.globalnews.ca

Chandler, M. J., & Dunlop, W. L. (2015). Cultural wounds demand cultural medicine. In M. Greenwood, S. de Leeuw, N. M. Lindsay, & C. Reading (Eds.), *Determinants of Indigenous peoples' health in Canada: Beyond the social* (pp. 78–89). Toronto, ON: Canadian Scholars Press Inc.

Canadian Institute for Health Information (CIHI). (2011). *Seniors and the health care system: What is the impact of multiple chronic conditions?* Ottawa, ON: Author.

Canadian Institute for Health Information (CIHI). (2016a). *National health expenditure trends, 1975 to 2016.* Ottawa, ON: Author.

Canadian Institute for Health Information (CIHI). (2016b). *Trends in income-related health inequalities in Canada* (Rev. ed.). Ottawa, ON: Author.

Clarke, J. N. (2016). *Health, illness, and medicine in Canada* (7th ed.). Don Mills, ON: Oxford University Press.

Claussen, B., Davey Smith, G., & Thelle, D. (2003). Impact of childhood and adulthood socioeconomic position on cause specific mortality: The Oslo Mortality Study. *Journal of Epidemiology and Community Health, 57*(1), 40–55.

Cockerham, W. C. (2007). Medical sociology. In G. Ritzer (Ed.), *Encyclopedia of sociology*. Retrieved from http://www.blackwellreferenceonline.com

Conrad, P. (2007). *The medicalization of society: On the transformation of human conditions into treatable disorders*. Baltimore, MD: Johns Hopkins University Press.

Decady, Y. (2016). Changes in causes of death, 1950 to 2012. *The Daily: Canadian Megatrends*. (Catalogue No. 11-630-X2016003). Ottawa, ON: Statistics Canada.

De Maio, F. (2010). *Health and social theory*. New York, NY: Palgrave Macmillan.

Eaton, W. W. (2001). *The sociology of mental disorders*. Westport, CT: Praeger.

Engels, F. (1985). *The condition of the working class in England*. Stanford, CA: Stanford University Press. (Original work published 1845)

Firestone, R., Rowe, C. J., Modi, S. N., & Sievers, D. (2017). The effectiveness of social marketing in global health: A systematic review. *Health Policy and Planning, 32*(1), 110–124.

Foucault, M. (1965). *Madness and civilization*. New York, NY: Random House.

Foucault, M. (1966). *Birth of the clinic*. New York, NY: Vintage.

Fox, N. J. (1993). Discourse, organisation and the surgical ward round. *Sociology of Health and Illness, 15*(1), 16–42.

Frailing, K., & Harper, D. W. (2010). The social construction of deviance, conflict and the criminalization of midwives, New Orleans: 1940s and 1950s. *Deviant Behavior, 31*, 729–755.

Garriguet, D. (2007). Canadians' eating habits. *Health Reports, 18*(2), 17–32. (Catalogue No. 82-003). Ottawa, ON: Statistics Canada.

Garriguet, D., Tremblay, S., & Colley, R. C. (2015). Comparison of physical activity questionnaire result with accelerometer data. *Health Reports*. (Catalogue No. 82-003-X). Ottawa, ON: Statistics Canada.

Ghirardelli, A., Quinn, V., & Foerster, S. B. (2010). Using geographic information systems and local food store data in California's low-income neighborhoods to inform community initiatives and resources. *American Journal of Public Health, 100*(11), 2156–2162.

Gionet, L., & Roshanafshar, S. (2013). Select health indicators of First Nations people living off reserve, Métis, and Inuit. *Health at a Glance*. (Catalogue No. 82-624-X). Ottawa, ON: Statistics Canada.

Greenberg, L., & Normandin, C. (2011). Disparities in life expectancy at birth. *Health at a Glance*. (Catalogue No. 82-624-X). Ottawa, ON: Statistics Canada.

Health Canada. (2017). Canadian Tobacco, Alcohol, and Drugs Survey (CTADS) 2015. Ottawa, ON: Author.

Heron, C. (2003). *Booze: A distilled history*. Downsview, ON: Between the Lines.

Hilmers, A. Hilmers, D. C., & Dave, J. (2012). Neighbourhood disparities in access to health food and their effects on environmental justice. *American Journal of Public Health, 102*(9), 1644–1654.

Historica Canada. (n.d.-a). Indigenous peoples: Uses of plants. In *The Canadian encyclopedia*. Retrieved from http://thecanadianencyclopedia.ca

Historica Canada. (n.d.-b). Influenza (flu). In *The Canadian encyclopedia*. Retrieved from http://thecanadianencyclopedia.ca

Johnson, L. (2011, June 30). *California teenagers to get whooping cough vaccinations*. Retrieved from http://www.reuters.com

Johnston, L. D., O'Malley, P. M., Bachman, J. G., Schelenberg, J. E., & Miech, R. A. (2016). *Monitoring the future. National survey on drug use, 1975-2015: Volume 2. College students and adults ages 19-55*. Ann Arbor, MI: University of Michigan.

Kempner, J. L. (2014). *Not tonight: Migraine and the politics of gender and health*. Chicago, IL: University of Chicago Press.

Le Vallée, J. C., MacLaine, C., Lalonde, M., & Grant, M. (2017). *Canada's food report card 2016: Provincial performance*. Ottawa, ON: Conference Board of Canada.

Lim, S. S., Vos, T., Flaxman, A. D., Danaei, G., Shibuya, K., Adair-Rohani, H., ... Ezzati, M. (2012). A comparative risk assessment of burden of disease and injury attributable to 67 risk factor clusters in 21 regions, 1990–2010: A systematic analysis for the Global Burden of Disease study 2010. *Lancet, 380*, 2224–2260.

MacNamara, N., & Parsons, H. (2016). "Everyone here wants everyone else to get better": The role of social identity in eating disorder recovery. *British Journal of Social Psychology, 55*(4), 662–680.

Markle, G. E., & McCrea, F. B. (2008). *What if medicine disappeared?* Albany, NY: New York University Press.

Marmot, M. G. (2005). Social determinants of health inequalities. *Lancet, 365*, 1099–1104.

McHugh, M. C., & Chrisler, J. C. (Eds.). (2015). *The wrong prescription for women: How medicine and media create a "need" for treatments, drugs, and surgery*. Santa Barbara, CA: Praeger.

McIntyre, L., & Anderson, N. (2016). Food insecurity. In D. Raphael (Ed.). *Social determinants of health: Canadian perspectives* (pp. 294–320). Toronto, ON: Canadian Scholars Press Inc.

Mehta, D. (2017, February 24). Canadians urged to update vaccines after mumps, measles cases reported. *Global News*. Retrieved from http://www.globalnews.ca

Millett, C., & Glantz, S. A. (2010). Assigning an "18" rating to movies with tobacco images is essential to reduce youth smoking. *Thorax, 65*, 377–378.

National Institute on Alcohol Abuse and Alcoholism. (2017). *Alcohol facts and statistics*. Retrieved from http://niaaa.nih.gov

Navarro, B. (1976). Social class, political power and the state and their implications for medicine. *Social Science and Medicine, 10*, 437–457.

Ni Mhurchu, C., Vandevijvere, S., Waterlander, W., Thornton, L. E., Kelly, B., Cameron, A. J., ... Swinburn, B. (2013). Monitoring the availability of healthy and unhealthy food and non-alcoholic beverages in community and consumer retail food environments globally. *Obesity Reviews, 14*(Supplement 1), 108–119.

Nunavut Bureau of Statistics. (2016). *Nunavut Food Price Survey, comparison of Nunavut & Canada CPI food price basket items*. Retrieved from http://www.stats.gov.nu.ca

Organisation for Economic Co-operation and Development (OECD). (2017). *OECD health statistics, 2017*. Paris, France: Author.

Parsons, T. (1951). *The social system*. Glencoe, IL: Free Press.

Perry, B. L. (2011). The labeling paradox: Stigma, the sick role, and social networks in mental illness. *Journal of Health and Social Behavior, 52*(4), 460–477.

Physical and Health Education Canada. (2017). *Quality daily physical education*. Retrieved from http://www.phecanada.ca

Picard, A. (2011, January 6). Medical fraud revealed in discredited vaccine-autism study. *The Globe and Mail*. Retrieved from http://www.globeandmail.com

Polansky, J. R., Titus, K., Atayeva, R., & Glantz, S. A. (2016). *Smoking in top-grossing US movies 2015*. (Series: Tobacco Control Policy Making: United States) Retrieved from www.scholarship.org.

Pryma, J. (2017). "Even my sister says I'm acting like a crazy to get a check": Race, gender, and moral boundary work in women's claims of disability, chronic pain. *Social Science and Medicine, 181*, 66–73.

Ramage-Morin, P. L., & Shields, M. (2010). Health-promoting factors and good health among Canadians in mid- to late life. *Health Reports, 21*(3). (Catalogue No. 82-003-X). Ottawa, ON: Statistics Canada.

Rao, M., Afshin, A., Singh, G., & Mozaffarian, D. (2013). Do healthier diets cost more than less healthy options? A systematic review and meta-analysis. *BMJ Open, 3*(12), 1–18.

Raphael, D. (2016). Social determinants of health: Key issues and themes. In D. Raphael (Ed.), *Social determinants of health: Canadian perspectives* (pp. 3–31). Toronto, ON: Canadian Scholars Press Inc.

Reading, C. (2015). Structural determinants of Aboriginal peoples' health. In M. Greenwood, S. de Leeuw, N. M. Lindsay, & C. Reading (Eds.), *Determinants of Indigenous peoples' health in Canada: Beyond the social* (pp. 3–15). Toronto, ON: Canadian Scholars Press Inc.

Reading, J., & Halseth, R. (2013). *Pathways to improving well-being for Indigenous peoples: How living conditions decide health*. Prince George, BC: National Collaborating Centre for Aboriginal Health.

Rindstedt, C. (2016). Negotiating illness in medical interactions: Narrative styles of two children with leukaemia. *Children and Society, 30*, 278–289.

Scales, K., Bailey, S., Middleton, J., & Schneider, J. (2017). Power, empowerment, and person-centred care: Using ethnography to examine the everyday practice of unregistered dementia care staff. *Sociology of Health and Illness, 39*(2), 227–243.

Schneider, J., & Conrad, P. (1983). *Having epilepsy: The experience and control of illness*. Philadelphia, PA: Temple University Press.

Statistics Canada. (2015). Food insecurity in Canada, 2007 to 2012. *The Daily*. (Catalogue No. 11-001-X). Ottawa, ON: Author.

Statistics Canada. (2017a). Age and sex, and type of dwelling data: Key results from the 2016 Census. *The Daily*. (Catalogue No. 11-001-X). Ottawa, ON: Author.

Statistics Canada. (2017b). *Age and sex highlight table, 2016 Census*. Ottawa, ON: Author.

Statistics Canada. (2017c). Canadian Health Measures Survey: Activity monitor data. *The Daily*. (Catalogue No. 11-001-X). Ottawa, ON: Author.

Statistics Canada. (2017d). Fruit and vegetable consumption, 2015. *Health Fact Sheets*. (Catalogue No. 82-625-X). Ottawa, ON: Author.

Statistics Canada. (2017e). *Leading causes of death, total population, by age group and sex, Canada, annual*. (CANSIM Table 102-0561). Ottawa, ON: Author.

Statistics Canada. (2017f). *Leading causes of death, total population, by sex, Canada, provinces and territories (age standardization using 2011 population)*. (CANSIM Table 102-0564). Ottawa, ON: Author.

Statistics Canada. (2017g). *Net income of liquor authorities and government revenue for the sale and control of alcoholic beverages*. (CANSIM Table 183-0025). Ottawa, ON: Author.

Statistics Canada. (2017h). *Sales and per capita sales of alcoholic beverages by liquor authorities and other retail outlets, by value, volume, and absolute volume*. (CANSIM Table 183-0023). Ottawa, ON: Author.

Strohschein, L., & Weitz, R. (2014). *The sociology of health, illness and health care in Canada: A critical approach*. Toronto, ON: Nelson.

Sturgeon, J. (2014, November 18). Here's who's really winning the grocery wars. *Global News*. Retrieved from http://www.globalnews.ca

Tarasuk, V. (2016). Health implications of food insecurity. In D. Raphael (Ed.), *Social determinants of health: Canadian perspectives* (pp. 321–342). Toronto, ON: Canadian Scholars Press Inc.

Teegee, T. (2015). Take care of the land and the land will take care of you: Resources, development, and health. In M. Greenwood, S. de Leeuw, N. M. Lindsay, & C. Reading (Eds.), *Determinants of Indigenous peoples' health in Canada: Beyond the social* (pp. 120–140). Toronto, ON: Canadian Scholars Press Inc.

Vang, Z., Sigouin, J., Flenon, A., & Gagnon, A. (2015). The healthy immigrant effect in Canada: A systematic review. *Population Changes and Lifecourse Strategic Knowledge Cluster Discussion Paper Series, 3*(1), Article 4.

Weeks, J. R. (2016). *Population: An introduction to concepts and issues* (12th ed.). Boston, MA: Cengage Learning.

White, B. (2017, June 20). 'Killing our youth': Natuashish leaders call for crackdown on bootlegging. CBC News. Retrieved from http://www.cbc.ca/news

World Health Organization. (1948). *Preamble to the Constitution of the World Health Organization as adopted by the International Health Conference, New York, 19 June–22 July 1946; signed on 22 July 1946 by the representatives of 61 states (Official Records of the World Health Organization, no. 2, p. 100) and entered into force on 7 April 1948*. Geneva, CH: World Health Organization.

World Health Organization. (2010). *Global strategy to reduce the harmful use of alcohol*. Geneva, CH: Author.

World Health Organization. (2013). Ban tobacco advertising to protect young people: World Tobacco Day 2013. Geneva, CH: Author.

World Health Organization. (2014). *Patterns of drinking score (15+). Global Information System on Alcohol and Health (GISAH)*. Retrieved from http://www.who.int

World Health Organization. (2015). *Alcohol. Fact Sheet*. Retrieved from http://www.who.int

World Health Organization. (2016). *Mental health: Strengthening our response. Fact Sheet.* Retrieved from http://www.who.int

World Health Organization. (2017a). *Noncommunicable diseases. Fact Sheet.* Retrieved from http://www.who.int

World Health Organization. (2017b). *Physical activity. Fact sheet.* Retrieved from http://www.who.int

World Health Organization. (2017c). *Prevalence of tobacco smoking. Global Health Observatory (GHO) Data.* Retrieved from http://www.who.int

World Health Organization. (2017d). *Tobacco and its environmental impact: An overview.* Geneva, CH: Author.

World Health Organization. (2017e). Tobacco control. *Global Health Observatory (GHO) Data.* Retrieved from http://www.who.int

World Health Organization. (2017f). *Unhealthy diet. Fact Sheet.* Retrieved from http://www.who.int

CHAPTER 13

Aberle, D. F. (1966). *The Peyote religion among the Navaho.* Chicago, IL: Aldine.

Alfred, G. R. (1995). *Heeding the voices of our ancestors: Kahnawake Mohawk politics and the rise of Native nationalism.* Toronto, ON: Oxford University Press.

Allport, G. W., & Postman, L. (1947). *The psychology of rumor.* New York, NY: Henry Holt.

BBC News. (2017, June 13). *Trump travel ban suffers new court defeat.* Retrieved from http://www.bbc.com

Benford, R. D., & Snow, D. A. (2000). Framing processes and social movements: An overview and assessment. *Annual Review of Sociology, 26,* 611–639.

Blumer, H. (1939). Collective behavior. In Robert E. Park (Ed.), *Outline of the principles of sociology* (pp. 221–279). New York, NY: Barnes & Noble.

Blumer, H. (1969). Collective behavior. In A. M. Lee (Ed.), *Principles of sociology* (3rd ed., pp. 67–120). New York, NY: Barnes & Noble.

Brunvand, J. H. (2003). *The choking doberman: And other urban legends.* New York, NY: W. W. Norton.

Brunvand, J. H. (2014a). *Dr. Jan Harold Brunvand: Frequently asked questions.* Retrieved from http://www.janbrunvand.com

Brunvand, J. H. (2014b). *Too good to be true: The colossal book of urban legends.* New York, NY: W. W. Norton.

Buechler, S. M. (2010). The strange career of strain and breakdown theories of collective action. In D. A. Snow, S. A. Soule, & H. Kriesi (Eds.), *The Blackwell companion to social movements* (pp. 47–66). Malden, MA: Blackwell Publishing.

Canadian Chiropractic Association. (2017). *About chiropractic care.* Toronto, ON: Author. Retrieved from http://www.chiropracticcanada.ca

(The) Canadian Press (2016, July 22). A look back at oil spills and leaks in prairies provinces. CTV News. Retrieved from http://www.ctvnews.ca

Carroll, W. K. (2016). Social movements and counter-hegemony. In W. K. Carroll & K. Sarker (Eds.), *A world to win: Contemporary movements and counter-hegemony* (pp. 9–60). Winnipeg, MB: ARP Books.

Castells, M. (2015). *Networks of outage and hope: Social movements in the internet age* (2nd ed.). Cambridge, UK: Polity Press.

Ciaccia, J. (2000). *The Oka crisis: A mirror of the soul.* Dorval, QC: Maren Publications.

Cohen, S. (1972). *Folk devils and moral panics.* London, UK: MacGibbon & Kee.

Cohen, S. (2002). *Folk devils and moral panics: The creation of the mods and rockers* (3rd ed.). New York, NY: Routledge.

Crawford, T. (2015, November 18). Stanley Cup riot investigation winds down as last two suspects charged. *Vancouver Sun.* Retrieved from http://www.vancouversun.com

CTV News. (2010, February 18). *Lightfoot very much alive, despite reports of death.* Retrieved from http://www.ctv.ca

della Porta, D., & Diani, M. (2008). *Social movements: An introduction* (2nd ed.). Malden, MA: Blackwell Publishing.

Deloitte. (2004, September). *Impact of delisting chiropractic services: Final report, Ontario Chiropractic Association.* Retrieved from http://www.chiropractic.on.ca

Eaves, S. (2011, May 4). *Alberta's biggest oil spill in 30 years is a call to action for Canadians.* Vancouver, BC: David Suzuki Foundation. Retrieved from http://www.davidsuzuki.org

Edwards, B., & McCarthy, J. D. (2004). Resources and social movement mobilization. In D. A. Snow, S. A. Soule, & H. Kriesi (Eds.), *The Blackwell companion to social movements* (pp. 116–152). Malden, MA: Blackwell Publishing.

Erikson, K. (1994). *A new species of trouble: The human experience of modern disasters.* New York, NY: W. W. Norton.

Erikson, K. (2012). *Everything in its path: Destruction of community in the Buffalo Creek flood.* New York, NY: Simon & Schuster Paperbacks. (Original work published 1976)

Festinger, L., Pepitone, A., & Newcomb, T. (1952). Some consequences of deindividuation in a group. *Journal of Abnormal and Social Psychology, 47,* 382–389.

Fisk, R., Cockburn, P, Sengupta, K., & *The Independent.* (2016). *Arab spring then and now: From hope to despair.* Coral Gables, FL: Mango Publishing Group.

Gamson, W. (1991). Commitment and agency in social movements. *Sociological Forum, 6,* 27–50.

Globe Staff and Canadian Press. (2017, January 5). The Fort McMurray fire: What's happening now, and what you've missed. *The Globe and Mail.* Retrieved from https://www.theglobeandmail.com

Goffman, E. (1974). *Frame analysis: An essay on the organization of experience.* New York, NY: Harper Colophon.

Goode, E. (1992). *Collective behavior.* Orlando, FL: Harcourt Brace Jovanovich.

Goode, E., & Ben-Yehuda, N. (2009). *Moral panics: The social construction of deviance* (2nd ed.). West Sussex, UK: Wiley-Blackwell.

Healthquotes.ca. (2015, January 9). *Chiropractic coverage and health insurance.* Retrieved from http://www.healthquotes.ca

Hier, S. P. (2002). Raves, risks and the ecstasy panic: A case study in the subversive nature of moral regulation. *Canadian Journal of Sociology, 27*(1), 33–57.

Hund, S. A., & Benford, R. D. (2010). Collective identity, solidarity, and commitment. In D. A. Snow, S. A. Soule, & H. Kriesi (Eds.), *The Blackwell companion to social movements* (pp. 433–457). Malden, MA: Blackwell Publishing.

Idle No More. (n.d.). *The manifesto*. Retrieved from http://www.idlenomore.ca

Khal. (2017). *Diehard Drake fans will love his new tattoo*. Retrieved from http://ca.complex.com

Kheraj, S. (2015, July 23). *The biggest oil spills in Canadian history*. Regina, SK: University of Saskatchewan and Heron University College. Retrieved from http://activehistory.ca

Laeeque, H., & Boon, H., (2004). Print media coverage on the Lana Dale Lewis inquest verdict: Exaggerated claims or accurate reporting? *Health Law Review, 13*(1), 7–26.

LaForme, H. S. (1991). Indian sovereignty: What does it mean? *Canadian Journal of Native Studies, 11*(2), 253–266.

Le Bon, G. (1895/2006). *The crowd: A study of the popular mind*. New York, NY: Cosimo Classics.

Lee, H., & Oh, H. J. (2017). Normative mechanism of rumor dissemination on Twitter. *CyberPsychology, Behavior and Social Networking, 20*(3), 164–171.

Lepisto, C. (2009, October 21). *8 worst man-made environmental disasters of all time*. Retrieved from http://www.treehugger.com

Lutz, J. M. & Lutz, B. J. (2013). *Global terrorism* (3rd ed.). Oxfordshire, UK: Routledge.

McAdam, D. (1982). *The political process and the development of Black insurgency*. Chicago, IL: University of Chicago Press.

McAdam, D., Tarrow, S., & Tilly, C. (2001). *Dynamics of contention*. Cambridge, UK: University Press.

McCarthy, J. D., & Zald, M. N. (1977). Resource mobilization and social movements: A partial theory. *American Journal of Sociology, 82*(6), 1212–1241.

McPhail, C. (1991). *The myth of the madding crowd*. New York, NY: Aldine de Gruyter.

Mellberg, C., Sandberg, S., Ryberg, M., Eriksson, M., Brage, S., Larsson, C., … Lindahl, B. (2014). Long-term effects of a Palaeolithic-type diet in obese postmenopausal women: A two-year randomized trial. *European Journal of Clinical Nutrition, 68*(3), 350–357.

Miller, D. L. (2000). *Introduction to collective behavior and collective action* (2nd ed.). Prospect Heights, IL: Waveland Publishing.

Natural Resources Canada. (2009). *The atlas of Canada: Natural hazards*. Ottawa, ON: Author. Retrieved from http://www.atlas.nrcan.gc.ca

Nurwisah, R. (2010, February 18). Gordon Lightfoot death rumours sparked by Internet hoax. *National Post*. Retrieved from http://www.network.nationalpost.com

Phillips, R. (2016, December 10). *Ranked: The five deadliest disasters of 2016*. London, UK: The Weather Company. Retrieved from https://weather.com

Roschke, R. (2016, April 30). *A step-by-step breakdown of the lemonade between Beyoncé, Rachel Roy, and Jay Z. Did Jay Z cheat on Beyoncé with Rachel Roy?* Retrieved from https://www.popsugar.com

Smelser, N. J. (1962). *Theory of collective behavior*. New York, NY: Free Press.

Snow, D. A. (2001). Collective identity and expressive forms. In N. J. Smelser & P. B. Baltes (Eds.), *International encyclopedia of the social and behavioral sciences* (pp. 196–254). London, UK: Elsevier Science.

Snow, D. A. (2007). Framing and social movements. In G. Ritzer (Ed.), *Blackwell encyclopedia of sociology*. Retrieved from http://www.blackwellreference.com

Snow, D. A., Rochford, B., Jr., Worden, S. K., & Benford, R. D. (1986). Frame alignment processes, micromobilization, and movement participation. *American Sociological Review, 51*, 464–481.

Staggenborg, S. (1998). *Gender, family, and social movements*. Thousand Oaks, CA: Pine Forge Press.

Staggenborg, S. (2008). *Social movements*. Toronto, ON: Oxford University Press.

Stokes Sullivan, D. (2010, October 2). The forgotten storm. *The Telegram*. Retrieved from http://www.thetelegram.com

Swain, H. (2010). *Oka*. Vancouver, BC: Douglas & McIntyre.

Taddese, Y. (2013, February 8). Idle No More "has it right": LaForme. Legal Feeds Blog. *Canadian Lawyer Magazine and Law Times Newspaper*. Retrieved from http://www.canadianlawermag.com

Tarrow, S. (1998). *Power in movement: Social movements and contentious politics* (2nd ed.). Cambridge, UK: Cambridge University Press.

Tilly, C., & Tarrow, S. (2015). *Contentious politics* (2nd ed.). New York, NY: Oxford University Press.

Tilly, C., & Wood, L. J. (2013). *Social movements, 1768-2012* (3rd ed.). Boulder, CO: Paradigm Publishers.

Turner, R. H., & Killian, L. M. (1987). *Collective behavior* (3rd ed.). Englewood Cliffs, NJ: Prentice-Hall.

Valverde, M. (1991). *The age of light, soap, and water: Moral reform in English Canada, 1885–1925*. Toronto, ON: McClelland & Stewart.

Villanueva-Russell, Y. (2009). Chiropractors as folk devils: Published and unpublished news coverage of a moral panic. *Deviant Behavior, 30*, 175–200.

West, D. (2013). *Social movements in global politics*. Cambridge, UK: Polity Press.

Whalen, K. A., McCullough, M. L., Flanders, W. D., Hartman, T. J., Judd, S., & Bostick, R. M. (2016). Paleolithic and Mediterranean diet pattern scores are inversely associated with biomarkers of inflammation and oxidative balance in adults. *Journal of Nutrition, 146*(6), 1217–1226.

Zajdow, G. (2008). Moral panics: The old and the new. *Deviant Behavior, 29*, 640–664.

CHAPTER 14

Agyeman, J., Cole, P., Haluza-DeLay, R., & O-Riely, P. (Eds.). (2009). *Speaking for ourselves: Environmental justice in Canada*. Vancouver, BC: University of Columbia Press.

Boano, C., Zetter, R., & Morris, T. (2008). Environmentally displaced people: Understanding the linkages between environmental change, livelihoods and forced migration. In *Forced migration policy briefing*. Oxford, UK: Refugee Studies Centre.

Buttel, F. H., & Humphrey, C. R. (2002). Sociological theory and the natural environment. In R. E. Dunlap & W. Michelson (Eds.), *Handbook of environmental sociology* (pp. 33–69). Westport, CT: Greenwood Press.

Catton, W. R., Jr. (1980). *Overshoot: The ecological basis of revolutionary change*. Urbana, IL: University of Illinois Press.

Catton, W. R., Jr., & Dunlap, R. E. (1978). Environmental sociology: A new paradigm. *American Sociologist, 13*, 41–49.

Catton, W. R., Jr., & Dunlap, R. E. (1980). A new ecological paradigm for post-exuberant sociology. *American Behavioral Scientist, 24,* 15–47.

Central Intelligence Agency. (2017a). Guide to country comparisons: Infant mortality rate. In *The world factbook*. Washington, DC: Office of Public Affairs. Retrieved from https://www.cia.gov

Central Intelligence Agency. (2017b). Guide to country comparisons: Median age. In *The world factbook*. Washington, DC: Office of Public Affairs. Retrieved from https://www.cia.gov

Central Intelligence Agency. (2017c). Guide to country comparisons: Total fertility rate. In *The world factbook*. Washington, DC: Office of Public Affairs. Retrieved from https://www.cia.gov

Cheremisinoff, P. N. (1992). Emissions control options for power plants. In D. G. Marowski (Ed.), *Environmental viewpoints: Selected essays and excerpts on issues in environmental protection* (pp. 43–49). Detroit, MI: Gale Research.

David Suzuki Foundation. (2017a). *Declaration of Interdependence*. Vancouver, BC: Author. Retrieved from http://www.davidsuzuki.org

David Suzuki Foundation. (2017b). *Help end food waste. Food and our planet*. Vancouver, BC: Author. Retrieved from http://www.davidsuzuki.org

Davies, K. (1988). What is ecofeminism? *Women and Environments, 10*(Spring), 4–6.

Dearing, S. (2010, August 31). Study finds Alberta's Athabasca River polluted by oil sands. In the Media. *Digital Journal*. Retrieved from http://www.digitaljournal.com

Dewis, G. (2014, March). *Uptake and disposal of compact fluorescent light bulbs by Canadian households*. (Catalogue No. 16-002-x). Ottawa, ON: Statistics Canada.

Diamond, J. (2000). *Ecological collapses of pre-industrial societies. The Tanner Lectures on Human Values*. (Lecture delivered at Stanford University, May 22–24, 2000) Retrieved from http://www.tannerlectures.utah.edu

Draper, D. (1998). *Our environment: A Canadian perspective*. Scarborough, ON: ITP Nelson.

Dunlap, R. E., & Catton, W. R., Jr. (1979). Environmental sociology. *Annual Review of Sociology, 5,* 243–273.

Dunlap, R. E., Michelson, W., & Stalkers, G. (2002). Environmental sociology: An introduction. In R. E. Dunlap & W. Michelson (Eds.), *Handbook of environmental sociology* (pp. 1–32). Westport, CT: Greenwood Press.

Environment Canada. (1998). *1997 Canadian acid rain assessment. Vol. 4. The effects on Canada's forests*. (Prepared for the Canadian Council of Ministers of the Environment) Ottawa, ON: Environment Canada, Atmospheric Environment Service.

Ewing, B., Moore, D., Goldfinger, S., Oursler, A., Reed, A., & Wackernagel, M. (2010). *The ecological footprint Atlas 2010*. Oakland, CA: Global Footprint Network.

Foster, J. B. (2009). *The ecological revolution*. New York, NY: Monthly Review Press.

Foster, J. B., Clark, B., & York, R. (2010). *The ecological rift: Capitalism's war on the Earth*. New York, NY: Monthly Review Press.

Global Footprint Network. (2017a). Biocapacity per capita. In *Ecological wealth of nations*. Oakland, CA: Author. Retrieved from http://www.footprintnetwork.org

Global Footprint Network. (2017b). *Ecological footprint*. Oakland, CA: Author. Retrieved from http://www.footprintnetwork.org

Global Footprint Network. (2017c). Ecological footprint per capita. In *Ecological wealth of nations*. Oakland, CA: Author. Retrieved from http://www.footprintnetwork.org

Gould, K., Pellow, D. N., & Schnaiberg, A. (2008). *The treadmill of production: Injustice and unsustainability in the global economy*. Boulder, CO: Paradigm.

Government of Canada. (2014). The safety of fluorescent lamps. In *Health: Healthy Canadians. Household products*. Ottawa, ON: Author. Retrieved from http://healthycanadians .gc.ca

Government of Ontario. (2016a, May 1). *Greater Golden Horseshoe growth forecasts to 2041*. Ottawa, ON: Queen's Printer for Ontario. Retrieved from https://www.ontario.ca

Grimm, N. B., Foster, D., Groffman, P., Grove, J. M., Hopkinson, C. S., Nadelhoffer, K. J., ... Peters, D. P. C. (2008). The changing landscape: Ecosystem responses to urbanization and pollution across climatic and societal gradients. *Frontiers in Ecology and the Environment, 6(5),* 264–272.

Harris, A. (2017). *Ecofeminism*. Retrieved from http://www.thegreenfuse.org

Hart, S. L. (1999). Business decision making about the environment: The challenge of sustainability. In *Better environmental decisions: Strategies for governments, businesses, and communities* (pp. 77–90). Washington, DC: Island Press.

Hernan, R. E. (2010). *This borrowed Earth: Lessons from the fifteen worst environmental disasters around the world*. New York, NY: Palgrave Macmillan.

Hitchcock, D., & Willard, M. (2009). *The business guide to sustainability: Practical strategies and tools for organizations*. Sterling, VA: AXIS Performance Advisors.

Houle, D. (2004). Effects on forests and soils. In *2004 Canadian acid deposition science assessment* (pp. 163–202). Downsview, ON: Environment Canada.

Indigenous Environmental Network. (2017). *Canadian Indigenous tar sands campaign*. Bermidji, MN: Author. Retrieved from http://www.ienearth.org

Intergovernmental Panel on Climate Change (IPCC). 2017. *IPCC fact sheet: What is the IPCC?* Geneva, CH: Author. Retrieved from http://www.ipcc

Internal Displacement Monitoring Centre. (2015, July). *Global estimates 2015: People displaced by disasters*. Geneva, CH: Author. Retrieved from http://www.internal-displacement.org

Kahan, A. M. (1986). *Acid rain: Reign of controversy*. Golden, CO: Fulcrum.

Kahaner, L. (1988). Something in the air: "Creeping degradation" joins the list of threats to the nation's parks and forests. *Wilderness, 52*(183), 18–27.

Kirk, D. (1996). Demographic transition theory. *Population Studies, 50,* 361–387.

Landry, A. (1934). *La révolution démographique*. Paris, France: Sirey.

Leaf, D. A. (1990). Acid rain and the clean air act. *Chemical Engineering Progress, 86*(5), 25–29.

Mackenzie River Basin Board. (2003). *Mackenzie River Basin state of the ecosystem report*. Ft. Smith, NT: Author. Retrieved from http://www.mrbb.ca

Malthus, T. (1998). *An essay on the principles of population*. London, UK: Printed for J. Johnson, in St. Paul's Church-Yard. Retrieved from http://www.esp.org/books (Original work published 1798)

Notestein, F. (1945). Population: The long view. In Theodore W. Schultz (Ed.), *Food for the world* (pp. 36–57). Chicago, IL: University of Chicago Press.

O'Sullivan, L. (2008, November 24). *Environmental hazards of electronic waste: The negative environmental impact of E-waste disposal. Waste reduction.* Retrieved from http://www.suite101.com

Park, C. C. (1992). The acid rain debate. In D. G. Marowski (Ed.), *Environmental viewpoints: Selected essays and excerpts on issues in environmental protection* (pp. 1–4). Detroit, MI: Gale Research.

Pecl, G. T., Araúgo, M. B., Bell, J. D., Blanchard, J., Bonebrake, T. C., Chen, I.-C., ... Williams, S. E. (2017). Biodiversity redistribution under climate change: Impacts on ecosystems and human well-being. *Science, 355*(6332), 1389–1399.

Plant, J. (1989). *Healing the wounds: The promise of ecofeminism.* Philadelphia, PA: New Society.

Pretty, J., Ball, A. S., Benton, T., Guivant, J. S., Lee., D. R., Orr, D., ... Ward, H. (2007). Introduction to environment and society. In J. Petty, A. S. Ball, T. Benton, J. S. Guivant, D. R. Lee, D. Orr, ... H. Ward (Eds.), *The Sage handbook of environment and society* (pp. 1–32). Thousand Oaks, CA: Sage Publications.

Raloff, J. (1988). New acid rain threat identified. *Science News, 133*(18), 275.

Rees, W. E. (2013). Ecological footprint, concept of. In S. A. Levin (Ed.), *Encyclopedia of biodiversity* (2nd ed., Vol. 2, pp. 701–713). Waltham, MA: Academic Press.

Robbins, P., Hintz, J., & Moore, S. A. (2010). *Environment and society: A critical introduction.* West Sussex, UK: John Wiley & Sons.

Sandler, C. (2010, April 21). Greenwashing meets disposable society. CBC News. Retrieved from http://www.cbc.ca

SaskPower. (2017, May 16). *Geothermal agreement signed.* Prince Albert, SK: Author. Retrieved from http://www.saskpower.com

Schindler, D. W. (1988). Effects of acid rain on freshwater ecosystems. *Science, 239*(4836), 149–157.

Schnaiberg, A. (1980). *The environment: From surplus to scarcity.* New York, NY: Oxford University Press.

Schnaiberg, A., Pellow, D. N., & Weinberg, A. S. (2002). The treadmill of production and the environmental state. In A. P. J. Mol & F. H. Buttel (Eds.), *The environmental state under pressure* (pp. 15–32). Amsterdam, NL: Elsevier Science.

Schlosser, C. A., Strzepek, K. M., Gao, X., Gueneau, A., Fant, C., Paltsev, S., ... Reilly, J. (2014). *The future of global water stress: An integrated assessment.* (Report No. 254). Cambridge, MA: MIT Joint Program on Science Policy of Global Change.

Statistics Canada. (2012). *Human activity and the environment: Waste management in Canada (2012 – updated).* (Catalogue No. 16-201-x). Ottawa, ON: Author.

Statistics Canada. (2015). *Total fertility rate of females.* Ottawa, ON: Author. Retrieved from http://www.statcan.gc.ca

Statistics Canada. (2017, February 8). *2016 Census: 150 years of urbanization in Canada.* (Catalogue No. 11-629-x). Ottawa, ON: Author.

Sustainable Europe Research Institute, Friends of the Earth Austria, and Friends of the Earth Europe. (2009, September). *Overconsumption? Our use of the world's natural resources.* Retrieved from http://www.foeeurope.org

TerraChoice. (2009, April). *The seven sins of greenwashing: Environmental claims in consumer markets. Summary report: North America.* Ottawa, ON: Author.

TerraChoice. (2010). *The sins of greenwashing home and family edition 2010: A report on environmental claims made in the North American consumer market.* Ottawa, ON: Author.

United Nations. (2009, February 5). *Majority of world population face water shortages unless action taken, warns Migiro.* New York, NY: Secretary of the Publications Board. Retrieved from http://www.un.org

United Nations. (2017). *Goal 13: Take urgent action to combat climate change and its impacts. Sustainable Development Goals.* Retrieved from http://www.un.org

United Nations Development Programme. (2017a, September 25). *World leaders adopt sustainable development goals.* Author. Retrieved from http://www.undp.org

United Nations Development Programme. (2017b). *Sustainable development goals: 17 goals to transform our world.* New York, NY: Author. Retrieved from http://www.undp.org

United Nations Environment Programme. (2000). *Montreal protocol on substances that deplete the ozone layer as adjusted and/ or amended in London 1990, Copenhagen 1992, Vienna 1995, Montreal 1997, and Beijing, 1999.* Nairobi, Kenya: Ozone Secretariat.

Wackernagel, M., & Rees, W. E. (1996). *Our ecological footprint: Reducing human impact on the earth.* Gabriola Island, BC: New Society.

Wali, M. K., Evrendilek, F., & Fennessy, M. S. (2010). *The environment: Science, issues, and solutions.* Boca Raton, FL: CRC Press.

Wildlife Conservation Society Canada. (2017). *Boreal birds.* Toronto, ON: Author. Retrieved from https://www.wcscanada.org

Williams, J. (2007). Thinking as natural: Another look at human exemptionalism. *Human Ecology Review, 14*(2), 130–139.

World Commission on Environment and Development. (1987, June 8). *Presentation of the report of the World Commission on Environment and Development to UNEP's 14th governing council session.* Nairobi, Kenya: G. H. Brundtland.

World Wild Fund. (2012). *Living Planet Report 2012: Biodiversity, biocapacity and better choices.* Retrieved from http://www.footprintnetwork.org

World Wildlife Fund. (2017). *Threats. Water scarcity.* Washington, DC: Author. Retrieved from https://www.worldwildlife.org

World Wildlife Fund for Nature–Canada (WWF-Canada). (2017a). *Largest land withdrawal for protection ever in Canada. Conservation successes in Canada.* Toronto, ON: Author. Retrieved from http://www.wwf.ca

World Wildlife Fund for Nature–Canada (WWF-Canada). (2017b). *MacKenzie gas pipeline.* Toronto, ON: Author. Retrieved from http://www.wwf.ca.

CHAPTER 15

Credit Suisse Research Institute. (2015). *Global wealth report 2015.* Retrieved from http://www.credit-suisse.com

Eitzen, D. S., & Zinn, M. B. (2012). Globalization: An introduction. In D. S. Eitzen & M. B. Zinn (Eds.), *Globalization: The transformation of social worlds* (3rd ed., pp. 1–9). Belmont, CA: Wadsworth Cengage Learning.

Faux, J. (2013). NAFTA at 20: State of the North American Worker. *Foreign Policy in Focus.* Retrieved from http://www.fpif.org

Finances Online. (n.d.). *How iPhone is made: The global assembly line*. Retrieved from http://www.financesonline.com

Frank, A. G. (1966). The development of underdevelopment. *Monthly Review, 18*(4), 17–31.

Furtado, C. (1984). *Recession and unemployment: An examination of the Brazilian economic crisis*. London, UK: TW Foundation.

Gachúz, J. C. (2016). *Globalization and organized crime: Challenges for international cooperation*. Retrieved from http://bakerinstitute.org

Hebron, L., & Stack, J. F. (2016). *Globalization* (3rd ed.). New York, NY: Rowman and Littlefield.

ICLEI (Local Governments for Sustainability). (n.d.). *Who we are*. Retrieved from http://www.iclei.org.

Inkeles, A., & Smith, D. H. (1976). *Becoming modern: Individual change in six developing countries*. Cambridge, MA: Harvard University Press.

International Labour Organization. (2008). *ILO declaration on social justice for a fair globalization*. Retrieved from http://www.ilo.org

International Labour Organization. (2017a). *Child labour*. Retrieved from http://www.ilo.org

International Labour Organization. (2017b). *ILO's five flagship programmes*. Retrieved from http://www.ilo.org

International Monetary Fund. (2017). *The IMF and the World Bank. Fact sheet*. Retrieved from http://www.imf.org

Jacobs, L. M., & Van Rossem, R. (2016). The rising powers of globalization: Structural change to the global system between 1965 and 2005. *Journal of World Systems Research, 22*(2), 373–403.

Kalaska, M., & Wites, T. (2015). Perception of the relations between former colonial powers and developing countries. *Third World Quarterly, 36*(10), 1809–1826.

Lee, S. H. (2007). World Bank. In G. Ritzer (Ed.), *Blackwell encyclopedia of sociology*. Retrieved from http://www.blackwellreferenceonline.com

Legrain, P. (2002). *Open world: The truth about globalization*. London, UK: Abacus.

Lerner, D. (1958). *The passing of tradition society: Modernity in the Middle East*. Glencoe, IL: Free Press.

Marks, R. B. (2012). The (modern) world since 1500. In J. R. McNeill & E. R. Mauldin (Eds.), *A companion to global environmental history* (pp. 57–78). Malden, MA: Blackwell Publishing.

Munck, R. (2016). Global sociology: Towards an alternative southern paradigm. *International Journal of Politics, Culture, and Society, 29*(3), 233–249.

Nikolayevna, P. N. (2013). Globalization as a trend of global development. *Society: Sociology, Psychology, Pedagogics, 4*, 1–5.

Parekh, S., & Wilcox, S. (2014). Feminist perspectives on globalization. In E. N. Zalta (Ed.), *The Stanford encyclopedia of philosophy*. Retrieved from http://www.plato.stanford.ed

Ritzer, G., & Stepnisky, J. (2017). *Modern sociological theory* (8th ed.). Thousand Oaks, CA: Sage Publications.

Routledge. (2011). *Critical race and postcolonial theory. Social theory re-wired*. Retrieved from http://www.routledgesoc.com

Shah, A. (2013). *Structural adjustment—A major cause of poverty*. Retrieved from http://www.globalissues.org

Steger, M. B. (2017). *Globalization: A very short introduction* (4th ed.). Oxford, UK: Oxford University Press.

Strohschein, L., & Weitz, R. (2014). *The sociology of health, illness and health care in Canada: A critical approach*. Toronto, ON: Nelson.

United Nations. (2013). *A new global partnership: Eradicate poverty and transform economies through sustainable development*. New York, NY: Author.

United Nations. (2017). *Sustainable development goals*. Retrieved from http://www.sustainabledevelopment.un.org

Wallerstein, I. M. (2000). *The essential Wallerstein*. New York, NY: New York University Press.

Wang, Y., & Zong, L. (2014). Temporary natives, perpetual foreigners: The secondary status of temporary foreign workers in Canada and structural barriers to their inclusion. In K. M. Kilbride (Ed.), *Immigrant integration: Research implications for future policy* (pp. 3–20). Toronto, ON: Canadian Scholars' Press.

World Bank. (2016). *Annual report 2016*. Washington, DC: Author.

World Health Organization. (2017). *Severe acute respiratory syndrome (SARS)*. Retrieved from http://www.who.int

World Social Forum. (2016). *What the World Social Forum is*. Retrieved from https://fsm2016.org/en

World Trade Organization. (2017). *The WTO ... In brief*. Retrieved from http://www.wto.org

Index

Note: Entries and page numbers in **bold** type refer to key terms and the pages in the text on which they are defined. Page numbers followed by *f* refer to figures; page numbers followed by *i* refer to illustrations or photographs; page numbers followed by *t* refer to tables.

G

H

U

V

W

X

Y

Z